BACTERIAL METABOLISM

BACTERIAL METABOLISM

by H. W. Doelle

DEPARTMENT OF MICROBIOLOGY
UNIVERSITY OF QUEENSLAND
BRISBANE, AUSTRALIA

 1969

ACADEMIC PRESS   New York and London

ACADEMIC PRESS, INC.
111 Fifth Avenue, New York, New York 10003

United Kingdom Edition published by
ACADEMIC PRESS, INC. (LONDON) LTD.
Berkeley Square House, London W.1

LIBRARY OF CONGRESS CATALOG CARD NUMBER: 68-26641

PRINTED IN THE UNITED STATES OF AMERICA

PREFACE

Microbial chemistry, which deals with the aspects of metabolic events occurring in microorganisms, has developed at a tremendous pace, from a mere diagnostic section of bacteriology to an independent branch that links the fields of microbiology and biochemistry. The work in this field is reflected by the large number of publications appearing in journals of biochemistry, microbiology, biological chemistry, and others.

There are a number of textbooks available on biochemistry, which deal with certain aspects of bacterial metabolism. However, since they are biochemically orientated, the microbial approach is very much neglected. In contrast to the biochemist whose main interest is directed toward the actual mechanism of reactions, and who therefore uses the microorganism more as a tool of convenience, the microbial chemist prefers to study the occurrence of biological reactions in the light of the particular microorganism and its environment, and to relate this information to biology as a whole. There are many problems which cannot be solved by the biochemist without the help of the microbiologist, and vice versa. Therefore, the aim of this book is to bring together the studies of microbial systematics and microbial chemistry with particular emphasis on catabolic events.

The importance of and the need for a work dealing specifically with bacterial metabolism are obvious, but its preparation has been a difficult task. I am well aware that certain sections may become outdated by the time the text reaches the bookstalls.

With perhaps questionable validity I have assumed that the person who will reach for this book will be a student who has had little or no training in the field of microbial chemistry, an advanced student or a teacher who would like additional information to enhance his present knowledge, or a research worker who will find himself confronted with problems in this field of study. This book should prove helpful to all of them.

v

The work begins with a chapter on thermodynamics and enzymes. Both of these topics are frequently neglected in metabolic studies, and yet they are particularly important, for example, in the evaluation of chemosynthetic pathways. With regard to enzymes, emphasis is given to the Commission Report on Enzyme Nomenclature of the International Union of Biochemists. I am very much in favor of a standardized system for the presentation of results. Where possible, the corresponding enzyme numbers are given; where this is not possible, suggestions are made as to which one of the known enzymes in the report could be responsible for the particular reaction.

The lack of uniform terminology is a problem in microbial chemistry. The second chapter of this book begins, therefore, with definitions of a number of terms used by the majority of research workers and which will be used throughout this work. In order to keep this list short, only the important terms are explained and defined. The second chapter of the book deals with the development of photosynthesis. As in all other chapters, the material is presented very generally at first and is then elaborated upon to include details and problems related to the various disciplines. A comprehensive general scheme will always be found at the beginning of a chapter, followed by a detailed treatment of the scheme. Metabolic events have been considered in the particular bacterial groups. It was the aim to stress not only the biochemical but also the biological problems facing the microbial chemist today.

Bacterial metabolism research includes studies of sources and storage of substances used for synthesis. These processes are intimately related to each other in the completion of overall metabolic events, but, for purposes of convenience, the main events leading to the production and storage of energy and the production of reducing substances have been dealt with under the titles of anaerobic respiration, aerobic respiration, and fermentation in Chapters 3, 5, and 6.

The metabolism of carbohydrates occurs through four major pathways all of which lead to pyruvate, and the principal energy-yielding reactions lead to the subsequent attack of this substrate. For this reason the pathways of carbohydrate catabolism have been treated separately (in Chapter 4) from that of pyruvate, which is dealt with under fermentation and respiration.

In the microbial world, a few organisms exist which may, under specific circumstances, behave quite differently from the general schemes discussed in Chapters 2–6. These organisms are the acetic acid bacteria, the lactic acid bacteria, and the pseudomonads, which are discussed in separate chapters in which only material supplementary to the general schemes has been added.

Bacterial metabolism, however, does not only comprise the carbon compounds but also, in some instances, nitrogenous compounds as energy sources. The last chapter, therefore, is devoted to the main events in this field.

In compiling this work, I am well aware that I may have overlooked publications or information not at my disposal. Criticism, information, or suggestions will, therefore, be very much appreciated.

I am deeply indebted to all those who helped me in the preparation of this book. The critical evaluation of the organization by my graduate and post-graduate students, in particular by Mr. G. J. Manderson, and of the text by Professor V. B. D. Skerman and Dr. I. C. MacRae are very much appreciated. Professor V. B. D. Skerman also gave valuable assistance not only in editorial but also in taxonomic problems. I would like to thank publishers and authors for permission to reproduce material, and all those who gave additional prepublished information. The valuable help of Mr. G. Heys in collecting the material, of Miss Barbara Heron in typing and correcting the manuscript, and of the photography section of the university is gratefully acknowledged.

Finally, I wish to express my sincere gratitude to Academic Press, who made this publication possible.

H. W. DOELLE

October, 1968

CONTENTS

BACTERIAL METABOLISM

1

THERMODYNAMICS OF BIOLOGICAL REACTIONS

FREE ENERGY

THERMODYNAMICS OF CHEMICAL REACTIONS

To synthesize the major chemical constituents of a living cell, microorganisms require a source of energy. Under normal cultural conditions, namely, an aqueous environment with a pH being almost neutral and relatively low temperatures, only energy-yielding (exergonic) reactions $(-\Delta F)$ can take place spontaneously. Synthetic reactions are endergonic. To synthesize new cell material, the individual chemical reactions involved must be linked or coupled with energy-yielding reactions. This is normally achieved through particular energy-rich compounds, several different types of which occur in microorganisms:

(1) derivatives of phosphoric acid, adenosine triphosphate (ATP), uridine triphosphate (UTP), acyl phosphates, and inorganic polyphosphates, and

(2) derivatives of carboxylic acids such as acetyl coenzyme A.

Before proceeding to investigate the mechanisms by which metabolic energy is generated in microorganisms, an appreciation of the basic principles of free energy is necessary.

The study of energy transactions is based upon thermodynamics, and it is only possible to explain and understand these transactions in terms of thermodynamics. To many students the field of thermodynamics often appears rather abstract because its principles are usually developed with idealized systems. However, the working philosophy and the approach taken by thermodynamicists are really very simple and logical and do not require special knowledge in chemistry or molecular theory. Apart from this, it is only necessary to deal with a small part of thermodynamic formalism in order to examine the nature of biological energy transfer. Thermodynamics deals with the properties of systems and with the changes in these properties when the system changes from one state into another. By properties such attributes as volume, pressure, temperature, and density are meant.

First and Second Law of Thermodynamics. All events in the physical world conform to and are determined by the two fundamental principles of thermodynamics known as the first and second law of thermodynamics(10):

First law: The total amount of energy in nature is constant.

Second law: The total amount of entropy in nature is increasing.

Energy is the term used to designate all forms of work and heat, whereas entropy may for the moment be described as disorder or randomness.

The first stage in analysis of energy changes is to specify exactly the collection of matter in which one wants to study these changes during some physical or chemical process. This collection of matter is generally called "the system." All other matter apart from the one studied is called "the surroundings." The next stage is to specify the total energy content of the system before the process takes place, which is called the "initial state," and then again after the process has taken place, which is called its "final state." As the system proceeds from its initial to its final state it may either absorb energy from or deliver energy to its surroundings. The difference in the energy content of the system during its process from initial to final state must, of course, be counterbalanced by a corresponding and inverse change in the energy content of the surroundings. In order to describe the total energy content of any isolated system, either in the initial or final state, the relevant macroscopic properties of the system such as pressure, volume, temperature, composition, and heat content must be specified by means of an equation called "the equation of state," which requires that the system be in equilibrium. In thermodynamics only the initial and final states matter, the pathway taken by the process being irrelevant.

Whereas the thermodynamics of chemical reactions in equilibrium are not primarily concerned with the time of the process, the newer field of thermodynamics of reactions which are not in equilibrium or are irreversible are concerned with time and rates.

When the thermodynamicist studies energy changes during a process he tries to reduce the number of variables to as few as possible. If, for example, volume or pressure or temperature of a system is held constant, it becomes easier to specify exactly the changes in energy content in going from the initial to the final state. This is the case in biological reactions, which normally take place in dilute aqueous solution under conditions where not just one but three of the most important variables—temperature, volume, and pressure—are all constant throughout the system. We can therefore leave aside the large part of thermodynamics which deals with gases, solids, and pressure–volume changes.

The first law of thermodynamics is essentially the law of conservation of energy. The most familiar form of energy is heat. Virtually every physical or chemical process either absorbs heat from or delivers heat to its surroundings. When a process occurs with loss of heat, it is called "exothermic" or "exergonic," and when it occurs with absorption of heat, it is called "endothermic" or "endergonic." Such transfer of heat or energy can take place only when there is a difference in temperature between the systems and the surroundings. Heat can only flow from a warmer to a cooler body.

If we take now an isolated system of a given energy content and give the symbol q to heat, the principle of conservation of energy says that the heat added to the system must appear as a "change in the internal energy" (ΔE) of the system, or in the amount of total work w done by the system on the surroundings. ΔE or w may be 0.

$$q = \Delta E + w \quad \text{or} \quad \Delta E = q - w$$

In many instances the addition of energy as heat to the system may result in a change of volume, the pressure remaining constant. This change $P\Delta V$ is a form of work.

$$\Delta E = q - P\Delta V - w'$$

where w' is useful work. Rarely is $P\Delta V$ a useful form of work, and it has been found convenient to combine it with ΔE so that

$$\Delta E + P\Delta V = q - w'$$

In chemical reactions occurring at constant pressure, the heat change ($\Delta E + P\Delta V$) is therefore called the "enthalpy change" and given the symbol ΔH.

$$\Delta H = q - w'$$
$$= \Delta E + P\Delta V$$

If the reaction occurs not only under constant pressure but also at constant volume, which means no work is done, then

$$\Delta H = \Delta E$$

The enthalpy change ΔH of a reaction is easily measured by direct calorimetry. The heat change of a chemical reaction under conditions of constant temperature and pressure can therefore give valuable information about the magnitude of the total energy change in this reaction. Each chemical reaction proceeds to completion with a definite heat of reaction, which is quantitatively related to the number of molecules reacting. The heat given off in the combustion of an organic compound such as glucose, will raise the temperature of the surrounding water in the jacket of the calorimeter to a degree that depends on the amount of water in the jacket and the number of molecules of glucose combusted. From such measurements, one can determine the molar enthalpy as

$$\Delta H = -673,000 \text{ cal/mole}$$

The negative sign indicates an exergonic reaction. A calorie is the amount of energy required to raise the temperature of one gram of water from 14.5° to 15.5°C. Heat is produced during combustion because complex organic molecules have a large potential energy of configuration and are degraded to simple, stable products, such as CO_2 and water, which have a much lower energy content. From elementary physics one knows that there exists an equivalence between heat and work, the so-called mechanical equivalence of heat. This "equivalence" suggests that heat and mechanical work are easily interconvertible, which, of course, is not the case. Mechanical work can be completely converted into heat, but the reverse process in practice is never complete. In biological systems, heat is not a useful way of transferring energy since the different components of living organisms are essentially isothermal. If there is no temperature differential at all, heat cannot be converted into work under any circumstances.

Spontaneous physical or chemical changes have a direction which cannot be explained by the first law of thermodynamics. All systems tend toward the equilibrium state in which temperature, pressure, and all other measurable parameters of state become uniform throughout. Once they reach such an equilibrium they no longer change back spontaneously to the nonuniform state.

One therefore comes to the second law of thermodynamics, which:

(1) defines entropy as a randomized state of energy that is unavailable to do work,
(2) states that all physical and chemical processes proceed in such a way that the entropy of the system becomes the maximum possible, at which point there is an equilibrium, and
(3) states that entropy or randomness in the universe always increases in irreversible processes. Under no circumstances does the entropy of the universe ever decrease.

Theoretically it is possible that the entropy of a system may remain constant during a process, whereby the process is reversible. Real processes are nearly always irreversible because they are usually accompanied by friction, which always leads to an increase in entropy. Entropy is expressed in calories per mole degree. At any given temperature, solids have relatively low entropy, liquids an intermediate amount, and gases the highest entropy. The gaseous state is the most disordered and chaotic state. Since there is great thermal motion with an increase of temperature, it is absolutely necessary to specify temperature when one specifies entropy changes. The entropy S is that fraction of the enthalpy, which may not be utilized for the performance of useful work, since, in most cases, it has increased the random motions of the molecules in the system. The product $T \times S$, in which T is the absolute temperature, represents energy that is wasted in the form of random molecule motions. In terms of S, the second law states that given the opportunity, any system will undergo spontaneous change in that direction which results in an increase in entropy. Equilibrium is attained when entropy has reached a maximum, and no further change may occur spontaneously unless additional energy is supplied from outside the system.

Since heat represents the kinetic energy of random molecular motion, the addition of heat increases the entropy. If the system is at equilibrium

$$q = T\Delta S$$

If the system is not at equilibrium, however, changes in the system may spontaneously increase the entropy even without addition of heat

$$T\Delta S > q$$

If one combines the equations for the first and the second law for a system at equilibrium, one finds that

$$\Delta H = T\Delta S - w'$$

The main interests in biological reactions, however, are in reactions proceeding in the direction which approaches equilibrium and at a single temperature. For such systems

$$\Delta H < T\Delta S - w'$$

The tendency to seek the position of maximum entropy is the driving force of all processes, and heat is either given up or absorbed by the system from the surroundings to allow the system plus surroundings to reach the state of maximum entropy. These changes of heat and entropy are related by a third dimension of energy: free energy.

Free Energy Change. The free energy of a system is denoted by the symbol F, although most textbooks of physical chemistry use the symbol G, after Willard Gibbs, the founder of chemical thermodynamics(19). It is a property of the system, which means it depends only upon the state of the system and not the path by which that state was reached. When the system undergoes a change of state, which takes place in most chemical reactions, a change in free energy occurs. It is in these changes in free energy rather than the absolute free energies of reactants and products that we are interested. Such a change is denoted by ΔF. Free energy is thus "useful" energy, whereas entropy is "degraded" energy. In general, the change in free energy, ΔF, is the energy that becomes available to be utilized for the accomplishment of work as a system *proceeds toward* equilibrium. For a process at a single temperature

$$\Delta F = \Delta H - T\Delta S$$

This is the form in which the laws of thermodynamics are most readily expressed for the description of biochemical systems. For such a system that is not at equilibrium

$$\Delta F = -w' \quad \text{(since} \quad \Delta H = T\Delta S - w')$$

Hence, systems not at equilibrium proceed spontaneously only in the direction of negative free energy changes.

In a chemical as in any other kind of system there is always a tendency for free energy to decrease when any change takes place in the system. A chemical change that is accompanied by a fall of free energy may therefore proceed spontaneously. However, in most biological systems, the reaction may need catalysis to proceed at a measurable rate (see section entitled "Enzymes," this chapter). On the other hand, a reaction involving an increase of free energy can only proceed if it is coupled to a suitable source of free energy. Chemical reactions in general are most commonly exothermic. The heat evolved during an exothermic process, however, does not correspond to the change in free energy. In an ordinary chemical reaction one can measure only ΔH directly. The determination of free energy ΔF depends upon accurate measurements of the equilibrium constant K of a reversible reaction.

The equilibrium constant K is the product of the active masses of the reaction products divided by the products of the active masses of reactants at equilibrium. For the reaction

$$A + B \rightleftharpoons C + D$$

the constant K can be calculated as follows

$$K = \frac{[C] \times [D]}{[A] \times [B]}$$

The more vigorously the reaction between substances A and B proceeds, the greater will be the proportion of reaction products in the equilibrium mixture and also the equilibrium constant K. One can then say that the reaction mixture possesses a high potential energy. During the course of the reaction this potential energy is reduced. Since this energy change is related quantitatively to the equilibrium constant, the constant K must be a mathematical function of the free energy change of the components of the reaction. This function can be expressed as

$$\Delta F^\circ = -RT \ln K$$

where R is the gas constant (1.987 cal/mole degree), T is the absolute temperature, and $\ln K$ is the natural logarithm of the equilibrium constant. The superscript "$\circ$" indicates the standard free energy change less the gain or loss of free energy in calories as one mole of the reactant is converted to one mole of product under conditions where each is maintained in its standard state. Since most biological reactions occur at or near pH 7.0, the symbol $\Delta F'$ is used to indicate the standard free energy change at pH 7.0. A chemical reaction is thermodynamically possible then if it is exothermic, i.e., is attended by a decrease of free energy. Whether or not it actually takes place, however, depends upon other factors. A body will not slide down a rough plane if the "frictional forces" are greater than the forces exerted by its free gravitational potential energy. Similarly, a chemical reaction can take place if it entails a fall of free energy, but it will not actually do so if the frictional forces tending to oppose it are too large. A chemical reaction requires for its accomplishment that the molecules shall be in a reactive state. Only those molecules with a high-energy content are likely to react to form the product. In order to make the reaction proceed one must raise the energy content of the entire population of molecules so that the activation energy barrier is overcome. Then the reaction proceeds quickly to its equilibrium. One way of doing this is to heat the mixture. In biological systems, however, enzymes, in their function as catalysts, take care of this requirement. The catalyst or enzyme lowers the activation energy of the reaction by allowing a much larger fraction of the molecular population to react at any one time. The catalyst can do this because it can form an unstable intermediate complex or compound with the substrate, which quickly decomposes to the product and thus provides a channel through the barrier which represents the activation energy. Once this channel of low activation energy is found, the reaction proceeds rapidly. Enzymes, however, merely accelerate the approach to equilibrium but do not influence the equilibrium point attained. The free energy change is the same whether the reaction is catalyzed by the enzyme or occurs slowly by itself, since time and rate do not enter into the calculation, only the final state. It follows from this that catalysts can only initiate and/or accelerate a reaction that is thermodynamically possible. As an example of a practical calculation of the equilibrium constant and the free energy change of a chemical reaction (19) consider the following:

Glucose 1-phosphate $\leftrightharpoons$ glucose 6-phosphate

is catalyzed by the enzyme phosphoglucomutase (α-D-glucose 1,6-diphosphate: α-D-glucose 1-phosphate phosphotransferase, E.C. 2.7.5.1.). If the reaction is started by adding the enzyme to 0.02 M glucose 1-phosphate solution at 25°C and at pH 7.0, it is found by chemical analysis that the reaction proceeds to an equilibrium at which the final concentration of glucose 1-phosphate is 0.001 M, whereas the final concentration of glucose 6-phosphate has risen from zero to 0.019 M. If one assumes that these measured concentrations are equal to the thermodynamically active masses,

$$K = \frac{[\text{glucose 6-phosphate}]}{[\text{glucose 1-phosphate}]}$$

Having the K value, one can calculate the standard free energy change of the above reaction:

$$\Delta F' = -RT\ln K$$

$$= -1.987 \times 298 \times \ln 19$$

$$= -1.987 \times 298 \times 2.303 \log_{10} 19$$

$$= -1745 \text{ cal/mole}$$

One has, in other words, a decline in free energy of 1745 cal when 1.0 mole of glucose 1-phosphate is converted to 1.0 mole of glucose 6-phosphate at 25°C.

Chemical reactions in living organisms, however, are in characteristically organized sequences called "metabolic pathways." These sequences have to be dealt with as a whole, i.e., the summation of the individual free energy steps:

$$A + B \overset{-6000}{\rightleftharpoons} C + D$$

$$D + E \overset{-4000}{\rightleftharpoons} G + H$$

$$H + I \overset{+3000}{\rightleftharpoons} J + K$$

The theoretical feasibility of the over-all reaction, from $A + B$ to $J + K$ can be assessed by algebraic summation of the individual free energy (ΔF) changes (e.g., $-6000 - 4000 + 3000 = -7000$ cal/mole of A). The whole sequence will therefore tend to move spontaneously from left to right. This example shows quite clearly why the microbial chemist should be familiar with the free energy changes of reactions. They can provide him with a rough check upon the accuracy of his idea about metabolic pathways. No system of coupled reactions will proceed spontaneously unless $\Delta F'$ is negative for the overall system. What happens now to the free energy, 7000 cal/mole of A, which is left? In a normal chemical reaction it is evolved as heat and is lost from the system to its surroundings. In biological systems, however, this need not be the case, as exergonic processes may be coupled or connected to endergonic processes so that the former delivers energy to the latter. In such coupled systems, the endergonic process will take place only if the decline in free energy of the exergonic process to which it is coupled is larger than the gain in free energy of the endergonic process. The algebraic sum of these processes must always be negative if the reaction sequences are to proceed.

The sequential steps in the oxidation of an organic substrate are aimed at the gradual liberation of energy which is either used directly in an endergonic reaction or is stored for subsequent release at a later stage of the pathway.

The most important mechanism of storage is the formation of an energy-rich intermediate. This compound has the role of conserving the free energy not as heat but as chemical energy. Of these energy carriers the most important is adenosine triphosphate (ATP), which is the carrier of chemical energy from the energy-yielding oxidation to those processes or reactions of the cell which cannot occur spontaneously and can proceed only if chemical energy is supplied. Adenosine triphosphate is formed from adenosine diphosphate (ADP) in coupled reactions. The many chemical steps in the charging and discharging of the ATP system in the cell are catalyzed by enzyme systems. The few examples given indicate that the concept of free energy plays a most important role in biological systems.

OXIDATIONS AND REDUCTIONS

Energy-yielding reactions within organisms are of the nature of oxidations. Oxidation may be defined in general as the loss of electrons and reductions as the gain of electrons. The oxidation of molecular hydrogen can therefore be expressed as

$$H_2 - 2e^- = 2H^+$$

The electrons from this oxidation must be accepted by an oxidizing agent. If one uses, for example, a ferric salt, the equation becomes

$$H_2 - 2e^- = 2H^+$$
$$\frac{2Fe^{3+} + 2e^- = 2Fe^{2+}}{H_2 + 2Fe^{3+} = 2H^+ + 2Fe^{2+}}$$

Molecular oxygen can act as an oxidizing agent, in a similar manner, picking up either two or four electrons

$$O_2 + 2e^- = O_2^{2-} \overset{+2H^+}{\underset{}{\rightleftharpoons}} H_2O_2$$

$$O_2 + 4e^- = 2O^{2-} \overset{+4H^+}{\underset{}{\rightleftharpoons}} 2H_2O$$

$$\Delta F = -57\,kcal/mole\,H_2O$$

According to modern theory, an electric current is essentially a transfer of electrons[21]. It should therefore be possible to obtain direct proof of the transfer of electricity in oxidation–reduction reactions under suitable experimental conditions.

When a pure zinc rod is immersed in distilled water, some of the zinc ionizes

$$Zn \rightleftharpoons Zn^{2+} + 2e^-$$

whereby Zn^{2+} passes into the solution and the freed electrons accumulate on the metal. The function of electrostatic forces is, however, responsible for the attraction of Zn^{2+} to the negatively charged electrons, which arranges the ions around the electrode in form of a boundary layer. Between the electrode and this boundary layer of ions exists therefore a certain difference of potential. If the distilled water is now replaced by a normal solution of a soluble zinc salt, such as zinc sulfate, the reaction would be driven to the left and a new equilibrium established between the electrode and the solution. The potential difference, which now exists between the zinc electrode and the normal solution of zinc ions is termed the "standard electrode potential" of zinc.

In a similar manner, if hydrogen gas at normal atmospheric pressure is adsorbed onto the surface of finely divided platinum and immersed in a normal solution of hydrochloric acid a *standard hydrogen electrode* is produced.

It is not possible to determine the absolute potential difference of either of these electrodes since they represent only half-cell reactions. When two half-cells are coupled, the electromotive force (emf) of the cell is the algebraic difference of the potentials of the two half-cells with the sign removed. By convention(6), the potential of the standard hydrogen electrode is equal to zero *at all temperatures*. Consequently, the potential of any other electrode system can then be determined with reference to the normal hydrogen electrode.

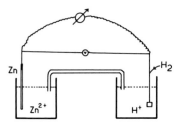

FIG. 1.1. An electrolytic cell consisting of a Zn and a H_2 half-cell.

If hydrogen and zinc electrodes are connected as in Fig. 1.1 the voltmeter will register the emf in volts, and the null point ammeter will indicate the direction of current flow (the reverse of the direction of electron flow). As the hydrogen potential is arbitrarily set at zero, the voltmeter measures equally arbitrarily the potential difference between the zinc and its ions. The sign which is placed before this potential difference is determined by the direction of the electron flow. Electrons will only flow from a place of low potential to one of high potential (from one potential to a more positive potential). Since the current flows from the hydrogen electrode to the zinc electrode, the electron flow is from the zinc to the hydrogen electrode. The potential difference between the zinc and its ions is more negative than that of the hydrogen and its ions and therefore carries a negative sign. Therefore, in this case

$$E_h(Zn \rightleftharpoons Zn^{2+}) = -0.77 \text{ V}$$

where E_h is the electrode potential with reference to the hydrogen electrode.

Although it is correct only to refer to the potential difference between a metal and its ions, the convention assigns the potential to the metal. One refers therefore to the "potential of the zinc electrode." This potential, however, varies with the concentration of the ions in solution. When the activity of the ion Zn^{2+} is equal to unity (approximately true for a 1 M solution), the electrode potential E_h is equal to the standard potential E_0.

In E_h the subscript "h" indicates a comparison with the standard hydrogen electrode. A standard hydrogen electrode, however, is very difficult to manipulate. It is therefore common to determine electrode potentials on the hydrogen scale indirectly by measuring the emf of a cell formed from the electrode in question and a convenient reference electrode whose potential with respect to the hydrogen electrode is accurately known. The reference electrodes generally used are the calomel electrode and the silver-silver chloride electrode. If the saturated calomel electrode with an $E_h = +0.246$ was substituted as a reference electrode, the emf between the zinc electrode and this reference electrode would be

$$-0.77 - (+0.246) = 1.046 \text{ V}$$

and would be expressed by

$$E_{s.c.e.}(Zn \rightleftharpoons Zn^{2+}) = -1.046 \text{ V}$$

since the ionization of zinc results in a loss of electrons, Zn^{2+} may thus be regarded as the oxidized form of zinc and the metal as the reduced form of zinc. The potential difference E between the zinc and its ions is expressed by the Nernst equation

$$E_h = E_0 + \frac{RT}{nF} \ln \frac{A_{ox}}{A_{red}}$$

where E_0 is the standard electrode potential, R is the gas constant equal to 8.314 J/degree/mole, T is the absolute temperature, n represents the valency of the ions involved in the reaction, F is the Faraday constant (equal to 96,494 C), which is necessary to convert one equivalent of an element to an equivalent of ions and A_{ox} and A_{red} are the activities of the oxidized and reduced forms of the oxidation–reduction system.

Where a metal ion exists in two oxidation states (e.g., ferric and ferrous ions) in solution, a potential difference exists between the two. If an inert electrode such as platinum is immersed in an oxygen-free solution of ferric and ferrous ions, electrons will accumulate on the metal and if coupled to a hydrogen electrode, electrons will flow from the hydrogen half-cell to the iron half-cell. This direction of electron flow indicates that the potential of the former is lower than that of the latter. Similarly, electrons would flow from a Zn/Zn^{2+} electrode to an Fe^{2+}/Fe^{3+} electrode.

In biological oxidation–reduction systems the interactions are governed by the same laws.

At 30°C, which is the temperature frequently employed for electrode measurements, the factor 2.303 RT/nF (converting natural logarithm to the base 10) has a value of 0.06 for $n = 1$ and 0.03 for $n = 2$. Thus, for $n = 1$

$$E_h = E_0 + 0.06 \log \frac{A_{ox}}{A_{red}}$$

When the activity of the oxidant and reductant are the same, the expression

$$+0.06 \log \frac{A_{ox}}{A_{red}} = 0$$

and

$$E_h = E_0$$

The standard electrode potential is therefore the potential of an electrode in equilibrium with a unit activity of its ions. In the case of an oxidation–reduction system involving a solution of two ions at different oxidation states, E_0 will be the potential at which the ratio of the activities of the two is one. This value is characteristic for each oxidation–reduction system and gives a measure of the relative ability of that system to accept or donate electrons in oxidation–reduction reactions; i.e., it has nothing to do with their concentration except insofar as concentration affects the activity. The redox potential is therefore a measure of oxidizing (or reducing) intensity and not capacity. The quantity of electrons which could be transferred would be dependent on the concentration of the components of the redox system.

If one examines the variations of E_0 for $Fe^{2+} - Fe^{3+}$ systems as a function of pH of the solution, it will be found that E_0 is the same over a wide range. Such constancy, however, is not found in systems in which hydrogen ions enter into the overall chemical reaction where the value varies with the pH.

Direct measurements of standard potentials are difficult to obtain because of the uncertainty of the exact concentration of the substances involved or the slowness of the establishment of equilibrium with the inert metal of the electrode (9).

Measurements of the Standard Potentials when Exact Concentration of the Substances Involved Are Uncertain. The pure oxidized form (100% oxidized and 0% reduced) of the system (e.g., a quinone) is first dissolved in a solution of definite hydrogen ion concentration such as a buffer solution. Known amounts of a reducing solution are then added in the absence of oxygen and the solution is kept agitated by means of a nitrogen stream. The potential of an inert electrode (e.g., platinum or gold) immersed in the reacting solution is measured after each addition of the titrant. The point at which the potential undergoes a rapid change is that corresponding to complete reduction, and the quantity of reducing solution (X_c) then added is equivalent to the whole of the oxidized organic compound originally present (see Fig. 1.2). From the amounts of reducing agent added at various stages the corresponding ratios

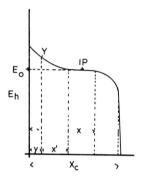

FIG. 1.2. A potentiometric titration curve.

of the concentrations of the oxidized form (A_{ox}) to the reduced form (A_{red}) may be calculated and from these the standard potential is derived for several values:

$$E_h = E_0 - \frac{RT}{nF} \ln \frac{(A_{ox})}{(A_{red})}$$

$$= E_0 - \frac{RT}{nF} \ln \frac{X_c - X}{X}$$

When a system is partially reduced the extent of reduction can be determined without any knowledge of the concentration of the reducing agent employed for titration provided the E_0 of the system is known.

Referring to Fig. 1.2 the initial point in the titration may be taken as point Y on the oxidation–reduction curve—equivalent to y ml of reductant. The curve is plotted commencing at Y with progressive additions of reductant. After the addition of X^1 ml of reductant

$$E_h = E_0 - \frac{RT}{nF} \ln \frac{(A_{ox})}{(A_{red})}$$

$$= E_0 - \frac{RT}{nF} \ln \frac{[X_c - (X^1 + y)]}{[X^1 + y]}$$

where the values of E_h, E_0, ($X_c - y$) and X^1 are known and y can be derived.

When the value of E_0 is not known for the system under investigation, and the initial state of reduction is not too great, the value of E_0 may be read from the inflection point (IP). From the value of X^1 at IP the value

$M[= X_c - (X^1 + y)]$ represents 50% reduction and

$$\frac{M - X^1}{2M} \times \frac{100}{1}$$

gives the percentage initial reduction.

Direct Measurements of the Standard Potentials in Relation to the Slowness of the Establishment of Equilibrium. The slower the equilibrium is obtainable the greater may be the error in measuring potential. This sluggishness of a system can be altered by accelerating the process with an electromotively active system which is called the "potential mediator." These mediators have been very useful in studying systems that are quite inactive by themselves. The mediator used should have a midpoint potential approximate to that of the mediated system. When active and inactive systems come to an equilibrium, the two systems should have the same potentials for the conditions used. It is therefore essential that the mediator system is well chosen and is not converted by the system too far toward 100% oxidation or reduction and should itself not be of sufficient concentration to materially alter the state of oxidation of the system being measured. Oxidation–reduction indicators have been used frequently as mediators since their color changes are helpful in rapidly selecting the mediator and their potentials are fairly well established.

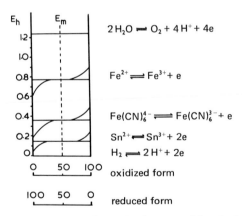

FIG. 1.3. The relation between oxidation–reduction potential and relative concentration of oxidized and reduced forms (19) (reprinted with permission of the authors and Cambridge Univ. Press).

A number of curves obtained by potentiometric titration are presented in Fig. 1.3. The position of the curve on the oxidation–reduction scale depends on the standard potential of the system, which corresponds to 50% reduction, while its slope is determined by the number of electrons by which the oxidized and reduced states differ. The majority of biological systems involve either a one or a two electron change and the potentials vary by 0.06 and 0.03 V, respectively, for each 10-fold change in ratio of oxidant to reductant.

The midpoint at 50% reduction is designated by E_m, the subscript "m" being a reminder of midpoint. A number of authors also use the designation E_0'.

TABLE 1.1

ELECTRODE POTENTIALS OF SOME O–R SYSTEMS[a]

	$E_0'(V)$	pH
H_2O/O_2	0.82	7.0
NO_2^-/NO_3^-	0.42	7.0
$H_2O_2/O_2 + H_2O$	0.30	7.0
Cytochrome a Fe^{2+}/Fe^{3+}	0.29	7.0
Cytochrome c Fe^{2+}/Fe^{3+}	0.22	7.0
Butyryl CoA/crotonyl CoA	0.19	7.0
Cytochrome b_2 Fe^{2+}/Fe^{3+}	0.12	7.4
Ubiquinone (red/ox)	0.10	7.4
Ascorbic acid/dehydroascorbic acid	0.08	6.4
Cytochrome b Fe^{2+}/Fe^{3+}	0.07	7.4
Succinic/fumaric acid	0.03	7.0
Methylene blue (red/ox)	0.01	7.0
Glutamic/α-oxoglutaric acid + NH_4	−0.14	7.0
Malic/oxalacetic acid	−0.17	7.0
Lactic/pyruvic acid	−0.19	7.0
Ethanol/acetaldehyde	−0.20	7.0
$NADH + H^+/NAD^+$	−0.32	7.0
Acetaldehyde + CoA/acetyl CoA	−0.41	7.0
H_2/H^+	−0.42	7.0
α-Oxoglutaric acid/succinic acid + CO_2	−0.67	7.0
Pyruvic acid/acetic acid + CO_2	−0.70	7.0

[a] From White et al. (22). Reprinted with permission of the authors and McGraw-Hill Book Co.

As the values for E_m vary in systems which vary with the hydrogen ion concentration (H^+), the particular pH is signified by the addition of a corresponding number, e.g., E_{m7} signifies the potential at 50% reduction at pH 7.0. The Nernst equation therefore in oxidation–reduction potential measurements would be

$$E_h = E_m \frac{RT}{nF} \ln \frac{[A_{ox}]}{[A_{red}]}$$

When reducing the oxidized form of one reversible system with the reduced form of another (or vice versa) the accuracy of the end point will be determined by the relative values of the E_m of each system. The potential before the equivalence point is determined by the titrated system since this is present in excess, and the potential after the equivalence point is determined by the titrant system. Where the respective standard potentials (midpoints) are reasonably far apart, a high accuracy can be assumed. The standard potentials should differ by at least 0.35 V if n is unity for both systems, 0.26 V if n is unity for one and two for the other, or 0.18 V if n is two for both.

Since E_m (E_0') is a measure of the oxidation or reduction intensity of a system, it is possible to draw up a list of oxidation–reduction (O–R) systems in order of their standard electrode potentials. Any given system will be theoretically capable of being oxidized by a system more positive and will in turn be reduced by any system more negative than itself (Table 1.1).

Energy Relations in Oxidative Reactions

Since oxidative reactions yield energy, some quantitative aspects of oxidative changes in relation to energy production will be considered.

It was stated earlier that the standard free energy change, in calories per mole, may be calculated from the equilibrium state in determining the equilibrium constant K. This determination of K depends on the availability of adequate analytical methods for the various components. When the difference in potential $\Delta E_0'$ between the two systems is large, equilibrium may lie so far in one direction that an accurate determination of the final concentration of the compound to be oxidized may be impossible. The free energy change associated with this reaction may, however, be calculated from the knowledge of the potentials of the two reacting systems

$$\Delta E_0' = (RT/nF)\ln K \quad \text{or} \quad nF\,\Delta E_0' = RT\ln K$$

Since
$$-\Delta F^\circ = RT\ln K \quad -\Delta F^\circ = nF\,\Delta E_0'$$

where ΔF° is the standard free energy of the reaction, n is the number of electrons (or hydrogen ions) involved, F is the Faraday constant (96,500 C), and $\Delta E_0'$ is the difference between the E_0' values of the two systems. The units of $F\,\Delta E_0'$ are coulomb-volts or joules, which can be converted to the usual units of free energy, since 4.18 J equal 1 gm-cal. The value obtained for ΔF° is that for the oxidation of one mole of reductant.

Example 1: Malate is oxidized to oxalacetate by cytochrome c under circumstances such that equimolar concentrations of each of the reactants initially exist. Since the E_0' value of the malate–oxalacetate system is −0.17 V and of the cytochrome c–reduced cytochrome c is 0.22 V:

$$\Delta F^\circ = -nF\,\Delta E_0'$$

$$= \frac{-2 \times 96,500 \times [0.22 - (-0.17)]}{4.18}$$

$$= -18,007 \text{ cal}$$

Theoretically, if molecular oxygen were substituted for cytochrome c, $-45,715$ cal would be released since the E_0' for the reduction of oxygen is $+0.82$ V. This amount of energy could then be available under physiological circumstances for doing useful work.

Example 2: Lactate + acetaldehyde $\rightleftharpoons$ pyruvate + ethanol. At pH 7.0, E_0' for the lactate/pyruvate system is -0.19 V and for the ethanol/acetaldehyde system is -0.20 V:

$$\Delta F° = -nF \Delta E_0'$$

For this reaction $n = 2$, and

$$\Delta E_0' = -0.20 - (-0.19)$$
$$= +0.01 \text{ V}$$

Hence
$$\Delta F° = \frac{-2 \times 96,500 \times 0.01}{4.18}$$
$$= 461.72 \text{ cal}$$

Energy Storage and Release

Within cells a mechanism exists by means of which the free energy available from oxidation reactions may be utilized to drive endergonic processes. This is done largely by trapping this energy through the formation of a special class of phosphate compounds. The terminal phosphate group of ATP may be transferred to a second molecule, a so-called phosphate acceptor, leaving behind ADP. The function of this reversible reaction will now be considered.

When ATP was first isolated from muscle, it was suspected to have something to do with the energy of muscle contraction. It was later found that when ATP is incubated with muscle fibres it undergoes enzymatic hydrolysis with the formation of ADP and inorganic phosphate

$$\text{ATP}^{4-} + H_2O \rightarrow \text{ADP}^{3-} + HPO_4^{2-} + H^+$$

During this hydrolysis a considerable amount of heat was liberated; since the free energy change of a chemical reaction can be determined from its equilibrium constant, by measuring this constant of enzymatic reaction in which the terminal phosphate group of ATP is transferred, an approximate value for the free energy change of hydrolysis of ATP has been obtained. If only one phosphate group is hydrolyzed, the free energy of hydrolysis of ATP at pH 7.0 and 25°C is

$$\Delta F° = -7000 \text{ cal/mole}$$

under standard conditions. It is, however, unlikely that this value of -7000 cal/mole represents the actual free energy released during the hydrolysis of ATP within the intact cell, because ADP and ATP are not present in the cell in equimolar concentrations. Furthermore, certain metal ions such as Mg^{2+} are able to shift the equilibrium of ATP hydrolysis. If one makes appropriate corrections(17), a free energy value of 12,000 cal/mole would be more likely. The free energy of ATP hydrolysis is significantly higher than that of simple esters or glycosides. This is one of the reasons why ATP has been called a high-energy phosphate compound. Why then does the equilibrium of ATP hydrolysis lie farther in the direction of completion than do those of so-called low-energy compounds? Briefly, the larger the equilibrium constant, the greater the decrease in the quantity of free energy. There are two basic features of the ATP molecule which endow it with a relatively high free energy of hydrolysis; both are properties of the highly charged polyphosphate structure (see Scheme 1.1). The chemical structure reveals three kinds of building blocks.

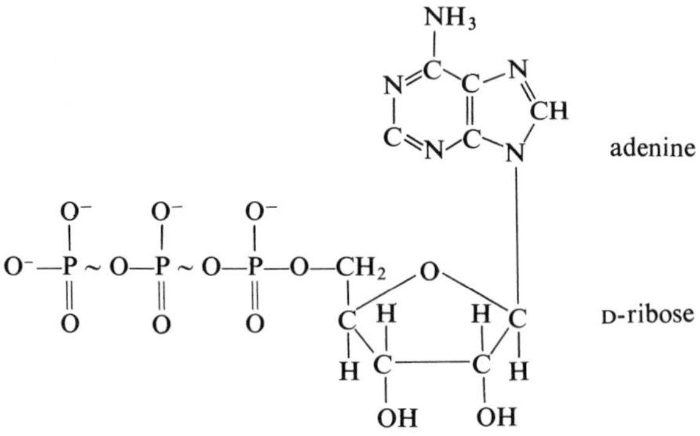

adenosine triphosphate (ATP)

SCHEME 1.1

First, there is a heterocyclic aromatic ring structure, called adenine, which is a derivative of 6-aminopurine. Attached to this base through a glycosidic linkage is a molecule of the five-carbon sugar D-ribose, to which is attached a phosphate group in ester linkage at the 5' position thus constituting adenosine monophosphate (AMP). This compound can contain a second (ADP) and a third (ATP) phosphate group in anhydric linkage with the 5'-phosphate, whereby the third phosphate group is in linear anhydric linkage to the second group. All these compounds fall into the category of mononucleotides, which occur in each microbial cell. At pH 7.0 the linear polyphosphate structure of ATP has four negative charges which are very close to each other and which also repel each other very strongly. When the terminal phosphate bond is hydrolyzed, some of this electrostatic stress is relieved. Once ADP^{3-} and phosphate^{2-} ions are separated they will have very little tendency to approach each other again because of the electrostatic repulsion. Low-energy phosphate bonds, on the other hand, have no such repulsive force at pH 7.0 between the products of hydrolysis, because one of these normally has no charge at all. In the case of ATP hydrolysis new arrangements of the electrons of the products is made as soon as the bond is broken. One product has a much lower energy content. This resonance stabilization of the hydrolysis is a major reason for the relatively high free energy of hydrolysis of this class of phosphate esters. It is quite common to use the term "high-energy phosphate bonds" for such bonds which are universally designated by the symbol ~P. Lehninger (17) warns, however, that this term may be taken wrongly and may be misleading. It implies that the energy spoken of is in the bond and that when the bond is split, energy is set free. In physical chemistry, the term "bond energy" means the energy required to break a given bond between two atoms. In other words, the free energy of hydrolysis is not localized in the actual chemical bond itself. In using the term "high-energy bond" as stated above, one should be aware that it means only that the difference in energy content between the reactants and product of hydrolysis is relatively high.

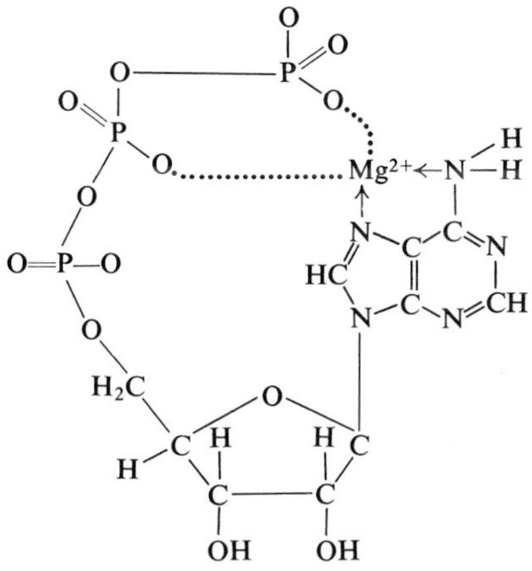

SCHEME 1.2

The ATP molecule as it exists in the intact cell is highly charged. At pH 7.0 each of the three phosphate groups is completely ionized so that ATP bears four negative charges. This fact leads to the assumption that ATP forms stable, soluble complexes with certain divalent cations such as Mg^{2+} and Ca^{2+} (see Scheme 1.2). This feature of ATP can also be related to its ability to act as an energy carrier. Because of this complex formation very little free ATP anion exists as such in the cell. This geometrical structure is of importance insofar as the enzymes that make and use ATP have active sites to which the ATP structure must fit exactly in order to be functional.

Reference to Table 1.2 makes one wonder why ATP is so unique if it is only one of many high-energy compounds in the cell, some of which have even greater free energy of hydrolysis than ATP. Generally speaking, it is the whole function of the ATP–ADP system to act as an intermediate bridge or linking system between phosphate compounds having a high transfer capacity, and other compounds having a low transfer capacity. Adenosine diphosphate serves in other words as the specific enzymatic acceptor of phosphate groups from cellular phosphate compounds of very high potential.

TABLE 1.2

FREE ENERGY OF HYDROLYSIS OF PHOSPHATE COMPOUNDS[a]

	$\Delta F'$ (cal/mole)	Phosphate transfer potential	Direction of P group transfer
Phosphoenol pyruvate	−12,800	12.8	
1,3-Diphosphoglycerate	−11,800	11.8	
Acetyl phosphate	−10,100	10.1	
ATP	−7,000	7.0	
Glucose 1-phosphate	−5,000	5.0	
Fructose 6-phosphate	−3,800	3.8	
Glucose 6-phosphate	−3,300	3.3	
3-Phosphoglycerate	−3,100	3.1	
Glycerol 1-phosphate	−2,300	2.3	

[a] From Lehninger (17). Reprinted with permission of the author and W. A. Benjamin, Inc.

The ATP so formed can then donate its terminal phosphate group enzymatically to certain specific phosphate acceptors such as glucose with the formation of the corresponding phosphate derivatives. Another reason for the uniqueness of ATP is that all the reactions in the cell which cause phosphorylation of ADP to ATP at the expense of phosphate compounds of very high potential, as well as the terminal phosphate transfer reactions, are catalyzed by enzymes. Nearly all of these enzymes are specific for ATP and ADP. These two compounds constitute virtually a shuttle service for phosphate groups from high-energy to low-energy compounds.

The Problem of Conservation of Energy of Oxidation as ATP Energy

Lehninger(17) demonstrated the foregoing by an actual reaction occurring in the cell as follows: The oxidation of an aldehyde to a carboxylic acid in aqueous solution is known to proceed with a large decline in free energy (see Scheme 1.3). In the cell the oxidation of certain aldehydes takes place enzymatically in such a way that this energy is not simply lost as heat but is largely conserved. For example 3-phosphoglyceraldehyde is oxidized to the acid 3-phosphoglycerate during glucose oxidation (see Scheme 1.4). This reaction does not take place in exactly this way but is coupled with the combination of one molecule of phosphate to one of ADP to form ATP (see Scheme 1.5).

$$R\text{—}C\text{—}H + H_2O \rightarrow 2\,H + R\text{—}C\text{—}O^- + H^+$$

$$\underset{O}{\overset{\|}{\phantom{R\text{—}C\text{—}H}}} \qquad \underset{O}{\overset{\|}{\phantom{R\text{—}C}}}$$

$$\Delta F' \cong -7000 \text{ cal/mole}$$

SCHEME 1.3

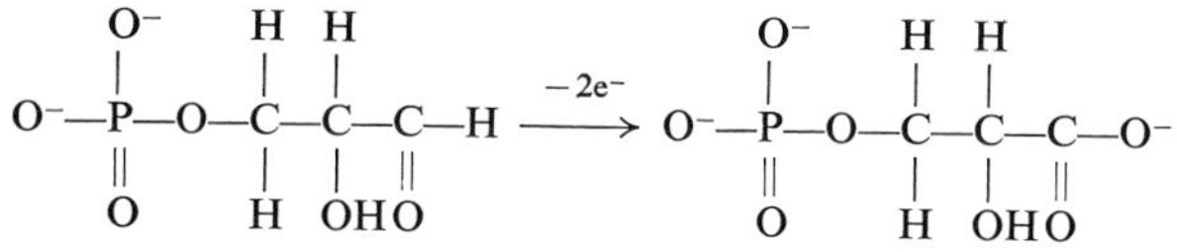

$$\underset{\underset{O}{\|}}{\overset{O^-}{|}}\text{P}\;\text{O}\;\underset{H}{\overset{H}{|}}\text{C}\;\underset{OH}{\overset{H}{|}}\text{C}\;\underset{O}{\overset{\|}{C}}\text{H} \xrightarrow{\;-2e^-\;} \underset{\underset{O}{\|}}{\overset{O^-}{|}}\text{P}\;\text{O}\;\underset{H}{\overset{H}{|}}\text{C}\;\underset{OH}{\overset{H}{|}}\text{C}\;\underset{O}{\overset{\|}{C}}\text{O}^-$$

SCHEME 1.4

$$RCHO + HPO_4^{2-} + ADP^{3-} \rightarrow 2\,H + RCOO^- + ATP^{4-}$$
$$\Delta F' = 0 \text{ cal/mole}$$

SCHEME 1.5

The potential energy of the aldehyde group is transformed into phosphate bond energy of the ATP formed. This conclusion can be drawn from the free energy change in the reaction, which is approximately zero. The free energy decline of ~7000 cal/mole from the aldehyde oxidation is absorbed in the formation of ATP from ADP and phosphate, which requires an input of ~7000 cal/mole (see Table 1.3). This phosphate transfer occurs in two separate steps, each catalyzed by a separate enzyme (see Scheme 1.6). When

TABLE 1.3

STANDARD FREE ENERGY OF HYDROLYSIS OF SOME ENERGY-RICH COMPOUNDS[a]

Compound	$\Delta F°$ (cal/mole)
ATP(−ADP + orthophosphate)	7,000
ATP(−AMP + pyrophosphate)	8,000
Pyrophosphate (−2 orthophosphate)	6,000
Creatine phosphate	8,000
Phosphoenol pyruvate	12,000
Phosphoglyceryl phosphate	11,000
Acetyl coenzyme A	8,000
Aminoacyl AMP	7,000

[a] From Karlson(16).

the aldehyde R–CHO was oxidized by the first enzyme, a large part of the free energy decline normally occurring when aldehydes are oxidized was conserved in the form of the phosphate derivative of the carboxylic acid. In the second reaction, the carboxyl phosphate group of the 1,3-diphosphoglycerate, the free energy of hydrolysis of which is substantially higher than that

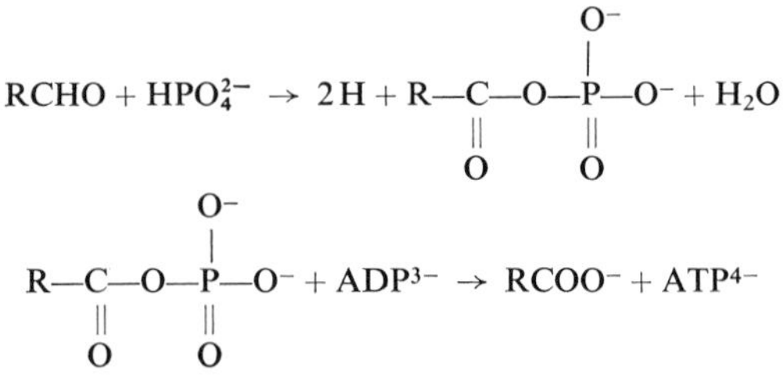

$$RCHO + HPO_4^{2-} \rightarrow 2\,H + R\!-\!\overset{\displaystyle O^-}{\underset{\displaystyle O}{\overset{|}{\underset{||}{C}}}}\!-\!O\!-\!\overset{}{\underset{\displaystyle O}{\overset{}{\underset{||}{P}}}}\!-\!O^- + H_2O$$

$$R\!-\!\overset{\displaystyle O^-}{\underset{\displaystyle O}{\overset{|}{\underset{||}{C}}}}\!-\!O\!-\!\overset{}{\underset{\displaystyle O}{\overset{}{\underset{||}{P}}}}\!-\!O^- + ADP^{3-} \rightarrow RCOO^- + ATP^{4-}$$

SCHEME 1.6

of ATP, is enzymatically transferred to ADP and ATP is formed. Thus the energy of oxidation of the aldehyde has been conserved in the form of ATP by two sequential reactions in which the high-energy phosphate derivative of a carboxylic acid is the common intermediate.

Uphill reactions, whereby ATP energy is utilized to do chemical work, are very similar and can be demonstrated in the reaction

$$glucose + fructose \rightarrow sucrose + water \qquad \Delta F' = +5500 \text{ cal/mole}$$

If one now dissects the sequence of reactions required to analyse the energy exchanges, one finds that the energy-yielding process is the hydrolysis of ATP and the energy-requiring process is the formation of sucrose. Adenosine triphosphate is the common intermediate linking the energy-yielding oxidation reaction and the energy-requiring synthesis of sucrose.

$$RCHO + HPO_4^{2-} \rightarrow 2\,H^+ + RCOOPO_3^{2-}$$

$$RCOOPO_3^{2-} + ADP \rightarrow RCOO^- + ATP$$

$$ATP + glucose \rightarrow\rightarrow ADP + glucose\ 1\text{-phosphate}$$

$$\underline{glucose\ 1\text{-phosphate} + fructose \rightarrow sucrose + phosphate}$$

sum: $RCHO + glucose + fructose \rightarrow 2H^+ + RCOO^- + sucrose$

This overall equation shows that the energy yielded by oxidation of aldehyde to an acid was used to form sucrose from glucose and fructose.

These examples illustrate the general working principle by which ATP is the energy carrier in sequential reactions involving flow of phosphate groups in coupled reactions.

ENZYMES

A high negative value of ΔF indicates that the reaction is likely to proceed spontaneously and that the products will greatly exceed the reactants at equilibrium (see Table 1.4). However, it does not guarantee that the reaction will proceed with measurable speed. There exists a kind of energy barrier which has to be overcome before the reaction can proceed. The important quantity is the free energy of activation. Reactions which fail to proceed notwithstanding a high negative value of ΔF can often be persuaded to do so

TABLE 1.4

REDOX POTENTIALS AT pH 7.0 (E_0') FOR SOME BIOCHEMICAL REDOX SYSTEMS

Coenzymes			Substrates	
$\Delta F°$ (kcal)	E_0' (V)	Substance	E_0' (V)	Substance
			−0.47	Acetaldehyde/acetate
			−0.42	$H_2/2H^+$
	−0.32	NADH + H$^+$/NAD$^+$		
			−0.20	Ethanol/acetaldehyde
	−0.185	Riboflavin-P·H$_2$/riboflavin −P		
−11.5			−0.18	Lactate/pyruvate
	−0.06	Flavoproteins		
	−0.05	Phyllohydroquinone/ phylloquinone		
	−0.04	Cytochrome b		
			0.0	Succinate/fumarate
−15.5			+0.01	Methylene blue/leukodye
			+0.20	Ascorbate/dehydro- ascorbate (pH 3.3)
	+0.26	Cytochrome c		
	+0.29	Cytochrome a		
−25.0			+0.81	$\frac{1}{2}O_2/O^{2-}$

in the presence of a catalyst. From the point of view of thermodynamics a catalyst is something which lowers the free energy of activation. From the physical point of view what probably happens is that the reactant combines temporarily with the catalyst and that as a result the energy of the reactant molecule is redistributed so that certain bonds become more liable to rupture by thermal agitation.

Enzymes are true catalysts since they do not influence the point of equilibrium of the reaction they catalyze, nor are they used up during catalysis. Like other catalysts, enzymes lower the activation energy of the reaction they catalyze.

All the enzymes whose chemical composition has been investigated are proteins. The methods which are used to separate and purify enzymes are the same methods as those used to separate and purify proteins. Enzymes are susceptible to influences and agents which are known to effect proteins. The molecules have a limited life within a cell—new enzymes being continually produced to replace the old. With exceptions they are rapidly denatured, and their catalytic properties destroyed, at temperatures of 50°C and over and by the ions of heavy metals. Their catalytic activities are notably affected by pH. Enzymes differ in several respects from inorganic catalysts: enzymes are more efficient than inorganic catalysts such as platinum, enzymes show much greater specificity, and enzymes are less stable.

It has already been mentioned that a great number of enzymes are complex proteins. They consist of a protein component and a "prosthetic group" which may be removed reversibly. In such cases the protein part is called "apoenzyme" and the prosthetic group "coenzyme"(16).

Much effort has been devoted to the study of enzymatic action(13). When an enzyme catalyzes a specific reaction, it first combines transiently with the substrate, the name given to the substance on which the enzyme acts, to form the enzyme-substrate complex. In this complex there is a "lock-and-key" fit of the substrate molecule to a "patch" on the surface of the very large enzyme molecule(17). This patch is called the "active site," and because of the specific geometrical relationship of the chemical groups which combine with the substrate, it can accept only molecules having a complementary fit. During the formation of the enzyme-substrate complex the enzyme molecule is somewhat twisted, placing some strain on the geometry of the substrate molecule. This renders it susceptible to attack by H^+ or OH^- ions, or by specific functional groups of the enzyme. In this manner the substrate molecule is converted to its products, which now diffuse away from the active site. The enzyme molecule returns to its native shape, combines with a second substrate molecule, and repeats the cycle. Most enzymes can be inhibited by specific poisons which may be structurally related to their normal substrate. Such inhibitors are very useful in analyzing enzyme-catalyzed reactions in cells and tissues. When enzymes act in a sequence so that the product of one enzyme becomes the substrate for the next, and so on, we have a multienzyme system and the chains of reactions are known as metabolic pathways.

Enzymes are not only chemically specific, they are also sterically specific when they act upon substances containing asymmetric centers. The substrate may contain an asymmetric carbon atom, in which case it is usually found that the enzyme acts on only one of the optical isomers. Specificity of this type appears usually to be absolute. A good example is the glyceraldehyde 3-phosphate dehydrogenase, which reacts only with the D-isomer of the DL-glyceraldehyde 3-phosphate.

Substrate concentration is one of the most important of the factors which determine the velocity of enzymatic reactions. The enzyme first forms a complex with its substrate, and this subsequently breaks down giving the free enzyme and the products of the reaction. One can therefore write:

$$\text{enzyme} + \text{substrate} \rightleftharpoons \text{enzyme--substrate}$$

$$E + S \rightleftharpoons ES$$

$$ES \rightarrow \underbrace{A + B + E}_{\text{products}}$$

If one starts with a given amount of enzyme and the substrate concentration is raised gradually, more and more enzyme will be converted into the complex ES and the rate of reaction will increase until finally virtually all the enzyme is in the form of ES, the equilibrium constant

$$K_{eq} = \frac{[E] \times [S]}{[ES]}$$

The enzyme·is then saturated and the reaction rate is maximal. In plotting velocity against substrate concentration a section of a rectangular hyperbole is obtained (Fig. 1.4), which may be owing to many factors such as inactivation

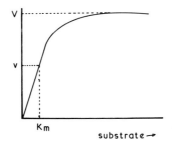

FIG. 1.4. Hyperbolic form of a typical substrate concentration curve.

at the temperature or the pH of the reaction. A different approach which is dependent on the measurement of initial velocity or half-maximal velocity is therefore adopted in the study of enzymatic action. At the point of half-maximal velocity, half of the entire enzyme is in form of the ES complex and the other half as free E. Since the reaction rate should be proportional to the ES concentration,

$$K_m = [S] \qquad \text{at half-maximal velocity.}$$

In other words, that substrate concentration at which half-maximal reaction velocity is reached equals the dissociation constant of the enzyme-substrate complex. This constant is named the "Michaelis constant," K_m. A large Michaelis constant means that a high substrate concentration is necessary or the enzyme possesses a low affinity for the substrate. Michaelis constants normally range between 10^{-2} and 10^{-5} mole/liter. A more detailed description of enzyme kinetics is given in Dixon and Webb(8) and Gutfreund(13).

The reaction rate of an enzyme-catalyzed reaction is also used to define "enzyme units." One unit (U) of any enzyme is defined as that amount which will catalyze the transformation of 1 μmole of substrate per minute, or, where more than one bond of each substrate molecule is attacked, 1 micro-equivalent of the group concerned per minute, under defined conditions. The temperature and all other conditions including pH and substrate concentration should be clearly stated. The International Union of Biochemists (IUB) recommends that where practicable the temperature should be 30°C and that enzyme assays be based wherever possible upon measurements of initial rates of reactions in order to avoid complications owing, for instance, to reversibility of reactions or to functions of inhibitory products. The substrate concentration should be, wherever possible, sufficient for saturation of the enzyme, so that the kinetics in the standard assay approach zero order. Where a distinct suboptimal concentration of substrate must be used, it is recommended that the Michaelis constant be determined where feasible so that the observed rate may be converted into that which would be obtained on saturation with substrate.

Specific activity is expressed as units of enzyme per milligram of protein.

Molecular activity is defined as units per micromole of enzyme at optimal substrate concentration, that is, as the number of molecules of substrate transformed per minute per molecule of enzyme. When the enzyme has a prosthetic group or catalytic center whose concentration can be measured, the catalytic power can be expressed as catalytic center activity, i. e., the number of molecules transformed per minute per catalytic center.

Concentration of an enzyme in solution should be expressed as units per milliliter.

These are the recommendations of the definitions of the IUB, which every microbial chemist should follow strictly in his biochemical work.

ENZYME CLASSIFICATION

It is also very important for a microbial chemist to know the principles on which the IUB based its classification scheme. Enzymes which have been known for a long time still have their trivial names, e.g., trypsin and pepsin. The more recent names, however, have been devised with the suffix "ase." This suffix is attached to the name of the reaction catalyzed. Enzymes that transfer groups are called "transferases"; dehydrogenating enzymes are called "dehydrogenases," etc. The IUB commission, however, recommended the use of this suffix only for single enzymes. A suffix should not be applied to systems containing more than one enzyme. When it is desired to name such a system on the basis of the overall reaction catalyzed by it, the word "system" should be included in the name, e.g., the "succinate oxidase system". Thus only actions of single enzyme entities, and not of composite enzyme systems, are considered for classification.

The enzymes are divided into groups on the basis of the type of reaction catalyzed and this, together with the name(s) of the substrate(s), provides a basis for naming individual enzymes. The IUB decided further to recommend that the over-all reaction, as expressed by the formal equation, should be taken as the basis, which means only the observed chemical change by the complete enzymatic reaction. In the case where a prosthetic group serves to catalyze transfer from a donor to an acceptor (biotin and pyridoxin enzymes) the name of the prosthetic group is not included in the name of the enzyme. In exceptional cases, where alternative names are possible, the mechanism may be taken into account in distinguishing between the enzymes involved.

As a part of its classification, each enzyme has a number. Each enzyme number contains four elements, separated by points. The first figure indicates to which of the six main divisions the particular enzyme belongs:

1. Oxidoreductases
2. Transferases
3. Hydrolases
4. Lyases
5. Isomerases
6. Ligases (synthetases)

The second figure indicates the sub-class and characterizes the type of group, bond, or link involved in the reaction. The third figure indicates the sub-subclass and specifies in more detail the type of donor or group involved in the reaction. The fourth figure is the serial number of the enzyme in its sub-subclass.

With this system it is possible to insert a new enzyme at the end of its sub-sub-class without disturbing any other numbers. Should it become necessary to create new classes, sub-classes, or sub-sub-classes, they can be added without disturbing those already defined. It is the aim of the IUB that even at revisions, the existing enzymes should not be renumbered to take account of any newly discovered enzyme. Such enzymes will be placed at the end of their respective sections and should be given new numbers. This should be done by some suitable authority and not by individuals.

In order to avoid the difficulties encountered by lengthy systematic names, the IUB adopted two kinds of names:

(1) the systematic name of an enzyme which will be formed in accordance with the above-mentioned definite rules;

(2) the trivial name which will be sufficiently short for general use, but not necessarily very exact or systematic.

The detailed rules for systematic and trivial nomenclature are outlined in Chapter 6 of the report of the IUB(15) and by Dixon and Webb(8) and by Karlson(16). In order to understand the nomenclature system, an example will be given with fructose 1,6-diphosphate aldolase, as it is known in literature. This enzyme has the systematic name fructose 1,6-diphosphate D-glyceraldehyde 3-phosphate-lyase with the code number E.C. 4.1.2.13, which means:

4.   the enzyme is a lyase, a group of enzymes which remove groups from their substrates (not by hydrolysis), leaving double bonds, or which conversely add groups to double bonds;

4.1.   the enzyme is a carbon–carbon lyase;

4.1.2. the enzyme is an aldehyde-lyase with a serial number 13. The reaction catalyzed by this enzyme is

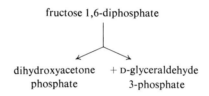

The recommended trivial name is fructose diphosphate aldolase. The names "zymohexase" and "aldolase" are no longer recommended.

COENZYMES

Many enzymes require the presence of certain organic substances as cofactors in order to function. The cofactors, or coenzymes, generally act as acceptors or donors of groups or of atoms that are removed from or contributed to the substrate. The terms "coenzyme" and "prosthetic group" are frequently used synonymously. Lately, the tendency has been to call the tightly bound groups that cannot be removed (e.g., by dialysis) "prosthetic groups," and those which dissociate easily, "coenzymes"(16,22). A third group of cofactors would be the activators, which are frequently of a very simple nature, e.g., inorganic ions, which bring the enzyme itself into a catalytically active state.

Since there is no definite classification scheme available as yet for the coenzymes, this particular field will be treated in a way similar to that used to classify enzymes, namely, according to the reactions in whose catalysis they are instrumental (see Table 1.5).

TABLE 1.5

COENZYMES[a]

Coenzymes	Usual abbreviation	Group transferred	Corresponding vitamins
1. Hydrogen-transferring coenzymes			
Nicotinamide-adenine dinucleotide	NAD	Hydrogen	Nicotinamide
Nicotinamide-adenine dinucleotide phosphate	NADP	Hydrogen	Nicotinamide
Nicotinamide mononucleotide	—	Hydrogen	Nicotinamide
Flavin mononucleotide (riboflavin phosphate)	FMN	Hydrogen	Riboflavin
Flavin adenine dinucleotide	FAD	Hydrogen	Riboflavin
Lipoic acid	Lip (S_2)	Hydrogen and acyl	—
Glutathione	GSH	Hydrogen	—
Ascorbate	—	—	—
Quinones	Q	Electrons	—
Cytochromes	cyt.	Electrons	—
2. Group-transferring coenzymes			
Adenosine triphosphate	ATP	Phosphate	—
Phosphoadenyl sulfate	PAPS	Sulfate	—
Uridine diphosphate	UDP	Sugar, uronic acid	—
Cytidine diphosphate	CDP	Phosphoryl choline	—
Coenzyme A	CoA	Acyl	Pantothenic acid
Tetrahydrofolic acid	THF	Formyl	Folic acid
Biotin	—	Carboxyl	Biotin
Thiamine pyrophosphate	TPP	C_2-aldehyde	Thiamine
Pyridoxal phosphate	PALP	Amino	Pyridoxine
3. Coenzymes of isomerases and lyases			
Uridine diphosphate	UDP	Sugar isomerization	—
Pyridoxal phosphate	PALP	Decarboxylation	Pyridoxine
Thiamine pyrophosphate	TPP	Decarboxylation	Thiamine
B_{12} coenzyme	—	Carboxyl displacement	Cobalamin

[a] From Karlson(16).

The most striking feature of these coenzymes is the close relationship of most of them to the vitamins. The majority are either actual nucleotides or have some structural analogy with nucleotides. Many have a nitrogeneous base at one end of the molecule and a phosphate group at the other, with or without a carbohydrate moiety between, or have two such structures joined in the form of a dinucleotide. The close relationship to vitamins is very interesting. The vitamins are necessary for the proper functioning of life processes and cannot be replaced by other substances. A biocatalytic function is known for many vitamins and generally a vitamin is the main or sole component of a coenzyme. A full understanding of coenzymes necessarily involves a detailed knowledge of the reactions in which they participate. However, a few introductory notes on their biochemistry will help in understanding their role in metabolism.

Nicotinamide Nucleotide Coenzymes. The hydrogen-transferring enzymes of fermentation, respiration, and many other reactions utilize as their coenzymes dinucleotides, one of whose bases is the pyridine derivative nicotinamide. These dinucleotides are therefore pyridine nucleotides (see Scheme 1.7). The nomenclature of the nicotinamide nucleotide coenzymes was, and partly is still, very much disputed. It is quite common to find in literature the names "diphosphopyridine nucleotide (DPN)" and "triphosphopyridine nucleotide

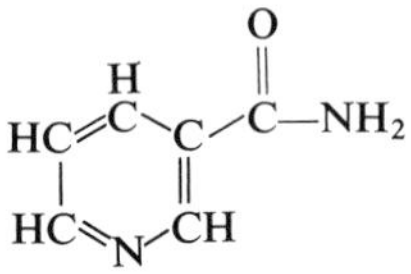

nicotinamide

SCHEME 1.7

(TPN)." Older literature contains a further number of names such as "cozymase," "phosphocozymase," "coenzyme I (Co I)," "coenzyme II (Co II)," "codehydrogenase I," and "codehydrogenase II." In order to eliminate this confusion in the terminology of pyridine nucleotides the IUB made the following recommendations: "The nicotinamide nucleotide coenzymes should in future be known by their chemical names 'nicotinamide-adenine dinucleotide (NAD)' and 'nicotinamide-adenine dinucleotide phosphate (NADP)' respectively. All other names should no longer be used. The mononucleotide should continue to be known as 'nicotinamide mononucleotide (NMN)'."

For the reduced form of NAD, the IUB allows two alternative abbreviations, namely, "reduced NAD" or, where it is desired to show the release of the H^+ ion in the reduction, "NADH + H^+."

If the latter form is used, the oxidized form should then be written "NAD^+." The reaction should never be written NAD $\rightarrow$ $NADH_2$. The same rules apply for NADP.

The pyridine ring in the coenzyme is attached in N-glycosidic linkage to ribose, which is possible only with the pyridinium cation, which bears one hydrogen atom on the nitrogen (see Scheme 1.8). Pyrophosphoric acid provides the linkage between nicotinamide riboside and adenosine.

In nicotinamide-adenine dinucleotide phosphate the adenosine moiety carries the additional phosphate group in the 2' position (see Scheme 1.9). Because of the positive charge in the pyridine ring these coenzymes are also abbreviated NAD^+ and $NADP^+$. Their function is the reversible uptake of hydrogen. The pyridine ring becomes reduced, retaining only two double bonds, while the nitrogen loses its positive charge. Details of these reactions will be found in Karlson(16) and Dixon and Webb(8).

With an enzyme E_1, NAD^+ can form a complex, and in this catalytic system the NAD^+ can oxidize a substrate and in so doing is reduced to NADH $+ H^+$. This reduced NAD can no longer form a complex with E_1 and is released.

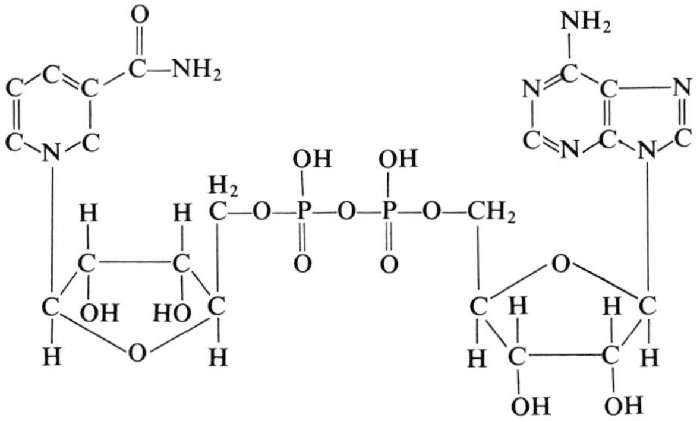

nicotinamide dinucleotide (NAD)

SCHEME 1.8

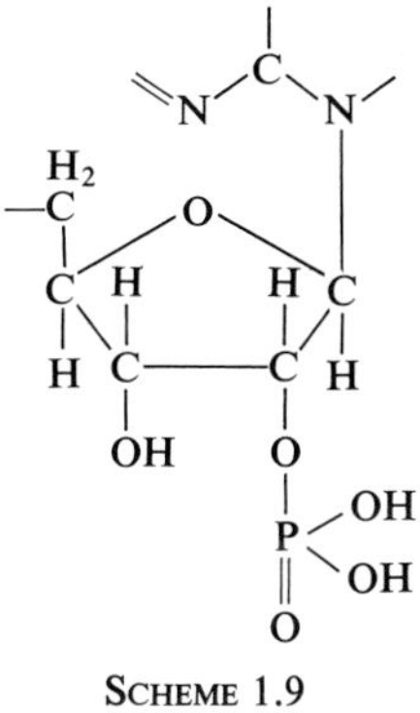

SCHEME 1.9

The NADH $+ H^+$ can then complex with an enzyme E_2 at some other stage in a metabolic pathway and in this complex can reduce another substrate, itself being reoxidized to NAD and again released, thus returning to the cycle. NAD^+ thus forms a link between two enzymes.

The production of NADH $+ H^+$ during a reaction, causes a rise in the spectrophotometer absorption band at 340 mμ. Since this rise in absorption can be followed quite easily, the transition can be followed with any spectrophotometer. The oxidation of reduced NAD, of course, can also be followed optically by way of the disappearance of the 340 mμ peak.

Since the reduction of NAD^+ occurs very frequently in biochemical systems, the reaction is symbolized in the following manner:

$$NAD^+ + CH_3\text{--}CH_2OH \rightleftharpoons CH_3CHO + NADH + H^+$$

This coenzyme functions particularly in dehydrogenation processes of primary and secondary alcohol groups and is associated mainly with a large number of dehydrogenases. Since these dehydrogenation reactions are generally reversible, the importance of this coenzyme rests on its role of reversibly transferring electrons (with associated protons). The coenzyme does not react catalytically by itself, but in association with the apoenzyme reacts with the substrate strictly stoichiometrically (see Scheme 1.10). The reoxidation of reduced NAD

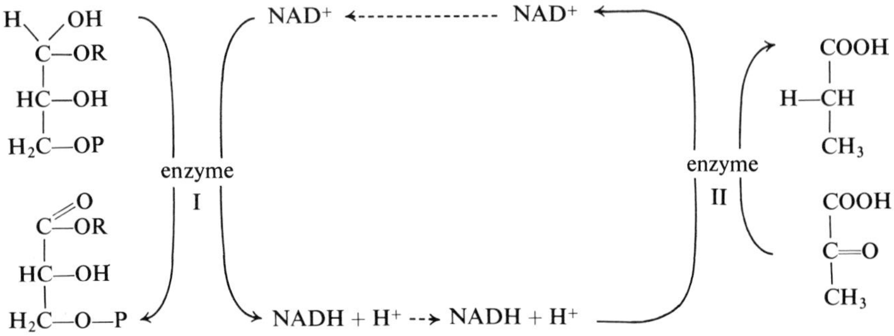

SCHEME 1.10

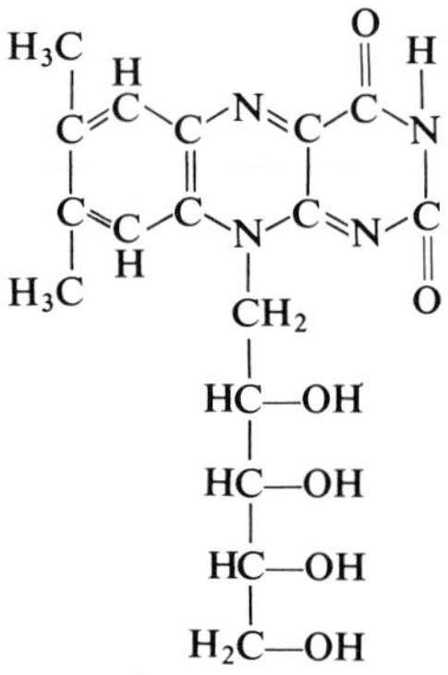

6,7-dimethyl-9-ribityl-
isoalloxazine (riboflavin)

SCHEME 1.11

also functions strictly stoichiometrically. Because coenzymes such as NAD can couple to different enzymes they are the links by means of which the exchange of material becomes possible; NAD occurs in all cells, and its role may be compared with that of ATP. Adenosine triphosphate is a universal phosphate carrier, and NAD is found universally as an electron carrier in cells.

Flavin Nucleotides. Flavoproteins are a class of oxidizing enzymes containing as electron acceptor flavin adenine dinucleotide (FAD), which is an electron carrier similar to NAD in its action. This molecule is remarkable for having as a building block the vitamin riboflavin or vitamin B_2 (see Scheme 1.11). In contrast to nicotinamide, riboflavin is an isoalloxazine derivative, which

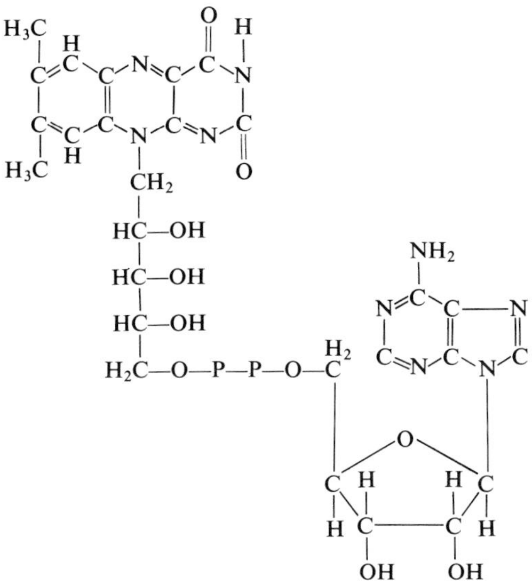

flavin adenine dinucleotide (FAD)

SCHEME 1.12

means a pteridine ring with benzene ring fused on it. The side chain is a five-carbon polyhydroxy group. It is not an *N*-glycoside of ribose, but rather a derivative of ribitol.

Most flavoproteins do not contain the mononucleotide, but rather the dinucleotide. The linkage between the two mononucleotides is the same as in the case of NAD, a pyrophosphate bond (see Scheme 1.12). The isoalloxazine ring acts here as a reversible redox system with the enzyme. Hydrogen is added to N^1 and N^{10} (see Scheme 1.13). For the enzyme to retain its catalytic power the flavin system must be reoxidized. This is usually accomplished by another enzyme system. A number of flavoproteins react directly with molecular oxygen reducing the oxygen molecule to H_2O_2, i.e., lactate oxidase (L-lactate: oxygen oxidoreductase, E.C. 1.1.3.2), pyruvate oxidase (pyruvate: oxygen oxidoreductase (phosphorylating), E.C. 1.2.3.3), and xanthine oxidase (xanthine: oxygen oxidoreductase, E.C. 1.2.3.2), whereas others use NAD(P)

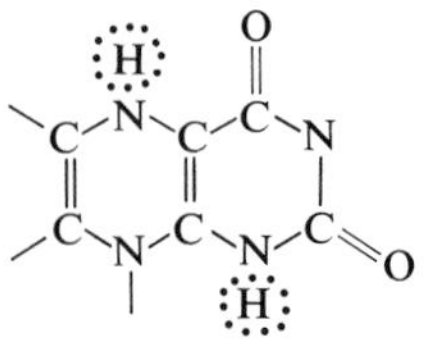

SCHEME 1.13

as acceptor. There is some evidence that in the reduction of several flavo-proteins only one electron is taken up(8). The result is a semiquinone with properties of radicals (unpaired electron). The semiquinone is very active and can easily donate the accepted electron, for example, to Fe^{3+} ions or to oxidized cytochromes. Some flavoproteins also contain tightly bound metal ions which probably participate in catalysis.

Cytochromes. At present the name "cytochromes" appears to include all intracellular hemoproteins with the exception of hemoglobin, myoglobin, peroxidase, and catalase. The group includes substances with many different functions, but they all appear to act by undergoing oxidation and reduction of iron. The nomenclature of individual cytochromes has become difficult owing to the isolation from different sources of cytochromes with similar properties. The recommendations of the IUB in regard to the classification and nomenclature can be found in Chapter 5 of the Commission's report(15). Four major groups of cytochromes have been established as follows.

(1) Cytochrome a: cytochromes in which the heme prosthetic group contains a formyl side chain, e.g., heme a.
(2) Cytochrome b: cytochromes with protoheme as prosthetic group (see Fig. 1.5).

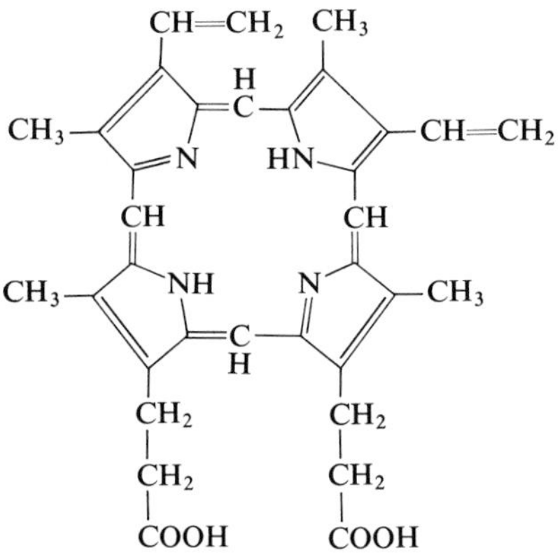

FIG. 1.5. Cytochrome b.

(3) Cytochrome c: cytochromes with covalent linkages between the heme side chains and protein. This group includes all cytochromes with prosthetic groups linked in this way. To date only thioether linkages are known.

The best means of assignment of these groups for the present may be the position of the α-spectroscopic absorption band of the pyridine ferrohemochrome (reduced cytochrome). This is for group a, 580–590 mμ; group b, 556–558 mμ; group c, 549–551 mμ; and group d, 600–620 mμ. The reaction mechanism of these cytochromes will be dealt with at a later stage.

Lipoic Acid. The name "lipoic acid" was first used by Reed *et al.*(20) for the crystalline organic acid isolated from an extract of beef liver which was highly active in assays for a substance which replaces acetate in lactic acid bacteria (acetate-replacing factor)(11,12). Bullock *et al.*(5) proposed the name "6-thioctic acid." However, lipoic acid has been adopted as the trivial name of 1,2-dithiolane-3-valeric acid (see Scheme 1.14). Lipoic acid exhibits a

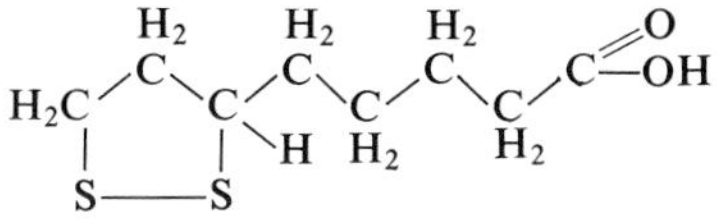

lipoic acid

SCHEME 1.14

spectrophotometric absorption maximum at 330 mμ and has been shown to be widely distributed among microorganisms, plants, and animals. The only well-defined role of lipoic acid is that of a prosthetic group in multienzyme complexes which catalyze an oxidative decarboxylation of pyruvate and α-oxoglutarate to yield acetyl CoA and succinyl CoA, respectively. Its prime role is in oxidative decarboxylation, which is a very complicated reaction and will be dealt with later. Its reactions are carried out together with NAD$^+$, thiamine pyrophosphate, and also with FAD.

Glutathione. Glutathione is a widely used and distributed sulfur-containing peptide, the functional group of which is the thiol group. It is oxidized by molecular oxygen under suitable conditions in the presence of traces of catalytic metals, and also by cytochrome c. In order to reduce the oxidized form back to the thiol form either powerful reducing agents are needed or the enzyme glutathione reductase (reduced NAD(P):oxidized glutathione oxidoreductase, E.C. 1.6.4.2) and NAD$^+$ or NADP$^+$. Since glutathione undergoes enzymatic oxidation and reduction, it can act as a biological hydrogen carrier particularly in the chemoautotrophs (see Chapter 5). Its function, however, is still obscure(8).

Ascorbic Acid. L-Ascorbic acid or vitamin C is an effective reducing agent useful in cultures of anaerobic bacteria. Although the substance exists in an oxidized and a reduced form, the name "ascorbic acid" is given to the reduced form only and the oxidized form is called "dehydroascorbic acid" (see Scheme 1.15). Being a good reducing agent, ascorbate, like glutathione, may play a part in maintaining the –SH enzymes active.

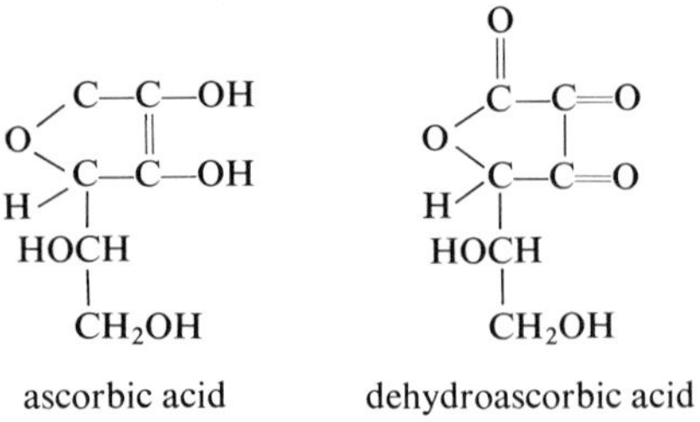

ascorbic acid   dehydroascorbic acid

SCHEME 1.15

Quinones. Quinones are widespread in living cells and some of them, mainly the methylated quinones with polyisoprenoid side chains, play an important part as intermediate hydrogen carriers in the respiratory system. These include two families, the ubiquinones and the vitamin K group. The vitamin K group consists of vitamin K, vitamin K_2, and menadione (see Schemes 1.16 and 1.17).

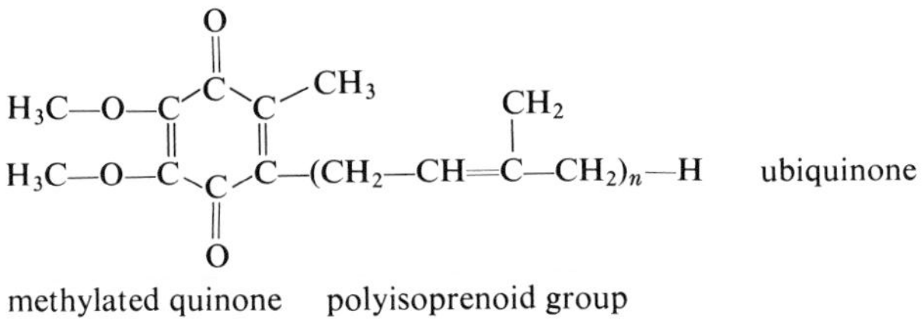

methylated quinone   polyisoprenoid group

SCHEME 1.16

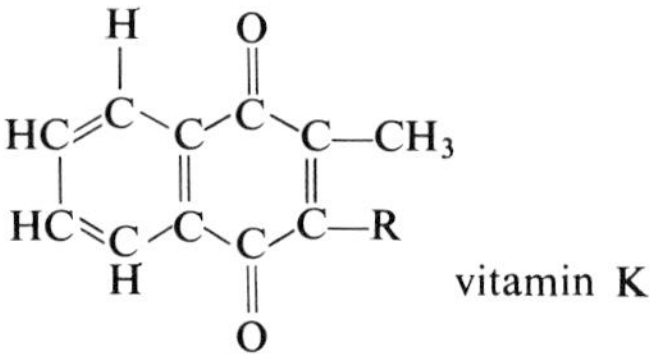

vitamin K

SCHEME 1.17

Ubiquinone was first discovered by Morton *et al.*(18). It has been variously known as "272 mμ substance," "SA," "coenzyme Q," and "Q_{275}," but the IUB recommended the term "ubiquinone," although "coenzyme Q" is still widely used. It is still difficult to say how many substrates depend for their oxidation on ubiquinone. The reduced form of ubiquinone (ubiquinol) is oxidized through the cytochrome system(14). The oxidation depends on cytochrome c and cytochrome oxidase and is quite often coupled to phosphorylation.

Vitamin K has been reported in the electron transport processes of photosynthetic phosphorylation in bacteria, although ferredoxin may replace it in this role as will be seen later.

Phosphate Carriers. The two most important types of transport reaction are electron transport and phosphate transport. The first type is concerned with the production of energy and the second with its transfer from one process to another. The biological carriers of phosphates are the nucleoside phosphates ADP and ATP, which act as cofactors in transphosphorylation processes. The enzymes which catalyze the transfer reactions to and from these phosphate carriers are the kinases (E.C.2.7.1-4). It is not clear how far other nucleoside phosphates such as inosine diphosphate (IDP), guanosine diphosphate (GDP), cytidine diphosphate (CDP), and uridine diphosphate (UDP) can act as phosphate carriers. The mechanism of formation of ATP as an energy-rich compound has been dealt with earlier. It contains two "energy-rich bonds" and has a high capacity for group transfers. One can differentiate ATP action into

(1) transfer of the terminal phosphate group with a release of ADP,
(2) transfer of the pyrophosphate group with a release of AMP,
(3) transfer of adenosyl monophosphate group with release of pyrophosphate, and
(4) transfer of the adenosyl group with release of both orthophosphate and pyrophosphate.

The transfer of a terminal phosphate group of ATP was explained earlier. In the case of pyrophosphate, however, this type of transfer cannot occur, since it cannot be used by the cell to participate in phosphorylation of ADP during oxidative phosphorylation or fermentation. It must first be enzymatically hydrolyzed to orthophosphate by an enzyme called "pyrophosphatase" (pyrophosphate phosphohydrolase, E.C. 3.6.1.1). This enzymatic hydrolysis of pyrophosphate proceeds with a large negative free energy change.

It is thought that ATP is the main line of transfer of bond energy, whereas all the other nucleoside 5'-triphosphates and the deoxynucleoside 5'-triphosphates are compounds which function to channel ATP energy into different biosynthetic pathways(17). Such a channeling process is made possible because the terminal phosphate group of ATP can be enzymatically transferred to the 5'-diphosphates of the other nucleosides by action of enzymes called "nucleoside diphosphokinases" (ATP: nucleoside diphosphate phosphotransferase, E.C. 2.7.4.6).

$$ATP + GDP \rightleftharpoons ADP + GTP$$

$$ATP + UDP \rightleftharpoons ADP + UTP$$

$$ATP + CDP \rightleftharpoons ADP + CTP$$

$$ATP + dADP \rightleftharpoons ADP + dATP$$

where dADP is deoxyadenine diphosphate.

All these mentioned phosphate carriers have about the same free energy of hydrolysis of the terminal phosphate group as ATP. However, only ADP can accept phosphate groups during oxidative phosphorylation. The ADP–ATP system is therefore necessary to phosphorylate GDP, UDP, etc., and fill each channel with high-energy phosphate groups. Lehninger(17) illustrated this as shown in Fig. 1.6.

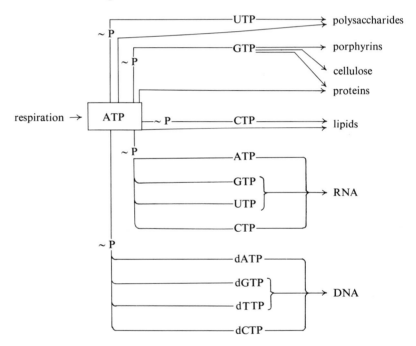

FIG. 1.6. Reprinted with permission of the authors and W. A. Benjamin Inc.

It appears probable that ATP occupies the central role in energy-transfer reactions because it may have been the first nucleoside 5′-triphosphate formed in the prebiotic era and thereby was selected for the role of energy carrier in the first primitive cell. Certain thiol esters, e.g., acetyl CoA, can be formed in cells without the intervention of ATP; in anaerobic glycolysis, probably a very primitive process of energy production, it serves as a precursor of ATP.

On these grounds the CoA derivatives could possibly represent the evolutionary ancestors of ATP.

Acyl-Group Carriers. Recent studies of intermediary metabolism of fats and carbohydrates drew attention to the acyl-group transfer, particularly by carriers containing thiol groups, with which they form thiol esters. These energy-rich compounds share with energy-rich phosphate compounds the important function of biological energy transfer.

Coenzyme A. This coenzyme was originally discovered by Lipman in 1947 and transfers carboxylic acids. The letter "A" stands for acylation. Acids bound to CoA have a high capacity for group transfer. The two-carbon fragment or "active acetyl" known to be involved in carbohydrate metabolism was identified as acetyl CoA. It was later found that not only acetyl CoA but also acyl CoA compounds generally are very important in metabolism, which is shown by the fact that over 60 enzymes act on acyl CoA compounds. Hydrolysis of acyl CoA compounds is exergonic to the extent of about 8000 cal/mole.

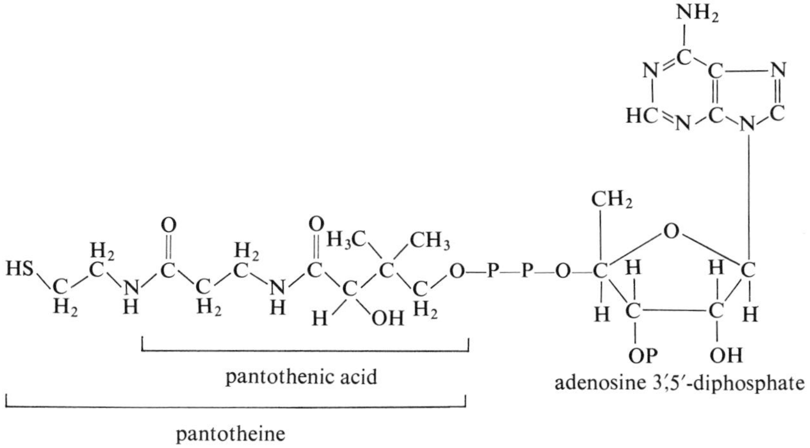

Coenzyme A

Scheme 1.18

The chemical structure of coenzyme A is considerably more complex than that of the cytochrome or NAD. It consists of adenosine 3',5'-diphosphate and panthotheine phosphate (see Scheme 1.18). Panthotheine is a growth factor for several microorganisms and consists of pantoic acid, β-alanine, and mercaptoethylamine. The combination of pantoic acid and β-alanine is also known under pantothenic acid, which is a B vitamin (1–4).

Acetyl CoA is undoubtedly the most important CoA compound. The acetyl residue CH_3CO- is bound to the free SH group, which constitutes a very reactive thio ester. In order to bring acetate or any other carboxylic acid into this compound, energy is required. This energy is most often derived from a strongly exergonic reaction such as oxidative decarboxylation. Another possibility is, of course, from cleavage of ATP, whereby an intermediate arises in the form of an anhydride with adenylic acid.

Coenzyme A is a colorless substance having a spectrophotometric absorption band in the region at 257 mμ owing to the adenine residue. All the enzymes of subgroup E.C. 6.2.1 (acid-thiol ligases) bring about the formation of CoA thiol esters from free acids, making use of the energy of ATP or GTP. All acyltransferases (E.C. 2.3.1) transfer acyl groups to or from CoA. The transfer may be from a combination with another S, N, O, or C atom or from phosphate. Acetyl CoA is also involved in reactions catalyzed by lyases. The acetyl group is added to a double bond in the acceptor molecule, either with or without hydrolysis of the thio ester bond. The three synthase reactions form the important metabolites citrate, malate, and hydroxymethylglutaryl CoA.

Coenzyme A is essential for the initiation of the tricarboxylic acid (TCA) cycle, for the oxidative breakdown of fatty acids, and for various biosynthetic processes.

Carrier of One-Carbon Groups. Just as acetyl CoA represents the active C_2 fragment of metabolism, so is formyltetrahydrofolic acid the active C_1

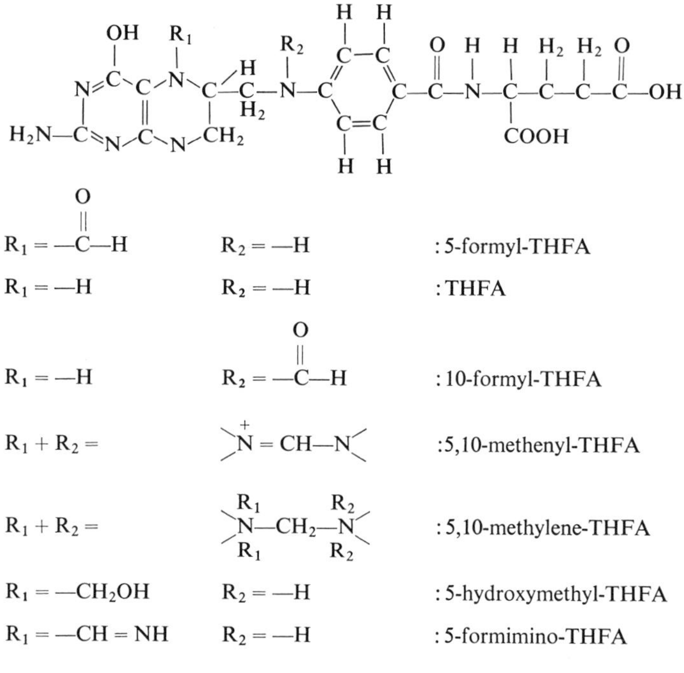

$R_1 = -\overset{\displaystyle O}{\overset{\|}{C}}-H$	$R_2 = -H$	: 5-formyl-THFA
$R_1 = -H$	$R_2 = -H$	: THFA
$R_1 = -H$	$R_2 = -\overset{\displaystyle O}{\overset{\|}{C}}-H$	: 10-formyl-THFA
$R_1 + R_2 =$	$\overset{+}{>}N = CH-N<$	: 5,10-methenyl-THFA
$R_1 + R_2 =$	$>\underset{R_1}{\overset{R_1}{N}}-CH_2-\underset{R_2}{\overset{R_2}{N}}<$	: 5,10-methylene-THFA
$R_1 = -CH_2OH$	$R_2 = -H$	: 5-hydroxymethyl-THFA
$R_1 = -CH = NH$	$R_2 = -H$	: 5-formimino-THFA

THFA and its derivatives

fragment. It has been known for some time that a folic acid derivative is important in one-carbon transfer reactions, but the exact nature of this factor was long in doubt and is still not entirely clear, although the nature of the reacting group is known. The active carrier is not folic acid itself, but tetrahydrofolate (THFA). In bacterial metabolism it is the polyglutamate derivative of folic acid which stimulates growth of a number of strains.

Tetrahydrofolate is highly autoxidizable, is rapidly converted into dihydrofolate by molecular oxygen, and is also oxidized enzymatically by NADP. Folate is reduced to di- and tetrahydrofolate by reduced NADP and the enzyme dihydrofolate dehydrogenase (7,8-dihydrofolate:NADP oxidoreductase, E.C. 1.5.1.4). THFA acts as carrier of methyl, hydroxymethyl, formyl, or formimino groups. Tetrahydrofolate differs from other carriers in that the group transported may undergo a change while attached to the carrier, so that the group which is given up to the acceptor may not be identical with that which was taken up by it.

Vitamin B_{12}. Vitamin B_{12} or cobalamin is a coenzyme of a rather complex structure which shows certain relationships to the hemin system. Coenzyme B_{12} acts also in isomerizations involving intramolecular transfer at C–C bonds. It can also act as a carrier of methyl groups.

Biotin. Biotin has long been known as an essential vitamin, but its function as a cofactor of enzymatic reactions involving incorporation or transfer of CO_2 has been discovered only recently. Biotin is linked to the enzyme protein by a peptide bond to the α-amino group of a lysyl residue (see Scheme 1.19). The

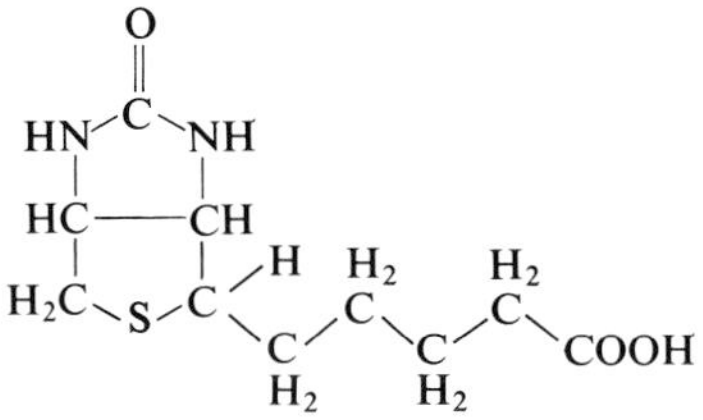

SCHEME 1.19

charging of biotin with carbon dioxide is an endergonic process which requires ATP. The CO_2 attached to the nitrogen of biotin is the "active form of carbon dioxide" which participates in numerous carboxylation reactions such as the formation of malonyl CoA from acetyl CoA (see Scheme 1.20). The very labile carboxy biotin has been isolated as a methyl ester.

Pyridoxal Phosphate. Pyridoxal phosphate is the coenzyme of amino acid metabolism. In some of its reactions which are transaminations it acts as an amino carrier. Pyridoxal phosphate is an excellent example of a single coenzyme capable of catalyzing completely different reactions (see Scheme 1.21). It is the active group not only for the aminotransferases but also for the decarboxylases and various lyases and synthetases. The mechanism of action is believed to be in all cases the formation of an azomethine (Schiff's base) by combination of its aldehyde group with the amino group of the substrate (see Scheme 1.22). The fate of this substance depends on the nature of the enzyme protein to which the pyridoxal phosphate is attached and on the group R.

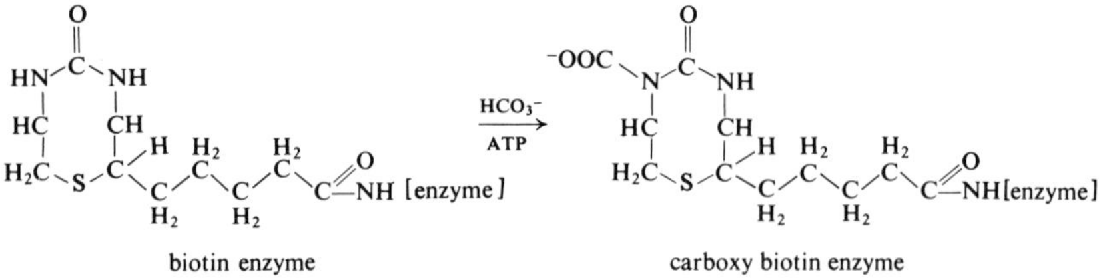

biotin enzyme   carboxy biotin enzyme

SCHEME 1.20

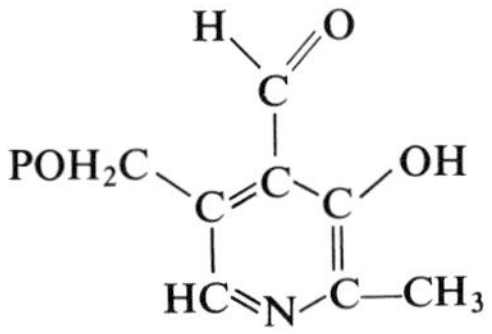

SCHEME 1.21

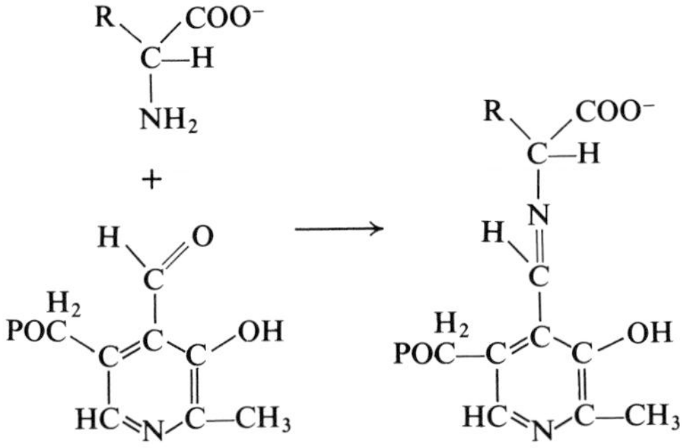

SCHEME 1.22

Thiamine Pyrophosphate. The coenzyme thiamine pyrophosphate (TPP) has also been called "cocarboxylase," "diphosphothiamine (DPT)," "aneurin pyrophosphate," and "vitamin B_1 pyrophosphate." The characteristic component is thiamine (vitamin B_1), the name referring to its sulfur content (see Scheme 1.23). The structural formula of thiamine has two heterocyclic rings which are not condensed: one pyrimidine and one thiazol ring. It therefore always carries a charge. It behaves as a prosthetic group since it remains bonded to the enzyme protein (see Scheme 1.24). In all reactions involving pyruvate, decarboxylation produces an "active acetaldehyde" which becomes attached to the reactive C atom between the S and the N of the thiazole ring (see Scheme 1.25).

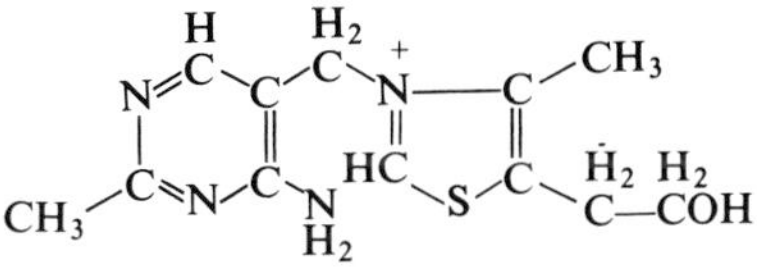

thiamine

SCHEME 1.23

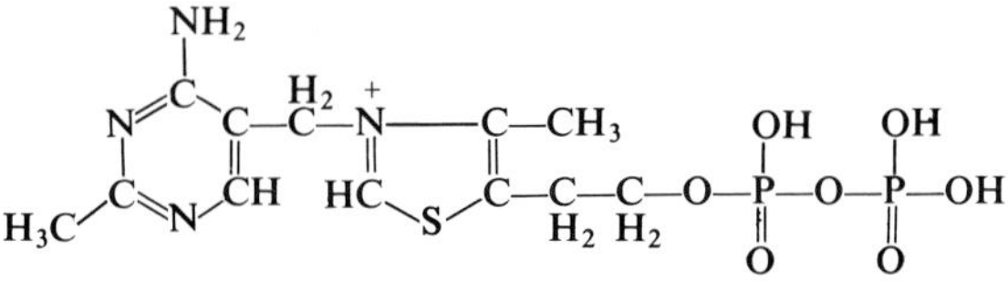

thiamine pyrophosphate
(TPP)

SCHEME 1.24

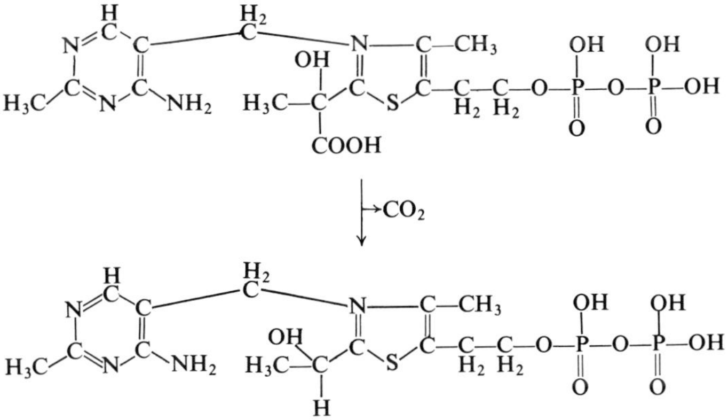

SCHEME 1.25

The enzyme first causes TPP to become attached to the pyruvate forming an intermediate, which undergoes rapid decarboxylation giving an α-hydroxy-ethyl-thiamine pyrophosphate. The fate of this compound depends on which enzyme is involved. The decarboxylase brings about the formation of free acetaldehyde. On the other hand, the aldehyde residue can be transferred to lipoic acid, which functions as an oxidizing reagent, and acetyl transfer can occur. The most important reaction in which TPP collaborates is therefore the oxidative decarboxylation of α-keto acids.

It is certainly not easy at the present moment to make a sharp distinction between a prosthetic group forming a part of the enzyme, a coenzyme distinct from the enzyme but forming a part of the catalytic mechanism, and a substrate acting purely as a reactant in the enzyme-catalyzed reaction. It has, however, been suggested(8) that firmness of combination with the enzyme protein should be used as a criterion for deciding whether a given substance is or is not a prosthetic group. This seems almost impracticable. There is, however, one definite difference between typical prosthetic groups and carriers such as NAD. True prosthetic groups undergo the whole catalytic cycle while attached to the same enzyme protein molecule. A carrier like NAD must migrate from one enzyme protein to another in order to fulfill its catalytic function. If this is adopted, hemes, flavins, biotin, and pyridoxal phosphate would be considered as prosthetic groups, while NAD, NADP, and coenzyme A would be considered as carrier substrates.

REFERENCES

1. Abiko, Y. (1967). Investigations on pantothenic acid and its related compounds. IX. Biochemical studies (4). Separation and substrate specificity of pantothenate kinase and phosphopantothenoylcysteine synthetase. *J. Biochem.* (*Tokyo*) **61**, 290.
2. Abiko, Y. (1967). Investigations on pantothenic acid and its related compounds. X. Biochemical studies (5). Purification and substrate specificity of phosphopanto-thenoylcysteine decarboxylase from rat liver. *J. Biochem.* (*Tokyo*) **61**, 300.
3. Abiko, Y., Suzuki, T., and Shimizu, M. (1967). Investigation on pantothenic acid and its related compounds. VI. Biochemical studies (2). Determination of Coenzyme A by the phosphotransacetylase system of *Escherichia coli* B. *J. Biochem.* (*Tokyo*) **61**,10.
4. Abiko, Y., Suzuki, T., and Shimizu, M. (1967). Investigations on pantothenic acid and its related compounds. XI. Biochemical studies (6). A final stage in the biosynthesis of CoA. *J. Biochem.* (*Tokyo*) **61**, 309.
5. Bullock, M. W., Brockman, J. A., Jr., Patterson, E. L., Pierce, J. V., and Stockstadt, E. L. R. (1952). Synthesis of compounds in the thioctic acid series. *J. Am. Chem. Soc.* **74**, 3455.
6. Clark, W. M. (1960). "Oxidation-Reduction Potentials of Organic Systems." Williams & Wilkins, Baltimore, Maryland.
7. Dawes, E. A. (1963). "Quantitative Problems in Biochemistry." Livingstone, Edinburgh and London.
8. Dixon, M., and Webb, E. C. (1964). "Enzymes," 2nd ed. Longmans, Green, New York.
9. Glasstone, S. (1954). "An Introduction to Electrochemistry," 6th printing. Van Nostrand, Princeton, New Jersey.
10. Glasstone, S. (1962). "Textbook of Physical Chemistry," 2nd ed. Macmillan, New York.
11. Guirard, B. M., Snell, E. E., and Williams, R. J. (1946). The nutritional role of acetate for lactic acid bacteria. I. The response to substances related to acetate. *Arch. Biochem.* **9**, 361.
12. Guirard, B. M., Snell, E. E., and Williams, R. J. (1946). The nutritional role of acetate for lactic acid bacteria. II. Fractionation of extracts of natural materials. *Arch. Biochem.* **9**, 381.
13. Gutfreund, H. (1965). "An Introduction to the Study of Enzymes." Blackwell, Oxford.
14. Hatefi, Y. (1959). Studies on the electron transport system. XXIII. Coenzyme Q oxidase. *Biochim. Biophys. Acta* **34**, 183.

15. International Union of Biochemistry Commission (1964). Enzyme Nomenclature: Recommendations of the International Union of Biochemistry on the nomenclature and classification of enzymes, together with their units and the symbols of enzyme kinetics. Elsevier Publ. Co., Amsterdam.
16. Karlson, P. (1965). "Introduction to Modern Biochemistry," 2nd ed. Academic Press, New York.
17. Lehninger, A. L. (1965). "Bioenergetics." Benjamin, New York.
18. Morton, R. L. (1953). As cited by Dixon and Webb (8).
19. Ramsay, J. A. (1965). "The Experimental Basis of Modern Biology." Cambridge Univ. Press, London and New York.
20. Reed, L. J., de Busk, B. G., Gunsalus, I. C., and Hornberger, C. S., Jr. (1957). Crystalline α-lipoic acid: A catalytic agent associated with pyruvate dehydrogenase. *Science* **114**, 93.
21. Vogel, A. I. (1961). "A Textbook of Quantitative Inorganic Analysis Including Elementary Instrumental Analysis," 3rd ed. Longmans, Green, New York.
22. White, A., Handler, P., and Smith, E. L. (1964). "Principles of Biochemistry," 3rd ed. McGraw-Hill, New York.

SUPPLEMENTARY READINGS

Chance, B. (1968). Cytochromes: chemical and structural aspects. *Science* **159**, 654.
Jacob, H. E. (1967). Zum Einfluss der Electrodenvorbehandlung auf die Redoxpotentialwerte von Bakterienkulturen. *Ztschr. allg. Mikrob.* **7**, 407.
Malhotra, O. P., and Bernhard, S. A. (1968). Spectrophotometric identification of an active site-specific acyl glyceraldehyde 3-phosphate dehydrogenase. The regulation of its kinetics and equilibrium properties by coenzymes. *J. Biol. Chem.* **243**, 1243.
McCormick, D. B., Koster, J. F., and Veeger, C. (1967). On the mechanism of photochemical reactions of FAD and FAD-dependent flavoproteins. *European J. Biochem.* **2**, 387.
Welch, W. H., Irwin, C. L., and Hines, R. H. (1968). Observations on the monovalent cation requirements of formyltetrahydrofolate synthetase. *Biochem. Biophys. Res. Commun.* **30**, 255.

2
PHOTOSYNTHESIS AND PHOTOMETABOLISM

TERMINOLOGY IN BACTERIAL METABOLISM

Under the term "metabolism" one understands all the anabolic and catabolic reactions which occur during the lifetime of a microorganism. Anabolism represents the biosynthetic build up of cell material from simple inorganic or organic compounds, whereas catabolism supplies all the energy, and in many cases the building blocks or precursors, for these essential biosynthetic reactions. Many of the terms used in microbial chemistry are unfortunately used as generalizations and have caused great confusion in terminology. In order to rectify this a number of the major terms which are essential in dealing with this subject matter are defined below.

Metabolism	Represents the overall chemical reactions which occur in microorganisms
Anabolism	Represents the biosynthetic reactions which lead to the buildup of cell material such as polymers, DNA, RNA, and lipids
Catabolism	Represents all chemical reactions which are involved in the breakdown of inorganic and organic material for the purpose of supplying energy and precursors for the biosynthesis of cell material
Autotroph	A microorganism, which is able to use CO_2 as sole carbon source for growth
Heterotroph	A microorganism which requires carbon sources more reduced than CO_2; the majority of microorganisms fall within this category
Photosynthetic microorganism	A microorganism which derives its energy from light quanta; it may be autotrophic or heterotrophic
Anaerobic or anoxybiontic respiration	The chemical energy-yielding reactions in which inorganic compounds other than oxygen act as the terminal electron acceptor
Aerobic or oxybiontic respiration	The chemical energy-yielding reactions which require molecular oxygen as the terminal electron acceptor

Fermentation	The chemical energy-yielding reactions which require organic compounds as electron acceptors
Photolithotroph	A microorganism which derives its energy from light and uses inorganic compounds as electron donors
Photoorganotroph	A microorganism which derives its energy from light and uses organic compounds as electron donors
Chemolithotroph	A microorganism which derives its energy from biochemical reactions and uses inorganic compounds as electron donors
Chemoorganotroph	A microorganism which derives its energy from biochemical reactions and uses organic compounds as electron donors

In regard to the relationship between bacteria and their oxygen requirement the definitions as set out by McBee *et al.* (93) as recommendations should be taken into serious consideration. Here, two distinct groupings are suggested:

(1) a description of the environment or atmosphere in which the bacteria can live, whereby the terms "aerobic" and "anaerobic" would be adequate; and

(2) a description of the metabolic use of gaseous oxygen by living bacteria, whereby the terms "oxybiontic" (oxybiotic) and "anoxybiontic" (anoxybiotic) should be introduced.

There are several reasons for this separation. Some organisms grow in the presence of oxygen but do not use it. Some cannot grow in the presence of molecular oxygen but are not killed by it. To some oxygen is lethal as a gas. Some organisms generally recognized as anaerobes, e.g., *Clostridium perfringens*, cannot only tolerate oxygen at partial pressures below that of the normal atmosphere but can actually metabolize it.

Liquid media are most unsuitable for defining oxygen relationships because of the difficulties associated with maintaining uniform distribution of oxygen throughout the fluid and exposed to air in the stationary state. Liquid media can often be internally deoxygenated.

Attempts to grow organisms on the surface of solid media where cells are freely exposed to air in the initial stages of growth is therefore a more reliable index of oxygen sensitivity.

The present recommendations are as follows: The terms "aerobic," "anaerobic," and "facultatively anaerobic" should be applied only to the description of practical cultural conditions used for the cultivation of bacteria or to the growth of bacteria under these conditions. Aerobic bacteria will grow on the surface of a solid medium exposed to air. Anaerobic bacteria will not grow on the surface of a solid medium freely exposed to air. Facultatively anaerobic bacteria are those aerobic bacteria which have the ability to grow anaerobically. The word "facultative" should not be used by itself. In order to cover microaerophilic bacteria, the term "aerotolerant" was proposed as an additional term to anaerobic. All bacteria, which are described as micro-aerophilic would thus be termed "anaerobic-aerotolerant." Aerobic incubation refers to incubation in the atmosphere of the laboratory and the medium used should not contain reducing substances added for the sole and specific purpose of reducing the oxidation–reduction potential.

The requirements for gaseous oxygen in the growth of an organism should be considered apart from the conditions of culture since they are not necessarily related. The term "oxybiontic" could be applied to those bacteria capable of using atmospheric oxygen in their growth, whereas "anoxybiontic" would apply to those bacteria not capable of using atmospheric oxygen in their growth. Many bacteria have not been studied adequately to permit their classification on the basis of oxygen utilization. It should, however, be included in the description of each new species and in studies which involve reexamination of a taxonomic group of bacteria. Exceptions which are not adequately covered under these terms need further description. Those clostridia, for example, which will grow to a limited extent under aerobic conditions should probably be defined as aerotolerant anaerobic anoxybiontic. This would give a better description than aerobic or microaerophilic.

In the case of so-called microaerophilic organisms actually requiring increased carbon dioxide tensions rather than reduced oxygen tension for growth, the term "microaerophilic" should not be used. Consideration should be given to the word "capneic" to describe these organisms.

The terms "oxybiontic" and "anoxybiontic" may be used without confusion to describe cultural habits as well as metabolism. Thus, *Pseudomonas aeruginosa* is aerobic with an oxybiontic metabolism. *Escherichia coli* is facultatively anaerobic and may be either oxybiontic or anoxybiontic depending on conditions of growth. *Streptococcus lactis* is facultative anaerobic with an anoxybiontic metabolism. *Clostridium histolyticum* is anaerobic, aerotolerant with an anoxybiontic metabolism, and *Clostridium tetani* is anaerobic with an anoxybiontic metabolism.

These major terms indicate that the nutritional classification in microbial chemistry is dependent upon two main factors: (1) source of energy, and (2) nature of the electron donor and acceptor.

A number of these terms come undoubtedly from animal biochemistry, but others had to be introduced in order to cope with significant differences which occur between mammalian tissues and bacteria.

PHOTOSYNTHESIS

HISTORICAL DEVELOPMENT

Rabinowitch(104), Bassham(12), and Arnon(4) have ably condensed the early history of photosynthesis. It commences in 1772 when Priestley discovered that green plants do not respire in the same way as animal cells, but seemed to use the reverse method(104) and thus discovered the capacity of plants to produce free oxygen. It was, however, Ingenhousz in 1779, who suggested a connection between sunlight and oxygen development and therefore discovered the necessity to photosynthesis of light and of the green pigment chlorophyll in the leaves. The importance of carbon dioxide in the air emerged a few years later when Ingenhousz and Senebier indicated that green plants exposed to light absorbed carbon dioxide and liberated oxygen. Saussure corrected this suggestion by indicating that water has to enter into the photosynthetic production of organic matter.

$$CO_2 + H_2O \xrightarrow{\text{light}} \text{organic matter} + O_2$$

This suggestion that air is absorbed, oxygen thrown out, and the carbon kept for its cell synthesis became a fixed principle of biology for the next 100 years.

Later investigators therefore divided all living organisms into two groups(4):

(1) green plants, which were regarded as the only carbon dioxide assimilators, and
(2) all other forms of life, which must consume the organic products of the photosynthetic group.

This led to the assumption that CO_2 assimilation was in fact photosynthesis. The role of light in photosynthesis became obvious as soon as von Mayer (ca. 1845) discovered the principle of conservation of energy, particularly the conversion of the light energy into chemical energy. A few years later (ca. 1880) Winogradsky started to shatter the firm belief that CO_2 assimilation was in fact photosynthesis when he discovered that certain microorganisms were also able to produce organic material by carbon dioxide assimilation without the influence of light. This finding was supported by Lebedev, who suggested further that all cells possess in one way or another the ability to assimilate carbon dioxide. Engelman also showed that purple bacteria perform a type of photosynthesis but do not evolve oxygen. These bacteria required light to metabolize sulfur compounds.

In measuring the rate of photosynthesis in plants under different conditions, Blackman (1905) suggested that photosynthesis cannot be a single photochemical reaction. He proposed that a "dark reaction"—a reaction which is not affected by light—must occur, and therefore divided photosynthesis into two steps: a photochemical step and a dark step, whereby the former produces unstable intermediates, which are stabilized by conversion into the final products oxygen and cellular material by the dark reaction.

The first work was done on the light or photochemical step in photosynthesis. It was known that in plant respiration carbon chains are broken down and hydrogen atoms are transferred to oxygen in order to produce water. In photosynthesis therefore, the same type of reactions must be involved, only in reverse. Hydrogen must therefore be transferred from water to carbon dioxide for the building of carbon chains. Since this transfer of hydrogen in respiration liberates energy, it must be the one that results in the ultimate storage of energy in photosynthesis. Since the energy comes from light, the light reaction was in all probability a hydrogen transfer from water to carbon against the gradient of chemical potential. The impact of light quanta adsorbed by chlorophyll would provide the necessary energy. This is approximately 112 kcal —the combustion heat of carbohydrate. Bohr and Einstein showed first in 1913 that light is adsorbed by atoms or molecules in the form of quanta of definite energy content, which is proportional to the wavelength of the light. The first attempt to measure the quanta required for photosynthesis was made by Warburg in 1923, who stated that four quanta of light energy were required per molecule oxygen produced. However, this value is considered as being too low and is still unsettled. The absorbing molecule was assumed to be chlorophyll, which was strongly supported by the fact that this pigment absorbs red light. However, other pigments are also able to absorb light energy (i.e., carotenoids).

The process at this period appeared to proceed in two separate sequences:

(1) the oxidation of water, which releases free oxygen, while hydrogen becomes attached to some acceptor, and
(2) the hydrogenation of carbon dioxide to produce carbohydrates.

A great step forward was made independently in the 1930's by Hill and van Niel and later by Calvin and his associates. Hill(104) found in 1937 that dried powdered leaves were still able to oxidize water and liberate oxygen, but could not reduce carbon dioxide to carbohydrate. This discovery separated the first sequence from the second. Van Niel and his associates obtained the converse, namely, organisms capable of reducing carbon dioxide in light, anaerobically, were dependent on hydrogen sulfide. From the H_2S, sulfur was deposited and a strict stoichiometric relationship was established between the amount of CO_2 reduced and H_2S oxidized. Van Niel was struck by the similarity of this process to plant photosynthesis. In the latter, O_2 is liberated and in the former S is liberated. At the same time Roelefson(107) and Gaffron(51, 52) showed that H_2 could replace H_2S, and Foster(43) demonstrated that hydrogen could be removed from alcohols by purple bacteria. The reader is referred to Foster's excellent review(43) on developments in research in photosynthesis to 1951. According to van Niel's ideas, water was split into $[H^+]$ and $[OH^-]$ radicals whereby $[H^+]$ supplies the reductant for the conversion of carbon dioxide to carbohydrates, and oxygen is derived from the [OH]. He suggested that bacteria lack the responsible enzyme involved in the photolytic process, and [OH] together with $[H^+]$ from an outside source reform water. In the case of photosynthetic bacteria the reductant is supplied by a compound other than water. Van Niel proposed therefore the following equation for photosynthesis

$$H_2A + CO_2 \xrightarrow{\text{light}} (CHO) + A^-$$

If A is taken to be an oxygen atom, we have plant photosynthesis, if it represents a sulfur atom, we have the photosynthesis of sulfur bacteria. With this great discovery van Niel removed photosynthesis by green plants from its unique position and placed it alongside other types of photosynthetic processes. He envisaged all photosynthetic processes as requiring therefore some source of hydrogen, released by light energy with the concomitant production of relatively oxidized substances (e.g., O_2 and S).

It appeared that the origin of oxygen (and sulfur) in photosynthesis had been resolved and it became necessary to trace the path of the reductant. It was mentioned before that carbon dioxide reduction was considered to be the reverse of the respiration. The reductant H^+ would then be responsible for the backward drive of the respiration—this type of synthesis does not require any light and represents therefore the dark step of photosynthesis. The energy was assumed to come from the adsorption of light quanta. The reduced pyridine nucleotides, however, were a problem since it was known already that these compounds were powerful biological reductants, which would force their hydrogen atoms on other molecules and so participate in oxidation–reduction reactions of the living cell. Studies on the dark reaction were undertaken by Calvin and his research group who confirmed that the carbon dioxide assimilation was the reverse of respiration and traced the pathway of carbon in photosynthesis along the "Calvin cycle" or "autotrophic CO_2 fixation mechanism"(12), which required the participation of ATP and reduced pyridine nucleotide. They also proved that ATP and reduced pyridine nucleotide formation requires light. This automatically suggested that the function of light must lie in the production of ATP and reduced pyridine nucleotides.

Meanwhile, Arnon and his associates were directing their attention to the light reaction. The results of their investigation may be integrated with the findings of Calvin under the name of "photophosphorylation."

PHOTOSYNTHETIC PHOSPHORYLATION

The basic requirements for photosynthesis are twofold:

(1) There has to be a production of energy (ATP) with the help of light quanta, which is called "photophosphorylation."
(2) Provision has to be made for the formation of a reductant, which is able to reduce high-energy compounds into cellular material.

Extensive research over the past decade, mainly by Arnon and co-workers (3,7,8), has made it quite clear that two different types of photophosphorylation exist which involve different pathways of electron transfer: (a) cyclic photophosphorylation and (b) noncyclic photophosphorylation.

Cyclic Photophosphorylation. This type is predominant in plants and used in a minor fashion in bacteria. Arnon(5) also distinguished between a noncyclic photophosphorylation of the plant type and one of the bacterial type.

On the present information all photosynthetic organisms whether bacteria, algae, or plants have one common denominator: ATP generation (see Fig. 2.1).

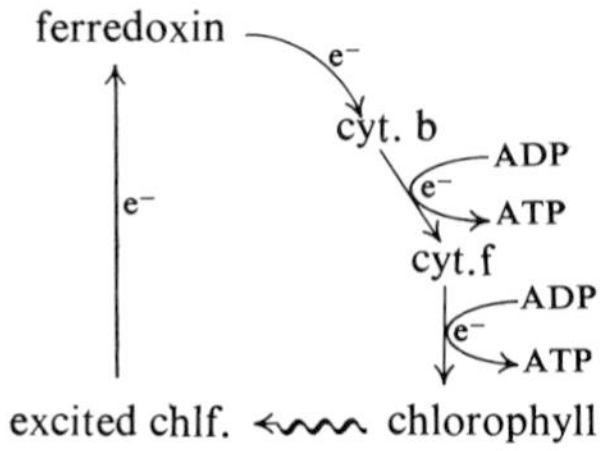

FIG. 2.1. Scheme for cyclic photophosphorylation(8) [reprinted with permission of Macmillan (Journals) Ltd.].

With the proposed model of the Calvin cycle (CO_2 fixation in the dark) the essence of photosynthesis—the conversion of light energy into physiologically useful chemical work or energy—must lie in the photochemical reaction which generates ATP. This involves cyclic photophosphorylation and the basic difference between this and respiration is that in the former electrons are *not* removed as they are in respiration where they are finally accepted by an electron acceptor. A light-absorbing molecule (chlorophyll or bacteriochlorophyll) becomes "excited" and acquires a tendency to expel an electron as well as a capacity to accept one as replacement for the expelled one. The expelled electron is raised to a high-energy potential as described earlier and is transferred to the special redox system ferredoxin. Ferredoxin is an iron-containing protein(80) with the unusual negative redox potential of -0.432 V, which is ~ 100 mV less than that of the $NAD^+/NADH + H^+$ system. This redox potential is similar to that of the hydrogen electrode at pH 7.0 (H_2/H^+ -0.42 V). From ferredoxin an electron pair goes via a number of redox systems before it finally returns to the chlorophyll, thus bringing it back to its ground state. The system is now ready again to accept a light quantum and repeat the process. In the course of this reaction it can be shown experimentally that 2 moles of ATP are generated. The catalytic action of ferredoxin in cyclic photophosphorylation can, however, only occur under strictly anaerobic conditions inside the cell.

$$n\text{ADP} + n\text{P}_i \xrightarrow[h\nu]{\text{Fd}} n\text{ATP}$$

The formation of ATP can therefore depend either on the availability of inorganic phosphate or pyrophosphate (9,10) or the availability of ADP (74). Whereas two possible mechanisms for the formation of inorganic pyrophosphate were described, the possibility of a high-energy intermediate in photosynthetic ATP formation has been postulated to be ADP-dependent in the photophosphorylation with chromatophores from *Rhodospirillum rubrum* (74). Figure 2.1 gives two sites for ATP generation in this electron transport chain, but this does not exclude the possibility of additional phosphorylation sites. Ferredoxin-catalyzed cyclic photophosphorylation will occur only under conditions when noncyclic photophosphorylation is excluded (8). This cycle has generated the necessary energy for use in the Calvin cycle, but the system lacks the necessary reducing power. The origin of ATP has been considered. For the operation of the Calvin cycle $NADH + H^+$ is required. The cyclic phosphorylation, however, cannot generate $NADH + H^+$ and dependence lies on the noncyclic phosphorylation.

Noncyclic Photophosphorylation. Van Niel's original concept was that CO_2 was reduced ultimately by hydrogen originating from the photolysis of water. However, CO_2 has been shown to be incorporated by fixation in the Calvin cycle. Hence any reduction effected by photolysis of water must be indirectly through another substance which has been shown to be NAD, involved in the Calvin cycle. Van Niel's concept was that photolysis of water was common to all photosynthetic organisms including plants and that the $[OH^-]$ released was enzymatically converted to molecular oxygen in plants and reduced to water by an external electron donor in bacteria. This, however, conflicts with a unified concept for all photosynthetic mechanisms.

Losada *et al.* (92) showed that photolysis of water occurs in plants but not in bacteria. It was assumed that the hydrogen evolved reduced the NAD.

A proposal that in bacteria a light independent reduction of NAD was effected by an external electron donor was supported by Ogata and co-workers (3). Thus in plant photosynthesis electrons resulting from quantum-activated chlorophyll are required for (*a*) production of ATP and (*b*) the reduction of NAD. The proton for the latter arises from the photolysis of water. In bacteria, electrons arising from chlorophyll are likewise involved in the production of ATP and the reduction of NAD, the proton for the latter, however, being donated by the external reducing agent (see Fig. 2.2).

The illuminated chromatophore does not react directly with NAD^+ or $NADP^+$, but first with ferredoxin, as explained in cyclic phosphorylation (8). The reduction of $NADP^+$ is the second of two dark reactions following the photochemical reduction of ferredoxin. The reoxidation, of reduced ferredoxin occurs with the help of a flavoprotein enzyme which is called "ferredoxin-NADP reductase" (reduced NADP:ferredoxin oxidoreductase, E.C. 1.6.99.4), and the reduced reductase is finally reoxidized by $NADP^+$. This flavoprotein enzyme, whose flavin is probably FAD, is very similar to the corresponding green plant enzyme. It is thought that it can act not only as an NADP reductase but also as a reduced NADP-cytochrome c-552 reductase, reduced NADP-DCIP (dichloroindophenol) reductase, and pyridine nucleotide transhydrogenase(141). This could be very important for the regulation of biosynthesis if the NADP reductase functions, for example, as reduced NADP-cytochrome c-552 reductase *in vivo* when a considerable amount of $NADP^+$, which is

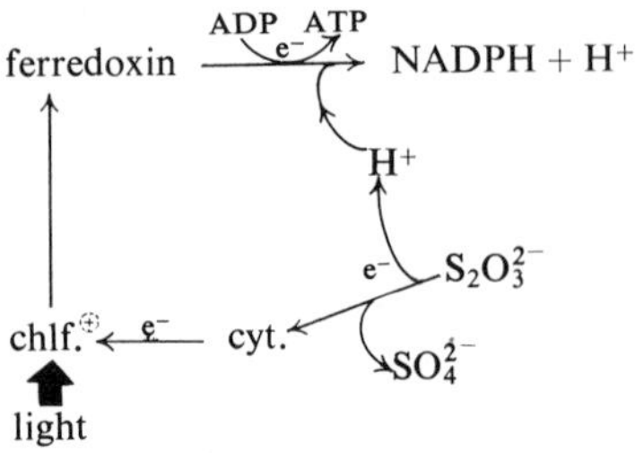

Fig. 2.2. Scheme for the photosynthetic $NADP^+$ reduction in sulfur bacteria.

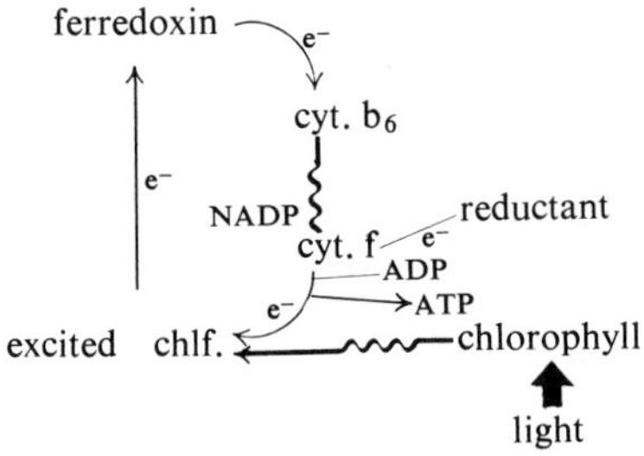

FIG. 2.3. Scheme for noncyclic photophosphorylation of the bacterial type(8) [reprinted with permission of Macmillan (Journals) Ltd.].

present in the chromatophores, is changed into $NADPH + H^+$ by a vigorous photosynthetic reduction of $NADP^+$ and could convert reduced $NADP^+$ to NAD^+. Cytochrome c-552 could in this case take the place of ferredoxin. The presence of a pyridine nucleotide transhydrogenase has been observed in *Rhodopseudomonas spheroides*(97), where the trapping of reduced NAD^+ completely inhibited the reduction of $NADP^+$ although $NADP^+$ was preferentially used over NAD^+. The oxidation–reduction reaction employing ferredoxin-NADP reductase transfers one electron.

Under strongly reducing conditions no cyclic electron flow is possible since the components of the cyclic chain will be kept in the reduced state. Electrons will flow unidirectionally via a portion of the cyclic chain to ferredoxin and to $NADP^+$. As long as this flow is maintained through a cytochrome, it would induce a phosphorylation at a cyclic site (see Fig. 2.3).

This noncyclic photophosphorylation of the bacterial type(8) explains

(1) the ATP formation at a cyclic site, and
(2) the dependence for the formation of reducing power on a noncyclic electron flow, as is indicated by the requirement for terminal acceptor (NADP).

As long as electrons flow from an external hydrogen donor to ferredoxin (via chlorophyll) and from there to NADP, cyclic photophosphorylation cannot proceed. Photosynthetic bacteria, in other words, are able to regulate ATP and reducing power production. If there is a great need for reducing power, the noncyclic photophosphorylation will operate with the help of an exogenous hydrogen donor. When the bacterium does not require reducing power, cyclic phosphorylation supplies the ATP required for cell synthesis. Studies in chloroplasts with ascorbate-dichloroindophenol as electron donor for $NADP^+$ reduction revealed that no indication could be obtained of a sharp transition from a nonphosphorylating to a phosphorylating system. Whenever a phosphorylation is observed in this system, cyclic phosphorylation systems operate simultaneously with two different sites of ATP formation. One site is located on the noncyclic pathway prior to the point of entry of electrons from the outside donor and the other on the pathway which is exclusive for the cyclic system and not shared by the noncyclic ones (66). Although this theory explains the simultaneous operation of both photophosphorylation systems, it requires two different systems (system I and system II) of light-absorbing pigments, one which excites the electrons from the photolysis of water and the second which absorbs and excites the electrons from the reductant(26). It is possible that system I and system II are similar if not identical with the short wavelength-sensitized and long wavelength-sensitized phosphorylation processes found in chloroplasts(111). A similar system has been indicated to exist in *Chromatium* sp. strain D(60).

Another hypothesis for a combined photophosphorylation was suggested after studies with *Rhodospirillum rubrum* chromatophores(11,110). When ascorbate-DCIP and fumarate were added as a redox couple, *R. rubrum* catalyzed an antimycin-insensitive photophosphorylation, which led to the proposal(110) shown in Fig. 2.4. Studies on the kinetics of an oxidase system(24), on the characteristics of heme pigments such as cytochrome c-552 and cytochromoid c(61,67,103) as well as a high-potential nonheme iron protein in photosynthetic bacteria(30) and coenzyme Q(101) appear to support this scheme, although it is almost certain that $NADP^+$ is preferentially used over NAD^+. Various photosynthetic bacteria, however, seem to use different combinations of cytochromes and proteins as is assumed to be the case in the respiratory chain of aerobic respiration (see Chapter 5).

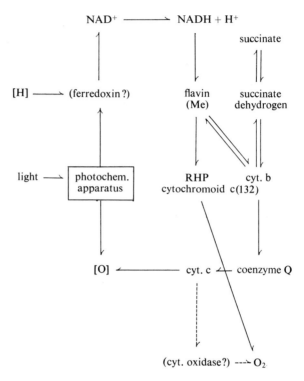

FIG. 2.4. Photophosphorylation (cyclic and noncyclic combined) in *Rhodospirillum rubrum* (reprinted with permission of Elsevier Publishing Co.).

AUTOTROPHY AND HETEROTROPHY IN BACTERIAL PHOTOSYNTHESIS

Most phototrophs perform a total synthesis of cell material from inorganic nutrients, whereby CO_2 serves as the sole carbon source. The gross conversion of CO_2 to cellular material required, however, in addition to ATP a source of reducing power. In green plants this reducing power comes from water linked with the photochemical process, which produces oxygen as a by-product. Green bacteria and many purple sulfur bacteria share with plants the use of CO_2 as sole carbon source, but because they are obligate anaerobes and lack the responsible enzyme, they cannot use water as a reductant and consequently depend on other inorganic reductants. They are also unable to use fermentative mechanisms to obtain the energy needed(121). This group would, in principle, follow the general scheme of plant photosynthesis. The other group of purple bacteria, which are categorized under photoorganotrophs, can make use of simple organic compounds as principal carbon sources and sources of reducing power. In such cases, the exogenous carbon source is similar in oxidation state to cell material, and the requirement for an exogenous inorganic reductant disappears. A strict overall oxidation–reduction balance must be maintained. When the organic substrate is more oxidized than cell material then this balance is achieved by anaerobic oxidation of part of the substrate to CO_2, and the energy released provides reducing power for the synthesis of cell material from CO_2 and other substrate molecules. If, on the other hand, the organic material is more reduced than cell material, then this balance is achieved by partial oxidation of the substrate, coupled with reduction and assimilation of CO_2. In other words, we have two exogenous carbon sources, and the assimilation of the organic substrate is mandatorily linked with CO_2 assimilation. Table 2.1 summarizes the differences between green plants,

TABLE 2.1

DIFFERENCES AMONG GREEN PLANTS, GREEN BACTERIA, AND PURPLE BACTERIA (121)[a]

	Green plants	Green bacteria	Purple bacteria
Source of reducing power	H_2O	H_2S, other inorganic compounds	As green; organic compounds
Photosynthetic O_2 evolution	Yes	No	No
Principal C source	CO_2	CO_2	CO_2; organic compounds
Relation to oxygen when photosynthesizing	Aerobic	Strictly anaerobic	Strictly anaerobic

[a] Reprinted with permission of the American Society of Microbiology.

green bacteria, and purple bacteria. The general principle of photochemical ATP generation and reducing power formation has been stated. The actual mechanisms depend entirely on the enzymatic outfit and environmental conditions required for the individual bacteria and will be dealt with under photometabolism of the photosynthetic bacteria.

PRIMARY PHOTOSYNTHETIC REACTION

One of the outstanding features of the process of photosynthesis is the ability of the organisms to utilize quanta of energy to accomplish an ordered chemical transformation with high efficiency.

Photosynthetic Apparatus. Electron microscopic studies of *Chlorobium* revealed (50) no vesicular or lamellar structure. The pigments seem to be readily dissociated and appear to be the equivalent of subunits of chromatophore fragments of a more highly organized system. It is therefore not possible to regard them as chromatophores, although the particles contain carotenoids, chlorophyll, cytochromes, quinones, and phospholipids. These particles are referred to as thylakoid structures(33). These observations are somewhat in contrast to investigations on *Chlorobium thiosulfatophilum* by Cohen-Bazire and co-workers(28) and on *Chloropseudomonas ethylicum*(72). In both cases it was found that the photosynthetic pigment is located in large peripheral vesicles. Electron micrographs of *Chloropseudomonas ethylicum* revealed vesicles 1300–1500 Å long and 300–500 Å wide along the cell periphery. All these vesicles seem to be interconnected at the apex. There is strong evidence that the chlorophyll in the green bacteria is contained as part of a structure which may be differentiated both structurally and functionally from the bacterial cytoplasmic membrane. The different opinions may result from the possibility that ballistic treatment of the cells causes disruption of the vesicles at their apparent interconnections(72).

Studies on the effect of light intensity on the formation of the photochemical apparatus in *Chloropseudomonas ethylicum*(73) supported the presence of vesicles and revealed that the formation of the photosynthetic vesicles is an inverse function of the light intensity at which cells were grown. However, not only the formation of these vesicles but also the specific chlorophyll content of isolated vesicles varied with light intensity, which has also been shown to be the case in *Rhodomicrobium vannielii*(129). These effects mean that in fact the regulation of chlorophyll content in *C. ethylicum* in response to light intensity changes is achieved both by a change in the specific chlorophyll content of the vesicles and by a change in the number of vesicles formed.

In green plants chlorophyll "a" and "b" are contained in plastids. The absorption bands for chlorophyll "a" are 683 and 695 mμ and for chlorophyll "b" 650 and 480 mμ. *In vivo* absorption measurements of the chlorophyll of the green sulfur bacteria revealed a maximum at 750 mμ which was different from the bacterio-chlorophyll found in the other two groups of photosynthetic bacteria and which showed maxima at 590 mμ and in the infrared region between 800 and 900 mμ (27, 136). The pigment of the green sulfur bacteria was therefore named "Chlorobium chlorophyll." *Chlorobium thiosulfatophilum* also accumulates large amounts of polymetaphosphates(75) in discrete intracellular granules, from which inorganic phosphate is released by an ADP-dependent and light-dependent reaction. It seems to be clear that these functional macromolecules can catalyze the light-dependent esterification of inorganic phosphate (P_i) into ATP in the absence of any artificial transport carriers. The structural formulae for chlorophyll "a" and bacteriochlorophyll are shown in Figs. 2.5 and 2.6.

The purple sulfur bacteria possess definitely circular vesicular chromatophores as has been shown in *Chromatium*, but the structure of these in a single species might be dependent on growth conditions and physiological age of the cell(18,46).

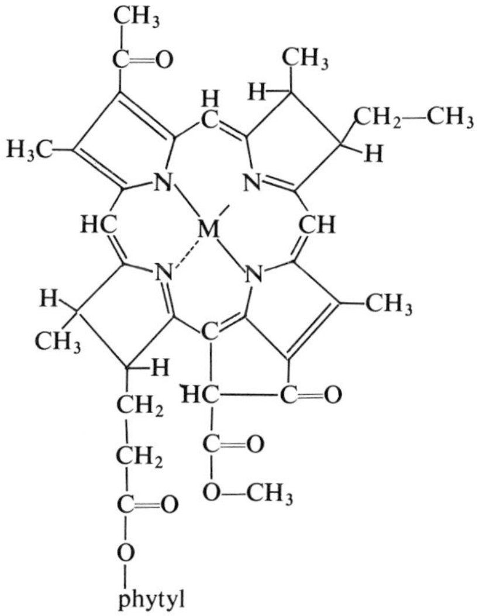

FIG. 2.5. Bacteriochlorophyll.

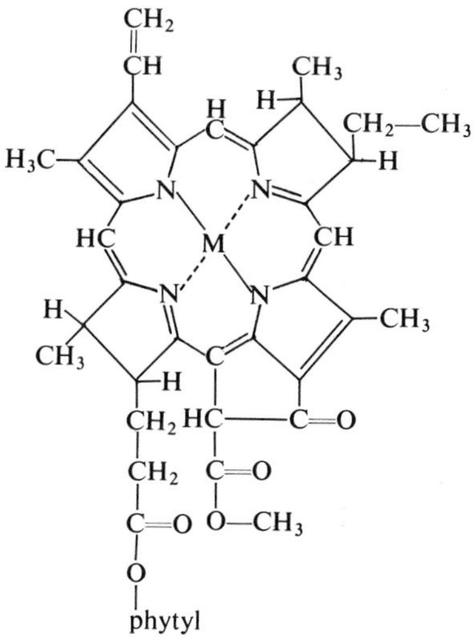

FIG. 2.6. Chlorophyll "a."

In lysates of *Rhodospirillum rubrum* prepared by osmotic shock of protoplasts it was found that all pigments sediment at a lower centrifugal force than the chromatophores after mechanical disruption(134). This result could be explained either by the size of the chromatophore or by the location of the photosynthetic apparatus in the membrane. It was Marr(94) and Stanier(122)

who postulated that the photosynthetic apparatus is part of the intracytoplasmic membrane since the differential release of chlorophyll during sonic
and ballistic disruption of the cells is not in agreement with the location of the
chlorophyll in independent vesicles. Direct electron microscopy of sonically
disrupted cells of R. *rubrum* as well as stereo-electron microscopy of osmotically
shocked cells revealed a network of tubules, which are attached to the enve-
lope(69). The micrographs suggest that the internal membranes containing
the photosynthetic pigments originate from the peripheral membrane in the
form of spherical vesicles that later develop into bulged and sometimes flattened
tubes. Holt and Marr(69) supported the idea that chromatophores are really
fragments of these tubular internal membranes, which represent the intra-
cytoplasmic membrane. The isolation and purification of this membrane(70)
revealed further that the fine structure of the "chromatophores" resembles
the fine structure of mitochondria and chloroplasts, or quantosomes. The
striking difference, however, is the small size of the units (approximately 50 Å
in diameter) compared with those in chloroplasts (185 × 155 × 100 Å). It has
been speculated by Holt and Marr(70) that these small units are the loci of the
photosynthetic pigments. A further support to the location of the photosynthetic pigments in intracytoplasmic membrane comes again from Holt and
Marr(71), who studied the effect of light on the formation of the intracytoplasmic membrane in R. *rubrum*. They demonstrated that highly purified
membranes (chromatophores) from cells grown at low to moderate light
intensity had a constant content of chlorophyll. It could be concluded therefore
that the regulation of the chlorophyll content in response to changes in light
depends upon the formation of greater or lesser amounts of membrane.

In *Rhodospirillum rubrum* it appears that protein and chlorophyll synthesis
(86,117) are coupled with an increased invagination of the intracytoplasmic
membrane into the cytoplasm of the cell, whereas with *Chloropseudomonas
ethylicum* this is not the case; C. *ethylicum* seems to couple its chlorophyll
synthesis with an increase or decrease in the number and the size of vesicles
formed(73). However, the change in the specific chlorophyll content in
C. *ethylicum* with light intensity changes does not occur in purple bacteria
and seems also not to be in agreement with the idea of a constant relationship
between the amount of internal membrane and the amount of pigment.
Whether or not this change in chlorophyll content is an artifact resulting from
extraction procedures remains to be seen. Another approach may lie in further
studies of the nature of the kinetics of proton movements in subcellular fractions of photosynthetic bacteria(25) since the rate of proton movement appears
to be more closely related to phosphorylation and ion movements in chromatophores than to their electron transport rate. A further problem also exists in
the isolation and determination of the chlorophyll content as the photochemical
pigment appears to change its spectrophotometric absorbance bands(2,62,63,

65) and its chemical constitution (17, 32, 34, 8 7, 118) under different environmental conditions.

The Physical Process of the Primary Reaction. Light in general is a form of electromagnetic radiation and consists of a wave of particles known as photons. It can be divided into three regions, namely, the ultraviolet, visible, and infrared regions. When light impinges on the surface of certain substances, electrons are ejected from the surface atoms. Einstein proposed first that photons are actually units of energy of light quanta and established the relation

$$E = hv - h(c/\lambda)$$

in which E is the energy of a light quantum, v the frequency in vibrations per second, h the Planck constant, c the velocity of light, and λ the wavelength (124).

The absorption of light and its energy varies greatly from substance to substance. This absorption ability is determined by the atomic structure of the substance, particularly by its surrounding electrons. It is in fact the electron of an atom which absorbs the photons. When these photons strike an atom or molecule which can absorb light, an electron in one of the orbitals may absorb it and thus gain its energy (23). This energy may be sufficient to move the electron farther away from the nucleus to an outer orbital with a higher energy level. The atom is said to be in the "excited state." This process can only happen when the electron and the photon have the exact energy to equal the energy difference between the initial orbital and the outer orbital to which the electron has been moved (89). Since the energy of a photon can only be used on an "all or none" basis, the term "quantum" was introduced. The excited atoms are very unstable.

Such a process seems certain to happen in the pigments of photosynthetic bacteria or plants. Chlorophyll is not the only light-absorbing molecule, but carotenoids are also able to absorb light. Purple bacteria and red algae, which are known for their high carotenoid content owe much of their color to such pigments. It seems certain that these carotenoids, although they possess a different absorption spectrum from chlorophyll (126), are able to supplement chlorophyll. However, the light energy absorbed by carotenoids has first to pass chlorophyll before it can be used to do photochemical work (89).

Photosynthetic bacteria can grow anaerobically under two markedly different conditions:

(1) CO_2 can serve as the sole carbon source, provided an inorganic electron donor is present.
(2) Simple organic compounds such as malate can serve as the sole carbon source instead of CO_2 provided an "accessory" electron donor is available.

There are, of course, certain species such as *Chromatium*, which can grow under both conditions. Fixation of CO_2 liberated during metabolic conversions of added organic substrates also occurs, but the extent of this process varies considerably depending on the nutritional conditions (41, 42, 55).

PHOTOMETABOLISM

Microorganisms, which are able to convert the energy of radiation directly into the energy-rich compound ATP, are called "photosynthetic bacteria" and are categorized into three major groups:

(1) the green sulfur bacteria, or *Chlorobacteriaceae*, represented by the genera *Chlorobium* and *Chloropseudomonas*;
(2) the purple sulfur bacteria, or *Thiorhodaceae*, among which the best known are species of *Chromatium* and *Thiospirillum*; and.
(3) the nonsulfur bacteria, *Athiorhodaceae*, with the genera *Rhodopseudomonas*, *Rhodospirillum*, *Rhodomicrobium*, and *Vannielia*.

Of the green sulfur bacteria or *Chlorobacteriaceae*, only the genus *Chlorobium* has been investigated.

These bacteria can use four different types of inorganic hydrogen donors (88):

(1) Sulfide. *Chlorobium thiosulfatophilum* will always oxidize sulfide to sulfate.

$$CO_2 + 2H_2S \xrightarrow{h\nu} (CH_2O) + 2S + H_2O$$

$$3CO_2 + 2S + 5H_2O \xrightarrow{h\nu} 3(CH_2O) + 2H_2SO_4$$

It was found that the rate of CO_2 assimilation diminished when all the sulfide had been converted to sulfur and the production of sulfate had begun. *Chlorobium limicola* converts sulfide to sulfur only which then accumulates outside the cell.

(2) Thiosulfate. *Chlorobium thiosulfatophilum* can oxidize thiosulfate to sulfate.

$$2CO_2 + Na_2S_2O_3 + 3H_2O \rightarrow 2(CH_2O) + Na_2SO_4 + H_2SO_4$$

(3) Hydrogen. Both *Chl. thiosulfatophilum* and *Chl. limicola* can use hydrogen as their hydrogen donor.

$$2H_2 + CO_2 \rightarrow (CH_2O) + H_2O$$

(4) Organic compounds. *Chlorobium thiosulfatophilum* is also able to use organic compounds under certain conditions as electron donors.

Of these electron donors, thiosulfate metabolism is the best studied and it is assumed that the other inorganic electron donors may serve in the same way (7).

The photosynthetic purple bacteria (*Thiorhodaceae* and *Athiorhodaceae*). The family *Thiorhodaceae* or purple sulfur bacteria behave similarly to the green sulfur bacteria in their use of inorganic compounds as hydrogen donors(120). In contrast, *Athiorhodaceae* or purple nonsulfur bacteria use organic compounds as hydrogen donors. Most of the work has been done with either *Rhodopseudomonas spheroides* or *Rhodospirillum rubrum*.

The separation of the green from the purple bacteria rests on the pigmentation of the respective organisms, whereas the subdivision of the latter into *Thiorhodaceae* and *Athiorhodaceae* is based on the fact that the former are predominantly autotrophic and the latter heterotrophic(136). This differentiation, however, is not sharp. Some purple sulfur bacteria can also grow in media devoid of H_2S but supplied instead with organic compounds and thus resemble the purple nonsulfur bacteria and vice versa. A further distinction between the two groups as to their growth factor requirement is not above criticism. *Rhodomicrobium*, which is classified with the *Athiorhodaceae* does not appear to require any vitamins for growth and can readily grow on purely mineral media containing H_2S, whereas *Chromatium* and *Thiospirillum* of the *Thiorhodaceae* seem to depend on an external supply of vitamin B_{12}. However, morphological differences can still support a differentiation between the two groups of purple bacteria.

Purple bacteria in general grow readily when illuminated under anaerobic conditions in synthetic media with malate and an ammonium salt as sole carbon and nitrogen source. With a suitable organic compound available, the presence of CO_2 or inorganic donors is unnecessary(99). Purple bacteria in fact seem to grow much more rapidly with organic carbon sources such as C_4-dicarboxylic acids than with CO_2. On media containing more oxidized substrates excellent growth is obtained in the absence or with evolution of CO_2 (54). These organic hydrogen donors do not undergo a simple one-step oxidation in order to furnish the cell with CO_2 for photochemical reduction (135) but generally supply carbon intermediates, other than CO_2, which are directly used by the cell for synthetic purposes (54). This, of course, led to the conclusion that under conditions in which organic compounds supply intermediates for direct assimilation, photosynthetic CO_2 fixation is not obligatory and may in fact be bypassed or suppressed (58, 78, 112–114, 116). The anaerobic utilization of organic compounds is therefore essentially of a heterotrophic character.

Photometabolism of Hydrogen. *Chromatium* cytochromes are reduced by thiosulfate and can serve therefore as a point of entry for electrons from this source. Apart from the reduction, gas, which was found to be hydrogen, was evolved in the light. This evolution of hydrogen occurred only in the light. The photoproduction of hydrogen is dependent on the thiosulfate concentration. In using one mole of thiosulfate, two electrons and two protons combine with the help of hydrogenase and hydrogen is evolved. This photoproduction of hydrogen can be viewed as a reduction of H^+ by a hydrogenase with the aid of electrons expelled from the excited chlorophyll molecules. The cyto-chrome system would thus become a gateway for the entry of electrons and for their transport to chlorophyll. The electron flow mechanism for the photoproduction of hydrogen from thiosulfate envisages the electron transfer shown in Fig. 2.7.

In other words, *Chromatium* raises electrons supplied by thiosulfate to chlorophyll, via cytochromes, to a reducing potential at least equal to that of molecular hydrogen. This hydrogen evolution is inhibited by nitrogen gas and ammonium ions as well as in the presence of organic electron donors (56,

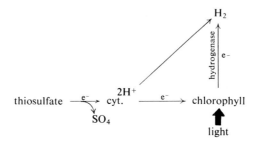

Fig. 2.7. The electron flow mechanism for the photoproduction of hydrogen from thiosulfate.

57). However, CO_2 fixation was not inhibited either by N_2 or NH_4 as long as thiosulfate was the electron donor, which indicates that only the flow of electrons to H^+, but not the flow of electrons for CO_2 fixation via NAD(P) is inhibited. The reaction sequence (see also Chapter 5) would therefore be

$$S_2O_3^{2-} + 2\,OH^- \;\rightarrow\; S + SO_4^{2-} + 2e^- + H_2O$$

$$S + 8\,OH^- \;\rightarrow\; SO_4^{2-} + 6e^- + 4\,H_2O$$

$$10\,H_2O \xrightarrow{\;dark\;} 10\,H^+ + 10\,OH^-$$

$$S_2O_3^{2-} + 5\,H_2O \;\rightarrow\; 2\,SO_4^{2-} + 8e^- + 10\,H^+$$

This evolution of hydrogen is quite common in photosynthetic bacteria (56, 57) (see Fig. 2.8).

The detailed properties of the hydrogenase are, however, still not well understood (99), particularly if one takes into consideration the possibilities of photoreduction of CO_2 with molecular hydrogen (45, 84, 95, 102, 109, 140). The finding that N_2 acts as a repressor to hydrogen evolution (79) led to the discovery that both purple and green bacteria are capable of nitrogen fixation under anaerobic conditions in the light (90). This nitrogen-fixing capability is another possible way of utilizing the electrons expelled from chlorophyll by light (6). This interrelationship between the photoproduction of hydrogen and photosynthetic N_2 fixation does not seem to be confined to the photosynthetic bacteria alone. For example, blue-green algae, which are known for their photosynthetic N_2-fixation ability, can be adapted also to hydrogen formation(1, 53).

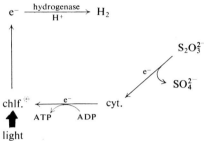

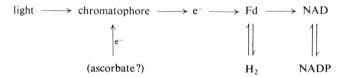

FIG. 2.8. The mechanism postulated by Losada, Nozaki, and Arnon to account for photohydrogen evolution from thiosulfate by purple bacteria(121) (reprinted with permission of the American Society for Microbiology).

If molecular hydrogen serves as electron donor instead of H_2S or thiosulfate, it can be used as a useful reductant in the reduction of NAD(138). Extracts of *Chromatium* and *Chlorobium* showed a ferredoxin-dependent reduction of NAD. The enzyme responsible for this step is called "ferredoxin–NAD reductase" and couples ferredoxin (Fd) with NAD (see Fig. 2.9). This Fd–NAD

FIG. 2.9. Hypothetical electron flow pattern of photosynthetic bacteria leading to PN reduction(138).

reaction is a so-called dark reaction(21, 41). The rate of NAD reduction is three to four times that of NADP, which indicates that NAD is the primary acceptor. It may therefore be that the enzyme Fd–NAD reductase could well play a key role in photochemical NAD reduction.

Photometabolism of Acetate. *Rhodospirillum rubrum* is able to assimilate acetate directly in the absence of CO_2(123). Acetate is converted to acetyl CoA by an acetate-activating enzyme(36, 37) with acetyl adenylate as the anhydride intermediate(15).

$$acetyl + ATP \rightleftharpoons acetyl\ adenylate + pyrophosphate$$

$$acetyl\ adenylate + CoA \rightleftharpoons acetyl\ CoA + AMP$$

The main assimilatory product formed is poly-β-hydroxybutyric acid. Since this synthesis is reductive, some acetate must be oxidized in order to provide the necessary reducing power. In this case the conversion of acetate to the polymer will compete with CO_2 fixation for the limiting reducing power available. In the absence of CO_2, poly-β-hydroxybutyric acid can be formed as a reserve product as shown in Fig. 2.10. The supply of reducing power is an anaerobic process also and probably proceeds via the tricarboxylic acid (TCA) cycle, as will be seen later.

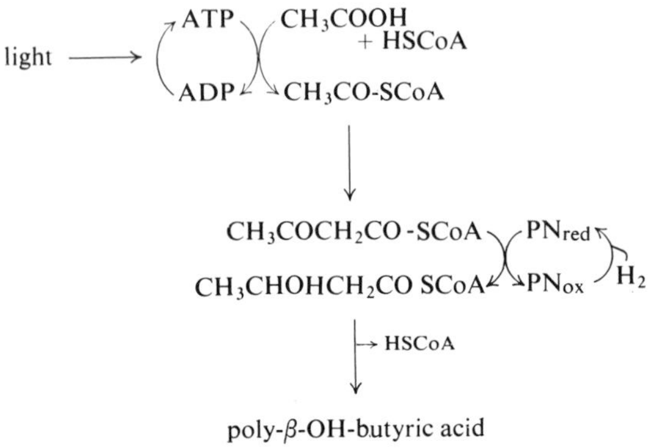

FIG. 2.10. The mechanism postulated by Stanier(121) to account for the acetate–hydrogen reaction in purple bacteria discovered by Gaffron in 1935 (reprinted with permission of the American Society of Microbiology).

The formation of poly-β-hydroxybutyric acid depends on the amount of CO_2 present, since CO_2 will swing the synthesis toward polysaccharide formation. The economics and usefulness of polymer formation as reserve products is quite remarkable, since the bacterial cell cannot accumulate free fatty acids to any extent without causing serious damage to the cell. By forming the polymer, these acids are neutralized and made osmotically inert and the cell is able to build up a reserve of reducing power, which can be used for subsequent CO_2 fixation. In the presence of sodium bicarbonate in addition to acetate, *Rhodospirillum rubrum*(106) performs a similar metabolism to *Chlorobium*(68). Studies with *R. rubrum* indicate that glutamate is synthesized from acetate and bicarbonate probably via a light-dependent anaerobic TCA cycle. *Rhodospirillum rubrum* can therefore assimilate acetate in the absence of bicarbonate to form poly-β-hydroxy butyrate and in the presence of bicarbonate to synthesize glutamate. *Chlorobium thiosulfatophilum*, although being a strict autotroph, assimilates acetate provided that bicarbonate and a source of reducing power (i.e., hydrogen gas) are present. There is no formation of the polymer poly-β-hydroxy butyrate. The pathways leading to glutamate are not known as yet although a hypothesis has been put forward (see Fig. 2.14). With the findings that even autotrophs may be able to assimilate organic compounds, the limitations of autotrophs may reside not in their capacity to assimilate or metabolize organic compounds, but in their capacity to oxidize them and so derive reducing power for biosynthetic reactions leading to cell growth. *Chloropseudomonas ethylicum* could play an intermediary role since this green obligately photosynthetic bacterium has a nutritional requirement for a 2-carbon compound(22) and most of the TCA cycle enzymes have been found to be present. Polymer synthesis from acetate requires only one mole of ATP per mole acetate. If therefore all the electrons needed for the reductive steps are transferred from hydrogen (reducing power) at the pyridine nucleotide level, no ATP can be formed as a result of hydrogen oxidation. The only function which could be attributed to light is the generation of ATP by cyclic photophosphorylation(121, 123). The two key enzymes for the formation and degradation of the polymer have been identified and purified as 3-hydroxy butyrate dehydrogenase(16) (D-hydroxy butyrate-NAD oxidoreductase, E.C. 1.1.1.30), which catalyzes the reaction

$$\text{acetoacetate} + \text{NADH} + \text{H}^+ \rightarrow \text{3-hydroxy butyrate} + \text{NAD}^+$$

and 3-hydroxy acid dehydrogenase (E.C. 1.1.1.45)(119) which can catalyze the reversible conversion of L(+)-3-hydroxy butyrate into acetoacetate.

Photometabolism of Butyrate. Butyrate is assimilated to poly-β-hydroxybutyric acid without CO_2 evolution(98). The CO_2 that is fixed photosynthetically with molecular hydrogen is converted to polysaccharides as indicated before:

$$2n\text{C}_4\text{H}_8\text{O}_2 \rightarrow 2(\text{C}_4\text{H}_6\text{O}_2)_n + 4n[\text{H}]$$

$$4n[\text{H}] + n\text{CO}_2 \rightarrow (\text{CH}_2\text{O})_n + n\text{H}_2\text{O}$$

$$2n\text{C}_4\text{H}_8\text{O}_2 + n\text{CO}_2 \rightarrow 2(\text{C}_4\text{H}_6\text{O}_2)_n + (\text{CH}_2\text{O})_n$$

Photometabolism of Succinate. The photometabolism of succinate is slightly more complicated than butyrate and acetate. Succinate as hydrogen donor transfers electrons at a potential which is lower than that of NAD. These electrons are therefore not able to reduce NAD directly. The bacterial chromatophore, however, is capable of performing a light-dependent reduction of NAD in order to overcome this problem. This reduction is coupled with the oxidation of either succinate or reduced flavin mononucleotides(47). Realizing that the photochemical reactions by *R. rubrum* chromatophores are couched in terms of only one electron transfer system(137), whereby part of this electron transfer scheme could be operative in the respiratory reaction which takes place in the dark with this organism, the reaction site should be as shown in Fig. 2.11. The result of the photometabolism is in principle the synthesis of polysaccharides. The substrate is oxidized via fumarate to pyruvate and a continuation of the reverse of the Embden-Meyerhof pathway. A small amount of substrate is also oxidized to acetate and forms the polymer poly-β-hydroxybutyric acid.

After having found a stoichiometric relationship between the amount of succinate and the NAD^+ reduced(39) and fumarate being the only product of succinate oxidation as well as succinate being the first detectable product of

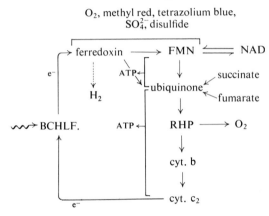

FIG. 2.11. Reaction sites for photochemical reactions observed with *Rhodospirillum rubrum* chromatophores(137) (reprinted with permission of The Antioch Press).

propionate oxidation followed by fumarate and malate(82), a pathway was proposed(40) leading from succinate to hexose (see Fig. 2.12). The enzymes involved in this pathway are:

E.C. 1.3.99.1:   succinate dehydrogenase (succinate- (acceptor) oxidoreductase)
E.C. 4.2.1.2:   fumarate hydratase (L-malate hydrolyase)
E.C. 1.1.1.37:   malate dehydrogenase (L-malate-NAD oxidoreductase)
E.C. 4.1.1.32:   phosphoenol pyruvate carboxylase (GTP-oxalacetate carboxylase (transphosphorylating))
E.C. 4.2.1.11:   phosphoenol pyruvate hydratase (D-2-phosphoglycerate hydrolyase)
E.C. 5.4.2.1:   phosphoglycerate phosphomutase (D-phosphoglycerate 2,3-phosphomutase)
E.C. 2.7.2.3:   phosphoglycerate kinase (ATP-D-3-phosphoglycerate 1-phosphotransferase)
E.C. 1.2.1.12:   triose phosphate dehydrogenase (D-glyceraldehyde 3 phosphate-NAD oxidoreductase (phosphorylating))
E.C. 5.3.1.1:   triose phosphate isomerase (D-glyceraldehyde 3-phosphate ketolisomerase)
E.C. 4.1.2.7:   aldolase (keto-1-phosphate aldehydelyase)

The aldolase, which catalyzes the reaction

dihydroxyacetone phosphate + aldehyde → ketose 1-phosphate

is mainly found in liver and has a wide specificity(31). The author wonders

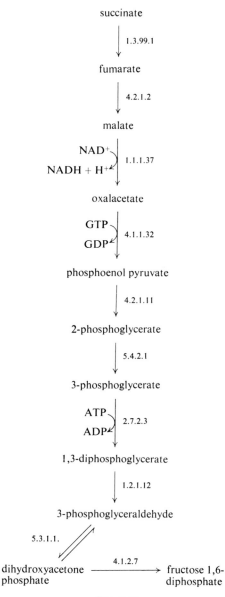

succinate

1.3.99.1

fumarate

4.2.1.2

malate

NAD+
NADH + H+   1.1.1.37

oxalacetate

GTP
GDP   4.1.1.32

phosphoenol pyruvate

4.2.1.11

2-phosphoglycerate

5.4.2.1

3-phosphoglycerate

ATP
ADP   2.7.2.3

1,3-diphosphoglycerate

1.2.1.12

3-phosphoglyceraldehyde

5.3.1.1.

dihydroxyacetone ————4.1.2.7————→ fructose 1,6-
phosphate   diphosphate

FIG. 2.12.

whether the more common aldolase, fructose diphosphate aldolase (fructose 1,6-diphosphate D-glyceraldehyde 3-phosphatelyase, E.C. 4.1.2.13) may be involved here catalyzing the reaction

dihydroxyacetone phosphate + 3-glyceraldehyde phosphate $\rightleftharpoons$ fructose 1,6-diphosphate

In comparing this pathway with the acetate metabolism and carbohydrate cycle in *Chromatium* (see Fig. 2.14) shows the similarities between the two systems. Earlier observations on the propionate fermentation(83) of *Rhodospirillum rubrum* would suggest that pyruvate is an intermediate, possibly instead of oxalacetate. The difference in the photometabolism of succinate and propionate is an additional carboxylation step which converts propionate to succinate(82), whereby propionyl CoA is the substrate for the carboxylation and methylmalonyl CoA the product of the reaction. As this propionate carboxylation resembles the ones in *Propionibacterium shermanii*, the detailed mechanism will be outlined in Chapter 6 under propionic acid metabolism.

If pyruvate is an intermediate, then part of the proposed pathway would have to be changed

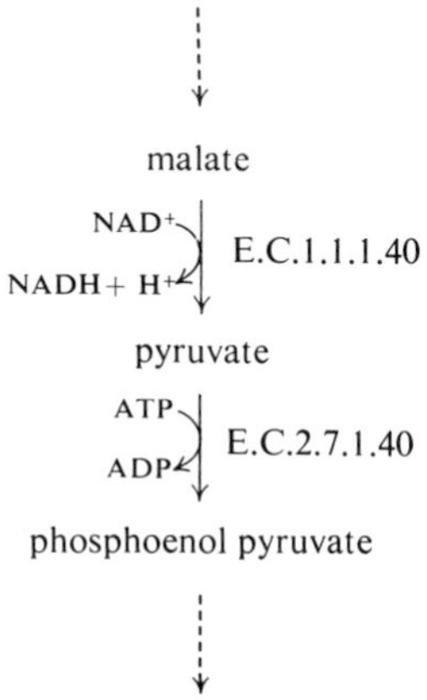

malate

NAD$^+$ ⟍
                    E.C.1.1.1.40
NADH + H$^+$ ⟋

pyruvate

ATP ⟍
                    E.C.2.7.1.40
ADP ⟋

phosphoenol pyruvate

Malate therefore would be converted to pyruvate instead of to oxalacetate by a reaction catalyzed by malate dehydrogenase (L-malate-NAD oxidoreductase (decarboxylating), E.C. 1.1.1.40) and phosphoenol pyruvate would be formed with the help of pyruvate kinase (ATP:pyruvate phosphotransferase, E.C. 2.7.1.40), which has been shown to be the case in enzyme fractions of *Chlorobium thiosulfatophilum*, *Chromatium*, and *Rhodospirillum rubrum*(20).

It can therefore be assumed that substrates which are convertible to acetyl units without forming pyruvate, i.e., acetate and butyrate, yield mostly poly-β-hydroxybutyric acid, whereas substrates which can be converted to pyruvate with an accompanying generation of reducing power, i.e., succinate, malate, and propionate, yield mostly polysaccharides. Synthesis of the latter follows a pathway similar to that of CO_2 fixation, which also leads to polysaccharide formation, but mainly via the Calvin cycle.

Hydrogen Evolution. All the previously mentioned dicarboxylic acids are members of the TCA cycle. It could therefore be expected that their photometabolism functions without hydrogen production if a suitable electron acceptor is provided or generated by the metabolism of the added substrate. Even CO_2 itself may act to some extent as an electron acceptor. Photoheterotrophically growing purple bacteria possess high levels of ribulose 1,5-diphosphate carboxylase (3-phospho-D-glycerate carboxylyase (dimerizing), E.C. 4.1.1.39) or carboxydismutase, the key enzyme for CO_2 fixation in the Calvin cycle for autotrophs(85). It can therefore be assumed that under certain conditions purple bacteria are able to simultaneously fix CO_2 via the autotrophic scheme (carboxylase reaction) and photoassimilate fragments derived from added organic compounds(130). It has been suggested that CO_2 may have the potentiality of influencing the direction of electron transfer(115). The presence of a certain steady-state concentration of CO_2 appears to be a major requirement for H_2 evolution also. A decreased yield of H_2 can certainly be correlated with the over-all oxidation level of the substrate, i.e., the higher the oxidation level, the smaller the effect. The mechanism, however, which is involved in the CO_2 stimulation of H_2 evolution is still obscure. In the presence of light as an energy source and substrates more reduced than CO_2, it may be assumed that the major function of the various metabolic cycles of photosynthetic bacteria is the synthesis of new cellular material rather than the production of energy(14). In *Chromatium* there exists a mechanism whereby an adequate supply of oxalacetate can be produced independently of the TCA cycle. The existence of enzymes which would bring about phosphoroclastic cleavage of pyruvate to acetylphosphate is now well established in anaerobes. This cleavage requires coenzyme A, P_i, and ferredoxin and results in the formation of a two-carbon unit, $H_2 + CO_2$, without formate as an intermediate. It was also shown that N_2 assimilation takes place at the expense of hydrogen evolution and is stimulated by pyruvate (see Fig. 2.13). Hydrogen evolution was strong in the dark, whereas in the light N_2 assimilation was favored. An enzyme was recently found(19) which can use ferredoxin directly as reductant in carbon assimilation. This enzyme was called "pyruvate synthase" and seems to catalyze a reductive synthesis of pyruvate from CO_2 and acetyl CoA. This mechanism can also function for the assimilation of acetate as well as of CO_2.

Illuminated cells of *R. rubrum* photometabolize 1 mole of malate to 3 moles of CO_2 and 3.8 moles of H_2. When H_2 is not produced, malate photodissimilation suggests that this C_4-dicarboxylic acid is converted to CO_2 and a C_3 fragment, which is then assimilated to carbohydrates(100). Hydrogen formation may represent an alternative electron transfer mechanism which comes into play when the metabolic energy balance is such that the ADP level has decreased to a critical level or, in other words, when the rate of ATP formation has exceeded the rate of utilization. The photoevolution of hydrogen via a terminal hydrogenase system can therefore be interpreted as the manifestation of an alternative pathway of electron transfer, which serves as a regulatory function in energy metabolism.

The Function of an Anaerobic TCA Cycle. The photometabolism of the organic acids mentioned above revealed that the role of ATP is twofold. It is either required for the formation of an "activated" substrate in order to bring about CO_2 fixation into the Calvin cycle, or it is required for the formation of an "activated" carbon source such as acetyl CoA from acetate(77) and CoA. The activated compounds are then ready for participation in the synthetic

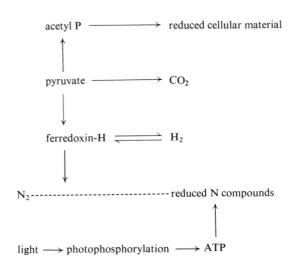

FIG. 2.13. The relationship between N_2 assimilation and evolution(14) (reprinted with permission of the National Academy of Sciences).

reactions that are catalyzed by a specific enzyme system, all of which function in the dark(91). It can therefore be stated that CO_2 assimilation is fundamentally only a special case of the use of light energy. The photosynthetic transformation of energy is more closely linked with phosphorus than with carbon assimilation.

It was mentioned earlier that the photometabolism of C_4-dicarboxylic acids such as malate and succinate form significant quantities of CO_2 and H_2. Because of this and the discovery of almost every enzyme of the TCA cycle in the cell-free extracts, it is now firmly believed that the photosynthetic bacteria use for their organic acid assimilation part of the TCA cycle, the glyoxylate cycle (see Fig. 2.14).

A mechanism of malate formation from acetate other than the TCA cycle functions in *Rhodopseudomonas spheroides* under light-anaerobic conditions (see Fig. 2.14). This route enables the continuous generation of malate from acetate through the action of malate synthase (L-malate glyoxylate lyase

(CoA acetylating), E.C. 4.1.3.2). Subsequent oxidation of malate to pyruvate would then become a site of acetate oxidation which does not pass through the stage of citrate(133). *Chromatium* and *Rhodospirillum rubrum* have a further

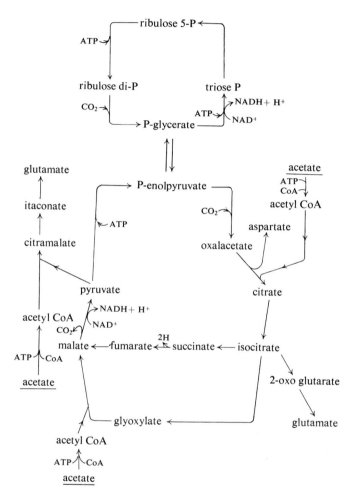

FIG. 2.14. Acetate metabolism and carbohydrate cycle in *Chromatium*(91) [reprinted with permission of Macmillan (Journals) Ltd.].

pathway of acetate transformation with the end products being citramalate and possibly glutamate(13,91).

In *Rhodospirillum palustris* one of the pathways from α-oxoglutarate via succinate, fumarate, malate, and pyruvate to cell material was confirmed, but the metabolism proceeds anaerobically in light, and only aerobically in the dark(96):

$$\alpha\text{-Oxoglutarate} + 1.5\,O_2 \longrightarrow 2.5\,(CH_2O) + 2.5\,CO_2 + 0.5\,H_2O \text{ (light)}$$

$$\alpha\text{-Oxoglutarate} + 2.0\,O_2 \longrightarrow 2.0\,(CH_2O) + 3\,CO_2 + H_2O \text{ (dark)}$$

$$\text{Succinate} + O_2 \longrightarrow 2.5\,(CH_2O) + 1.5\,CO_2 + 0.5\,H_2O \text{ (light)}$$

$$\text{Succinate} + 1.5\,O_2 \longrightarrow 2\,(CH_2O) + 2\,CO_2 + H_2O \text{ (dark)}$$

$$\text{Fumarate} + 0.5\,O_2 + 0.5\,H_2O \rightarrow 2.5\,(CH_2O) + 1.5\,CO_2 \text{ (light)}$$

$$\text{Fumarate} + O_2 + 0.5\,H_2O \longrightarrow 2\,(CH_2O) + 2\,CO_2 \text{ (dark)}$$

$$\text{Malate} + 0.5\,O_2 \longrightarrow 2.5\,(CH_2O) + 1.5\,CO_2 + 0.5\,H_2O$$

$$\text{Malate} + O_2 \longrightarrow 2\,(CH_2O) + 2\,CO_2 + H_2O$$

$$\text{Lactate} + 0.5\,O_2 \longrightarrow 2.5\,(CH_2O) + 0.5\,CO_2 + 0.5\,H_2O \text{ (light)}$$

$$\text{Lactate} + O_2 \longrightarrow 2(CH_2O) + CO_2 + H_2O \text{ (dark)}$$

$$\text{Pyruvate} + 0.5\,O_2 \longrightarrow 2.5\,(CH_2O) + 0.5\,CO_2 \text{ (light)}$$

$$\text{Pyruvate} + 0.5\,O_2 \longrightarrow 2\,(CH_2O) + CO_2$$

The molar amounts of oxygen uptake for one mole of each substrate consumed was as shown in the accompanying tabulation.

	Light	Dark
α-Oxoglutarate	1.13	1.51
Succinate	0.73	1.45
Malate	0.45	0.92

The higher rate of oxygen uptake in the dark reaction results in a higher rate of CO_2 formation [see also Stoppani et al.(125) for R. capsulatus].

The oxidation of citric, isocitric, and α-oxoglutaric acids did not occur in living cells but in dried cells or cell-free extracts(35). It is assumed that permeability barriers rather than lack of enzymes may be the reason for this situation. The presence of all the required enzymes, however, indicate that this TCA cycle may be the pathway for the terminal oxidation of the organic acid in a number of purple bacteria such as Chromatium and Rhodospirillum rubrum. The metabolism of organic acids under anaerobic conditions via the TCA cycle appears to be best in the dark. Light-anaerobic conditions, however, seem to suppress somewhat the activity of the TCA cycle having it only partly functioning(81). This suppression could be caused indirectly by a stimulation of the citrate cleavage reaction, which increases the levels of ATP and NADH + H^+ in the cell(131).

The observations on the photometabolism of acetate and the various dicarboxylic acids with *Rhodospirillum rubrum*(83) and *Chromatium*(91, 130) could be summarized by the comprehensive scheme shown in Fig. 2.15.

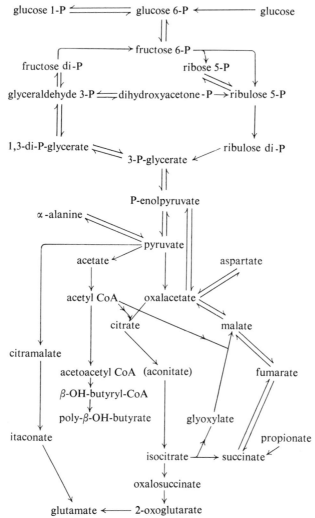

Fig. 2.15. Photometabolism of acetate and dicarboxylic acids in *Rhodospirillum rubrum* and *Chromatium*.

Coupled oxidation–reduction reactions between carboxylic acids of oxidatively different levels are favored as was indicated when the photometabolism of succinate in *Rhodospirillum rubrum*, for example, increased threefold when CO_2 was present, suggesting that CO_2 played the role of a hydrogen acceptor

(38). The CO_2 evolution was dependent on the oxidation level of the acids to be metabolized. In the case of *Chromatium* sp. strain *D* 2-oxoglutarate dehydrogenase (2-oxoglutarate:lipoate oxidoreductase (acceptor acylating), E.C. 1.2.4.2) and malate dehydrogenase (E.C. 1.1.1.37) are absent and substituted by malic enzyme (E.C. 1.1.1.40) and pyruvate carboxylase (E.C. 2.7.1.40)(48,49) which would give the modified glyoxylate cycle. The *Athiorhodaceae*, on the other hand, possess a complete TCA cycle, which functions oxidatively in the dark(29,35,38,125) as well as anaerobically in the light(59). The question whether aconitate is an intermediate of the TCA cycle will be

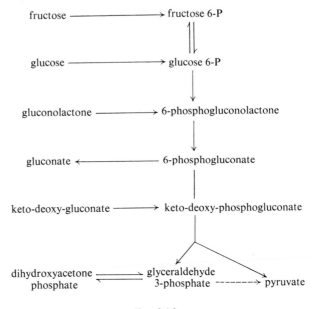

FIG. 2.16

discussed in Chapter 5. The presence of fructose diphosphate aldolase is still in dispute since its activity was found to be very low(130). This observation coincides with those made in *Hydrogenomonas H 16*(64), *Anacystis nidulans* (105), and *Rhodopseudomonas spheroides*(127). It is therefore suggested that the rapid and efficient utilization of glucose and fructose without acid production is dependent on the mutational acquisition of the enzyme phosphogluconic acid dehydrase or mannose isomerase, which is inducible in *Rhodopseudomonas spheroides*. The detailed descriptions of the individual reactions are given in Chapters 4 and 9. However, the reductive pentose cycle seems to be preferred for all those photosynthetic organisms which possess in addition to a weak fructose diphosphate aldolase activity also a weak ribulose diphosphate carboxylase (E.C. 4.1.1)(76, 108) (see Fig. 2.16).

Photometabolism of Acetone and Alcohols. A number of the *Athiorhodaceae* or nonsulfur purple bacteria are able to utilize various alcohols for the photosynthetic reduction of CO_2(44). Some species seem to specialize on primary, others on secondary alcohols. In many cases induced enzymes are required. The general reactions are

$$CH_3CH_2OH + 3H_2O \rightarrow 2CO_2 + 12H^+$$

$$3CO_2 + 12H^+ \rightarrow 3(CH_2O) + 3H_2O$$

$$CH_3CH_2CH_2OH + 5H_2O \rightarrow 3CO_2 + 18H^+$$

$$4.5CO_2 + 18H^+ \rightarrow 4.5(CH_2O) + 4.5H_2O$$

The photometabolism of acetone to products other than cell material is possible with *Rhodopseudomonas gelatinosa*(112). Since there were no intermediates found to accumulate, the following mechanism is postulated (reprinted with the permission of the American Society of Microbiologists):

isopropanol
$\downarrow$
(I)   acetone $\rightarrow$ acetoacetate $\rightarrow$ acetate $\rightarrow$ cell material
$\downarrow$
(II) acetol $\rightarrow$ methylglyoxal $\rightarrow$ pyruvate $\rightarrow$ cell material
$\downarrow$
(III) dihydroxyacetone $\rightarrow$ glyceraldehyde $\rightarrow$ glycerate $\rightarrow$ pyruvate
$\downarrow$
cell material

This scheme indicates that acetone condenses with CO_2 to form acetoacetate, but is governed by induced enzymes. Photophosphorylation, however, seem to be strongly inhibited by these lower aliphatic alcohols as could be shown with chromatophores of *Rhodospirillum rubrum*(128).

Metabolism of Glycine. *Rhodopseudomonas spheroides* is able to metabolize glycine almost exclusively through the glyoxylate cycle under both, light-anaerobic and dark-aerobic conditions(132). It has been demonstrated that the conversion of glycine into glyoxylate occurred mainly by transamination reactions, whereby pyruvate and oxalacetate act as amino acceptors.

Metabolism of Methane. A recent report(139) brought the first evidence that a strain of *Rhodopseudomonas gelatinosa* is able to utilize methane. This bacterium was found to grow with methane as sole electron donor and can incorporate CH_4– carbon into cellular material as well as oxidize methane to carbon dioxide. Details of the pathway are not available as yet.

The Electron Acceptor in Purple Bacteria. Throughout the chapter the main emphasis has been placed on the metabolism of the various photosynthetic bacteria with regard to their ATP formation and hydrogen donors, but little has been said about the hydrogen or electron acceptors. It was stated before that ATP plays a dual function, that there exists a relation between CO_2

concentration and H_2 evolution as well as a competition between H_2 evolution and nitrogen fixation. Assuming that the electrons (or hydrogen) required for the net generation of reduced NAD are derived from an accessory inorganic or organic compound, which would therefore serve as hydrogen donors, the mechanism shown in Fig. 2.17 would be possible (55). Depending on the redox potential of the donor, or on the steady-state concentration of the reduced and oxidized form of donor and NAD, the formation of reduced NAD may be promoted by energy-rich intermediates created by the action of

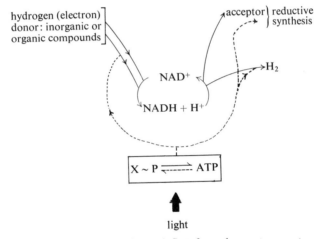

FIG. 2.17. Scheme for hydrogen (electron) flow from donors to acceptors and photo-production of bacterial photosynthesis(55) (reprinted with permission of The Antioch Press).

light on the photochemical apparatus. Reduced NAD would then be available for a great variety of reductive syntheses such as conversion of CO_2 to cell material, transformation of C_2 and C_3 compounds to reserve materials, or even reductive aminations to provide the protein synthesis with amino acid precursors. In the case of an excess production of ATP and reduced NAD in relation to the biosynthetic machinery, reduced NAD can be reoxidized through liberation of molecular hydrogen, by an energy-dependent process. The evolution of H_2 therefore can be interpreted as a sort of regulatory device which maintains ATP and reduced NAD at levels which are consistent with the over-all rate of biosynthetic activity(99).

The only common event left in all types of photosynthesis is the primary photochemical reaction which leads to ATP formation that includes the transfer of electrons through a closed carrier system coupled to chlorophyll. The use that a photosynthetic cell makes of the ATP generated is determined in part by its inherited enzymatic constitution and in part by environmental conditions. In green plants, green bacteria, and some of the purple sulfur bacteria, major portions of ATP go into CO_2 reduction to drive cell synthesis. In purple nonsulfur bacteria and some of the purple sulfur bacteria it is used to drive cell synthesis from externally provided organic substrates. The use of CO_2 as a sole source in photosynthesis is, in other words, not a fundamental feature of this process, but is restricted to those organisms which are called "autotrophs."

EVOLUTION OF PHOTOSYNTHESIS

Arnon and co-workers (7) proposed a very good theory on the evolution and development of photosynthesis. The first step is considered to be an emergence of a porphyrin that gave rise to chlorophyll. Primitive photosynthesis was probably limited to anaerobic cyclic photophosphorylation because there was no need for a photochemically formed reductant as long as H_2 was present. *Chromatium* has still this type of photosynthesis. As H_2 vanished from the atmosphere, the photosynthetic cell probably became dependent on the photosynthetic apparatus for generating photochemically a strong reductant from such electron donors as succinate or thiosulfate. In organisms which contain or can form adaptively hydrogenase or nitrogenase, this place of photosynthesis can be served today as photoproduction of molecular hydrogen or a photofixation of nitrogen. Water became an electron donor only with the emergence of plant photosynthesis. The difference between bacterial and plant photosynthesis seems to center on the electron donors that are consumed in the reduction of NAD.

REFERENCES

1. Allen, M. B. (1956). Photosynthetic nitrogen fixation by blue-green algae. *Sci. Monthly* **83**, 100; as cited by Stanier (121).
2. Amesz, J., and Vredenberg, W. J. (1966). Absorbance changes of photosynthetic pigments in various purple bacteria. *Proc. 2nd Western-Europe Conf. Photosyn., Zeist, Netherlands, 1965* p. 75. Donker, Rotterdam, Netherlands; *Chem. Abstr.* **65**, 19018 (1966).
3. Arnon, D. I. (1959). Conversion of light into chemical energy in photosynthesis. *Nature* **184**, 10.
4. Arnon, D. I. (1965). The role of light in photosynthesis. *In* "Readings from Scientific American: The Living Cell," p. 97. Freeman, San Francisco, California.
5. Arnon, D. I. (1966). The photosynthetic energy conversion process in isolated chloroplasts. *Experientia* **22**, 273.
6. Arnon, D. I., Losada, M., Nozaki, M., and Tagawa, K. (1960). Photofixation of nitrogen and photoproduction of hydrogen by thiosulfate during bacterial photosynthesis. *Biochem. J.* **77**, 23P.
7. Arnon, D. I., Losada, M., Nozaki, M., and Tagawa, K. (1961). Photoproduction of hydrogen, photofixation of nitrogen and a unified concept of photosynthesis. *Nature*, **190**, 601.
8. Arnon, D. I., Tsujimoto, H. Y., and McSwain, B. D. (1965). Photosynthetic phosphorylation and electron transport. *Nature* **207**, 1367.

9. Baltscheffsky, H., and von Stedingk, L. V. (1966). Bacterial photophosphorylation in the absence of added nucleotide. A second intermediate stage of energy transfer in light induced formation of ATP. *Biochem. Biophys. Res. Commun.* **22**, 722.

10. Baltscheffsky, H., von Stedingk, L. V., Heldt, H. W., and Klingenberg, M. (1966). Inorganic pyrophosphate: Formation in bacterial photophosphorylation. *Science* **153**, 1120.

11. Baltscheffsky, M., and Baltscheffsky, H. (1963). Photophosphorylation in *Rhodospirillum rubrum*. About the electron transport chain and the phosphorylation reactions. *In* "Bacterial Photosynthesis" (H. Gest, A. S. Pietro, and L. P. Vernon, eds.), p. 195. Antioch Press, Yellow Springs, Ohio.

12. Bassham, J. A. (1962). The path of carbon on photosynthesis. *Sci. Am.* **206**, 88.

13. Benedict, C. R. (1962). Early products of ^{14}C-acetate incorporation in resting cells of *Rhodospirillum rubrum*. *Biochim. Biophys. Acta* **56**, 620.

14. Bennett, H. R., Rigopoulos, N., and Fuller, R. C. (1964). The pyruvate phosphoroclastic reaction and light-dependent N_2-fixation in bacterial photosynthesis. *Proc. Nat. Acad. Sci. U.S.* **52**, 762.

15. Berg, P. (1955). Participation of adenyl-acetate in the acetate-activating system. *J. Am. Chem. Soc.* **77**, 3163.

16. Bergmeyer, H. W., Gawehn, K., Klotzsch, H., Krebs, H. A., and Williamson, D. H. (1967). Purification and properties of crystalline 3-hydroxybutyrate dehydrogenase from *Rhodopseudomonas spheroides*. *Biochem J.* **102**, 423.

17. Biedermann, M., Drews, G., Marx, R., and Schröder, J. (1967). Der Einfluß des Sauerstoffpartialdruckes und der Antibiotica Actinomycin und Puromycin auf das Wachstum, die Synthese von Bakteriochlorophyll und die Thylakoidmorphogenese in Dunkelkulturen von *Rhodospirillum rubrum*. *Arch. Mikrobiol.* **56**, 133.

18. Bril, C. (1963). Studies on bacterial chromatophores. II. Energy transfer and photooxidative bleaching of bacteriochlorophyll in relation to structure in normal and carotinoid-depleted *Chromatium*. *Biochim. Biophys. Acta* **66**, 50.

19. Buchanan, B. B., and Arnon, D. I. (1965). Ferredoxin-dependent synthesis of labelled pyruvate from labelled acetyl-CoA and CO_2. *Biochem. Biophys. Res. Commun.* **20**, 163.

20. Buchanan, B. B., and Evans, M. C. W. (1966). The synthesis of phosphoenolpyruvate from pyruvate and ATP by extracts of photosynthetic bacteria. *Biochem. Biophys. Res. Commun.* **22**, 484.

21. Buchanan, B. B., Bachofen, R., and Arnon, D. I. (1964). Role of ferredoxin in the reductive assimilation of CO_2 and acetate by extracts of the photosynthetic bacterium, *Chromatium*. *Proc. Natl. Acad. Sci. U.S.* **52**, 829.

22. Callely, A. G., and Fuller, R. C. (1967). Carboxylic acid cycle enzymes in *Chloropseudomonas ethylicum*. *Biochem. J.* **103**, 74P.

23. Calvin, M., and Androes, G. M. (1962). Primary quantum conversion in photosynthesis. *Science* **138**, 867.

24. Chance, B., Horio, T., Kamen, M. D., Taniguchi, S. (1965). Kinetic studies on the oxidase systems of photosynthetic bacteria. *Biochim. Biophys. Acta* **112**, 1.

25. Chance, B., Nishimura, M., Avron, M., and Baltscheffsky, M. (1966). Light-induced intravesicular changes pH in *Rhodospirillum rubrum* chromatophores. *Arch. Biochem. Biophys.* **117**, 158.

26. Clayton, R. K. (1962). Symposium on Autotrophy. III. Recent developments in photosynthesis. *Bacteriol. Rev.* **26**, 151.

27. Clayton, R. K. (1963). Toward the isolation of a photochemical reaction center in *Rhodopseudomonas spheroides*. *Biochim. Biophys. Acta* **75**, 312.

28. Cohen-Bazire, G., Pfennig, N., and Kunisawa, R. (1964). The fine structure of green bacteria. *J. Cell Biol.* **22**, 207.
29. Crook, P. G., and Lindstrom, E. S. (1956). A comparison of the oxidative metabolism of light and dark grown *Rhodospirillum rubrum. Can. J. Microbiol.* **2**, 427.
30. de Klerk, H., and Kamen, M. D. (1966). A high-potential non-haem iron protein from the facultative photoheterotroph *Rhodopseudomonas gelatinosa. Biochim. Biophys. Acta* **112**, 175.
31. Dixon, M., and Webb, E. C. (1964). "Enzymes," 2nd ed. Longmans, Green, New York.
32. Drews, G. (1965). Untersuchungen zur Regulation der Bakteriochlorophyll-Synthese bei *Rhodospirillum rubrum. Arch. Mikrobiol.* **51**, 186.
33. Drews, G., and Giesebrecht, P. (1965). Die Thylakoidstrukturen von *Rhodopseudomonas* sp. *Arch. Mikrobiol.* **52**, 242.
34. Drews, G., and Oelze, J. (1966). Regulation of bacteriochlorophyll synthesis in *Rhodospirillum rubrum. Zentr. Bakteriol., Parasitenk., Abt. II* **120**, 1; *Chem. Abstr.* **65**, 4298 (1966).
35. Eisenberg, M. A. (1953). The tricarboxylic acid cycle in *Rhodospirillum rubrum. J. Biol. Chem.* **203** 815.
36. Eisenberg, M. A. (1955). The acetate-activating enzyme of *Rhodospirillum rubrum. Biochim. Biophys. Acta* **16**, 58.
37. Eisenberg, M. A. (1957). The acetate-activating enzyme of *Rhodospirillum rubrum. Biochim. Biophys. Acta* **23**, 327.
38. Elsden, S. R., and Ormerod, J. G. (1956). The effect of monofluoroacetate on the metabolism of *Rhodospirillum rubrum. Biochem. J.* **63**, 691.
39. Evans, M. C. W. (1965). The photooxidation of succinate by chromatophores of *Rhodospirillum rubrum. Biochem. J.* **95**, 661.
40. Evans, M. C. W. (1965). The photoassimilation of succinate to hexose by *Rhodospirillum rubrum. Biochem. J.* **95**, 669.
41. Evans, M. C. W., and Buchanan, B. B. (1965). Photoreduction of ferredoxin and its use in carbon dioxide by a subcellular system from a photosynthetic bacterium. *Proc. Natl. Acad. Sci. US.* **53**, 1420.
42. Evans, M. C. W., Buchanan, B. B., and Arnon, D. I. (1966). A new ferredoxin-dependent carbon reduction cycle in a photosynthetic bacterium. *Federation Proc.* **25**, 226.
43. Foster, J. W. (1951). Autotrophic assimilation of carbon dioxide. *In* "Bacterial Physiology" (C. H. Werkman and P. W. Wilson, eds.), p. 361. Academic Press, New York.
44. Foster, J. W. (1944). Oxidation of alcohols by non-sulfur photosynthetic bacteria. *J. Bacteriol.* **47**, 355.
45. French, C. S. (1937). The quantum yield of hydrogen and carbon dioxide assimilation in purple bacteria. *J. Gen. Physiol.* **20**, 711; as cited by Ormerod and Gest (99).
46. Frenkel, A. W., and Hickman, D. D. (1959). *J. Biophys. Biochem. Cytol.* **6**, 284; as cited by Fuller *et al.* (50).
47. Frenkel, H. (1958). *Brookhaven Symp. Biol.* **11**, 276; as cited by Stanier (121).
48. Fuller, R. C., and Kornberg, H. L. (1961). A possible route for malate oxidation by *Chromatium. Biochem. J.* **79**, 8P.
49. Fuller, R. C., Smillie, R. M., Sisler, E. C., and Kornberg, H. L. (1961). Carbon metabolism in *Chromatium. J. Biol. Chem.* **236**, 2140.
50. Fuller, R. C., Conti, S. F., and Mellin, D. B. (1963). The structure of the photosynthetic apparatus in the green and purple sulfur bacteria. *In* "Bacterial Photosynthesis" (H. Gest, A. S. Pietro, and L. P. Vernon, eds.), p. 71. Antioch Press, Yellow Springs, Ohio.

51. Gaffron, H. (1935). Uber den Stoffwechsel der Purpurbakterien. II. *Biochem. Z.* 275, 301; as cited by Stanier (121).
52. Gaffron, H. (1935). Uber den Stoffwechsel der Purpurbakterien. II. *Biochem. Z.* 275, 301; as cited by Foster (43).
53. Gaffron, H., and Rubin, J. (1942). Fermentative and photochemical production of hydrogen in algae. *J. Gen. Physiol.* 26, 129; as cited by Stanier (121).
54. Gest, H. (1951). Metabolic pattern in photosynthetic bacteria. *Bacteriol. Rev.* 15, 183.
55. Gest, H. (1963). Metabolic aspects of bacterial photosynthesis. *In* "Bacterial Photosynthesis" (H. Gest, A. S. Pietro, and L. P. Vernon, eds.), p. 129. Antioch Press, Yellow Springs, Ohio.
56. Gest, H., and Kamen, M. D. (1949). Photoproduction of molecular hydrogen by *Rhodospirillum rubrum*. *Science* 109, 558.
57. Gest, H., and Kamen, M. D. (1949). Studies on the metabolism of photosynthetic bacteria. IV. Photochemical production of H$_2$ by growing cultures of photosynthetic bacteria. *J. Bacteriol.* 58, 239.
58. Gest, H., Kamen, M. D., and Bregoff, H. M. (1950). Studies on the metabolism of photosynthetic bacteria. V. Photoproduction of hydrogen and nitrogen fixation by *Rhodospirillum rubrum*. *J. Biol. Chem.* 182, 153.
59. Gest, H., Ormerod, J. G., and Ormerod, K. S. (1962). Photometabolism of *Rhodospirillum rubrum*: Light-dependent dissimilation of organic compounds to carbon dioxide and molecular hydrogen by an anaerobic citric acid cycle. *Arch. Biochem. Biophys.* 97, 21.
60. Gibson, J., and Morita, S. (1967). Changes in adenine nucleotides of intact *Chromatium* D by illumination. *J. Bacteriol.* 93, 1544.
61. Gibson, K. D. (1955). Nature of the insoluble pigmented structures (chromatophores) in extracts and lysates of *Rhodopseudomonas spheroides*. *Biochemistry* 4, 2027.
62. Gibson, K. D. (1965). Isolation and characterization of chromatophores from *Rhodopseudomonas spheroides*. *Biochemistry* 4, 2042.
63. Gibson, K. D. (1965). Structure of chromatophores of *Rhodopseudomonas spheroides;* removal of a non-pigmented outer layer of lipid. *Biochemistry* 4, 2052.
64. Gottschalk, G. (1964). Die Biosynthese der Poly-β-hydroxy-buttersäure durch Knallgasbakterien. III. Synthese aus Kohlendioxyd. *Arch. Mikrobiol.* 47, 236.
65. Gould, E. S., Kuntz, I. D., Jr., and Calvin, M. (1965). Absorption changes in bacterial chromatophores. II. A new chlorophyll-like pigment from the oxidation of chromatophores from *Rhodospirillum rubrum*. *Photochem. Photobiol.* 4, 482; *Chem. Abstr.* 63, 13617 (1965).
66. Gromet-Elhanan, Z. (1967). The relationship of cyclic and non-cyclic electron flow patterns with reduced indophenols to photophosphorylation. *Biochim. Biophys. Acta* 131, 526.
67. Henderson, R. W., and Nankiville, D. D. (1966). Electrophoretic and other studies on haem pigments from *Rhodopseudomonas palustris:* Cytochrome 552 and cytochromoid c. *Biochem. J.* 98, 587.
68. Hoare, D. S., and Gibson, J. (1964). Photoassimilation of acetate and the biosynthesis of amino acids by *Chlorobium thiosulfatophilum*. *Biochem. J.* 91, 546.
69. Holt, S. C., and Marr, A. G. (1965). Location of chlorophyll in *Rhodospirillum rubrum*. *J. Bacteriol.* 89, 1402.
70. Holt, S. C., and Marr, A. G. (1965). Isolation and purification of the intra-cytoplasmic membrane of *Rhodospirillum rubrum*. *J. Bacteriol.* 89, 1413.
71. Holt, S. C., and Marr, A. G. (1965). Effect of light intensity on the formation of intra-cytoplasmic membrane in *Rhodospirillum rubrum*. *J. Bacteriol.* 89, 1421.

72. Holt, S. C., Conti, S. F., and Fuller, R. C. (1966). Photosynthetic apparatus in the green bacterium *Chloropseudomonas ethylicum. J. Bacteriol.* **91**, 311.

73. Holt, S. C., Conti, S. F., and Fuller, R. C. (1966). Effect of light intensity on the formation of the photochemical apparatus in the green bacterium *Chloropseudomonas ethylicum. J. Bacteriol.* **91**, 349.

74. Horio, T., Nishikawa, K., and Yamashita, J. (1966). Synthesis and possible character of a high-energy intermediate in bacterial photophosphorylation. *Biochem. J.* **98**, 321.

75. Hughes, D. E., Conti, S. F., and Fuller, R. C. (1963). Inorganic polyphosphate metabolism in *Chlorobium thiosulfatophilum. J. Bacteriol.* **85**, 577.

76. Hurlbert, R. E., and Lascelles, J. (1963). Ribulosediphosphate carboxylase in Thiorhodaceae. *J. Gen. Microbiol.* **33**, 445.

77. James, A. T., Harris, R. V., Hitchcock, C., Wood, B. J. B., and Nichols, B. W. (1965). The biosynthesis and degradation of unsaturated fatty acids in higher plants and photosynthetic bacteria. *Fette, Seifen, Anstrichmittel* **67**, 393; *Chem. Abstr.* **63**, 15154 (1965).

78. Kamen, M. D. (1950). Hydrogenase activity and photoassimilation. *Federation Proc.* **9**, 543.

79. Kamen, M. D., and Gest, H. (1949). Evidence for a nitrogenase system in the photosynthetic bacterium *Rhodospirillum rubrum. Science* **109**, 560.

80. Karlson, P. (1965). "Introduction to Modern Biochemistry" 2nd ed. Academic Press, New York.

81. Kikuchi, G., Abe, S., and Muto, A. (1961). Carboxylic acid metabolism and its relation to porphyrin biosynthesis in *Rhodopseudomonas spheroides* under light-anaerobic conditions. *J. Biochem. (Tokyo)* **49**, 570.

82. Knight, M. (1962). The photometabolism of propionate by *Rhodospirillum rubrum. Biochem. J.* **84**, 170.

83. Kohlmiller, E. F., and Gest, H. (1951). A comparative study of the light and dark fermentations of organic acids by *Rhodospirillum rubrum. J. Bacteriol.* **61**, 269.

84. Korkes, S. (1955). Enzymatic reduction of pyridine nucleotides by molecular hydrogen. *J. Biol. Chem.* **216**, 737.

85. Lascelles, J. (1960). The formation of ribulose 1:5-diphosphate carboxylase by growing cultures of Athiorhodaceae. *J. Gen. Microbiol.* **23**, 499.

86. Lascelles, J. (1962). The chromatophores of photosynthetic bacteria. *J. Gen. Microbiol.* **29**, 47.

87. Lascelles, J. (1966). The accumulation of bacteriochlorophyll precursors by mutant and wild-type strains of *Rhodopseudomonas spheroides. Biochem. J.* **100**, 175.

88. Lees, H. (1955). The photosynthetic bacteria. *In* "Biochemistry of Autotrophic Bacteria," p. 61. Butterworth, London and Washington, D.C.

89. Lehninger, A. L. (1965). "Bioenergetics." Benjamin, New York.

90. Lindstrom, E. S., Burris, R. H., and Wilson, P. W. (1949). Nitrogen fixation by photosynthetic bacteria. *J. Bacteriol.* **58**, 313.

91. Losada, M., Trebst, A. V., Ogata, S., and Arnon, D. I. (1960). Equivalence of light and ATP in bacterial photosynthesis. *Nature* **186**, 753.

92. Losada, M., Whatley, F. R., and Arnon, D. I. (1961). Separation of two light reactions in non-cyclic photophosphorylation of green plants. *Nature* **190**, 606.

93. McBee, R. H., Lamanna, C., and Weeks, O. B. (1955). Definitions of bacterial oxygen relationship. *Bacteriol. Rev.* **19**, 45.

94. Marr, A. G. (1960). Localization of enzymes in bacteria. *In* "The Bacteria" (I. C. Gunsalus and R. Y. Stanier, eds.), Vol. 1, p. 443. Academic Press, New York.

95. Mechalas, B. J., and Rittenber, S. C. (1960). Energy coupling in *Desulfovibrio desulfuricans. J. Bacteriol.* **80**, 501.

96. Morita, S. (1961). Metabolism of organic acids in *Rhodopseudomonas palustris* in light and dark. *J. Biochem. (Tokyo)* **50**, 190.

97. Orlando, J. A., Sabo, D., and Curnyn, C. (1966). Photoreduction of pyridine nucleotide by subcellular preparations from *Rhodopseudomonas spheroides. Plant Physiol.* **41**, 937.

98. Ormerod, J. G. (1956). The use of radioactive CO_2 in the measurement of CO_2 fixation in *Rhodospirillum rubrum. Biochem. J.* **64**, 373.

99. Ormerod, J. G., and Gest, H. (1962). Symposium on metabolism of inorganic compounds. IV. Hydrogen photosynthesis and alternative pathways metabolic in photosynthetic bacteria. *Bacteriol. Rev.* **26**, 51.

100. Ormerod, J. G., Ormerod, K. S., and Gest, H. (1961). Light-dependent utilization of organic compounds and photoproduction of molecular hydrogen by photosynthetic bacteria; relationships with nitrogen metabolism. *Arch. Biochem. Biophys.* **94**, 449.

101. Park, C., and Berger, L. R. (1967). Fatty acids of extractable and bound lipids of *Rhodomicrobium vannielii. J. Bacteriol.* **93**, 230.

102. Peck, H. D. (1960). Evidence for oxidative phosphorylation during the reduction of sulfate with hydrogen by *Desulfovibrio desulfuricans. J. Biol. Chem.* **235**, 2734.

103. Porva, R. J., and Lascelles, J. (1965). Haemoproteins and haem-synthesis in facultative photosynthetic and denitrifying bacteria. *Biochem. J.* **94**, 120.

104. Rabinowitch, E. I. (1948). Photosynthesis. *Sci. Am.* **179**, 24.

105. Richter, G. (1959). Comparison of enzymes of sugar metabolism in two photosynthetic algae: *Anacystis nidulans* and *Chlorella pyrenoidosa. Nature* **46**, 604.

106. Rinne, R. W., Buckman, R. W., and Benedict, C. R. (1965). Acetate and bicarbonate metabolism in photosynthetic bacteria. *Plant Physiol.* **40**, 1066.

107. Roelefson, P. A. (1934). On the metabolism of the purple sulfur bacteria. *Koninkl. Ned. Akad. Wetenschap., Proc.* **37**, 660; as cited by Foster (43).

108. Rolls, J. P., and Lindstrom, E. S. (1966). Coupling of thiosulfate oxidation with CO_2 fixation in *Rhodopseudomonas palustris. Federation Proc.* **25**, 739.

109. Rose, I. A., and Ochoa, S. (1956). Phosphorylation by particulate preparations of *Azotobacter vinelandi. J. Biol. Chem.* **220**, 307.

110. Sato, H., Takahashi, K., and Kikuchi, G. (1966). Inhibition studies of photophosphorylation by *Rhodospirillum rubrum* chromatophores with particular concerns to antimycin-resistant photophosphorylation in the presence of artificial electron carriers. *Biochim. Biophys. Acta* **112**, 8.

111. Schwartz, M. (1967). Wavelength-dependent quantum yields of chloroplast phosphorylation catalyzed by phenazine methosulphate. *Biochim. Biophys. Acta* **131**, 548.

112. Siegel, J. M. (1950). The metabolism of acetone by the photosynthetic bacterium *Rhodopseudomonas gelatinosa. J. Bacteriol.* **60**, 595.

113. Siegel, J. M. (1954). The photosynthetic metabolism of acetone by *Rhodopseudomonas gelatinosa. J. Biol. Chem.* **208**, 205.

114. Siegel, J. M. (1957). The dark anaerobic metabolism of acetone and acetate by the photosynthetic bacterium *Rhodopseudomonas gelatinosa. J. Biol. Chem.* **228**, 41.

115. Siegel, J. M., and Kamen, M. D. (1951). Studies on the metabolism of photosynthetic bacteria. VII. Comparative studies on the photoproduction of hydrogen by *Rhodopseudomonas gelatinosa* and *Rhodospirillum rubrum. J. Bacteriol.* **61**, 215.

116. Siegel, J. M., and Smith, A. M. (1955). The dark aerobic metabolism of acetone by the photosynthetic bacterium *Rhodopseudomonas gelatinosa. J. Biol. Chem.* **214**, 475.

117. Sistrom, W. R. (1962). Observations on the relationship between formation of photo-pigments and the synthesis of protein in *Rhodopseudomonas spheroides*. *J. Gen. Microbiol.* **28**, 599.

118. Sistrom, W. R. (1965). Effect of oxygen on growth and the systhesis of bacteriochloro-phyll in *Rhodospirillum molischianum*. *J. Bacteriol.* **89**, 403.

119. Smiley, J. D., and Ashwell, G. (1961). Purification and properties of β-L-hydroxy acid dehydrogenase. II. Isolation of β-keto-L-gluconic acid, an intermediate in L-xylulose biosynthesis. *J. Biol. Chem.* **236**, 357.

120. Smith, A. J., and Lascelles, J. (1966). Thiosulphate metabolism and rhodanese in *Chromatium sp.* strain *D. J. Gen. Microbiol.* **42**, 357.

121. Stanier, R. Y. (1961). Photosynthetic mechanisms in bacteria and plants. Development of a unitary concept. *Bacteriol. Rev.* **25**, 1.

122. Stanier, R. Y. (1963). The organization of photosynthetic apparatus in purple bacteria. *In* "The General Physiology of Cell Specialization" (D. Mazie and A. Tyler, eds.), p. 242. McGraw-Hill, New York.

123. Stanier, R. Y., Doudoroff, M., Kunisawa, R., and Contopoulos, R. (1959). The role of organic substrates in bacterial photosynthesis. *Proc. Natl. Acad. Sci. U.S.* **45**, 1246.

124. Stern, H., and Nanney, D. L. (1965). "The Biology of Cells." Wiley, New York.

125. Stoppani, A. O. M., Fuller, R. C., and Calvin, M. (1955). Carbon dioxide fixation by *Rhodopseudomonas capsulatus*. *J. Bacteriol.* **61**, 491.

126. Sybesma, C., and Beugeling, T. (1967). Light-induced absorbance changes in the green photosynthetic bacterium *Chloropseudomonas ethylicum*. *Biochim. Biophys. Acta* **131**, 357.

127. Szymona, M., and Doudoroff, M. (1960). Carbohydrate metabolism in *Rhodopseudomonas spheroides*. *J. Gen. Microbiol.* **22**, 167.

128. Thore, A., and Baltscheffsky, H. (1965). Inhibitory effect of lower aliphatic alcohols on electron transport phosphorylation systems. I. Straightchain primary alcohols. *Acta Chem. Scand.* **19**, 1591; *Chem. Abstr.* **64**, 5316 (1966).

129. Trentini, W. C., and Starr, M. P. (1967). Growth and ultrastructure of *Rhodomicrobium vannielii* as a function of light-intensity. *J. Bacteriol.* **93**, 1699.

130. Trüper, H. G. (1964). CO₂-fixierung und Intermediärstoffwechsel bei *Chromatium okenii* Perty. *Arch. Mikrobiol.* **49**, 23.

131. Tsuboi, S., and Kikuchi, G. (1966). Regulation by illumination of the citric acid cycle activity in *Rhodopseudomonas spheroides*. *J. Biochem. (Tokyo)* **59**, 456.

132. Tsuiki, S., and Kikuchi, G. (1962). Catabolism of glycine by *Rhodopseudomonas spheroides*. *Biochim. Biophys. Acta* **64**, 514.

133. Tsuiki, S., Muto, A., and Kikuchi, G. (1963). A possible route of acetate oxidation in *Rhodopseudomonas spheroides*. *Biochim. Biophys. Acta* **69**, 181.

134. Tuttle, A. L., and Gest, H. (1959). Subcellular particulate systems and the photo-chemical apparatus of *Rhodospirillum rubrum*. *Proc. Natl. Acad. Sci. U.S.* **45**, 1261.

135. van Niel, C. B. (1941). The bacterial photosynthesis and their importance for the general problem of photosynthesis. *Advan. Enzymol.* **1**, 263.

136. van Niel, C. B. (1963). A brief survey of the photosynthetic bacteria. *In* "Bacterial Photosynthesis" (H. Gest, A. S. Pietro, and L. P. Vernon, eds.), p. 459. Antioch Press, Yellow Springs, Ohio.

137. Vernon, L. P. (1963). Photooxidation and photoreduction reactions catalyzed by chromatophores of purple photosynthetic bacteria. *In* "Bacterial Photosynthesis" (H. Gest, A. S. Pietro, and L. P. Vernon, eds.), p. 235. Antioch Press, Yellow Springs, Ohio.

138. Weaver, P., Tinker, K., and Valentine, R. C. (1965). Ferredoxin-linked DPN reduction by the photosynthetic bacteria *Chromatium* and *Chlorobium*. *Biochem. Biophys. Res. Commun.* **21**, 195.
139. Wertlieb, D., and Vishniac, W. (1967). Methane utilization by a strain of *Rhodopseudomonas gelatinosa*. *J. Bacteriol.* **93**, 1722.
140. Whittenberger, C. C., and Repaske, R. (1961). Studies on hydrogen oxidation in cell-free extracts of *Hydrogenomonas eutropha*. *Biochim. Biophys. Acta* **47**, 542; as cited by Ormerod and Gest (99).
141. Yamanaka, T., and Kamen, M. D. (1967). An NADP reductase and a non-haem iron protein isolated from a facultative photoheterotroph, *Rhodopseudomonas palustris*. *Biochim. Biophys. Acta* **131**, 317.

SUPPLEMENTARY READINGS

Bachofen, R., and Neeracher, H. (1968). Glutamatdehydrogenase im photosynthetischen Bakterium *Rhodospirillum rubrum*. *Arch. Mikrobiol.* **60**, 235.
Barker, H. A. (1967). Citramalate lyase of *Clostridium tetanomorphum*. *Arch. Mikrobiol.* **59**, 4.
Beugeling, T. (1968). Photochemical activities of $K_3Fe(CN)_6$-treated chromatophores from *Rhodospirillum rubrum*. *Biochim. Biophys. Acta* **153**, 143.
Biedermann, M., and Drews, G. (1968). Trennung der Thylakoidbausteine einiger Athiorhodaceae durch Gelelektrophorese. *Arch. Mikrobiol.* **61**, 48.
Black, C. C. (1967). Evidence supporting the theory of two sites of photophosphorylation in green plants. *Biochem. Biophys. Res. Commun.* **28**, 985.
Buchanan, B. B., Evans, M. C. W., and Arnon, D. I. (1967). Ferredoxin-dependent carbon assimilation in *Rhodospirillum rubrum*. *Arch. Mikrobiol.* **59**, 32.
Calleby, A. G., Rigopoulos, N., and Fuller, R. C. (1968). The assimilation of carbon by *Chloropseudomonas ethylicum*. *Biochem. J.* **106**, 615.
Carmeli, C., and Avron, M. (1967). A light-triggered adenosine triphosphate-phosphate exchange reaction in chloroplasts. *European J. Biochem.* **2**, 318.
Cox, R. M., and Fay, P. (1967). Nitrogen fixation and pyruvate metabolism in cell-free preparations of *Anabaena cylindrica*. *Arch. Mikrobiol.* **58**, 357.
Cusanovich, M. A., and Kamen, M. D. (1968). Light-induced electron transport in *Chromatium* strain D. I. Isolation and characterization of *Chromatium* chromatophores. *Biochim. Biophys. Acta* **153**, 376.
Cusanovich, M. A., Bartsch, R. G., and Kamen, M. D. (1968). Light-induced electron transport in *Chromatium* strain D. II. Light-induced absorbance changes in *Chromatium* chromatophores. *Biochim. Biophys. Acta* **153**, 387.
Cusanovich, M. A., and Kamen, M. D. (1968). Light-induced electron transport in *Chromatium* strain D. III. Photophosphorylation by *Chromatium* chromatophores. *Biochem. Biophys. Acta* **153**, 418.
Czygan, F.-Ch. (1968). Sekundär-Carotinoide in Grünalgen. I. Chemie, Vorkommen und Faktoren, welche die Bildung dieser Polyene beeinflussen. *Arch. Mikrobiol.* **61**, 81.
Del Campo, F. F., Ramirez, J. M., and Arnon, D. I. (1968). Stoichiometry of photosynthetic phosphorylation. *J. Biol. Chem.* **243**, 2805.
Gajdos, A., Gajdos-Török, M., Gorchein, A., Neuberger, A., and Tait, G. H. (1968). The effect of adenosine triphosphate on porphyrin excretion and on glycine metabolism in *Rhodopseudomonas spheroides*. *Biochem. J.* **106**, 185.
Graham, D., Grieve, A. M., and Smillie, R. M. (1968). Phytochrome as the primary photoregulator of the synthesis of Calvin cycle enzymes in etiolated pea seedlings. *Nature* **218**, 89.

Gray, E. D. (1967). Studies on the adaptive formation of photosynthetic structures in *Rhodopseudomonas spheroides*. I. Synthesis of macromolecules. *Biochim. Biophys. Acta* **138**, 550.

Gibson, J. (1967). Aerobic metabolism of *Chromatium* sp. strain *D*. *Arch. Mikrobiol.* **59**, 104.

Hatch, M. D., and Slack, C. R. (1968). A new enzyme for the interconversion of pyruvate and phosphopyruvate and its role in the C_4-dicarboxylic acid pathway of photosynthesis. *Biochem. J.* **106**, 141.

Hegeman, G. D. (1967). The metabolism of p-hydroxybenzoate by *Rhodopseudomonas palustris* and its regulation. *Arch. Microbiol.* **59**, 143.

Hirsch, P. (1968). Photosynthetic bacterium growing under carbon monoxide. *Nature* **217**, 555.

Hoare, D. S., Hoare, S. L., and Moore, R. B. (1967). The photoassimilation of organic compounds by autotrophic blue-green algae. *J. Gen. Microbiol.* **49**, 351.

Hurlbert, D. R. E. (1968). Effect of thiol-binding reagents on the metabolism of *Chromatium* *D*. *J. Bacteriol.* **95**, 1706.

Jensen, R. G., and Bassham, J. A. (1968). Photosynthesis by isolated chloroplasts. III. Light activation of the carboxylation reaction. *Biochim. Biophys. Acta* **153**, 227.

Joliot, P., Joliot, A., and Kok, B. (1968). Analysis of the interactions between the two photosystems in isolated chloroplasts. *Biochim. Biophys. Acta* **153**, 635.

Karlander, E. P., and Kraus, R. W. (1968). The laser as a light source for the photosynthesis and growth of *Chlorella vannielia*. *Biochim. Biophys. Acta* **153**, 312.

Kassner, R. D., and Kamen, M. D. (1968). Trace metal composition of photosynthetic bacteria. *Biochim. Biophys. Acta* **153**, 270.

Klemme, J.-H., and Schlegel, H. G. (1967). Photoreduction of pyridine nucleotide by chromatophores of *Rhodopseudomonas capsulata* by molecular hydrogen. *Arch. Mikrobiol.* **59**, 185.

Lascelles, J. (1968). The bacterial photosynthetic apparatus. *In* "Advances in Microbial Physiology" (A. H. Rose and J. F. Wilkinson, eds.), Vol. 2. p. 1. Academic Press, New York.

Loach, P. A. (1966). Primary oxidation-reduction changes during photosynthesis in *Rhodospirillum rubrum*. *Biochemistry*, **5**, 592; *Chem. Abstr.* **64**, 13117 (1966).

Lundegardh, H. (1967). Role of carotenoids in photosynthesis of green plants. *Nature* **216**, 981.

Morita, S. (1968). Evidence for three photochemical systems in *Chromatium D*. *Biochim. Biophys. Acta* **153**, 241.

Nelson, N., and Neumann, J. (1968). Interaction between ferredoxin and ferredoxin-NADP reductase from chlorophlasts. *Biochem. Biophys. Res. Commun.* **30**, 142.

Nishimura, M., Kadota, K., and Chance, B. (1968). Light-induced electron transfer, internal and external hydrogen ion changes, and phosphorylation in chormatophores of *Rhodospirillum rubrum*. *Arch. Biochem. Biophys.* **125**, 308.

Ohashi, A., Ishihava, N., and Kikuchi, G. (1967). Pyruvate metabolism in *Rhodopseudomonas spheroides* under light-anaerobic conditions. *J. Biochem.* (*Tokyo*) **62**, 497.

Olsen, I., and Merrick, J. M. (1968). Identification of propionate as an endogenous CO_2 acceptor in *Rhodospirillum rubrum* and properties of purified propionyl-coenzyme CoA carboxylase. *J. Bacteriol.* **95**, 1774.

Orlando, J. A. (1968). Light-dependent reduction of nicotinamide adenine dinucleotide phosphate by chromatophores of *Rhodopseudomonas spheroides*. *Arch. Biochem. Biophys.* **124**, 413.

Parson, W. W. (1968). The role of P_{870} in bacterial photosynthesis. *Biochim. Biophys. Acta* **153**, 248.

Ramirez, J., and Smith, L. (1968). Synthesis of adenosine triphosphate in intact cells of *Rhodospirillum rubrum* and *Rhodopseudomonas spheroides* on oxygenation or illumination. *Biochim. Biophys. Acta* **153**, 466.

Redfearn, E. R., and Powls, R. (1968). The quinones of green photosynthetic bacteria. *Biochem. J.* **106**, 50P.

Roles, J. P., and Lindstrom, E. S. (1967). Induction of a thiosulfate-oxidizing enzyme in *Rhodopseudomonas palustris*. *J. Bacteriol.* **94**, 784.

Roles, J. P., and Lindstrom, E. S. (1967). Effect of thiosulfate on the photosynthetic growth of *Rhodopseudomonas palustris*. *J. Bacteriol.* **94**, 860.

Schleyer, H. (1968). Electron paramagnetic resonance studies on photosynthetic bacteria. I. Properties of photo-induced EPR-signals of *Chromatium* D. *Biochim. Biophys. Acta* **153**, 427.

Sojka, G. A., Din, G. A., and Gest, H. (1967). Integration of energy conversion and biosynthetic processes in bacterial photosynthesis. *Nature* **216**, 1021.

Stedingk, L. V. van (1967). Light-induced reversible pH changes in chromatophores from *Rhodospirillum rubrum*. *Arch. Biochem. Biophys.* **120**, 537.

Tagawa, K., and Arnon, D. I. (1968). Oxidation-reduction potentials and stoichiometry of electron transfer in ferredoxins. *Biochim. Biophys. Acta* **153**, 602.

Terpstra, W. (1968). Interaction of a spinach protein factor with bacteriochlorophyll. *Biochim. Biophys. Acta* **153**, 675.

Thiele, H. H. (1968). Die Verwertung einfacher Substrate durch Thiorhodaceae. *Arch. Mikrobiol.* **60**, 124.

Yamada, T., and Kikuchi, G. (1968). Inhibition of the metabolism of carboxylic acids and amino acids by citramalate and other related compounds in *Rhodopseudomonas spheroides*. *J. Biochem.* (*Tokyo*) **63**, 462.

Yamanaka, T., and Okumuki, K. (1968). Comparison of *Chlorobium thiosulfatophilum* cytochrome C-555 with c-type cytochromes derived from algae and nonsulphur purple bacteria. *J. Biochem.* (*Tokyo*) **63**, 341.

3

CHEMOSYNTHESIS—ANAEROBIC RESPIRATION

CHEMOSYNTHESIS

It has been shown that photosynthetic bacteria obtain their energy from light, transfer it via cytochromes, and store it as ATP. They obtain their reducing power from the substrate, i.e., the exogenous hydrogen donor supplied. On comparative biochemical grounds therefore the energy system of the chemosynthetic bacteria would consist of a cytochrome system coupled to phosphorylation which generates ATP. In the case of chemolithotrophs, the whole system would be driven by the oxidation of inorganic compounds whereas in chemoorganotrophs this system would be driven by the oxidation of organic compounds. As in photosynthesis, three general processes have to be considered in the study of biological oxidations(35):

(1) the dehydrogenation of a substrate, followed by transfer of the hydrogen, or electron, to an ultimate acceptor;
(2) conservation of the energy released in step 1; and
(3) the subsequent metabolism of the dehydrogenated (oxidized) substrate.

In biological oxidations the energy present in an organic substrate is released by successive dehydrogenations of the carbon chain. Hereby the reducing equivalents are removed, normally two at a time, and transferred to a final acceptor, which may be oxygen in the case of aerobic respiration, inorganic compounds except oxygen in the case of anaerobic respiration, and organic compounds in the case of fermentation. This transfer proceeds via a potentially graded series of reversible oxidation–reduction systems known as electron transport systems. Although the electron transport mechanisms in mammalian systems are well studied, the knowledge of bacterial electron transport mechanisms has lagged well behind. The main reason for this is the great diversity of metabolic types among bacteria which thus provides a far greater diversity in composition of the electron transport chains. A generalized scheme of the presently understood electron transport system was well summarized by Dolin

(35) (see Scheme 3.1). The donated hydrogen is transferred from the substrate to NAD^+, which itself then donates electrons to the cytochrome system via a flavoprotein (FP). The identity and number of cytochrome components involved in bacterial systems are very difficult to specify as has been done in mammalian systems. In bacteria the cytochrome components vary from species to species and also with growth conditions. Bacteria may contain pigments

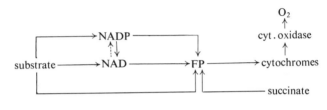

SCHEME 3.1

like the cytochrome a, a_3, b, c, and c_1 and others in a number of combinations. Some of the cytochromes have only been observed in bacteria. The main difference, however, between the mammalian and the bacterial cytochrome system seems to be the presence of several oxidases in bacteria. The possible pathway observed among the different bacteria could be summarized as shown in Scheme 3.2(148). The cytochromes of the bacterial systems, which are

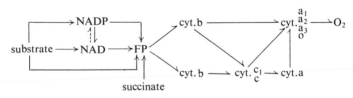

SCHEME 3.2

attached to insoluble particulate matter within the cell, can have very high turnover rates. The numerous combinations of cytochrome components of different bacteria led to the conclusion that the only requirement is for a mixture of several cytochromes with appropriately separated redox potentials. The most common ones are presented in Table 3.1 together with some electron donors and acceptors and carriers. After the enzyme-catalyzed dehydrogenation of a substrate, two electrons pass through the components of the electron transfer chain. This chain forms a transport sequence in which there occurs a stepwise increase in potential from that of $NADH + H^+/NAD^+$ to that of the oxygen electrode. Most substrates (e.g., lactate) are electromotively passive. In the presence of the appropriate dehydrogenase the oxidation of the substrate is catalyzed and the resulting two-component system (e.g., lactate–pyruvate) establishes the potential of the lower end of the electron transport chain.

The oxidized substrate (e.g., pyruvate) may enter a metabolic system while the released electrons proceed independently along the transport system. From Table 3.1 and Fig. 3.1, it can be seen that glyceraldehyde, α-ketoglutaric acid, and pyruvic acid—carbonyl and carboxyl compounds—are the most potent electron donors. Electrons from substrates usually enter the electron transport system through a carrier whose potential lies in the vicinity of, or

TABLE 3.1

SOME ELECTRODE POTENTIALS OF BIOLOGICAL INTEREST[a]

Couple	E_0' (V at pH 7.0)
$2H_2O \rightleftharpoons O_2 + 4H^+ + 4e$	+0.816
$NO_2^- + H_2O \rightleftharpoons NO_3^- + 2H^+ + 2e$	+0.421
$H_2O_2 \rightleftharpoons O_2 + 2H^+ + 2e$	+0.295
Cyt. $a_3^{2+} \rightleftharpoons$ cyt. $a_3^{3+} + 1e$	+0.285
Cyt. $a^{2+} \rightleftharpoons$ cyt. $a^{3+} + 1e$	+0.290
Cyt. $c^{2+} \rightleftharpoons$ cyt. $c^{3+} + 1e$	+0.250
Succinate $\rightleftharpoons$ fumarate + $2H^+ + 2e$	+0.031
Leucomethylene blue $\rightleftharpoons$ methylene blue + $2H^+ + 2e$	+0.011
$H_2 \rightleftharpoons 2H^+ + 2e$ (pH 0)	0.0
Cyt. $b^{2+} \rightleftharpoons$ cyt. $b^{3+} + 1e$ (pH 7.4)	−0.040
Lactate $\rightleftharpoons$ pyruvate + $2H^+ + 2e$	−0.19
$FADH_2 \rightleftharpoons FAD^+ + 2H^+ + 2e$	−0.22
$FMNH_2 \rightleftharpoons FMN^+ + 2H^+ + 2e$	−0.22
$NADH + H^+ \rightleftharpoons NAD^+ + 2H^+ + 2e$	−0.32
$NADPH + H^+ \rightleftharpoons NADP^+ + 2H^+ + 2e$	−0.324
$H_2 \rightleftharpoons 2H^+ + 2e$	−0.414
Glyceraldehyde 3-P + $H_2O \rightleftharpoons$ 3-phosphoglycerate + $3H^+ + 2e$	−0.57
α-Ketoglutarate + $H_2O \rightleftharpoons$ succinate + $CO_2 + 2H^+ + 2e$	−0.673
Pyruvate + $H_2O \rightleftharpoons$ acetate + $CO_2 + 2H^+ + 2e$	−0.699

[a] From Dolin(35).

higher than, the potential for the substrate dehydrogenation. In the presence of the appropriate catalyst, electron flow will take place from the system of lower potential to the system of higher potential (more positive). The greater the difference in voltage, the farther the reactions will go toward completion.

The formation of energy-rich phosphate compounds (ATP, etc.) was described earlier. The yield of ~P depends upon the ΔF of the reaction and upon the number of steps that may be available for energy conservation. Where oxygen is the final electron acceptor, the results are expressed usually as P/O ratios. This ratio represents the equivalents of phosphate esterified per atom of oxygen taken up. There also exist reactions which have no need for further hydrogen transfer reactions. These types of reactions are called "substrate phosphorylation," because they are coupled to the formation of ATP. This type of phosphorylation will be treated under "fermentation."

A number of bacteria are able to form high molecular weight polyphosphates or metaphosphates. This process appears to be a form of "high-energy" phosphate storage generated in oxidative phosphorylation. This polyphosphate is formed solely from the terminal phosphate group of ATP.

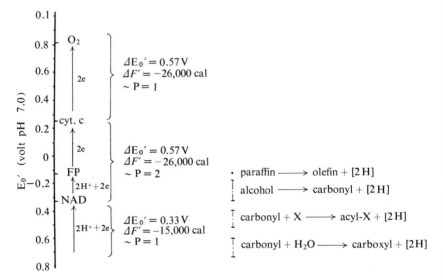

FIG. 3.1. Comparison of electrode potentials of coenzymes and substrate systems(35).

Although the division of the bacteria into aerobes and anaerobes cannot be rigidly maintained from the point of view of comparative biochemistry, it still plays an important role in bacterial nutrition and classification. Among the chemosynthetic bacteria in general those which reduce inorganic sulfur compounds in various oxidation states are anaerobes, those which reduce nitrogen compounds in various oxidation states are facultative anaerobes, and those which oxidize reduced sulfur and nitrogen compounds are obligate aerobes. It is possible to estimate the maximum energy available for biochemical use in the electron systems which may be encountered in anaerobes. However, information on phosphorylations coupled to the electron transport systems in anaerobic bacteria is very scattered and will be considered with the individual bacterial groups. In general, there is no justification for assuming that the electron transport systems of anaerobic bacteria differ in principle or even in any major way from that of aerobes. There is almost no difference in the cytochrome-dependent electron transport systems of facultative anaerobes when grown aerobically and anaerobically since both terminate in cyto-chromes. There are intermediate systems in which the bacteria have become less dependent on cytochromes and more dependent on flavoproteins. Finally there are organisms which, like the *Lactobacillaceae*, while growing aerobically, are completely independent of cytochromes. Systems in obligate anaerobes will be discussed elsewhere. With all the presently available information, the tentative scheme for electron systems used by various microorganisms has been postulated by Dolin(35) and may function as a guide throughout bacterial metabolic studies (see Scheme 3.3).

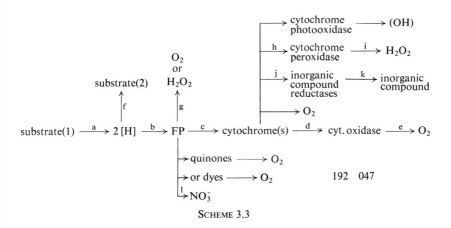

SCHEME 3.3

Depending upon the pathway under consideration in Scheme 3.3 (2 H) may represent (1) reducing equivalents, (2) reduced pyrimidine nucleotides, or (3) reduced flavoprotein. Cytochrome photooxidase is used by photosynthetic bacteria. Dolin provides the following definitions in relation to Scheme 3.3.

Obligate aerobes: Cannot grow in absence of O_2. Presumably no functional fermentative metabolism. Pathway of electron transport—a, b, c, d, e.
Facultative anaerobes: Can grow in presence and absence of O_2 (in absence of O_2 they use fermentative pathways). There are two groups:

(1) cytochrome-independent (e.g., lactic acid bacteria). Pathway of electron transport:
     aerobic—a, b, g
     anaerobic—a, f (may be sole pathway of some representatives of this class);
(2) cytochrome-dependent (e.g., coliforms). Pathway of electron transport:
     aerobic a, b, c, d, e; a, b, g
     anaerobic—a, f; a, b, c, j (nitrate reduction); a, b, l.

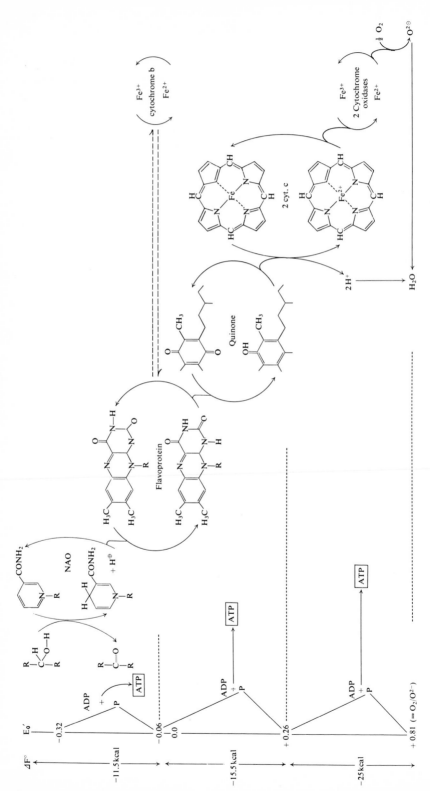

Fig. 3.2. Sequence of redox systems in the respiratory chain [from Karlson(71)].

Obligate anaerobes: Cannot grow aerobically. There are two groups:

(1) cytochrome-independent (e.g., *Clostridium*). Pathway of electron transport—a, f; a, b, g (not used under physiological conditions);
(2) cytochrome-dependent (e.g., *Desulfovibrio desulfuricans*). Pathway of electron transport—a, b, c, j (reduction of sulfur anions—step c obscure). Quinones such as menaquinone seem to play an important role in electron transfer in *Mycobacterium*(21) and *Corynebacterium*(82) (see Fig. 3.2).

ANAEROBIC RESPIRATION

Three main groups of bacteria are known which use an inorganic compound as terminal electron acceptors.

(1) SO_4^{2-}:   *Desulfovibrio* and *Desulfotomaculum*
(2) NO_3^-:   denitrifying bacteria
(3) CO_2:   *Methanobacterium*

The first two groups of bacteria are very closely related in their electron transport systems but differ in that the sulfate-reducing bacteria do not possess NAD (arrows indicate the direction of electron flow):

$$\text{[2H]} \rightarrow \text{cytochrome(s)} \rightarrow \begin{array}{l} \text{sulfate reductase} \rightarrow SO_4^{2-} \\ \text{thiosulfate reductase} \rightarrow S_2O_3^{2-} \end{array}$$

$$\text{NAD} \rightarrow \text{FD} \rightarrow \text{cytochrome(s)} \rightarrow \begin{array}{l} \text{nitrate reductase} \rightarrow NO_3^- \\ \text{nitrite reductase} \rightarrow NO_2^- \\ \text{nitric oxide reductase} \rightarrow NO^- \end{array}$$

Although the chemical nature of the reductases is not as yet precisely known(35), they have a function similar to that of cytochrome oxidase as the final electron transferring enzyme.

Sulfur Compounds as Electron Acceptors

The number of microorganisms utilizing sulfate as the terminal electron acceptor is very small. They are divided into the two following groups(25).

(1) Nonsporing sulfate-reducing bacteria:

   (a) *Desulfovibrio desulfuricans*, and

   (b) *Desulfovibrio gigas*(86).

(2) Sporing sulfate-reducing bacteria(128):

   (a) *Desulfotomaculum nigrificans* (syn. *Clostridium nigrificans*, *Desulfovibrio thermodesulfuricans*(105), *Sporovibrio thermodesulfuricans*),

   (b) *Desulfotomaculum orientis* (syn. *Desulfovibrio orientis*), and

   (c) *Desulfotomaculum ruminis* (Coleman's organism).

Most studies of sulfate reduction have been done, however, on the classic sulfate reducer *Desulfovibrio desulfuricans*.

Desulfovibrio desulfuricans is an obligately anaerobic organism that can be grown autotrophically with sulfate, hydrogen, and carbon dioxide(24) and also heterotrophically with sulfate and an organic hydrogen (electron) donor. The presence of sulfate is obligatory for growth both with hydrogen and organic electron donors except in the case of pyruvate(125). During growth large amounts of sulfide are produced from the sulfate (126).

Autotrophic Sulfate Reduction. Whole cells of *Desulfovibrio desulfuricans* reduce sulfate very rapidly in the presence of hydrogen

$$4\,H_2 + SO_4^{2-} \;\rightarrow\; S^{2-} + 4\,H_2O$$

Most of the strains studied so far contain a very active hydrogenase, which was found(113) to require Fe^{2+}. This dependence on iron led to the discovery

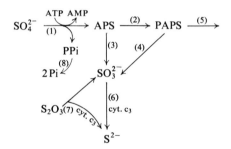

SCHEME 3.4. (1) ATP sulfurylase, (2) APS kinase, (3) APS reductase, (4) PAPS reductase, (5) sulfokinase, (6) sulfite reductase, (7) thiosulfate reductase, (8) inorganic pyrophosphatase.

of cytochrome c_3 which was in fact the first cytochrome discovered in a non-photosynthetic anaerobic microorganism. Cytochrome c_3 is a soluble autoxidizable hemoprotein(126), which has reduction bands at 553, 525, and 419 mμ. It has also a very low redox potential of -250 mV, a high isoelectric point (IEP) at >pH 10 and contains 0.9 % Fe. Cytochrome c_3 can act as carrier in reactions which have oxygen as the terminal acceptor, and it is assumed therefore that it could provide a mechanism by which the organism could remove traces of oxygen from its environment. The E_m of cytochrome c_3 of -250 mV is related to the free energy of its oxidation at pH 7.0

$$Fe_2^{4+} + 2\,H^+ = Fe_2^{6+} + H_2 \qquad \Delta F = -9500 \text{ cal}$$

Cytochrome c_3 may also be responsible for the low oxidation-reduction potential required for the growth of *Desulfovibrio desulfuricans*. This organism therefore conducts its oxidation reactions at the strongly reducing potential of about -200 mV. The function of cytochrome c_3 is, of course, mainly as an electron carrier.

Stoichiometric investigations as well as studies with cell-free extracts indicated that *Desulfovibrio desulfuricans* reduces sulfate in a number of steps, using organic sulfur compounds such as adenosine 5'-phosphosulfate (APS) as an intermediate (see Scheme 3.4).

It was Bernstein and McGilverey(13) who established the participation of ATP in enzymatic activation of sulfate. This activation energy, however, is very minute and regarded as being at the catalytic level. Segal(141) indicated that pyrophosphate (PP$_i$) is eliminated from ATP during this activation reaction. It is therefore possible to assume that the initial reaction in the presence of sulfate, sulfurylase, ATP, and pyrophosphatase is a complex one. This liberation of inorganic phosphate (P$_i$) from ATP is very rapid (171). With this system the initial step in sulfate reduction first creates a high-energy sulfate

$$ATP + SO_4^{2-} \rightleftharpoons APS + PP_i$$
$$\longrightarrow 2P_i$$

compound in APS and, second, causes a cleavage of PP$_i$ from ATP. This cleavage ultimately causes the hydrolysis of two high-energy phosphate bonds of ATP(88), which evidently confers in a much larger thermodynamic pull(117) on such coupled reactions than is the case for reactions in which only the terminal phosphate group of ATP is lost. The split of PP$_i$ → 2P$_i$ in the presence of pyrophosphatase is therefore equivalent to another ATP → ADP step as far as energy is concerned. The enzyme catalyzing this reaction is ATP sulfurylase.

Since the organism is able to grow autotrophically on H$_2$, CO$_2$, and sulfate, it must derive its energy from the oxidation of molecular hydrogen by sulfate (111). The second step in sulfate reduction would therefore be:

$$APS + \text{cytochrome } c_3 \text{ (red.)} \rightarrow AMP + SO_3^{2-} + \text{cytochrome } c_3 \text{ (oxid.)}$$

The enzyme responsible for this reaction is APS reductase. The final reduction to S^{2-} occurs then in the presence of cytochrome c$_3$, hydrogenase, and sulfite reductase.

$$SO_3^{2-} + 3H_2 \rightarrow S^{2-} + 3H_2O$$

The autotrophic reduction of sulfate is unique insofar as the metabolism combines phosphorylation and electron transport via cytochrome c$_3$. Peck(113) demonstrated that the reduction of sulfate to sulfite under a hydrogen atmosphere involves the transfer of electrons by cytochrome c$_3$ and a preliminary activation of the sulfate molecule by ATP with formation of APS and PP_i as follows:

$$H_2 + cyt.\ 2\,Fe^{3+} \xrightarrow{\ hydrogenase\ } cyt.\ 2Fe^{2+} + 2\,H^+$$

$$SO_4^{2-} + ATP \underset{\ }{\overset{ATP\ sulfurylase}{\rightleftharpoons}} APS + PP_i$$

$$APS + cyt.\ 2Fe^{2+} + 2H^+ \xrightarrow{\ APS\ reductase\ } AMP + SO_3^{2-} + H_2O + cyt.\ 2Fe^{3+}$$

This summary of reactions shows why it has been considered that in the oxidation of hydrogen with sulfate a generation of high-energy phosphate coupled with electron transport occurs(111). The reduction of sulfate with

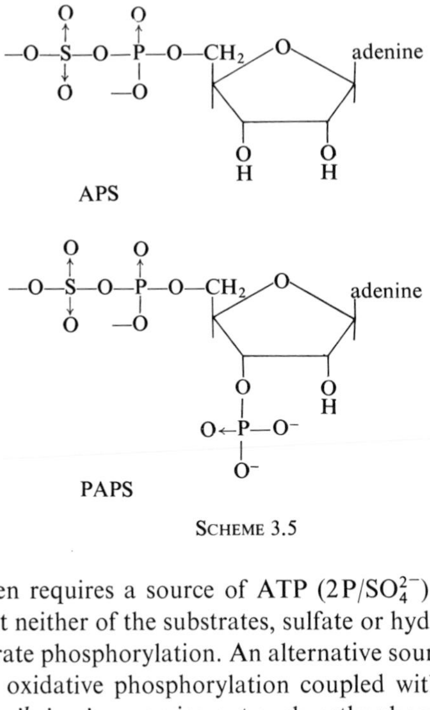

APS

PAPS

SCHEME 3.5

molecular hydrogen requires a source of ATP ($2P/SO_4^{2-}$) for the activation of sulfate(114) that neither of the substrates, sulfate or hydrogen, can provide by means of substrate phosphorylation. An alternative source for the required ATP could be an oxidative phosphorylation coupled with the oxidation of hydrogen. *Desulfovibrio gigas* carries out such orthophosphate esterification (115) which is dependent on hydrogen oxidation with either sulfite or thio-sulfate as electron acceptor. It appears therefore that *Desulfovibrio* is able to carry out an oxidative phosphorylation comparable to the one in aerobic bacteria, but with a single cytochrome only. This organism is therefore in the unique position to carry out a single oxidative phosphorylation with a single cytochrome. If one draws a parallel to yeasts, which work on the same substrates, the difference becomes quite clear since the pathway proceeds via PAPS (see Scheme 3.5). This yeast type of sulfate reduction requires, in addition to the enzyme and ATP, reduced NADP or reduced lipoic acid as electron donor(54). It involves first the formation of the sulfur-containing nucleotide 3'-phospho-adenosine 5'-phosphosulfate (PAPS):

$$ATP + SO_4^{2-} \rightleftharpoons APS + PP_i$$

$$ATP + APS \rightleftharpoons ADP + PAPS$$

Apart from the already mentioned ATP sulfurylase, which catalyzes the first part of the reaction, a second enzyme in form of a kinase, APS kinase, is necessary to transfer a second phosphate group to APS(113). The final step to sulfite is a reduction step with reduced NADP as electron donor

$$(NADPH + H^+) + PAPS \rightarrow NADP^+ + PAP + HSO_3^-$$

The catalyzing enzyme has been given the name PAPS reductase. This reduction of PAPS is thought to involve a thiolytic split by dihydrolipoic acid(55) via the following proposed mechanism(54):

$$PAP\!-\!O\!-\!SO_3^- + lip\!\!\begin{array}{c} {\nearrow SH} \\ {\searrow SH} \end{array} \rightleftharpoons PAP\!-\!OH + lip\!\!\begin{array}{c} {\nearrow S\!-\!SO_3} \\ {\searrow SH} \end{array}$$

$$lip\!\!\begin{array}{c} {\nearrow S\!-\!SO_3} \\ {\searrow SH} \end{array} \rightleftharpoons lip\!\!\begin{array}{c} {\nearrow SH} \\ {\searrow SH} \end{array} + HSO_3^-$$

The postulated intermediate "lipothiosulfate," however, has not yet been isolated.

This reduction of PAPS is paralleled in the case of *Desulfovibrio desulfuricans* to a certain extent since APS is reduced(59) with APS reductase(20,117) as the catalyzing enzyme but no lipoic acid involvement

$$APS + 2e \rightleftharpoons AMP + SO_3^{2-}$$

Recent chromatographic observations led to the discovery of yet another organic sulfur compound, which was tentatively named "adenosine 5'-phospho-dithionate(18) (APSS) and detected when crude extracts of *Thiobacillus denitrificans* were incubated in the presence of AMP, sulfite, and ferricyanide. Autoradiography also showed the production of APSS from APS and sulfite in the presence and absence of ferricyanide(30).

The existence of these two different pathways of sulfate reduction(55, 172) appears to separate all those organisms, which use thiosulfate reduction as dissimilatory pathway(127) from all those which use it as an assimilatory pathway. The dissimilatory pathway is taken by those microorganisms which reduce sulfate in great excess of nutritional requirements and therefore produce large amounts of sulfide by using sulfate as terminal electron acceptor. The amount of sulfide produced is proportional to the amount of H_2 or organic material dissimilated(154). Yeasts, *Escherichia coli* (27) and *Salmonella typhimurium* (37,89), on the other hand, have the ability to grow on sulfate as their sole source of sulfur(140) and use the sulfite or sulfide produced for assimilation. The H_2S produced by these organisms is far in excess of the sulfate reduced and must therefore come from the metabolism of sulfur-containing amino acids(112). The formation of PAPS separates these two pathways clearly and distinctively.

The reduction of thiosulfate ($S_2O_3^{2-}$) to sulfite and sulfide is very similar to the reverse reaction occurring in thiobacilli (see Chapter 5). In this reduction a stereospecific enzymatic reaction is coupled with lipoate or lipoamide(161).

$$S_2O_3^{2-} + CN^- \rightleftharpoons SCN^- + SO_3^{2-}$$

The enzyme responsible for this reaction has been isolated(136) from anaerobically grown *Thiobacillus denitrificans* and is known under the name "rhodanese" (thiosulfate:cyanide sulfurtransferase, E.C. 2.8.1.1). The detailed mechanism of Scheme 3.6 resembles somehow the mammalian enzyme. This

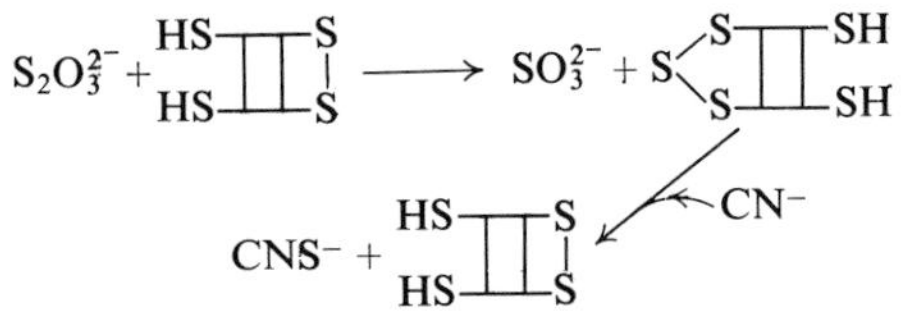

SCHEME 3.6. (Reprinted with permission of The Biochemical Journal, London.).

bacterial rhodanese has, however, been regarded as a distinct enzyme in regard to its unique combination of properties(19) and may therefore occupy a transitional position among sulfurtransferases.

Rhodanese-S_2 reacts with dihydrolipoate and sulfide is produced. The overall reaction mechanism can be summarized (162) as shown in Scheme 3.7.

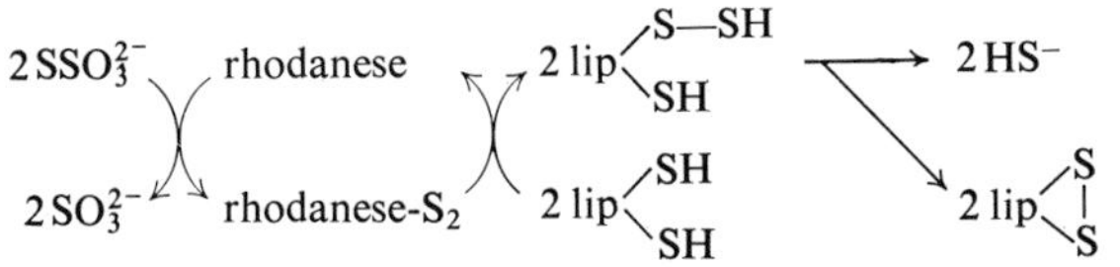

SCHEME 3.7. (Reprinted with permission of the American Society of Biological Chemists.)

In this reaction sequence the outer sulfur atom of thiosulfate is transferred to dihydrolipoate(163) via an enzyme-sulfur intermediate. This intermediate transfers its sulfur to dihydrolipoate with the formation of lipoate persulfide, which in turn is highly active and breaks down immediately to HS^- and lip–S_2. Apart from being a double displacement mechanism(51, 79, 166), the reaction is very similar to the one known for the oxidative decarboxylation of pyruvate and 2-oxoglutarate (see Chapter 5) with acetyl CoA being substituted by rhodanese-S_2.

The electron transfer system is the same as given for the sulfate reduction. *Heterotrophic Sulfate Reduction.* Hydrogen can be replaced by simple organic compounds such as acetate, formate, lactate, and pyruvate(149). Whenever the organic compound serves as carbon source, hydrogen and carbon dioxide are evolved. The best studied system is the oxidation of lactate, which forms acetate, carbon dioxide, and hydrogen sulfide(111) as end products (see Scheme 3.8).

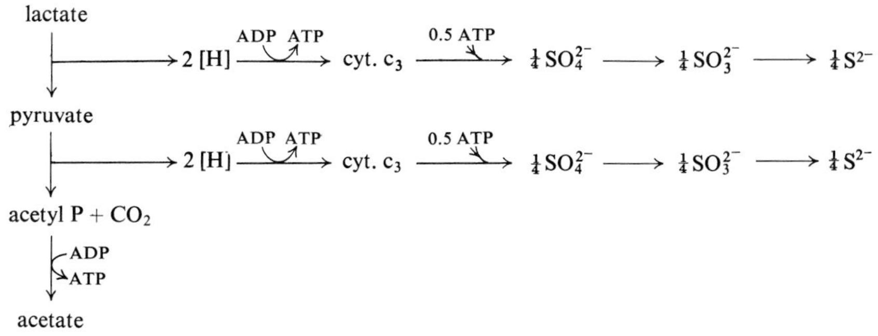

lactate

$$\longrightarrow 2\,[H] \xrightarrow{\text{ADP ATP}} \text{cyt. } c_3 \xrightarrow{\text{0.5 ATP}} \tfrac{1}{4}SO_4^{2-} \longrightarrow \tfrac{1}{4}SO_3^{2-} \longrightarrow \tfrac{1}{4}S^{2-}$$

pyruvate

$$\longrightarrow 2\,[H] \xrightarrow{\text{ADP ATP}} \text{cyt. } c_3 \xrightarrow{\text{0.5 ATP}} \tfrac{1}{4}SO_4^{2-} \longrightarrow \tfrac{1}{4}SO_3^{2-} \longrightarrow \tfrac{1}{4}S^{2-}$$

acetyl P + CO$_2$

$$\begin{array}{l} \text{\Large\textcorner}\text{ADP} \\ \text{\Large\textcorner}\text{ATP} \end{array}$$

acetate

SCHEME 3.8. (Reprinted with permission of the American Society of Microbiologists.)

The initial step is from lactate to pyruvate. The following phosphoroclastic split of pyruvate to acetylphosphate, carbon dioxide, and hydrogen occurs in many anaerobes(98). The pyruvate–carbon dioxide exchange reaction in cell-free extracts of *Desulfovibrio desulfuricans* showed a definite requirement for P_i and coenzyme A(156). It can also be assumed that thiamine diphosphate (98) is required. The initial ATP expenditure in sulfate reduction is finally regenerated by the conversion of acetyl phosphate to acetate and ATP. The enzyme acetokinase involved in this reaction has been purified(23) and appears to be no different from the one in *Escherichia coli* as it is not dependent on coenzyme A. This enzyme is specific for acetate and inactive against formate, propionate, butyrate, and succinate. Adenosine triphosphate has a stimulatory effect on this pyruvate phosphoroclastic split(182). This stimulatory effect might be attributed to the formation of ADP, which by simple mass reaction accelerates the removal of acetylphosphate and pulls the whole reaction sequence

$$2CH_3CHOHCOOH \rightarrow 2\,CH_3COCOOH + 4\,H^+$$

$$2CH_3COCOOH + 2\,HOPO_3^{2-} \rightarrow 2\,CH_3COOPO_3 + 2\,CO_2 + 4\,H^+$$

$$2\,CH_3COOPO_3 + AMP + 2\,H^+ \rightarrow 2\,CH_3COOH + ATP$$

$$SO_4^{2-} + ATP + 8\,H^+ \rightarrow S^{2-} + 2\,H_2S + AMP + 2\,HOPO_3^{2-} + 2\,H^+$$

$$2CH_3CHOHCOOH + SO_4^{2-} \rightarrow 2\,CH_3COOH + 2\,CO_2 + S^{2-} + 2\,H_2S$$

The classical phosphoroclastic mechanism produces formate in addition to acetyl phosphate (see Chapter 6). Formate, however, has never been isolated as an intermediate in the pyruvate metabolism of *Desulfovibrio desulfuricans* (156). It is possible that the formate exchange proceeds via cytochrome c_3– mediated breadkdown to H_2 and CO_2, the latter subsequently exchanging with pyruvate. Since cytochrome c_3 was found to participate as electron carrier for the formic hydrogenlyase system it is assumed that the *Desulfovibrio desulfuricans* may have a clostridial type of phosphoroclastic reaction combined with a coli type of formic hydrogenlyase system (49) (see Chapter 6).

The overall ATP balance is very similar to the one in autotrophic sulfur reduction. The four electron pairs originating from the oxidation of two molecules of lactate to two molecules of acetyl phosphate and carbon dioxide, plus the two high-energy phosphates of acetyl phosphates formed are utilized for the conversion of one molecule of sulfate to sulfide. Since there would be no net production of ATP from substrate phosphorylation, the same scheme as for the autotrophic *Desulfovibrio desulfuricans* has been suggested. With this the organism obtains its energy required for growth from phosphate esterification (142) or oxidative phosphorylation coupled with the electron transport from lactate and pyruvate to sulfate.

If pyruvate replaces lactate as sole energy source, *Desulfovibrio desulfuricans* can grow without sulfate but evolves hydrogen instead. The finding of ferredoxin (99) in *Desulfovibrio desulfuricans* (158) as well as cytochrome c_3 explained the process of molecular hydrogen evolution (3). Electrons released from pyruvate are accepted by ferredoxin, transferred to cytochrome c_3, and the latter donates the electrons finally to a hydrogenase (116) (see Scheme 3.9). In the absence of cytochrome c_3, for instance, in *Desulfotomacu-*

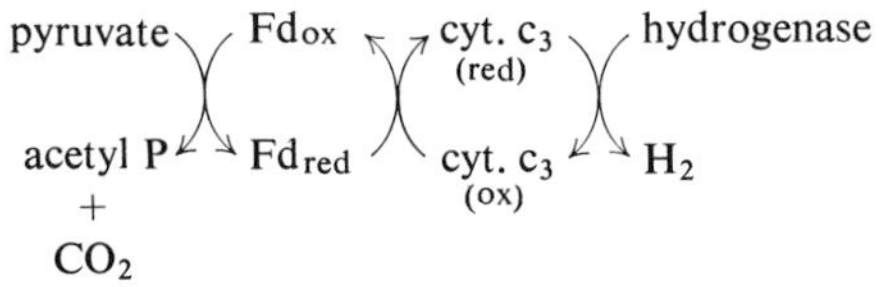

SCHEME 3.9. (Reprinted with permission of the American Society of Biological Chemists.)

lum, ferredoxin donates the electrons to the hydrogenase. In the case of pyruvate metabolism sulfate is not required since hydrogen is produced and evolved by the function of hydrogenase. The formation of hydrogen and acetyl phosphate is proportional to the ferredoxin concentration (1). It is also assumed that ferredoxin is closely associated with the sulfite reductase system (87).

Desulfovibrio and *Desulfotomaculum* appear to differ in the length of their electron transport systems. Whereas the former possesses either cytochrome c_3 alone or together with ferredoxin, *Desulfotomaculum* has no cytochrome c_3

but contains ferredoxin alone. In general the electron transport system could be expressed as in Scheme 3.10. The potential difference of 0.2 V is not sufficient

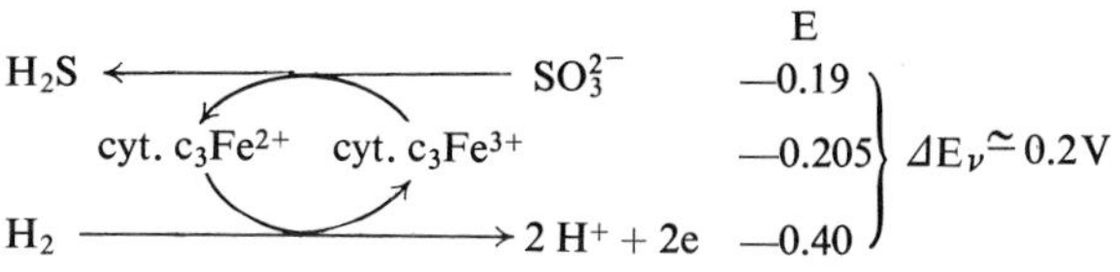

$$\begin{array}{ll}
\text{E} \\
\text{H}_2\text{S} \longleftarrow \quad\quad \text{SO}_3^{2-} & -0.19 \\
\quad\quad \text{cyt. c}_3\text{Fe}^{2+} \quad \text{cyt. c}_3\text{Fe}^{3+} & -0.205 \\
\text{H}_2 \longrightarrow \quad\quad 2\,\text{H}^+ + 2e & -0.40
\end{array} \Bigg\} \; \Delta E_\nu \simeq 0.2\,\text{V}$$

SCHEME 3.10

for the generation of one molecule of ATP. Therefore two electrons must be transferred together; NAD^+, $NADP^+$ or flavins cannot replace cytochrome c_3.

Apart from growth investigations (5, 58, 60, 95) studies on the deoxyribonucleic acid (DNA) base composition of *Desulfovibrio* (138) and *Desulfotomaculum* (137) showed the diversity of these sulfate-reducing bacteria. Thirty strains of *Desulfovibrio desulfuricans* fell into three groups judged on their DNA base composition

> Group I   contained 60–62% guanine + cytosine
>
> Group II contained 54–56% guanine + cytosine
>
> Group III contained 46–47% guanine + cytosine

The sulfate-reducing strains of *Desulfotomaculum* showed a base composition of 42–46% guanine + cytosine.

There is also some evidence (9) that *Desulfovibrio desulfuricans* is able to metabolize choline in the absence of sulfate. It is, however, not clear as yet whether this organism is *Desulfovibrio desulfuricans* or *Vibrio cholinicus* (52).

Nitrate as Final Electron Acceptor

Chemolithotrophic Reduction of Nitrate. A small number of bacteria are able to reduce nitrate by using molecular hydrogen as the electron donor

$$5\,\text{H}_2 + 2\,\text{NO}_3^- \rightarrow \text{N}_2 + 4\,\text{H}_2\text{O} + 2\,\text{OH}^-$$

The end product of this reaction is molecular nitrogen. Certain species of hydrogen bacteria are able to use this reaction as a source of energy for their anaerobic growth in a strictly mineral medium.

Micrococcus denitrificans, a facultative autotroph, grows in air or anaerobically with either organic compounds or molecular hydrogen as the source of energy and molecular oxygen or nitrate as electron acceptor (10).

The utilization of the carbon source by *Micrococcus* is very similar to that of the chemoorganotrophic sulfate reducer *Desulfotomaculum* (2). Apart from lactate (109) and pyruvate, *Micrococcus denitrificans* can also use glycollate as sole source of carbon. With glycollate as substrate this denitrifying bacterium is able to synthesize a C_4-dicarboxylic acid by the condensation of two C_2-compounds without a prior activation to CoA derivatives (78) in order to yield a C_4-dicarboxylic acid precursor of a TCA cycle intermediate. This new pathway goes via erythro-β-hydroxyaspartate, which plays a key role in glycollate utilization of *Micrococcus denitrificans* (see Scheme 3.11). Glycollate

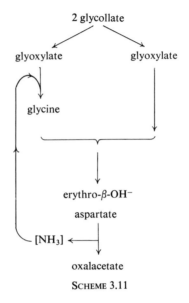

SCHEME 3.11

is first converted to glyoxylate by the NAD-dependent glyoxylate reductase (glycollate:NAD oxidoreductase, E.C. 1.1.1.26). The amination of glyoxylate

$$
\begin{array}{ccc}
\underset{\text{glycollate}}{\begin{array}{c} \text{CH}_2\text{OH} \\ | \\ \text{COOH} \end{array}}
&
\xrightarrow[]{\text{NAD}^+ \quad \text{NADH}+\text{H}^+}
&
\underset{\text{glyoxylate}}{\begin{array}{c} \text{COOH} \\ | \\ \text{CHO} \end{array}}
\end{array}
$$

in the following step to form glycine is not yet definitely solved, but it is thought that a specific aminotransferase might be involved (44).

$$
\begin{array}{ccc}
\underset{\text{glyoxylate}}{\begin{array}{c} \text{COOH} \\ | \\ \text{CHO} \end{array}}
&
\xrightarrow[2\text{ H} \quad \text{H}_2\text{O}]{\text{NH}_3}
&
\underset{\text{glycine}}{\begin{array}{c} \text{COOH} \\ | \\ \text{CH}_2\text{—NH}_2 \end{array}}
\end{array}
$$

The following cleavage reaction of glyoxylate and glycine in order to produce erythro-β-hydroxyaspartate is very similar to the known aldolase cleavages (see Chapter 4) and the name "erythro-β-hydroxyaspartate aldolase" has been given to the enzyme catalyzing this reaction. The final step toward the

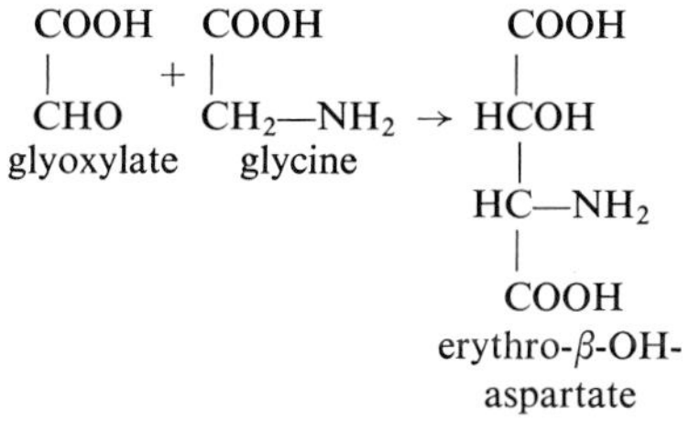

$$\begin{matrix} \text{COOH} & \text{COOH} \\ | & + & | \\ \text{CHO} & \text{CH}_2\!-\!\text{NH}_2 \\ \text{glyoxylate} & \text{glycine} \end{matrix} \rightarrow \begin{matrix} \text{COOH} \\ | \\ \text{HCOH} \\ | \\ \text{HC}\!-\!\text{NH}_2 \\ | \\ \text{COOH} \\ \text{erythro-}\beta\text{-OH-} \\ \text{aspartate} \end{matrix}$$

TCA cycle precursor, oxalacetate, is a dehydratase action of which the enzyme has been purified and named "erythro-β-hydroxyaspartate dehydratase" [erythro-3-hydroxyaspartate hydrolyase (deaminating)](43). The liberated

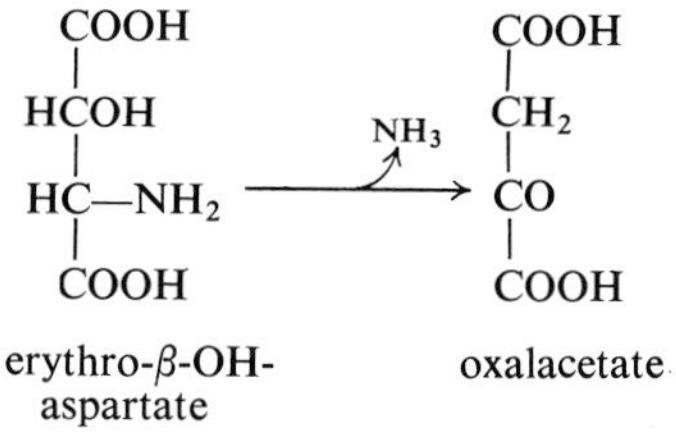

$$\begin{matrix} \text{COOH} \\ | \\ \text{HCOH} \\ | \\ \text{HC}\!-\!\text{NH}_2 \\ | \\ \text{COOH} \\ \text{erythro-}\beta\text{-OH-} \\ \text{aspartate} \end{matrix} \xrightarrow{\ \ \text{NH}_3\ \ } \begin{matrix} \text{COOH} \\ | \\ \text{CH}_2 \\ | \\ \text{CO} \\ | \\ \text{COOH} \\ \text{oxalacetate} \end{matrix}$$

ammonia is thought to reenter the metabolism in the conversion of glyoxylate to glycine.

Thiobacillus denitrificans. Elemental sulfur or thiosulfate, both of which are converted to sulfate, are the energy sources for this organism. It is therefore a sulfur-oxidizing chemoautotroph:

$$5S + 6NO_3^- + 2H_2O \rightarrow 5SO_4^{2-} + 3N_2 + 4H^+$$

In each of these chemolithotrophic cases, molecular nitrogen is evolved (179). *Chemoorganotrophic Reduction of Nitrate.* The great majority of nitrate-reducing bacteria, however, are chemoorganotrophs. In the reduction of nitrate to nitrite there are two types of microbial enzymes in existence:

(1) the assimilatory enzyme, which contains flavin and molybdenum and usually utilizes reduced NAD or reduced NADP as an hydrogen donor; and
(2) the dissimilatory enzyme, which has an additional iron requirement.

During assimilation, NO_3^- is reduced and incorporated into cellular nitrogenous material, whereas in the dissimilatory process or nitrate respiration, nitrate serves as an alternative hydrogen acceptor to oxygen. Only the dissimilatory section or anaerobic respiration will be dealt with. In the dissimilatory reduction of nitrate there are three microbiological reactions(4):

(1) a complete reduction to ammonium, frequently with the transitory appearance of nitrite;
(2) an incomplete reduction and an accumulation of nitrite in the medium; and
(3) a reduction to nitrite followed by the evolution of gaseous compounds, or denitrification.

Regardless of their other physiological characteristics, microorganisms that use NO_3^- as a nitrogen source carry out reaction (1), whereas cultures incapable of the complete reduction must be supplied with ammonium or other reduced nitrogen compounds for growth to proceed.

Denitrification. Anaerobic respiration that results in the conversion of nitrate to N_2, N_2O, or a mixture of these two gases is known as denitrification(131). The first step in denitrification is the addition of two electrons to the nitrate with the formation of nitrite. All denitrifying bacteria can use nitrite in place of nitrate for denitrification. Molecular nitrogen is the usual major end product of denitrification, but under certain conditions, large amounts of N_2O can be formed from NO_2^-, which represents the addition of two further electrons per nitrogen atom:

$$2NO_2^- + 4[H] \rightarrow N_2O + H_2O + 2OH^-$$

Nitrous oxide, on the other hand, can also be reduced by denitrifiers to N_2:

$$N_2O + 2H^+ \rightarrow N_2 + H_2O$$

It is therefore possible that denitrifying bacteria can either form N_2O or N_2 directly from nitrite or N_2 via nitrous oxide. Because of this fact it has been suggested that an intermediate of the elementary composition of $N_2O_2H_2$ may be involved(75):

$$N_2O_2H_2 \rightarrow N_2O + H_2O \quad \text{or} \quad N_2O_2H_2 + 2H^+ \rightarrow N_2 + H_2O$$

This intermediate can be formed relatively easily from nitrite via a free radical:

$$NO_2^- + 2H^+ \rightarrow {>}NOH + H_2O$$

$$2NOH \rightarrow N_2O_2H_2$$

When acetic acid is the carbon source, its oxidation in the presence of nitrate can occur in two ways

$$CH_3COOH + 2NO_3^- \rightarrow 2CO_2 + N_2O + H_2O + 2OH^-$$

$$5CH_3COOH + 8NO_3^- \rightarrow 10CO_2 + 4N_2 + 6H_2O + 8OH^-$$

A comparison of these reactions shows that in the case of N_2 formation one mole of acetate more can be metabolized if the same eight moles of NO_3^-

are available in both cases. The suitability of nitrite for N_2 formation and its utilization in ammonia formation suggests that it is an intermediate in both cases. On the basis of current knowledge, the biochemical pathway given in Scheme 3.12 is likely. This pathway assumes that the reduction of nitrate to

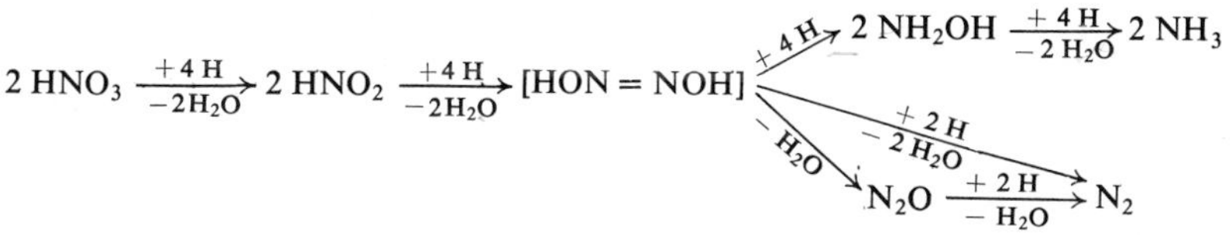

$$2\,HNO_3 \xrightarrow[-2H_2O]{+4H} 2\,HNO_2 \xrightarrow[-2H_2O]{+4H} [HON=NOH]$$

$$\xrightarrow[]{+4H} 2\,NH_2OH \xrightarrow[-2H_2O]{+4H} 2\,NH_3$$

$$\xrightarrow[-2H_2O]{+2H} N_2O \xrightarrow[-H_2O]{+2H} N_2$$

SCHEME 3.12

ammonia proceeds by a sequence of two-electron changes from the +5 oxidation state of nitrate to the −3 of ammonia, a shift of eight electrons. The responsible enzymes are termed the "nitrate," "nitrite," "hyponitrite," and "hydroxylamine" reductases. This scheme postulates two-electron steps: (1) in the conversion of $NO_3^- \rightarrow NO_2^-$ (nitrate reductase), and (2) in the reduction of nitrite by two possible pathways. Nitrate reductase is the most common and important enzyme in nitrate reduction and will be dealt with later.

The electron transport systems in denitrifying bacteria are just as obscure as is our present knowledge of the denitrification scheme. Over the past years many suggestions have been put forward for different organisms and will be dealt with briefly. More details can be found in publications of Nason(103).

Micrococcus Nitrite Reductase. By using a partially purified enzyme preparation of a halotolerant *Micrococcus* (*strain 203*), Asano(6,7) showed that the electron transport system functioning in the reduction of nitrite was similar to that for oxygen. The *Micrococcus* sp. converted all nitrite to nitrogen with one mole molecular nitrogen being formed for every two moles of nitrite reduced. The preparation possessed a reduced NAD-nitrite reductase activity in the presence of 0.6 M NaCl and was stimulated by FAD and menadione. A cytochrome b_4 seemed to function as an electron carrier [from Nason(103), reprinted with permission of the American Society of Microbiology]:

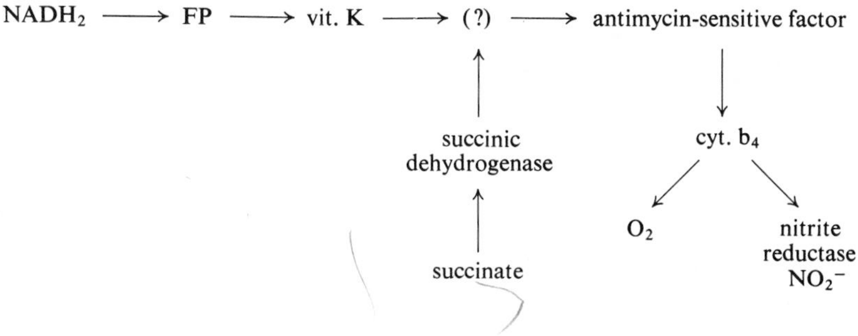

$$NADH_2 \longrightarrow FP \longrightarrow vit.\ K \longrightarrow (?) \longrightarrow antimycin\text{-}sensitive\ factor$$

succinic dehydrogenase   cyt. b_4

succinate O_2 nitrite reductase NO_2^-

This preparation also possessed a powerful hydroxylamine reductase activity, which was found in the soluble protein component, whereas the nitrite reductase was part of the particulate protein fraction. Neither fraction, however, contained a cytochrome.

Pseudomonas denitrificans Nitrite Reductase. Iwasaki(61) purified two fractions from *Pseudomonas denitrificans.* One of these fractions had the typical absorption spectrum of a cytochrome c type, and was considered to be an electron carrier to the denitrifying or "cytochrome c" system with the latter also mediating the conversion of nitrite and hydroxylamine to molecular nitrogen [from Nason(103), reprinted with permission of the American Society of Microbiology]:

H donor $\longrightarrow$ cyt. c $HNO_2 + NH_2OH$

cryptocytochrome c

N_2

Pseudomonas stutzeri Nitrite Reductase. Using crude ammonium sulfate fractions of *Pseudomonas stutzeri* extract, Najjar and Chung(101) showed that reduced NADP and reduced NAD served as electron donors and FAD and FMN gave a stimulation to nitrite reduction [from Nason(103), reprinted with permission of the American Society of Microbiology]. Nitrite reductase

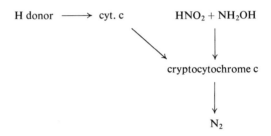

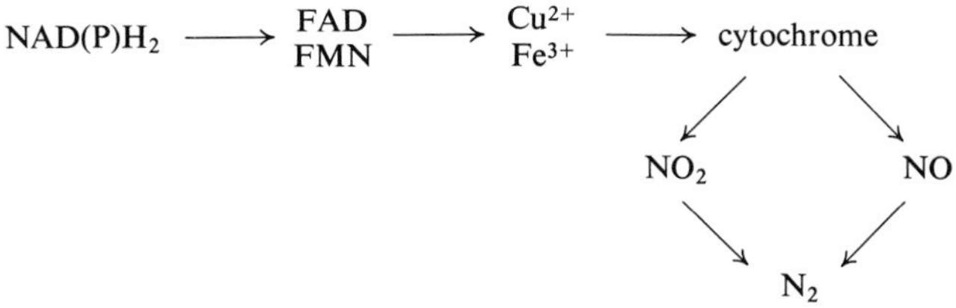

$NAD(P)H_2 \longrightarrow \begin{matrix} FAD \\ FMN \end{matrix} \longrightarrow \begin{matrix} Cu^{2+} \\ Fe^{3+} \end{matrix} \longrightarrow$ cytochrome

NO_2 NO

N_2

and nitric oxide reductase exhibited almost identical properties and both led to the formation of molecular nitrogen.

Hydroxylamine Reductase. It was mentioned earlier that *Micrococcus* sp. (strain *203*) possessed a very active hydroxylamine reductase. Kono and Taniguchi(77) supported this evidence and found that this enzyme is active even when the bacteria are strongly denitrifying. The reduced enzyme was also reacting with molecular oxygen [from Nason(103), reprinted with permission of the American Society of Microbiology]:

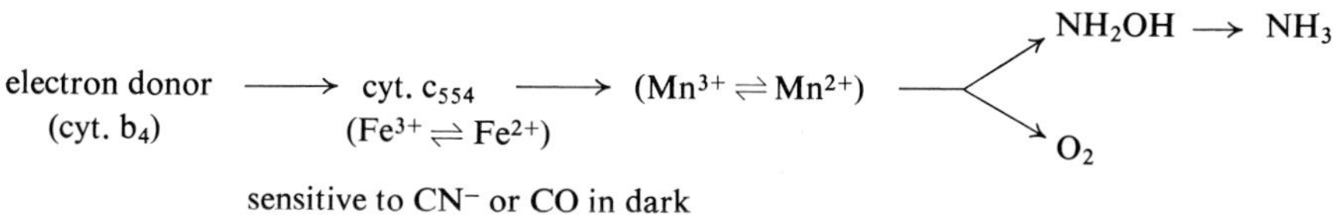

$$\text{electron donor} \longrightarrow \text{cyt. } c_{554} \longrightarrow (Mn^{3+} \rightleftharpoons Mn^{2+}) \underset{\searrow O_2}{\overset{\nearrow NH_2OH \longrightarrow NH_3}{}}$$

(cyt. b_4) $(Fe^{3+} \rightleftharpoons Fe^{2+})$

sensitive to CN^- or CO in dark

This halotolerant strain of *Micrococcus* is able to grow under aerobic and anaerobic conditions. A similar arrangement functions in *Pseudomonas aeruginosa*(164) and *Bacterium anitratum*(70). To date, five chromoproteins have been isolated: cytochrome b_4 (I), cytochrome b_4 (II), cytochrome $c_{625,553}$ (HR), cytochrome c_{551}, and a "brown protein"(56,57). Whereas cytochrome$_{560}$, cytochrome b_4 (I), and cytochrome b_4 (II) can function in both anaerobic and aerobic cells, it is thought that cytochrome c_{551} may function in a role similar to that of mammalian cytochrome c and brown

TABLE 3.2

PROPERTIES OF CYTOCHROME b_4 (I) AND CYTOCHROME b_4 (II)[a]

	Cytochrome b_4 (I)	Cytochrome b_4 (II)
$S_{20;20}$	2.20 S	2.17 S
$D_{20,w}$	10.2×10^{-7} cm^{2}sec^{-1}	—
Minimum molecular weight	9,300	14,800
Molecular weight	18,000	18,000
Electrophoretic mobility	-9.6×10^{-5} cm^{2}sec^{-1} V^{-1}	-12.7×10^{-5} cm^{2}sec^{-1} V^{-1}
E_0' 9 (pH 7)	+0.113 V	+0.180 V
Iron content (%)	0.61	0.38

[a] From Hori(57). Reprinted with permission of the Japanese Biochemical Society.

protein may function as a direct electron donor to the nitrate reductase(56,57). The electron transfer sequence would then be as given in Scheme 3.13. No definite conclusion of phosphorylation coupled to electron transport can yet be reached. If it is assumed that the starting potential for nitrate reduction is near the $NAD^+/NADH + H^+$ system and that the potential for the NO_3^-/NO_2^- system is +0.5 V, then the potential change is reduced to approximately 0.9 V.

For *Micrococcus denitrificans*, Naik and Nicholas(100) showed that phosphorylation is associated with the reduction of nitrate to nitrite, but not with the reduction of nitric oxide, nitrous oxide, or hydroxylamine. This suggests that esterification of phosphorus occurs only when inorganic nitrogen compounds containing at least two atoms of oxygen are used as terminal acceptors. This phosphorylation was considerably greater in the case of nitrate reduction than in nitrite reduction.

The nitrite-reducing system in *Micrococcus denitrificans* seems to be different from that of *Pseudomonas denitrificans* (62), since there was no phosphorylation observed with nitrite as terminal acceptor with the former. This would support the findings of Yamanaka (180), who suggested that cytochrome oxidase and nitrite reductase are identical in *Pseudomonas*.

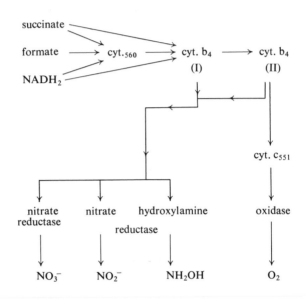

SCHEME 3.13. [From Hori (57)]. Reprinted with permission of the Japanese Biochemical Society.

On the other hand, there is a possibility that there are two types of cytochrome oxidases (8):

(1) Cytochrome c_2:oxygen oxidoreductase, E.C. 1.9.3.2 (syn. *Pseudomonas* cytochrome oxidase; cytochrome cd; cytochrome oxidase/nitrite reductase; *Pseudomonas* cytochrome c_{551}:nitrite, oxygen, oxidoreductase), which does not act on mammalian cytochrome c.

(2) Cytochrome c:oxygen oxidoreductase, E.C. 1.9.3.1 (syn. cytochrome a_3; cytochrome oxidase; *Pseudomonas* cytochrome c_{551}/O_2 oxidoreductase), which can reduce mammalian cytochrome c, but does not reduce nitrite.

A similar finding was observed in *Micrococcus denitrificans* (160). Denitrification plays an important role in soil metabolism (4, 130). A high rate of denitrification occurs only when oxygen tension is very low. About 1 % oxygen will suppress denitrification to about 12%. It is therefore suggested that the amount of oxygen present serves to control the denitrification rate. The first gaseous product is nitric oxide (approximately 5% of nitrate in soil) with nitrous oxide being next and finally molecular nitrogen appears and accounts for 83–95% of the nitrate present in soil. The author states that only in the presence of appreciable concentrations of organic matter and low oxygen levels (7%) will an appreciable reduction of nitrate to nitrite occur [cf. Quastel(130)].

Many bacteria that normally respire aerobically grow anaerobically by substituting nitrate for oxygen as the final hydrogen acceptor. The products formed are characteristic of a given species. The respiratory mechanism involved in these reductions utilizes an electron transport system(42). Whereas three moles of ATP are formed per atom oxygen, only two moles of ATP are formed per mole of nitrate(150). The most common product of nitrate reduction is nitrite. Using acetate as substrate and nitrate as hydrogen acceptor, the reaction would be as follows:

$$CH_3COOH + 4NO_3^- \rightarrow 2CO_2 + 4NO_2^- + 2H_2O$$

Nitrite, however, is toxic to a number of bacteria and consequently a reduction of nitrate with the accumulation of nitrite is not a reaction that supports extensive anaerobic growth. Therefore, further reduction of nitrite to nontoxic products generally occurs. These further reductions also permit a greater amount of substrate to be oxidized per mole of nitrate reduced.

The enzyme responsible for this nitrate reduction is a nitrate reductase. The versatility of nitrate reduction can easily be seen by the number of enzymes available. At the present state of our knowledge, there are four nitrate reductases in existence(34):

(1) reduced NAD: nitrate oxidoreductase, E.C. 1.6.6.1, which catalyzes the reaction

reduced NAD + nitrate $\rightarrow$ NAD$^+$ + nitrite + water

and requires a metalloflavoprotein for its function.
(2) reduced NAD(P): nitrate oxidoreductase, E.C. 1.6.6.2, which catalyzes the reaction

reduced NAD(P) + nitrate $\rightarrow$ NAD(P)$^+$ + nitrite + water

and requires only a simple flavoprotein.
(3) reduced NADP: nitrate oxidoreductase, E.C. 1.6.6.3, which catalyzes the reaction

reduced NADP + nitrate $\rightarrow$ NADP$^+$ + nitrite + water

and requires a flavoprotein containing molybdenum.
(4) cytochrome: nitrate oxidoreductase, E.C. 1.9.6.1, which catalyzes the reaction

ferrocytochrome + nitrate $\rightarrow$ ferricytochrome + nitrite

and has no further requirements.

The existence of these four nitrate reductases gives some indication of the variation that can be expected in the electron transport system of bacteria using nitrate as final hydrogen acceptor.

The respiratory nitrate reductase is bound to subcellular particles which are themselves intimately involved in aerobic respiration. Nitrate respiration is competitively inhibited by molecular oxygen. This competition between nitrate and oxygen reduction in cells of *Pseudomonas denitrificans*, for example, led to the conclusion that nitrate reduction can only occur when the oxygen concentration is below the critical level at which the oxygen utilizing enzymes are saturated(56). It appears that the competition between oxygen and nitrate for the donor electrons favors the oxygen so much that nitrate reduction only occurs when the oxygen supply is completely inadequate to meet the demand (144). However, there exists a direct relationship between nitrate reduction and oxygen solution rate. No reduction was detectable at an oxygen concentration above 0.2 ppm. Similar results were obtained with *Achromobacter* sp. (91). This competition seems to be restricted to the nitrate reductase and does not necessarily apply to the nitrite reductase. Nitrite reduction was observed with *Achromobacter liquefaciens*, which reduces nitrite but not nitrate(146) in solutions in which the oxygen concentration was in equilibrium with air. Sachs and Barker(132), however, with *Ps. stutzeri* recorded high oxygen sensitivity of nitrite reduction. *Escherichia coli* possesses a nitrite reductase specific for reduced NAD(72).

Taking these studies into consideration, there exist two electron transport schemes which have been established using different bacteria (reprinted with permission of the authors and the Elsevier Publishing Co.):

(1) *Achromobacter fisheri*(107, 108, 133)

$$\text{reduced NAD(P)} \rightarrow \text{FMN (FAD)}$$
$$\downarrow$$
$$Fe^{3+}$$
$$\downarrow$$

$$O_2 \leftarrow \text{cytochrome} \leftarrow \text{bacterial}$$
$$\text{oxidase} \qquad \text{cytochrome}$$
$$\downarrow$$
$$\text{nitrate}$$
$$\text{reductase}$$
$$\downarrow$$
$$NO_3^-$$

(2) *Pseudomonas aeruginosa*(42)

$$\text{reduced NAD} \rightarrow \text{FAD} \rightarrow \text{cyt.c} \rightarrow Mo \rightarrow NO_3$$
$$\downarrow$$
$$\text{cytochrome} \rightarrow O_2$$
$$\text{oxidase}$$

The main difference between the electron transport systems of *Achromobacter* and *Pseudomonas* appears to be in the electron carrier immediately before the enzyme. In the case of nitrite reductase, *Achromobacter fisheri* possessed a heme-containing protein with only a c-type spectrum(129), whereas *Pseudomonas aeruginosa* has been shown to have a cytochrome(181). In contrast *Neurospora*(104,106), soybean leaves(104), *E. coli*(73) and *Azotobacter agile*(151) are believed to possess metalloflavoproteins.

Whether or not nitrate reductase is an adaptive or constitutive enzyme is still under dispute. Whereas it has been claimed that it is adaptive in *Escherichia coli*(93,94), *Aerobacter aerogenes*, and *Bacillus stearothermophilus*(36), Nicholas *et al.*(108) claim it to be a constitutive enzyme for *Achromobacter fisheri* [Photobacterium sepia (*sic*)].

The apparent oxygen toxicity found in some facultatively anaerobic bacteria can represent a disturbance of metabolism, since it can be reversed nutritionally(45).

A recent discovery is that oxygen may not always influence nitrate reductase but the formation of cytochromes, which form the electron carrier system to nitrate reductase. Extracts of *Micrococcus denitrificans* showed a higher cytochrome content of b and c type if the organism was grown anaerobically on nitrate compared with those from aerobically grown cells(124). On the other hand, some strains of *Staphylococcus epidermidis*(65) produced nitrite from nitrate when grown in air, but failed to do so during growth under anaerobic conditions although nitrate reductase was present but remained nonfunctional under anaerobic conditions. These observations clearly indicate that some electron carrier of the respiratory system must be affected by the anaerobic conditions(28,139,147). Although it is not known what role oxygen plays in the development of the respiratory systems(66) in these facultative anaerobes, a parallel could be drawn to the yeast, *Saccharomyces cerevisiae*. It has been shown quite clearly here that oxygen induces the formation of respiratory enzymes, cytochrome pigments, and even mitochondrial structures(123,165). *Staphylococcus epidermidis* shows a decreased cytochrome content as a result of anaerobiosis, which was also found in the case of *Pasteurella pestis*(38,39), *Proteus vulgaris*(81), and *Staphylococcus aureus*(46,84). This deficiency of nitrate reduction could be compensated by the addition of hemin(64). Since the enzyme nitrate reductase does not contain a heme component(26), the effect of hemin in nitrate reduction must result from its conversion into a cytochrome that mediates in electron transfer to nitrate. It can therefore be said that all those bacteria which reduce nitrate under aerobic conditions do possess the nitrate reductase and require oxygen not as terminal electron acceptor but for the biosynthesis of a heme-containing cytochrome, which mediates in the electron carrier system to nitrate reduction. Whereas in other facultative anaerobes such as *Saccharomyces cerevisiae, Pasteurella pestis,* and *Bacillus cereus* oxygen is required for the synthesis of the complete respiratory system (40), the major role oxygen seems to play in *Staphylococcus epidermidis* and *Staphylococcus aureus* (157) is as a requirement for heme biosynthesis (63).

One possible explanation for this requirement is suggested by the finding with beef liver mitochondria that one of the oxidative steps in heme biosynthesis exhibits a requirement for molecular oxygen and no other electron acceptor will substitute (135). This reaction converts coproporphyrinogen to proto-porphyrin, which would support the finding that *Staphylococcus epidermidis*

protoporphyrin IX

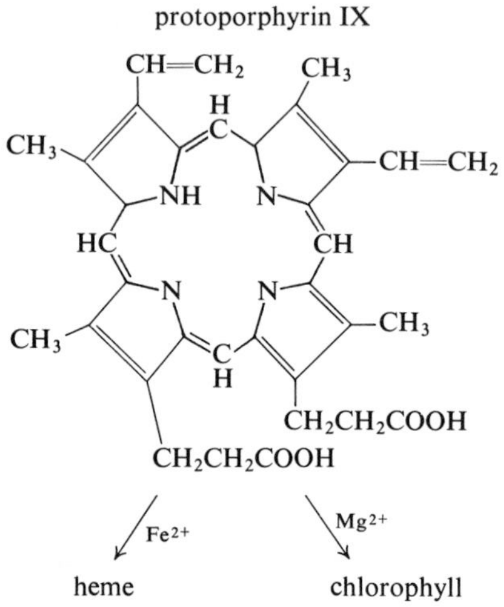

FIG. 3.3

accumulates large amounts of coproporphyrinogen during anaerobic growth (53). In the heme biosynthesis protoporphyrin IX (Fig. 3.3)(135) is the key porphyrin in animal and plant cells. From this porphyrin two branches of the biosynthetic chain are postulated, namely, an "iron branch" and a "magnesium branch." The former arises by the insertion of Fe^{2+} into the ring of proto-porphyrin IX to form heme. This is the prosthetic group of hemoglobin, catalase, peroxidase, and some cytochromes. The "magnesium branch" on the other hand, leads toward chlorophyll. The details of heme biosynthesis will not be given here, but could be followed up in a series of publications (12, 16, 17, 46–48, 74, 85, 90, 96, 97, 110, 135, 168).

It has been concluded that hemin combines with the protein component of cytochrome b to form cytochrome b_1 (26, 32), which participates in the electron transfer to nitrate, mediated by nitrate reductase.

The observation, however, that other bacteria such as *Escherichia coli* form cytochromes during anaerobic growth suggests that not all bacteria exhibit an oxygen requirement for heme biosynthesis(50). In summarizing our present knowledge on facultative anaerobes, one could divide these into two groups. The first group comprises all those which use nitrate as terminal electron acceptor under aerobic and anaerobic conditions without heme requirements. Their cytochrome system consists of metalloflavoproteins, i.e., *Escherichia coli* and *Pseudomonas*. The second group includes those facultative anaerobes which use only nitrate as their final electron acceptor but require either oxygen or heme for their growth. The cytochrome sytem of this group contains heme as prosthetic group for at least one of their cytochromes, i.e., *Pasteurella pestis*, *Staphylococcus aureus*, *Staphylococcus epidermidis*, and *Haemophilus parainfluenzae*.

Aerobacter aerogenes was found to utilize nitrate as a sole source of nitrogen for the synthesis of cell material(118) and also as hydrogen acceptor under anaerobic conditions(121), and is thought to have one nitrate reductase(120). This organism would therefore belong to the group which has metalloflavo-protein-containing cytochromes. The indication that *Micrococcus denitrificans* possesses two nitrate reductases(119) may suggest that its cytochromes require heme when grown under anaerobic conditions.

Aerobacter aerogenes has probably a unique nitrate reductase since it can use molecular hydrogen as an electron source for nitrate reduction to nitrite as well as ammonia. *Vibrio sputorum*(92) also seems to possess a nitrate reductase since it reduces nitrate beyond nitrite under anaerobic conditions. For detailed information refer to the excellent review by Taniguchi(159).

Additional studies on the effect of glucose on the formation of cytochromes have been started(167), but no conclusion can be drawn as yet.

Carbon Dioxide Reduction

Carbon dioxide is used by a small group of bacteria as their final electron acceptor, the reduction product being methane. These are the "methane bacteria." These bacteria are entirely different from the aerobic methane-oxidizing bacteria as will be seen later (Chapter 5). The former produce methane from various organic and inorganic compounds, whereas the latter oxidize methane to carbon dioxide and water.

The methane bacteria have not been studied as extensively as most other groups of bacteria. The reason for this is most likely the extreme difficulty experienced in isolating and maintaining pure cultures. All of the species are strict anaerobes and therefore develop only in the absence of oxygen and in the presence of a suitable reducing agent. The methane bacteria are much more sensitive to oxygen or certain other oxidizing agents, such as nitrate, than are most other anaerobic bacteria. Their energy metabolism is specialized for a process that produces methane as the only major product. They also specialize in respect to the type of substrates utilized for energy and carbon sources. They have not been reported to utilize carbohydrates or amino acids. The substrates utilized by the methane bacteria fall into three categories:

(1) the lower fatty acids containing from one to six carbon atoms;
(2) the normal and iso-alcohols containing from one to five carbon atoms; and
(3) the three inorganic gases hydrogen, carbon monoxide, and carbon dioxide.

Each species therefore is restricted to the use of a few compounds.

The methane bacteria are represented by *Methanobacterium*, *Methanobacillus*, *Methanococcus*, and *Methanosarcina*(11,179).

Barker(11) reviewed the literature on methane production. Early theories have proposed that organic compounds metabolized by methane bacteria are oxidized completely to carbon dioxide and this oxidation is coupled with a reduction of some or all of the carbon dioxide to methane:

$$\text{oxidation} \quad CH_3COOH + 2H_2O \rightarrow 2CO_2 + 8[H]$$
$$\text{reduction} \quad 8[H] + CO_2 \rightarrow CH_4 + 2H_2O$$

$$\text{net} \quad CH_3COOH \rightarrow CH_4 + CO_2$$

Coupled reactions were cited for (a) *Methanobacterium omelianski*:

$$(1) \quad 2CH_3CH_2OH + 2H_2O \rightarrow 2CH_3COOH + 8[H]$$
$$8[H] + CO_2 \rightarrow CH_4 + 2H_2O$$

$$2CH_3CH_2OH + CO_2 \rightarrow 2CH_3COOH + CH_4$$
$$(2) \quad 4H_2 \rightarrow 8[H]$$
$$8[H] + CO_2 \rightarrow CH_4 + 2H_2O$$

$$4H_2 + CO_2 \rightarrow CH_4 + 2H_2O$$
$$(3) \quad 4CH_3OH + 4H_2O \rightarrow 4CO_2 + 24[H]$$
$$24[H] + 3CO_2 \rightarrow 3CH_4 + 6H_2O$$

$$4CH_3OH \rightarrow 3CH_4 + 2H_2O + CO_2$$

The first reaction was quite distinct from the third reaction. The oxidation of ethanol was strictly CO_2 dependent. When the CO_2 was completely consumed the oxidation of ethanol stopped(76). During the third reaction CO_2 was first formed and then reduced to methane. It was therefore not necessary to supply the medium with CO_2 continuously.

(b) *Methanobacterium formicicum*:

$$CO + H_2O \rightarrow CO_2 + H_2$$
$$CO_2 + 4H_2 \rightarrow CH_4 + 2H_2O$$

$$CO + 3H_2 \rightarrow CH_4 + H_2O$$

(c) *Methanobacillus suboxydans*:

$$2CH_3CH_2CH_2COOH + 4H_2O \rightarrow 4CH_3COOH + 8[H]$$

$$8[H] + CO_2 \rightarrow CH_4 + 2H_2O$$

$$2CH_3CH_2CH_2COOH + 2H_2O + CO_2 \rightarrow 4CH_3COOH + CH_4$$

(d) *Methanobacterium propionicum*:

$$4CH_3CH_2COOH + 8H_2O \rightarrow 4CH_3COOH + 4CO_2 + 24[H]$$

$$3CO_2 + 24[H] \rightarrow 3CH_4 + 6H_2O$$

$$4CH_3CH_2COOH + 2H_2O \rightarrow 4CH_3COOH + CO_2 + 3CH_4$$

In cases (a)(1), (b), and (c), acetate was an additional end product. The substrates were not converted completely into methane as in the other coupled reactions. These are called the "fermentative type" because the substrate is not completely oxidized.

In at least two cases tracer experiments on the metabolism of acetate and methanol by methane bacteria suggested that the carbon dioxide reduction theory was not tenable in all cases. Stadtman and Barker(152,153) showed that the methane is formed entirely from the methyl carbon, and the carbon dioxide exclusively from the carboxyl carbon of acetate, while Pine and Barker (122) found similar results for methanol. These results suggested then that the methane formation from methanol and acetate was independent of CO_2. To provide for the various modes of methane production Barker(11) postulated possible pathways as follows, whereby XH represents an unknown carrier (see Scheme 3.14). The reduction steps require energy which probably come from ATP. The detailed mechanism of CO_2 reduction is therefore still obscure(173), but a hydrogen atmosphere was found essential for optimal methane formation. Cell-free extracts of *Methanobacterium omelianski* produced methane when H_2, CO_2, CoA and ATP were in the reaction mixture, which suggests that the oxidation of H_2, coupled with the reduction of carbon dioxide to methane, involves CoA and ATP(173). Pyruvate, serine, and *o*-phosphoserine could substitute for ATP and CO_2. The search for a methyl transfer enzyme in methane formation has led to comparisons with a cobamide enzyme, which is involved in a similar step during methionine biosynthesis of *Escherichia coli*(22). It was found that methyl cobalamine was an excellent substrate for the methane-forming reaction(173,174). This formation of methane from methyl cobalamine by extracts of *Methanobacterium omelianski* was ATP-dependent and in extracts of *Methanosarcina barkeri*(15) also CoA-dependent. With the purification of the methane-forming system of *M. omelianski*, it was possible to support the concept that a cobamide moiety of the methane-forming enzyme exists(176). The site of participation of ATP is still obscure, although it is known that 1 μmole of ATP is required for each micromole of methane evolved. The strong adenosine triphosphatase activity seems to indicate that the products ADP and AMP somehow regulate methane formation(177). This discovery was interesting insofar as the presence or absence of ATP regulates C_1 transfer in the methane formation from N^5,

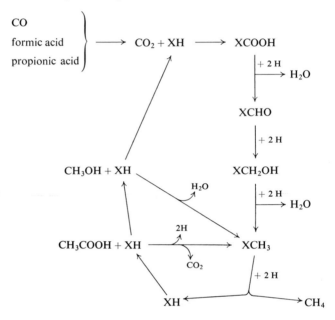

SCHEME 3.14. (Reprinted with permission of John Wiley and Sons.)

N^{10}-methylenetetrahydrofolate in extracts of *Methanobacterium omelianski*(178).

Our present state of knowledge concerning the methane formation from carbon dioxide and substrates such as pyruvate or serine under hydrogen atmosphere is:

(1) that with some substrates (e.g., ethanol, butyrate, and hydrogen) methane is formed by CO_2 reduction, if CO_2 is added to the atmosphere;
(2) that methane is formed by CO_2 reduction, if CO_2 is formed during the oxidation of the substrate (e.g., CO and propionate); and
(3) that methane is formed via a methyl transfer using either methyl cobalamine or N^5, N^{10}-methylenetetrahydrofolate as cofactors, but without carbon dioxide (e.g., acetate and methanol).

In the latter case there is a requirement for 1 μmole of ATP for each micromole of methane formed. It is possible that further ATP may be required to generate a reducing potential. This role of ATP and the presence of an active adenosine triphosphatase may lead to the assumption that ADP and AMP as products of this enzyme could regulate methane formation.

REFERENCES

1. Akagi, J. M. (1965). The participation of a ferredoxin of *Clostridium nigrificans* in sulphite reduction. *Biochem. Biophys. Res. Commun.* **21**, 72.
2. Akagi, J. M. (1965). Phosphoroclastic reaction of *Clostridium nigrificans*. *J. Bacteriol.* **88**, 813.
3. Akagi, J. M. (1967). Electron carriers for the phosphoroclastic reaction of *Desulfovibrio desulfuricans*. *J. Biol. Chem.* **242**, 2478.
4. Alexander, M. (1964). "Introduction to Soil Microbiology." Wiley, New York.
5. Alico, R. K., and Liegey, R. W. (1966). Growth of *Desulfovibrio desulfuricans* under heterotrophic and anaerobic conditions. *J. Bacteriol.* **91**, 1112.
6. Asano, A. (1959). Studies on enzymic nitrite reduction. I. Properties of the enzyme system involved in the process of nitrite reduction. *J. Biochem. (Tokyo)* **46**, 781.
7. Asano, A. (1959). Studies on enzymic nitrite reduction. II. Separation of nitrite reductase to particulate and soluble components. *J. Biochem. (Tokyo)* **46**, 1235.
8. Azoulay, E. (1964). Influence des conditions de culture sur la respiration de *Pseudomonas aeruginosa*. *Biochim. Biophys. Acta* **92**, 458.
9. Baker, F. D., Papiska, H. R., and Campbell, L. L. (1962). Choline fermentation by *Desulfovibrio desulfuricans*. *J. Bacteriol.* **84**, 973.
10. Banerje, A. K. (1966). Physiologische Untersuchungen an *Micrococcus denitrificans* Beijerinck und auxotrophen Mutanten. Isolierung auxotropher Mutanten und Spaltung des Cystathionins. *Arch. Mikrobiol.* **53**, 107.
11. Barker, H. A. (1956). "Bacterial Fermentations," CIBA Lectures in Microbial Biochemistry. Wiley, New York.
12. Barrett, J. (1956). The prosthetic group of cytochrome a_2. *Biochem. J.* **64**, 626.
13. Bernstein, S., and McGilverey, R. W. (1952). Substrate activation in the synthesis of phenylsulfate. *J. Biol. Chem.* **199**, 745.
14. Bieberstein, E. L., and Gills, M. (1961). Catalase activity of *Haemophilus* species grown with graded amounts of hemin. *J. Bacteriol.* **81**, 380.
15. Blaylock, B. A., and Stadtman, T. C. (1966). Methane biosynthesis by *Methanosarcina barkeri*. Properties of the soluble enzyme system. *Arch. Biochem. Biophys.* **116**, 138.
16. Bogorad, L. (1958). The enzymatic synthesis of porphyrins from porphobilinogen I, uroporphyrin I. *J. Biol. Chem.* **233**, 501.
17. Bogorad, L. (1958). The enzymatic synthesis of porphyrins from porphobilinogen II, uroporphyrin II. *J. Biol. Chem.* **233**, 510.
18. Bowen, T. J., and Cook, W. T. (1966). *J. Chromatog.* **22**, 488; as cited by Cook (30).
19. Bowen, T. J., Butler, P. J., and Happold, F. C. (1965). Some properties of the rhodanese system of *Thiobacillus denitrificans*. *Biochem. J.* **97**, 651.
20. Bowen, T. J., Happold, F. C., and Taylor, B. F. (1966). Studies on adenosine-5'-phosphosulfate reduction from *Thiobacillus denitrificans*. *Biochim. Biophys. Acta* **118**, 566.
21. Brodie, A. F., and Adelson, J. (1965). Respiratory chains and sites of coupled phosphorylation. Studies in a bacterial system give further evidence of a basic biochemical unity between different forms. *Science* **149**, 265.
22. Brot, N., and Weissbach, H. (1966). The role of cobamides in methionine synthesis. Enzymatic formation of holoenzyme. *J. Biol. Chem.* **241**, 2024.

23. Brown, M. S., and Akagi, J. M. (1966). Purification of acetokinase from *Desulfovibrio desulfuricans. J. Bacteriol.* **92**, 1273.
24. Butlin, K. R., Adams, M. E., and Thomas, M. (1949). The isolation and cultivation of sulphate-reducing bacteria. *J. Gen. Microbiol.* **3**, 46.
25. Campbell, L. L., and Postgate, J. R. (1965). Classification of the spore-forming sulphate-reducing bacteria. *Bacteriol. Rev.* **29**, 359.
26. Chang, J. P., and Lascelles, J. (1963). Nitrate reductase in cell-free extracts of a haemin-requiring strain of *Staphylococcus aureus. Biochem. J.* **89**, 503.
27. Chaste, J., and Pierfitte, M. (1965). Sulfur metabolism of *Escherichia coli. Bull. Soc. Pharm. Nancy* **64**, 13; *Chem. Abstr.* **63**, 13723 (1965).
28. Chin, C. H. (1950). Effect of aeration on the cytochrome systems of the resting cells of brewer's yeast. *Nature* **165**, 926.
29. Clayton, R. K. (1960). Protein synthesis in the induced formation of catalase in *Rhodopseudomonas spheroides. J. Biol. Chem.* **235**, 405.
30. Cook, W. K. T. (1967). Aspects of dithionate metabolism in *Thiobacillus denitrificans. Biochem. J.* **102**, 5P.
31. Dacre, J. C., and Sharpe, M. E. (1956). Catalase production by lactobacilli. *Nature* **178**, 700.
32. Deeb, S. S., and Hager, L. P. (1964). Crystalline cytochrome b_1 from *E. coli. J. Biol. Chem.* **239**, 1024.
33. Delwiche, E. A. (1961). Catalase of *Pediococcus cerevisiae. J. Bacteriol.* **81**, 416.
34. Dixon, M., and Webb, E. C. (1964). "Enzymes," 2nd ed. Longmans, Green, New York.
35. Dolin, M. I. (1961). Survey of microbial electron transport mechanisms. *In* "The Bacteria" (I. C. Gunsalus and R. Y. Stanier, eds.), Vol. 2, p. 341. Academic Press, New York.
36. Downey, R. J. (1966). Nitrate reductase and respiratory adaption in *Bacillus stearothermophilus. J. Bacteriol.* **91**, 634.
37. Dreyfuss, J., and Monty, K. J. (1963). Coincident repression of the reduction of 3'-phosphoadenosine 5'-phosphosulfate, sulfite and thiosulfate in the cysteine pathway of *Salmonella typhimurium. J. Biol. Chem.* **238**, 3781.
38. Englesberg, E., Gibor, A., and Levy, J. B. (1954). Adaptive control of terminal respiration in *Pasteurella pestis. J. Bacteriol.* **68**, 146.
39. Englesberg, E., Levy, J. B., and Gibor, A. (1954). Some enzymatic changes accompanying the shift from anaerobiosis to aerobiosis in *Pasteurella pestis. J. Bacteriol.* **68**, 178.
40. Ephrussi, B., and Slonimski, P. P. (1950). La synthese adaptative des cytochrome chez la levure de boulangerie. *Biochim. Biophys. Acta* **6**, 256.
41. Felton, E. A., Evans, J. B., and Niven, C. F. (1953). Production of catalase by the pediococci. *J. Bacteriol.* **65**, 481.
42. Fewson, C. A., and Nicholas, D. J. D. (1961). Nitrate reductase from *Pseudomonas aeruginosa. Biochim. Biophys. Acta* **49**, 335.
43. Gibbs, R. G., and Morris, J. G. (1965). Purification and properties of erythro-β-hydroxyaspartate dehydratase from *Micrococcus denitrificans. Biochem. J.* **97**, 547.
44. Gibbs, R. G., and Morris, J. G. (1966). Formation of glycine from glyoxylate in *Micrococcus denitrificans. Biochem. J.* **99**, 27P.
45. Gottlieb, S. F. (1966). Bacterial nutritional approach to mechanisms of oxygen toxicity. *J. Bacteriol.* **92**, 1021.
46. Granick, S. (1958). Porphyrin biosynthesis in erythrocytes. I. Formation of α-aminolevulinic acid in erythrocytes. *J. Biol. Chem.* **232**, 1101.

47. Granick, S., and Mauzerall, D. (1958). Porphyrin biosynthesis in erythrocytes. II. Enzymes converting α-aminolevulinic acid to coproporphyrinogen. *J. Biol. Chem.* **232**, 1119.
48. Granick, S., and Mauzerall, D. (1961). The metabolism of heme and chlorophyll. *Metab. Pathways* **3**, 525–625.
49. Gray, C. T., and Gest, H. (1965). Biological function of molecular hydrogen. *Science* **148**, 186.
50. Gray, C. T., Wimpenny, J. W. T., Hughes, D. E., and Mossman, M. R. (1966). Regulation of metabolism in facultative bacteria. I. Structural and functional changes in *Escherichia coli* associated with shifts between the aerobic and anaerobic states. *Biochim. Biophys. Acta* **117**, 22.
51. Green, J. R., and Westley, J. (1961). Mechanism of rhodanese action: Polarographic studies. *J. Biol. Chem.* **236**, 3047.
52. Hayward, H. R., and Stadtman, T. C. (1959). Anaerobic degradation of choline. I. Fermentation of choline by an anaerobic, cytochrome-producing bacterium, *Vibrio cholinicus* n. sp. *J. Bacteriol.* **78**, 557.
53. Heady, R. E., Jacobs, N. J., and Deibel, R. H. (1964). Effect of haemin supplementation on porphyrin accumulation and catalase synthesis during anaerobic growth of *Staphylococcus. Nature* **203**, 1285.
54. Hilz, H., and Kittler, M. (1960). Reduction of active sulfate (PAPS) by diphydrolipoic acid. *Biochem. Biophys. Res. Commun.* **3**, 140.
55. Hilz, H., Kittler, M., and Knape, G. (1959). Die Reduktion von Sulfat in der Hefe. *Biochem. Z.* **332**, 151.
56. Hori, K. (1961). Electron transport components participating in nitrate and oxygen respiration from a halotolerant *Micrococcus.* I. Purification and properties of cytochromes b_4 (I) and b_4 (II). *J. Biochem. (Tokyo)* **50**, 440.
57. Hori, K. (1961). Properties of cytochrome c_{551} and brown protein. *J. Biochem. (Tokyo)* **50**, 481.
58. Hutchinson, M., Johnstone, K. I., and White, D. (1967). Taxonomy of anaerobic thiobacilli. *J. Gen. Microbiol.* **47**, 17.
59. Ishimoto, M. (1959). Sulfate reduction in cell-free extracts of *Desulfovibrio. J. Biochem. (Tokyo)* **46**, 105.
60. Iverson, W. P. (1966). Growth of *Desulfovibrio* on the surface of agar media. *Appl. Microbiol.* **14**, 529.
61. Iwasaki, H. (1960). Studies on denitrification. IV. Participation of cytochromes in the denitrification. *J. Biochem (Tokyo)* **47**, 174.
62. Iwasaki, H., Shidara, S., Suzuki, H., and Mori, T. (1963). Studies on denitrification. VII. Further purification and properties of denitrifying enzyme. *J. Biochem. (Tokyo)* **53**, 299.
63. Jacobs, N. J., and Conti, S. (1965). Effect of hemin on the formation of the cytochrome system of anaerobically grown *Staphylococcus epidermidis. J. Bacteriol.* **89**, 675.
64. Jacobs, N. J., and Deibel, R. H. (1963). Effect of anaerobic growth on nitrate reduction by staphylococci. *Bacteriol. Proc.* p. 124.
65. Jacobs, N. J., Johantges, J., and Deibel, R. H. (1963). Effect of anaerobic growth on nitrate reduction by *Staphylococcus epidermidis. J. Bacteriol.* **85**, 782.
66. Jacobs, N. J., Maclosky, E. R., and Conti, S. F. (1967). Effects of oxygen and heme on the development of a microbial respiratory system. *J. Bacteriol.* **93**, 278.
67. Jensen, J. (1957). Biosynthesis of hematin compounds in a hemin requiring strain of *Micrococcus pyogenes* var. aureus. I. The significance of coenzyme A for the terminal synthesis of catalase. *J. Bacteriol.* **73**, 324.

68. Jensen, J., and Hyde, M. O. (1963). "Apocatalase" of catalase-negative staphylococci. *Science* **141**, 45.
69. Johnston, M. A., and Delwiche, E. A. (1962). Catalase of the *Lactobacillaceae*. *J. Bacteriol.* **83**, 936.
70. Jyssum, K., and Joner, P. E. (1966). Hydroxylamine as a possible intermediate in nitrate reduction by *Bacterium anitratum* (B5W). *Acta Pathol. Microbiol. Scand.* **67**, 139.
71. Karlson, P. (1965). "Introduction to Modern Biochemistry," 2nd ed. Academic Press, New York.
72. Kemp, J. D., and Atkinson, D. E. (1966). Nitrite reductase of *Escherichia coli* specific for NADH$_2$. *J. Bacteriol.* **92**, 628.
73. Kemp, J. D., Atkinson, D. E., Ehret, A., and Lazzarini, R. A. (1963). Evidence for the identity of the nicotinamide adenine dinucleotide phosphate-specific sulfite and nitrite reduction of *Escherichia coli*. *J. Biol. Chem.* **238**, 3466.
74. Kikuchi, G., Kumar, A., Talmage, P., and Shemin, D. (1958). The enzymatic synthesis of α-aminolevulinic acid. *J. Biol. Chem.* **233**, 1214.
75. Kluyver, A. J., and Verhoeven, W. (1954). Studies on two dissimilatory nitrate reduction. II. The mechanism of denitrification. *Antonie van Leeuwenhoek, J. Microbiol. Serol.* **20**, 241.
76. Knight, M., Wolfe, R. S., and Elsden, S. R. (1966). The synthesis of amino acids by *Methanobacterium omelianski*. *Biochem. J.* **99**, 76.
77. Kono, M., and Taniguchi, S. (1960). Hydroxylamine reductase of a halotolerant *Micrococcus*. *Biochim. Biophys. Acta* **43**, 419.
78. Kornberg, H. L., and Morris, J. G. (1965). The utilization of glycollate by *Micrococcus denitrificans*: β-Hydroxyaspartate pathway. *Biochem. J.* **95**, 577.
79. Koshland, D. E., Jr. (1954). *In* "The Mechanism of Enzyme Action" (W. D. McElroy and B. Glass, eds.), p. 608. Johns Hopkins Press, Baltimore, Maryland; as cited by Green and Westley (51).
80. Kovacs, E., Mazarean, H. H., and Jaki, A. (1965). Relation between the synthesis of catalase and the intensity of respiration in cultures of *Staphylococcus aureus*. *Enzymologia* **28**, 316; *Chem. Abstr.* **63**, 8761 (1965).
81. Krasna, A. I., and Rittenberg, D. (1954). Reduction of nitrate with molecular hydrogen by *Proteus vulgaris*. *J. Bacteriol.* **68**, 53.
82. Krogstad, D. J., and Howland, J. L. (1966). Role of menaquinone in *Corynebacterium diphtheriae* electron transport. *Biochim. Biophys. Acta* **118**, 189.
83. Lamanna, C., and Malette, M. F. (1965). "Basic Bacteriology," p. 846. Williams & Wilkins, Baltimore, Maryland.
84. Lascelles, J. (1956). An assay of iron protoporphyrin based on the reduction of nitrate by a variant strain of *Staphylococcus aureus*: Synthesis of iron protoporphyrin by suspensions of *Rhodopseudomonas spheroides*. *J. Gen. Microbiol.* **15**, 404.
85. Lascelles, J. (1960). The synthesis of enzymes concerned in bacteriochlorophyll formation in growing cultures of *Rhodopseudomonas spheroides*. *J. Gen. Microbiol.* **23**, 487.
86. LeGall, J. (1963). A new species of *Desulfovibrio*. *J. Bacteriol.* **86**, 1120.
87. LeGall, J., and Dragoni, N. (1966). Dependence of sulfite reduction on a crystallized ferredoxin from *Desulfovibrio gigas*. *Biochem. Biophys. Res. Commun.* **23**, 145.
88. Lehninger, A. C. (1965). "Bioenergetics." Benjamin, New York.
89. Leinweber, F. J., and Monty, K. J. (1963). The metabolism of thiosulfate in *Salmonella typhimurium*. *J. Biol. Chem.* **238**, 3775.

90. Lemberg, R. (1961). Cytochromes of group a and their prosthetic groups. *Advan. Enzymol.* **23**, 265.

91. Lindeberg, G., Lode, A., and Somme, R. (1963). Effect of oxygen on formation and activity of nitrate reductase in a halophilic *Achromobacter* species. *Acta Chem. Scand.* **17**, 232.

92. Loesche, W. J., Gibbons, R. J., and Socransky, S. S. (1965). Biochemical characteristics of *Vibrio sputorum* and relationship to *Vibrio bubulus* and *Vibrio fetus. J. Bacteriol.* **89**, 1109.

93. McNall, E. G., and Atkinson, D. E. (1956). Nitrate reduction. I. Growth of *Escherichia coli* with nitrate as sole source of nitrogen. *J. Bacteriol.* **72**, 226.

94. McNall, E. G., and Atkinson, D. E. (1957). Nitrate reduction. II. Utilization of possible intermediates as nitrogen sources and as electron acceptors. *J. Bacteriol.* **74**, 60.

95. MacPherson, R., and Miller, J. D. A. (1963). Nutritional studies on *Desulfovibrio desulfuricans* using chemically defined media. *J. Gen. Microbiol.* **31**, 365.

96. Mauzerall, D. (1960). The thermodynamic stability of the porphyrinogens. *J. Am. Chem. Soc.* **82**, 2601.

97. Mauzerall, D., and Granick, S. (1958). Porphyrin biosynthesis in erythrocytes. III. Uroporphyrinogen and its decarboxylase. *J. Biol. Chem.* **232**, 1141.

98. Millet, J. (1954). *Compt. Rend.* **238**, 408; as cited by Peck (111).

99. Mortensen, L. E., Valentine, R. C., and Carnahan, J. E. (1962). An electron transport factor from *Clostridium pasteurianum. Biochem. Biophys. Res Commun.* **7**, 448.

100. Naik, M. S., and Nicholas, D. J. D. (1966). Phosphorylation associated with nitrate and nitrite reductions in *Micrococcus denitrificans* and *Pseudomonas denitrificans. Biochim. Biophys. Acta* **113**, 490.

101. Najjar, V. A., and Chung, C. W. (1956). Enzymatic steps in denitrification. *In* "Inorganic Nitrogen Metabolism" (W. D. McElroy and B. Glass, eds.), p. 260. Johns Hopkins Press, Baltimore, Maryland; as cited by Nason (103).

102. Nakajima, O., and Gray, C. H. (1967). Studies on haem α-methyl oxygenase. Isomeric structure of formylbiliverdin, a possible precursor of biliverdin. *Biochem. J.* **104**, 20.

103. Nason, A. (1962). Symposium on metabolism of inorganic compounds. II. Enzymatic pathways of nitrate, nitrite and hydroxylamine metabolism. *Bacteriol. Rev.* **26**, 16.

104. Nason, A., Abraham, R. C., and Averbach, B. C. (1954). *Biochim. Biophys. Acta* **15**, 159; as cited by Prakash *et al.* (129).

105. Newton, J. W., and Kamen, M. D. (1961). Cytochrome systems in anaerobic electron transport. *In* "The Bacteria" (I. C. Gunsalus and R. Y. Stanier, eds.), Vol. 2, p. 397. Academic Press, New York.

106. Nicholas, D. J. D., Medina, A., and Jones, O. T. G. (1960). *Biochim. Biophys. Acta* **37**, 478; as cited by Prakash *et al.* (129).

107. Nicholas, D. J. D., Redmond, W. J., and Wright, M. A. (1963). Mo and Fe requirements for nitrate reductase in *Photobacterium sepia. Nature* **200**, 1125.

108. Nicholas, D. J. D., Redmond, W. J., and Wright, M. A. (1964). Effects of cultural conditions in *Photobacterium sepia. J. Gen. Microbiol.* **35**, 401.

109. Pascal, M. C., Pichinoty, F., and Bruno, V. (1965). Sur les lactate-déhydrogènases d'une bactérie dénitrifiante. *Biochim. Biophys. Acta* **99**, 543.

110. Paul, K. G. (1951). The porphyrin component of cytochrome c and its linkage to the protein. *Acta Chem. Scand.* **5**, 389.

111. Peck, H. D., Jr. (1960). Evidence for oxidative phosphorylation during the reduction of sulfate with hydrogen by *Desulfovibrio desulfuricans. J. Biol. Chem.* **235**, 2734.

112. Peck, H. D., Jr. (1961). Enzymatic basis for assimilatory and dissimilatory sulfate reduction. *J. Bacteriol.* **82**, 933.

113. Peck, H. D., Jr. (1962). Symposium on metabolism on inorganic compounds. V. Comparative metabolism of inorganic sulfur compounds in microorganisms. *Bacteriol. Rev.* **26**, 67.
114. Peck, H. D., Jr. (1962). The role of adenosine-5′phosphosulfate in the reduction of sulfate to sulfite by *Desulfovibrio desulfuricans. J. Biol. Chem.* **237**, 198.
115. Peck, H. D., Jr. (1966). Phosphorylation coupled with electron transfer in extracts of the sulfate-reducing bacterium *Desulfovibrio gigas. Biochem. Biophys. Res. Commun.* **22**, 112.
116. Peck, H. D., Jr., and Gest, H. (1956). A new procedure for assay of bacterial hydrogenases. *J. Bacteriol.* **71**, 70.
117. Peck, H. D., Jr., Deacon, T. E., and Davidson, J. T. (1965). Studies on adenosine 5′-phosphosulfate reductase from *Desulfovibrio desulfuricans* and *Thiobacillus thioparus*. I. The assay and purification. *Biochim. Biophys. Acta* **96**, 429.
118. Pichinoty, F. (1960). Reduction assimilative du nitrate par les cultures aérobies d'*Aérobacter aérogènes*. Influence de la nutrition azotée sur la croissance. *Folia Microbiol. (Prague)* **5**, 165.
119. Pichinoty, F. (1964). A propos des nitrate-reductases d'une bactérie dénitrificante. *Biochim. Biophys. Acta* **89**, 378.
120. Pichinoty, F. (1965). L'effet oxygène de la biosynthèse des enzymes d'oxydoreduction bactériens. *In* "Mécanismes de regulation des activites cellulaires chez les microorganismes," pp. 507–520. C.N.R.S., Paris; as cited in Stouthamer (155).
121. Pichinoty, F., and d'Ornano, L. (1961). Sur le mécanisme de l'inhibition par l'oxygène de la dénitrification bactérienne. *Biochim. Biophys. Acta* **52**, 386.
122. Pine, M. S., and Barker, H. A. (1954). *Bacteriol. Proc.* p. 98.
123. Polakis, E. S., Bartley, W., and Meek, G. A. (1964). Changes in the structure and enzyme activity of *Saccharomyces cerevisiae* in response to changes in the environment. *Biochem. J.* **90**, 369.
124. Porva, R. J., and Lascelles, J. (1965). Haemoproteins and haemsynthesis in facultative photosynthetic and denitrifying bacteria. *Biochem. J.* **94**, 120.
125. Postgate, H. D. (1952). J. Res. **5**, 189; as cited by Peck (111).
126. Postgate, J. (1956). Cytochrome c₃ and desulphoviridin; pigments of the anaerobe *Desulphovibrio desulphuricans. J. Gen. Microbiol.* **14**, 545.
127. Postgate, J. (1959). Sulphate reduction by bacteria. *Ann. Rev. Microbiol.* **13**, 505.
128. Postgate, J. (1965). Recent advances in the study of the sulphate reducing bacteria. *Bacteriol. Rev.* **29**, 425.
129. Prakash, O., Rao, R. R., and Sadana, J. C. (1966). Purification and characterization of nitrite reductase from *Achromobacter fisheri. Biochim. Biophys. Acta* **118**, 426.
130. Quastel, J. H. (1965). Soil metabolism. *Ann. Rev. Plant Physiol.* **16**, 217.
131. Rose, A. H. (1965). "Chemical Microbiology," p. 108. Butterworth, London and Washington, D.C.
132. Sachs, L. E., and Barker, H. A. (1949). The influence of oxygen on nitrate and nitrite reduction. *J. Bacteriol.* **58**, 11.
133. Sadana, J. C., and McElroy, W. D. (1957). Nitrate reductase from *Achromobacter fisheri*. Purification and properties: Function of flavines and cytochromes. *Arch. Biochem. Biophys.* **67**, 16.
134. Sands, D. C., Gleason, F. H., and Hildebrand, D. C. (1967). Cytochromes of *Pseudomonas syringae. J. Bacteriol.* **94**, 1785.
135. Sano, S., and Granick, S. (1961). Mitochondrial coproporphyrinogen oxidase and protoporphyrin formation. *J. Biol. Chem.* **236**, 1173.

136. Sargeant, K., Buck, P. W., Ford, J. W. S., and Yeo, R. G. (1966). Anaerobic production of *Thiobacillus denitrificans* for the enzyme rhodanese. *Appl. Microbiol.* **14**, 998.

137. Saunders, G. F., and Campbell, L. L. (1966). Deoxyribonucleic acid base composition of *Desulfotomaculum nigrificans*. *J. Bacteriol.* **92**, 515.

138. Saunders, G. F., Campbell, L. L., and Postgate, J. R. (1964). Base composition of DNA of sulfate-reducing bacteria deduced from buoyant density measurements in cesium chloride. *J. Bacteriol.* **87**, 1073.

139. Schaeffer, P. (1952). Recherches sur la métabolisme bactérien des cytochromes et des porphyrins. I. Disparition partielle des cytochromes par culture anaérobie chez certaines bactéries aérobies facultative. *Biochim. Biophys. Acta* **9**, 261.

140. Schultz, A. S., and McManus, D. K. (1949). Amino acids and inorganic sulfur as sulfur source for the growth of yeasts. *Arch. Biochem. Biophys.* **25**, 401.

141. Segal, H. L. (1956). Sulfate-dependent exchange of pyrophosphate with nucleotide phosphate. *Biochim. Biophys. Acta* **21**, 194.

142. Senez, J. C. (1962). Some considerations of the energetics of bacterial growth. *Bacteriol. Rev.* **26**, 95.

143. Skerman, V. B. D. (1967). "A Guide to the Identification of the Genera of Bacteria," 2nd ed. Williams & Wilkins, Baltimore, Maryland.

144. Skerman, V. B. D., and MacRae, I. C. (1957). The influence of oxygen on the reduction of nitrate by adapted cells of *Pseudomonas denitrificans*. *Can. J. Microbiol.* **3**, 215.

145. Skerman, V. B. D., and MacRae, I. C. (1957). The influence of oxygen availability in the degree of nitrate reduction by *Pseudomonas denitrificans*. *Can. J. Microbiol.* **3**, 506.

146. Skerman, V. B. D., Carey, B. J., and MacRae, I. C. (1958). The influence of oxygen on the reduction of nitrite by washed suspensions of adapted cells of *Achromobacter liquefaciens*. *Can. J. Microbiol.* **4**, 243.

147. Slonimski, P. P. (1953). "La formation des enzymes respiratoires chez la levure." Masson, Paris; as cited by Jacobs *et al.* (66).

148. Smith, L. (1961). Cytochrome systems in aerobic electron transport. *In* "The Bacteria" (I. C. Gunsalus and R. Y. Stanier, eds.), Vol. 2, p. 365. Academic Press, New York.

149. Sorokin, Y. I. (1966). Role of CO_2 and acetate in biosynthesis by sulfate-reducing bacteria. *Nature* **210**, 551.

150. Spangler, W. J., and Gilmour, C. M. (1966). Biochemistry of nitrate respiration in *Pseudomonas stutzeri*. I. Aerobic and nitrate respiration routes of carbohydrate catabolism. *J. Bacteriol.* **91**, 245.

151. Spencer, D., Takahashi, H., and Nason, A. (1957). Relationship of nitrite and hydroxylamine reductases to nitrate assimilation and nitrogen fixation in *Azotobacter agile*. *J. Bacteriol.* **73**, 553.

152. Stadtman, T. C., and Barker, H. A. (1949). Studies on the methane fermentation. VII. Tracer experiments on the mechanism of methane formation. *Arch. Biochem.* **21**, 256.

153. Stadtman, T. C., and Barker, H. A. (1951). Studies on the methane fermentation. IX. The origin of methane in the acetate and methanol fermentation by *Methanosarcina*. *J. Bacteriol.* **61**, 81.

154. Starkey, L. R. (1960). Sulfate-reducing bacteria—physiology and practical significance. Lectures on theoretical and applied aspects of modern microbiology. University of Maryland, College Park, NID; as cited by Peck (113).

155. Stouthamer, A. H. (1967). Nitrate reduction in Aerobacter aerogenes. I. Isolation and properties of mutant strains blocked in nitrate assimilation and resistant against chlorate. *Arch. Mikrobiol.* **56**, 68.

156. Suh, B., and Akagi, J. M. (1966). Pyruvate-carbon dioxide exchange reaction of *Desulfovibrio desulfuricans. J. Bacteriol.* **91**, 2281.

157. Taber, H. W., and Morrison, M. (1964). Electron transport in staphylococci. Properties of a particle preparation from exponential phase *Staphylococcus aureus. Arch. Biochem. Biophys.* **105**, 367.

158. Tagawa, K., and Arnon, D. I. (1962). Ferredoxins as electron carriers in photosynthesis and in the biological production and consumption of hydrogen gas. *Nature* **195**, 537.

159. Taniguchi, S. (1961). Comparative biochemistry of nitrate metabolism. *Zt. Mikrobiol.* **1**, 341.

160. Vernon, L. P., and White, F. G. (1957). *Biochim. Biophys. Acta* **25**, 321; as cited by Dolin (35).

161. Villarejo, M., and Westley, J. (1963). Rhodanese-catalyzed reduction of thiosulphate by reduced lipoic acid. *J. Biol. Chem.* **238**, PC1185.

162. Villarejo, M., and Westley, J. (1963). Mechanism of rhodanese catalysis of thiosulphate-lipoate oxidation-reduction. *J. Biol. Chem.* **238**, 4016.

163. Volini, M., and Westley, J. (1966). The mechanism of the rhodanese-catalyzed thio-sulfate-lipoate reaction. Kinetic analysis. *J. Biol. Chem.* **241**, 5168.

164. Walker, G. C., and Nicholas, D. J. D. (1961). Hydroxylamine reductase from *Pseudomonas aeruginosa. Biochim. Biophys. Acta* **49**, 361.

165. Wallace, P. G., and Linnane, A. W. (1964). Oxygen-induced synthesis of yeast mitochondria. *Nature* **201**, 1191.

166. Westley, J., and Nakamoto, T. (1962). Mechanism of rhodanese action: Isotopic tracer studies. *J. Biol. Chem.* **237**, 547.

167. White, D. C. (1967). Effect of glucose on the formation of the membrane-bound electron transport system in *Haemophilus parainfluenzae. J. Bacteriol.* **93**, 567.

168. White, D. C., and Granick, S. (1963). Hemin biosynthesis in *Haemophilus. J. Bacteriol.* **85**, 842.

169. Whittenbury, R. (1960). Two types of catalase-like activity in lactic acid bacteria. *Nature* **187**, 433.

170. Whittenbury, R. (1964). Hydrogen peroxide formation and catalase activity in the lactic acid bacteria. *J. Gen. Microbiol.* **35**, 13.

171. Wilson, L. G., and Bandurski, R. S. (1958). Enzymatic reactions involving sulfate, sulfite, selanete and molybdate. *J. Biol. Chem.* **233**, 975.

172. Wilson, L. G., and Bandurski, R. C. (1958). Enzymatic reduction of sulfate. *J. Am. Chem. Soc.* **80**, 5576.

173. Wolin, M. J., Wolin, E. A., and Wolfe, R. S. (1963). ATP-dependent formation of methane from methylcobalamin by extracts of *Methanobacillus omelianski. Biochem. Biophys. Res. Commun.* **12**, 464.

174. Wolin, M. J., Wolin, E. A., and Wolfe, R. S. (1964). The cobalamin product of the conversion of methylcobalamin to methane by extracts of *Methanobacillus omelianskii. Biochem. Biophys. Res. Commun.* **15**, 420.

175. Wood, J. M., and Wolfe, R. S. (1965). The formation of methane from N^5-methyl-tetrahydrofolate monoglutamate by cell-free extracts of *Methanobacillus omelianskii. Biochem. Biophys. Res. Commun.* **19**, 306.

176. Wood, J. M., and Wolfe, R. S. (1966). Alkylation of an enzyme in the methane-forming system of *Methanobacillus omelianskii. Biochem. Biophys. Res. Commun.* **22**, 119.

177. Wood, J. M., and Wolfe, R. S. (1966). Components required for the formation of CH_4 from methylcobalamin by extracts of *Methanobacillus omelianski. J. Bacteriol.* **92**, 698.

178. Wood, J. M., Allan, A. M., Brill, W. J., and Wolfe, R. S. (1965). Formation of methane from serine by cell-free extracts of *Methanobacillus omelianskii*. *J. Biol. Chem.* **240**, 4564.

179. Wood, W. A. (1961). Fermentation of carbohydrates and related compounds. In "The Bacteria" (I. C. Gunsalus and R. Y. Stanier, eds.), Vol. 2, p. 59. Academic Press, New York.

180. Yamanaka, T. (1964). Identity of *Pseudomonas* cytochrome oxidase with *Pseudomonas* nitrite reductase. *Nature* **204**, 458.

181. Yamanaka, T., Ota, A., and Okumuki, K. (1961). *Biochim. Biophys. Acta* **53**, 294; as cited by Prakash *et al.* (129).

182. Yates, M. G. (1967). Stimulation of the phosphoroclastic system of *Desulfovibrio* by nucleotide triphosphate. *Biochem. J.* **103**, 32C.

SUPPLEMENTARY READINGS

Akagi, J. M., and Jackson, G. (1967). Degradation of glucose by proliferating cells of *Desulfotomaculum nigrificans*. *Appl. Microbiol.* **15**, 1427.

Amarger, N., and Alexander, M. (1968). Nitrite formation from hydroxylamine and oximes by *Pseudomonas aeruginosa*. *J. Bacteriol.* **95**, 1651.

Asano, A., Imai, K., and Sato, R. (1967). Oxidative phosphorylation in *Micrococcus denitrificans*. III. ATP-supported reduction of NAD⁺ by succinate. *J. Biochem.* (*Tokyo*) **62**, 210.

Bovell, C. (1967). The effect of sodium nitrite on the growth of *Micrococcus denitrificans*. *Arch. Mikrobiol.* **59**, 13.

Broberg, P. L., and Smith, L. (1967). The cytochrome system of *Bacillus megaterium* KM. The presence and some properties of two CO-binding cytochromes. *Biochim. Biophys. Acta* **131**, 479.

Bryant, M. P., Wolin, E. A., Wolin, M. J., and Wolfe, R. S. (1967). *Methanobacillus omelianski*, a symbiotic association of two species of bacteria. *Arch. Mikrobiol.* **59**, 20.

Clark-Walker, G. D., Rittenberg, B., and Lascelles, J. (1967). Cytochrome synthesis and its regulation in *Spirillum itersonii*. *J. Bacteriol.* **94**, 1648.

Connell, W. E., and Patrick, W. H., Jr. (1968). Sulfate reduction in soil: Effects of redox-potential and pH. *Science* **159**, 86.

Dunphy, P. J., Gutnick, D. L., Phillips, P. G., and Brodie, A. F. (1967). Naturally occurring isomers of a bacterial menaquinone. *Arch. Biochem. Biophys.* **122**, 252.

Ehteshamuddiu, A. F. M. (1968). Anaerobic formation of protoporphyrin from copro-porphyrinogen III by bacterial preparations. *Biochem. J.* **107**, 446.

Imai, K., Asano, A., and Sato, R. (1968). Oxidative phosphorylation in *Micrococcus denitrificans*. IV. Further characterization of electron-transfer pathway and phosphorylation activity in NADH oxidation. *J. Biochem.* (*Tokyo*) **63**, 207.

Imai, K., Asano, A., and Sato, R. (1968). Oxidative phosphorylation in *Micrococcus denitrificans*. V. Effects of iron deficiency on respiratory components and oxidative phosphorylation. *J. Biochem.* (*Tokyo*) **63**, 219.

Jones, C. W., and Redfearn, E. R. (1966). Electron transport in *Azotobacter vinelandii*. *Biochim. Biophys. Acta* **113**, 467.

Jurtshuk, P., and Old, L. (1968). Cytochrome c oxidation by the electron transport fraction of *Azotobacter vinelandii*. *J. Bacteriol.* **95**, 1790.

Knowles, C. J., and Redfearn, E. R. (1966). Ubiquinone in the electron transport system of *Azotobacter vinelandii*. *Biochem. J.* **99**, 33P.

Radcliffe, B. C., and Nicholas, D. J. D. (1968). Some properties of a nitrate reductase from *Pseudomonas denitrificans. Biochim. Biophys. Acta* **153**, 545.

Sabater, F. (1966). Phosphorylation coupled with nitrite and nitrate reductase in *Micrococcus denitrificans. Rev. Espan. Fisiol.* **22**, 1; *Chem. Abstr.* **65**, 10827 (1966).

SanMartin de Viale, L. C., and Grinstein, M. (1968). Porphyrin biosynthesis. IV. 5- and 6-COOH porphyrinogens (type III) as normal intermediates in haem biosynthesis. *Biochim. Biophys. Acta* **158**, 79.

Scholes, P. B., and Smith, L. (1968). Composition and properties of the membrane-bound respiratory chain system of *Micrococcus denitrificans. Biochim. Biophys. Acta* **153**, 363.

Showe, M. K., and DeMoss, J. A. (1968). Localization and regulation of synthesis of nitrate reductase in *Escherichia coli. J. Bacteriol.* **95**, 1305.

Stouthamer, A. H., Bettenhansen, C., and van Hartingsveldt, J. (1967). Nitrate reduction in *Aerobacter aerogenes.* III. Nitrate reduction, chlorate resistance and formate metabolism in mutant strains. *Arch. Mikrobiol.* **58**, 228.

Subramanian, K. N., Padmarsaban, G., and Sarma, P. S. (1968). Control of nitrate reductase by iron in *Neurospora crassa. Arch. Biochem. Biophys.* **124**, 535.

Tagawa, K., and Arnon, D. I. (1968). Oxidation-reduction potentials and stoichiometry of electron transfer in ferredoxins. *Biochim. Biophys. Acta.* **153**, 602.

van Droogenbroeck, R., and Laudelout, H. (1967). Phosphate requirements of the nitrifying bacteria. *Ant. v. Leeuwenhoek J. Microbiol. and Ser.* **33**, 287.

Villarejo, M., and Westley, J. (1966). Sulfur metabolism of *Bacillus subtilis. Biochim. Biophys. Acta* **117**, 209.

Yoshimoto, A., and Sato, R. (1968). Studies on yeast sulfite reductase. I. Purification and characterization. *Biochim. Biophys. Acta* **153**, 555.

4

CHEMOSYNTHESIS—PATHWAYS OF CARBOHYDRATE BREAKDOWN

CARBOHYDRATE METABOLISM

Pyruvate has been established as the key intermediate substance in the metabolism of carbohydrates by bacteria. Almost all 6-carbon compounds are converted initially to pyruvate from which substance further catabolic or synthetic reactions proceed. Before discussing the ways in which carbohydrates are metabolized the origin of pyruvate will be considered.

The main carbohydrate compound which serves as carbon source for bacteria is glucose. Glucose is converted to pyruvate via four different pathways which have been named after those researchers who discovered and established them or according to their main components:

(1) Embden-Meyerhof-Parnas (EMP) pathway
(2) Warburg-Dickens or hexose monophosphate (HMP) pathway
(3) Entner-Doudoroff (ED) pathway
(4) Phosphoketolase pathway

The first two pathways are also functional in mammalian tissue and in yeasts. There are, however, significant differences between the terminology used by biochemists and microbiologists. The EMP pathway is very often referred to as "glycolysis" or the "glycolytic" pathway. As recognized by mammalian biochemists the term "glycolysis" refers to the pathway by which glycogen or glucose is converted anaerobically via pyruvate to lactate. Only in the homo-fermentative lactobacilli is the complete cycle, including the conversion of pyruvate to lactate found. In several other lactobacilli the pathway to pyruvate is followed, but the subsequent metabolism of pyruvate varies from one group to another. The term "glycolysis" would best be restricted to its mammalian biochemical usage.

Another term which needs clarification is the word "fermentation." Anaerobiosis is often considered as synonymous with fermentation and all the different anaerobic pathways as "fermentative pathways"(1).

The term "ferment" has an ancient history and with progress and biochemical knowledge it has assumed various meanings. As defined in this book (see Chapter 6) "fermentative" is restricted to those pathways in which the terminal electron acceptor is an organic compound. Where the terminal acceptor is oxygen or an inorganic compound the pathway is regarded as oxidative and

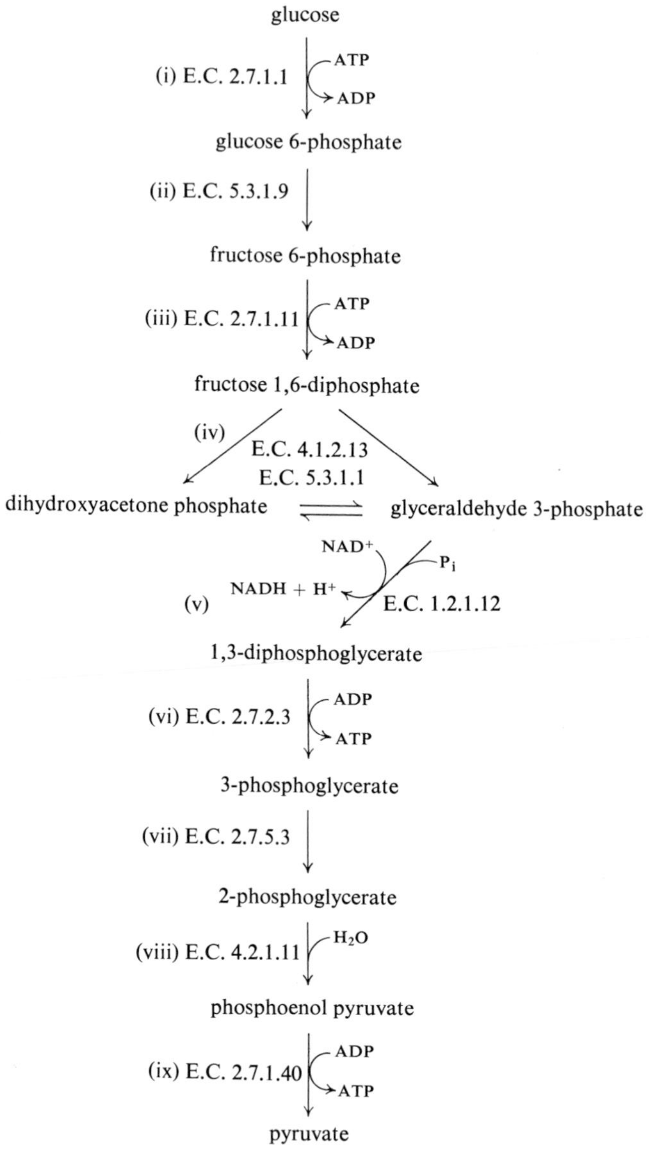

glucose

(i) E.C. 2.7.1.1   ATP → ADP

glucose 6-phosphate

(ii) E.C. 5.3.1.9

fructose 6-phosphate

(iii) E.C. 2.7.1.11   ATP → ADP

fructose 1,6-diphosphate

(iv)   E.C. 4.1.2.13   E.C. 5.3.1.1

dihydroxyacetone phosphate ⇌ glyceraldehyde 3-phosphate

NAD^+ P_i

(v) $NADH + H^+$ E.C. 1.2.1.12

1,3-diphosphoglycerate

(vi) E.C. 2.7.2.3   ADP → ATP

3-phosphoglycerate

(vii) E.C. 2.7.5.3

2-phosphoglycerate

(viii) E.C. 4.2.1.11 H_2O

phosphoenol pyruvate

(ix) E.C. 2.7.1.40   ADP → ATP

pyruvate

the process one of respiration. The latter is either aerobic (using oxygen) or anaerobic (using inorganic compounds other than oxygen).

Disregarding for the moment whether the various pathways are functional under aerobic or anaerobic conditions, each will be traced to the level of the production of pyruvate, which is an intermediate common to them all (40).

GLUCOSE METABOLISM

Embden-Meyerhof-Parnas Pathway

Glucose metabolism, via the EMP pathway, is as outlined on page 130.

The EMP pathway to pyruvate is widely distributed among bacteria (*Enterobacteriaceae*, *Lactobacillaceae*, and *saccharoylytic clostridia*) and shows the over all reaction

$$\text{glucose} + 2\,\text{ATP} + 2\,\text{NAD}^+ \rightleftharpoons 2\,\text{pyruvate} + 4\,\text{ATP} + 2(\text{NADH} + \text{H}^+)$$

The first step (i) in the glucose breakdown is a phosphorylation step, which requires one mole of ATP and the enzyme hexokinase (ATP:D-hexose 6-phosphotransferase, E.C. 2.7.1.1).

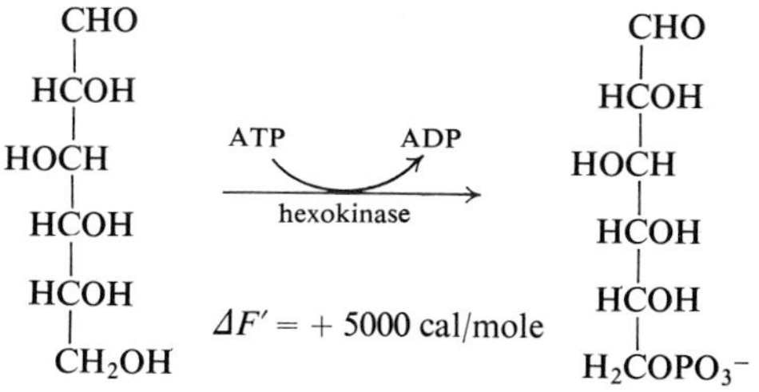

glucose $\xrightarrow[\text{hexokinase}]{\text{ATP} \quad \text{ADP}}$ glucose 6-phosphate

$\Delta F' = +5000$ cal/mole

D-Mannose, D-fructose, and D-glucosamine can replace D-glucose. Inosine triphosphate (ITP) and deoxy-ATP could replace ATP as phosphate donors.

The isomerization (ii) of glucose 6-phosphate is catalyzed by the enzyme glucose phosphate isomerase (D-glucose-6-phosphate ketol isomerase, E.C. 5.3.1.9).

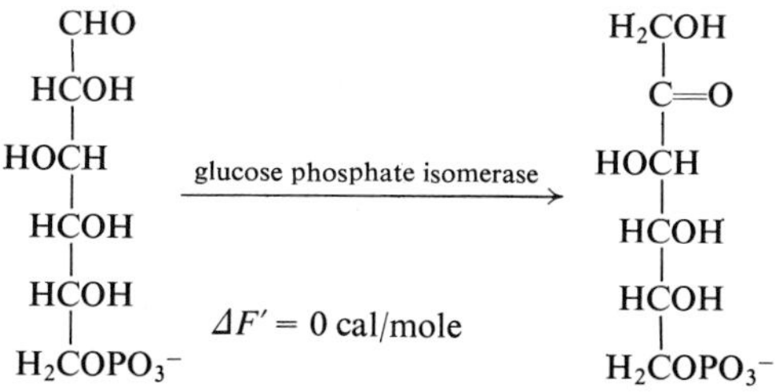

glucose 6-phosphate $\xrightarrow[\Delta F' = 0 \text{ cal/mole}]{\text{glucose phosphate isomerase}}$ fructose 6-phosphate

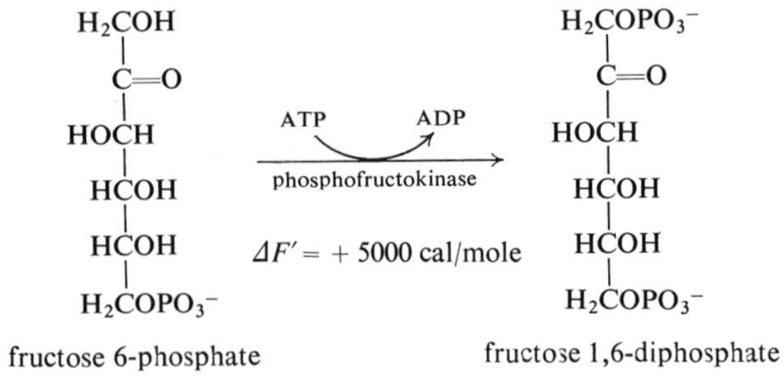

$$
\begin{array}{ccc}
\begin{array}{c}
H_2COH \\
| \\
C{=}O \\
| \\
HOCH \\
| \\
HCOH \\
| \\
HCOH \\
| \\
H_2COPO_3^-
\end{array}
&
\xrightarrow[\text{phosphofructokinase}]{\text{ATP} \quad \text{ADP}}
&
\begin{array}{c}
H_2COPO_3^- \\
| \\
C{=}O \\
| \\
HOCH \\
| \\
HCOH \\
| \\
HCOH \\
| \\
H_2COPO_3^-
\end{array}
\end{array}
$$

$$\Delta F' = +5000 \text{ cal/mole}$$

fructose 6-phosphate   fructose 1,6-diphosphate

The second phosphorylation step (iii) requires a second molecule of ATP and is catalyzed by probably the most important enzyme in the pathway, phosphofructokinase (ATP:D-fructose 6-phosphate 1-phosphotransferase, E.C. 2.7.1.11). The second key enzyme of the EMP pathway is fructose diphosphate aldolase (fructose 1,6-diphosphate:D-glyceraldehyde 3-phosphate-lyase, E.C. 4.1.2.13) which forms two molecules of triose phosphates (iv).

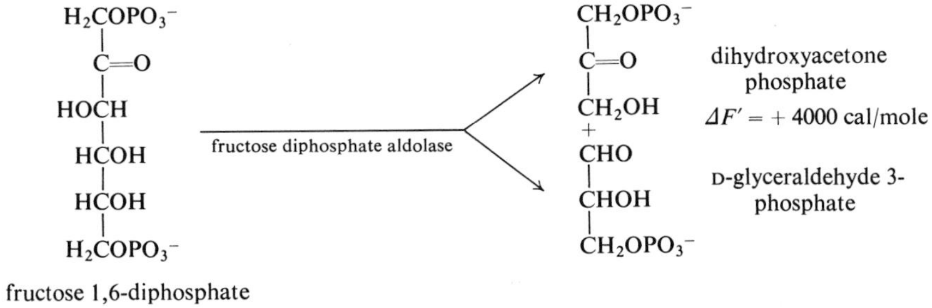

$$
\begin{array}{c}
H_2COPO_3^- \\
| \\
C{=}O \\
| \\
HOCH \\
| \\
HCOH \\
| \\
HCOH \\
| \\
H_2COPO_3^-
\end{array}
\xrightarrow{\text{fructose diphosphate aldolase}}
\begin{array}{c}
CH_2OPO_3^- \\
| \\
C{=}O \\
| \\
CH_2OH \\
+ \\
CHO \\
| \\
CHOH \\
| \\
CH_2OPO_3^-
\end{array}
$$

dihydroxyacetone phosphate

$$\Delta F' = +4000 \text{ cal/mole}$$

D-glyceraldehyde 3-phosphate

fructose 1,6-diphosphate

A triose phosphate isomerase (D-glyceraldehyde 3-phosphate ketol isomerase, E.C. 5.3.1.1) ensures that neither of the two products accumulate.

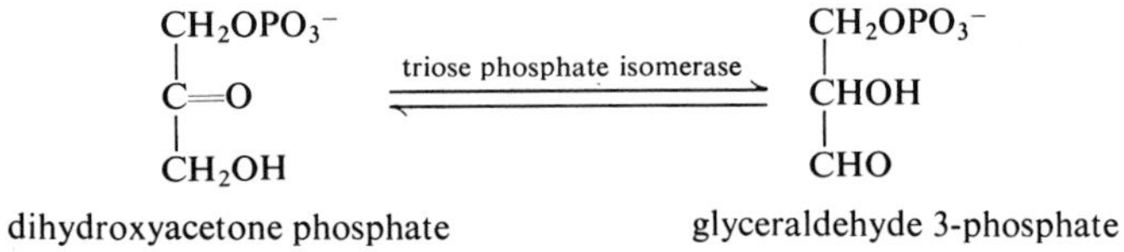

$$
\begin{array}{c}
CH_2OPO_3^- \\
| \\
C{=}O \\
| \\
CH_2OH
\end{array}
\xrightleftharpoons{\text{triose phosphate isomerase}}
\begin{array}{c}
CH_2OPO_3^- \\
| \\
CHOH \\
| \\
CHO
\end{array}
$$

dihydroxyacetone phosphate   glyceraldehyde 3-phosphate

The equilibrium lies toward the right (glyceraldehyde 3-phosphate) as long as the EMP pathway functions in the proper way.

The next step (v) is a combined oxidation and phosphorylation step, which is catalyzed by the enzyme glyceraldehyde phosphate dehydrogenase (D-glyceraldehyde 3-phosphate:NAD oxidoreductase (phosphorylating), E.C. 1.2.1.12). This complex reaction can be separated into two steps(47). The

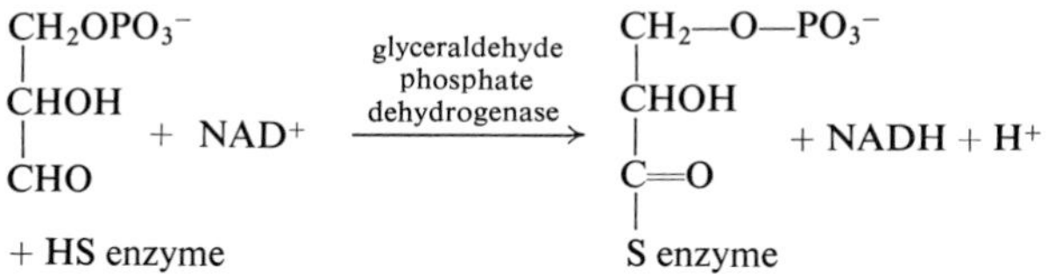

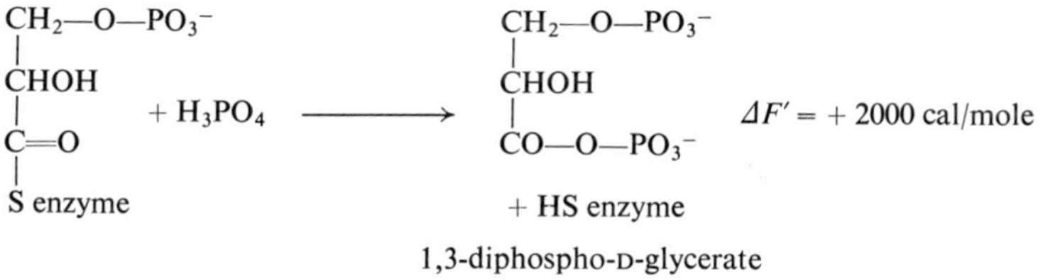

$$\begin{array}{l}
CH_2OPO_3^- \\
| \\
CHOH \\
| \\
CHO \\
\end{array} + NAD^+ \quad \xrightarrow{\substack{\text{glyceraldehyde} \\ \text{phosphate} \\ \text{dehydrogenase}}} \quad \begin{array}{l}
CH_2{-}O{-}PO_3^- \\
| \\
CHOH \\
| \\
C{=}O \\
\end{array} + NADH + H^+$$

$+ \text{ HS enzyme}$
S enzyme

$$\begin{array}{l}
CH_2{-}O{-}PO_3^- \\
| \\
CHOH \\
| \\
C{=}O \\
\end{array} + H_3PO_4 \quad \longrightarrow \quad \begin{array}{l}
CH_2{-}O{-}PO_3^- \\
| \\
CHOH \\
| \\
CO{-}O{-}PO_3^- \\
\end{array} \quad \Delta F' = +2000 \text{ cal/mole}$$

S enzyme
$+ \text{ HS enzyme}$

1,3-diphospho-D-glycerate

high-energy compound 1,3-diphospho-D-glycerate now releases one phosphate group to form one mole of ATP (vi) under the catalytic action of phospho-glycerate kinase (ATP:3-phospho-D-glycerate-1-phosphotransferase, E.C.

$$\begin{array}{l}
CH_2{-}O{-}PO_3^- \\
| \\
CHOH \\
| \\
CO{-}O{-}PO_3^- \\
\end{array} + ADP \quad \xrightarrow{\substack{\text{phosphoglycerate} \\ \text{kinase}}} \quad \begin{array}{l}
CH_2{-}O{-}PO_3^- \\
| \\
CHOH \\
| \\
COO^- \\
\end{array} + ATP \quad \Delta F' = -27,000 \text{ cal/mole}$$

1,3-diphospho-D-glycerate   3-phosphoglycerate

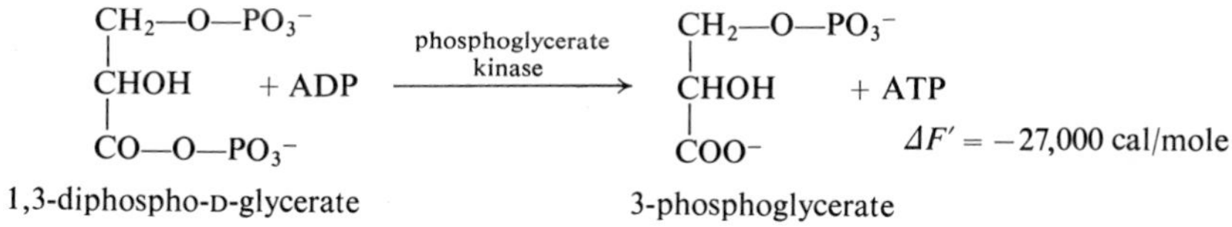

2.7.2.3). The conversion of 3-phosphoglycerate to 2-phosphoglycerate (vii) results from the interaction of 2,3-diphosphoglycerate and the enzyme phosphoglucomutase (2,3-diphospho-D-glycerate phosphotransferase, E.C. 2.7.5.3). The phosphate group is transferred to the 2 position in the molecule.

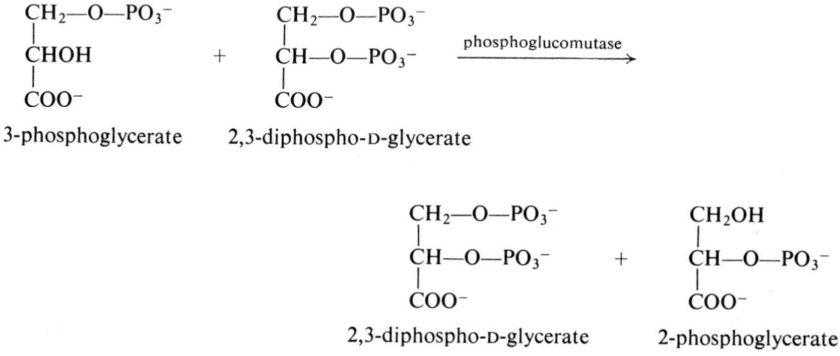

$$\begin{array}{l}
CH_2{-}O{-}PO_3^- \\
| \\
CHOH \\
| \\
COO^- \\
\end{array} + \begin{array}{l}
CH_2{-}O{-}PO_3^- \\
| \\
CH{-}O{-}PO_3^- \\
| \\
COO^- \\
\end{array} \quad \xrightarrow{\text{phosphoglucomutase}}$$

3-phosphoglycerate   2,3-diphospho-D-glycerate

$$\begin{array}{l}
CH_2{-}O{-}PO_3^- \\
| \\
CH{-}O{-}PO_3^- \\
| \\
COO^- \\
\end{array} + \begin{array}{l}
CH_2OH \\
| \\
CH{-}O{-}PO_3^- \\
| \\
COO^- \\
\end{array}$$

2,3-diphospho-D-glycerate   2-phosphoglycerate

Since 2,3-diphospho-D-glycerate is regenerated during this reaction, it is used in a cycling process by this particular reaction. The formation of phosphoenol pyruvate (viii) is obtained by the action of a hydratase (2-phospho-D-glycerate hydrolyase, E.C. 4.2.1.11), which is very often referred to as enolase.

$$
\begin{array}{c}
\text{CH}_2\text{OH} \\
| \\
\text{CH—O—PO}_3^- \\
| \\
\text{COO}^-
\end{array}
\qquad
\xrightarrow[\text{hydratase}]{\text{P-enolpyruvate}}
\qquad
\begin{array}{c}
\text{CH}_2 \\
\| \\
\text{C—O—PO}_3^- \\
| \\
\text{COO}^-
\end{array}
+ \text{H}_2\text{O}
$$

$$\Delta F' = 0 \text{ cal/mole}$$

2-phosphoglycerate   phosphoenol pyruvate

The final action (ix) of pyruvate kinase (ATP:pyruvate phosphotransferase E.C. 2.7.1.40) completes the pathway with the formation of pyruvate and an additional molecule ATP. The EMP pathway thus produces two molecules

$$
\begin{array}{c}
\text{CH}_2 \\
\| \\
\text{C—O—PO}_3^- \\
| \\
\text{COO}^-
\end{array}
+ \text{ADP}
\qquad
\xrightarrow{\text{pyruvate kinase}}
\qquad
\begin{array}{c}
\text{CH}_3 \\
| \\
\text{CO} \\
| \\
\text{COO}^-
\end{array}
+ \text{ATP}
$$

$$\Delta F' = -27,000 \text{ cal/mole}$$

phosphoenol pyruvate   pyruvate

of ATP and two molecules of $NADH + H^+$, which are used for biosynthesis and as hydrogen donor, respectively, in the further breakdown of pyruvate. The two molecules of $NADH + H^+$ are formed during the production of two moles of pyruvate from one mole of glucose at the 1,3-diphosphoglycerate level. This metabolic breakdown of glucose to pyruvate can be used by most of the anaerobic microorganisms such as yeast and fermentative bacteria since no oxygen is necessary. We know, however, that it is not restricted to these particular groups (9, 137, 148).

Hexose Monophosphate or Warburg-Dickens Pathway. The hexose monophosphate pathway of glucose metabolism carries a number of names, i.e. "shunt" and "pentose cycle." It comprises a rather complicated series of reactions which can be carried out by many organisms that metabolize glucose via the EMP or ED pathway (26, 30, 70, 124, 137). The process of conversion of glucose to glucose 6-phosphate is identical to that of the EMP pathway (i). From here, however, the HMP pathway departs from the EMP pathway. A NADP-linked glucose 6-phosphate dehydrogenase (D-glucose 6-phosphate: NADP oxidoreductase, E.C. 1.1.1.49) catalyzes the production of D-glucono-δ-lactone 6-phosphate (ii). The product of this reaction is hydrolyzed (iii)

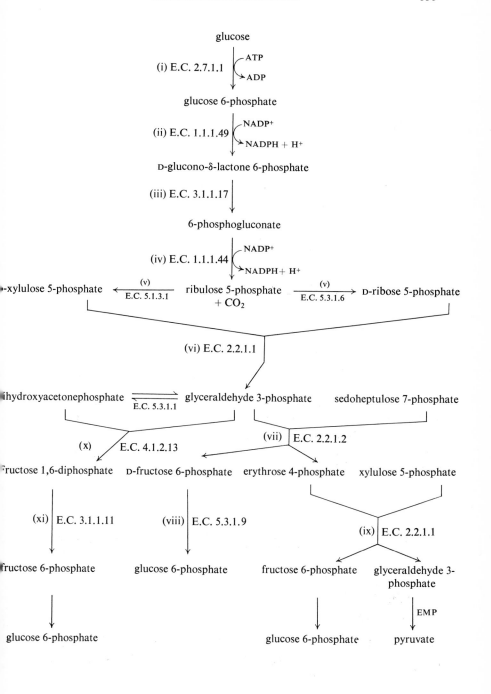

$$
\begin{array}{c}
\text{H} \quad \text{OH} \\
\diagdown \diagup \\
\text{C} \\
| \\
\text{HCOH} \\
| \\
\text{HOCH} \quad \text{O} \\
| \\
\text{HCOH} \\
| \\
\text{HC} \\
| \\
\text{CH}_2\text{—O—H}_2\text{PO}_3
\end{array}
\quad + \text{ NADP}^+ \quad \xrightarrow[\substack{\text{glucose 6-}\\\text{phosphate}\\\text{dehydrogenase}}]{} \quad
\begin{array}{c}
\text{O} \\
\| \\
\text{C} \\
| \\
\text{HCOH} \\
| \\
\text{HOCH} \quad \text{O} \\
| \\
\text{HCOH} \\
| \\
\text{HC} \\
| \\
\text{CH}_2\text{—O—H}_2\text{PO}_3
\end{array}
\quad + \text{ NADPH} + \text{H}^+
$$

glucose 6-phosphate   D-glucose-δ-lactone 6-phosphate

almost immediately to 6-phosphogluconate by gluconolactonase (D-glucono-δ-lactone hydrolase, E.C. 3.1.1.17).

$$
\begin{array}{c}
\text{O} \\
\| \\
\text{C} \\
| \\
\text{HCOH} \\
| \\
\text{HOCH} \quad \text{O} \\
| \\
\text{HCOH} \\
| \\
\text{HC} \\
| \\
\text{CH}_2\text{—O—H}_2\text{PO}_3
\end{array}
\quad + \text{ H}_2\text{O} \quad \xrightarrow{\text{gluconolactonase}} \quad
\begin{array}{c}
\text{COOH} \\
| \\
\text{HCOH} \\
| \\
\text{HOCH} \\
| \\
\text{HCOH} \\
| \\
\text{HCOH} \\
| \\
\text{CH}_2\text{—O—H}_2\text{PO}_3
\end{array}
$$

D-glucono-δ-lactose 6-phosphate   6-phosphogluconate

A second NADP-linked oxidation (iv) leads to D-ribulose 5-phosphate. The reaction is catalyzed by phosphogluconate dehydrogenase (6-phospho-D-gluconate:NADP oxidoreductase (decarboxylating), E.C. 1.1.1.44) which is responsible for a concomitant decarboxylation. D-Ribulose 5-phosphate is then converted (v) partly to D-xylulose 5-phosphate by the action of ribulose

$$
\begin{array}{c}
\text{COOH} \\
| \\
\text{HCOH} \\
| \\
\text{HOCH} \\
| \\
\text{HCOH} \\
| \\
\text{HCOH} \\
| \\
\text{CH}_2\text{—O—H}_2\text{PO}_3
\end{array}
\quad \xrightarrow[\substack{\text{phosphogluconate}\\\text{dehydrogenase}}]{+ \text{ NADP}^+} \quad
\begin{array}{c}
\text{CH}_2\text{OH} \\
| \\
\text{C}{=}\text{O} \\
| \\
\text{HCOH} \\
| \\
\text{HCOH} \\
| \\
\text{CH}_2\text{—OH}_2\text{PO}_3
\end{array}
\quad
\begin{array}{c}
+ \text{ NADPH} + \text{H}^+ \\
+ \text{ CO}_2
\end{array}
$$

6-phosphogluconate   ribulose 5-phosphate

phosphate 3-epimerase (D-ribulose 5-phosphate 3-epimerase, E.C. 5.1.3.1) and partly to D-ribose 5-phosphate by the action of ribose phosphate isomerase (D-ribose 5-phosphate ketol isomerase, E.C. 5.3.1.6).

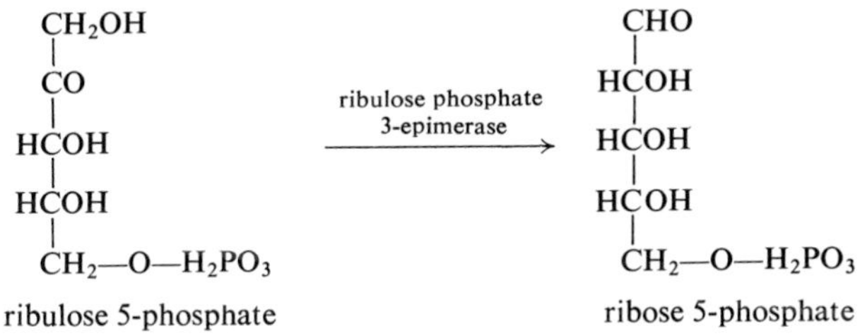

$$
\begin{array}{ccc}
\begin{array}{l}
CH_2OH \\
| \\
CO \\
| \\
HCOH \\
| \\
HCOH \\
| \\
CH_2-O-H_2PO_3
\end{array}
&
\xrightarrow[\text{3-epimerase}]{\text{ribulose phosphate}}
&
\begin{array}{l}
CHO \\
| \\
HCOH \\
| \\
HCOH \\
| \\
HCOH \\
| \\
CH_2-O-H_2PO_3
\end{array}
\\
\text{ribulose 5-phosphate} & & \text{ribose 5-phosphate}
\end{array}
$$

D-Xylulose 5-phosphate and D-ribose 5-phosphate are then condensed and the product cleaved by transketolase (sedoheptulose 7-phosphate: D-glyceraldehyde 3-phosphate glycolaldehyde transferase, E.C. 2.2.1.1) (vi) yielding glyceraldehyde 3-phosphate and sedoheptulose 7-phosphate. Both products from this transketolase reaction immediately react to form D-fructose 6-phosphate and D-erythrose 4-phosphate (vii). The reaction is catalyzed by

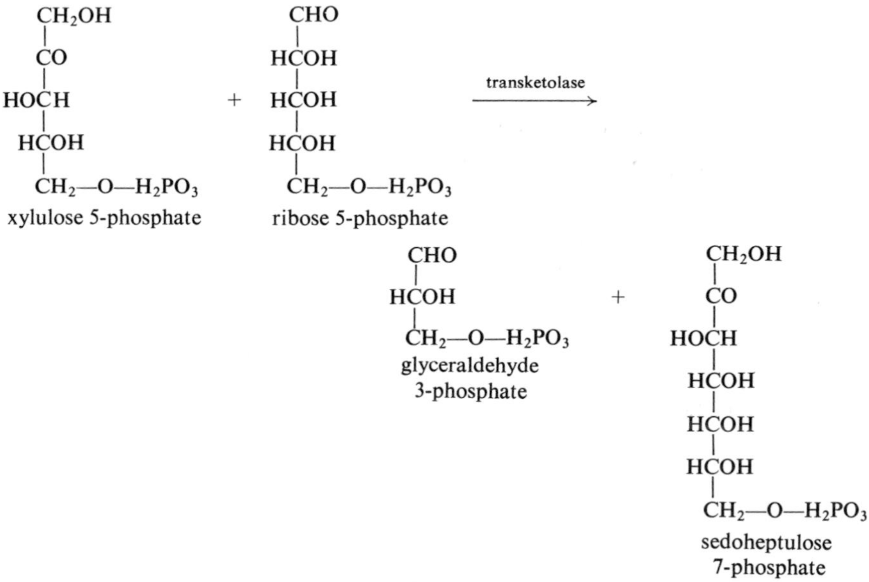

$$
\begin{array}{l}
CH_2OH \\
| \\
CO \\
| \\
HOCH \\
| \\
HCOH \\
| \\
CH_2-O-H_2PO_3
\end{array}
\quad + \quad
\begin{array}{l}
CHO \\
| \\
HCOH \\
| \\
HCOH \\
| \\
HCOH \\
| \\
CH_2-O-H_2PO_3
\end{array}
\quad \xrightarrow{\text{transketolase}}
$$

xylulose 5-phosphate   ribose 5-phosphate

$$
\begin{array}{l}
CHO \\
| \\
HCOH \\
| \\
CH_2-O-H_2PO_3
\end{array}
\quad + \quad
\begin{array}{l}
CH_2OH \\
| \\
CO \\
| \\
HOCH \\
| \\
HCOH \\
| \\
HCOH \\
| \\
HCOH \\
| \\
CH_2-O-H_2PO_3
\end{array}
$$

glyceraldehyde   sedoheptulose
3-phosphate   7-phosphate

transaldolase (sedoheptulose 7-phosphate: D-glyceraldehyde 3-phosphate dihydroxyacetonetransferase, E.C. 2.2.1.2). Whereas (viii) D-fructose 6-phosphate forms D-glucose 6-phosphate with a glucose phosphate isomerase (D-glucose 6-phosphate ketol isomerase, E.C. 5.3.1.9), D-erythrose 4-phosphate undergoes with D-xylulose 5-phosphate a second transketolase (E.C. 2.2.1.1) reaction (ix) with the production of fructose 6-phosphate and glyceraldehyde

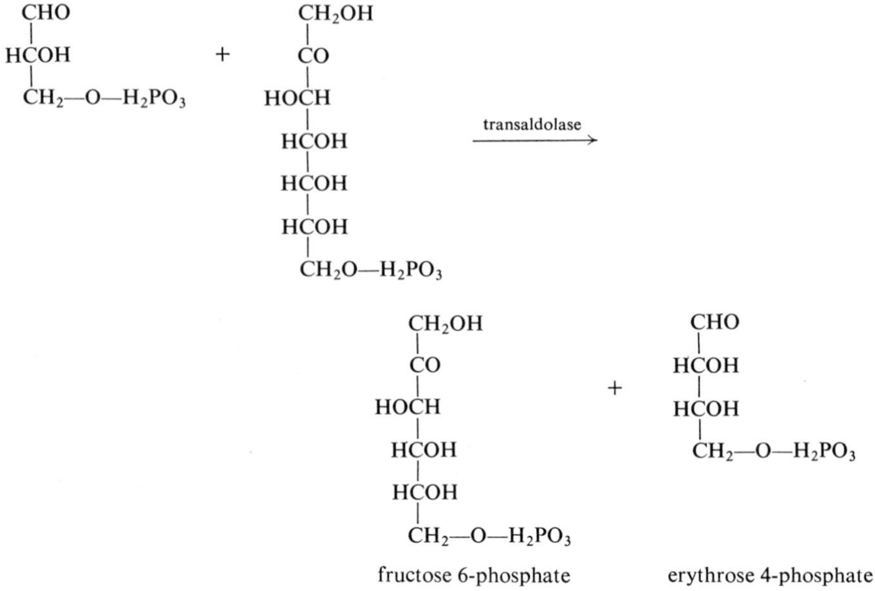

CHO
|
HCOH   +
|
CH₂—O—H₂PO₃

CH₂OH
|
CO
|
HOCH
| transaldolase
HCOH   ────────────→
|
HCOH
|
HCOH
|
CH₂O—H₂PO₃

CH₂OH
|
CO
|
HOCH
| +
HCOH
|
HCOH
|
CH₂—O—H₂PO₃
fructose 6-phosphate

CHO
|
HCOH
|
HCOH
|
CH₂—O—H₂PO₃
erythrose 4-phosphate

3-phosphate thus providing a link between the HMP pathway and the EMP pathway at the glyceraldehyde 3-phosphate level.

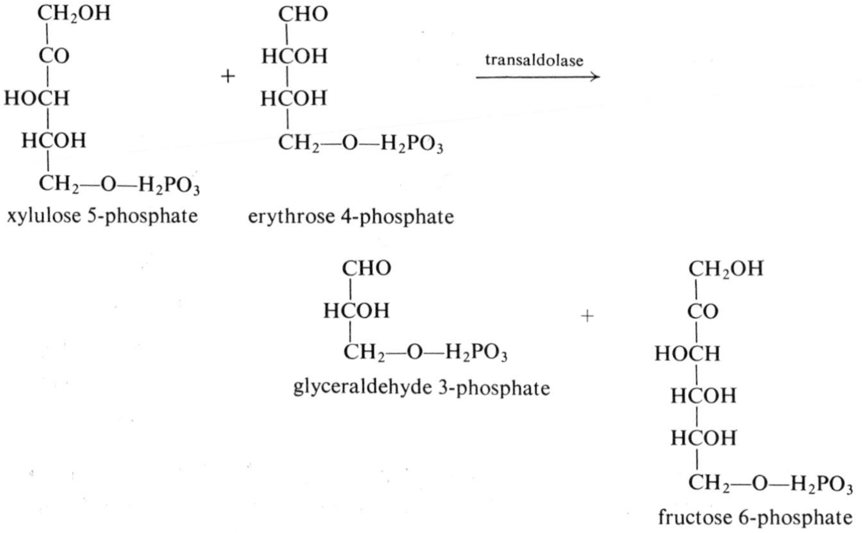

CH₂OH
|
CO
|
HOCH
|
HCOH
|
CH₂—O—H₂PO₃
xylulose 5-phosphate

+

CHO
|
HCOH
| transaldolase
HCOH   ────────────→
|
CH₂—O—H₂PO₃
erythrose 4-phosphate

CHO
|
HCOH
|
CH₂—O—H₂PO₃
glyceraldehyde 3-phosphate

+

CH₂OH
|
CO
|
HOCH
|
HCOH
|
HCOH
|
CH₂—O—H₂PO₃
fructose 6-phosphate

The cycle can be partly complete, since D-fructose 6-phosphate can again be converted to D-glucose 6-phosphate as mentioned earlier, or fully complete, as D-glyceraldehyde 3-phosphate can follow the reverse EMP-like pathway and

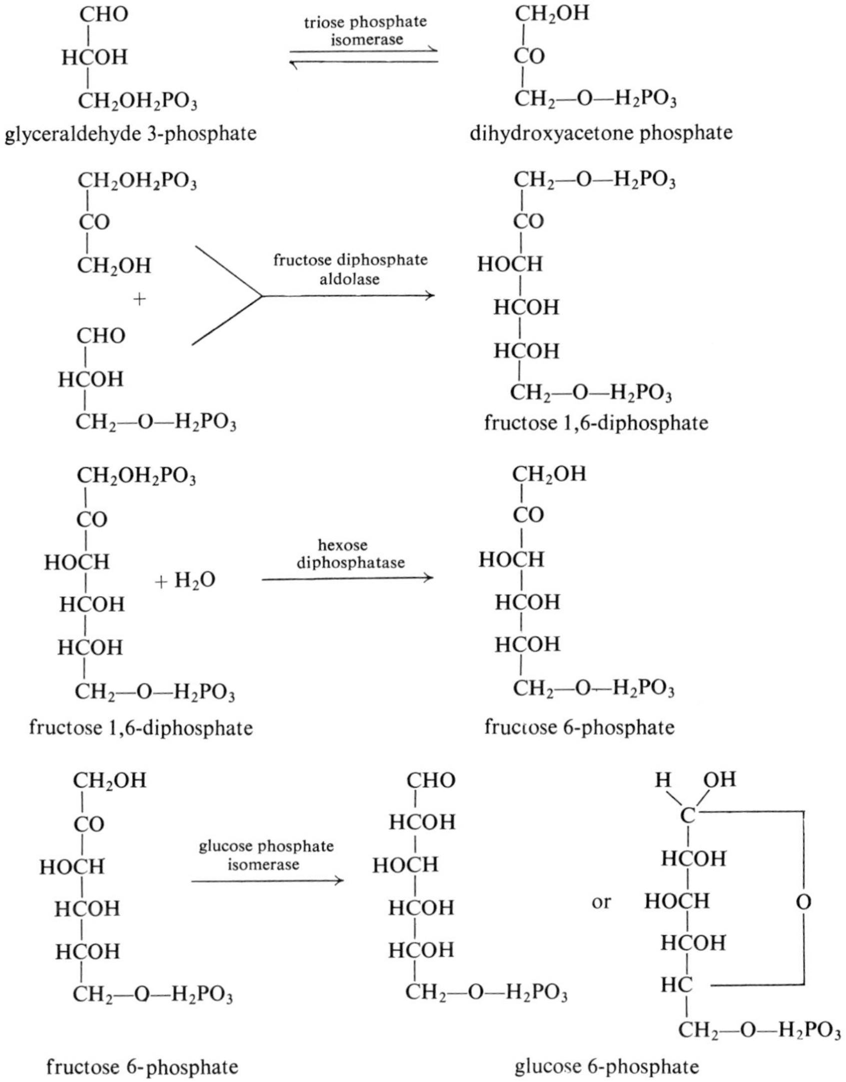

CHO
|
HCOH   —— triose phosphate isomerase ⇌ ——
|
$CH_2OH_2PO_3$
glyceraldehyde 3-phosphate

CH_2OH
|
CO
|
CH_2—O—H_2PO_3
dihydroxyacetone phosphate

$CH_2OH_2PO_3$
|
CO
|
CH_2OH
+
CHO
|
HCOH
|
CH_2—O—H_2PO_3

—— fructose diphosphate aldolase ——→

CH_2—O—H_2PO_3
|
CO
|
HOCH
|
HCOH
|
HCOH
|
CH_2—O—H_2PO_3
fructose 1,6-diphosphate

$CH_2OH_2PO_3$
|
CO
|
HOCH   + H_2O
|
HCOH
|
HCOH
|
CH_2—O—H_2PO_3
fructose 1,6-diphosphate

—— hexose diphosphatase ——→

CH_2OH
|
CO
|
HOCH
|
HCOH
|
HCOH
|
CH_2—O—H_2PO_3
fructose 6-phosphate

CH_2OH
|
CO
|
HOCH
|
HCOH
|
HCOH
|
CH_2—O—H_2PO_3
fructose 6-phosphate

—— glucose phosphate isomerase ——→

CHO
|
HCOH
|
HOCH
|
HCOH
|
HCOH
|
CH_2—O—H_2PO_3
glucose 6-phosphate

or

H   OH
 \ /
  C
  |
  HCOH
  |
  HOCH   O
  |
  HCOH
  |
  HC ————
  |
  CH_2—O—H_2PO_3

also form D-glucose 6-phosphate. The latter pathway represents what is called the "pentose cycle" or "shunt". Oxidative microorganisms, however, use the partly complete cycle in order to produce pyruvate. Returning to the glyceraldehyde 3-phosphate resulting from step (iv)—provided the enzyme triose phosphate isomerase (E.C. 5.3.1.1) is present—an equilibrium will be established between the glyceraldehyde 3-phosphate and dihydroxyacetone phosphate. This could lead to the condensation of the two, catalyzed by fructose 1,6-diphosphate aldolase (E.C. 4.1.2.13) to form fructose 1,6-diphosphate from which D-fructose 6-phosphate may be formed by dephosphorylation by the enzyme hexose diphosphatase (D-fructose 1,6-diphosphate 1-phosphohydrolase, E.C. 3.1.3.11)(60,62). The "end product" glucose 6-phosphate is obtained by the action of glucose phosphate isomerase (E.C. 5.3.1.9) as mentioned earlier.

The sum of reactions for the complete HMP cycle would then be

$$\text{glucose} + 12\,\text{NADP}^+ + 7\,\text{H}_2\text{O} \rightleftharpoons 6\,\text{CO}_2 + 12\,(\text{NADPH} + \text{H}^+) + \text{H}_3\text{PO}_4$$

and for the noncomplete HMP cycle

$$3\ \text{glucose} + 6\ \text{NADP}^+ \rightleftharpoons$$
$$2\ \text{fructose 6-phosphate} + \text{glyceraldehyde 3-phosphate} + 3\,\text{CO}_2 + 6\,(\text{NADPH} + \text{H}^+)$$

The HMP pathway does not require ATP and produces only one mole of ATP in the formation of pyruvate. However, reduced pyridine nucleotides are formed. At least one of these reduced pyridine nucleotides could also function as H donor for reduction of an organic compound. The pathway has therefore not necessarily to be dependent on oxygen in order to function. Apart from forming pyridine nucleotides, the HMP pathway provides a means of forming pentoses which are necessary for the biosynthesis of nucleic acids and the prosthetic groups of many enzymes. Erythrose 4-phosphate is also used as a precursor for certain aromatic amino acids, e.g, tyrosine and phenylalanine, in combination with phosphoenol pyruvate. The functioning of this cycle is also of great importance to photosynthetic and chemosynthetic autotrophs since all their cellular carbon is derived by condensing CO_2 with ribulose 1,5-diphosphate which is derived from ribulose 5-phosphate.

Although the pathway does not necessarily depend on oxygen, it has in comparison with the EMP pathway the great advantage of being able to produce all precursors for pyridine and pyrimidine requirements, which the EMP pathway is not able to do, and has no oxygen-sensitive enzyme. Microorganisms such as homofermentative lactobacilli (see Chapter 8) which grow only on complex media, must therefore only be able to use the EMP pathway.

A slight variation of the HMP pathway has been found to occur in *Pseudomonas methanica*. As will be mentioned under aerobic respiration, *Pseudomonas methanica* oxidizes methane stepwise via methanol, formaldehyde, and formate to CO_2 (see Chapter 5). It was thought that methane and methanol were rapidly assimilated by growing cell suspensions into sugar phosphates whereas CO_2 was incorporated mainly into C_4-dicarboxylic acids(95). Tracer element work, however, revealed that it is the formaldehyde which is incorporated into phosphorylated compounds, whereas formate is assimilated into serine and malate(100).

It appears that high fixation occurs between the oxidation levels of methane and formaldehyde and low fixation between formate and CO_2. This means that formaldehyde must be the oxidation level at which most of the carbon is assimilated into cell constituents. With the observation that all the pentose phosphate cycle intermediates occur in *Ps. methanica* and the identification of a new hexose phosphate, namely, allulose 6-phosphate(99), the mechanism for

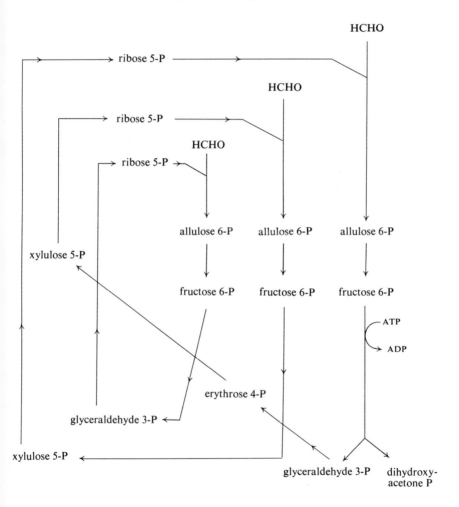

formaldehyde incorporation has been suggested, whereby the first reaction involves a hydroxymethylation of ribose 5-phosphate and formaldehyde to allulose 6-phosphate.

With this mechanism functioning, *Pseudomonas methanica* is able to produce most of the intermediates required for cell material synthesis.

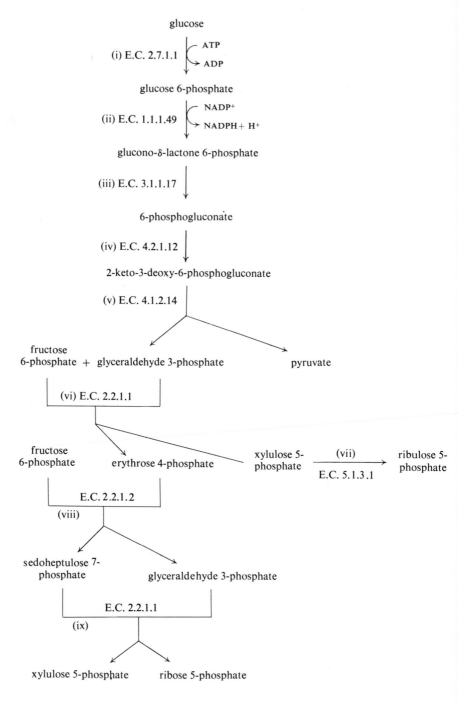

Entner-Doudoroff Pathway. This pathway is one of the most recently described pathways discovered by Entner and Doudoroff during metabolic studies of *Pseudomonas saccharophila.* It has since been found in a number of other bacteria (30, 38, 73, 102, 103, 164, 176). The marked differences of this pathway

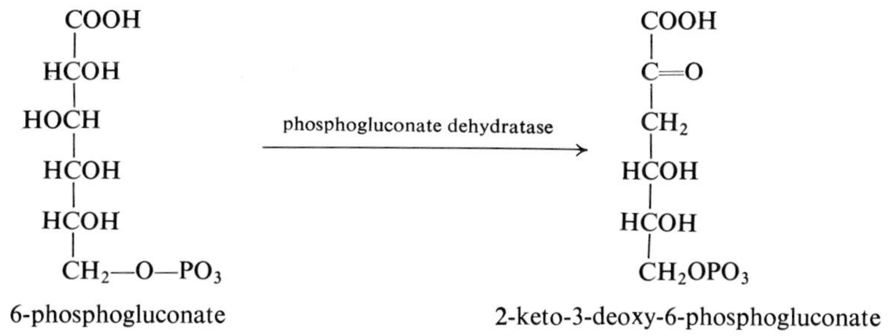

$$
\begin{array}{ccc}
\text{COOH} & & \text{COOH} \\
| & & | \\
\text{HCOH} & & \text{C}=\!\text{O} \\
| & & | \\
\text{HOCH} & \xrightarrow{\text{phosphogluconate dehydratase}} & \text{CH}_2 \\
| & & | \\
\text{HCOH} & & \text{HCOH} \\
| & & | \\
\text{HCOH} & & \text{HCOH} \\
| & & | \\
\text{CH}_2\!-\!\text{O}\!-\!\text{PO}_3 & & \text{CH}_2\text{OPO}_3 \\
\end{array}
$$

6-phosphogluconate   2-keto-3-deoxy-6-phosphogluconate

from the other two is the dehydration of 6-phosphogluconate (iv)(102) to form 2-keto-3-deoxy-6-phosphogluconate by a phosphogluconate dehydratase (6-phosphogluconate hydrolyase, E.C. 4.2.1.12). A subsequent cleavage by 2-phospho-2-keto-3-deoxygluconate aldolase (6-phospho-2-keto-3-deoxy-D-gluconate: D-glyceraldehyde-3-phosphatelyase, E.C. 4.1.2.14), which is similar

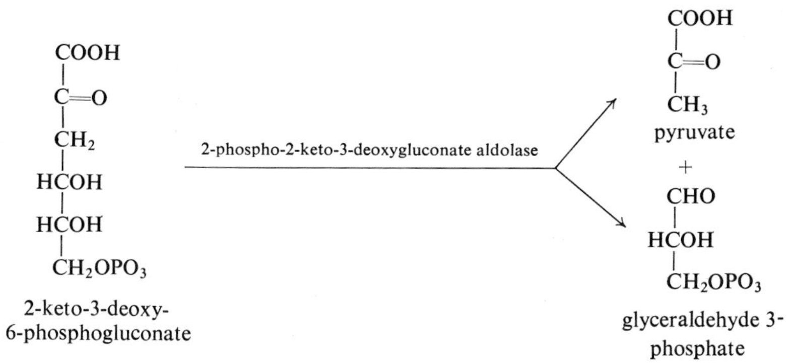

2-phospho-2-keto-3-deoxygluconate aldolase

$$
\begin{array}{c}
\text{COOH} \\
| \\
\text{C}=\!\text{O} \\
| \\
\text{CH}_2 \\
| \\
\text{HCOH} \\
| \\
\text{HCOH} \\
| \\
\text{CH}_2\text{OPO}_3 \\
\end{array}
$$

2-keto-3-deoxy-
6-phosphogluconate

$$
\begin{array}{c}
\text{COOH} \\
| \\
\text{C}=\!\text{O} \\
| \\
\text{CH}_3 \\
\text{pyruvate} \\
+ \\
\text{CHO} \\
| \\
\text{HCOH} \\
| \\
\text{CH}_2\text{OPO}_3 \\
\end{array}
$$

glyceraldehyde 3-
phosphate

to that described for fructose diphosphate aldolase, splits the 2-keto-3-deoxy-6-phosphogluconate into glyceraldehyde 3-phosphate and pyruvate (v).

The triose phosphate is free for use in the EMP pathway to pyruvate. Where this pathway is followed it yields two moles of ATP per mole substrate (glucose), and one mole each of reduced NADP and NAD. Two moles of $NADH + H^+$ are later used in the further breakdown of pyruvate.

Another important feature of this pathway is that it enables organisms to produce their pentose precursors for pyridine and pyrimidine biosynthesis by a reversed hexose monophosphate pathway. Glyceraldehyde 3-phosphate may condense (vi) with fructose 6-phosphate yielding erythrose 4-phosphate and xylulose 5-phosphate. The reaction is catalyzed by transketolase (E.C. 2.2.1.1). Ribulose phosphate 3-epimerase (E.C. 5.1.3.1) converts (vii) xylulose 5-phosphate into ribulose 5-phosphate, whereas a transaldolase (E.C. 2.2.1.2) forms (viii) glyceraldehyde 3-phosphate and sedoheptulose 7-phosphate from erythrose 4-phosphate and fructose 6-phosphate. Ribose 5-phosphate and xylulose 5-phosphate (ix) are the products from a second transketolase (E.C. 2.2.1.1) reaction. Depending upon the environmental conditions, microorganisms are able to use the reversed pentose cycle to meet their pyridine and pyrimidine requirement or alternatively, use this cycle only partially and form pyruvate from glyceraldehyde 3-phosphate. Pyruvate can then be metabolized in ways to be considered later.

In comparing the three different pathways, each of them could serve certain aspects of metabolic activities. The EMP pathway provides the greatest amount of ATP, namely, two moles, but does not produce the most important precursors for purine and pyrimidine synthesis, ribose 5-phosphate and erythrose 4-phosphate. Therefore it could be assumed that microorganisms using this pathway must have specific growth requirements for pentoses, purines, or pyrimidines in order to build, for example, their nucleic acids. In general, organisms which grow only on complex media, e.g., media containing meat extract and yeast extract, use this particular pathway (143).

The HMP pathway, on the other hand, produces all the precursors necessary for purine and pyrimidine biosynthesis but produces only half the amount of ATP. This pathway does not produce pyruvate directly so that the organism must have at least part of the EMP pathway enzyme complex from glyceraldehyde 3-phosphate onward to form pyruvate. It is therefore not surprising that both pathways may be present in those organisms which do possess the HMP pathway (see Table 4.1) and therefore are independent in regard to their purine and pyrimidine requirements. There is as yet no known microorganism able to use solely the HMP pathway. The ratio of usage of the EMP and HMP pathways can vary greatly depending upon environmental conditions.

The Entner-Doudoroff pathway is at the other extreme where the reverse HMP pathway may be present but the direct formation of pyruvate makes it possible to be independent of the other two pathways. The production of one mole of ATP and all necessary pentoses makes it very similar to the HMP, particularly since a number of enzymes are the same. There are some groups of bacteria which are able to use this pathway alone. Table 4.1 indicates the percentage distribution of these pathways in some microorganisms. The reasons for the individual choices are not yet quite clear. It was thought that oxygen may play an important role in the selection of pathway usage. The majority of anaerobic bacteria were found to contain the EMP pathway, those which are facultative aerobes found to contain a combination of EMP and

HMP pathway, and strict aerobes found to contain almost exclusively the ED pathway. However, the finding that the strict anaerobe *Zymomonas mobilis* can use only the ED pathway and that homofermentative lactobacilli can use the EMP pathway even under aerobic conditions cast doubt upon the early assumptions.

A few examples of the participation of mixed pathways and the problems involved for metabolic studies and evaluation in general will now be given.

TABLE 4.1

ESTIMATION OF CATABOLIC PATHWAYS OF GLUCOSE PATHWAY ESTIMATION[a]

Microorganisms	EMP	HMP	ED
Saccharomyces cerevisiae	88	12	
Candida utilis	66–81	19–34	
Streptomyces griseus	97	3	
Penicillium chrysogenum	77	23	
Fusarium lini	83	17	
Escherichia coli	72	28	
Sarcina lutea	70	30	
Bacillus subtilis	74	26	
Pseudomonas aeruginosa		29	71
Acetomonas oxydans		100	
Zymomonas mobilis			100
Pseudomonas saccharophilus			100

[a] From Cheldelin(29). Reprinted with permission of John Wiley and Sons.

The pathway of D-glucose metabolism in *Salmonella typhimurium*(59) can follow either a combination of EMP and HMP or the ED pathway. Investigations on a wild and mutant strain of *S. typhimurium* showed that the wild type utilized 20% of the glucose via the HMP and metabolized the remainder via the EMP pathway. Although the mutant was deficient in the enzyme phosphoglucose isomerase, it was not possible to adapt the strain to the HMP to a greater extent than the wild type despite the greater need of the mutant for this particular pathway. On gluconate as substrate, however, both the wild type and the mutant utilized gluconate via the ED pathway and not via the EMP or HMP pathway.

Gluconokinase and gluconate 6-phosphate dehydrase were found to be inducible.

A similar arrangement of glucose utilization was found in *Haemophilus parainfluenzae*(178), where the EMP and HMP are functional. Evidence has been given for the need of a functioning electron transport system. The growth of this bacterium depends on the presence of electron acceptors such as oxygen, nitrate, pyruvate, fumarate, NAD^+, and $NADP^+$ in the media. Such an obligatory requirement of oxygen for glucose catabolism via the EMP pathway has also been demonstrated for *Pasteurella tularensis*, *Agrobacterium tumefaciens*(91), and *Streptomyces coelicolor*(31). Whether or not oxygen may be required for the biosynthesis of cofactors, an example of which has been given in Chapter 3 for heme biosynthesis, has to be left for further studies. A good example for the dependence of end products on cultural conditions has been demonstrated with the facultative anaerobe, *Actinomyces naeslundii* (23). This organism is pathogenic and ferments sugar but requires carbon dioxide for maximal growth. Without the addition of carbon dioxide, growth was limited and the fermentation product was lactic acid. Addition of carbon dioxide caused a change in end product formation, and formate, acetate, and succinate were found in addition to lactate in a ratio dependent upon the carbon dioxide concentration(22, 139). The major pathway used was the EMP pathway although the presence of most of the enzymes of the HMP pathway indicates a small participation of this pathway as well.

Carbohydrate metabolism can also occur when an organism is unable to grow in the presence of nonphosphorylated sugars as sole source of carbon and energy, but require permeable intermediates of the TCA cycle(13). The parent strain of *Mima polymorpha*, for example, is lacking some kinases and therefore requires additional energy. The enzymes found in this organism(123) i.e., glucose dehydrogenase, 6-phosphogluconate dehydrogenase, FDP aldolase, and 2-keto-3-deoxy-6-phosphogluconate aldolase indicate the functioning of the HMP and ED pathways.

Another combination of pathways appears to exist in *Microbacterium lacticum*(170), where the HMP and EMP seem to function under anaerobic conditions and the phosphoketolase pathway under aerobic conditions.

Most changes in pathways appear to be attributed to oxygen availability. The most interesting materials for this type of study are certainly the facultative anaerobes(107). The available evidence suggests that these bacteria use preferentially an oxygen-linked electron transport mechanism and therefore develop control mechanisms triggered by oxygen for repressing the synthesis of systems unnecessary for aerobic growth. In other words, facultative aerobes may retain anaerobic mechanisms for the synthesis of certain metabolites, but use aerobic energy-yielding mechanisms preferentially to anaerobic ones. Very little is known at the present moment whether the available oxygen or the nutritional changes influence the carbohydrate utilization. Oxygen availability certainly changes the end products formed (see Chapters 5 and 6), but uncertainty exists whether it influences the pathways.

Studies with *Bacillus subtilis* revealed that oxygen has no effect on the ratio of participation of EMP and HMP during glucose catabolism(76) when the radiorespirometric method(174) was employed in the study. With resting cells of *Bacillus cereus*(16) only 1–2% of the glucose was utilized by the HMP and the remainder by the EMP pathway. During sporulation, however, this ratio changed(50,75,82) but eventually returned to the previous level. The EMP pathway appears to occupy the key position of glucose catabolism at all stages of development of *Bacillus cereus*(77). Similar studies have been carried out with *Clostridium botulinum*(157).

The only occasion on which a genus of bacteria has been classified according to the pathway of glucose breakdown is *Arthrobacter*(188). *Arthrobacter ureofaciens* and *Arthrobacter globiformis*(131) use primarily the EMP and to some extent the HMP pathway, whereas *A. simplex*, *A. pascens*, and *A. atrocyaneus* catabolize glucose mainly via the ED and HMP pathway. The presence and absence of the ED pathway has been used as the differential criterion. Much more work has to be done in this field to find out whether the use of one or another pathway is dependent upon nutritional requirements or oxygen availability.

Pasteur Effect. The finding of Pasteur that glycolysis is linked to respiration and that oxygen consumption inhibits glycolysis has not been fully explored. This is known as "Pasteur effect." The vital importance of oxygen lies in the conservation of nutrient while the useful energy yield per molecule of glucose is rendered large. Although we know about the benefits, the mechanism is still obscure. There are a few proposed hypotheses in existence which will be mentioned briefly:

(1) Yeasts grown aerobically exhibit full mitochondrial structures, which disappear under anaerobic conditions. By changing back to aerobic conditions these mitochondria reappear (139a). Since the mitochondria are responsible for the oxidation of citric acid cycle intermediates and phosphorylation (173a, 173b), a lack of these structures in yeasts causes inhibition of oxidative phosphorylation and a change from respiration to fermentation.

(2) There is growing evidence which suggests that phosphofructokinase may be affected under anaerobic conditions(68,130,167,169). This enzyme is activated by inorganic phosphate, AMP and ADP, but is inhibited by relatively low concentrations of ATP. The latter can be bound at an effector site, which leads to conformation changes that modify both the affinity of the enzyme for its substrate and the maximal rate of reaction catalyzed(7).

(3) The oxidation of 3-phosphoglyceraldehyde requires inorganic ortho-phosphate and also a supply of ADP. Orthophosphate and ADP are, on the other hand, also consumed in the oxidation of pyruvate via the tricarboxylic acid cycle, while generating ATP. There may exist true competition between these reactions. When respiration is low, ample phosphate and ADP are provided for a rapid use of the EMP pathway, whereas in the reverse case,

they may diminish to the level of nonavailability(141). This leads to the proposal that the control of the rate of anaerobic metabolism is mediated by intracellular orthophosphate or feedback mechanisms involving ATP and ADP(57).

(4) A number of the enzymes involved in the EMP pathway contain SH groups, i.e., phosphoglyceraldehyde dehydrogenase, and phosphofructokinase, which may be oxidized and thus decrease their enzyme activity.

These are a few of the complex questions which surround the Pasteur effect. It may be even that there is no general Pasteur effect, but this effect may be different from one species to another. The increasing work with continuous culture systems should provide more information in this field in the near future.

Closely related with the Pasteur effect is the finding that high concentrations of glucose will inhibit cellular respiration(177, 185). This effect is generally known as the "Crabtree effect."

Phosphoketolase Pathway. Apart from the well known EMP, HMP, and ED pathways, there are two other pathways which are possessed by only a small group of bacteria(41, 44, 45, 48, 108), the heterofermentative lactobacilli and the *Bifidobacteria*. These pathways can be regarded as a branch or a variation of the HMP pathway, since a part of these pathways is identical with the HMP pathway. Because of this, they are referred to as the pentose phosphoketolase and the hexose phosphoketolase pathways.

The Pentose Phosphoketolase Pathway. Glucose can also serve as a carbon

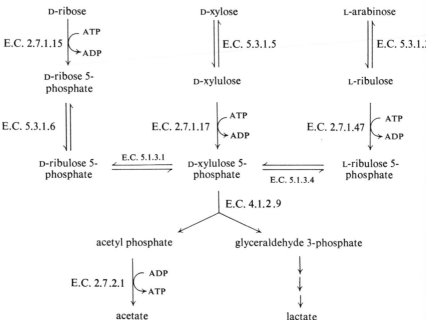

source in which case D-ribose 5-phosphate, D-ribulose 5-phosphate, or D-xylulose 5-phosphate are formed via the HMP pathway, but these bacteria lack the enzyme transketolase (E.C. 2.2.1.1). If supplied with the pentose D-ribose, a ribokinase (ATP:D-ribose 5-phosphotransferase, E.C. 2.7.1.15) transfers one phosphate group from ATP to ribose, forming D-ribose 5-phosphate:

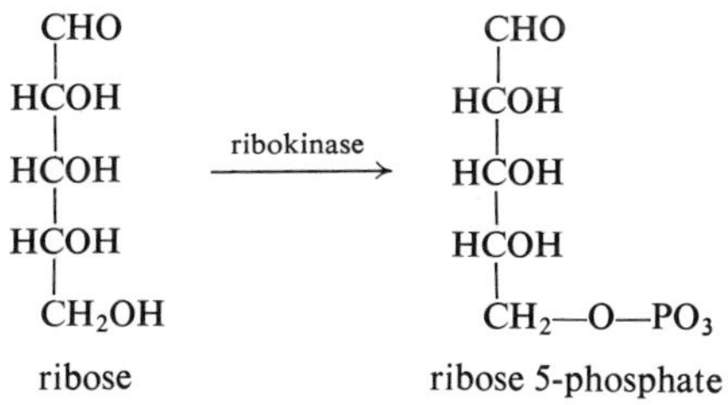

$$
\begin{array}{ccc}
\text{CHO} & & \text{CHO}\\
\text{HCOH} & & \text{HCOH}\\
\text{HCOH} & \xrightarrow{\text{ribokinase}} & \text{HCOH}\\
\text{HCOH} & & \text{HCOH}\\
\text{CH}_2\text{OH} & & \text{CH}_2\text{—O—PO}_3\\
\text{ribose} & & \text{ribose 5-phosphate}
\end{array}
$$

The product of this reaction is then isomerized to D-ribulose 5-phosphate by ribose phosphate isomerase (D-ribose 5-phosphate ketol isomerase, E.C. 5.3.1.6). Ribulose phosphate 3-epimerase (D-ribulose 5-phosphate 3-epimerase,

$$
\begin{array}{ccc}
\text{CHO} & & \text{CH}_2\text{OH}\\
\text{HCOH} & & \text{C}{=}\text{O}\\
\text{HCOH} & \xrightarrow{\text{ribose phosphate isomerase}} & \text{HCOH}\\
\text{HCOH} & & \text{HCOH}\\
\text{CH}_2\text{—O—PO}_3 & & \text{CH}_2\text{—O—PO}_3\\
\text{ribose 5-phosphate} & & \text{ribulose 5-phosphate}
\end{array}
$$

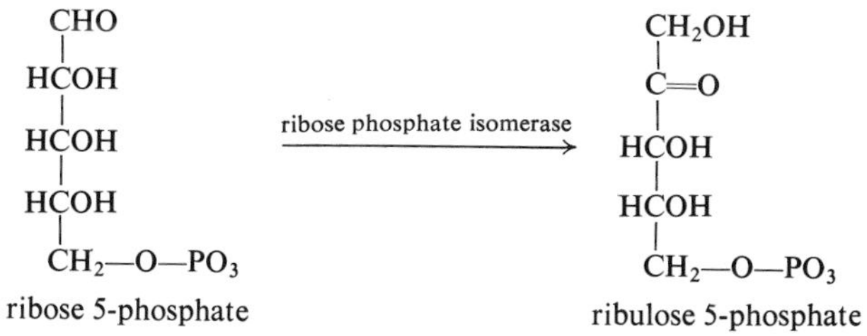

E.C. 5.1.3.1) converts the D-ribulose 5-phosphate to D-xylulose 5-phosphate.

$$
\begin{array}{ccc}
\text{CH}_2\text{OH} & & \text{CH}_2\text{OH}\\
\text{C}{=}\text{O} & & \text{C}{=}\text{O}\\
\text{HCOH} & \xrightarrow{\text{ribulose 5-phosphate 3-epimerase}} & \text{HOCH}\\
\text{HCOH} & & \text{HCOH}\\
\text{CH}_2\text{—O—PO}_3 & & \text{CH}_2\text{—O—PO}_3\\
\text{ribulose 5-phosphate} & & \text{xylulose 5-phosphate}
\end{array}
$$

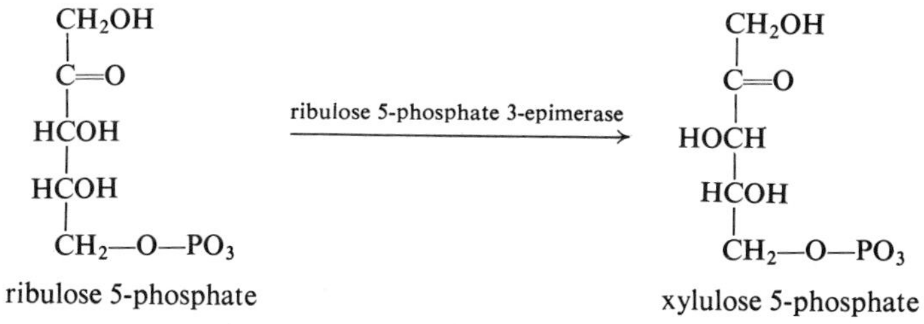

This newly formed phosphate ester plays a key role in this pathway. All other pentoses, such as D-xylose or L-arabinose have first to be converted to D-xylulose 5-phosphate, since the key enzyme of this pathway, phosphoketolase (D-xylulose 5-phosphate:D-glyceraldehyde 3-phosphatelyase (phosphate acetylating), E.C. 4.1.2.9) reacts only on this compound. D-Xylose, for example, undergoes first an isomerization catalyzed by D-xylose isomerase

(D-xylose ketol isomerase, E.C. 5.3.1.5) to D-xylulose. After this conversion, D-xylulose kinase (ATP:D-xylulose-5-phosphotransferase, E.C. 2.7.1.17) phosphorylates D-xylulose to D-xylulose 5-phosphate:

$$
\begin{array}{ccc}
\text{CH}_2\text{OH} & & \text{CH}_2\text{OH} \\
| & & | \\
\text{C}=\text{O} & & \text{C}=\text{O} \\
| & \xrightarrow{\text{xylulose kinase}} & | \\
\text{HOCH} & & \text{HOCH} \\
| & & | \\
\text{HCOH} & & \text{HCOH} \\
| & & | \\
\text{CH}_2\text{OH} & & \text{CH}_2\text{—O—PO}_3 \\
\text{xylulose} & & \text{xylulose 5-phosphate}
\end{array}
$$

Another well-known pentose attacked by heterofermentative lactobacilli is L-arabinose, which also undergoes first an isomerization (D-arabinose ketol isomerase, E.C. 5.3.1.3) to D-ribulose and, second, a phosphorylation to

$$
\begin{array}{ccccc}
\text{CHO} & & \text{CH}_2\text{OH} & & \text{CH}_2\text{OH} \\
| & & | & & | \\
\text{HOCH} & & \text{C}=\text{O} & & \text{C}=\text{O} \\
| & \xrightarrow[\text{isomerase}]{\text{arabinose}} & | & \xrightarrow{\text{ribulokinase}} & | \\
\text{HCOH} & & \text{HCOH} & & \text{HCOH} \\
| & & | & & | \\
\text{HCOH} & & \text{HCOH} & & \text{HCOH} \\
| & & | & & | \\
\text{CH}_2\text{OH} & & \text{CH}_2\text{OH} & & \text{CH}_2\text{OPO}_3 \\
\text{arabinose} & & \text{ribulose} & & \text{ribulose 5-phosphate}
\end{array}
$$

D-ribulose 5-phosphate with the help of ribulokinase(24) (ATP:D-ribulose 5-phosphotransferase, E.C. 2.7.1.47). The conversion of ribulose 5-phosphate to xylulose 5-phosphate is catalyzed by ribulose phosphate 4-epimerase(25) (L-ribulose-5-phosphate 4-epimerase, E.C. 5.1.3.4):

$$
\begin{array}{ccc}
\text{CH}_2\text{OH} & & \text{CH}_2\text{OH} \\
| & & | \\
\text{C}=\text{O} & & \text{C}=\text{O} \\
| & \xrightarrow{\text{ribulose phosphate 4-epimerase}} & | \\
\text{HCOH} & & \text{HOCH} \\
| & & | \\
\text{HCOH} & & \text{HCOH} \\
| & & | \\
\text{CH}_2\text{—O—PO}_3 & & \text{CH}_2\text{—O—PO}_3 \\
\text{ribulose 5-phosphate} & & \text{xylulose 5-phosphate}
\end{array}
$$

Having formed D-xylulose 5-phosphate, phosphoketolase splits the pentose molecule into acetyl phosphate and glyceraldehyde 3-phosphate. This reaction requires a thiamine pyrophosphate protein as well as inorganic phosphate.

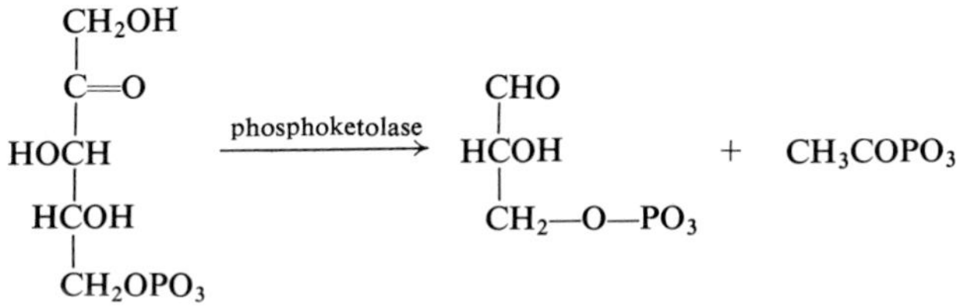

$$
\begin{array}{c}
CH_2OH \\
| \\
C{=}O \\
| \\
HOCH \\
| \\
HCOH \\
| \\
CH_2OPO_3
\end{array}
\quad\xrightarrow{\text{phosphoketolase}}\quad
\begin{array}{c}
CHO \\
| \\
HCOH \\
| \\
CH_2{-}O{-}PO_3
\end{array}
\quad + \quad CH_3COPO_3
$$

xylulose 5-phosphate   glyceraldehyde   acetylphosphate
                              3-phosphate

Whereas glyceraldehyde 3-phosphate may continue via the EMP pathway to pyruvate, acetyl phosphate is converted to acetate with acetokinase (ATP: acetate phosphotransferase, E.C. 2.7.2.1) and the formation of one molecule of ATP. From the point of view of ATP formation, the phosphoketolase pathway behaves similarly to the HMP pathway. The net production is one molecule of ATP. The main difference, of course, is that the phosphoketolase

$$
CH_3COPO_3 \quad\xrightarrow{\text{acetokinase}}\quad CH_3COOH + H_3PO_4
$$

acetyl phosphate   acetate

pathway substitutes for the transketolase–transaldolase reaction of the HMP pathway a phosphoketolase reaction. The other difference can be found in the cycling mechanism of the HMP pathway, which according to the carbon balance sheet seems not to occur (see Chapter 8).

Hexose Phosphoketolase Pathway. The occurrence of a specific catabolic route in a group of bacteria, the genus *Bifidobacterium* (*Lactobacillus bifidus*) has been reported recently(46). This group of bacteria was found to lack fructose diphosphate aldolase as well as glucose 6-phosphate dehydrogenase. They ferment glucose via a pathway which is different from those found in homo- and heterofermentative lactic acid bacteria, which means that none of the EMP, HMP, ED, or phosphoketolase pathways could operate. The key

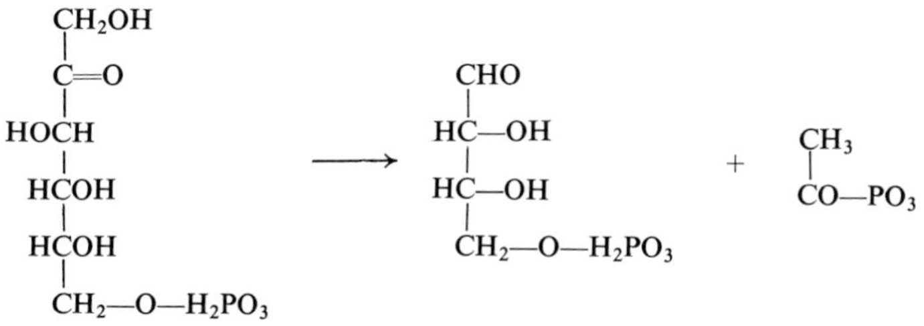

$$
\begin{array}{c}
CH_2OH \\
| \\
C{=}O \\
| \\
HOCH \\
| \\
HCOH \\
| \\
HCOH \\
| \\
CH_2{-}O{-}H_2PO_3
\end{array}
\quad\longrightarrow\quad
\begin{array}{c}
CHO \\
| \\
HC{-}OH \\
| \\
HC{-}OH \\
| \\
CH_2{-}O{-}H_2PO_3
\end{array}
\quad + \quad
\begin{array}{c}
CH_3 \\
| \\
CO{-}PO_3
\end{array}
$$

fructose 6-phosphate   erythrose 4-phosphate   acetylphosphate reaction in the fermentation of glucose appears to be a phosphoketolase cleavage of fructose 6-phosphate into acetyl phosphate and erythrose 4-phosphate. Pentose phosphates are thus formed in a reverse HMP pathway by the action of transaldolase (E.C. 2.2.1.2) and transketolase (E.C. 2.2.1.1). The product of this sequence, xylulose 5-phosphate can then be split into acetyl phosphate and glyceraldehyde 3-phosphate as described earlier. Hexose phosphoketolase was not found in *Lactobacillus, Ramibacterium, Arthrobacter, Propionibacterium, Corynebacterium,* and *Actinomyces*(149). All hexose phosphoketolase positive strains of *Bifidobacterium* form more acetic than lactic acid.

All five pathways have a great number of intermediates and enzymes in common. However, there are some which are characteristic for each pathway. The HMP, for example, does not possess the enzymes phosphofructokinase and often fructose diphosphate aldolase, whereas the EMP pathway does not have a transketolase–transaldolase reaction as well as no glucose 6-phosphate dehydrogenase. The ED pathway has 2-keto-3-deoxy-6-phosphogluconate aldolase, which is not present in any of the other pathways. In the two phosphoketolase pathways, the characteristic enzyme is the xylulose 5-phosphate ketolase which both have in common. The pentose phosphoketolase pathway, however, lacks fructose diphosphate aldolase, transketolase, transaldolase, whereas the hexose phosphoketolase pathway did not show any glucose 6-phosphate dehydrogenase activity, but does possess phosphofructokinase, transaldolase, and transketolase. These enzymes are so-called key enzymes for the particular pathways and may be of great importance for the distinction between the pathways. Their reactions and characteristics together with those enzymes, which may play an important role in the investigations of the Pasteur effect, will therefore be discussed further.

The Calvin Cycle or Autotrophic Mechanism of CO_2 fixation. Although this cycle is not a catabolic event, a knowledge of the cycle is necessary for the understanding of many metabolic reactions in a number of photo- and chemolithotrophic bacteria which live autotrophically. These interaction of anabolic and catabolic reactions are sometimes linked to such an extent that they have to be considered together.

Autotrophic microorganisms are all those which are able to use carbon dioxide as the only carbon source for synthesizing cell material. These organisms are able to reduce carbon dioxide to cell material. This is done in a cycling reaction sequence as outlined in Fig. 4.1. The sum of the reaction sequence is

$$6\,CO_2 + 18\,ATP + 12\,(NADPH + H^+) \rightarrow 1\,F\,6\text{-}P + 18\,ADP + 12\,NADP^+$$

Carbon dioxide is incorporated with ribulose 1,5-diphosphate by the enzyme ribulose   diphosphate   carboxylase   (3-phospho-D-glycerate-carboxylyase

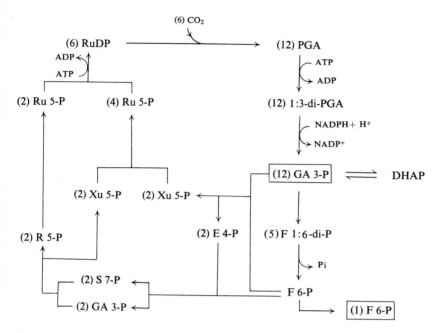

FIG. 4.1. Carbon dioxide assimilation via the Calvin cycle in autotrophic microorganisms.

(dimerizing), E.C. 4.1.1.39) in the formation of two moles of 3-phospho-glycerate. The first energy-requiring step follows as 3-phosphoglycerate is

$$
\begin{array}{ccc}
\begin{array}{l}
CH_2{-}O{-}H_2PO_3 \\
|\ \\
CO \\
|\ \\
HCOH \\
|\ \\
HCOH \\
|\ \\
CH_2{-}O{-}H_2PO_3
\end{array}
& + CO_2 \longrightarrow &
\begin{array}{l}
CH_2{-}O{-}H_2PO_3 \\
|\ \\
HCOH \\
|\ \\
COOH \\
+ \\
COOH \\
|\ \\
HCOH \\
|\ \\
CH_2{-}O{-}H_2PO_3
\end{array}
\end{array}
$$

D-ribulose 1,5-diphosphate (RuDP)　　(2)　　3-phosphoglycerate (PGA)

converted to a diphosphoglycerate in a reaction catalyzed by phosphoglycerate kinase (ATP: 3-phospho-D-glycerate 1-phosphotransferase, E.C. 2.7.2.3).

$$
\begin{array}{ccc}
\begin{array}{l}
CH_2{-}O{-}H_2PO_3 \\
|\ \\
CHOH \\
|\ \\
COOH
\end{array}
& + ATP \longrightarrow &
\begin{array}{l}
CH_2{-}O{-}H_2PO_3 \\
|\ \\
CHOH \\
|\ \\
CO{-}O{-}H_2PO_3
\end{array}
& + ADP
\end{array}
$$

3-phospho-D-glycerate　　　1,3-diphospho-D-glycerate (1,3-diPGA)

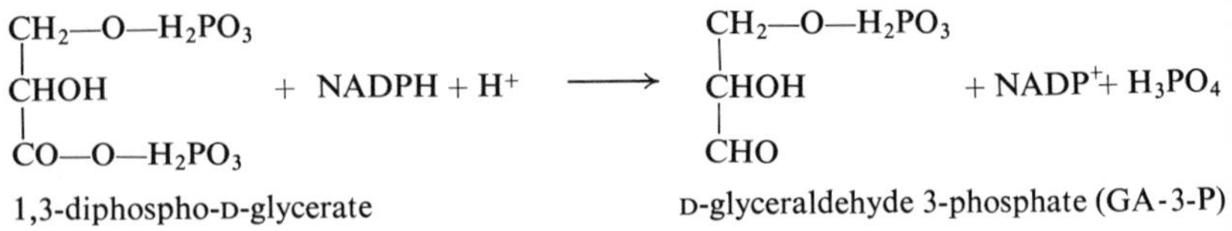

$$
\begin{array}{l}
CH_2\!-\!O\!-\!H_2PO_3 \\
| \\
CHOH \\
| \\
CO\!-\!O\!-\!H_2PO_3
\end{array}
\; + \; NADPH + H^+ \;\longrightarrow\;
\begin{array}{l}
CH_2\!-\!O\!-\!H_2PO_3 \\
| \\
CHOH \\
| \\
CHO
\end{array}
\; + NADP^+ + H_3PO_4
$$

1,3-diphospho-D-glycerate   D-glyceraldehyde 3-phosphate (GA-3-P)

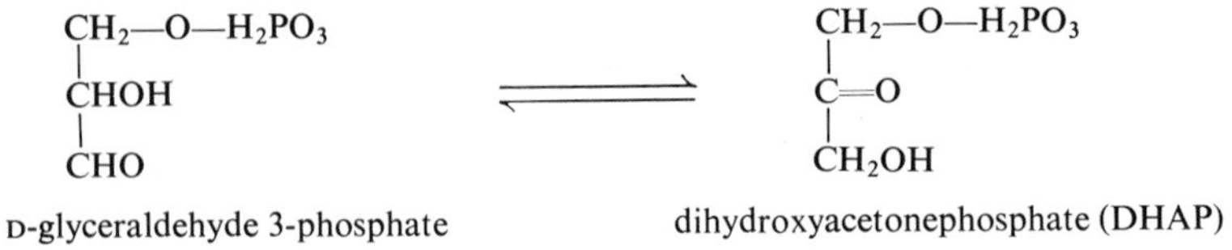

$$
\begin{array}{l}
CH_2\!-\!O\!-\!H_2PO_3 \\
| \\
CHOH \\
| \\
CHO
\end{array}
\;\rightleftharpoons\;
\begin{array}{l}
CH_2\!-\!O\!-\!H_2PO_3 \\
| \\
C\!=\!O \\
| \\
CH_2OH
\end{array}
$$

D-glyceraldehyde 3-phosphate   dihydroxyacetonephosphate (DHAP)

A further oxidation with a NADP-linked dehydrogenase [D-glyceraldehyde 3-phosphate: NADP oxidoreductase (phosphorylating) E.C. 1.2.1.13] produces glyceraldehyde 3-phosphate, which is held in an equilibrium with dihydroxyacetone phosphate by the triose phosphate isomerase (D-glyceraldehyde 3-phosphate ketol isomerase, E.C. 5.3.1.1). Fructose diphosphate aldolase

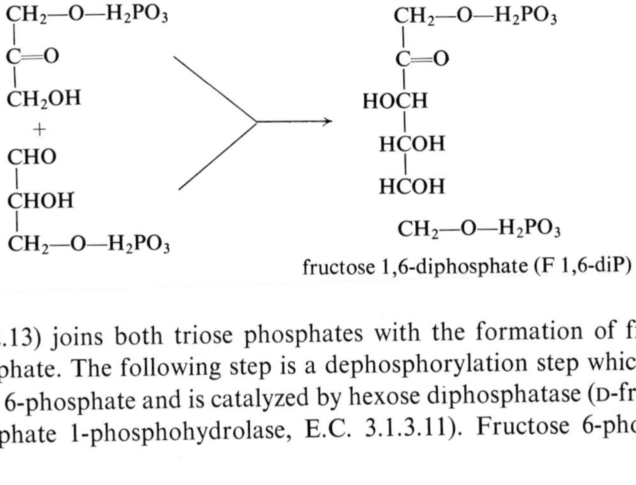

$$
\begin{array}{l}
CH_2\!-\!O\!-\!H_2PO_3 \\
| \\
C\!=\!O \\
| \\
CH_2OH \\
+ \\
CHO \\
| \\
CHOH \\
| \\
CH_2\!-\!O\!-\!H_2PO_3
\end{array}
\;\longrightarrow\;
\begin{array}{l}
CH_2\!-\!O\!-\!H_2PO_3 \\
| \\
C\!=\!O \\
| \\
HOCH \\
| \\
HCOH \\
| \\
HCOH \\
| \\
CH_2\!-\!O\!-\!H_2PO_3
\end{array}
$$

fructose 1,6-diphosphate (F 1,6-diP)

(E.C. 4.1.2.13) joins both triose phosphates with the formation of fructose 1,6-diphosphate. The following step is a dephosphorylation step which leads to fructose 6-phosphate and is catalyzed by hexose diphosphatase (D-fructose-1,6-diphosphate 1-phosphohydrolase, E.C. 3.1.3.11). Fructose 6-phosphate

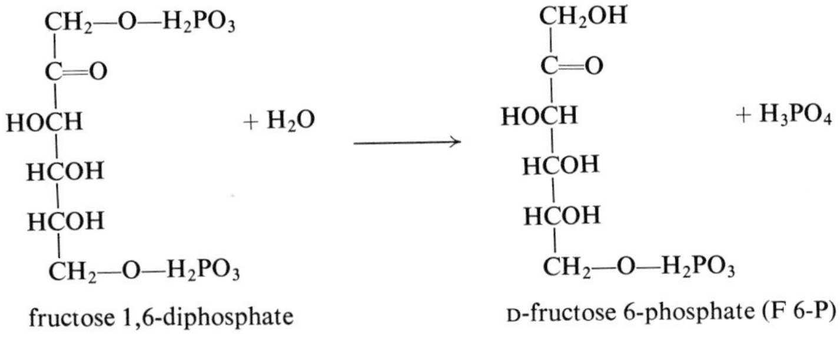

$$
\begin{array}{l}
CH_2\!-\!O\!-\!H_2PO_3 \\
| \\
C\!=\!O \\
| \\
HOCH \\
| \\
HCOH \\
| \\
HCOH \\
| \\
CH_2\!-\!O\!-\!H_2PO_3
\end{array}
\; + H_2O \;\longrightarrow\;
\begin{array}{l}
CH_2OH \\
| \\
C\!=\!O \\
| \\
HOCH \\
| \\
HCOH \\
| \\
HCOH \\
| \\
CH_2\!-\!O\!-\!H_2PO_3
\end{array}
\; + H_3PO_4
$$

fructose 1,6-diphosphate   D-fructose 6-phosphate (F 6-P) can now be converted in two different ways. It can either produce sucrose or pentoses. In autotrophic microorganisms the latter is the case, since pentoses provide the organisms with vital precursors for the formation of cell material such as RNA and DNA and also close the cyclic reaction sequence by forming again ribulose 1,5-diphosphate.

In order to obtain such pentoses, transketolase (E.C. 2.2.1.1) first cleaves D-glyceraldehyde 3-phosphate and D-fructose 6-phosphate with the formation of D-erythrose 4-phosphate and D-xylulose 5-phosphate. The reaction sequence continues as in the HMP pathway with transaldolase reaction producing sedoheptulose 7-phosphate and glyceraldehyde 3-phosphate from erythrose

$$
\begin{array}{cccc}
\mathrm{CH_2OH} & & & \mathrm{CH_2OH} \\
| & & & | \\
\mathrm{C{=}O} & & & \mathrm{C{=}O} \\
| & & & | \\
\mathrm{HOCH} & \mathrm{CHO} & \mathrm{CHO} & \mathrm{HOCH} \\
| & | & | & | \\
\mathrm{HCOH} + & \mathrm{HCOH} \longrightarrow & \mathrm{HCOH} + & \mathrm{HCOH} \\
| & | & | & | \\
\mathrm{HCOH} & \mathrm{CH_2{-}O{-}H_2PO_3} & \mathrm{HCOH} & \mathrm{CH_2{-}O{-}H_2PO_3} \\
| & & | & \\
\mathrm{CH_2{-}O{-}H_2PO_3} & & \mathrm{CH_2{-}O{-}H_2PO_3} & \\
\text{fructose 6-P} & \text{GA 3-P} & \text{erythrose 4-P} & \text{xylulose 5-P} \\
& & \text{(E 4-P)} & \text{(Xu 5-P)}
\end{array}
$$

4-phosphate and fructose 6-phosphate. This reaction is followed by a second transketolase (E.C. 2.2.1.1) cleavage of sedoheptulose 7-phosphate and glyceraldehyde 3-phosphate, which forms ribose 5-phosphate and xylulose 5-phosphate. The products ribose 5-phosphate and xylulose 5-phosphate are

$$
\begin{array}{cccc}
\mathrm{CH_2OH} & & & \mathrm{CH_2OH} \\
| & & & | \\
\mathrm{C{=}O} & & & \mathrm{C{=}O} \\
| & & & | \\
\mathrm{HOCH} & \mathrm{CHO} & \mathrm{CHO} & \mathrm{HOCH} \\
| & | & | & | \\
\mathrm{HCOH} + & \mathrm{HCOH} \longrightarrow & \mathrm{HCOH} + & \mathrm{HCOH} \\
| & | & | & | \\
\mathrm{HCOH} & \mathrm{CH_2{-}O{-}H_2PO_3} & \mathrm{HCOH} & \mathrm{CH_2{-}O{-}H_2PO_3} \\
| & & | & \\
\mathrm{HCOH} & & \mathrm{HCOH} & \\
| & & | & \\
\mathrm{CH_2{-}O{-}H_2PO_3} & & \mathrm{CH_2{-}O{-}H_2PO_3} & \\
\text{sedoheptulose 7-P} & \text{GA 3-P} & \text{ribose 5-P (R 5-P)} & \text{Xu 5-P}
\end{array}
$$

both converted in two separated reactions into ribulose 5-phosphate. In the first instance, ribose 5-phosphate ketol isomerase (E.C. 5.3.1.6) and in the latter, ribulose 5-phosphate 3-epimerase (E.C. 5.1.3.1) are the responsible enzymes.

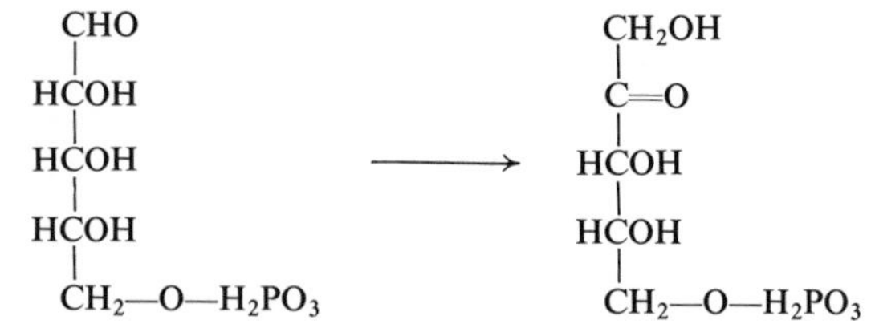

$$
\begin{array}{c}
CHO \\
| \\
HCOH \\
| \\
HCOH \\
| \\
HCOH \\
| \\
CH_2\text{—}O\text{—}H_2PO_3
\end{array}
\quad\longrightarrow\quad
\begin{array}{c}
CH_2OH \\
| \\
C\text{=}O \\
| \\
HCOH \\
| \\
HCOH \\
| \\
CH_2\text{—}O\text{—}H_2PO_3
\end{array}
$$

R 5-P   ribulose 5-P (Ru 5-P)

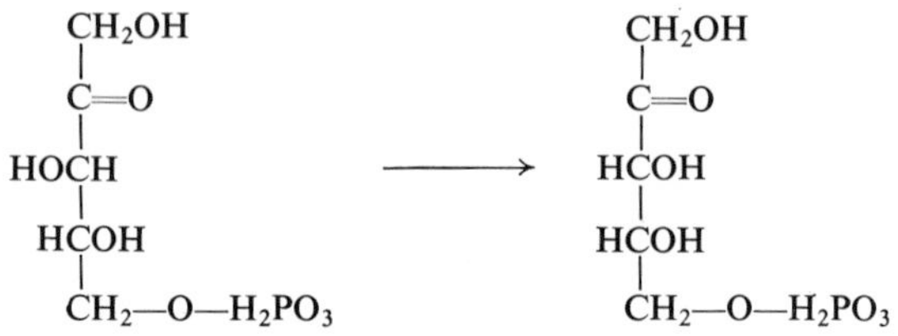

$$
\begin{array}{c}
CH_2OH \\
| \\
C\text{=}O \\
| \\
HOCH \\
| \\
HCOH \\
| \\
CH_2\text{—}O\text{—}H_2PO_3
\end{array}
\quad\longrightarrow\quad
\begin{array}{c}
CH_2OH \\
| \\
C\text{=}O \\
| \\
HCOH \\
| \\
HCOH \\
| \\
CH_2\text{—}O\text{—}H_2PO_3
\end{array}
$$

Xu 5-P   Ru 5-P

The second unique enzyme of the Calvin cycle closes the cyclic mechanism by phosphorylating ribulose 5-phosphate to ribulose 1,5-diphosphate, which is required for autotrophic carbon dioxide fixation. This enzyme is known to be phosphoribulokinase (ATP: D-ribulose 5-phosphate 1-phosphotransferase, E.C. 2.7.1.19). The presence or absence of this autotrophic carbon dioxide fixation mechanism of the Calvin cycle is quite commonly determined by testing the activity of ribulose diphosphate carboxylase (E.C. 4.1.1.39). In older literature this enzyme is referred to under the name "carboxydismutase."

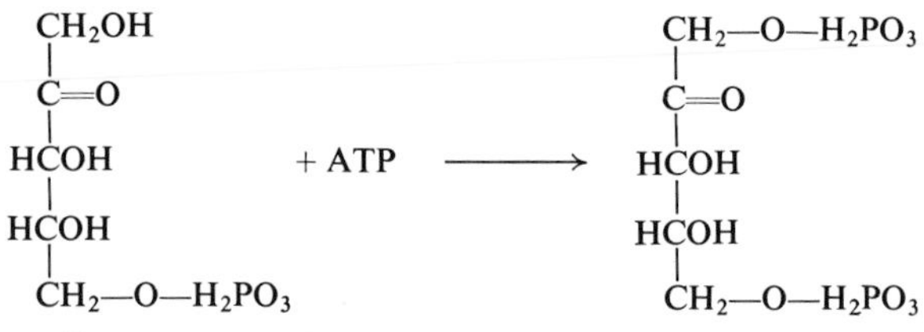

$$
\begin{array}{c}
CH_2OH \\
| \\
C\text{=}O \\
| \\
HCOH \\
| \\
HCOH \\
| \\
CH_2\text{—}O\text{—}H_2PO_3
\end{array}
\quad + ATP \quad\longrightarrow\quad
\begin{array}{c}
CH_2\text{—}O\text{—}H_2PO_3 \\
| \\
C\text{=}O \\
| \\
HCOH \\
| \\
HCOH \\
| \\
CH_2\text{—}O\text{—}H_2PO_3
\end{array}
$$

ribulose 5-phosphate   ribulose 1,5-diphosphate
                                (Ru diP)

With this mechanism working in most autotrophic microorganisms, these organisms are also able to draw on each of the intermediates for further synthetic reactions of all types of cell material. The claim that these organisms are able to form hexoses from carbon dioxide could be misleading since they do not accumulate hexoses, but draw on the intermediates rather than form sugars.

Not all autotrophic microorganisms, however, possess this Calvin cycle as described above. There are a number of microorganisms known which follow a slightly altered mechanism depending on whether they require two carbon dioxide fixation steps or only one.

Radioautographs of reaction products in *Chromatium*(67) indicated that phosphoglycerate and aspartic acid were the earliest stable products of carbon dioxide fixation. The high initial incorporation of carbon dioxide into aspartic acid was found to be owing to a second carboxylation step at the phosphoenol pyruvate level(67, 114), which in turn was formed from phosphoglycerate (Fig. 4.2). Oxalacetate was produced in the presence of phosphoenol pyruvate carboxylase and aspartate probably formed via transamination. It has therefore been postulated that *Chromatium* might use this pathway of a "double carbon dioxide" fixation as a rapid method for incorporating carbon into organic acids and amino acids for the production of new cellular material and may also explain the function of the TCA cycle in autotrophs. It is apparently not solved yet whether part of the phosphoglycerate produces ribulose 5-phosphate via glyceraldehyde 3-phosphate or through the intact Calvin cycle.

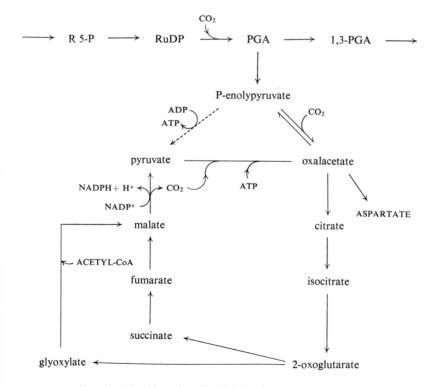

FIG. 4.2. "Double carbon dioxide" fixation in *Chromatium*.

A similar two cycle system has recently been found also in sugarcane leaves(84,85). In these leaves the first product of the major carboxylation reaction is either malate or oxalacetate and aspartate is formed by a side reaction. The nature of this carboxylation reaction is considered to be either malate dehydrogenase (E.C. 1.1.1.40) or phosphopyruvate carboxylase (E.C. 4.1.1.31). The additional cycle seems to operate in order to regenerate the carboxyl acceptor for a transcarboxylation reaction (see Fig. 4.2).

KEY ENZYMES IN THE CARBOHYDRATE METABOLISM

Hexokinase. Under the terms "hexokinase" and "pentokinase" fall all enzymes which catalyze the transfer of the terminal phosphoryl residue of ATP to any one of the hydroxyl groups of a carbon-5- or carbon-6-monosaccharide. In actual fact, however, only the terminal –OH group of the free sugar seems to be involved in the reaction(34). Enzyme-catalyzed phosphorylation of hydroxyl groups occupying other positions on the sugar molecule have been observed only in the case of the ribose moiety of certain coenzymes and cofactors.

Hexokinase, the prototype of this group of enzymes was first described in yeasts, catalyzing the following reaction:

$$\text{hexose} + \text{ATP} \rightarrow \text{hexose 6-phosphate} + \text{ADP}$$

It is likely that cells capable of metabolizing hexoses or pentoses contain at least one such enzyme. The distribution of these enzymes among microorganisms is shown in Table 4.2.

TABLE 4.2

HEXOKINASES AND PENTOKINASES OF MICROBIAL ORIGIN[a]

Enzyme	Substrate	Product	Source
Hexokinase	Glucose, mannose, fructose, 2-deoxyglucose, etc.	Hexose 6-phosphate	Yeast *Neurospora crassa, Ps. putrefaciens, Borrelia recurrentis*
Glucokinase	Glucose	Glucose 6-phosphate	*Ps. saccharophila Staph. aureus*
Mannokinase	Mannose	M 6-P	*Ps. saccharophila*
Galactokinase	Galactose	Ga 6-P	*Sacchar. fragilis*
Fructokinase	Fructose	F 6-P	*Ps. saccharophila*
Ribokinase	Ribose, 2-deoxyribose	R 5-P	Yeast bacteria
Ribulokinase	L-Ribulose, arabitol	Ru 5-P	Bacteria
Xylulokinase	D-Xylulose	Xu 5-P	Bacteria
N-Acetyl glucosamine kinase	N-Acetyl glucosamine	N-Acglu-6-P	General bacterial distribution

[a] From Crane(34).

In regard to specificity, the hexokinases of bacterial origin appear to have a far greater substrate specificity than those of mammalian or yeast origin. The yeast hexokinase is capable of phosphorylating a number of different sugars and appears to be specific for the 3,4,5,6 region of the molecule but not for the 1,2 part, provided, of course, that no larger groups are attached to them (47). Brain and aspergillus hexokinases are broadly similar but differences occur between the two, e.g., brain enzyme is much less exacting with regard to substitution on carbon-5, and aspergillus enzyme with regard to the carbon-4 atom. Because of this, galactose can serve almost as well as glucose as a substrate. The phosphorylation of hexoses and pentoses in bacteria, however, is governed by more specific enzymes, glucose by glucokinase (E.C. 2.7.1.2), fructose by ketohexokinase (E.C. 2.7.1.3), etc. In many cases, kinases are quite specific for a particular sugar structure, e.g., ribulokinase (E.C. 2.7.1.16) of *Aerobacter aerogenes* phosphorylates only D- and L-ribulose.

All kinases require the participation of ATP as the phosphate donor and also a metal, normally Mg^{2+}. The actual number of hexokinases continues to grow, as can well be expected from the almost universal occurrence of glucose throughout the living forms.

Hexokinases, with the exception of glucokinase, are inhibited by glucose 6-phosphate (172, 173). A mechanism for ADP control of hexokinases in yeast was proposed (28) by invoking an ATP compartment. Adenosine diphosphate enters the compartment and is also phosphorylated there, which means that ATP must be compartmented either with or without hexokinase.

The rate of glucose utilization in a cell which has rapid glucose transport and which has little glucose 6-phosphate hydrolysis has been shown to depend on the hexokinase step which has been located in soluble and mitochondrial fractions of mammalian cells (116) and is strongly inhibited by glucose 6-phosphate (35). This inhibition is competitive (65) with ATP in the presence of excess Mg^{2+}. However, van Tiedemann and Born (171) observed that inorganic phosphate offsets the inhibitory effect of glucose 6-phosphate in Ehrlich ascites cell homogenates and concluded that the specific inhibition of glucose 6-phosphate is overcome by inorganic phosphate. They also suggested that this might have an important relation to the Pasteur effect. Rose et al. (145) traced the effect of inorganic phosphate in stimulating glucose utilization in red blood cells to this property of inorganic phosphate.

On the other hand, it is possible that glucose 6-phosphate, as a regulatory substance of hexokinase, might be a consequence rather than a cause of metabolic control, whereby hexokinase could effect a limitation on the size of the glucose 6-phosphate pool only.

Assay Methods. Two assay methods are available, established with yeast and with animal tissues, which have the same basic principle, but differ in their approach.

The methods are based on the facts that hexose disappears and that for each mole of phosphate transferred from ATP, one acid equivalent is liberated. The formation of hexose 6-phosphate can also be determined. There are two assay methods for animal tissue hexokinase. One measures the glucose 6-phosphate formed by the action of hexokinase on glucose. The other measures the NADP reduction following the action of glucose 6-phosphate dehydrogenase and hexokinase on glucose. The production of phosphoric acid was found most convenient for the yeast hexokinase.

ANIMAL TISSUE HEXOKINASE ASSAY METHOD(36).

Reagents:

(1) ATP–Mg^{2+} mixture—A solution of ATP and MgCl$_2$ of appropriate strength are mixed, neutralized to pH 7.0, and diluted to the final concentrations of 0.075 M ATP and 0.04 M MgCl$_2$. This solution is stable at −15°C for limited periods only.
(2) Buffer mixture—solutions of histidine, tris(hydroxylmethyl)amino methane, EDTA and MgCl$_2$ of appropriate strength are mixed, neutralized to pH 7.0 and diluted to the respective concentrations of 0.1, 0.1, 0.01, and 0.01 M.
(3) Glucose solution—0.01 M.
(4) Enzyme—the stock enzyme is diluted with 0.002 M EDTA, 0.002 M MgCl$_2$, at pH 7.0 to obtain 5 to 25 units/ml.

Procedure: 0.2 ml of each of the ATP–Mg^{2+} mixture, buffer mixture, and glucose solution together with 0.3 ml of water are mixed and warmed up to 30°C. Diluted enzyme (0.01 ml) is added, the solution mixed and the mixture is incubated at 30°C for 15 minutes. The reaction is stopped by the addition of the appropriate chemical to the procedure chosen. In the case of the determination of hexose 6-phosphate formation by assaying the stable phosphorus, the reaction is terminated by the addition of 4 ml of 5% trichloroacetic acid (w/v) and 0.3–0.5 gm of Norit-A charcoal is stirred in, and mixture is filtered. Analysis is then made for stable phosphorus(109), according to Fiske and Subbarow(56) or Lowry and Lopez(115).

Definition of unit activity: One unit of enzyme is that amount which can catalyze the phosphorylation of 1 μmole of glucose at 30°C for 15 minutes under optimal conditions.

METHOD ACCORDING TO JOSHI AND JAGANNATHAN(96)

Reagents:

(1) Glucose, 0.15 M
(2) MgCl$_2$ × 6 H$_2$O, 0.2 M

(3) Tris-HCl buffer, 0.2 M, pH 7.6
(4) NADP, 0.0013 M
(5) Disodium ethylenediaminetetraacetate (EDTA), 0.0001 M
(6) ATP, sodium salt, 0.3 M, pH 7.6
(7) Glucose 6-phosphate dehydrogenase, 2 units/ml

Procedure: Mix 0.3 ml each of glucose, $MgCl_2$, tris, EDTA, NADP, and glucose 6-phosphate dehydrogenase and 1.0 ml of water in a cuvette with a 1-cm light path, add 0.1 ml of hexokinase and then 0.1 ml of ATP. The rate of change in optical density at 340 mμ is noted and should be between 0.005 and 0.020 per minute. This rate is measured from the second to the tenth minute after adding ATP. The controls contain no ATP and no hexokinase.

If crude hexokinase has to be diluted, a 0.1 M phosphate buffer, pH 7.6, is recommended.

Definition of unit activity: One unit is defined as that amount of enzyme which catalyzes the formation of 1 μmole of glucose 6-phosphate—which corresponds to the reduction of 1 μmole of NADP per minute at 30°C.

YEAST HEXOKINASE ASSAY METHOD (117)

Reagents:

(1) 0.01 M NaOH containing 6.25 ml of 0.1 % phenol red per liter of solution
(2) 0.01 M HCl
(3) Solution A—20 ml of 0.045 M ATP and 3 ml of 0.05 M $MgCl_2$ are stored with thymol at 0° to 5°C
(4) Solution B—8 ml of 5 % glucose and 3 ml of 0.05 M Sørensen's buffer (pH 7.5) are mixed and made up to 25 ml with water. This solution is stored with thymol at 0° to 5°C
(5) Solution C—0.0025 % phenol red
Standard: 2.5 ml 0.1 M phosphate buffer (pH 7.5) and 0.5 ml 0.0025 % phenol red.

Reaction mixture: 0.5 ml of solution A, 0.5 ml of solution B, and 0.5 ml of solution C are mixed in 1.5 × 12 cm test tubes.

Procedure: Add 0.5 ml of an ice-cold aqueous hexokinase reaction to the reaction mixture, which had been cooled to 5°C beforehand. Titrate the mixture immediately with 0.01 M NaOH or HCl from a microburette to the color of the standard. Leave the adjusted mixture at 5°C for 30 minutes and retitrate with 0.01 M NaOH.

Definition of unit activity: One unit of hexokinase is defined as the amount of enzyme which catalyzes the formation of 1×10^{-8} acid equivalents per minute at 5°C and pH 7.5 in the standard reaction mixture.

Phosphofructokinase. Phosphofructokinase must be a most complex enzyme, both in terms of kinetics and in terms of physical structure since it is inhibited by ATP(106), by citrate(135, 136), and to a lesser degree by Mg^{2+}. On the other hand, phosphofructokinase is activated or reactivated by NH_4^+, K^+, P_i, ADP, 3'-AMP, 5'-AMP, and fructose 6-phosphate(135,136). There is strong evidence that each of these activators act at a different site on the enzyme molecule.

In considering possible structures that might give the kinetic properties of phosphofructokinase, it is important to have in mind the fact that citrate and ATP are synergistic in action, each lowering the inhibition constant of the other. Also, fructose 6-phosphate is antagonistic to both citrate and ATP since it raises the apparent inhibition constants for both.

Phosphofructokinase, belonging to the phosphohexokinases, was discovered by Harden and Young in 1914 and the reaction catalyzed was described in 1935(66):

$$\text{fructose 6-phosphate} + \text{ATP} \rightarrow \text{fructose 1,6-diphosphate} + \text{ADP}$$

Shortly after this reaction was known, two different kinds of phosphohexokinases were observed in yeasts and liver slices, which catalyze the reactions

$$\alpha\text{-glucose 1-phosphate} + \text{ATP} \rightarrow \text{D-glucose 1,6-diphosphate} + \text{ADP}$$

$$\text{fructose 1-phosphate} + \text{ATP} \rightarrow \text{fructose 1,6-diphosphate} + \text{ADP}$$

respectively. It was therefore decided to name the Harden and Young enzyme "6-phosphofructokinase."

Phosphofructokinase is a unique enzyme of the EMP pathway, whereas other enzymes of this pathway may be involved in the many other types of carbohydrate degradations as well, or they may be involved in the synthesis of carbohydrate from smaller fragments.

Hexose monophosphate can increase in considerable amounts under certain experimental conditions without any increase in the formation of lactic acid. This indicates that the reaction between fructose 6-phosphate and ATP

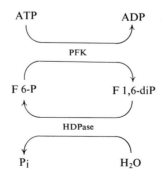

is a limiting factor in the oxidation of glucose. In cells containing both phospho-fructokinase and hexose diphosphatase such a control is needed to prevent loss of energy by a cyclic process. One possible means of control occurs since phosphofructokinase has its activity depressed by ATP when ATP concentration exceeds Mg^{2+} concentration. It is known that the molar concentration of Mg^{2+} exceeds that of ATP under normal conditions by several fold. However, much of this Mg^{2+} is probably protein-bound to nucleotides other than ATP. In muscle tissue, a low activity of phosphofructokinase has been observed, presumably because of high ATP concentrations. But in working muscle ATP concentration diminishes and phosphofructokinase becomes more active than in resting muscle.

Evidence indicates that phosphofructokinase may be the rate-limiting factor of the EMP pathway and that it may be inactivated by oxidation has led to proposals that the enzyme is the mediator of the Pasteur effect because:

(1) phosphofructokinase, like the overall EMP pathway, is inactivated by oxidation and reactivated by reduction.

(2) inhibition of phosphofructokinase does not depress oxidation of carbohydrate by the glucose 6-phosphate dehydrogenase pathways.

(3) glycolysis is limited by the amount of phosphofructokinase present and the rate can be enhanced by adding purified enzyme preparations.

(4) depression of lactic acid formation can be relieved by adding fructose diphosphate.

(5) depression of phosphofructokinase activity may also account for the depression of glucose utilization in cells, for hexokinase is inhibited by its product glucose 6-phosphate and inactivation of phosphofructokinase would prevent the removal of glucose 6-phosphate.

There is also other evidence which indicates that phosphofructokinase is endowed with many properties, which make it well adapted for regulation in the cell. Three such properties can be recognized: (a) kinetic properties of the enzyme (7), (b) reversible dissociation of the active enzyme to an inactive enzyme (120), and (c) aggregation of the enzyme in a monomer–polymer system in equilibrium. These three properties are dependent on adenylic nucleotides and the hexose phosphates which induce a primary change in the molecular configuration of the enzyme (119). After such structural change, the enzyme may become more susceptible to the formation of inactive sub-units (186).

A fourth phenomenon observed in yeast (173) is the (d) transformation of the enzyme from the active (a) form to a still active (b) form. Only the (b) form is susceptible to ATP inhibition.

In summary, phosphofructokinase is influenced by no less than eight metabolites, seven of which (viz., ATP, ADP, AMP, F 6-P, FDP, P_i, citrate) are all affected, or capable of being affected, by phosphofructokinase activity. Many of these in turn determine through equilibria the level of other metabolites. Consequently, cell composition may be determined to a considerable extent by the kinetic parameter of the particular brand of phosphofructokinase present in the cell.

Assay methods. Principle: The formation of fructose 1,6-diphosphate is followed by a spectrophotometric method involving the conversion of FDP to triose phosphate and the oxidation or reduction of the latter by pyridine nucleotide requiring enzymes. In tissue systems two methods are used whereby fructose 6-phosphate and ATP are the substrates, whereas in yeasts ATP is replaced by GTP.

ASSAY FOR TISSUES (120)

Reagents:

(1) Glycylglycine-KOH buffer, 0.5 M (pH 8.2)
(2) Tris-HCl buffer, 1.0 M (pH 8.0)
(3) Fructose 6-phosphate, 0.01 M (pH 8.2, adjusted with KOH)
(4) Glycylglycine-KOH buffer, 0.01 M (pH 7.5)
(5) MgCl$_2$, 0.1 M
(6) Bovine serum albumin, 0.1 %
(7) NADH + H$^+$, 1 mg/ml
(8) Cysteine-HCl, 0.1 M (pH 8.2), prepared freshly each day
(9) ATP, K salt, 0.01 M, pH 8.2
(10) α-Glycerol-1-phosphate dehydrogenase (GDH)/triose phosphate isomerase mixture, 10 mg/ml (specific activity 67.8 GDH units/mg protein)
(11) Fructose diphosphate aldolase suspension, 10 mg/ml
(12) Reduced glutathion, 0.1 M (pH 8.0, adjusted with KOH)

From these reagents, the following stock solutions are prepared:

(1) Solution A—2 ml of reagent 1, 0.2 ml of reagent 5, 2 ml of reagent 6, 1.6 ml of reagent 7, 2.8 ml of reagent 8, and 3.4 ml of distilled water. This solution may be used for one day if kept in ice.
(2) Solution B—0.2 ml of reagent 3, 1 ml of reagent 9, and 2 ml of distilled water. This solution can be stored frozen for one month.
(3) Solution C—1.88 ml of reagent 4, 0.02 ml of reagent 10, and 0.1 ml of reagent 11, which must be prepared daily.

The enzyme dilution fluid consists of 10 ml of reagent 12, 10 ml of reagent 6, 1 ml of reagent 2, and makes up to 100 ml. This solution should be made up at least once a week.

Procedure: Add to a 1-cm cuvette 0.6 ml of solution A, 0.16 ml of solution B, 0.05 ml of solution C, 0.29 ml of distilled water, and appropriate enzyme diluted in 0.2 ml enzyme dilution fluid. After mixing the content, the optical density is read at 340 mμ every minute. A change in optical density of 0.310 in a 5-minute period corresponds to an enzyme activity of 0.005 unit.

Definition of unit activity: A unit of phosphofructokinase is the amount of enzyme that catalyzes the formation of 1 μmole of fructose 1,6-phosphate per minute.

ASSAY FOR YEAST(163). The assay mixture contains in 2.0 ml: 1 mmole of fructose 6-phosphate, 1 mmole of GTP, 5 mmoles of $MgCl_2$, 25 mmoles of K phosphate (pH 6.5), 5 mmoles of ethanethiol, 0.15 mmole of NADH + H$^+$, 0.2 unit/2 ml of fructose diphosphate aldolase, 1 unit/2 ml of glycerolphosphate dehydrogenase, and 3 units/2 ml of triose phosphate isomerase.

Add all these components to a 1-cm cuvette. The reaction is started with the addition of the phosphofructokinase and the decrease in optical density read at 340 mμ. The blank should not contain GTP.

A unit is the amount of enzyme that phosphorylates 1 μmole of fructose 6-phosphate per minute. For each mole of fructose 6-phosphate phosphorylated, two moles of NADH + H$^+$ are consumed.

Glucose 6-Phosphate Dehydrogenase. The enzymes glucose 6-phosphate dehydrogenase and 6-phosphogluconate dehydrogenase are associated with the initial steps of an oxidative pathway known as the HMP pathway. The enzyme glucose 6-phosphate dehydrogenase was discovered in 1933 by Warburg and Christian(174a) who found that yeast preparations were capable of carrying out the oxidation of glucose 6-phosphate to 6-phosphogluconate. They called this enzyme "Zwischenferment." The discovery of this enzyme is important historically, because it led directly to the discovery of the coenzyme NADP.

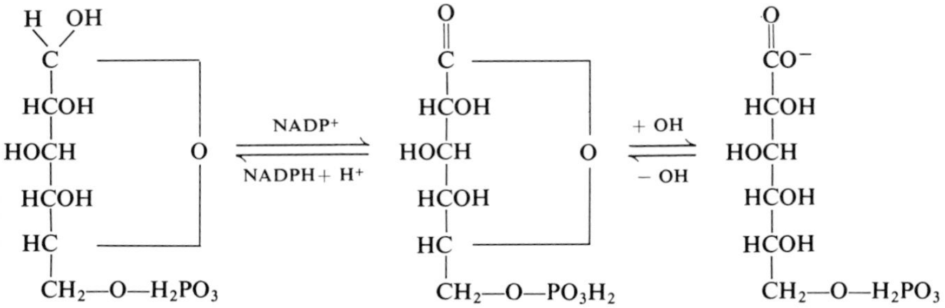

Glucose 6-phosphate dehydrogenase catalyzes the oxidation of glucose 6-phosphate to 6-phospho-δ-gluconolactone, which is spontaneously hydrolyzed to 6-phosphogluconate. This hydrolysis is accelerated by a specific delactonizing enzyme 6-phosphoglucone lactonase. The equilibrium for the over-all reaction is far to the right but the oxidative step is readily reversible in the presence of reduced NADP, 6-phospho-δ-gluconolactone and glucose 6-phosphate dehydrogenase.

Glucose 6-phosphate dehydrogenase is localized exclusively in the soluble fraction of the cell and has been detected in a wide variety of cells and tissues in the plant and animal kingdoms (yeast, *Escherichia coli, Bacillus subtilis, Bacillus megaterium, Pseudomonas fluorescens, Zymomonas mobilis, Leuconostoc mesenteroides*, red, blue-green, green algae, and higher plants). The enzyme of yeast, *Escherichia coli*, and mammalian tissues origin is specific for NADP. However, it has been reported in some cases, e.g., *Zymomonas mobilis* and *Leuconostoc mesenteroides*, that the enzyme lacks coenzyme specificity and is also active with NAD. This lack of specificity could also be owing to a transhydrogenase(32), which catalyzes the reaction

$$NADPH + H^+ + NAD^+ \rightarrow NADP^+ + NADH + H^+$$

as is the case in *Pseudomonas fluorescens*(183). The enzyme in *Aspergillus flavus-oryzae* is specific for both NADP and NAD. In *Bacterium anitratum*(86) glucose dehydrogenase catalyzes the reduction of glucose without the intervention of pyridine or flavin nucleotides. It is therefore assumed that a novel prosthetic group may be involved.

Glucose 6-phosphate dehydrogenase is inhibited by inorganic phosphate, high concentration of Mg^{2+}, and heavy metal ions such as Cu^{2+}, Zn^{2+}, and Hg^{2+}.

Assay method. The determination of glucose 6-phosphate (G 6-P) dehydrogenase activity is most conveniently done spectrophotometrically by measuring the rate of formation of NADPH + H$^+$ at 340 mμ. A great number of different assay methods are available, which work on the same principle, but vary more or less in their composition. From the methods used most frequently for yeast(101,104), *Escherichia coli*(152), *Bacillus subtilis*, and *Bacillus megaterium*(37), *Pseudomonas fluorescens*(183), *Zymomonas mobilis* (43), and *Leuconostoc mesenteroides*(45), the one by DeMoss(42) has been selected.

Reagents:

(1) Glucose 6-phosphate, 0.2 M
(2) Tris buffer, 0.1 M, pH 7.8
(3) NAD$^+$, 0.0027 M
(4) MgCl$_2$, 0.1 M
(5) The enzyme to be assayed is diluted either with tris buffer or water to an activity of 1 to 5 units/ml.

Procedure: To a spectrophotometric cuvette with a 1-cm light path add 1.5 ml of reagent 2, 0.2 ml of reagent 3, 0.1 ml of reagent 4, 0.1 ml of enzyme, and 1.05 ml of distilled water. Take readings at 340 mμ before and at 15 seconds intervals after mixing with 0.05 ml of reagent 1.

Definition of unit activity: A unit is defined as that amount of enzyme which effects a rate of change of optical density of 1.0 per minute during the 15- to 30-second interval.

A reinvestigation of the determination methods of glucose 6-phosphate dehydrogenase using cell-free extracts of *Zymomonas mobilis* gave the following new method as being optimal(161).

Reagents:

(1) Tris buffer, 0.5 M
(2) NADP$^+$, 0.001 M
(3) MgCl$_2$, 0.21 M
(4) Glucose 6-phosphate, 0.006 M

Buffer mixture: Mix 12.5 ml of reagent 1 with 9.0 ml of reagent 2, and 5.95 ml of reagent 3; adjust the pH to 8.7. Dilute this solution to 100 ml with glass-distilled water.

Procedure: To a 1-cm quartz cuvette containing 0.1 ml of cell-free extract add 2.4 ml of buffer mixture. Start the reaction by the addition of 0.5 ml of reagent 4 and follow the initial rate of reduction of NADP$^+$ at 340 mμ in a spectrophotometer for 5 minutes.

Definition of unit activity: One unit of enzyme activity is defined as that amount of enzyme which shows an optical change of 1.0 per minute at 30°C.

6-Phosphogluconate Dehydrogenase. The degradation of 6-phosphogluconate was first shown in yeast by Warburg and Christian in 1933(174a). They obtained evidence that the product was a C-5 compound, most likely to be a pentose phosphate, which we now know to be ribulose 5-phosphate. Recent investigations suggest that 3-keto-6-phosphogluconate may be an intermediate in the reaction, but this compound has not yet been isolated or even detected.

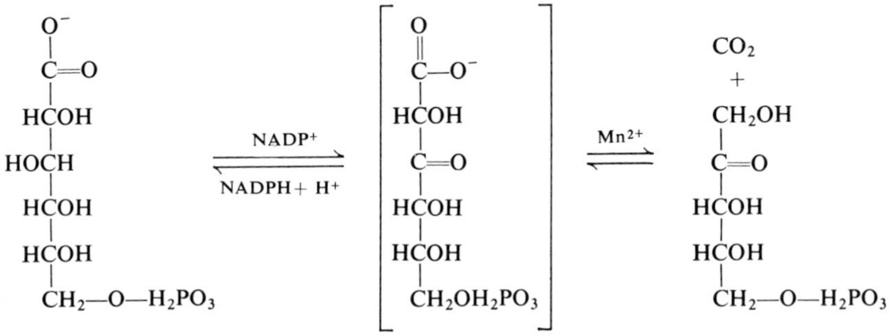

Although the equilibrium of 6-phosphogluconate oxidation favors oxidative decarboxylation, the reaction is reversible as demonstrated by the enzymatic fixation of $^{14}CO_2$ into the C-1 atom of 6-phosphogluconate and by the reductive carboxylation of ribulose 5-phosphate in the presence of NADPH $+$ H$^+$ and CO_2.

Although the majority of workers report 6-phosphogluconate dehydrogenase to be exclusively in the soluble fraction of the cell, there is evidence that the enzyme is associated with a particulate fraction in *Pseudomonas fluorescens*(182). 6-Phosphogluconate dehydrogenase is similar in its distribution in the animal and plant kingdom to glucose 6-phosphate dehydrogenase.

The mammalian and *Escherichia coli* enzymes are specific for NADP, but the enzyme obtained from *Leuconostoc mesenteroides* reduces NAD at 25 times the rate of NADP. As seen with glucose 6-phosphate dehydrogenase, *Aspergillus flavus-oryzae* contains two 6-phosphogluconate dehydrogenases which are specific for either NAD or NADP. The inhibition pattern of 6-phosphogluconate dehydrogenase is also very similar to glucose 6-phosphate dehydrogenase, since Cu^{2+}, Zn^{2+}, and Hg^{2+} inhibit enzyme activity.

Assay Method. The method of determination of 6-phosphogluconate dehydrogenase is based on the spectrophotometric measurements of NADPH $+$ H$^+$ at 340 mμ(140).
Reagents:

(1) Glycylglycine buffer, 0.05 M, pH 7.6
(2) NADP$^+$, 0.01 M
(3) MgCl$_2$, 0.1 M
(4) D-Gluconate 6-phosphate, Na salt, 0.15 M

Procedure: Add to a spectrophotometric cuvette with a 1-cm light path 0.26 ml of distilled water, 0.5 ml of reagent 1, 0.2 ml of reagent 3, 30 μl of reagent 2, 10 μl of reagent 4, and a quantity of enzyme to produce an optical density change of 0.01 to 0.025 per minute at 340 mμ.

Definition of unit activity: A unit of enzyme activity is defined as that quantity which would result in an optical density change of 1.0 per minute.

Investigations into the determination of 6-phosphogluconate dehydrogenase, which included studies on the optimal conditions in regard to pH, NADP$^+$, MgCl$_2$ and substrate concentration, in bacterial cell-free extracts of *Escherichia coli*(160) led to the following assay method.
Reagents:

(1) Glycylglycine, 0.5 M
(2) NADP$^+$, 0.001 M
(3) MgCl$_2'$, 0.21 M
(4) 6-Phosphogluconate, 0.003 M

Buffer mixture: Mix 13 ml of reagent 1 with 6.25 ml of reagent 2, and 5.95 ml of reagent 3; adjust the pH to 9.5 and dilute with distilled water to 100 ml.

Procedure: To a 1-cm quartz cuvette containing 0.1 ml of cell-free extract add 2.4 ml of buffer mixture. Start the reaction by the addition of 0.5 ml of reagent 4 and follow the initial rate of $NADP^+$ reduction at 340 mμ in a spectrophotometer for 5 minutes.

The final reaction mixture contains therefore glycylglycine buffer, pH 9.5, 0.052 M; $NADP^+$ 0.00005 M; $MgCl_2$ 0.01 M, and 6-phosphogluconate, 0.0005 M.

One unit of enzyme activity is defined as that quantity which would result in an optical density change of 1.0 per minute at 30°C.

TABLE 4.3

DISTRIBUTION OF 6-PHOSPHOGLUCONATE SPLITTING SYSTEM AND 2-KETO-3-DEOXY-PHOSPHOGLUCONATE ALDOLASE IN BACTERIA[a]

| | Pyruvate per mg protein/hr | |
Organism	6-PG (μmole)	KDPG (μmole)
Pseudomonas fluorescens A-3.12	3.3	6.6
Pseudomonas aeruginosa ATCC 9027	2.5	6.1
Pseudomonas fragi UIDS 215	2.5	0.3
Pseudomonas putrefaciens UI 206	0	0.1
Acetobacter suboxydans NRRL 6-72	1.9	6.6
Escherichia coli ATCC 9739	1.0	6.6
Proteus vulgaris WDB 47	0	0.2

[a] Data obtained from Kovachevich and Wood(103).

2-Keto-3-Deoxy-6-Phosphogluconate Aldolase. Entner and Doudoroff(55) reported that *Pseudomonas saccharophila* metabolizes 6-phosphogluconate to pyruvate and triose phosphate in a two step reaction

$$6\text{-PG} \rightarrow 2\text{-KDPG (enol form)} + H_2O$$

$$2\text{-KDPG} \rightarrow \text{pyruvate} + \text{D-glyceraldehyde 3-P}$$

These reaction steps have been further separated by Kovachevich and Wood (103). Later Meloche and Wood(127) solved the mechanism of the first step, which was found to be catalyzed by a different enzyme, 6-phosphogluconate dehydratase (E.C. 4.2.1.12). The separation of the reaction forming KDPG and the isolation, characterization, and quantitative conversion of KDPG to pyruvate and glyceraldehyde 3-phosphate brought the evidence for the mechanism postulated by Entner and Doudoroff(55). Not many organisms are known to possess this enzyme(39) and Table 4.3 gives some indications of the distribution of this enzyme among bacteria.

Apart from the cleavage reaction, 2-KDPG aldolase catalyzes also the enolization of pyruvate(127). It is therefore assumed that KDPG aldolase

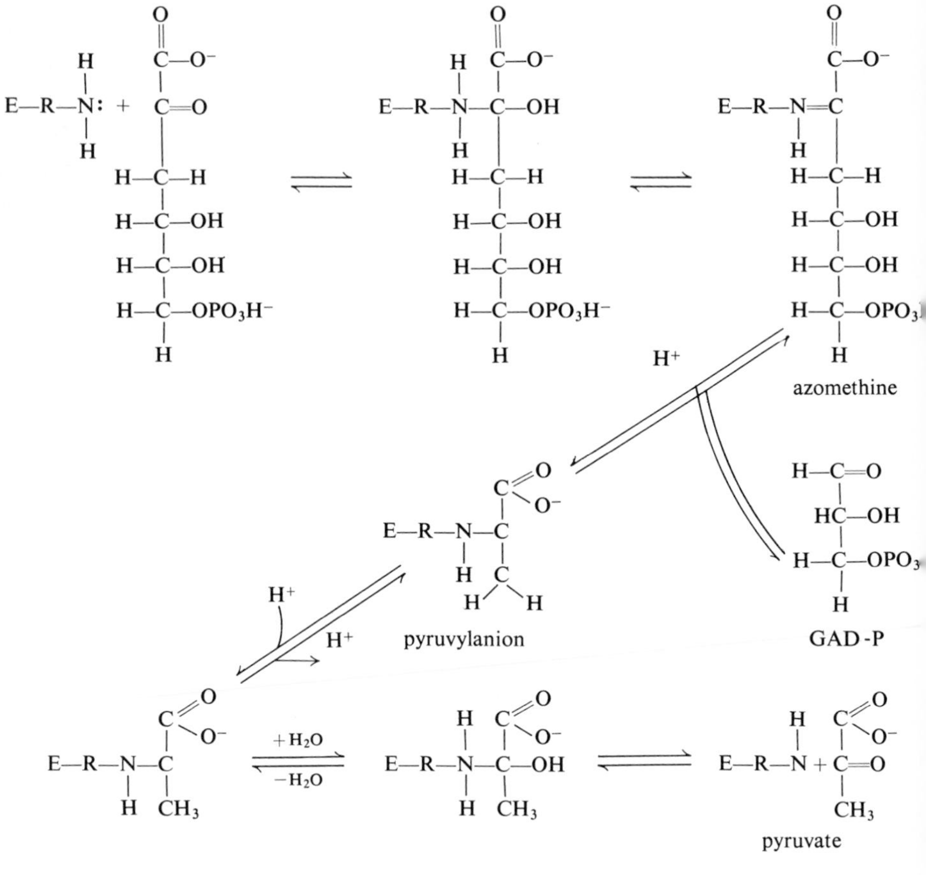

$$
\begin{array}{ccc}
& \text{O} & \\
& \| & \\
\text{H} & \text{C—O}^- & \\
| & | & \\
\text{E—R—N: +} & \text{C=O} & \\
| & & \\
\text{H} & \text{H—C—H} & \\
& | & \\
& \text{H—C—OH} & \rightleftharpoons \\
& | & \\
& \text{H—C—OH} & \\
& | & \\
& \text{H—C—OPO}_3\text{H}^- & \\
& | & \\
& \text{H} & \\
\end{array}
$$

$$
\begin{array}{c}
\text{O} \\
\| \\
\text{H   C—O}^- \\
|\ \ \ | \\
\text{E—R—N—C—OH} \\
|\ \ \ | \\
\text{H   H—C—H} \\
|\ \ \ \ \ | \\
\text{H—C—OH} \\
| \\
\text{H—C—OH} \\
| \\
\text{H—C—OPO}_3\text{H}^- \\
| \\
\text{H} \qquad \text{H}^+ \\
\end{array}
\rightleftharpoons
\begin{array}{c}
\text{O} \\
\| \\
\text{C—O}^- \\
| \\
\text{E—R—N=C} \\
|\ \ \ \ \ | \\
\text{H   H—C—H} \\
| \\
\text{H—C—OH} \\
| \\
\text{H—C—OH} \\
| \\
\text{H—C—OPO}_3\text{J} \\
| \\
\text{H} \\
\text{azomethine}
\end{array}
$$

$$
\begin{array}{c}
\text{C}{\Large{<}}^{\text{O}}_{\text{O}^-} \\
| \\
\text{E—R—N—C} \\
|\ \ \ | \\
\text{H   C} \\
\quad \text{H} \diagup\diagdown \text{H} \\
\text{pyruvylanion}
\end{array}
$$

$$
\begin{array}{c}
\text{H—C=O} \\
| \\
\text{HC—OH} \\
| \\
\text{H—C—OPO}_3 \\
| \\
\text{H} \\
\text{GAD-P}
\end{array}
$$

$$
\begin{array}{c}
\text{C}{\Large{<}}^{\text{O}}_{\text{O}^-} \\
|\ \ \ | \\
\text{E—R—N—C} \\
|\ \ \ | \\
\text{H   CH}_3 \\
\end{array}
\underset{-\text{H}_2\text{O}}{\overset{+\text{H}_2\text{O}}{\rightleftharpoons}}
\begin{array}{c}
\text{H   C}{\Large{<}}^{\text{O}}_{\text{O}^-} \\
|\ \ \ | \\
\text{E—R—N—C—OH} \\
|\ \ \ | \\
\text{H   CH}_3 \\
\end{array}
\rightleftharpoons
\begin{array}{c}
\text{H   C}{\Large{<}}^{\text{O}}_{\text{O}^-} \\
|\ \ \ | \\
\text{E—R—N + C=O} \\
| \\
\text{CH}_3 \\
\text{pyruvate}
\end{array}
$$

FIG. 4.3. Proposed mechanism of α-keto-3-deoxy-6-phosphogluconic acid aldolase [Meloche and Wood(127), reprinted with the permission of the Journal of Biological Chemistry].

binds pyruvate by formation of a Schiff's base (azomethine)(81) between the ε-amino group of lysine and the carbonyl carbon of the substrate (see Fig. 4.3). The attack on the substrates therefore is initiated by the electron pair of an amino nitrogen forming a KDPG-lysine azomethine, which is rearranged with the elimination of glyceraldehyde 3-phosphate, and yields a pyruvyl anion. The pyruvyl anion can then either be attacked by a proton or by a tautomeric form of glyceraldehyde 3-phosphate, yielding pyruvate in the former and KDPG in the latter case. The over-all system is completely reversible. *Acetobacter melanogenum* and *Azotobacter vinelandii* also show KDPG aldolase activity as well as 6-phosphogluconate dehydrase; KDPG aldolase was not detected in *Leuconostoc mesenteroides 8081*, *Corynebacterium creatinovorans 7562*, *Microbacterium lacticum 8081*, *Lactobacillus arabinosus 8014*, and brewer's yeast.

Assay Method. The activity of 2-keto-3-deoxy-6-phosphogluconate aldolase can be measured either by a colorimetric or by a spectrophotometric method.

COLORIMETRIC METHOD (103). The enzyme is determined in the presence of an excess of 6-phosphogluconate dehydrase by the rate of pyruvate production from 6-phosphogluconate, which is linear and dependent upon the amount 2-keto-3-deoxy-6-phosphogluconate aldolase present.

Procedure: Mix in a 3-ml cuvette the following reaction mixture—200 μmoles of tris buffer, pH 7.65; 3 μmoles of glutathion; 6 μmoles of $FeSO_4$; and 0.7 unit 6-phosphogluconate dehydrase together with the enzyme to be assayed. After 10 minutes equilibration at 37°C and 10 minutes incubation with 6-phosphogluconate, the reaction is stopped by adding 2,4-dinitrophenylhydrazine reagent of Friedeman and Haugen (63).

SPECTROPHOTOMETRIC METHOD (128). 2-Keto-3-deoxy-6-phosphogluconate aldolase is assayed spectrophotometrically at 340 mμ. The enzyme produces pyruvate and GAP. The pyruvate is then reduced by NADH + H$^+$ in the presence of lactic dehydrogenase. The rate of oxidation of NADH + H$^+$ is proportional to enzyme concentration.

Reagents:

(1) Assay solution containing 4 mg of NADH + H$^+$-sodium salt; 0.25 ml of 1.0 M imidazole, pH 8; 0.05 ml of a commercial suspension of crystalline muscle lactic dehydrogenase and water to make up to 5.0 ml volume.

(2) Sodium or potassium salt of KDPG, 0.05 M, pH 6.0

Procedure: Pipet into a microcuvette 0.05 ml of reagent 1, 0.015 ml of reagent 2, and 0.085 ml of water. Upon addition of the enzyme to be assayed, the absorbancy is measured.

Definition of unit activity: One unit of KDPG aldolase is defined as an absorbance change of 1.0 per minute. This is equivalent to the cleavage of 0.0241 μmole of KDPG per minute.

Phosphoketolase. The reaction of this enzyme is the simplest of a series known as phosphoroclastic cleavages (88, 89, 150). When *Lactobacillus plantarum* was grown in the presence of xylose, cells contained an enzyme which cleaved xylulose 5-phosphate phosphorolytically to glyceraldehyde 3-phosphate and acetyl phosphate. The action of this enzyme phosphoketolase is dependent on TPP and Mg^{2+} and is stimulated by SH compounds. Since acetyl phosphate is the product, the reaction resembles the phosphoroclastic split with pyruvate; since xylulose 5-phosphate is the substrate and glyceraldehyde 3-phosphate is a product, the reaction also resembles a transketolase reaction. This reaction described for *Lactobacillus plantarum* was found to be identical to *Leuconostoc mesenteroides*(87). In these organisms the usual pathways, i.e., EMP, HMP, and ED are absent(87). The enzyme phosphoketolase is produced by *Lactobacillus plantarum* when grown in a xylose-containing medium (induced enzyme) or the enzyme is constitutive as in *Leuconostoc mesenteroides* and *Acetobacter xylinum*(150).

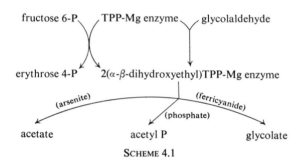

SCHEME 4.1

In essence the reaction is none other than a substrate level phosphorylation —one carbon of the substrate becoming "more" oxidized, while the other carbon of the substrate becomes "more" reduced. The conservation of energy is at the carbon which becomes more oxidized.

Another reaction catalyzed by phosphoketolase is that given in Scheme 4.1. The first step of this reaction is the formation of 2-(α,β-dihydroxyethyl) TPP-Mg^{2+} enzyme intermediate(92). This reaction is followed by an active interaction of the glycolaldehyde enzyme with arsenate that yields acetate, or with phosphate that yields acetyl phosphate or with ferricyanide that yields glycolate. Other details of this mechanism can be obtained from articles by Breslow(18) and Breslow and McNelis(19).

It was mentioned earlier that *Acetobacter xylinum* has a functional phosphoketolase, which is, however, less apparent. It is thought that a cyclic process is involved, which can be called the phosphoketolase shunt and summarized as shown in Scheme 4.2. The formulation of this cycle represents a short circuit pathway for the production of acetate in *Acetobacter xylinum*. The function may be important since this organism lacks phosphofructokinase. The energy yield of the short circuit in terms of ATP is 3 moles per mole of fructose 6-phosphate or 2 moles of ATP per mole of glucose; a yield identical with that of the EMP system and the cycle is considerably simpler. The energy yield is low, however, compared to that obtained by oxidation of acetate in the tricarboxylic acid cycle. The phosphoketolase shunt therefore probably functions as a short circuit to acetate rather than an important contributor to the energy budget of this microorganism.

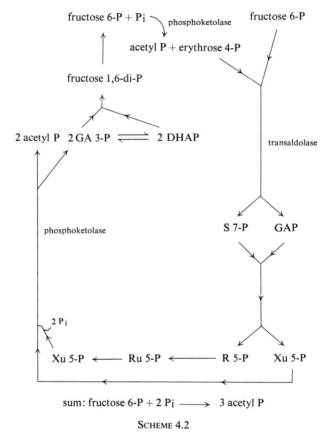

SCHEME 4.2

Assay method for pentose-phosphoketolase. This phosphoketolase can be estimated in two ways:

(1) The formation of glyceraldehyde 3-phosphate is measured by the oxidation of NADH + H$^+$ in the presence of triose phosphate isomerase and glycerophosphate dehydrogenase.
(2) The formation of acetyl phosphate is measured as hydroxamic acid.

METHOD (1)(74).

Reagents:

(1) Potassium phosphate, 0.1 M, pH 6.0
(2) Glutathione, 0.3 M, pH 6.0

(3) Triethanolamine, $1M$, pH 7.5
(4) Xylulose 5-phosphate, 20 mmoles
(5) $MgCl_2$, 0.1 M
(6) Thiamine pyrophosphate, 0.03 M
(7) $NADH + H^+$, 0.001 M
(8) Triose phosphate isomerase/glycerophosphate dehydrogenase mixture (Boehringer) diluted with distilled water to 0.2 mg/ml
(9) Fructose diphosphate aldolase (Boehringer) diluted with distilled water to 1 mg/ml

Procedure: Mix in a final volume of 0.3 ml: 0.1 ml of reagent 1; 0.1 ml of reagent 4; 0.01 ml of reagent 2; 0.01 ml of reagent 5; 0.01 ml of reagent 6; 0.01 ml of reagent 8; 0.01 ml of reagent 9; and 0.01–0.05 ml of dilute enzyme (approximately 200 μg/ml). After incubation for 15 minutes at 37°C, the mixture is placed in a boiling water bath for 1 minute to terminate the reaction. After centrifugation, 0.05–0.15 ml of the supernatant is assayed for the presence of fructose 1,6-diphosphate by addition to the following reagents in a quartz cuvette of 1-cm light path in a final volume of 1ml—0.05 ml of reagent 3 and 0.01 ml of reagent 7. On addition of 0.01 ml of reagent 8 and 0.01 ml of reagent 9 the change in optical density at 340 mμ is followed until no further change occurs.

METHOD (2)

Reagents:

(1) Succinate, 0.2 M, pH 6.2
(2) Potassium phosphate, 0.5 M, pH 6.1
(3) Sodium acetate buffer, 0.1 M, pH 5.4
(4) NH_2OH-HCl, 28%, brought to pH 6.4 with an equal volume of 15% NaOH
(5) Thioglycerol, 0.6 M
(6) $MgCl_2$, 0.1 M
(7) Thiamine pyrophosphate, 0.05 M
(8) Xylulose 5-phosphate, 20 mmoles
(9) HCl, 6 N
(10) Trichloroacetic acid, 28% (w/v)
(11) $FeCl_3$, 20% in 0.1 N HCl

Procedure: Pipet 0.05 ml of reagent 1; 0.05 ml of reagent 2; 0.01 ml of reagent 5; 0.01 ml of reagent 6; 0.02 ml of reagent 7; 0.1 ml of reagent 8; and 0.01–0.1 ml of phosphoketolase into a final volume of 0.5 ml. Incubate at 37°C for 15 minutes, remove an aliquot of 0.2 ml and add to this aliquot 0.3 ml of reagent 4; 0.3 ml of reagent 3; and 0.1 ml of distilled water. Keep this mixture at 23°C for 10 minutes. Add after this period 0.1 ml of reagent 9;

0.1 ml of reagent 10; and 0.1 ml of reagent 11. After 5 minutes the reading is taken at 540 mμ with succinic anhydride as a standard.

Definition of unit activity: A unit of enzyme is defined as the amount of enzyme which catalyzes the formation of 1 μmole of acetyl phosphate per minute.

Assay method for hexose phosphoketolase (fructose 6-phosphate phosphoketolase). The determination of hexose phosphoketolase is based on the formation of acetyl phosphate from fructose 6-phosphate(46,150).

Procedure: The reaction mixture contains per 0.75 ml—45 μmoles of histidine buffer, pH 6.0; 18 μmoles of potassium phosphate buffer, pH 6.0; 0.25 μmoles of thiamine pyrophosphate; 15 μmoles of fructose 6-phosphate. After addition of the enzyme to be assayed, the incubation was carried out at 37°C for 30 minutes and the reaction terminated by the addition of 0.75 ml of 2 *M* hydroxylamine (pH 5.4). The substrate was added to the controls after addition of hydroxylamine. The determination of the hydroxamic acid of acetyl phosphate is done according to Lipmann and Tuttle(112).

Definition of unit activity: A unit of enzyme activity is defined as the amount of enzyme that catalyzes the formation of 1 μmole of acetyl phosphate per minute.

Fructose Diphosphate Aldolase. In discovering "zymohexase," an enzyme of wide distribution which catalyzed the cleavage of one mole of fructose 1,6-diphosphate to two moles of triphosphate, Meyerhof and Lohmann in 1934 (129a) proposed the reaction

fructose 1,6-diphosphate → 2 dihydroxyacetone phosphate

and thus confirmed, experimentally, a view expressed by Embden in 1913(66). The term "zymohexase" has been used to connote the combined activity of two independent catalysts, fructose diphosphate aldolase and triose phosphate isomerase(129) although the name has been used to refer to aldolase free of isomerase(90).

Warburg and Christian(175), who first reported the purification and crystallization of the aldolase from rat muscle, brought the first evidence that there exist differences between the mammalian and the yeast aldolases. Investigations into the nature of bacterial aldolases indicated that these enzymes were inhibited by chelating agents (e.g., EDTA) and that this inhibition could be overcome with metal ions(9,10,69,162,179). The accumulation of these and other differences led Richards and Rutter(142) to consider aldolase to be the prototype of metal-ion-independent (class I) enzymes while yeast aldolase was considered the prototype of metal-ion-dependent (class II) aldolases (Table 4.4). Differences between the class I and class II aldolases were considered to be owing either to the existence of dissimilarities in the over-all protein molecule with the active site in each case remaining equivalent or to the existence of different active sites. It was also found that yeast aldolase had only half the molecular weight of the muscle aldolase.

A concise idea of the active site of aldolase has been possible as a result of the discovery that a stable, inert dihydroxyacetone phosphate aldolase compound could be formed by treating rabbit muscle or *Candida utilis*

$$
\begin{array}{c}
\text{CH}_2\text{OH} \\
| \\
\text{C}=\text{O} \\
| \\
\text{CH}_2-\text{O}-\textcircled{P}
\end{array}
\quad + \quad
\begin{array}{c}
\text{R}_1 \\
| \\
\text{O}=\text{C} \\
| \\
\text{H}_2\text{N}-(\text{CH}_2)_4-\text{CH} \\
| \\
\text{NH} \\
| \\
\text{R}_2
\end{array}
\quad \rightleftharpoons \quad
\left[
\begin{array}{cc}
\text{CH}_2\text{OH} & \text{C}=\text{O} \\
| & | \\
\text{C}=\text{N}-(\text{CH}_2)_4-\text{CH} \\
| & | \\
\text{CH}_2-\text{O}-\textcircled{P} & \text{NH}
\end{array}
\right]
$$

dihydroxyacetonephosphate

$\downarrow$ NaBH$_4$ reduction

$$
\begin{array}{cc}
\text{CH}_2-\text{OH} & \text{O}=\text{C} \\
| & | \\
\text{HC}-\text{NH}-(\text{CH}_2)_4-\text{CH} \\
| & | \\
\text{CH}_2-\text{O}-\textcircled{P} & \text{NH}
\end{array}
$$

DHAP aldolase

aldolases with borohydride in the presence of dihydroxyacetone phosphate (79, 80). It was shown that the linkage of the substrate carbonyl group to the enzyme involved the formation of a Schiff base intermediate with the ε-amino group of lysine residue of the enzyme protein. Grazi *et al.* (79, 80) concluded that the lysine was located at the active site of the protein and that the Schiff base formation occurs during the enzyme-catalyzed aldol condensation and the transfer reactions.

Both yeast and muscle aldolase have been shown to proceed almost exclusively by an ordered reaction sequence

enzyme + FDP $\rightleftharpoons$ GAP + enzyme − DHAP (lacking a proton on α-carbon) $\rightleftharpoons$
enzyme + DHAP (146)

Details of this reaction sequence have indicated the following steps

$$E + DH \rightleftharpoons E-DH \rightleftharpoons E-D^\ominus \rightleftharpoons E'D \rightleftharpoons E\!\!\stackrel{D^\ominus}{\underset{G}{\diagup}}$$

$$E\!\!\stackrel{D^\ominus}{\underset{G}{\diagdown}} \rightleftharpoons E-DG \rightleftharpoons E + DG$$

whereby DH indicates dihydroxyacetone phosphate; E, enzyme; E-DH, Schiff base intermediate; and E-D⁻, intermediate after loss of proton on α-carbon; E'D, product following isomerization step; G, glyceraldehyde 3-phosphate; and DG, condensation product, i.e., FDP.

Rose *et al.*(146) considered that the rate-limiting step involves the –C–H bond formation, i.e., the proton exchange reaction.

TABLE 4.4

SOME DIFFERENCES BETWEEN CLASS I AND CLASS II ALDOLASES

Source	Metal ion reversal of inhibition	Chelation inhibition	Optimal pH range
Class I			
Muscle	—	No	6.7–8.5
Liver	—	No	
bovine			7.2–9.2
rabbit			7.5–8.0
Green pea	—	No	5.9–8.8
Class II			
Anacystis nidulans	Fe^{2+}	Yes	8.0–8.5
Clostridium perfringens	Fe^{2+} Co^{2+}	Yes	7.5–7.9
Lactobacillus bifidus	Zn^{2+}; Fe^{2+} Co^{2+}	Yes	No data
Brucella suis	Fe^{2+}; Mn^{2+}	Yes	7.0–7.5
Aspergillus niger	Zn^{2+}; Fe^{2+} Co^{2+}; Mn^{2+}	Yes	7.6–7.9
Bacillus stearothermophilus	—	No	7.2–7.5

The enzyme is generally intracellular and found in the soluble fraction of the cytoplasm(144) although there have been a number of reports indicating the association of the enzyme with certain intracellular structures(20, 155). In microorganisms, the enzyme has been observed in the soluble fraction(9, 53, 77). At high concentrations of fructose 1,6-diphosphate a 6-fold augmentation of aldolase activity was observed(105), which may result from a specific interaction of ionized FDP and the enzyme molecule rather than a nonspecific anion stimulation.

Assay method. Principle: Several methods for the assay of FDP aldolase have been reported(9, 11, 12, 14, 17, 21, 33, 52, 147, 156). Most of these methods estimate the triose phosphates formed from FDP, in the presence of cyanide or hydrazine or by rate measurements (340 mμ) employing triose phosphate isomerase and the NAD-linked α-glycerophosphate dehydrogenase.

CHROMOGEN METHOD ACCORDING TO SIBLEY AND LEHNINGER(156) AND MODIFIED BY DOELLE AND MANDERSON(49,118) FOR BACTERIA.

Reagents:

(1) Tris buffer, 0.1 M, pH 8.3
(2) Hydrazine sulfate, 0.56 M, pH 8.3
(3) Fructose 1,6-diphosphate, 0.05 M, pH 8.3
(4) Trichloroacetic acid, 10% (w/v)
(5) NaOH, 0.75 N
(6) 2,4-Dinitrophenylhydrazine, 0.1%

Procedure: One milliliter of the enzyme sample to be assayed was added to a 15-ml test tube at 30°C, containing 1.0 ml of reagent 1, 0.25 ml of reagent 2, and 0.25 ml of reagent 3. Thirty minutes after the addition of the enzyme, the reaction was terminated by adding 2.0 ml of reagent 4. A 1.0-ml aliquot was used for the chromogen development assay. After the addition of 1.0 ml of reagent 5 the solution was allowed to stand for 10 minutes after which time 1.0 ml of reagent 6 was added. This solution was allowed to stand for a further 10 minutes at 37°C. After the addition of 7.0 ml of reagent 5 the color development took 10 minutes at room temperature and the optical density was read at 540 mμ. The amount of triose phosphate formed in the enzymatic reaction was proportional to the color developed in the reaction.

Definition of unit activity: The enzyme activity, as recommended by the IUB Enzyme Commission is expressed in international units (I.U.) 1 I.U. = 1 mole substrate split per milliliter enzyme per minute at 30°C. The milliunit activity of the enzyme can be obtained by the following calculation

$$\frac{270 \times v \times E_{540}}{t}$$

where t is the incubation time, v is the volume of the assay mixture, and E is the extinction value read at 540 mμ.

COUPLED ENZYMATIC ASSAY FOR YEAST(147)

Reagents:

(1) Buffer K-SH solution—Glycylglycine, 0.1 M, pH 7.5 (neutralized with NaOH), potassium acetate, 0.2 M, β-mercaptoethanol 0.05 M. This solution should only be used for 72 hours.
(2) FDP, sodium salt, 0.02 M, pH 7.5
(3) NADH + H$^+$, sodium salt, 0.002 M in 0.001 M NaOH stored at 0–4°C for a period not to exceed 2 weeks.
(4) α-Glycerophosphate dehydrogenase/triose phosphate isomerase (Boehringer) 10 mg/ml, diluted 1:5 in distilled water at 0°C.

Procedure: 0.5 ml of reagent 1, 0.1 ml of reagent 2, 0.1 ml of reagent 3, and 10 μl of reagent 4 are diluted to 1.0 ml with distilled water in a 1.0-ml cuvette with a 1.0-cm light path. Ten microliters of enzyme are added to start the reaction. Measurements are made at 340 mμ at 10–15 second intervals until a linear rate is obtained (3–5 minutes). It is assumed that the oxidation of 2 μmoles of NADH + H$^+$ (12.44 absorbance units) reflects the cleavage of 1 μmole of FDP under these conditions.

Definition of unit activity: A unit of aldolase activity is defined as that amount of enzyme which catalyzes the cleavage of 1 μmole of FDP per minute.

COUPLED ENZYMATIC ASSAY FOR *Clostridium Perfringens*(78). Unlike the yeasts and some fungal aldolases, the *Cl. perfringens* enzyme requires Fe^{2+} or Co^{2+} for optimal activity. It is therefore necessary to replace the buffer mixture only with a buffer Co^{2+}-K$^+$ cysteine solution, which contains tris-(hydroxylmethyl)amino methane, 0.1 M, pH 7.5 (with acetic acid), potassium acetate, 0.2 M, CoCl$_2$, 0.0014 M, L-cysteine-HCl, 0.0002 M. All other reagents are the same and also the procedure if the change in buffer solution has been made.

GLUCONATE METABOLISM

Not only glucose is used for catabolism of carbohydrates. The lack of the enzyme gluconokinase prevents a number of bacteria from utilizing glucose.

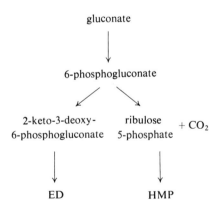

Gluconate can be attacked instead of being broken down via the ED or HMP pathway(54). In most cases the diversion from glucose to the gluconate metabolism is caused by the lack of either glucokinase, which phosphorylates glucose, or of phosphoglucoisomerase, which converts glucose 6-phosphate to fructose 6-phosphate. *Escherichia coli*(61) and *Salmonella typhimurium*(59) are able to (*1*) utilize gluconate as substrate and in the case of *E. coli* preferably via the ED pathway(187) and (*2*) utilize glucose via the HMP pathway.

FRUCTOSE METABOLISM

The utilization of fructose is known to occur particularly in *Alcaligenes*(51) and *Aerobacter*(83). Fructose can be phosphorylated to fructose 1-phosphate by a kinase (ATP: D-fructose 1-phosphotransferase, E.C. 2.7.1.3). An inducible

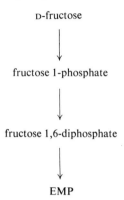

D-fructose

↓

fructose 1-phosphate

↓

fructose 1,6-diphosphate

↓

EMP

enzyme, which has been named D-fructose 1-phosphate kinase(83), phosphorylates fructose 1-phosphate to fructose 1,6-diphosphate and further utilization follows the EMP pathway.

MANNOSE METABOLISM

The catabolism of mannose in *Aerobacter aerogenes* follows a cyclic mechanism with connections into the EMP and HMP pathway(97) as shown in Scheme 4.3.

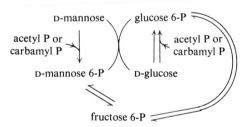

SCHEME 4.3. (Reprinted with permission of the American Society of Biological Chemists.)

D-Mannose is first phosphorylated with glucose 6-phosphate to yield mannose 6-phosphate and D-glucose by a phosphotransferase. This enzyme can also phosphorylate mannose with acetyl phosphate or carbamyl phosphate. There is no D-mannokinase present. Glucose 6-phosphate can now be regenerated by the isomerization of D-mannose 6-phosphate to fructose 6-phosphate, which is catalyzed by mannose phosphate isomerase (D-mannose 6-phosphate ketol isomerase, E.C. 5.3.1.8). Fructose 6-phosphate is now converted to glucose 6-phosphate by a second isomerase (D-glucose 6-phosphate ketol isomerase, E.C. 5.3.1.9). *Aerobacter aerogenes PRL-R3* can also regenerate glucose 6-phosphate by phosphorylating the formed glucose with a stereo-specific glucokinase. Fructose 6-phosphate is further metabolized via the EMP pathway.

The apparent epimerization of D-mannose to D-glucose may be explained by a cyclic process involving D-mannose 6-phosphate isomerase, D-glucose 6-phosphate isomerase and acyl phosphate: hexose phosphotransferase (97).

ALLOSE METABOLISM

The catabolism of glucose and allose follow independent paths until they merge and join the EMP pathway at the fructose 6-phosphate level (72).

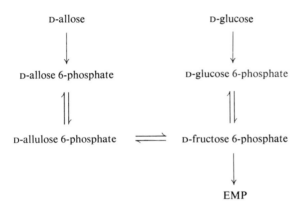

Since *Aerobacter aerogenes* has been shown to metabolize allose (2) under both aerobic and anaerobic conditions, most of this study has been conducted with this microorganism. D-Allose is phosphorylated in the first step by a specific kinase, D-allose 6-kinase, to D-allose 6-phosphate. The kinase has been purified and characterized (71). The second step is performed by an inducible isomerase, D-allose 6-phosphate ketol isomerase (126), and D-allulose 6-phosphate is formed. This inducible enzyme nonspecifically also isomerizes ribulose 5-phosphate to ribose 5-phosphate but does not act on other phosphorylated aldoses. The interconversion of D-allulose 6-phosphate to D-fructose 6-phosphate is thought to be catalyzed by a 3-epimerase. *Aerobacter aerogenes* is also able to metabolize glucose since it possesses the glucose phosphate isomerase (E.C. 5.3.1.9) (125) as well as a stereospecific D-gluco-kinase (E.C. 2.7.1.2) (98).

MANNITOL AND SORBITOL METABOLISM

Bacterial species can be divided into two groups with respect to their mode of catabolism of mannitol(165): (*a*) those which initiate its metabolism by a phosphorylation, and (*b*) those which initiate its metabolism by a dehydrogenation. In both cases the mannitol metabolism joins the EMP pathway at the fructose 6-phosphate level. The division into these two groups can be made

I	II
mannitol	mannitol
↓	↓
mannitol 1-phosphate	fructose
↓	↓
fructose 6-phosphate	fructose 6-phosphate
↓	↓
EMP	EMP

on the ability of the organisms to form an NAD-dependent mannitol 1-phosphate dehydrogenase (D-mannitol 1-phosphate:NAD oxidoreductase, E.C. 1.1.1.17). With this criterion *Aerobacter aerogenes*(113,180), *Bacillus subtilis* (93), *Diplococcus pneumoniae*(122), *Escherichia coli*(180,181), *Lactobacillus*

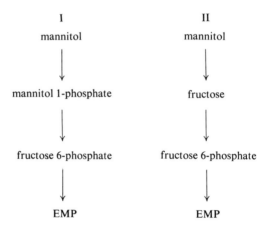

mannitol   mannitol 1-phosphate

plantarum(27,180), and *Staphylococcus aureus* (134) would follow scheme I, whereas *Acetobacter suboxydans*(6,138), *Azotobacter agilis*(121), *Cellvibrio polyoltrophicus*(151), and *Pseudomonas fluorescens*(153) possess a mannitol dehydrogenase and follow scheme II.

The first step in scheme I is the phosphorylation of mannitol by a mannitol-1-phosphotransferase which is phosphoenol-pyruvate dependent(165) and converts mannitol to mannitol 1-phosphate which can accumulate(8). The latter compound is now converted to the EMP pathway intermediate fructose 6-phosphate with the enzyme D-mannitol 1-phosphate dehydrogenase (E.C. 1.1.1.17) as catalyst, which is NAD-linked.

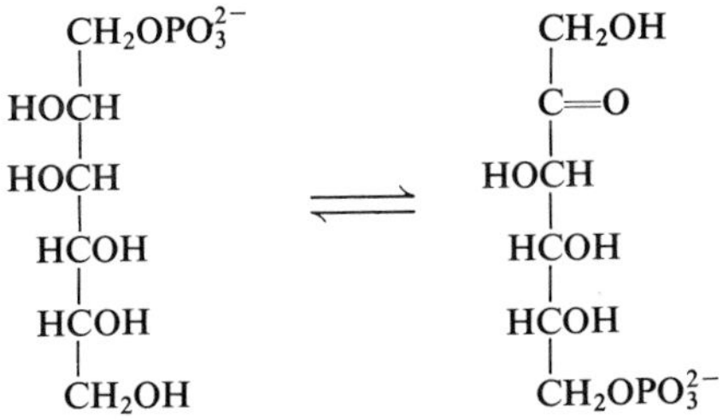

$$
\begin{array}{ccc}
CH_2OPO_3^{2-} & & CH_2OH \\
| & & | \\
HOCH & & C{=}O \\
| & & | \\
HOCH & \rightleftharpoons & HOCH \\
| & & | \\
HCOH & & HCOH \\
| & & | \\
HCOH & & HCOH \\
| & & | \\
CH_2OH & & CH_2OPO_3^{2-}
\end{array}
$$

mannitol 1-phosphate   fructose 6-phosphate

Those microorganisms which will metabolize D-mannitol to D-fructose at a nonphosphorylated level(6, 154) possess a NAD-linked mannitol dehydrogenase and carry out an oxidative dissimilation of mannitol(153). This enzyme has been reported to be NAD-linked. Whether or not it may be identical with the cytochrome-linked mannitol dehydrogenase (D-mannitol: cytochrome oxidoreductase, E.C. 1.1.2.2) is not known. The similarity is,

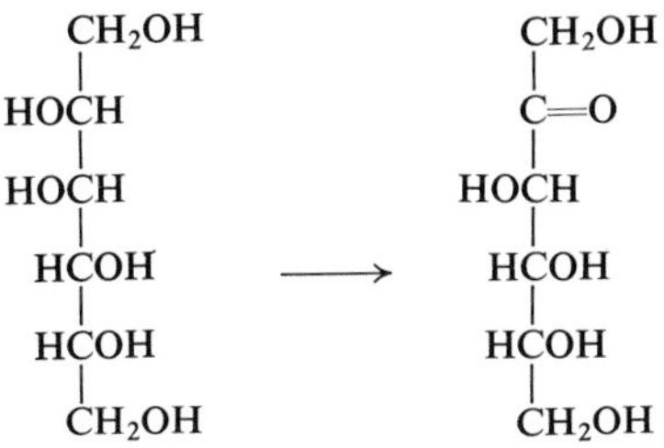

$$
\begin{array}{ccc}
CH_2OH & & CH_2OH \\
| & & | \\
HOCH & & C{=}O \\
| & & | \\
HOCH & & HOCH \\
| & \longrightarrow & | \\
HCOH & & HCOH \\
| & & | \\
HCOH & & HCOH \\
| & & | \\
CH_2OH & & CH_2OH
\end{array}
$$

D-mannitol   D-fructose

however, striking since the latter also oxidizes D-sorbitol as has been reported for the NAD-linked enzyme(153). Fructose can either be phosphorylated by fructose kinase (E.C. 2.7.1.3) and join the EMP pathway at the fructose 1,6-diphosphate level as described under fructose metabolism or be converted to glucose and gluconic acid(153, 166), which is characteristic for the *Pseudomonadaceae* and will be discussed in Chapter 9. The metabolism of sorbitol is almost identical to the one just described since only the arrangement on carbon-2 differentiates between mannitol and sorbitol. The only difference occurs in the phosphorylation of sorbitol with a sorbitol kinase to sorbitol 6-phosphate(113) and subsequently a NAD-linked sorbitol 6-phosphate dehydrogenase converts sorbitol 6-phosphate into fructose 6-phosphate. Both enzymes mannitol 1-phosphate dehydrogenase and sorbitol 6-phosphate dehydrogenase have been purified and found to be completely different enzymes(113). Sorbitol itelf, on the other hand, can induce the formation of mannitol 1-phosphate dehydrogenase in *Bacillus subtilis*(93) although sorbitol 6-phosphate is inactive as substrate.

PENTOSE AND PENTITOL METABOLISM

Aerobacter aerogenes grows very well on a variety of pentoses and pentitols which lead to an extensive elaboration of their metabolism. The overall scheme could be summarized as follows(132, 133):

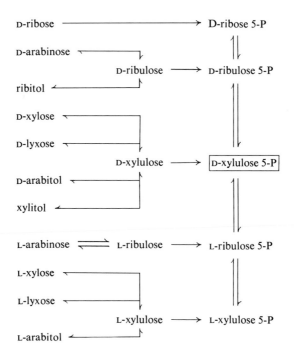

The reaction of D-ribose to D-ribose 5-phosphate and further to D-xylulose 5-phosphate has been described in detail under the phosphoketolase pathway and function in the same way in *Aerobacter aerogenes*.

The other straightforward reaction is the metabolism of L-arabinose(159), which first produces L-ribulose by an isomerase reaction (L-arabinose ketol isomerase, E.C. 5.3.1.4) which is then followed by a phosphorylation step. The acting enzyme in this reaction is L-ribulokinase(158) [ATP:L(or D)-ribulose

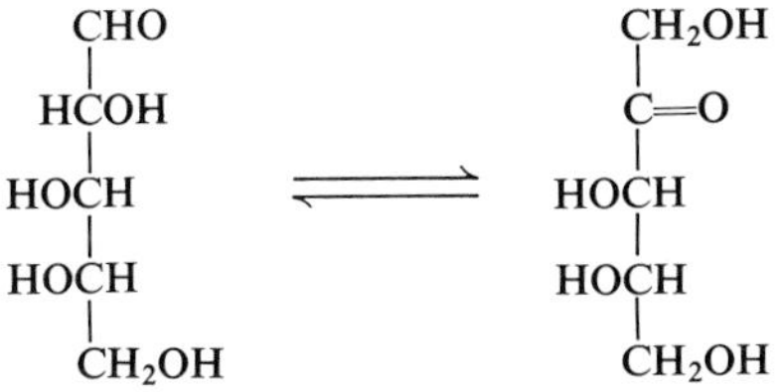

```
      CHO                         CH₂OH
       |                            |
      HCOH                         C=O
       |                            |
      HOCH        ⇌             HOCH
       |                            |
      HOCH                         HOCH
       |                            |
      CH₂OH                        CH₂OH
```

$$\text{CHO} \quad \text{CH}_2\text{OH}$$

L-arabinose   L-ribulose

5-phosphotransferase, E.C. 2.7.1.16] and the product formed L-ribulose 5-phosphate. The latter is now acted upon by a ribulose phosphate 4-epimerase

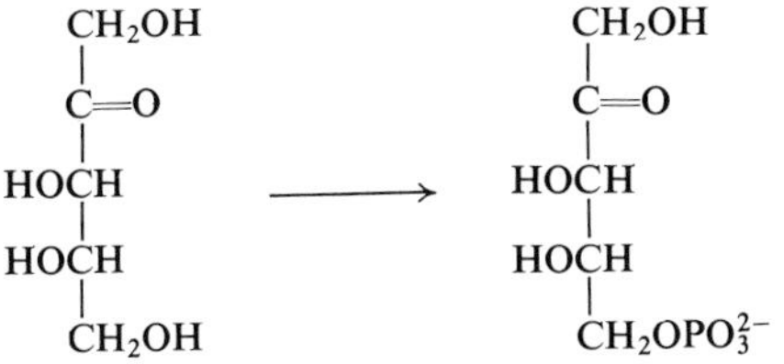

```
      CH₂OH                       CH₂OH
       |                            |
      C=O                          C=O
       |                            |
      HOCH        ⟶            HOCH
       |                            |
      HOCH                         HOCH
       |                            |
      CH₂OH                        CH₂OPO₃²⁻
```

L-ribulose   L-ribulose 5-phosphate

(L-ribulose 5-phosphate 4-epimerase, E.C. 5.1.3.4) which converts L-ribulose 5-phosphate to the key intermediate D-xylulose 5-phosphate.

```
      CH₂OH                       CH₂OH
       |                            |
      C=O                          C=O
       |                            |
      HOCH        ⇌            HOCH
       |                            |
      HOCH                         HCOH
       |                            |
      CH₂OPO₃²⁻                    CH₂OPO₃²⁻
```

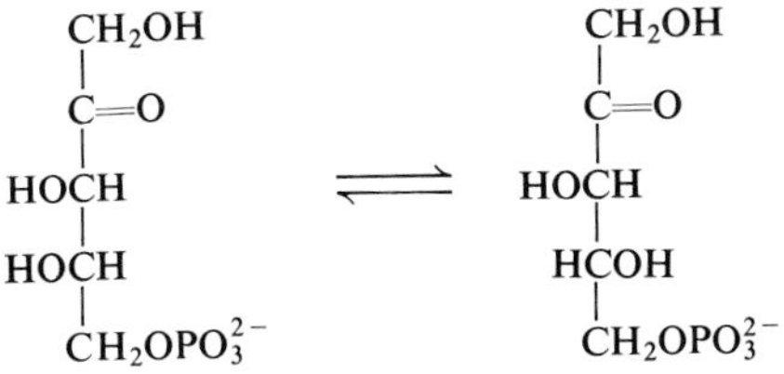

L-ribulose 5-phosphate   D-xylulose 5-phosphate

The metabolism of D-arabinose is very similar to that of L-arabinose, but since most of the enzymes are substrate and stereospecific, different enzymes are involved. D-Arabinose is attacked by an arabinose isomerase (D-arabinose ketol isomerase, E.C. 5.3.1.3), which converts D-arabinose to D-ribulose, which in turn is phosphorylated by a specific D-ribulokinase (ATP:D-ribulose 5-phosphotransferase, E.C. 2.7.1.47) to D-ribulose 5-phosphate. This specific D-ribulokinase has also been found in *Escherichia coli*(110) and appears to be different from the other ribulokinase (E.C. 2.7.1.16). The conversion of D-ribulose 5-phosphate to D-xylulose 5-phosphate is the same as that described for the D-ribose metabolism. The other two pentoses which undergo isomerizations are xylose and lyxose(4).

The conversion of D-xylose to D-xylulose is catalyzed by xylose isomerase (D-xylose ketol isomerase, E.C. 5.3.1.5), whereas D-lyxose is isomerized by

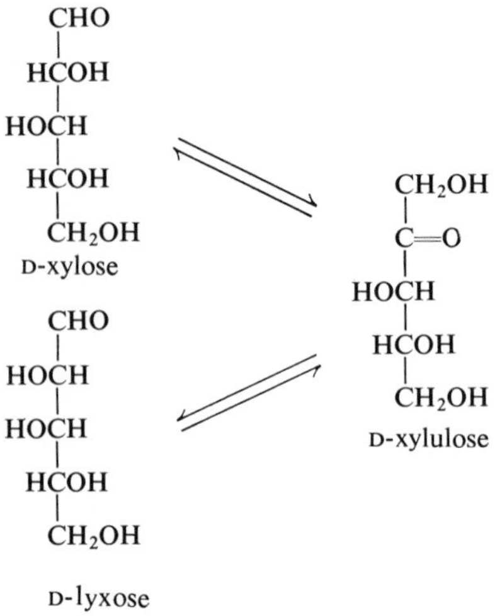

D-lyxose isomerase (D-lyxose ketol isomerase), which has been purified (3). The common product of both isomerization reactions, D-xylulose is subsequently phosphorylated by xylulokinase (ATP:D-xylulose 5-phosphotransferase, E.C. 2.7.1.17)(15). The pathways of the L-isomers of these two pentoses have

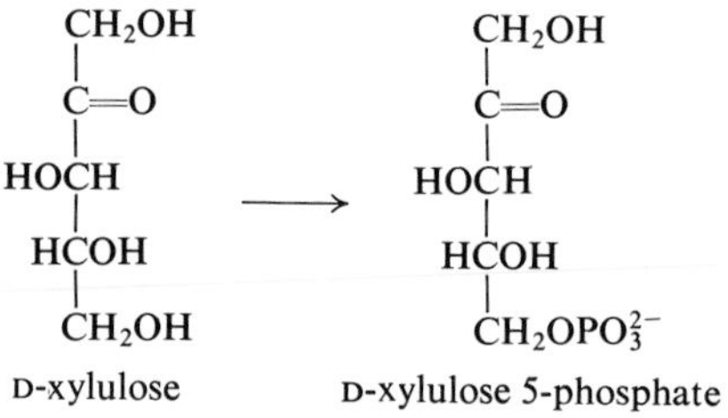

also been evaluated (4), but none of the isomerases is reported in the Enzyme Commission's Report. It appears that the main difference between the isomerases of the D- and L-isomers lies in the cofactor requirements. Whereas the D-isomerases require Mg^{2+}, the L-isomerases are reported to require Co^{2+} for their activity.

The isomerization of L-xylose and L-lyxose to L-xylulose is followed by a phosphorylation reaction, which requires ATP and Mg^{2+}, to L-xylulose 5-phosphate. The enzyme involved in this reaction is named "L-xylulokinase" (ATP:L-xylulose 5-phosphotransferase, E.C. 2.7.1)(5). The conversion of L-xylulose 5-phosphate to D-xylulose 5-phosphate includes two enzymatic steps involving a 3- and a 4-epimerase. The first step involves a ribulose phosphate 3-epimerase, which converts L-xylulose 5-phosphate to L-ribulose

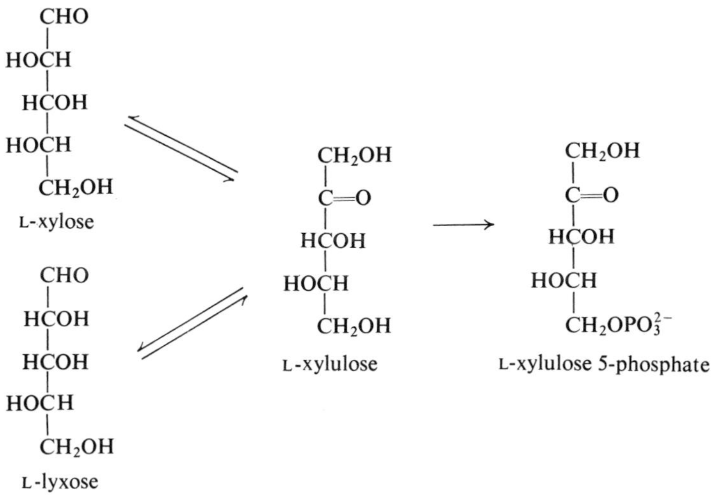

CHO
|
HOCH
|
HCOH
|
HOCH
|
CH$_2$OH
L-xylose

CHO
|
HCOH
|
HCOH
|
HOCH
|
CH$_2$OH
L-lyxose

CH$_2$OH
|
C=O
|
HCOH
|
HOCH
|
CH$_2$OH
L-xylulose

CH$_2$OH
|
C=O
|
HCOH
|
HOCH
|
CH$_2$OPO$_3^{2-}$
L-xylulose 5-phosphate

5-phosphate. Whether this enzyme is identical to E.C. 5.1.3.1 or not could not be clarified. The second stage with the formation of D-xylulose 5-phosphate is the action of ribulose phosphate 4-epimerase (E.C. 5.1.3.4).

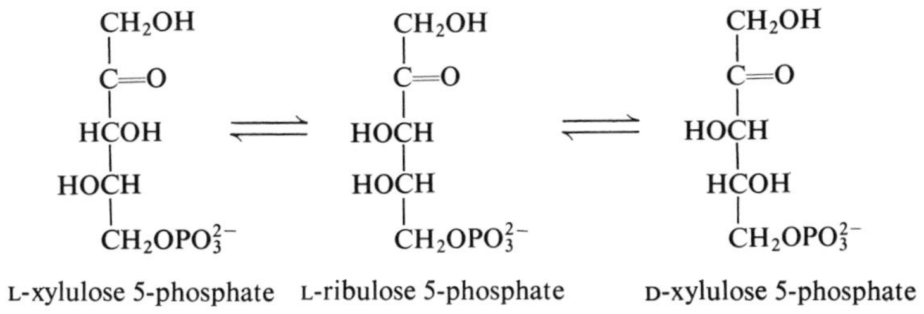

CH$_2$OH
|
C=O
|
HCOH
|
HOCH
|
CH$_2$OPO$_3^{2-}$
L-xylulose 5-phosphate

$\rightleftharpoons$

CH$_2$OH
|
C=O
|
HOCH
|
HOCH
|
CH$_2$OPO$_3^{2-}$
L-ribulose 5-phosphate

$\rightleftharpoons$

CH$_2$OH
|
C=O
|
HOCH
|
HCOH
|
CH$_2$OPO$_3^{2-}$
D-xylulose 5-phosphate

If the metabolism of pentoses involve mainly isomerases, the metabolism of pentitols requires NAD-linked dehydrogenases. Ribitol is acted upon by a NAD-specific ribitol dehydrogenase(94,184), which converts ribitol to D-ribulose.

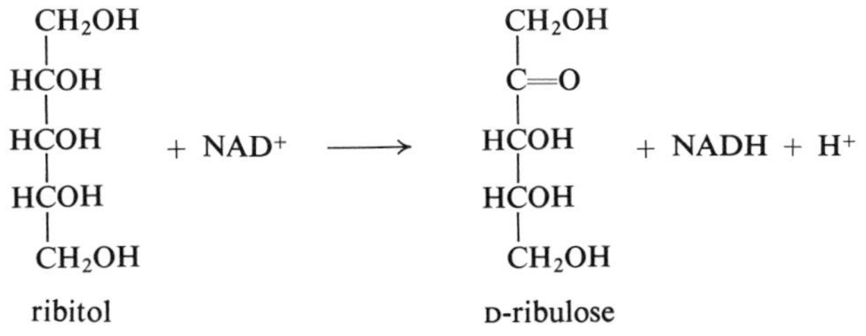

CH$_2$OH
|
HCOH
|
HCOH   + NAD$^+$ $\longrightarrow$
|
HCOH
|
CH$_2$OH
ribitol

CH$_2$OH
|
C=O
|
HCOH   + NADH + H$^+$
|
HCOH
|
CH$_2$OH
D-ribulose

This enzyme appears to be specific for the substrate(64), whereas D-arabitol dehydrogenase, which converts D-arabitol to D-xylulose, also acted upon D-mannitol to form D-fructose(111).

In the case of xylitol metabolism, only D-xylulose could be identified as reaction product of a NAD-dehydrogenase reaction(58) and never L-xylulose, as yet.

The NAD-dependent dehydrogenases of L- and D-arabitol oxidation(58, 184) have also been identified and the reaction products identified as L- and D-xylulose, respectively. The key intermediate D-xylulose 5-phosphate is now able to undergo transketolase and transaldolase reactions as described in the HMP pathway to produce fructose 6-phosphate. From here most of the bacteria, in particular *Aerobacter*, follow the Embden-Meyerhof-Parnas pathway for their further metabolism.

REFERENCES

1. Aiba, S., Humphrey, A. E., and Millis, N. F. (1965). "Biochemical Engineering," p. 42ff. Univ. of Tokyo Press, Tokyo, Japan.
2. Altermatt, H. A., Simpson, F. J., and Neish, A. C. (1955). The fermentation of D-allose and D-glucose by *Aerobacter aerogenes*. *Can. J. Microbiol.* **1**, 473.
3. Anderson, R. L., and Allison, D. P. (1965). Purification and characterization of D-lyxose isomerase. *J. Biol. Chem.* **240**, 2367.
4. Anderson, R. L., and Wood, W. A. (1962). Pathway of L-xylose and L-lyxose degradation in *Aerobacter aerogenes*. *J. Biol. Chem.* **237**, 296.
5. Anderson, R. L., and Wood, W. A. (1962). Purification and properties of L-xylulokinase. *J. Biol. Chem.* **237**, 1029.
6. Arcus, A. C., and Edson, N. L. (1956). Polyol dehydrogenases. 2. The polyol dehydrogenase of *Acetobacter suboxydans* and *Candida utilis*. *Biochem. J.* **64**, 385.
7. Atkinson, D. E., and Walton, G. M. (1965). Kinetics of regulatory enzymes. *Escherichia coli* phosphofructokinase. *J. Biol. Chem.* **240**, 757.
8. Baddiley, J., Buchanan, J. G., Carss, B., Mathies, A. P., and Sanderson, A. R. (1956). The isolation of cytidine diphosphate glycerol, cytidine diphosphate ribitol and mannitol-1-phosphate from *Lactobacillus arabinosus*. *Biochem. J.* **64**, 599.
9. Bard, R. C., and Gunsalus, I. C. (1950). Glucose metabolism of *Clostridium perfringens*. Existence of a metallo-aldolase. *J. Bacteriol.* **59**, 387.
10. Bastarracea, F., Anderson, D. G., and Goldman, D. S. (1961). Enzyme systems in mycobacteria. XI. Evidence for a functional glycolytic system. *J. Bacteriol.* **82**, 94.
11. Beck, W. S. (1955). The determination of triosephosphate and proposed modification in the aldolase method of Sibley and Lehninger. *J. Biol. Chem.* **212**, 847.
12. Beck, W. S. (1963). Assay of triosephosphates. *Methods Enzymol.* **3**, 201.
13. Bell, E. J., and Marus, A. (1966). Carbohydrate catabolism of *Mima polymorpha*. I. Supplemental energy from glucose added to a growth medium. *J. Bacteriol.* **91**, 2223.
14. Bergmeyer, H. U. (1963). Fructose-1,6-diphosphate aldolase (spectrophotometric assay). *In* "Methods of Enzymatic Analysis" (H. U. Bergmeyer, ed.), p. 728. Verlag Chemie, Weinheim.
15. Bhuyan, B. K., and Simpson, F. J. (1962). Some properties of the D-xylulokinase of *Aerobacter aerogenes*. *Can. J. Microbiol.* **8**, 737.

16. Blumenthal, H. J. (1961). *In* "Spore II" (H. O. Halvorson, ed.), pp. 120–126. Burgess, Minneapolis, Minnesota.

17. Boehringer, C. F. (1964). Aldolase. Colorimetric determinations. *In* "General Instructions," TC-O Art. No. 15961. Boehringer, Mannheim, Germany.

18. Breslow, R. (1959). Discussion part in "Aldol and Ketol condensation" by B. L. Horecker. *J. Cellular Comp. Physiol.* **54**, 100.

19. Breslow, R., and McNelis, E. (1960). On the mechanism of thiamine action. VI. 2-acetylthrazolium salts as "active acetate." *J. Am. Chem. Soc.* **82**, 2394.

20. Brumgraber, E., and Abood, G. (1960). Mitochondrial glycolysis of rat brain to its relationship to the remainder of cellular glycolysis. *J. Biol. Chem.* **235**, 1847.

21. Bruns, F. (1954). Bestimmung und Eigenschaften der Serum-aldolase. *Biochem. Z.* **325**, 156.

22. Buchanan, B. B., and Pine, L. (1963). Factors influencing the fermentation and growth of an atypical strain of *Actinomyces naeslundii*. *Sabouraudia* **3**, 26.

23. Buchanan, B. B., and Pine, L. (1967). Path of glucose breakdown and cell yields of a facultative anaerobe, *Actinomyces naeslundii*. *J. Gen. Microbiol.* **46**, 225.

24. Burma, D. P., and Horecker, B. L. (1958). Pentose fermentation by *Lactobacillus plantarum*. III. Ribulokinase. *J. Biol. Chem.* **231**, 1039.

25. Burma, D. P., and Horecker, B. L. (1958). Pentose fermentation by *Lactobacillus plantarum*. IV. L-Ribulose-5-phosphate-4-epimerase. *J. Biol. Chem.* **231**, 1053.

26. Campbell, J. J. R., and Norris, F. C. (1950). The intermediary metabolism of *Pseudomonas aeruginosa*. IV. The absence of an Embden-Meyerhof system as evidenced by phosphorus distribution. *Can. J. Res.* **C28**, 203.

27. Chakravorty, M. (1964). Metabolism of mannitol and induction of mannitol-1-phosphate dehydrogenase in *Lactobacillus plantarum*. *J. Bacteriol.* **87**, 1246.

28. Chance, B., and Hess, B. (1959). Spectroscopic evidence of metabolic control. *Science* **129**, 700.

29. Cheldelin, V. H. (1961). "Metabolic Pathways in Microorganism," E. R. Squibb lectures on chemistry of microbial products. Wiley, New York.

30. Claridge, C. A., and Werkman, C. H. (1954). Evidence for alternate pathways for the oxidation of glucose by *Pseudomonas aeruginosa*. *J. Bacteriol.* **68**, 77.

31. Cochrane, V. W. (1955). The metabolism of species of streptomyces. VIII. Reactions of the Embden-Meyerhof-Parnas sequence in *Streptomyces coelicolor*. *J. Bacteriol.* **69**, 256.

32. Colowick, S. P., Kaplan, N. O., Neufeld, E. F., and Ciotti, M. M. (1952). Pyridine nucleotide transhydrogenase. I. Indirect evidence for the reaction and purification of the enzyme. *J. Biol. Chem.* **195**, 95.

33. Cook, J. L., and Dounce, A. L. (1954). Determination of serum aldolase. *Proc.Soc. Exptl. Biol. Med.* **87**, 349.

34. Crane, R. K. (1962). Hexokinases and pentokinases. *In* "The Enzymes" (P. D. Boyer, H. Lardy, and K. Myrbäck, eds.), 2nd ed., Vol. 6, p. 47. Academic Press, New York.

35. Crane, R. K., and Sols, A. (1953). The association of hexokinase with particulate fractions of brain and other tissue homogenates. *J. Biol. Chem.* **203**, 273.

36. Crane, R. K., and Sols, A. (1962). Animal tissue Hexokinases. *Methods Enzymol.* **1**, 277.

37. Dedonder, R., and Noblesse, C. (1953). Deshydrogenases du glucose-6-phosphate et de l'acide 6-phosphogluconique des *B. subtilis* et *B. megatherium*. *Ann. Inst. Pasteur* **85**, 71.

38. DeLey, J. (1960). Comparative carbohydrate metabolism and localization of enzymes in *Pseudomonas* and related microorganisms. *J. Appl. Bacteriol.* **23**, 400.

39. DeLey, J. (1962). Comparative biochemistry and enzymology in bacterial classification. *Symp. Soc. Gen. Microbiol.* **12**, 190.
40. DeMoss, R. D. (1953). Routes of ethanol formation in bacteria. *J. Cellular Comp. Physiol.* **41**, Suppl. 1, 207.
41. DeMoss, R. D. (1954). Oxidation of 6-phosphogluconate by *Leuconostoc mesenteroides. Bacteriol. Proc.* p. 109.
42. DeMoss, R. D. (1955). Glucose-6-phosphate and 6-phosphogluconic dehydrogenases from *Leuconostoc mesenteroides. Methods Enzymol.* **1**, 328.
43. DeMoss, R. D., and Gibbs, M. (1952). Mechanism of ethanol formation by *Pseudomonas lindneri. Bacteriol. Proc.* p. 146.
44. DeMoss, R. D., Bard, R. C., and Gunsalus, I. C. (1951). The mechanism of the heterolactic fermentation: A new route of ethanol formation. *J. Bacteriol.* **62**, 499.
45. DeMoss, R. D., Gunsalus, I. C., and Bard, R. C. (1953). A glucose-6-phosphate dehydrogenase in *Leuconostoc mesenteroides. J. Bacteriol.* **66**, 10.
46. DeVries, W., and Stouthamer, A. H. (1967). Pathway of glucose fermentation in relation to the taxonomy of Bifidobacteria. *J. Bacteriol.* **93**, 574.
47. Dixon, M., and Webb, E. C. (1964). "Enzymes," 2nd ed. Longmans, Green, New York.
48. Dobrogosz, W. J., and DeMos, R. D. (1963). The regulation of ribose phosphate isomerase activity in *Pediococcus pentosaceus. Biochim. Biophys. Acta* **77**, 629.
49. Doelle, H. W., and Manderson, G. (1967). Bacterial FDP-Aldolase. I. Considerations for obtaining enzyme activity as a mathematical function of optical density using stable triosephosphates and the chromogen method, p. 154. *Australian Biochem. Soc.*, Sydney.
50. Doi, R., Halvorson, H., and Church, B. D. (1959). Intermediate metabolism of aerobic spores. III. The mechanism of glucose and hexose phosphate oxidation in extracts of *Bacillus cereus* spores. *J. Bacteriol.* **77**, 43.
51. Domagk, G. F., and Horecker, B. L. (1965). Fructose and erythrose metabolism in *Alcaligenes faecalis. Arch. Biochem. Biophys.* **109**, 342; *Chem. Abstr.* **62**, 8145 (1965).
52. Dounce, A. L., Barnett, S. R., and Beyer, G. T. (1950). Further studies on the kinetics and determination of aldolase. *J. Biol. Chem.* **185**, 769.
53. Eagon, R. G., and Wang, C. H. (1961). Dissimilation of glucose and gluconic acid by *Pseudomonas natriegens. J. Bacteriol.* **83**, 879.
54. Eisenberg, R. C., and Dobrogosz, W. J. (1967). Gluconate metabolism in *Escherichia coli. J. Bacteriol.* **93**, 941.
55. Entner, N., and Doudoroff, M. (1952). Glucose and gluconic acid oxidation by *Pseudomonas saccharophila. J. Biol. Chem.* **196**, 853.
56. Fiske, C. H., and Subbarow, Y. (1925). The colorimetric determination of phosphorus. *J. Biol. Chem.* **66**, 375; as cited by Leloir and Cardini (109).
57. Forrest, W. W., and Walker, D. J. (1965). Control of glycolysis in washed suspensions of *Streptococcus faecalis. Nature* **207**, 46.
58. Fossitt, D., Mortlock, R. P., Anderson, R. L., and Wood, W. A. (1964). Pathways of L-arabitol and xylitol metabolism in *Aerobacter aerogenes. J. Biol. Chem.* **239**, 2110.
59. Fraenkel, D. G., and Horecker, B. L. (1964). Pathways of D-glucose metabolism in *Salmonella typhimurium.* A study of a mutant lacking phosphoglucose isomerase. *J. Biol. Chem.* **239**, 2765.
60. Fraenkel, D. G., and Horecker, B. L. (1965). Fructose-1, 6-diphosphatase and acid hexose phosphatase of *Escherichia coli. J. Bacteriol.* **90**, 837.
61. Fraenkel, D. G., and Levisohn, S. R. (1967). Glucose and gluconate metabolism in an *Escherichia coli* mutant lacking phosphoglucose isomerase. *J. Bacteriol.* **93**, 1571.

62. Fraenkel, D. H., Pontremoli, S., and Horecker, B. L. (1966). The specific fructose diphosphatase of *Escherichia coli*. Properties and partial purification. *Arch. Biochem. Biophys.* **114**, 4; *Chem. Abstr.* **64**, 17926 (1966).

63. Friedeman, T. E., and Haugen, G. E. (1943). *J. Biol. Chem.* **147**, 415; as cited by Kovachevich and Wood (103).

64. Fromm, H. J. (1958). Ribitol dehydrogenase. I. Purification and properties of the enzyme. *J. Biol. Chem.* **233**, 1049.

65. Fromm, H. J., and Zewe, V. (1962). Kinetic studies of brain hexokinase reaction. *J. Biol. Chem.* **237**, 1661.

66. Fruton, J. S., and Simmons, S. (1959). Fermentation and glycolysis. *In* "General Biochemistry," 2nd ed., p. 468. Wiley, New York.

67. Fuller, R. C., Smillie, R. M., Sisler, E. C., and Kornberg, H. L. (1961). Carbonmetabolism in *Chromatium. J. Biol. Chem.* **236**, 2140.

68. Garfinkel, D. (1965). A computer simulation study of the metabolic control behaviour of phosphofructokinase. *Control Energy Metab., Colloq., Philadelphia*, 1965 p. 101. Academic Press, New York; *Chem. Abstr.* **65**, 12489 (1966).

69. Gary, N. D., Kupferberg, L. L., and Graf, L. H. (1955). Demonstration of an iron activated aldolase in some extracts of *Brucella suis. J. Bacteriol.* **69**, 478.

70. Ghuretti, F., and Barron, E. S. G. (1954). Der Gang der Glukose-Oxydation in *Corynebacterium creatinovorum. Biochim. Biophys. Acta* **15**, 445.

71. Gibbins, L. N., and Simpson, F. J. (1963). The purification and properties of D-allose-6-kinase from *Aerobacter aerogenes. Can. J. Microbiol.* **9**, 769.

72. Gibbins, L. N., and Simpson, F. J. (1964). The incorporation of D-allose into the glycolytic pathway by *Aerobacter aerogenes. Can. J. Microbiol.* **10**, 829.

73. Gibbs, M., and DeMoss, R. D. (1954). Anaerobic dissimilation of C^{14}-labelled glucose and fructose by *Pseudomonas lindneri. J. Biol. Chem.* **207**, 689.

74. Goldberg, M., Fessenden, J. M., and Racker, E. (1966). Phosphoketolase. *Methods Enzymol.* **9**, 515.

75. Goldman, M., and Blumenthal, H. J. (1960). Pathway of glucose catabolism in intact heat-activated spores of *Bacillus cereus. Biochem. Biophys. Res. Commun.* **3**, 164.

76. Goldman, M., and Blumenthal, H. J. (1963). Pathways of glucose catabolism in *Bacillus subtilis. J. Bacteriol.* **86**, 303.

77. Goldman, M., and Blumenthal, H. J. (1964). Pathways of glucose catabolism in *Bacillus cereus. J. Bacteriol.* **87**, 377.

78. Gorves, W. E., Calder, J., and Rutter, W. J. (1966). Fructose diphosphate aldolase. II. *Clostridium perfringens. Methods Enzymol.* **9**, 486.

79. Grazi, E., Cheng, T., and Horecker, B. L. (1962). The formation of a stable aldolase-DHAP complex. *Biochem. Biophys. Res. Commun.* **7**, 250.

80. Grazi, E., Rowley, P. T., Cheng, T., Tchola, O., and Horecker, B. L. (1962). The mechanism of action of aldolases. III. Schiff base formation with lysine. *Biochem. Biophys. Res. Commun.* **9**, 38.

81. Grazi, E., Meloche, H., Martinez, G., Wood, W. A., and Horecker, B. L. (1963). Evidence for Schiff base formation in enzymatic aldol condensations. *Biochem. Biophys. Res. Commun.* **10**, 4.

82. Halvorson, H., and Church, B. D. (1957). Intermediate metabolism of aerobic spores. II. The relationship between oxidative metabolism and germination. *J. Appl. Bacteriol.* **20**, 359.

83. Hanson, T. E., and Anderson, R. L. (1966). D-Fructose-1-phosphate kinase, a new enzyme instrumental in the metabolism of D-fructose. *J. Biol. Chem.* **241**, 1644.

84. Hatch, M. D., and Slack, C. R. (1966). Photosynthesis by sugarcane leaves. A new carboxylation reaction and the pathway of sugar formation. *Biochem. J.* **101**, 103.
85. Hatch, M. D., Slack, C. R., and Johnson, H. S. (1967). Further studies on a new pathway of photosynthetic CO_2-fixation in sugarcane and its occurrence in other plant species. *Biochem. J.* **102**, 417.
86. Hauge, J. G. (1964). Glucose dehydrogenase of *Bacterium anitratum:* an enzyme with a novel prosthetic group. *J. Biol. Chem.* **239**, 3630.
87. Heath, E. C., Hurnitz, J., and Horecker, B. L. (1956). Acetyl phosphate formation in the phosphorolytic cleavage of pentose phosphate. *J. Am. Chem. Soc.* **78**, 5449.
88. Heath, E. C., Hurnitz, J., Horecker, B. L., and Ginsburg, A. (1958). Pentose fermentation by *Lactobacillus plantarum.* I. The cleavage of xylulose-5-phosphate by phosphoketolase. *J. Biol. Chem.* **231**, 1009.
89. Heath, E. C., Horecker, B. L., Smyrniotis, P. Z., and Takagi, Y. (1958). Pentose fermentation by *Lactobacillus plantarum.* II. L-Arabinose isomerase. *J. Biol. Chem.* **231**, 1031.
90. Herbert, D., Gordon, V., Subrahmanyan, V., and Green, D. E. (1940). Zymohexase. *Biochem. J.* **34**, 1108.
91. Hill, R. L., and Mills, R. C. (1954). The anaerobic glucose metabolism of *Bacterium tularense. Arch. Biochem. Biophys.* **53**, 174.
92. Holzer, H., and Schröter, W. (1962). Zum Wirkungsmechanismus der Phosphoketolase. I. Oxydation verschiedener Substrate mit Ferricyanid zu Glycolsäure. *Biochim. Biophys. Acta* **65**, 271.
93. Horwitz, S. B., and Kaplan, N. O. (1964). Hexitol dehydrogenase of *Bacillus subtilis. J. Biol. Chem.* **239**, 830.
94. Hulley, S. B., Jorgensen, S. B., and Lin, E. C. C. (1963). Ribitol dehydrogenase in *Aerobacter aerogenes* 1033. *Biochim. Biophys. Acta* **67**, 219; as cited by Mortlock and Wood (132).
95. Johnson, P. A., and Quayle, J. R. (1965). Microbial growth on C_1-compounds. Synthesis of cell constituents by methane- and methanol-grown *Pseudomonas methanica. Biochem. J.* **95**, 859.
96. Joshi, M. D., and Jagannathan, V. (1966). Hexokinase. I. Brain. *Methods Enzymol.* **9**, 371.
97. Kamel, M. Y., and Anderson, R. L. (1966). Metabolism of D-mannose in *Aerobacter aerogenes.* Evidence for a cyclic pathway. *J. Bacteriol.* **92**, 1689.
98. Kamel, M. Y., Allison, D. P., and Anderson, R. L. (1966). Stereospecific D-glucokinase of *Aerobacter aerogenes.* Purification and properties. *J. Biol. Chem.* **241**, 690.
99. Kemp, M. B., and Quayle, J. R. (1966). Microbial growth on C_1-compounds. Incorporation of C_1 units into allulose-phosphate by extracts of *Pseudomonas methanica. Biochem. J.* **99**, 41.
100. Kemp, M. B., and Quayle, J. R. (1967). Microbial growth on C_1-compounds. Uptake of ^{14}C formaldehyde and ^{14}C formate by methane-grown *Pseudomonas methanica* and determination of the hexose labelling pattern after brief incubation with ^{14}C methanol. *Biochem. J.* **102**, 94.
101. Kornberg, A. (1950). Enzymatic synthesis of triphosphopyridine nucleotide. *J. Biol. Chem.* **182**, 805.
102. Kovachevich, R., and Wood, W. A. (1955). Carbohydrate metabolism of *Pseudomonas fluorescens.* III. Purification and properties of a 6-phosphogluconate dehydrase. *J. Biol. Chem.* **213**, 745.
103. Kovachevich, R., and Wood, W. A. (1955). Carbohydrate metabolism of *Pseudomonas fluorescens.* IV. Purification and properties of 2-keto-3-deoxy-6-phosphogluconate aldolase. *J. Biol. Chem.* **213**, 757.

104. Kuby, S. A., and Noltmann, E. A. (1966). Glucose-6-phosphate dehydrogenase (crystalline) from Brewer's yeast. *Methods Enzymol.* **9**, 116.

105. Kwon, T. W., and Brown, W. D. (1966). Augmentation of aldolase activity by high concentration of fructose-1,6-diphosphate. *J. Biol. Chem.* **241**, 1509.

106. Lardy, H. A., and Parks, R. E., Jr. (1956). Influence of ATP concentration on rates of some phosphorylation reactions. *In* "Enzymes: Units of Biological Structure and Function" (O. H. Gaebler, ed.), p. 584. Academic Press, New York.

107. Lascelles, J. (1964). Oxygen and the evolution of biochemical pathways. *Proc. Symp. Oxygen Animal Organism*, London, 1964 p. 657. Pergamon Press, Oxford.

108. Lee, C. K., and Dobrogosz, W. J. (1965). Oxidative metabolism in *Pediococcus pentosaceus*. III. Glucose dehydrogenase system. *J. Bacteriol.* **90**, 653.

109. Leloir, L. F., and Cardini, C. E. (1957). Characterization of phosphorus compounds by acid lability. *Methods Enzymol.* **3**, 840.

110. Lim, R., and Cohen, S. S. (1966). D-Phosphoarabinoisomerase and D-ribulokinase in *Escherichia coli*. *J. Biol. Chem.* **241**, 4304.

111. Lin, E. C. C. (1961). An inducible D-arabitol dehydrogenase from *Aerobacter aerogenes*. *J. Biol. Chem.* **236**, 31.

112. Lipmann, F., and Tuttle, L. C. (1945). A specific micromethod for the determination of acylphosphates. *J. Biol. Chem.* **159**, 21.

113. Liss, M., Horwitz, S. B., and Kaplan, N. O. (1962). D-Mannitol-1-phosphate dehydrogenase and D-sorbitol-6-phosphate dehydrogenase in *Aerobacter aerogenes*. *J. Biol. Chem.* **237**, 1342.

114. Losada, M., Trebst, A. V., Ogata, S., and Arnon, D. I. (1960). Equivalence of light and adenosine triphosphate in bacterial photosynthesis. *Nature* **186**, 753.

115. Lowry, O. H., and Lopez, J. A. (1946). *J. Biol. Chem.* **162**, 421; as cited by Leloir and Cardini (109).

116. McComb, B. B., and Yushok, W. D. (1959). Properties of particulate hexokinase of the Krebs-2-Ascites tumor. *Biochim. Biophys. Acta* **34**, 515.

117. McDonald, M. R. (1962). Yeast Hexokinase. *Methods Enzymol.* **1**, 269.

118. Manderson, G., and Doelle, H. W. (1967). Bacterial FDP-Aldolase. II. The establishment of a routine assay method for cell-free extracts, p. 155. *Australian Biochem. Soc.*, Sydney.

119. Mansour, T. E. (1965). Studies on heart phosphofructokinase. Active and inactive forms of the enzyme. *J. Biol. Chem.* **240**, 2165.

120. Mansour, T. E. (1966). Phosphofructokinase. II. Heart muscle. *Methods Enzymol.* **9**, 340.

121. Marcus, L., and Marr, A. G. (1961). Polyol dehydrogenase of *Azotobacter agilis*. *J. Bacteriol.* **82**, 224.

122. Marmur, J., and Hotchkiss, R. D. (1955). Mannitol metabolism, a transferable property of *Pneumococcus*. *J. Biol. Chem.* **214**, 383.

123. Marus, A., and Bell, E. J. (1966). Carbohydrate catabolism of *Mima polymorpha*. II. Abortive catabolism of glucose. *J. Bacteriol.* **91**, 2229.

124. Mastroni, P., and Contadini, V. (1965). Incubation temperature and metabolism of glucose in *Serratia marcescens*. *Riv. Ist. Sieroterap. Ital.* **40**, 90; *Chem. Abstr.* **63**, 15252 (1965).

125. Matsushima, K., and Simpson, F. J. (1965). The ribosephosphate and glucosephosphate isomerases of *Aerobacter aerogenes*. *Can. J. Microbiol.* **11**, 967.

126. Matsushima, K., and Simpson, F. J. (1966). The purification and properties of D-allosephosphate isomerase of *Aaerobacter aerogenes*. *Can. J. Microbiol.* **12**, 313.

127. Meloche, H. P., and Wood, W. A. (1964). The mechanism of 2-keto-3-deoxy-6-phosphogluconate aldolase. *J. Biol. Chem.* **239**, 3511.

128. Meloche, H. P., Ingram, J. M., and Wood, W. A. (1966). 2-Keto-3-deoxy-6-phospho-gluconic aldolase (crystalline). *Methods Enzymol.* **9**, 520.
129. Meyerhof, O. (1951). Aldolase and isomerase. *In* "The Enzymes" (J. B. Sumner and K. Myrbäck, eds.), 1st ed., Vol. 2, Part 1, p. 162. Academic Press, New York.
129a. Meyerhof, O., and Lohmann, K. (1934). *Biochem. Z.* **271**, 89; as cited by Fruton and Simmons (66).
130. Moore, C. C. (1965). Control properties of phosphofructokinase from *Saccharomyces cerevisiae. Control Energy Metab., Colloq., Philadelphia*, 1965 p. 97. Academic Press, New York; *Chem. Abstr.* **65**, 12490 (1966).
131. Morris, J. G. (1960). Studies on the metabolism of *Arthrobacter globiformis. J. Gen. Microbiol.* **22**, 564.
132. Mortlock, R. P., and Wood, W. A. (1964). Metabolism of pentoses and pentitols by *Aerobacter aerogenes.* I. Demonstration of pentose isomerase, pentolokinase and pentitol dehydrogenase enzyme families. *J. Bacteriol.* **88**, 838.
133. Mortlock, R. P., and Wood, W. A. (1964). Metabolism of pentoses and pentitols by *Aerobacter aerogenes.* II. Mechanism of acquisition of kinase, isomerase and dehydrogenase activity. *J. Bacteriol.* **88**, 845.
134. Murphy, W. H., and Rosenblum, E. D. (1964). Mannitol catabolism by *Staphylococcus aureus. Arch. Biochem. Biophys.* **107**, 292.
135. Passonneau, J. V., and Lowry, O. H. (1962). Phosphofructokinase and the Pasteur effect. *Biochem. Biophys. Res. Commun.* **7**, 10.
136. Passoneau, J. V., and Lowry, O. H. (1963). Phosphofructokinase and the control of the citric acid cycle. *Biochem. Biophys. Res. Commun.* **13**, 372.
137. Pepper, R. E., and Costilow, R. N. (1964). Glucose catabolism by *Bacillus popilliae* and *Bacillus lentimorbus. J. Bacteriol.* **87**, 303.
138. Peterson, M. H., Friedland, W. C., Denison, F. W., Jr., and Sylvester, J. C. (1956). The conversion of mannitol to fructose by *Acetobacter suboxydans. Appl. Microbiol.* **4**, 316.
139. Pine, L., and Howell, A., Jr. (1956). Comparison of physiological and biochemical characters of *Actinomyces* spp. with those of *Lactobacillus bifidus. J. Gen. Microbiol.* **15**, 428.
139a. Polakis, E. S., Bartley, W., and Meek, G. A. (1964). Changes in the structure and enzyme activity of *Saccharomyces cerevisiae* in response to changes in the environment. *Biochem. J.* **90**, 369.
140. Pontremoli, S., and Grazi, E. (1966). 6-phosphogluconate dehydrogenase-crystalline. *Methods Enzymol.* **9**, 137.
141. Pye, K. (1965). The control of glycolysis in yeast. *Control Energy Metab. Colloq., Philadelphia*, 1965, p. 193. Academic Press, New York; *Chem. Abstr.* **65**, 11002 (1966).
142. Richards, O. C., and Rutter, W. J. (1961). Comparative properties of yeast and muscle aldolase. *J. Biol. Chem.* **236**, 3185.
143. Rogosa, M., Krichevsky, M. I., and Bishop, F. S. (1965). Truncated glycolytic system in *Veillonella alkalescens. J. Bacteriol.* **90**, 164.
144. Roodyne, D. B. (1957). The binding of aldolase to isolated nuclei. *Biochim. Biophys. Acta* **25**, 128.
145. Rose, I. A., Warms, J. V. B., and O'Connell, E. L. (1964). Role of inorganic phosphate in stimulation of glucose utilization of human red blood cells. *Biochem. Biophys. Res. Commun.* **15**, 33.
146. Rose, I. A., O'Connell, E. L., and Mehler, A. H. (1965). Mechanism of the aldolase reaction. *J. Biol. Chem.* **240**, 1758.

147. Rutter, W. J., and Hunsley, J. R. (1966). Fructose diphosphate aldolase. I. Yeast. *Methods Enzymol.* 9, 480.

148. Saito, N. (1965). Contribution of glucose phosphorylation to glucose metabolism in *Brevibacterium fuscum. Agr. Biol. Chem. (Tokyo)* 29, 621.

149. Scardovi, V., and Trovatelli, L. D. (1965). Fructose-6-phosphate shunt as peculiar pattern of hexose degradation in the genus *Bifidobacterium. Ann. Microbiol. Enzimol.* 15, 19.

150. Schramm, M., Klybas, V., and Racker, E. (1958). Phosphorolytic cleavage of fructose-6-phosphate by fructose-6-phosphate phosphoketolase from *Acetobacter xylinum. J. Biol. Chem.* 233, 1283.

151. Scolnick, E. M., and Linn, E. C. C. (1962). Parallel induction of D-arabitol and D-sorbitol dehydrogenases. *J. Bacteriol.* 84, 631.

152. Scott, D. B. M., and Cohen, S. S. (1953). The oxidative pathway of carbohydrate metabolism in *Escherichia coli.* I. The isolation and properties of glucose-6-phosphate dehydrogenase and 6-phosphogluconate dehydrogenase. *Biochem. J.* 55, 23.

153. Sebek, O. K., and Randles, C. I. (1952). The oxidative dissimilation of mannitol and sorbitol by *Pseudomonas fluorescens. J. Bacteriol.* 63, 693.

154. Shaw, D. R. D. (1956). Polyol dehydrogenases. 3. Galactitol dehydrogenase and D-iditol dehydrogenase. *Biochem. J.* 64, 394.

155. Shaw, W. N., and Stadie, W. C. (1959). Two identical Embden-Meyerhof enzyme systems in normal rat diaphagm differing in cytological location and response to insulin. *J. Biol. Chem.* 234, 2491.

156. Sibley, J. A., and Lehninger, A. L. (1949). Determination of aldolase in animal tissues. *J. Biol. Chem.* 177, 859.

157. Simmons, R. I., and Costilow, R. N. (1962). Enzymes of glucose and pyruvate catabolism in cells and spores and germinated spores of *Clostridium botulinum. J. Bacteriol.* 84, 1274.

158. Simpson, F. J., and Wood, W. A. (1958). Degradation of L-arabinose by *Aerobacter aerogenes.* II. Purification and properties of L-ribulokinase. *J. Biol. Chem.* 230, 473.

159. Simpson, F. J., Wolin, M. J., and Wood, W. A. (1958). Degradation of L-arabinose by *Aerobacter aerogenes.* I. A pathway involving phosphorylated intermediates. *J. Biol. Chem.* 230, 457.

160. Sly, L. I., and Doelle, H. W. (1968). 6-Phosphogluconate dehydrogenase in cell free extracts of *Escherichia coli K-12. Arch. Mikrobiol.* 63, 214.

161. Sly, L. I., and Doelle, H. W. (1968). Glucose-6-phosphate dehydrogenase in cell free extracts of *Zymomonas mobilis. Arch. Mikrobiol.* 63, 197.

162. Smith, P. J. C. (1960). Carbohydrate metabolism in *Spirochaeta recurrentis.* III. Properties of aldolase in spirochaetes. *Biochem. J.* 76, 508.

163. Sols, A., and Salas, M. L. (1966). Phosphofructokinase. III. Yeast. *Methods Enzymol.* 9, 436.

164. Stern, I. J., Wang, C. H., and Gilmour, C. M. (1960). Comparative catabolism of carbohydrates in *Pseudomonas* species. *J. Bacteriol.* 79, 601.

165. Tanaka, S., Lerner, S. A., and Lin, E. C. (1967). Replacement of a phosphoenolpyruvate-dependent phosphotransferase by a nicotinamide adenine dinucleotide-linked dehydrogenase for the utilization of mannitol. *J. Bacteriol.* 93, 642.

166. Tsumura, N., and Sato, T. (1965). Enzymic conversion of D-glucose to D-fructose. V. Partial purification and properties of the enzyme from *Aerobacter cloaceae. Agr. Biol. Chem. (Tokyo)* 29, 1123; *Chem. Abstr.* 64, 8551 (1966).

167. Ui, M. (1966). A role of phosphofructokinase in pH-dependent regulation of glycolysis. *Biochim. Biophys. Acta* 124, 310.

168. Utter, M. F. (1947). *Federation Proc.* **6**, 299; as cited by Mansour (119).
169. Uyeda, K., and Racker, E. (1965). Coordinated stimulation of hexokinase and phosphofructokinase by phosphate in a reconstituted system of glycolysis. *Control Energy Metab. Colloq., Philadelphia,* 1965 p. 127. Academic Press, New York; *Chem. Abstr.* **65**, 12489 (1966).
170. Vandemark, P. J., and Wood, W. A. (1956). The pathways of glucose dissimilation by *Microbacterium. lacticum. J. Bacteriol.* **71**, 385.
171. van Thiedemann, H., and Born, J. (1959). Versuche zum Mechanismus der Pasteur-Reaktion. Der Einfluss von Phosphationen auf die Aktivität der struktur-gebundenen Hexokinase. *Z. Naturforsch.* **14b**, 447; as cited by Crane (34).
172. Veste, J., and Reino, M. L. (1963). Hepatic glucokinase in a direct effect of insulin. *Science* **142**, 590.
173. Vinuela, E., Salas, M. L., Salas, M., and Sols, A. (1964). Two interconvertible forms of yeast phosphofructokinase with different sensitivity to endproduct inhibition. *Biochem. Biophys. Res. Commun.* **5**, 243.
173a. Vitols, E., and Linnane, A. W. (1961). Studies on the oxidative metabolism of *Saccharomyces cerevisiae*. II. Morphology and oxidative phosphorylation capacity of mitochondria and derives particles from Baker's yeast. *J. Biophys. Biochem. Cytology* **9**, 701.
173b. Vitols, E., North, R. F., and Linnane, A. W. (1961). Studies on the oxidative metabolism of *Saccharomyces cerevisiae*. I. Observations on the fine structure of the yeast cell. *J. Biophys. Biochem. Cytology* **9**, 689.
174. Wang, C. H., Stern, I., Gilmour, C. M., Klungsoyr, S., Reed, D. J., Bialy, J. J., Christensen, B. E., and Cheldelin, V. H. (1958). Comparative studies of glucose catabolism by the radiorespirometric method. *J. Bacteriol.* **76**, 207.
174a. Warburg, O., and Christian, W. (1933). Über das gelbe Oxydationsferment. *Biochem. Z.* **257**, 492.
175. Warburg, O., and Christian, W. (1943). Isolierung und Kristallisierung des Gärungs-fermentes Zymohexase. *Biochem. Z.* **314**, 149.
176. Warburton, R. H., Eagles, B. A., and Campbell, J. J. R. (1951). The intermediate metabolism of *Pseudomonas aeruginosa*. V. The identification of pyruvate as an intermediate in glucose oxidation. *Can. J. Botany* **29**, 143.
177. White, A., Handler, P., and Smith, E. L. (1964). "Principles of Biochemistry." McGraw-Hill, New York.
178. White, D. C. (1966). The obligatory involvement of the electron transport system in the catabolic metabolism of *Haemophilus parainfluenzae. Antonie van. Leeuwenhoek, J. Microbiol. Serol.* **32**, 139.
179. Willard, J. M., Schulman, M., and Gibbs, H. (1965). Aldolase in *Anacystis nidulans* and *Rhodopseudomonas spheroides. Nature* **206**, 195.
180. Wolff, J. B., and Kaplan, N. O. (1956). Hexitol metabolism in *Escherichia coli. J. Bacteriol.* **71**, 557.
181. Wolff, J. B., and Kaplan, N. O. (1956). D-Mannitol-1-phosphate dehydrogenase from *Escherichia coli. J. Biol. Chem.* **218**, 849.
182. Wood, W. A., and Schwerdt, R. F. (1952). Evidence for alternate routes of carbo-hydrate oxidation in *Pseudomonas fluorescens. Bacteriol. Proc.* p. 138.
183. Wood, W. A., and Schwerdt, R. F. (1954). Carbohydrate oxidation by *Pseudomonas fluorescens*. II. Mechanism of hexose phosphate oxidation. *J. Biol. Chem.* **206**, 625.
184. Wood, W. A., McDonough, M. J., and Jacobs, B. L. (1961). Ribitol and D-arabitol utilization by *Aerobacter aerogenes. J. Biol. Chem.* **236**, 2190.

185. Wright, D. N, and Lockhart, W. R. (1965). Effects of growth rate and limiting substrate on glucose metabolism in *Escherichia coli. J. Bacteriol.* **89**, 1082.
186. Wu, R. (1966). Further analysis of the mode of inhibition and activation of Novikoff Ascites tumor phosphofructokinase. *J. Biol. Chem.* **241**, 4680.
187. Zablotny, R., and Fraenkel, D. G. (1967). Glucose and gluconate metabolism in a mutant of *Escherichia coli* lacking gluconate-6-phosphate dehydrase. *J. Bacteriol.* **93**, 1579.
188. Zagallo, A. C., and Wang, C. H. (1962). Comparative carbohydrate catabolism in *Arthrobacter. J. Gen. Microbiol.* **29**, 389.

SUPPLEMENTARY READINGS

Berman, T., and Magasanik, B. (1966). The pathway of myo-inositol degradation in *Aerobacter aerogenes*. Dehydrogenation and dehydration. *J. Biol. Chem.* **241**, 800.
Berman, K., Itada, N., and Cohn, M. (1967). On the mechanism of ATP cleavage in phospho-enolpyruvate synthase reaction of *E. coli. Biochim. Biophys. Acta* **141**, 214.
Betz, A. (1968). Pulsed incorporation of ^{32}P by the soluble oscillating glycolytic system from *Saccharomyces carlsbergensis. European J. Biochem.* **4**, 354.
Bisson, T. M., and Mortlock, R. P. (1968). Regulation of pentitol metabolism by *Aerobacter aerogenes*. I. Coordinate control of ribitol dehydrogenase and D-ribulokinase activities. *J. Bacteriol.* **95**, 925.
Bisson, T. M., Oliver, E. J., and Mortlock, R. P. (1968). Regulation of pentitol metabolism by *Aerobacter aerogenes*. II. Induction of the ribitol pathway. *J. Bacteriol.* **95**, 932.
Bowman, J. E., Brubaker, R. R., Frischer, H., and Carson, P. E. (1967). Characterization of enterobacteria by starch-gel electrophoresis of glucose 6-P dehydrogenase and 6-phosphogluconate dehydrogenase. *J. Bacteriol.* **94**, 544.
Brand, K., and Horecker, B. L. (1968). Reaction of cyanide with the transaldolase-dihydroxy-acetone complex. *Arch. Biochem. Biophys.* **123**, 312.
Brady, R. J., and Chambliss, G. H. (1967). The lack of phosphofructokinase activity in several species of *Rhodotorula. Biochem. Biophys. Res. Commun.* **29**, 343.
Brubaker, R. R. (1968). Metabolism of carbohydrates by *Pasteurella pseudotuberculosis. J. Bacteriol.* **95**, 1698.
Buchanan, B. B., Kalberer, P. B., and Arnon, D. I. (1967). Ferredoxin-activated fructose diphosphatase in isolated chloroplasts. *Biochim. Biophys. Res. Commun.* **29**, 76.
Canovas, J. L., and Kornberg, H. L. (1966). Properties and regulation of phosphopyruvate carboxylase activity in *Escherichia coli. Proc. Royal Soc. (London),* Ser. B **165**, 189; *Chem. Abstr.* **65**, 10875 (1966).
Dobrogosz, W. J. (1968). Effect of amino sugars on catabolite repression in *Escherichia coli. J. Bacteriol.* **95**, 578.
Duntze, W., Atzpodien, W., and Holzer, H. (1967). Glucose-dependent enzyme activities in different yeast species. *Arch. Mikrobiol.* **58**, 296.
Egan, B., and Morse, M. C. (1966). Carbohydrate transport in *Staphylococcus aureus*. III. Studies of the transport process. *Biochim. Biophys. Acta* **112**, 63.
Fernandez, Ma J., Medrano, L., Ruiz-Arnil, M., and Losada, M. (1967). Regulation and function of pyruvate kinase and malate enzyme in yeast. *European J. Biochem.* **3**, 11.
Forrest, W. W. (1967). Energies of activation and uncoupled growth in *Streptococcus faecalis* and *Zymomonas mobilis. J. Bacteriol.* **94**, 1459.
Frerman, F. E., and White, D. C. (1967). Membrane lipid changes during formation of a functional electron transport system in *Staphylococcus aureus. J. Bacteriol.* **94**, 1868.

Görtz, C. P. M. (1967). Effect of different carbon sources on the regulation of carbohydrate metabolism in *Saccharomyces cerevisiae*. *Ant. v. Leeuwenhoek J. Microbiol. Serol.* **33**, 451.

Griffin, C. C., Hoock, B. N., and Brand, L. (1967). Purification of *Escherichia coli* phosphofructokinase. *Biochem. Biophys. Res. Commun.* **27**, 287.

Gunsalus, I. C., Bertland, A. U., II, and Jacobson, L. A. (1967). Enzyme induction and repression in anabolic and catabolic pathways. *Arch. Mikrobiol.* **59**, 113.

Hempfling, W. P., and Gibson, J. (1966). Multisite control of glycolysis and K^+ uptake by *Escherichia coli* B. *Fed. Proc.* **25**, 583.

Hempfling, W. P., Höfer, M., Harris, E. J., and Pressman, B. C. (1967). Correlation between changes in metabolite concentrations and rate of ion transport following glucose addition to *Escherichia coli* B. *Biochim. Biophys. Acta* **141**, 391.

Hill, W. M., Fields, M. L., and Tweedy, B. G. (1967). Pathways of glucose metabolism by rough and smooth variants of *Bacillus stearothermophilus*. *Appl. Microbiol.* **15**, 556.

Hsie, A. W., and Rickenberg, H. V. (1967). Catabolite repression in *Escherichia coli*: The role of glucose 6-phosphate. *Biochem. Biophys. Res. Commun.* **29**, 303.

Johnson, M. J. (1967). Aerobic microbial growth at low oxygen concentrations. *J. Bacteriol.* **94**, 201.

Kelly, G. J., and Turner, J. F. (1968). Inhibition of pea-seed phosphofructokinase by phosphoenolpyruvate. *Biochem. Biophys. Res. Commun.* **30**, 195.

Lee, N., and Bendet, I. (1967). Crystalline L-ribulokinase from *Escherichia coli*. *J. Biol. Chem.* **242**, 2043.

Lee, C. K., and Ordal, Z. J. (1967). Regulatory effect of pyruvate on the glucose metabolism of *Clostridium thermosaccharolyticum*. *J. Bacteriol.* **94**, 530.

Maeba, P., and Sanwal, B. D. (1968). The regulation of pyruvate kinase of *Escherichia coli* by fructose diphosphate and adenylic acid. *J. Biol. Chem.* **243**, 448.

Moss, F. J., and Bush, F. (1967). Working design for a 5-liter controlled continuous culture apparatus. *Biotech. Bioengineering* IX, 585.

Nishikido, T., Izui, K., Iwatani, A., Katsuki, H., and Tanaka, S. (1968). Control of the carbon dioxide fixation in *Escherichia coli* by the compounds related to TCA cycle. *J. Biochem.* (*Tokyo*) **63**, 532.

Novello, F., and McLean, P. (1968). The pentose phosphate pathway of glucose metabolism. Measurement of the non-oxidative reactions of the cycle. *Biochem. J.* **107**, 775.

Raj, H. D. (1967). Radiorespirometric studies of *Leucothrix mucor*. *J. Bacteriol.* **94**, 615.

Sel'kov, E. E. (1968). Self-oscillations in glycolysis. 1. A simple kinetic model. *European J. Biochem.* **4**, 79.

Slezak, J., and Sikyta, B. (1967). Growth of *Escherichia coli* B in a continuous culture under limitation by inorganic phosphate. *Folia Microbiologica* **12**, 441.

Staub, M., and Denes, G. (1967). A kinetic study of the mechanism of action of 3-deoxy-D-arabino-heptulosonate-7-phosphate synthase in *Escherichia coli* K 12. *Biochim. Biophys. Acta* **132**, 428.

Vender, J., and Moulder, J. W. (1967). Initial step in catabolism of glucose by the Meningopneumonitis agent. *J. Bacteriol.* **94**, 867.

Wawszkiewicz, E. J., and Barker, H. A. (1968). Erythritol metabolism by *Propionibacterium pentosaceum*. The over-all reaction sequence. *J. Biol. Chem.* **243**, 1948.

5

CHEMOSYNTHESIS—AEROBIC RESPIRATION

AEROBIC RESPIRATION

Aerobic or oxidative respiration involves a considerably greater number of processes than in fermentation. It is the enzymatic oxidation of fuel molecules by molecular oxygen. A great number of books and reviews on this subject deal only with the tricarboxylic acid cycle (TCA) as the image of aerobic respiration. In microbiology, however, we have a complex group of organisms which are not able to use the TCA cycle, but use molecular oxygen as their final hydrogen acceptor. These microorganisms are the chemolithotrophic bacteria, which are mainly autotrophs and derive their energy by oxidizing inorganic compounds and incorporate CO_2 into the Calvin cycle for cellular biosynthesis (30, 36, 48, 140, 185). In contrast to this group of microorganisms stands the vast majority which are called the "chemoorganotrophs" and which use organic compounds such as carbohydrates as electron donors.

Chemolithotrophic Bacteria

There are only a few bacterial groups that are able to oxidize an inorganic compound for production of energy:

(1) the "nitroso" group of genera—*Nitrosomonas, Nitrosococcus, Nitrosocystis, Nitrosogloea*, and *Nitrosospira*—which oxidize ammonia;
(2) the "nitro" group of genera—*Nitrobacter* and *Nitrocystis*—which oxidize nitrite;
(3) the genus *Hydrogenomonas* or hydrogen bacteria (*Knallgas* bacteria), which oxidize hydrogen;
(4) the "ferrous iron oxidizing bacteria" *Ferrobacillus* and *Thiobacillus ferrooxidans*;
(5) the methane-oxidizing bacteria *Methanomonas methanooxidans* and *Pseudomonas methanica*; and
(6) the sulfur-oxidizing bacteria *Thiobacillus*.

Most of these bacteria are strict autotrophs. The composition of their cells is similar to that of heterotrophs. They possess similar enzymes and require similar cofactors and vitamins as the heterotrophs. They also have a phosphorylation system for ATP formation. Autotrophs have, however, a number of additional enzymes which enable them to oxidize inorganic salts and to reduce carbon dioxide for synthesis of cell material. While they may differ with regard to the former they all use a common way of fixing carbon dioxide via the Calvin cycle (see Chapter 4).

Why then are autotrophs unable to grow heterotrophically? It will be shown later that they can, on occasions, utilize glucose, but not as an energy source.

Umbreit(198) attempts to answer the question by stating that "the strict autotroph is adapted to life in what is essentially a toxic environment and that it has therefore so changed its permeability properties that all but a few essential materials are excluded." This is a hypothesis and not an answer and ignores the question of which came first—the autotrophs or the heterotrophs. It also fails to explain why the heterotrophs have not found the environment toxic. [For more information on membrane potentials and permeability see Cirillo(50).]

In search of an explanation of autotrophy one should accept first the possibility that there may be no single explanation for all autotrophs. Kelly(104) states six factors which may be responsible either individually or in combination. These factors are as follows:

(1) Limited permeability to organic nutrients, which has been mentioned before, but appears to be losing its significance on evidence which will be presented later.

(2) Inability to oxidize organic nutrients or to obtain energy from their oxidation, thus making chemo- or photosynthetic energy indispensable. This factor may be the most attractive explanation because the membrane of the organism could be permeable to organic nutrients and yet the organism be unable to obtain sufficient energy for its oxidation.

(3) A limited ability to synthesize all the compounds necessary for growth from all or most carbon sources other than carbon dioxide. This may be owing to a lack of a number of key enzymes(158) which are necessary for the synthesis of essential metabolites for biosynthetic reactions. This has recently been explained(175) in some blue-green algae and thiobacilli on the basis of a defective metabolism because of the absence of $NADH_2$ oxidase, α-ketoglutarate dehydrogenase, and unusually low levels of malic and succinic dehydrogenase enzymes. Such an explanation is not in harmony, however, with the observations that the electron transport particles from *Nitrobacter* actively oxidize $NADH_2$ involving normal carriers of the electron transport chain. Moreover, this process is coupled to the generation of adenosine triphosphate

(10). The missing metabolites, on the other hand, could be formed in the presence of carbon dioxide via the Calvin cycle (see Chapter 4). In spite of all this, the specificity toward an inorganic energy-yielding substrate for autotrophic growth and metabolism remains a mystery which might perhaps lie in the specific nature of the cellular proteins. Perhaps the sequence of amino acids in protein fractions catalyzing inorganic oxidations might reflect their unusual characteristics which might otherwise be different from those catalyzing organic oxidations in chemoorganotrophs(9).

(4) Some biochemical block of growth on excess external organic nutrients, related in some way to the carbon dioxide–based metabolism.

(5) Self-inhibition by products of the metabolism of organic compounds. It will be shown later that pyruvic acid, a metabolite of glucose breakdown, inhibits the growth of *Thiobacillus* quite strongly.

(6) Some special dependence either on an intermediate of the inorganic respiratory processes in the chemoautotroph, or on light in the photoautotrophs, for some specific reactions in the cells.

Whatever factor(s) may be involved no conclusion can be drawn at the present state of knowledge and more study of the regulatory mechanisms of the carbon dioxide–based metabolism of autotrophs is necessary.

Notwithstanding their origin, the ability to derive energy from an inorganic substance, to convert carbon dioxide to cellular material, and to wall off virtually all the rest of their environment seems to be the unique character of autotrophs(198).

Nitrosomonas. The bacterial species which are involved in the oxidation of ammonia and which have been studied belong to the genus *Nitrosomonas.* They oxidize ammonia as follows:

$$NH_4^+ + \tfrac{3}{2}O_2 + H_2O \rightarrow NO_2^- + 2H_3O^+$$

In exposing this reaction to hydrazine, the oxidation of ammonia does not proceed to nitrite, but hydroxylamine accumulates instead(113):

$$NH_4^+ + \tfrac{1}{2}O_2 \rightarrow NH_2OH + H^+$$

Lees(118) indicated that the metabolism must go via hydroxylamine and postulated a series of three two-electron steps in which energy and reducing power released would be efficiently used by the cell (see also 163).

Since *Nitrosomonas* is also able to oxidize hydroxylamine with the formation of nitrite, it has been assumed that hydroxylamine must be one of the intermediates of ammonia oxidation(209). The free energy changes (ΔF) at pH 7.0 were calculated(23) by reducing the standard free energy change in kilocalories by 9.7 kcal (= 7 pH units $\times$ 1.38 kcal) for each H^+ ion appearing on the right-hand side of the equations:

$$NH_4^+(-19.0) + \tfrac{1}{2}O_2(0.0) = NH_2OH(-5.6) + H^+(0.0)$$
$$\Delta F = +13.4 \text{ kcal}$$

$$NH_2OH(-5.6) + O_2(0.0) = NO_2^-(-8.25) + H_2O(-56.7) + H^+$$
$$\Delta F = -59.4 \text{ kcal}$$

$$N_2H_4(30.6) + O_2(0.0) = N_2(0.0) + 2 H_2O(-113.4)$$
$$\Delta F = -144.0 \text{ kcal}$$

At pH 7.0 the oxidations of hydroxylamine and hydrazine are exergonic, whereas the oxidation of ammonia to hydroxylamine requires energy. These energetics request that the oxidation of hydroxylamine (NH_2OH) must be connected with a respiratory chain system. Nicholas and Jones[139] showed that cell-free extracts of *Nitrosomonas* were able to produce nitrite from hydroxylamine aerobically in the presence of mammalian cytochrome c and flavin. Aleem and Lees[13] concluded that the oxidation of NH_2OH to NOH and of the latter to NO_2^- might be a semicyclic process involving an initial oxidative condensation between the two products of ammonium oxidation, i.e., NH_2OH and NO_2^- with nitrohydroxylamine as the "unknown" intermediate as indicated by the occurrence of the following reactions catalyzed by the *Nitrosomonas* cell-free extracts:

$$NH_2OH \rightarrow (NOH) + 2 H^+$$

$$2 H^+ + 2 \text{ cytochrome c } Fe^{3+} \rightarrow 2 \text{ cytochrome c } Fe^{2+} + 2 H^+$$

$$(NOH) + HNO_2 \rightarrow NO_2 \cdot NHOH$$

$$NO_2 \cdot NHOH + \tfrac{1}{2}O_2 \rightarrow 2 HNO_2$$

Although NH_2OH oxidation involved the mediation of cytochrome systems, the oxidation of $NO_2 \cdot NHOH$ proceeded stoichiometrically without the involvement of cytochromes. It is probable that this reaction is catalyzed by a mixed function oxidase or more likely an oxygenase[9]. Anderson[22] observed that under anaerobic conditions the metabolism of hydroxylamine was accompanied by the formation of nitrogenous gas and not nitrite.

In the light of the observations of Aleem and Lees[13], Anderson[22], and Nicholas and Jones[139], the reactions involved in hydroxylamine oxidation appear to be as follows:

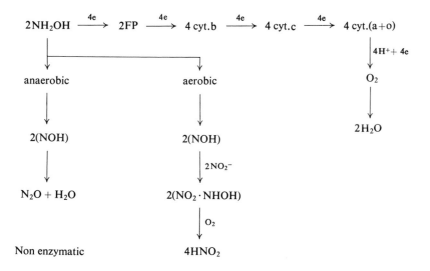

This suggested that the aerobic metabolism of hydroxylamine to nitrite must at least occur in two steps:

(1) a dehydrogenation of hydroxylamine with the formation of an intermediate in the same oxidation state as nitroxyl, and
(2) a conversion of nitroxyl to nitrite by an enzyme requiring oxygen.

The proposed scheme of hydroxylamine oxidation was therefore as shown in Fig. 5.1 (Reprinted with permission of The Biochemical Journal, London). Since this process requires oxygen, the dehydrogenation of hydroxylamine by the cell would be inhibited under anaerobic conditions when the bacterial

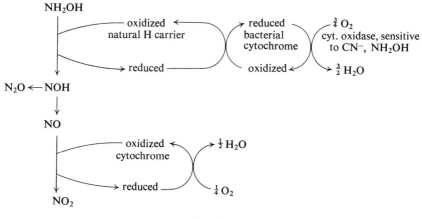

FIG. 5.1

cytochrome was reduced. Under aerobic conditions the mammalian cytochrome c replaced the natural carrier and bacterial cytochrome. It is possible that FAD is the natural carrier and is oxidized by cytochrome c. The formation of nitric oxide from hydroxylamine would involve the production of three equivalents of reducing power, which can be channeled through the respiratory chain, and probably provides most of the energy released by ammonia oxidation. In order to do this it must be coupled with systems that generate ATP. There is no reduced NAD formation, which is thought to be necessary for the reduction of carbon dioxide. The relationship between the intermediate of ammonia oxidation to nitrite is therefore as shown in Scheme

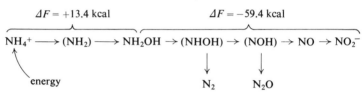

$$\Delta F = +13.4 \text{ kcal} \qquad\qquad \Delta F = -59.4 \text{ kcal}$$

$$NH_4^+ \longrightarrow (NH_2) \longrightarrow NH_2OH \rightarrow (NHOH) \rightarrow (NOH) \rightarrow NO \rightarrow NO_2^-$$

energy N_2 N_2O

SCHEME 5.1. (Reprinted with permission of The Biochemical Journal, London.)

5.1(24). The hydroxylamine-cytochrome c reductase(89) was found to be a complex of associated proteins, activators, and lipids rather than a single protein. Whether or not glutamate dehydrogenase (E.C. 1.4.1.4) participates in the ammonia to hydroxylamine sequence(88) is not known as yet. Difference spectra of whole cells obtained gave rise to an electron transport in hydroxylamine-cytochrome c reductase:

$$NH_2OH \rightarrow \text{flavin (Fe}^{3+}) \rightarrow \text{cyt. b} \rightarrow \text{cyt. c}$$

The terminal oxidase is apparently of cytochrome c type and soluble rather than particulate.

The finding of a cytochrome P-450-like pigment(159) poses the question of whether this pigment may be an oxygenase in one of the several presumed steps of ammonia oxidation. It was found by radioactive tracer work that at least one of the oxygen atoms in nitrite comes from atmospheric oxygen. This would mean the participation of such an oxygenase system in *Nitrosomonas* (160). However, there is still the possibility that the additional oxygen may be derived from water if the oxidation of ammonia to nitrite involves the ultimate transfer of electrons to atmospheric oxygen via a cytochrome oxidase type of system exclusively. If, however, one or more steps in the oxidation of ammonia to nitrite is mediated by an oxygenase type of enzymatic system, then at least one of the oxygen atoms of nitrite would be derived from atmospheric oxygen(170).

The fixation of carbon dioxide and the formation of cell material also requires reducing power in the form of $NADH + H^+$. Thermodynamically it is impossible for the generation of the whole of this reducing power through the electron transport chain

$$NH_2OH \rightarrow cyt.\ b \rightarrow cyt.\ c \rightarrow cyt.\ oxidase \rightarrow O_2$$

This problem seems to be characteristic for all chemoautotrophic bacteria (121). It is therefore thought that a reversed electron flow from ferrocytochrome c to NAD^+ or $NADP^+$ with the possible mediation of flavoproteins may occur. This system, however, would require an input of energy (5–7). The fact that a 5-minute lag occurs in the ATP-dependent reduction of $NAD(P)^+$ indicates the possible formation of a high-energy compound effective in this reduction:

$$ATP + X \rightarrow {\sim}X + ADP + P_i$$

$$AH_2 + {\sim}X + NAD(P)^+ \rightarrow A + NAD(P)H + H^+ + X$$

where AH_2 may be either hydroxylamine or succinate or even reduced cytochrome c. Since cytochrome c appears to be rather an intermediate between the electron transfer chain and the formation of a high-energy intermediate utilized by energy-requiring processes than a component part of an intermediate that functions between the breakdown of ATP and the formation of the high-energy intermediate (131), the electron transport system would then be similar to Scheme 5.2. (Reprinted with permission of Elsevier Publ. Co., Amsterdam).

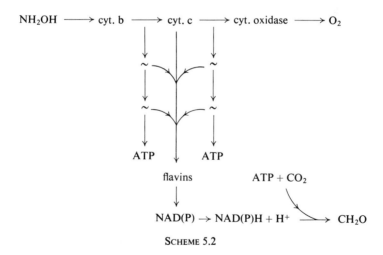

SCHEME 5.2

The electrons donated by hydroxylamine are ultimately accepted by oxygen. This path is certainly mediated by cytochromes of the b, c, and oxidase type (a or o) (13). From cytochrome c branches the pathway of energy transfer "$\sim$" involving hypothetical high-energy intermediates generated either in the electron transport chain or from externally supplied ATP. This possible formation of an high-energy intermediate supports in some ways the observation by Burge et al.(44) of a strong phosphatase activity which results in a net loss of organic phosphate and an incorporation of $^{32}P_i$ into organic fractions including ATP and ADP. However, no such high-energy intermediate has yet been found in Nitrosomonas.

Nitrobacter. The genus Nitrobacter oxidizes nitrite to nitrate and is generally found in association with Nitrosomonas. Whereas Nitrosomonas requires intermediate steps for its oxidation, Nitrobacter oxidizes nitrite directly to nitrate. It is therefore necessary that phosphorylation and NAD^+ reduction be coupled to this oxidation step. The problem in the formation of reducing power is similar to Nitrosomonas since the potential of $NO_2^- NO_3^-$ system is $+0.421$ against -0.32 of the $NAD^+/NADH + H^+$ system(12). It is therefore assumed that Nitrobacter has the same general scheme of electron transport as Nitrosomonas. Reduction level measurements of cytochromes c and a_1 in intact cells and cell-free extracts of Nitrobacter(201) revealed an activation energy of the over all nitrite oxidation process of approximately 15 kcal as shown in Scheme 5.3. [Reprinted with permission of Macmillan (Journals) Ltd., London].

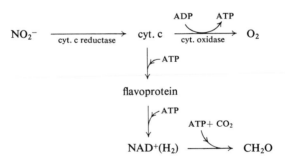

SCHEME 5.3. [Reprinted with permission of Macmillan (Journals) Ltd., London.]

There are, however, a number of other differences in comparison with Nitrosomonas. Ions, similar in structure to nitrite, e.g., nitrate, arsenite, cyanate, and even nitrite itself, inhibit the nitrite oxidation at normal oxygen concentrations(47) and stimulate it at decreased oxygen concentrations. Inhibition by nitrite could be explained if it is assumed that a transport system carries nitrite into the cell as indicated in the following (reprinted with permission of the Biochemical Journal).

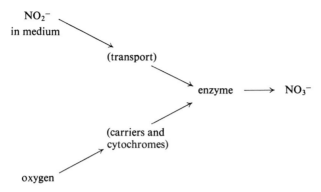

At moderate nitrite concentrations (up to approximately 20 mM) and normal oxygen concentrations (20 % in the gas phase), the influence of the two on the rate of nitrite oxidation via a carrier–cytochrome system can be assumed to be roughly equal. If this is so, then at lower oxygen concentrations a lower nitrite concentration is necessary to obtain optimal oxidation rates. *Nitrobacter* seems to have therefore a regulatory mechanism for its oxidation rate, probably to cope with the various oxygen levels in the environment. This is different from *Nitrosomonas*, since in the latter the outlet is the formation of nitrous gas.

The enzymatic oxidation of nitrite is catalyzed by cytochrome-containing electron transport particles via cytochrome c and cytochrome oxidase-like components(14, 16). This oxidation is coupled with the generation of ATP:

$$NO_2^- + \tfrac{1}{2}O_2 + nADP + nP_i \rightarrow NO_3^- + nATP$$

This liberated energy is utilized in part to drive endergonic reduction and assimilation of carbon dioxide and in part to produce reduced NAD(P). There is no evidence yet for the presence of an oxygenase type of mechanism as in *Nitrosomonas*. With the regulatory mechanism of nitrite oxidation mentioned above, an oxygenase functional system would hardly work. Aleem *et al.*(16) and Aleem(3) demonstrated for the first time in *Nitrobacter* that water and not molecular oxygen participated in the oxidation of nitrite to nitrate and that the hydrogen donor for the concomitant reduction of NAD^+ was also water(3, 16).

$$NO_2^- + nADP + nP_i + H_2O \xrightarrow{\text{cyt. chain}} NO_3^- + nATP + 2\,H^+ \quad (1)$$

$$NAD^+ + 2\,H^+ + 2e + \text{energy} \longrightarrow NADH + H^+ \quad (2)$$

$$NADH + H^+ + ADP + P_i + \tfrac{1}{2}O_2 \longrightarrow NAD^+ + ATP + H_2O \quad (3)$$

Nitrite first donates electrons to the cytochrome–electron transport chain [reaction (1)], which are ultimately accepted by molecular oxygen [reaction (3)].

This reaction is coupled with ATP formation. One part of this energy is required for reaction (2), which is the reduction of NAD^+. This reduction involves the participation of electrons from a reduced component such as ferrocytochrome c of the respiratory chain and protons donated by water. Reaction (3) gives the energy required to fulfill the requirement of this reduction. The use of water as a source of hydrogen for the reducing power in the system was discovered in studies of cell-free preparations in the presence of tritiated H_2O. Aleem(3) used a pyruvate-lactate dehydrogenase (L-lactate: NAD oxidoreductase, E.C: 1.1.1.27) trapping system for his experiment. If the following reactions take place then the $NADH + H^+$ generated in the presence of ^3H_2O when trapped by pyruvate and lactate dehydrogenase should yield labeled lactate. Since this proved to be the case, the role of water as the

$$NO_2^- + ADP + P_i + \tfrac{1}{2}O_2 \xrightarrow[\text{transport chain}]{\text{cytochrome-electron}} NO_3^- + ATP$$

$$NAD^+ + NO_2^- + H_2O + ADP + P_i + \tfrac{1}{2}O_2 \longrightarrow NADH + H^+ + ATP + NO_3^-$$

$$NAD^+ + ATP + H_2O \longrightarrow NADH + H^+ + AMP + PP_i$$

$$CH_3COCOOH + NADH^+ + H^+ \xrightarrow[\text{dehydrogenase}]{\text{lactate}} CH_3CHOHCOOH + NAD^+$$

source of a reductant was established. There is no necessity for other types of high-energy intermediates as in the case of *Nitrosomonas*. The energy metabolism of *Nitrobacter* in comparison has some similarities with photosynthesis and seems to stand between that of photosynthesis and that in *Nitrosomonas*. During the autotrophic oxidation of 1 gm mole of nitrite approximately 17.5 kcal of energy becomes available. It is therefore quite reasonable to assume that at least part of this energy is dissipated in other reactions such as ATP formation. Consideration of the over-all yield suggests that 2 ATP might be expected(132), which supports the findings of Aleem and Nason(14). The enzyme ATPase is also present and might regulate the ATP requirement as outlined earlier.

In 1965, Schön(171) discovered that the inhibition of the nitrite oxidation at normal oxygen concentration did not result from the NO_2^- inhibiting its own oxidation or from the influence of oxygen on the nitrite oxidation, but resulted from the effect of oxygen on the carbon dioxide assimilation. The presence of 95% (v/v) oxygen inhibited the carbon dioxide assimilation completely but did not affect the nitrite oxidation in *Nitrobacter winogradskyi*. These findings provide firm evidence that the energy metabolism must be independent of the carbon dioxide assimilation. During the same investigations it was shown that a decrease in soluble oxygen to 2 mg of O_2/liter (approximately 27% saturation) was harmful for the growth of *Nitrobacter*, whereas the limiting concentration for *Nitrosomonas* was 0.9 mg of O_2/liter. *Nitroso-cystis oceanus*(82) was found to react similarly to *Nitrobacter winogradskyi*.

This separation of energy metabolism from the carbon dioxide assimilation was supported by the finding of cytochromes c, b, a, and two components of a_1(181), which suggests that *Nitrobacter* must have a respiratory chain which functions independently from the reducing power production and subsequent carbon dioxide assimilation.

Further studies on the electron transport system came from studies of nitrate reduction by *Nitrobacter*. Spectral studies indicate that the pathway of this nitrate reduction involves cytochrome c and one of the a_1 components, whereas

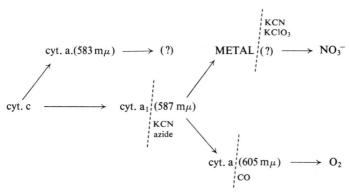

SCHEME 5.4. (Reprinted with permission of the American Society of Biological Chemists.)

the pathway for cytochrome oxidase activity (occurring in nitrite oxidation) involves the same cytochromes and in addition cytochrome a at 605 mμ(181). The electron transport scheme (Scheme 5.4) would thus comprise these new discoveries. According to this scheme electrons are transferred from bacterial cytochrome c to both cytochrome a_1 components, namely, those which absorb at 583 and 587 mμ. The function of the former is still unknown, whereas the latter is definitely involved in electron transport. Since nitrate as well as oxygen oxidizes bacterial cytochrome c and a_1 at 587 mμ, these two components are placed in a position common to both nitrate reductase and cytochrome oxidase. From cytochrome a_1 (587 mμ) electrons may be donated either directly to nitrate or through cytochrome a (605 mμ) to oxygen. The requirement of molybdenum for growth of *Nitrobacter* seems to be well established(67) and is required in nitrate reduction.

Of particular interest is the fact that oxygen is not inhibitory to nitrate reduction in preparations of *Nitrobacter agilis*(181) which is in contrast to all other respiratory nitrate reductases. In fact, the addition or accumulation of nitrate prevents or inhibits the oxygen uptake.

We have in the chemoautotrophic *Nitrobacter* a unique example of metabolism whereby *Nitrobacter* growth depends on the oxidation of nitrite to nitrate with oxygen as terminal electron acceptor and possesses also an enzyme capable of reducing nitrate to nitrite. Any accumulation of nitrate inhibits the production of nitrate as the oxygen uptake is inhibited. In this case *Nitrobacter* may be able to reduce nitrate to nitrite, and this could mean a recycling process of the nitrite used for nitrite oxidation. If this new discovery proves to be functional in *Nitrobacter* it would be a better regulatory mechanism than that mentioned earlier(47). There exists, however, insufficient evidence for

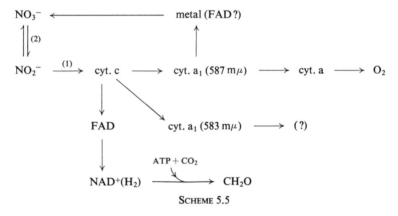

SCHEME 5.5

either of the two mechanisms, although *Nitrobacter* seems to have a high cytochrome concentration(200).

In summarizing the present state of knowledge in *Nitrobacter* metabolism, the electron transport chain together with the formation of ATP and reduced NAD gives Scheme 5.5, where (1) is catalyzed by a cytochrome c reductase which is coupled with a phosphorylation and (2) by nitrate reductase. The nitrate reductase may be of the type of cytochrome:nitrate oxidoreductase (E.C. 1.9.6.1), although Straat and Nason(181) do not specify any NAD-linked or flavoprotein-linked reaction. Since there is a metal-containing flavoprotein as prosthetic group, it is anticipated that the nitrate reductase could also be reduced NAD:nitrate oxidoreductase (E.C. 1.6.6.1). The electron transfer from nitrite to cytochrome c is almost certainly catalyzed by reduced NAD: (acceptor) oxidoreductase (E.C. 1.6.99.3) since cytochrome c may act as acceptor instead of NAD, if the preparation has been subjected to certain treatments. Now that the nature and function of the electron transport chain and the important part played by water as the reductant have been established the question as to whether *Nitrobacter* really had two phosphorylation sites as has *Nitrosomonas* will be discussed. Using substrate quantities of cytochrome c no phosphorylation could be obtained under anaerobic conditions with NO_2^- as the electron donor(9). However, the site between cytochrome c and molecular oxygen was operative. Therefore, with NO_2^- as the electron donor, ATP can be visualized as being generated in the cytochrome oxidase region of the electron transport chain. Preliminary evidence, based on spectrophotometry, and use of uncouplers indicated that nitrite enters first at the level of cytochrome a_1 and the reduction of cytochrome c involves an energy-dependent reversal of electron transfer from cytochrome a_1-like component(10). Thus only one phosphorylation site is so far in evidence. In view of these observations the electron transport from nitrite to molecular oxygen as well as to NAD may be presented as follows(9):

$$H_2O \cdot NO_2^- \longrightarrow \text{cyt. } a_1 \longrightarrow \text{cyt. } a_3 \longrightarrow Fe^{2+}(?) \longrightarrow O_2$$

ADP + Pi

ATP

NAD $\xleftarrow{\text{ATP}}$ FP $\longleftarrow$ cyt. b $\xleftarrow{\text{ATP}}$ cyt. c

The nature of substrate specificity of *Nitrobacter* species is also uncertain since it was found that they can metabolize a large variety of organic compounds(57). However, neither cell development nor nitrification took place unless carbon dioxide was provided. These organic compounds were metabolized and also incorporated into cell material but they were unable to serve either as sole source of carbon or as energy substrates for cell development.

Hydrogenomonas. Members of this genus use for their energy-yielding process the reaction between molecular hydrogen and molecular oxygen. Since this reaction is also called "the *Knallgas* reaction" one finds these bacteria quite commonly referred to as "*Knallgas* bacteria." The word "*Knallgas*" is German and means something like "explosive gas."

Species of *Hydrogenomonas* are able to live autotrophically or heterotrophically and are chemolithotrophs as well as strict aerobes.

In common with all bacteria which utilize molecular hydrogen in one way or another, *Hydrogenomonas* species possess hydrogenase activity. Cells reduce nitrate and methylene blue at the expense of hydrogen and can assimilate one mole of CO_2 for every two moles of O_2 reduced in the *Knallgas* reaction(29). As autotrophs, the organisms need ATP and reducing power for the assimilation of carbon dioxide via the Calvin cycle. This CO_2 fixation is very rapid(36). Very little work has been done to date on the energy metabolism of these bacteria. Cell-free extract studies, however, on *Hydrogenomonas H 16* revealed that the hydrogenase activity can be separated into a soluble and a particulate fraction(64). The soluble fraction is able to reduce methylene blue, NAD^+, FMN, FAD, and oxygen, but not $NADP^+$. The particulate fraction is more limited in its action and reduces methylene blue and apparently only oxygen as a physiological hydrogen acceptor. The soluble hydrogenase would be sufficient to provide the cell with reduced NAD and ATP for carbon dioxide reduction and Eberhardt(64) suggested that the second hydrogenase may be the first member of the electron transport chain which is coupled with oxidative phosphorylation. There is also some evidence for the presence of a reduced NAD oxidase, which could oxidize $NADH + H^+$ with oxygen.

$$NADH + H^+ + O_2 \rightarrow NAD^+ + H_2O_2$$
$$\text{or} \quad 2\,NADH + 2\,H^+ + O_2 \rightarrow 2\,NAD^+ + 2\,H_2O$$

This enzyme could be reduced NAD:(acceptor) oxidoreductase (E.C. 1.6.99.3), which is synonymous with reduced-NAD dehydrogenase and cytochrome reductase. It is a flavoprotein and after purification can be coupled with cytochrome c as an acceptor. There is no ATP formation in this transfer. The formation of H_2O_2 presents no problem since *Hydrogenomonas H 16* exhibits a strong catalase activity.

Hydrogenomonas H 16 has therefore two hydrogenases which have different functions. These functions may be similar to those of the two hydrogenases of the photosynthetic bacteria. Since one enzyme is obligately coupled with the phosphorylation of ADP to ATP(33), its function is controlled by the relative concentrations of ADP and ATP, being retarded by a deficiency of the former or an excess of the latter. Excess ATP may occur when there is a deficiency of carbon dioxide. The second hydrogenase transfers the electrons to oxygen via reduced NAD and is not necessarily affected by excess ATP, but possibly by reduced NAD(2). This control mechanism would in this case be similar to the one of APS reductase in *Desulfovibrio desulfuricans*, where the reaction product AMP carries this regulatory function. The over-all scheme has been described by Packer and Vishniac(145) and Repaske(161).

Very little information is available in regard to the oxidation of reduced NAD by hydrogenomonads. Investigations with *Hydrogenomonas eutropha* revealed two possible pathways(162), one which has a menadione-dependent reductase and the other a menadione-independent cytochrome c reductase. With quinones being found in a number of microorganisms(100, 123) the following scheme (reprinted with permission of American Society of Microbiology) has been proposed to exist in cell-free extracts of hydrogen bacteria(41):

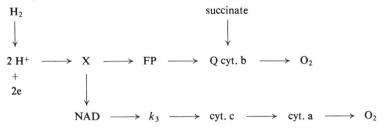

The oxidative phosphorylation of hydrogen is thought of being limited to between hydrogen and cytochrome b.

With carbon dioxide as the sole carbon source and hydrogen as the sole electron donor, *Hydrogenomonas ruhlandii*(145) performs as follows:

$$CO_2 + H_2 \rightarrow (CH_2O) + H_2O \qquad \Delta F = +8.2 \text{ kcal}$$

$$H_2 + O_2 \rightarrow H_2O \qquad \Delta F = -56.5 \text{ kcal}$$

$$CO_2 + 2H_2 + O_2 \rightarrow (CH_2O) + 2H_2O$$

Similar results have been obtained with *Hydrogenomonas facilis*(155).

When *Hydrogenomonas facilis* is grown heterotrophically, the hydrogenase, although present, is not functional(125). Its function, however, recovers almost immediately if cells are washed and exposed to an atmosphere of 95% (v/v) hydrogen and 5% (v/v) air. *Hydrogenomonas facilis* can develop heterotrophically, as an obligate aerobe, on many substrates(164). Using acetate as substrate, *Hydrogenomonas H 16 G* is able to use the complete TCA cycle (197). *Hydrogenomonas facilis* may use the glyoxylate bypass (see Chapter 9) since it lacks aconitate hydratase (citrate (isocitrate) hydrolyase, E.C. 4.2.1.3). Whichever pathway is used, the *Knallgas* reaction is certainly no longer required, since both cycles yield the energy and reducing power necessary for biosynthesis.

Autotrophically and heterotrophically, cells of the *Hydrogenomonas* species are able to synthesize poly-β-hydroxybutyric acid, not only heterotrophically from pyruvate or acetate but also autotrophically from carbon dioxide (71, 72, 169).

Since acetate from the Calvin cycle is the precursor of the polymer, Schlegel and Gottschalk(168) postulated two pathways:

(1) Acetyl CoA could be formed from 3-phosphoglycerate via pyruvate and a decarboxylation reaction.

(2) Acetyl CoA could be formed from fructose 6-phosphate or xylulose 5-phosphate via a phosphoketolase reaction.

Since there was no phosphoketolase reaction detectable in *Hydrogenomonas H 16*(165), the first reaction from 3-phosphoglycerate via pyruvate is the only possible mechanism. Acetyl CoA is formed from pyruvate by a catalyzed reaction which requires pyruvate dehydrogenase (pyruvate:lipoate oxidoreductase (acceptor-acetylating), E.C. 1.2.4.1), CoA, NAD^+, and thiamine pyrophosphate:

$$\text{pyruvate} + \text{CoA-SH} + NAD^+ \xrightarrow{\text{+ TPP, Mg}^{2+}} \text{acetyl CoA} + CO_2 + \text{NADH} + H^+$$

The details of the formation of acetyl CoA will be dealt with in the section entitled "Chemoorganic, Heterotrophic Microorganisms and the Tricarboxylic Acid Cycle." Acetyl CoA may be carboxylated to malonyl CoA, which requires as cofactor, biotin, or may condense for the formation of poly-β-hydroxybutyric acid. The formation of malonate is assumed to be the introductory step toward lipid biosynthesis.

The speed of formation of poly-β-hydroxybutyric acid is far greater under heterotrophic than under autotrophic conditions. The polymer is normally utilized again in the absence of a carbon source and can be used for protein synthesis in the presence of an N source (169).

Apart from metabolic acids, *Hydrogenomonas facilis* and *H 16* can utilize certain carbohydrates such as glucose (55) or fructose (73) whereas *H. eutropha* utilizes fructose and gluconic acid (53). The fructose metabolism follows the Entner-Doudoroff pathway. *Hydrogenomonas H 16* exhibits a strong fructose 1,6-diphosphate phosphatase and only a weak phosphofructokinase, which makes the reverse reaction

$$\text{triose phosphate} \rightarrow \text{FDP} \rightarrow \text{F 6-P}$$

virtually impossible. The reaction

$$\text{6-phosphogluconate} \rightarrow \text{2-keto-3-deoxy-6-phosphogluconate}$$

thus becomes irreversible and the subsequent metabolic steps are to pyruvate and 3-phosphoglyceraldehyde. The activity of the ribulose diphosphate carboxylase is reduced by up to 75 % if cells of *Hydrogenomonas H 16* are grown on carbohydrates. *Hydrogenomonas facilis* and *H 16* are versatile bacteria as far as their metabolism is concerned.

Whenever the heterotrophically grown *Hydrogenomonas* spp. are grown under hydrogen atmosphere they exhibit a rapid and linear oxygen uptake (28), which means that they can grow almost immediately under autotrophic conditions again. *Hydrogenomonas* is also able to form urea as a storage product (112) with NH_4Cl as nitrogen source. As soon as the nitrogen source is exhausted, urease activity is observed which indicates a possible breakdown of endogenous nitrogen compounds, thus resembling the breakdown of poly-β-hydroxybutyric acid under similar conditions. Urease activity (111) is strongly inhibited by ammonium ions.

For further detailed studies on *Hydrogenomonas* refer to the comprehensive review by Schlegel (167).

The Iron Bacteria. The microbial transformation of iron is brought about in two ways (46):

(1) By specific organisms which use the oxidation of ferrous ion to ferric ion as a source of energy for growth: (a) some blue-green algae and (b) the "true iron bacteria," e.g., *Ferrobacillus ferrooxidans* and *Thiobacillus ferrooxidans.*

(2) By non-specific organisms. These may act by metabolizing the organic substances which chelate with iron and hold it in solution at pH 7.0. Removal of the chelate releases the Fe^{3+} which precipitates as $Fe(OH)_3$ or chelates with the substances of the bacterial cell resulting in iron encrustation on cell sheaths or capsules. We shall only deal with the specific organisms which use iron oxidation as a source of energy because the second group transform iron only as result of their metabolism, but do not require iron specifically for their energy metabolism.

Ferrobacillus ferrooxidans. Information concerning the metabolism of this bacterium is very limited, probably because of the lack of suitable methods for obtaining mass growth of cells. Observed yields of only one to two grams of cells per 18 liters of medium(38) do not encourage metabolic studies. *Ferrobacillus ferrooxidans* derives its energy from the following reaction:

$$4\,FeCO_3 + O_2 + 6\,H_2O \;\rightarrow\; 4\,Fe(OH)_3 + 4\,CO_2 \qquad \Delta F = -40\ kcal$$

Although 92 % of the theoretical amount of oxygen required for the oxidation of iron has been accounted for(120), the efficiency during the oxidation of 50 μmoles of iron was $20.5 \pm 4.3\,\%$.

Despite the higher efficiency, *Ferrobacillus* has the same problems with regard to the formation of ATP and reducing power as shown with the other chemolithotrophs. The preliminary findings of Aleem *et al.*(15) did in fact reflect the energy-dependent reversal of electron transport transfer from ferrocytochrome c to NAD^+ in cell-free extracts of this chemoautotroph. It contains cytochromes of the b, c, and a types and the E_m of Fe^{2+}/Fe^{3+} is 0.77 V. It was, however, observed(38) that this potential could be reduced when iron was complexed with an ion, for example, iron oxalate. The potential of iron oxalate is approximately zero at pH 4–7. It also seems possible that the enzymatic reduction of cytochrome c by ferrous ions under these conditions could prove to be an energy-yielding reaction, provided the potential of Fe^{2+}/Fe^{3+} was sufficiently lowered. This was found to be the case with iron–cytochrome c reductase(208) which was found to be capable of transferring electrons from ferrous ion to cytochrome c. The oxidation of $Fe^{2+} \rightarrow Fe^{3+}$ is accompanied by the production of an acid, which seems to be always H_2SO_4(61). In formulating any scheme for iron oxidation this requirement of SO_4^{2-} together with the fact that the ferrous ion must either enter the cell or be attached to a binding site at the surface of the cell in order to couple its oxidation with the carbon reduction mechanism within the cell, has to be taken into account. The scheme shown in Fig. 5.2 has been proposed(61).

The oxidation of iron is linked to an energy source where an iron–oxygen complex is formed. The iron in this complex is oxygenated, but not oxidized since no electron flow has taken place. The complex can be formed either in solution or on the cell surface where it reacts with iron oxidase (or oxygenase). This reaction releases an electron which is transported into the cell via sulfate or flavoprotein (FP). In the cell, this electron is assumed to go via an ubiquinone to cytochrome c, cytochrome a, and finally to oxygen as final acceptor. It is presumed that the electron transfer to cytochrome c is coupled to a phosphorylation step as in *Nitrobacter* and *Nitrosomonas*.

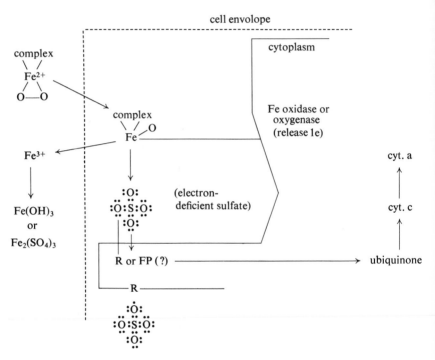

FIG. 5.2. Sulfate may be bound to an R group or else electrons flow directly to Flavoprotein; R may be a Flavoprotein. (Reprinted with permission of the American Society of Microbiologists.)

The source of reducing power is also sought in a reverse electron flow since it seems impossible to form an iron complex which would lower the potential to the E_m (−0.32 V) of the $NAD^+/NADH + H^+$ system. This would mean that one would have the same electron transport chain as outlined in *Nitrosomonas*, which would support the findings of Dugan and Lundgren (61). *Ferrobacillus ferrooxidans* is also able to grow on elemental sulfur (134). The oxidation of iron was as rapid by sulfur-grown cells as by iron-grown cells. It is suggested that the different oxidative capacities are owing to the heterogenous mixture of cell types in the culture population.

Thiobacillus ferrooxidans. The metabolism of *Thiobacillus ferrooxidans* has not been studied as extensively as that of *Ferrobacillus ferrooxidans.* The sulfate requirement(116), the effect of phosphate(35), and the rate of iron oxidation(114) give the impression that the metabolism of *Thiobacillus ferrooxidans* must be very similar to or even the same as that observed in *Ferrobacillus ferrooxidans.*

As the name indicates, *Thiobacillus ferrooxidans* is also able to oxidize reduced sulfur compounds. This oxidation, of course, is at a far slower rate than the oxidation of iron(115). Expressed on a molar basis, the organism can oxidize approximately 180 moles of ferrous iron in the same time as is required for the oxidation of one mole of sulfur. Both oxidations have been shown to occur simultaneously(115).

Other iron bacteria. A number of bacteria have been described in literature which can also oxidize ferrous and even manganous compounds(37) and which deposit these compounds in the form of a colloidal sheath. However, the taxonomy of these organisms is very complex and disputed at the moment. A number of species have been found to be cultural variants of two species, *Sphaerotilus discophorus* (*Leptothrix discophorus*) and *Sphaerotilus natans.*

A very interesting genus is *Gallionella* which deposits ferric hydroxide on the surface of a stalk. The absence of pure cultures of species of genera such as *Gallionella, Siderocapsa, Siderophaera, Siderobacter, Sideromonas,* and *Ferribacterium* has delayed biochemical investigation of these groups. For a review of iron bacteria in general, see Schlegel(166).

The Methane-Oxidizing Bacteria. The main representative of this group of bacteria is *Methanomonas methanooxidans* (*Pseudomonas methanica*). There is a possibility that the name "*Methanomonas methanooxidans*" was given to the autotrophic strains and "*Pseudomonas methanica*" to the heterotrophic strains of the same species(94) since *Pseudomonas methanica* oxidizes methanol, methane, formaldehyde, and formate as does *M. methanooxidans,* but it has a growth factor requirement for calcium pantothenate(63, 117).

Methane-oxidizing bacteria appear to occur quite commonly in the topmost layer of marine sedimentary materials and in soil, being particularly abundant where methane and free oxygen are present(90). Carbon dioxide is required for growth initiation and these bacteria are able to utilize almost equally well ammonium chloride, potassium nitrate, and peptone or glutamic acid as nitrogen sources(91). A most rapid utilization of methane occurred under an atmosphere of 10–40% oxygen, up to 70% methane and 5–20% carbon dioxide.

Methane oxidation by *Pseudomonas methanica*(63, 96) and *Methanomonas methanooxidans*(43) proceeds as follows:

$$CH_4 \rightarrow CH_3OH \rightarrow HCHO \rightarrow HCOOH \rightarrow CO_2$$

Resting cells of *M. methanooxidans* are capable of oxidizing methanol, formaldehyde, and formic acid, but there is no oxygen uptake with ethanol, propanol, butanol, acetaldehyde, propionaldehyde, butyraldehyde, acetate, propionate, or butyrate. Respiratory quotient values were found to be 0.59 for methanol, 0.73 for formaldehyde, and 1.33 for formate.

A suggestion that methanol is oxidized by *Ps. methanica* via a catalase-linked peroxidase to formaldehyde which in turn is oxidized by a substrate specific aldehyde dehydrogenase requiring NAD and glutathion[83] was partly opposed by Anthony and Zatman[25] and Johnson and Quayle[95] who showed that methanol oxidation was independent of catalase. However, *Ps. methanica* contains a high concentration of NAD^+-linked formaldehyde dehydrogenase (formaldehyde:NAD oxidoreductase, E.C. 1.2.1.1) which requires reduced glutathion (GSH). The subsequent reaction could be catalyzed by formate:NAD oxidoreductase (E.C. 1.2.1.2), which produces carbon dioxide and a further molecule of $NADH + H^+$. Although two molecules of $NADH + H^+$ are formed together with carbon dioxide for CO_2 fixation, the formation of ATP has not been solved. An alternative mechanism for formaldehyde oxidation was therefore proposed[95].

$$\text{formaldehyde} + \text{tetrahydrofolate} \rightleftharpoons N_{5,\,10}\text{-methylenetetrahydrofolate}$$

$$N_{5,\,10}\text{-methylene tetrahydrofolate} + NADP^+ \rightleftharpoons$$
$$N_{5,\,10}\text{-methylenetetrahydrofolate} + NADPH + H^+$$

$$N_{5,\,10}\text{-methylenetetrahydrofolate} + H_2O \rightleftharpoons N_{10}\text{-formyltetrahydrofolate} + H^+$$

$$N_{10}\text{-formyltetrahydrofolate} + ADP + P_i \rightleftharpoons \text{tetrahydrofolate} + \text{formate} + ATP$$

This proposed reaction sequence results in one mole of ATP and one mole of reduced NADP per mole of formaldehyde. It is, however, not known which scheme functions and whether the methane-oxidizing bacteria have a cytochrome system and another way of producing ATP. The purification of a methanol-oxidizing system of *Pseudomonas M 27*[26] showed that it reduces cytochrome c and is independent of NAD(P). Despite the fact that the enzyme appears to be NAD(P) independent, Anthony and Zatman[26] called it alcohol dehydrogenase with a specificity to primary alcohols. This enzyme seems to be alcohol:NADP oxidoreductase (E.C. 1.1.1.2), which requires NADP, whereas alcohol:NAD oxidoreductase (E.C. 1.1.1.1) acts also on secondary alcohols. The methanol-oxidizing step is probably the energy-yielding step which is coupled to a phosphorylation at cytochrome c level. Studies on the synthetic pathway revealed that the autotrophic CO_2 fixation mechanism does not apply (as the methane-oxidizing bacteria are heterotrophs). It therefore follows that the C_1 units are assimilated at reduction levels between methanol and formate by one pathway and as carbon dioxide by another. The mechanism of carbon dioxide incorporation may be mainly concerned with the synthesis of C_4 compounds from C_3 compounds. The C_1 incorporation appears to go via a modified pentose phosphate cycle(109), which involves the condensation of ribose 5-phosphate with formaldehyde to produce allulose 6-phosphate. This condensation is an hydroxymethylation reaction(110) of ribose 5-phosphate with formaldehyde (see Chapter 4) and appears to be the key reaction. There also appears to be a quantitative difference in the paths of carbon fixation from C_1 units on the one hand and carbon dioxide on the other, since high fixation occurs between the oxidation levels CH_4–HCHO, and low fixation between HCOOH–CO_2. If one makes the assumption that the conversions from methane to carbon dioxide are irreversible, then the evidence points to formaldehyde as the oxidation level at which most of the carbon is assimilated into cell constituents.

Pseudomonas methanica stores poly-β-hydroxybutyric acid, and 8% of the total lipid is in the form of monopalmitin(98). As in the other bacteria the polymer can serve as a substrate for endogenous metabolism in the absence of an exogenous carbon source(60).

The Sulfur Bacteria. Members of the genus *Thiobacillus*, generally called the "nonphotosynthetic sulfur bacteria," are known to oxidize thiosulfate to sulfate via various pathways. Thiosulfate, however, is not the only sulfur compound they are able to oxidize (see Table 5.1). This great versatility makes it difficult to map a general metabolic pathway for these organisms, particularly since the permeability problem, as in the discussion of iron bacteria, is an important factor in the metabolism of *Thiobacillus* species.

The four general pathways recognized at the present moment by taxonomists are the following(146):

(1) Here thiosulfate is oxidized first to the tetrathionate, which in turn is reoxidized to sulfate. However, the organisms which apparently perform this reaction are not able to oxidize tetrathionate alone: *Th. concretivorus* and *Th. thiooxidans. Thiobacillus neapolitanus* is the only bacterium in this group which oxidizes tetrathionate:

$$6Na_2S_2O_3 + 5O_2 \rightarrow 4Na_2SO_4 + 2Na_2S_4O_6$$

$$2Na_2S_4O_6 + 6H_2O + 7O_2 \rightarrow 2Na_2SO_4 + 6H_2SO_4$$

(2) *Thiobacillus thioparus* oxidizes thiosulfate first to sulfur, which in turn is oxidized to sulfate:

$$5Na_2S_2O_3 + H_2O + 4O_2 \rightarrow 5Na_2SO_4 + H_2SO_4 + 4S$$

$$2S + 3O_2 + 2H_2O \rightarrow 2H_2SO_4$$

(3) The facultative autotroph *Th. novellus* is able to oxidize thiosulfate directly to sulfate(4):

$$Na_2S_2O_3 + 2O_2 + H_2O \rightarrow Na_2SO_4 + H_2SO_4$$

TABLE 5.1

The Sulfur Bacteria

Thiobacillus	\$S_2O_3^{2-}\$ oxidized to:					Oxidation of:			pH (1% \$S_2O_3^{2-}\$)		Strict auto-troph	Utilizes		Motility
	\$S_4O_6^{2-}\$	\$S_5O_6^{2-}\$	\$S_3O_6^{2-}\$	\$SO_4^{2-}\$	\$S^0\$	\$S_4O_6^{2-}\$	\$S^0\$	\$H_2S\$	Initial	Final		\$NH_3\$	\$NO_3^-\$	
Concretivorus	+			+	+	−	+ (\$SO_4^{2-}\$)	+ \$SO_4^{2-}\$	4.4	2.3	+	+	+	+
Thiooxidans	+	+		+	+	−	+ \$SO_4^{2-}\$	+ \$SO_4^{2-}\$	4.4	2.2	+	+	−	+
Thioparus	−		+	+	+	−	+ \$SO_4^{2-}\$	−	6.6	4.5	+	+	+	±
X	+	+		+	+	+	+ \$SO_4^{2-}\$	+ \$SO_4^{2-}\$	6.6	3.3 → 3.0	+	+	+ +\$NO_2\$	−
Novellus	−	−		+		−	−	−	7.8	5.8	−			−
\$M_{20}\$, \$M_{77}\$, \$M_{79}\$	+	+		+	+	−	+ \$SO_4^{2-}\$	−	6.6	7.8 → 7.0	−			
T (Trautwein)	+	+	+	+		−	−	+ \$S_2O_3^{2-}\$ \$SO_4^{2-}\$	6.6	Slight rise then slight fall	−			
B (Waksman)	+	+	+	+	+	−	−	−						
K (Trautwein)	+	+	+	+	+	−	−	−	6.6	Slight rise then slight fall	−			+ +
Ferrooxidans	−			+	+		Poor	+	5.8	2.0	+	+	+	+ +
Caprolytiens				+	+		+ \$SO_4^{2-}\$	−	7.6	6.1	−			+ +
Denitrificans				+			+ (\$SO_4^{2-}\$)	+ \$SO_4^{2-}\$			?	+	+	+

(4) Some facultative autotrophs are able to perform this reaction which is coupled with a rise in pH that is sometimes followed by a return to the original value:

$$2\,Na_2S_2O_3 + H_2O + \tfrac{1}{2}O_2 \rightarrow Na_2S_4O_6 + 2\,NaOH$$

Although some of the thiobacilli are able to form elemental sulfur, they never seem to store it, but rather oxidize it further or excrete it(178).

The early work with *Thiobacillus* therefore revealed thiosulfate as playing a key role in sulfur metabolism. Studies on the reduction of elemental sulfur S^0 to S^{2-} with a reduced glutathion requirement(184,193,202) suggested

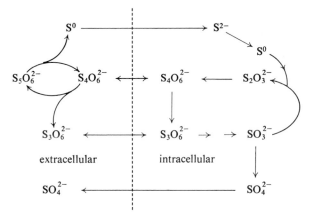

SCHEME 5.6. (Reprinted with permission of the American Society of Microbiology.)

a possible permeability barrier. This function, although possibly nonenzymatic, appears very similar to the oxidation of iron by *Ferrobacillus* which requires sulfate for its electron transport into the cell. A path of sulfur oxidation was therefore postulated(202) as shown in Scheme 5.6. The extracellular circular reactions are thiosulfate-dependent. The discovery(173) that only the outer S atom of $S_2O_3^-$ is metabolized to form SO_3^{2-}, does not agree with the postulated scheme. It was therefore suggested, that only S^{2-} can enter the cell, whereas all other reactions occur on the cell surface(119, 120) as shown in Scheme 5.7. This mechanism would also explain the GSH requirement for sulfur oxidation and would be very similar to, although probably more complex than, the GSH requirement of the iron bacteria. If these oxidations occur on the cell surface, the reactions within the cell would be reduced to that of oxidation of S^{2-} to SO_4^{2-}.

This mechanism corresponds with the findings of tracer element work(108) on *Thiobacillus* strain C; ^{35}S-thiosulfate was completely oxidized to sulfate, whereby ^{35}S sulfate was formed more rapidly from $^{35}S\cdot SO_3^{2-}$ as substrate

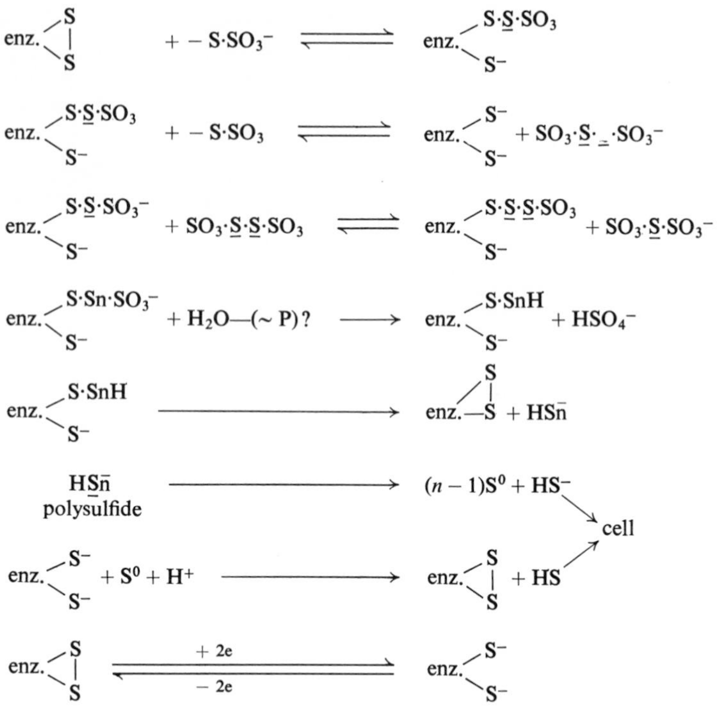

$$\text{enz.}\underset{\diagdown S}{\overset{\diagup \overset{\displaystyle S}{|}}{<}} \quad + - S \cdot SO_3^- \quad \rightleftharpoons \quad \text{enz.}\underset{\diagdown S^-}{\overset{\diagup S \cdot \underline{S} \cdot SO_3}{<}}$$

$$\text{enz.}\underset{\diagdown S^-}{\overset{\diagup S \cdot \underline{S} \cdot SO_3}{<}} \quad + - S \cdot SO_3 \quad \rightleftharpoons \quad \text{enz.}\underset{\diagdown S^-}{\overset{\diagup S^-}{<}} + SO_3 \cdot \underline{S} \cdot {}_{=} \cdot SO_3^-$$

$$\text{enz.}\underset{\diagdown S^-}{\overset{\diagup S \cdot \underline{S} \cdot SO_3^-}{<}} + SO_3 \cdot \underline{S} \cdot S \cdot SO_3 \quad \rightleftharpoons \quad \text{enz.}\underset{\diagdown S^-}{\overset{\diagup S \cdot \underline{S} \cdot S \cdot SO_3}{<}} + SO_3 \cdot \underline{S} \cdot SO_3^-$$

$$\text{enz.}\underset{\diagdown S^-}{\overset{\diagup S \cdot Sn \cdot SO_3^-}{<}} + H_2O—(\sim P)? \quad \longrightarrow \quad \text{enz.}\underset{\diagdown S^-}{\overset{\diagup S \cdot SnH}{<}} + HSO_4^-$$

$$\text{enz.}\underset{\diagdown S^-}{\overset{\diagup S \cdot SnH}{<}} \quad \longrightarrow \quad \text{enz.}—\underset{}{\overset{\diagup \overset{\displaystyle S}{|}}{S}} + HS\bar{n}$$

$$\begin{array}{l}\text{HS}\bar{\text{n}} \\ \text{polysulfide}\end{array} \quad \longrightarrow \quad (n-1)S^0 + HS^- \searrow \text{cell}$$

$$\text{enz.}\underset{\diagdown S^-}{\overset{\diagup S^-}{<}} + S^0 + H^+ \quad \longrightarrow \quad \text{enz.}\underset{\diagdown S}{\overset{\diagup \overset{\displaystyle S}{|}}{<}} + HS \nearrow$$

$$\text{enz.}\underset{\diagdown S}{\overset{\diagup \overset{\displaystyle S}{|}}{<}} \quad \underset{-2e}{\overset{+2e}{\rightleftharpoons}} \quad \text{enz.}\underset{\diagdown S^-}{\overset{\diagup S^-}{<}}$$

SCHEME 5.7. (Reprinted with permission of Annual Reviews, Inc.)

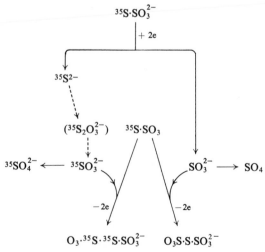

SCHEME 5.8. (Reprinted with permission of Biochemical Journal.)

than with $S \cdot ^{35}SO_2^-$ (see Scheme 5.8). The elemental sulfur produced could then penetrate the cell membrane.

This permeability barrier theory has received more support(194, 195) since it was found that SO_3^{2-} inhibits thiosulfate oxidation in cell-free extracts. Work with thiol-binding reagents indicated the existence of thiol groups on the membrane. Sulfite reacts readily with disulfide groups to form sulphenyl sulfites. It is therefore quite possible that SO_3^{2-} can displace $S_2O_3^{2-}$ from a sulfenyl thiosulfate and thus inhibits thiosulfate oxidation. It is therefore assumed that $S_2O_3^{2-}$ is carried into the cell with its S–S bond intact. The competition for the binding site on the membrane(192) between $S_2O_3^{2-}$ and SO_3^{2-} therefore occurs only outside the bacterial cell. This, however, opens the question of S^0 oxidation of $S_2O_3^{2-}$ which was thought to occur with the help of GSH on the cell membrane, since it was also shown that $S_2O_3^{2-}$ is an intermediate of S^{2-} formation. Adair(1) has provided evidence that the oxidation of S^0 to $S_2O_3^{2-}$ which may involve a glutathione polysulfide as intermediate(182) occurs only in the presence of GSH and may be linked to the cell wall membrane complex.

The initial product of sulfur oxidation by *Th. thioparus* and *Th. thiooxidans* was identified as being sulfite(183). The enzyme catalyzing this reaction (sulfur-oxidizing enzyme) has been purified and proposed to be an iron-containing oxygenase, which requires reduced glutathion as cofactor

$$S + O_2 + H_2O \rightarrow H_2SO_3$$

while thiosulfate is formed through a secondary, nonenzymatic reaction

$$H_2SO_3 + S \rightarrow H_2S_2O_3$$

This purified sulfur-oxidizing enzyme is a nonheme iron oxygenase which possibly contains labile sulfide. If it is assumed that the initial scission of thiosulfate by GSH leads to sulfur and sulfite instead of sulfide and sulfite, then this oxygenase could play an important role in the oxidation of the other sulfur atom of thiosulfate:

$$S \cdot SO_3^{2-} + GS^- \rightarrow GSS^- + SO_3^{2-}$$

$$GSS^- + O_2 + H_2O \rightarrow GS^- + SO_3^{2-} + 2H^+$$

$$2SO_3^{2-} + 2H_2O \rightarrow 2SO_4^{2-} + 4e + 4H^+$$

$$4e + O_2 + 4H^+ \rightarrow 2H_2O$$

$$\overline{}$$

$$S \cdot SO_3^{2-} + 2O_2 + H_2O \rightarrow 2SO_4^{2-} + 2H^+$$

In summarizing the present state of knowledge on the sulfur metabolism by thiobacilli, it can be said that all sulfur compounds in the culture medium have to be reduced or oxidized to $S_2O_3^{2-}$ first because of the permeability barrier occurring in the cell membrane. Elemental sulfur (S^0) is converted to $S_2O_3^{2-}$ with the help of GSH probably via a glutathione polysulfide; $S_2O_3^{2-}$ is transported across the membrane with the help of GSH and with its disulfide bond still intact. Within the cell, $S_2O_3^{2-}$ can undergo a great variety of oxidations. It can form polythionates and S^{2-} but the key intermediate to sulfate seems to be sulfite. Two different pathways for oxidizing sulfite to sulfate are functional. The first is coupled to photophosphorylation and forms energy-rich sulfur compounds such as APS, and the second is a direct oxidation of sulfite. The permeability barrier theory, however, is in contrast to the findings that *Thiobacillus* is able to utilize organic compounds, which will be dealt with at a later stage in this Chapter. The observations (39) made with regard to the growth of *Thiobacillus thiooxidans*, leaves doubt also on the validity of this permeability theory. It was found that keto acids accumulate in media of strictly autotrophically grown *Thiobacillus thiooxidans*. The keto acids, after having reached a certain level, inhibit further growth of the organism. The involvement of inorganic phosphate (P_i) in thiosulfate oxidation suggested that organic sulfur compounds may be involved in the reaction sequence (147, 148) which may be the same as, or similar to, that observed in *Desulfovibrio desulfuricans*. Studies with *Th. thioparus* revealed the following sequence:

$$4H^+ + 4e + 2S_2O_3^{2-} \rightarrow 2SO_3^{2-} + 2H_2S \tag{1}$$

$$2H_2S + O_2 \rightarrow 2S^0 + 2H_2O \tag{2}$$

$$2SO_3^{2-} + 2AMP \rightleftharpoons 2APS + 4e \tag{3}$$

$$2APS + 2P_i \rightleftharpoons 2ADP + 2SO_4^{2-} \tag{4}$$

$$2ADP \rightleftharpoons AMP + ATP \tag{5}$$

$$2S_2O_3 + O_2 + AMP + 2P_i + 4H^+ \rightarrow 2S^0 + 2SO_4 + ATP + 2H_2O$$

The first reaction is catalyzed by a thiosulfate reductase, which may be the thiosulfate:cyanide sulfurtransferase (E.C. 2.8.1.1), and forms sulfite and hydrogen sulfide. A sulfide oxidase oxidizes H_2S to elemental sulfur and a APS reductase forms APS from sulfite and AMP. In reaction (4) the enzyme ADP:sulfate adenylyltransferase (E.C. 2.7.7.5) or ADP sulfurylase catalyzes this reaction before ATP is formed in reaction (5) which is catalyzed by ATP:AMP phosphotransferase (E.C. 2.7.4.4) or adenylate kinase.

With GSH, $S_2O_3^{2-}$ is always reductively cleaved to S^0 or SO_3^{2-}. The oxidation reaction of SO_3^{2-} to SO_4^{2-} results, in other words, in the production of one mole of ATP per mole sulfate formed. From the oxidation of reduced sulfur compounds, thiobacilli can produce a high-energy sulfate at the substrate level and all indications are that SO_3^{2-} is the key intermediate.

Tetrathionate cannot function as a substrate for formation of ATP unless

GSH is present(142, 143); $S_4O_6^{2-}$ is rapidly reduced nonenzymatically to $S_2O_3^{2-}$ in the presence of GSH. At high cell concentration, however, tetra-thionate oxidation could take place after the addition of a trace amount of thiosulfate in *Thiobacillus X* and *Thiobacillus thioparus*(191) This oxidation of tetrathionate did not take place at low cell concentration and was also inhibited by 100% oxygen. Decreased oxygen concentrations allowed tetra-thionate oxidation to proceed even without the addition or presence of thio-sulfate. Tetrathionate can be metabolized best anaerobically. It is therefore

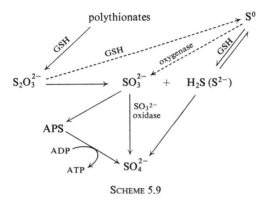

SCHEME 5.9

suggested that under aerobic conditions tetrathionate can be oxidized depend-ing upon age, strain, and cell concentration. Elementary sulfur (S^0) seems to be reduced first to H_2S with GSH before further oxidation to sulfate takes place, although *Thiobacillus* strain C appears to possess an Fe-containing oxygenase(183) whereby S^0 is oxidized to SO_3^{2-}.

The initial attack on $S_2O_3^{2-}$ is the reductive cleavage to S^{2-} and SO_3^{2-} or S^0 and SO_3^{2-}, whereby SO_3^{2-} can be oxidized via two different pathways: (*a*) a phosphorylation pathway involving APS, and (*b*) a nonphosphorylating pathway involving sulfite oxidase(49) (see Scheme 5.9). If one now combines the whole sulfur cycle known in nature, including dissimilatory sulfate reducers (*Desulfovibrio desulfuricans*), assimilatory sulfur reduction and sulfur oxidation (*Thiobacillus*, mammals, and plants), Scheme 5.10 can be drawn(147, 148). Reactions (1), (5), and (6) are dissimilatory sulfite reducers, (2), (3), and (4) are used by assimilatory sulfate reducers, (7) to (12) and (14) by thiobacilli, and (13) by most organisms. The individual reactions are catalyzed as follows: (1) ATP sulfurylase; (2) APS kinase; (3) sulfokinase; (4) PAPS reductase; (5) APS reductase; (6) sulfite reductase; (7) sulfide oxi-dase; (8) thiosulfate reductase; (9) APS reductase; (10) ADP sulfurylase; (11) sulfite oxidase; (12) tetrathionase, GSH requirement; (13) serine sulf-hydrase; (14) nonenzymatic, but GSH is required; and (15) Fe-containing oxygenase.

There seems to be hardly any doubt that thionate and sulfide oxidation are coupled with ATP formation(105).

Low aeration inhibits the completion of thiosulfate oxidation by *Thiobacillus X*, and tetrathionate is formed instead(190). Thiosulfate can also function as an intermediate in the oxidation of S^0 by *Thiobacillus X*(183).

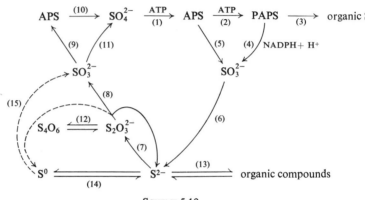

SCHEME 5.10

Over the recent years the postulated oxidation mechanisms of sulfur compounds have, however, become more complicated. It was shown that cell-free extracts of *Th. thioparus* and *Th. thiooxidans* catalyze the complete oxidation of S^{2-}, $S_2O_3^{2-}$, $S_4O_6^{2-}$, $S_3O_6^{2-}$ to sulfate, and it was demonstrated that tetra- and trithionate are formed during thiosulfate oxidation(127).

$$4\,S^{2-} \longrightarrow 2\,S_2O_3^{2-} \longrightarrow S_4O_6^{2-} \longrightarrow \begin{cases} SO_3^{2-} \\ \\ S_3O_6^{2-} \end{cases} \longrightarrow 4\,SO_3^{2-} \longrightarrow 4\,SO_4^{2-}$$

Autotrophic carbon dioxide fixation, which occurs in the thiobacilli, requires reduced NAD or NADP and ATP(11,106). The discovery of cytochromes of the c type(126,188) and a thiosulfate-oxidizing system(189) connected the $S_2O_3^{2-}$ transfer across the cell membrane with its subsequent oxidation together with an electron transfer. The thiosulfate-oxidizing system is a thiosulfate-activating enzyme called "thiosulfate–cytochrome c reductase"(6) which is not involved in an oxidative phosphorylation process(86). However, the transfer of electrons to molecular oxygen is mediated by cytochromes of b, c, o, and a type(9). This process does generate energy which could be utilized to drive the reverse electron flow for the reduction of NAD(P)(5,8):

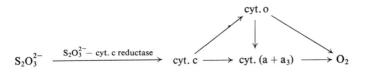

The direct reduction of pyridine nucleotides by inorganic sulfur compounds is thermodynamically infeasible and involves highly endergonic reactions(70):

$$(S^{2-} + HS^+ + H_2S) + 3\,H_2O + 3\,NAD(P) \rightarrow SO_3^{2-} + 3\,NAD(P)H + 5\,H^+$$
$$\varDelta F = +186\;\text{kcal/mole}$$

$$SO_3^{2-} + H_2O + NAD(P) \rightarrow SO_4^{2-} + NAD(P)H + H^+$$
$$\varDelta F = +33.7\;\text{kcal/mole}$$

The mode of formation of reducing power necessary for carbon dioxide fixations is therefore the same as in the other autotrophs(5, 107) (reprinted with permission of the American Society of Microbiology):

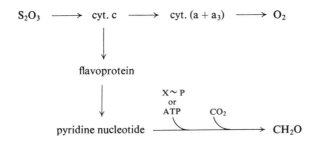

We have therefore an electron pathway toward oxygen and an energy-dependent reverse electron flow system which forms reduced $NAD(P)^+$ necessary for carbon dioxide fixation. During the SO_3^{2-} oxidation there is a coupled phosphorylation with the formation of AMP and ATP. The ATP- and NADH-dependent CO_2 assimilation is markedly inhibited by AMP(93). Likewise, AMP inhibits the CO_2 fixation when cell-free extracts are primed with ribose 5-phosphate and ATP. The fixation of CO_2 with ribulose diphosphate as acceptor is not very sensitive to AMP and the phosphoenol pyruvate carboxylation is hardly affected by AMP. These observations indicate therefore that AMP causes a competitive inhibition in systems where ATP is involved (11). This competitive inhibition could possibly represent a basic control mechanism. There appears to exist an AMP regulation of CO_2 fixation which could possibly represent a basic control mechanism.

Some species of *Thiobacillus* are able to utilize organic material such as aspartic acid(45), yeast extract, glucose(40), glutamate, acetate(102), and other organic materials(128), but no growth occurred in the absence of thiosulfate. In all cases ribulose 1,5-diphosphate carboxylase synthesis is repressed.

The assimilation of these organic compounds(102) provided the evidence for the presence of TCA cycle enzymes in *Th. thioparus*(54). Thiobacilli appear to require certain organic compounds for their assimilation(101) despite the functioning of the Calvin cycle. Provided that energy is available from thiosulfate oxidation *Thiobacillus neapolitanus* strain C(103) is able to activate exogeneous amino acids, incorporate them together with carbon dioxide into protein, and also synthesize proline and arginine from glutamate and adenine

TABLE 5.2

FREE ENERGY EFFICIENCY OF CHEMOLITHOTROPHIC BACTERIA[a]

Organism	Reaction	$-\Delta F°$ 298°C (kcal)	Free energy efficiency (%)
Hydrogenomonas sp.	$H_2 + \frac{1}{2}O_2 = H_2O$	57.4	30
Thiobacillus thiooxidans	$S^0 + \frac{3}{2}O_2 = H_2SO_4$	118	max. 50
Thiobacillus denitrificans	$5\,Na_2S_2O_3 + 8\,KNO_3 + 2\,NaHCO_3 =$ $6\,Na_2SO_4 + 2\,K_2SO_4 + 4\,N_2 + 2\,CO_2 + H_2O$	893	max. 25
Thiobacillus thiocyanooxidans	$NH_4CNS + 2\,O_2 + 2\,H_2O = (NH_4)_2SO_4 + CO_2$	40	25
Thiobacillus ferrooxidans	$Fe^{2+} = Fe^{3+} + e$	11.3	3
Nitrosomonas sp.	$NH_4^+ + \frac{3}{2}O_2 = NO_2^- + H_2O + 2\,H^+$	66.5	max. 20

[a] From Senez(172). Reprinted with permission of the American Society of Microbiology.

and guanine from glycine. Its biosynthesis depends almost on mechanisms like those of heterotrophs but requires a chemolithotrophic energy supply (see Table 5.2).

Thiobacillus novellus can also grow heterotrophically without a chemolithotrophic energy supply(8). Organic (succinate) oxidations yield high-energy cellular intermediates such as ATP or precursors of it (~X) and then ATP or (~X) reverses the normal electron flow in the respiratory chain so that NAD^+ is reduced by cytochrome c as demonstrated in the other chemolithotrophs:

$$\text{succinate} + FP \rightarrow \text{fumarate} + FPH + H^+$$

$$FPH + H^+ + 2\ \text{cyt. } Fe^{3+} + (X) \rightarrow (\sim X) + FP + 2\ \text{cyt. } Fe^{2+} + 2\,H^+$$

$$(\sim X) + 2\ \text{cyt. } Fe^{2+} + NAD^+ + 2\,H^+ \rightarrow (X) + 2\ \text{cyt. } Fe^{3+} + NADH + H^+$$

On the other side of the chain, cytochrome c is oxidized by molecular oxygen under the production of a high-energy compound.

$$2 \text{ cyt. Fe}^{2+} + 2H^+ + \tfrac{1}{2}O_2 + (X) \rightarrow 2 \text{ cyt. Fe}^{3+} + H_2O + (\sim X)$$

The ($\sim$X) generated at the terminal or cytochrome oxidase site can also be used for the reversal of electron transfer to reduce NAD(P)(8). Thus the microorganism appears in principle not to change its respiratory chain when inorganic compounds are replaced by organic compounds as electron donors. There are no reports of poly-β-hydroxybutyric acid formation. The thiobacilli do not require this polymer because of their ability to use organic sulfur compounds or polythionates as storage products.

For the purpose of completion, mention should be made that for many years not only autotrophic but also heterotrophic bacteria [which can oxidize inorganic sulfur compounds(79–81)] have been known to exist. Some workers even consider that heterotrophs may play the dominant role in the oxidation of sulfur compounds in soil. Microorganisms such as *Pseudomonas fluorescens*, *Ps. aeruginosa*, and *Achromobacter stutzeri* represent some of the identified organisms which can oxidize thiosulfate to tetrathionate(179,180). There is, however, little information available as yet in regard to their requirements and metabolic activities(196).

Chemoorganotrophic, Heterotrophic Microorganisms and the Tricarboxylic Acid Cycle

A great number of microorganisms and other living cells meet their energy needs with the oxidation of organic compounds by molecular oxygen and liberation of free energy. An appropriate group of enzymes catalyze a series of consecutive transformations, including dehydrogenations, of these substrates resulting in their complete oxidation to carbon dioxide and water. The electrons removed from the substrates during these oxidations flow through an organized arrangement of electron carriers from the lowest to the highest potential and finally to oxygen. In the course of this energy flow ATP is generated and becomes available for biosynthesis. Processes which lead to pyruvate from carbohydrates or polysaccharides or lipids have been considered in Chapter 4. The complete oxidation of pyruvate will be considered in this section.

The conversion of pyruvate into water and carbon dioxide occurs by means of a series of reactions called the "tricarboxylic acid cycle" (TCA), "Krebs cycle," or, since citrate holds a key position among the intermediates, "citric acid cycle." Enzymes catalyzing the reactions of the TCA cycle have been found in extracts of a wide range of microorganisms. Thus, there is no doubt that this cycle is the main pathway of oxidative respiration in microorganisms. The operation of this cycle also provides the microorganisms with a number of precursors for biosynthetic reactions as will be indicated.

The TCA cycle itself can, however, accept only acetic acid in the form of an activated derivative. Pyruvate must first be broken down to yield a two-carbon acid. This conversion is achieved enzymatically with the help of a complex system consisting of not less than five different enzymes, the cofactors thiamine pyrophosphate and lipoic acid, as well as $NADH + H^+$. The detailed reaction is as follows:

$$
\begin{array}{c}
CH_3 \\
| \\
CO \\
| \\
COOH
\end{array}
\ + \ \text{thiamine PP} \ \xrightarrow{\ \ \textcircled{1}\ \ } \
\begin{array}{c}
CH_3 \\
| \\
CHOH \\
| \\
\text{thiamine PP}
\end{array}
\ + \ CO_2
$$

$$\alpha\text{-OH-ethyl thiamine PP}$$

$$
\begin{array}{c}
CH_3 \\
| \\
CHOH \\
| \\
\text{thiamine PP}
\end{array}
\ + \
\begin{array}{c}
S\!-\!CH_3 \\
| \ \ \ CH_2 \\
S\!\diagdown\ | \\
CH \\
| \\
(CH_2)_4 \\
| \\
COOH
\end{array}
\ \xrightarrow{\ \ \textcircled{1}\ \ } \
\begin{array}{c}
HS\!\diagdown\!CH_2 \\
| \\
CH_3 \quad CH_2 \\
| \quad\quad | \\
CO\!-\!S\!-\!CH \\
| \\
(CH_2)_4 \\
| \\
COOH
\end{array}
\ + \ \text{thiamine PP}
$$

$$\text{oxid. lipoate} \qquad\qquad \text{6-S-acetylhydrolipoate}$$

$$
\begin{array}{c}
HS\!-\!CH_2 \\
| \\
CH_3 \quad CH_2 \\
| \quad\quad | \\
CO\!-\!S\!-\!CH \\
| \\
(CH_2)_4 \\
| \\
COOH
\end{array}
\ + \ CoA \ \xrightarrow{\ \ \textcircled{2}\ \ } \ CH_3\!-\!CO\!-\!CoA \ + \
\begin{array}{c}
HS\!-\!CH_2 \\
| \\
CH_2 \\
| \\
HS\!-\!CH \\
| \\
(CH_2)_4 \\
| \\
COOH
\end{array}
$$

$$\text{dihydrolipoate}$$

$$
\begin{array}{c}
HS\!-\!CH_2 \\
| \\
CH_2 \\
| \\
HS\!-\!CH \\
| \\
(CH_2)_4 \\
| \\
COOH
\end{array}
\ + \ NAD^+ \ \xrightarrow{\ \ \textcircled{3}\ \ } \
\begin{array}{c}
S\!-\!CH_2 \\
| \ \ \ \ | \\
CH_2 \\
| \\
S\!-\!CH \\
| \\
(CH_2)_4 \\
| \\
COOH
\end{array}
\ + \ NADH + H^+
$$

$$NADH + H^+ + \tfrac{1}{2}O_2 \ \xrightarrow{\ \ \textcircled{4}\ \textcircled{5}\ \ } \ NAD^+ + H_2O$$

The enzymes involved in this complex system of acetyl CoA formation are:

(1) pyruvate dehydrogenase (pyruvate:lipoate oxidoreductase (acceptor-acetylating), E.C. 1.2.4.1)

(2) lipoate acetyltransferase (acetyl CoA: dihydrolipoate-S-acetyltransferase, E.C. 2.3.1.12)
(3) lipoamide dehydrogenase (reduced NAD: lipoamide oxidoreductase, E.C. 1.6.4.3)
(4) reduced NAD cytochrome c reductase (reduced NAD: (acceptor) oxido-reductase, E.C. 1.6.99.3; or reduced NAD dehydrogenase)
(5) cytochrome oxidase (cytochrome c: oxygen oxidoreductase, E.C. 1.9.3.1)

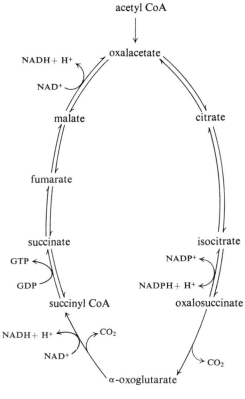

SCHEME 5.11

The role of coenzyme A has been discussed earlier and should be regarded as a carrier of acetyl groups (31), just as ATP is a carrier of phosphate groups and NAD^+ is a carrier of electrons in the cell. The free energy of acetyl CoA hydrolysis

$$CH_3CO—S—CoA + H_2O \rightarrow CH_3COO^- + H^+ + CoA—SH$$

is about $\Delta F = -8800$ cal/mole, which is somewhat higher than the free energy of ATP hydrolysis (122). The acetyl group of acetyl CoA is therefore the immediate fuel for the TCA cycle, and is made available to the cycle by an enzymatic transfer reaction. The TCA cycle will now be considered in toto and then step by step (see Scheme 5.11). In the first step of the cycle, acetyl CoA donates the acetyl group to the four-carbon dicarboxylic acid oxalacetic acid to form citric acid, a six-carbon tricarboxylic acid.

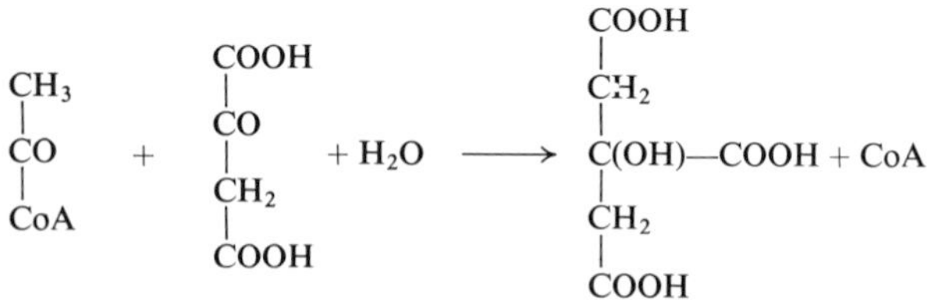

$$
\begin{array}{c}
CH_3 \\
| \\
CO \\
| \\
CoA
\end{array}
\quad + \quad
\begin{array}{c}
COOH \\
| \\
CO \\
| \\
CH_2 \\
| \\
COOH
\end{array}
\quad + H_2O \longrightarrow
\begin{array}{c}
COOH \\
| \\
CH_2 \\
| \\
C(OH)—COOH \\
| \\
CH_2 \\
| \\
COOH
\end{array}
\quad + CoA
$$

acetyl CoA   oxalacetic   citric acid
                    acid

During this reaction, catalyzed by the enzyme citrate synthase [citrate oxaloacetatelyase (CoA-acetylating), E.C. 4.1.3.7](187), free CoA is generated and can reenter in the formation of acetyl CoA. Citrate synthase is a condensing enzyme and may appear also under the names of "citrate condensing enzyme," "citrogenase," or, "oxalacetate transacetase(92)." The next two steps are disputable at the moment, since one single enzyme forms two other tricarboxylic acids. First, cis-aconitate and then isocitrate are formed with the enzyme

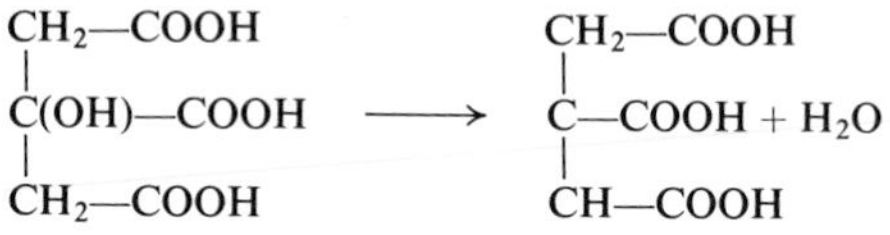

$$
\begin{array}{c}
CH_2—COOH \\
| \\
C(OH)—COOH \\
| \\
CH_2—COOH
\end{array}
\longrightarrow
\begin{array}{c}
CH_2—COOH \\
| \\
C—COOH \\
| \\
CH—COOH
\end{array}
+ H_2O
$$

           citric acid   cis-aconitate

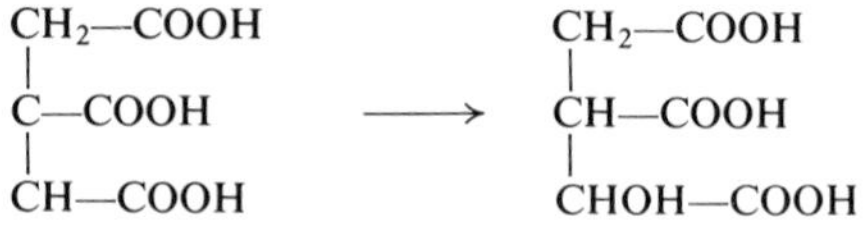

$$
\begin{array}{c}
CH_2—COOH \\
| \\
C—COOH \\
| \\
CH—COOH
\end{array}
\longrightarrow
\begin{array}{c}
CH_2—COOH \\
| \\
CH—COOH \\
| \\
CHOH—COOH
\end{array}
$$

        cis-aconitate   isocitrate

aconitate hydratase [citrate(isocitrate)hydrolyase, E.C. 4.2.1.3] catalyzing both reactions. Investigations by Speyer and Dickman(176) and Englard and Colowick(66), however, showed that cis-aconitate cannot be an intermediate of the TCA cycle, although it is in equilibrium with both citrate and isocitrate. The single intermediate which is common to all three substrates in the aconitase reaction is now believed(99) to be a carbonium ion with an intramolecular hydrogen transfer system. The actual reaction therefore would be

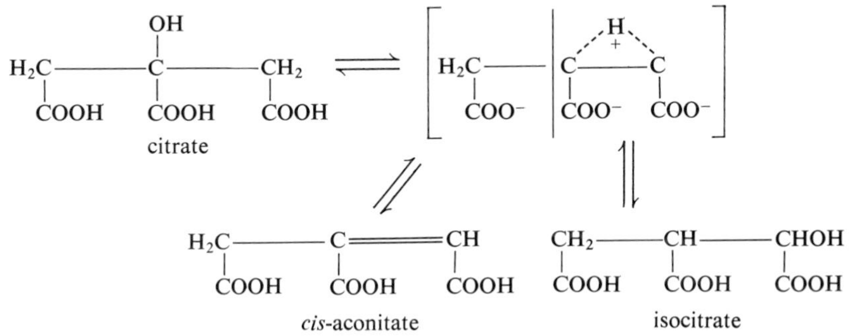

Speyer and Dickman(176) regard this carbonium ion as being different from the classical carbonium ion, because it occurs as a constituent of an enzyme-metal-substrate complex and it is formed and directed under the influence of an enzyme. This intermediate could therefore never occur free but only as part of a complex.

All three acids, citrate, *cis*-aconitate, and isocitrate form an equilibrium mixture.

Isocitrate is converted into oxalosuccinate by an enzyme isocitrate dehydrogenase (threo-D_S-isocitrate: NADP oxidoreductase (decarboxylating), E.C. 1.1.1.42) and is $NADP^+$-dependent. Consequently, a reduced NADP:

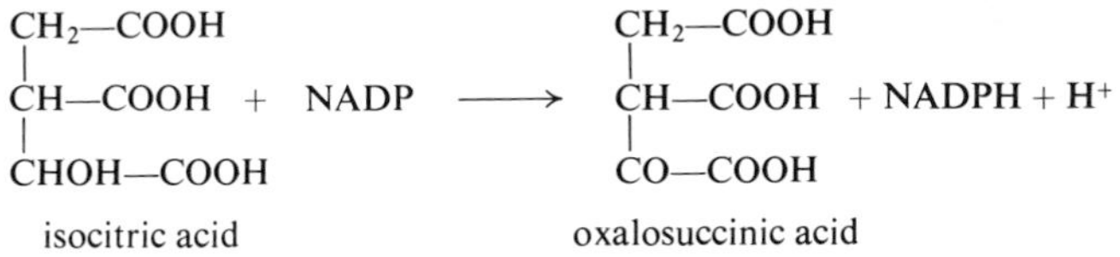

(acceptor) oxidoreductase (E.C. 1.6.99.1) and a cytochrome oxidase (E.C. 1.9.3.1) react in the reduction of NADP. The same enzyme (E.C. 1.1.1.42), which converts isocitrate to oxalosuccinate catalyzes the subsequent decarboxylation step to form 2-oxoglutarate and evolves one molecule of CO_2.

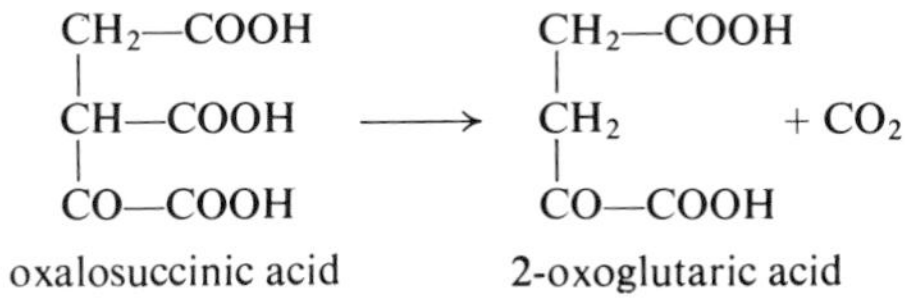

This molecule of CO_2 is the first of the two which arise from the two-carbon acetic acid fed into the cycle. The second molecule of CO_2 arises in the following step, which requires two enzymes, oxoglutarate dehydrogenase [2-oxoglutarate: lipoate oxidoreductase (acceptor-acylating), E.C. 1. 2.4.2] and lipoate acetyltransferase (acetyl CoA: dihydrolipoate-S-acetyltransferase, E.C. 2.3.1.12), and the cofactors thiamine pyrophosphate, coenzyme A, and lipoic acid. It is not clear yet whether the lipoate acetyltransferase reaction, which transfers acetyl groups, takes place or whether a similar enzyme is involved. The reaction complex and sequence, however, is very similar indeed to the one which transforms pyruvate into acetyl CoA. In the initial event, 2-oxo-glutarate reacts with thiamine pyrophosphate to form an "active succinic

$$
\begin{array}{l}
\text{CH}_2\text{—COOH} \\
| \\
\text{CH}_2 \\
| \\
\text{CO—COOH}
\end{array}
\;+\;
\begin{array}{l}
\text{S—CH}_2 \\
| \quad | \\
\text{S} \;\; \text{CH}_2 \\
\backslash \; | \\
\quad \text{CH} \\
\quad | \\
\text{(CH}_2)_4\text{—COOH}
\end{array}
\;\longrightarrow\;
\begin{array}{l}
\text{CH}_2\text{—COOH} \quad \text{HS—CH}_2 \\
| \qquad\qquad\qquad | \\
\text{CH}_2 \qquad\qquad\quad \text{CH}_2 \\
| \qquad\qquad\qquad\quad | \\
\text{CO———S———CH} \\
\qquad\qquad\qquad\quad | \\
\qquad\qquad\qquad \text{(CH}_2)_4\text{—COOH}
\end{array}
\;+\; \text{CO}_2
$$

2-oxoglutaric acid   lipoic acid   6-S-succinyl hydrolipoate

$$
\begin{array}{l}
\text{CH}_2\text{—COOH} \quad \text{HS—CH}_2 \\
| \qquad\qquad\qquad | \\
\text{CH}_2 \qquad\qquad\quad \text{CH}_2 \\
| \qquad\qquad\qquad\quad | \\
\text{CO———S———CH} \;+\; \text{CoA} \\
\qquad\qquad\qquad\quad | \\
\qquad\qquad\qquad \text{(CH}_2)_4 \\
\qquad\qquad\qquad\quad | \\
\qquad\qquad\qquad \text{COOH}
\end{array}
\;\longrightarrow\;
\begin{array}{l}
\\
\text{CH}_2\text{—COOH} \\
| \\
\text{CH}_2 \\
| \\
\text{CO—CoA}
\end{array}
\;+\;
\begin{array}{l}
\text{HS—CH}_2 \\
| \\
\text{CH}_2 \\
| \\
\text{HS—CH} \\
| \\
\text{(CH}_2)_4 \\
| \\
\text{COOH}
\end{array}
$$

6-S-succinyl hydrolipoate   succinyl CoA   dihydrolipoate

semialdehyde." By analogy with the mechanism for pyruvate oxidation, the intermediate is inferred to be α-hydroxy-γ-carboxypropyl thiamine pyro-phosphate(203). This derivative of thiamine pyrophosphate formed during the decarboxylation reaction is the succinic semialdehyde addition compound of the coenzyme. On the surface of the same protein, the four-carbon chain is transferred to enzyme-bound lipoic acid, forming a succinyl lipoamide compound. The succinyl group is then transferred to coenzyme A and the dihydro-lipoamide is reoxidized by NAD^+ as in the case of the pyruvate oxidation.

Thiamine pyrophosphate is required for the function of the enzyme oxoglutarate dehydrogenase. During the conversion of 2-oxoglutarate to succinyl CoA, one mole of NAD^+ is reduced to $NADH + H^+$ as well. For the formation of succinate, succinyl CoA is hydrolyzed by the enzyme succinyl CoA hydrolase (E.C. 3.1.2.3). The next step is a dehydrogenation of succinate,

$$
\begin{array}{l}
\text{CH}_2\text{—COOH} \\
| \\
\text{CH}_2 \\
| \\
\text{CO—CoA}
\end{array}
\;+\; \text{H}_2\text{O} \;\longrightarrow\;
\begin{array}{l}
\text{CH}_2\text{—COOH} \\
| \\
\text{CH}_2\text{—COOH}
\end{array}
\;+\; \text{CoA}
$$

succinyl CoA   succinic acid whereby succinate is oxidized to fumarate by the enzyme succinate dehydro-

$$\begin{array}{c} CH_2\text{---}COOH \\ | \\ CH_2\text{---}COOH \end{array} + \tfrac{1}{2}O_2 \longrightarrow \begin{array}{c} CH\text{---}COOH \\ \| \\ CH\text{---}COOH \end{array} + H_2O$$

succinic acid   fumaric acid

genase [succinate:(acceptor) oxidoreductase, E.C. 1.3.99.1]. The active group of this enzyme accepts the hydrogen atoms and becomes reduced. *Escherichia coli* as a facultative anaerobe has in addition to this succinate-oxidizing enzyme also a fumarate-reducing activity catalyzed by fumarate reductase, which is distinctly different from succinate dehydrogenase(87). Fumarate itself is now hydrated at the double bond to form malate by the action of the

$$\begin{array}{c} CH\text{---}COOH \\ \| \\ CH\text{---}COOH \end{array} + H_2O \longrightarrow \begin{array}{c} CH_2\text{---}COOH \\ | \\ CHOH\text{---}COOH \end{array}$$

fumaric acid   malic acid

enzyme fumarate hydratase (L-malate hydrolyase, E.C. 4.2.1.2). The final reaction in the TCA cycle is the dehydrogenation of malate to oxalacetate, catalyzed by malate dehydrogenase (L-malate:NAD oxidoreductase, E.C. 1.1.1.37). Some bacteria such as *Serratia*(85) have a malate dehydrogenase

$$\begin{array}{c} CH_2\text{---}COOH \\ | \\ CHOH\text{---}COOH \end{array} + NAD^+ \longrightarrow \begin{array}{c} CH_2\text{---}COOH \\ | \\ CO\text{---}COOH \end{array}$$

malic acid   oxalacetic acid

(D-malate:NAD oxidoreductase) which oxidizes malate to pyruvate. This enzyme is also known under the name "malic enzyme" and could be either E.C. 1.1.1.38 or 1.1.1.39, depending whether it also decarboxylates oxalacetate or not.

   The various possibilities of malate utilization make the oxidation of malate to oxalacetate a key step in the TCA cycle, but this step can be carried out in different ways by different microorganisms:

   (1) The most common situation is the presence of the soluble NAD-linked dehydrogenase (E.C. 1.1.1.37) as it occurs in *Escherichia coli*.

   (2) In addition to the soluble NAD-linked dehydrogenase, some bacteria possess a particulate oxidation system as it occurs in *Azotobacter agilis*(18) and *Micrococcus lysodeikticus*(51).

   (3) The soluble NAD-linked dehydrogenase can be absent and the oxidation of malate is coupled to oxygen and brought about by a particulate system as in *Serratia marcescens*(85), *Pseudomonas fluorescens*(177), or *Pseudomonas ovalis*

(68). These microorganisms require also cytochrome c, which may be similar to *Pseudomonas* cytochrome c-511(20,21,76) since nicotinamides and nucleotides did not show any influence. This enzyme, known under the name "malic enzyme" was also found in a number of *Lactobacillaceae*(156,157).

(4) The fourth possible mode of malate conversion to oxalacetate is achieved by a sequential oxidative decarboxylation of malate to pyruvate with a subsequent recarboxylation of pyruvate to oxalacetate. This mechanism has only been found so far in *Chromatium*, which lacks both the soluble and particulate malate dehydrogenases(69).

The cycling reactions of the TCA cycle will now be evaluated. One molecule of acetyl CoA and one molecule of oxalacetate are fed into the cycle. The reaction yields two molecules of carbon dioxide and one molecule of oxalacetate. It is therefore possible to write the over-all equation

$$\text{acetate} + \text{oxalacetate} \rightarrow 2CO_2 + \text{oxalacetate}$$

As one molecule of oxalacetate was supplied and received, the formula could be simplified to

$$\text{acetate} \rightarrow 2CO_2$$

In addition, there were four dehydrogenation steps in the TCA cycle which extract four pairs of electrons enzymatically from the intermediates of the cycle, to which reference will be made shortly. There is also the possibility of gaining one molecule of ATP from ADP, if the enzyme succinyl CoA synthetase or succinic thiokinase (succinate:CoA ligase (GDP), E.C. 6.2.1.4) replaces the enzyme succinyl CoA hydrolase (E.C. 3.1.2.3). This reaction would then be as follows(58):

$$\begin{array}{l} CH_2-COOH \\ | \\ CH_2-CO-CoA \end{array} + GDP + H_3PO_4 \longrightarrow \begin{array}{l} CH_2-COOH \\ | \\ CH_2-COOH \end{array} + GTP + CoA$$

succinyl CoA   succinic acid

$$GTP + ADP \longrightarrow GDP + ATP$$

A nucleoside diphosphate kinase (ATP:nucleoside-diphosphate phosphotransferase, E.C. 2.7.4.6) forms GDP and ATP from GTP and ADP. On the other hand, GTP could be used also for the biosynthesis of ribonucleic acid (RNA) as shown earlier (Chapter 7). It seems that this alternative way of succinyl CoA conversion to succinate may function in microorganisms. The metabolism of C_2 compounds as well as TCA cycle intermediates will be discussed in Chapter 9. It was mentioned earlier that pyruvate is completely broken down to carbon dioxide and water. So far only the carbon dioxide formation has been evaluated. Attention will now be paid to the system which produces the water. When molecular oxygen is available as final electron acceptor aerobic respiration takes place and the oxygen is reduced to water. Water is therefore the end product of the electron transport chain.

The TCA cycle primarily describes only the fate of the carbon skeleton of acetic acid, but it is not involved in energy conservation. From the four dehydrogenation steps in each revolution of the cycle, three are connected to NAD^+, thus forming three molecules of $NADH + H^+$. In the fourth step, the pair of electrons removed from succinate are accepted by the active group of succinate dehydrogenase, a so-called flavoprotein. These flavoproteins are a class of oxidizing enzymes that contain FAD as electron acceptor, which is an electron carrier similar to NAD^+ in its action. All four molecules donate their electrons to another series of enzymes, which constitute the respiratory chain (77) (see Scheme 5.12). Electrons can enter the chain of cytochromes only via one of two flavoproteins. One of these accepts electrons from $NADH + H^+$ and the other from succinate. The connection of the TCA cycle to the respiratory chain can be seen in Scheme 5.12.

The two carriers in the chain—coenzyme Q and cytochrome c—are thought to be relatively free moving molecules and can be transferred from one protein molecule to another. This multiplicity of catalysts provides a device for tapping or bleeding off the energy. It also takes into account the great variety of cytochrome pathways in microorganisms (see Chapter 3).

A molecule of cytochrome can carry only one electron at a time, whereas those of NAD and flavoprotein can carry two at a time. Therefore, each cytochrome has to react twice

$$NADH + H^+ + FAD^+ \rightarrow NAD^+ + FADH + H^+$$

$$FADH + H^+ + 2\ \text{cyt.}\ b_{ox} \rightarrow FAD^+ + 2\ \text{cyt.}\ b_{red}$$

$$2\ \text{cyt.}\ b_{red} + 2\ \text{cyt.}\ c_{ox} \rightarrow 2\ \text{cyt.}\ b_{ox} + 2\ \text{cyt.}\ c_{red}$$

$$2\ \text{cyt.}\ c_{red} + 2\ \text{cyt.}\ a_{ox} \rightarrow 2\ \text{cyt.}\ c_{ox} + 2\ \text{cyt.}\ a_{red}$$

$$2\ \text{cyt.}\ a_{red} + \tfrac{1}{2}O_2 \rightarrow 2\ \text{cyt.}\ a_{ox} + H_2O$$

When electrons are transferred from one compound to another, an oxidation–reduction reaction takes place, whereby the electron donor is the reducing agent and the electron acceptor the oxidizing agent.

During complete oxidation of one mole of glucose, twelve pairs of electrons pass down the respiratory chain with each pair giving a free energy of $\Delta F' = -52,000$ cal/mole. This means a total of $\Delta F' = -624,000$ cal/mole of glucose oxidized against a free energy of combustion of glucose of $\Delta F' = -686,000$ cal/mole. In order to bring about phosphorylation, the formation of one mole of ATP requires an input of at least 7,000 cal. Since it is assumed that three moles of ATP are formed, and the oxidation of $NADH + H^+$ delivers 52,000 cal, we can deduce that the oxidative phosphorylation of three moles of ADP

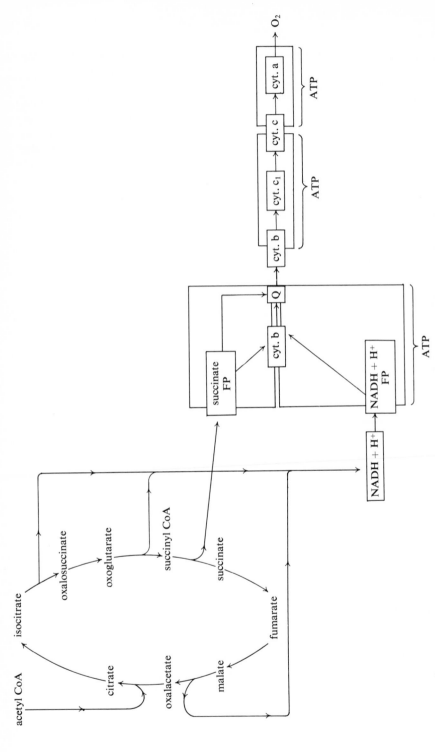

Scheme 5.12. (Reprinted with the permission of Business Publications, Ltd.)

conserves $3(7,000/52,000) \times 100 = 41\%$ of the total energy yield when one mole of $NADH + H^+$ is oxidized by oxygen (122). This high delivery of energy by reduced NAD oxidation makes it also clear why a respiratory chain has to have so many carriers acting in sequence and not just one or two. The standard biological energy currency is in the form of "packets" of 7,000 cal, the free energy of the formation of ATP from ADP and phosphate. The electron transport chain is therefore really a molecular device for delivering the 52,000 cal of energy in a series of small packets, three of which are energetically equivalent to ATP. This is only possible by lowering the energy of the electrons gradually in a series of small steps. It is now possible to write the equation for the oxidation of two molecules of pyruvate to acetyl CoA

$$2 \text{ pyruvate} + 2\,NAD^+ + CoA \rightarrow 2 \text{ acetyl CoA} + 2CO_2 + 2\,NAD_{red}$$

$$2\,NAD_{red} + 6\,P_i + 6\,ADP + O_2 \rightarrow 2\,NAD^+ + 8\,H_2O + 6\,ATP$$

and also for the coupled oxidation of two moles of acetate via two operations of the TCA cycle

$$2 \text{ acetate} + 24\,P_i + 24\,ADP + 4\,O_2 \rightarrow 4\,CO_2 + 28\,H_2O + 24\,ATP$$

The complete oxidation of two moles of pyruvate to carbon dioxide and water results in the formation of 30 moles of ATP. This figure looks very impressive since it conserves 42% of the energy produced. It is, however, very likely that this figure is only a minimum one, since cells are open systems and the efficiency may be more likely around the 60% mark. Open systems in general exist in a dynamic steady state. It has been recognized that many enzyme systems in the cell have self-adjusting and self-regulating features; thus, the rate of the over-all process being catalyzed is geared to the needs of the cell for the products of the system. The ADP:ATP ratio, for example, is very critical for the rate of respiration. If this ratio is low, the rate of respiration is low because it is limited by the supply of ADP. The amount of ADP available represents therefore the dynamic balance of the system if there are no restrictions on acetate or oxygen supplies. The actual coupling mechanism which conserves energy by converting ADP to ATP is still obscure in microorganisms (113). It is assumed that it may be the same as studied in mitochondria. There is some evidence (42, 163) that in bacteria the chain may be shorter with fewer catalysts since P/O ratios of 1.0 and below are usually obtained with bacterial cell-free extracts. This small ratio suggests that there is only one phosphorylation site in the electron transport chain. It is, however, possible that the chain operates only in whole cells. It is also possible that bacterial cytochromes may have different oxidation–reduction potentials since their absorption bands differ often from those of animal cells. This is probably one of the reasons why the cytochrome oxidase reaction is not, in all circumstances,

$$O_2 + 4H^+ \rightarrow 2H_2O$$

Some cytochrome oxidases transfer only one pair of hydrogen atoms to molecular oxygen, thus forming hydrogen peroxide

$$O_2 + 2H^+ \rightarrow H_2O_2$$

Hydrogen peroxide, however, is extremely toxic to bacteria and needs to be removed rapidly. This can be accomplished in the presence of two iron porphyrin enzymes, catalase (hydrogen peroxide:hydrogen peroxide oxidoreductase, E.C. 1.11.1.6) and either

(1) peroxidase (donor:hydrogen peroxide oxidoreductase, E.C. 1.11.1.7) or
(2) reduced NAD:hydrogen peroxide oxidoreductase, E.C. 1.11.1.1 or
(3) reduced NADP:hydrogen peroxide oxidoreductase, E.C. 1.11.1.2 or
(4) cytochrome c:hydrogen peroxide oxidoreductase, E.C. 1.11.1.5 or
(5) glutathione:hydrogen peroxide oxidoreductase, E.C. 1.11.1.9

$$\text{catalase} \qquad 2H_2O_2 \rightarrow 2H_2O + O_2$$

$$\text{peroxidase} \qquad H_2A + H_2O_2 \rightarrow A + 2H_2O$$

where A may be an electron donor, cytochrome c, reduced NAD, reduced NADP, or glutathion. The enzyme catalase is found in most cytochrome-containing aerobic microorganisms, whereas most anaerobic microorganisms seem to possess peroxidase or substrate peroxidase. This generalization, however, is still disputed, since it was found that the catalase test carried out on microorganisms is not specific, but could interfere with peroxidases present. Electrochemical analysis of enzymatic reactions(78, 124) could help to solve these difficulties. A new approach in studying electron transfer and metabolism called the "coulokinetic" technique should give a better insight into the present problems in this field(19).

The respiratory components of *Mycobacterium phlei*, for example, contain bound NAD, flavins, a naphthoquinone (K_9H), and cytochromes b, c_1, c, a, and a_3. Three distinct respiratory chains were revealed(27), namely, one with succinic oxidase, one with malate, and one with an NAD^+-linked mechanism whereby X represents a light sensitive component (360 mμ) (see Scheme 5.13). The oxidation of $NADPH + H^+$ was mediated by the particulate transhydrogenase reaction to NAD^+. The phosphorylation associated with the oxidation of $NADPH + H^+$ arises from the NAD^+-linked pathway(138). In *Mycobacterium phlei* there exist also so-called nonphosphorylative bypass enzymes which are capable of oxidizing reduced NADP. The existence of these latter enzymes may contribute to the lowering of the P/O ratio in bacteria. A similar respiratory chain involving membrane-bound dehydrogenases, quinones, cytochromes, and cytochrome oxidase appears to function in *Escherichia coli*(138) and *Haemophilus parainfluenzae*(204). The arrangement of this respiratory chain is variable particularly in the cytochrome section according to environmental conditions(205). *Proteus vulgaris* possesses such an adjustment since it is extremely rich on flavoproteins(97), which suggests that a terminal flavoprotein oxidase may carry some of the respiratory load in the cells. A cytochrome and a direct flavin link for the electrons from reduced NAD to oxygen occurs also in *Bacillus popilliae*(150) which has in addition a diaphorase activity, but is devoid of cytochrome c and possesses only cytochrome b_1 consistently.

In order to possess an intact Krebs cycle and an array of terminal respiratory enzymes, the heterotrophic microorganism has to be strictly aerobic. It is also

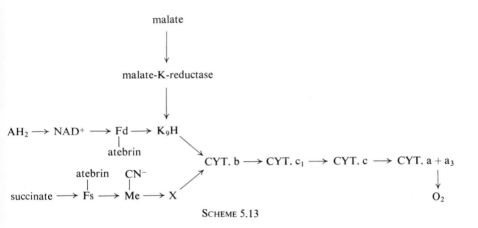

SCHEME 5.13

known that strictly aerobic microorganisms(17,135) have many more membrane-bound systems than are formed in obligate anaerobic bacteria. This led to the tendency to localize in membranes enzymatic activities that link with molecular oxygen(205), since anaerobic electron transport and the associated energy-yielding reactions are mediated by soluble enzymes. In the case of facultative bacteria such as *Escherichia coli,* this would mean that aerobically grown cells would resemble strict aerobes and anaerobically grown cells would resemble strict anaerobes. This, however, would demand large alterations and expenditure of energy when adjusting from one type of growth to another. *Escherichia coli* grown aerobically corresponds closely to a strict aerobe in that it has an intact TCA cycle and a similar array of terminal respiratory enzymes(74). In contrast to strict anaerobes, however, anaerobically grown *Escherichia coli* contains many membrane-bound enzymes. In some instances *Escherichia coli* showed a complete and functional correspondence with both strict aerobes and anaerobes since it possesses, for example, a membrane-bound formate dehydrogenase aerobically and in addition a soluble formate dehydrogenase anaerobically. Studies in regard to the levels of Krebs cycle enzymes(75) in aerobically and anaerobically grown cells revealed that at least three factors were found to influence their biosynthesis:

(1) the presence or absence of molecular oxygen(65, 189, 206),
(2) the repressive effect of glucose(59, 141), and
(3) the balance between catabolic and anabolic demands in the cycle which is dictated by the nutritional background(52, 75).

The existence of qualitative differences between the metabolic response of growing (multiplying) and nongrowing bacteria to oxygen tension was mentioned before. It has been known for a long time(186) that the oxygen demand of aerobic microorganisms is of zero order above a critical oxygen tension, whereas below this tension, the demand becomes first order(207). The introduction of continuous culture techniques opened a new era for this type of investigation, particularly since the development of oxygen electrodes (129) has made measurements of dissolved oxygen concentrations over long periods much more feasible. With a continuous culture technique(84, 129, 130, 133, 151–154) it is possible to maintain microorganisms at a certain growth stage under constant environmental conditions for a long period of time. By the continued use of the new oxygen electrode and continuous culture it was found that a decrease in the dissolved oxygen tension resulted in an increase in the cytochrome a_2 which reached a maximum at about 0.2 mm Hg(136, 137). It was known that facultative bacteria go through three stages in their metabolism: a fully aerobic, a partially aerobic, and an anaerobic stage(151). An additional phase has just recently been detected between the fully aerobic and partially aerobic phase(84). The change from growth in the presence of excess oxygen to growth with limited oxygen occurred quite readily, whereas the reverse reaction took several days to reach a steady state. When oxygen tension is decreased below a certain minimum level there is a marked increase in the cytochrome content which increases the potential respirational capacity. Thus, with further decrease in the oxygen tension, increase in cytochrome content is reversed. It is therefore necessary to change the definition of "critical" oxygen tension to that oxygen tension above which the respiration capacities of an organism is independent of changes in dissolved oxygen tension. At oxygen tensions above this "critical" value the oxygen uptake rate is therefore constant and independent of oxygen tension. This switch over is very rapid. This change may support the theory that ADP and ATP concentrations are important in the control of glucose utilization(32). It is proposed (84) that the stimulation of respiration in *Aerobacter aerogenes* by low oxygen tension may be caused by a decreased ATP yield which accompanies either a change to an alternative electron transport pathway or the uncoupling of oxidative phosphorylation. Very small amounts of fermentation products were found in the excess oxygen state, whereas they increased with the lowering of oxygen tension in the medium.

The most dramatic nutritional effects are related to glucose metabolism. Glucose markedly represses the formation of Krebs cycle enzymes in cells grown on a complex medium, where the TCA cycle is not required for anabolic purposes. It has been suggested that the enzymes of the TCA cycle must be controlled by a number of separated but interrelated mechanisms and should therefore not be called constitutive enzymes.

Facultative anaerobes which possess the TCA cycle under certain environmental conditions (34, 56, 62, 144, 199) are very suitable for this type of investigation.

REFERENCES

1. Adair, F. W. (1966). Membrane-associated sulphur oxidation by the autotroph *Thiobacillus thiooxidans. J. Bacteriol.* **92**, 899.
2. Ahrens, J., and Schlegel, H. G. (1966). Zur Regulation der NAD-abhängigen Hydrogenase-Aktivität. *Arch. Mikrobiol.* **55**, 257.
3. Aleem, M. I. H. (1965). Path of carbon and assimilatory power in chemosynthetic bacteria. I. *Nitrobacter agilis. Biochim. Biophys. Acta* **107**, 14.
4. Aleem, M. I. H. (1965). Thiosulphate oxidation and electron transport in *Thiobacillus novellus. J. Bacteriol.* **90**, 95.
5. Aleem, M. I. H. (1966). Generation of reducing power in chemosynthesis. III. Energy-linked reduction of pyridine nucleotides in *Thiobacillus novellus. J. Bacteriol.* **91**, 729.
6. Aleem, M. I. H. (1966). Electron transfer pathways in *Thiobacillus novellus. J. Bacteriol.* **91**, 735.
7. Aleem, M. I. H. (1966). Generation of reducing power in chemosynthesis. II. Energy-linked reduction of pyridine nucleotides in the chemoautotroph *Nitrosomonas europaea. Biochim. Biophys. Acta* **113**, 216.
8. Aleem, M. I. H. (1966). Generation of reducing power in chemosynthesis. IV. Energy-linked reduction of pyridine nucleotides by succinate in *Thiobacillus novellus. Biochim. Biophys. Acta* **128**, 1.
9. Aleem, M. I. H. (1967). Personal communication.
10. Aleem, M. I. H. (1967). Energy conversions in the chemoautotroph *Nitrobacter agilis. Bacteriol. Proc.* p. 112.
11. Aleem, M. I. H., and Huang, E. (1965). CO_2 fixation and carboxydismutase in *Thiobacillus novellus. Biochem. Biophys. Res. Commun.* **20**, 515.
12. Aleem, M. I. H., and Lees, H. (1963). ATP-dependent reduction of NAD by ferrocytochrome c in chemoautotrophic bacteria. *Nature* **200**, 759.
13. Aleem, M. I. H., and Lees, H. (1963). Autotrophic enzyme systems. I. Electron transport systems concerned with hydroxylamine oxidation in *Nitrosomonas. Can. J. Biochem. Physiol.* **41**, 763.
14. Aleem, M. I. H., and Nason, A. (1960). Phosphorylation coupled to nitrite oxidation by particles from the chemoautotroph, *Nitrobacter agilis. Proc. Natl. Acad. Sci. U.S.* **46**, 763.
15. Aleem, M. I. H., Lees, H., and Nicholas, D. J. D. (1963). ATP-dependent reduction of NAD by ferrocytochrome c in chemoautotrophic bacteria. *Nature* **200**, 759.

16. Aleem, M. I. H., Hock, G. E., and Vanner, J. E. (1965). Water as the source of oxidant and reductant in bacterial chemosynthesis. *Proc. Natl. Acad. Sci. U.S.* **54**, 869.
17. Alexander, M. (1955). Localization of enzymes in the microbial cell. *Bacteriol. Rev.* **20**, 67.
18. Alexander, M., and Wilson, P. W. (1956). Intracellular distribution of tricarboxylic acid cycle enzymes in *Azotobacter vinelandii*. *J. Bacteriol.* **71**, 252.
19. Allen, M. J. (1966). Symposium on Bioelectrochemistry of microorganisms. II. Electrochemical aspects of metabolism. *Bacteriol. Rev.* **30**, 80.
20. Ambler, R. P. (1963). The purification and amino acid composition of *Pseudomonas* cytochrome c-551. *Biochem. J.* **89**, 341.
21. Ambler, R. P. (1963). The amino acid sequence of *Pseudomonas* cytochrome c-551. *Biochem. J.* **89**, 349.
22. Anderson, J. H. (1964). The metabolism of hydroxylamine to nitrite by *Nitrosomonas*. *Biochem. J.* **91**, 8.
23. Anderson, J. H. (1964). Studies on the oxidation of ammonia to hydroxylamine by *Nitrosomonas*. *Biochem. J.* **92**, 16.
24. Anderson, J. H. (1965). Studies on the oxidation of ammonia by *Nitrosomonas*. *Biochem. J.* **95**, 688.
25. Anthony, C., and Zatman, L. J. (1964). Microbial oxidation of methanol. The methanol-oxidizing enzyme of *Pseudomonas M 27*. *Biochem. J.* **92**, 614.
26. Anthony, C., and Zatman, L. J. (1965). Microbial oxidation of methanol. The alcohol dehydrogenase of *Pseudomonas* sp. *M 27*. *Biochem. J.* **96**, 808.
27. Asano, A., and Brodie, A. F. (1964). Oxidative phosphorylation in fractionated bacterial systems. XIV. Respiratory chain of *Mycobacterium phlei*. *J. Biol. Chem.* **239**, 4280.
28. Atkinson, D. E. (1955). The Biochemistry of *Hydrogenomonas*. II. The adaptive oxidation of organic substrates. *J. Bacteriol.* **69**, 310.
29. Atkinson, D. E., and McFadden, B. A. (1954). The Biochemistry of *Hydrogenomonas*. I. The hydrogenase of *Hydrogenomonas facilis* in cell-free preparations. *J. Biol. Chem.* **210**, 885.
30. Aubert, J. P., Milhaud, G., and Millet, J. (1957). L'assimilation de l'anhydride carbonique par les bactéries chimiautotrophes. *Ann. Inst. Pasteur* **92**, 515.
31. Baddiley, J. (1955). The structure of coenzyme A. *Advan. Enzymol.* **16**, 1.
32. Barker, J., Khan, M. A. A., and Solomos, T. (1964). Mechanism of the Pasteur effect. *Nature* **201**, 1126.
33. Bartha, R. (1962). Physiologische Untersuchungen über den chemolithotrophen Stoffwechsel neu isolierter Hydrogenomonas-Stämme. *Arch. Mikrobiol.* **41**, 313; as cited by Eberhardt (64).
34. Basu, S. K., and Chakrabartz, A. M. (1965). Tricarboxylic acid cycle activity in pseudomonads. *Indian J. Biochem.* **2**, 230; *Chem. Abstr.* **64**, 16310 (1966).
35. Beck, J. V., and Hafia, F. M. (1964). Effect of phosphate ions and 2,4-dinitrophenol on the activity of intact cells of *Thiobacillus ferrooxidans*. *J. Bacteriol.* **88**, 850.
36. Bergmann, F. H., Towne, J. C., and Burris, R. H. (1958). Assimilation of CO_2 by hydrogen bacteria. *J. Biol. Chem.* **230**, 13.
37. Bisset, K. A., and Grace, J. B. (1954). Iron and manganese oxidizing bacteria. *Symp. Soc. Gen. Microbiol.* **4**, 44.
38. Blaylock, B. A., and Nason, A. (1963). Electron transport systems of the chemoautotroph *Ferrobacillus ferrooxidans*. I. Cytochrome c-containing iron-oxidase. *J. Biol. Chem.* **238**, 3453.

39. Borischewski, R. M. (1967). Keto acids as growth-limiting factors in autotrophic growth of *Thiobacillus thiooxidans*. *J. Bacteriol.* **93**, 597.
40. Borischewski, R. M., and Umbreit, W. W. (1966). Growth of *Thiobacillus thiooxydans* on glucose. *Arch. Biochem. Biophys.* **116**, 97; *Chem. Abstr.* **65**, 15816 (1966).
41. Bongers, L. (1967). Phosphorylation in hydrogen bacteria. *J. Bacteriol.* **93**, 1615.
42. Brodie, A. F., and Adelson, J. (1965). Respiratory chains and sites of coupled phosphorylation. *Science* **149**, 265.
43. Brown, L. R., Strawinski, R. J., and McCleskey, C. S. (1964). The isolation and characterization of *Methanomonas methanooxidans* Brown and Strawinski. *Can. J. Microbiol.* **10**, 791.
44. Burge, W. D., Malavolta, E., and Delwiche, C. C. (1963). Phosphorylation by extracts of *Nitrosomonas europaea*. *J. Bacteriol.* **85**, 106.
45. Butler, R. G., and Umbreit, W. W. (1966). Absorption and utilization of organic matter by the strict autotroph *Thiobacillus thiooxidans*, with special reference to aspartic acid. *J. Bacteriol.* **91**, 661.
46. Butlin, K. R., and Postgate, J. B. (1954). Microbial transformation of inorganic iron. *Symp. Soc. Gen. Microbiol.* **4**, 294.
47. Butt, W. D., and Lees, H. (1960). The Biochemistry of the nitrifying organisms. 6. The effect of oxygen on nitrite oxidation in the presence of different inorganic ions. *Biochem. J.* **76**, 425.
48. Campbell, A. E., Hellebust, J. A., and Watson, S. W. (1966). Reductive pentose phosphate cycle in *Nitrosocystis oceanuns*. *J. Bacteriol.* **91**, 1178.
49. Charles, A. M., and Suzuki, I. (1965). Sulfite oxidase of the facultative autotroph *Thiobacillus novellus*. *Biochem. Biophys. Res. Commun.* **19**, 686.
50. Cirillo, V. P. (1966). Symposium on bioelectrochemistry of microorganisms. 1. Membrane potentials and permeability. *Bacteriol. Rev.* **30**, 68.
51. Cohn, D. V. (1958). The enzymatic formation of oxalacetic acid by nonpyridine nucleotide malic dehydrogenase of *Micrococcus lysodeikticus*. *J. Biol. Chem.* **233**, 299.
52. Cole, H., Wimpenny, J. W. T., and Hughes, D. E. (1966). The adenosine triphosphate pool in *Escherichia coli*. *Biochem. J.* **100**, 81P.
53. Cook, D. W., Tischer, R. G., and Brown, C. R. (1967). Carbohydrate metabolism in *Hydrogenomonas eutropha*. *Can. J. Microbiol.* **13**, 701.
54. Cooper, R. C. (1964). Evidence for presence of certain TCA cycle enzymes in *Thiobacillus thioparus*. *J. Bacteriol.* **88**, 624.
55. Crouch, D. J., and Ramsay, H. H. (1962). Oxidation of glucose by *Hydrogenomonas facilis*. *J. Bacteriol.* **84**, 1340.
56. Delwich, E. A., and Carson, S. F. (1953). A citric acid cycle in *Propionibacterium pentosaceum*. *J. Bacteriol.* **65**, 318.
57. Delwiche, C. C., and Finstein, M. S. (1965). Carbon and energy sources for the nitrifying autotroph *Nitrobacter*. *J. Bacteriol.* **90**, 102.
58. Dixon, M., and Webb, E. C. (1964). "Enzymes," 2nd ed. Longmans, Green, New York.
59. Dobrogosz, W. J. (1966). Altered end-product patterns and catabolite repression in *Escherichia coli*. *J. Bacteriol.* **91**, 2263.
60. Doudoroff, M., and Stanier, R. Y. (1959). Role of poly-β-hydroxy-butyric acid in assimilation of organic carbon by bacteria. *Nature* **183**, 1440.
61. Dugan, P., and Lundgren, D. G. (1965). Energy supply for the chemoautotroph *Ferrobacillus ferrooxidans*. *J. Bacteriol.* **89**, 825.
62. Durye, F. L., Faj, H. D., Wang, C. H., Anderson, A. W., and Elliker, P. R. (1961). Carbohydrate metabolism in *Micrococcus radiodurans*. *Can. J. Microbiol.* **7**, 799.

63. Dworkin, M., and Foster, J. W. (1956). Studies on *Pseudomonas methanica* (Söhngen) nov. comb. *J. Bacteriol.* **72**, 646.

64. Eberhardt, W. (1966). Über das Wasserstoff aktivierende System von *Hydrogenomonas H 16*. I. Verteilung der Hydrogenase-Aktivität auf zwei Zellfraktionen. *Arch. Mikrobiol.* **53**, 288.

65. Ehrlich, H. L., and Segel, I. H. (1959). Carbon balance for *Bacillus megaterium* growing in a glucose-mineral medium. *J. Bacteriol.* **77**, 110.

66. England, S., and Colowick, S. P. (1957). On the mechanism of the aconitase and isocitric dehydrogenase reaction. *J. Biol. Chem.* **226**, 1047.

67. Finstein, M. S., and Delwiche, C. C. (1965). Molybdenum as a micronutrient for *Nitrobacter*. *J. Bacteriol.* **89**, 123.

68. Francis, M. J. O., Hughes, D. E., and Phizackerley, P. J. R. (1963). The oxidation of L-malate by *Pseudomonas* sp. *Biochem. J.* **89**, 430.

69. Fuller, R. C., and Kornberg, H. L. (1961). A possible route for malate oxidation by *Chromatium*. *Biochem. J.* **79**, 8P.

70. Gibbs, M., and Schiff, J. A. (1960). Chemosynthesis: The energy of chemoautotrophic organisms. *Plant Physiol.* **1B**, 27.

71. Gottschalk, G. (1964). Die Biosynthese der Poly-β-hydroxy-buttersäure durch Knallgasbakterien. III. Synthese aus CO_2. *Arch. Mikrobiol.* **47**, 236.

72. Gottschalk, G., and Schlegel, H. G. (1965). Preparation of ^{14}C-D(-)-β-hydroxybutyric acid from $^{14}CO_2$ using "Knallgas" bacteria (*Hydrogenomonas*). *Nature* **205**, 308.

73. Gottschalk, G., Eberhardt, U., and Schlegel, H. G. (1964). Verwertung von Fructose durch *Hydrogenomonas H 16* (1.). *Arch. Mikrobiol.* **48**, 95.

74. Gray, C. T., Wimpenny, J. W. T., Hughes, D. E., and Mossman, M. R. (1966). Regulation of metabolism in facultative bacteria. I. Structural and functional changes in *Escherichia coli* associated with shifts between the aerobic and anaerobic states. *Biochim. Biophys. Acta* **117**, 22.

75. Gray, C. T., Wimpenny, J. W. T., and Mossman, M. R. (1966). Regulation of metabolism in facultative bacteria. II. Effects of aerobiosis, anaerobiosis and nutrition on the formation of Krebs cycle enzymes in *Escherichia coli*. *Biochim. Biophys. Acta* **117**, 33.

76. Gray, W. R., and Hartley, B. S. (1963). The structure of a chymotryptic peptide from *Pseudomonas* cytochrome c-551. *Biochem. J.* **89**, 379.

77. Green, D. E. (1962). Power from the mitochondrion. *Discovery* **23**, 32.

78. Guilbault, G. (1966). Symposium on bioelectrochemistry of microorganisms. III. Electrochemical analysis of enzymatic reactions. *Bacteriol. Rev.* **30**, 94.

79. Guittonneau, G. (1925). Sur la transformation du soufre en sulfate per voie d'association microbienne. *Compt. Rend.* **181**, 261; as cited by Trudinger (196).

80. Guittonneau, G. (1927). Sur l'oxydation microbienne du soufre an cours de l'ammonisation. *Compt. Rend.* **184**, 45; as cited by Trudinger (196).

81. Guittonneau, G., and Keilling, J. (1932). L'évolution et la solubilisation du soufre élémentaire dans la terre avable. *Ann. Agron.* [N.S.] **2**, 690; as cited by Trudinger (196).

82. Gundersen, K. (1966). The growth and respiration of *Nitrosocystis oceanus* at different partial pressures of oxygen. *J. Gen. Microbiol.* **42**, 387.

83. Harrington, A. A., and Kallio, R. E. (1960). Oxidation of methanol and formaldehyde by *Pseudomonas methanica*. *Can. J. Microbiol.* **6**, 1.

84. Harrison, D. E. F., and Pirt, S. J. (1967). The influence of dissolved oxygen concentration on the respiration and glucose metabolism of *Klebsiella aerogenes* during growth. *J. Gen. Microbiol.* **46**, 193.

85. Hayashi, M., Hayashi, M., and Unemoto, T. (1966). The presence of D-malate dehydrogenase (D-malate: NAD oxidoreductase) in *Serratia marcescens*. *Biochim. Biophys. Acta* **124**, 374.

86. Hempfling, W. P., and Vishniac, W. (1965). Oxidative phosphorylation in extracts of *Thiobacillus X*. *Biochem. Z.* **342**, 272; *Chem. Abstr.* **63**, 12020 (1965).

87. Hirsch, C. A., Rasminsky, M., Davis, B. D., and Lin, E. C. C. (1963). A fumarate reductase in *Escherichia coli* distinct from succinate dehydrogenase. *J. Biol. Chem.* **238**, 3770.

88. Hooper, A. B., Hansen, J., and Bell, R. (1967). Characterization of glutamate dehydrogenase from the ammonia-oxidizing chemoautotroph *Nitrosomonas europaea*. *J. Biol. Chem.* **242**, 288.

89. Hooper, A. B., and Nason, A. (1965). Characterisation of hydroxylamine-cytochrome c reductase from the chemoautotrophs *Nitrosomonas europaea* and *Nitrosocystis oceanus*. *J. Biol. Chem.* **240**, 4044.

90. Hutton, W. E., and Zobell, C. E. (1949). The occurrence and characteristic of methane-oxidizing bacteria in marine sediments. *J. Bacteriol.* **58**, 463.

91. Hutton, W. E., and Zobell, C. E. (1963). Production of nitrite from ammonia by methane-oxidizing bacteria. *J. Bacteriol.* **65**, 217.

92. International Union of Biochemistry Commission. (1964). Enzyme Nomenclature: Recommendations of the International Union of Biochemistry on the nomenclature and classification of enzymes, together with their units and the symbols of enzyme kinetics. Elsevier Publ. Co., Amsterdam.

93. Johnson, E. U., and Peck, H. D., Jr. (1965). Coupling of phosphorylation and CO_2 fixation in extracts of *Thiobacillus thioparus*. *J. Bacteriol.* **89**, 1041.

94. Johnson, J. L., and Temple, K. L. (1962). Some aspects of methane oxidation. *J. Bacteriol.* **84**, 456.

95. Johnson, P. A., and Quayle, J. R. (1964). Microbial growth on C_1-compounds. 6. Oxidation of methanol, formaldehyde and formate by methanol-grown *Pseudomonas AM 1*. *Biochem. J.* **92**, 281.

96. Johnson, P. A., and Quayle, J. R. (1965). Microbial growth on C_1-compounds. Synthesis of cell constituents by methane and methanol-grown *Pseudomonas methanica*. *Biochem. J.* **95**, 859.

97. Jones, C. W., and King, H. K. (1964). Electron transport in cell fractions of *Proteus vulgaris*. *Biochem. J.* **91**, 10P.

98. Kallio, R. E., and Harrington, A. A. (1960). Sudanophilic granules and lipid of *Pseudomonas methanica*. *J. Bacteriol.* **80**, 321.

99. Karlson, P. (1965). "Introduction to Modern Biochemistry," 2nd ed. Academic Press, New York.

100. Kashket, E. R. and Brodie, A. F. (1963). Oxidative phosphorylation in fractionated bacterial systems. X. Different roles for the natural quinones of *Escherichia coli* W in oxidative metabolism. *J. Biol. Chem.* **238**, 2564.

101. Kelly, D. P. (1965). Assimilation of organic compounds by a strictly chemoautotrophic *Thiobacillus*. *J. Gen. Microbiol.* **41**, v.

102. Kelly, D. P. (1966). Influence of organic compounds on *Thiobacillus*. *Biochem. J.* **100**, 9P.

103. Kelly, D. P. (1967). Influence of amino acids and organic antimetabolites on growth and biosynthesis of the chemoautotroph *Thiobacillus neapolitanus* Strain C. *Arch. Mikrobiol.* **56**, 91.

104. Kelly, D. P. (1967). Problems of the autotrophic microorganisms. *Sci. Progr.* (*London*) **55**, 35.

105. Kelly, D. P., and Syrett, P. J. (1964). The effects of uncoupling agents on CO_2 fixation by a *Thiobacillus*. *J. Gen. Microbiol.* **34**, 307.
106. Kelly, D. P., and Syrett, P. J. (1964). Inhibition of formation of ATP in *Thiobacillus thioparus* by 2,4-dinitrophenol. *Nature* **202**, 597.
107. Kelly, D. P., and Syrett, P. J. (1966). Energy coupling during sulphur compound oxidation by *Thiobacillus* sp. strain C. *J. Gen. Microbiol.* **43**, 109.
108. Kelly, D. P., and Syrett, P. J. (1966). ^{35}S Thiosulphate oxidation by *Thiobacillus* strain C. *Biochem. J.* **98**, 537.
109. Kemp, M. B., and Quayle, J. R. (1966). Microbial growth on C-1 compounds. Incorporation of C-1 units into allulose phosphate by extracts of *Pseudomonas methanica*. *Biochem. J.* **99**, 41.
110. Kemp, M. B., and Quayle, J. R. (1967). Microbial growth on C-1 compounds. Uptake of ^{14}C formaldehyde and ^{14}C formate by methane-grown *Pseudomonas methanica* and determination of the hexose labelling pattern after brief incubation with ^{14}C methanol. *Biochem. J.* **102**, 94.
111. König, C., and Schlegel, H. G. (1967). Oscillationen der Ureaseaktivität von *Hydrogenomonas H 16* in statischer Kultur. *Biochim. Biophys. Acta* **139**, 182.
112. König, C., Kaltwasser, H., and Schlegel, H. G. (1966). Die Bildung von Urease nach Verbrauch der aüßeren N-Quelle bei *Hydrogenomonas H 16*. *Arch. Mikrobiol.* **53**, 231.
113. Lamanna, C., and Mallette, M. F. (1965). "Basic Bacteriology," 3rd ed., p. 842. Williams & Wilkins, Baltimore, Maryland.
114. Landesman, J., Duncan, D. W., and Walden, C. C. (1966). Iron oxidation by washed cell suspensions of the chemoautotroph *Thiobacillus ferrooxidans*. *Can. J. Microbiol.* **12**, 25.
115. Landesman, J., Duncan, D. W., and Walden, C. C. (1966). Oxidation of inorganic sulfur compounds by washed cell suspensions of *Thiobacillus ferrooxidans*. *Can. J. Microbiol.* **12**, 957.
116. Lazaroff, N. (1963). Sulphate requirement for iron oxidation by *Thiobacillus ferrooxidans*. *J. Bacteriol.* **85**, 78.
117. Leadbetter, E. R., and Foster, J. W. (1958). Studies on some methane-utilizing bacteria. *Arch. Mikrobiol.* **30**, 91.
118. Lees, H. (1954). The Biochemistry of the nitrifying bacteria. *Symp. Soc. Gen. Microbiol.* **4**, 84.
119. Lees, H. (1960). Energy metabolism of thiobacilli. *Ann. Rev. Microbiol.* **14**, 83.
120. Lees, H. (1960). Energy metabolism in chemolithotrophic bacteria. *Ann. Rev. Microbiol.* **14**, 91.
121. Lees, H. (1962). Some thoughts on the energetics of chemosynthesis. *Bacteriol. Rev.* **26**, 165.
122. Lehninger, A. L. (1965). "Bioenergetics." Benjamin, New York.
123. Lester, R. L., and Crane, F. L. (1959). The natural occurrence of coenzyme Q and related compounds. *J. Biol. Chem.* **234**, 2169.
124. Lewis, K. (1966). Symposium on bioelectrochemistry of microorganisms. IV. Biochemical fuel cells. *Bacteriol. Rev.* **30**, 101.
125. Linday, E. M., and Syrett, P. J. (1958). The induced synthesis of hydrogenase by *Hydrogenomonas facilis*. *J. Gen. Microbiol.* **19**, 223.
126. London, J. (1963). Cytochrome in *Thiobacillus thiooxidans*. *Science* **140**, 409.
127. London, J., and Rittenberg, R. C. (1964). Path of sulfur in sulphide and thiosulfate oxidation by thiobacilli. *Proc. Natl. Acad. Sci. U.S.* **52**, 1183.
128. London, J., and Rittenberg, R. C. (1966). Effects of organic matter on growth of *Thiobacillus intermedians*. *J. Bacteriol.* **91**, 1062.

129. Mackereth, F. J. H. (1964). An improved galvanic cell for determination of oxygen concentration in fluids. *J. Sci. Instr.* **41**, 38.

130. MacLennan, D. G. and Pirt, S. J. (1966). Automatic control of dissolved oxygen tension in stirred microbial cultures. *J. Gen. Microbiol.* **45**, 289.

131. MacLennan, D. G., Lenaz, G., and Szarkowska, L. (1966). Studies on the mechanism of oxidative phosphorylation. IV. Effect of cytochrome c on energy-linked processes. *J. Biol. Chem.* **241**, 5251.

132. Malavolta, E., Delwiche, C. C., and Burge, W. D. (1960). CO_2 fixation and phosphorylation by *Nitrobacter agilis*. *Biochem. Biophys. Res. Commun.* **2**, 445.

133. Malek, L., and Fencl, Z. (1966). "Theoretical and Methodological Basis of Continuous Culture of Microorganisms." Academic Press, New York.

134. Margalith, P., Silver, M., and Lundgre, D. G. (1966). Sulfur oxidation by the iron bacterium *Ferrobacillus ferrooxidans*. *J. Bacteriol.* **92**, 1706.

135. Marr, A. G. (1960). Enzyme localization in bacteria. *Ann. Rev. Microbiol.* **14**, 241.

136. Moss, F. (1952). The influence of oxygen tension on respiration and cytochrome a_2 formation of *Escherichia coli*. *Australian J. Exptl. Biol. Med. Sci.* **30**, 531.

137. Moss, F. (1956). Adaptation of the cytochromes of *Aerobacter aerogenes* in response to environmental oxygen tension. *Australian J. Exptl. Biol. Med. Sci.* **34**, 395.

138. Murthy, P. S., and Brodie, A. F. (1964). Oxidative phosphorylation in fractionated bacterial systems. XV. Reduced nicotinamide adenine phosphate-linked phosphorylation. *J. Biol. Chem.* **239**, 4292.

139. Nicholas, D. J. D., and Jones, O. T. G. (1960). Oxidation of hydroxylamine in cell-free extracts of *Nitrosomonas europaea*. *Nature* **185**, 512.

140. Nicholas, D. J. D., and Rao, P. S. (1964). The incorporation of labelled CO_2 into cells and extracts of *Nitrosomonas europaea*. *Biochim. Biophys. Acta* **82**, 394.

141. Okinaka, R. T., and Dobrogosz, W. J. (1967). Catabolite repression and pyruvate metabolism in *Escherichia coli*. *J. Bacteriol.* **93**, 1644.

142. Okuzumi, M. (1966). Biochemistry of thiobacilli. VIII. Dismutation of tetrathionate by *Thiobacillus thiooxydans*. *Agr. Biol. Chem.* (*Tokyo*) **30**, 313; *Chem. Abstr.* **65**, 1068 (1966).

143. Okuzumi, M. (1966). Biochemistry of thiobacilli. IX. Reduction of trithionate by *Thiobacillus thiooxydans*. *Agr. Biol. Chem.* (*Tokyo*) **30**, 713; *Chem. Abstr.* **65**, 1068 (1966).

144. Otsuka, S., Miyajima, R., and Shio, I. (1965). Comparative studies on the mechanisms of microbial glutamate formation. I. Pathways of glutamate formation from glucose in *Brevibacterium flavum* and in *Micrococcus glutamicus*. *J. Gen. Appl. Microbiol.* (*Tokyo*) **11**, 285; *Chem. Abstr.* **65**, 9376 (1966).

145. Packer, L., and Vishniac, W. (1955). Chemosynthetic fixation of CO_2 and characteristics of hydrogenase in resting cells suspensions of *Hydrogenomonas ruhlandii nov. spec.* *J. Bacteriol* **70**, 216.

146. Parker, C. D., and Prisk, J. (1953). The oxidation of inorganic compounds of sulphur by various sulphur bacteria. *J. Gen. Microbiol.* **8**, 344.

147. Peck, H. D. (1962). Comparative metabolism of inorganic sulfur compounds in microorganisms. *Bacteriol Rev.* **26**, 67.

148. Peck, H. D. (1962). The oxidation of reduced sulfur compounds. *Bacteriol. Rev.* **26**, 83.

149. Pepper, R. E., and Costilow, R. N. (1964). Glucose catabolism by *Bacillus popilliae* and *Bacillus lentimorbus*. *J. Bacteriol.* **87**, 303.

150. Pepper, R. E., and Costilow, R. N. (1965). Electron transport in *Bacillus popilliae*. *J. Bacteriol.* **89**, 271.

151. Pirt, S. J. (1957). The oxygen requirement of growing cultures of an *Aerobacter* species determined by means of the continuous culture technique. *J. Gen. Microbiol.* **16**, 59.

152. Pirt, S. J., and Callow, D. S. (1958). Exocellular product formation by microorganisms in continuous cultures. I. Production of 2:3-butanediol by *Aerobacter aerogenes* in a single-stage process. *J. Appl. Bacteriol.* **21**, 188.
153. Pirt, S. J., and Callow, D. S. (1958). Observations on foaming and its inhibition in a bacterial culture. *J. Appl. Bacteriol.* **21**, 211.
154. Pirt, S. J., and Callow, D. S. (1959). Exocellular product formation by microorganisms in continuous culture. II. Production of 2,3-butanediol from sucrose by *Aerobacter aerogenes* in a two-stage process. *Sci. Rept. Ist. Super. Sanita* **2**, 292; as cited by Harrison and Pirt (84).
155. Pugh, L. H., and Umbreit, W. W. (1966). Anaerobic CO_2 fixation by autotrophic bacteria, *Hydrogenomonas* and *Ferrobacillus*. *Arch. Biochem. Biophys.* **115**, 122; *Chem. Abstr.* **65**, 5901 (1966).
156. Radler, F. (1962). Uber die Milchsäurebakterien des Weines und den biologischen Säureabbau. Übersicht. I. Systematik und chemische Grundlagen. *Vitis* **3**, 144.
157. Radler, F. (1962). Uber die Milchsäurebakterien des Weines und den biologischen Säureabbau. Übersicht. II. Physiologie und Okologie der Bakterien. *Vitis* **3**, 207.
158. Raw, P. S., and Nicholas, D. J. D. (1966). Studies on the incorporation of CO_2 by cells and cell-free extracts of *Nitrosomonas europaea*. *Biochim. Biophys. Acta* **124**, 221.
159. Rees, M., and Nason, S. (1965). A P-450-like cytochrome and a soluble terminal oxidase identified as cytochrome *o* from *Nitrosomonas europaea*. *Biochem. Biophys. Res. Commun.* **21**, 248.
160. Rees, M., and Nason, A. (1966). Incorporation of atmospheric oxygen into nitrite formed during ammonia oxidation by *Nitrosomonas europaea*. *Biochim. Biophys. Acta* **113**, 398.
161. Repaske, R. (1962). The electron transport system of *Hydrogenomonas eutropha*. I. Diphosphopyridine nucleotide reduction by hydrogen. *J. Biol. Chem.* **237**, 1351.
162. Repaske, R., and Lizotte, C. L. (1965). The electron transport system of *Hydrogenomonas eutropha*. II. Reduced nicotinamide adenine dinucleotide-menadione reductase. *J. Biol. Chem.* **240**, 4774.
163. Rose, A. H. (1965). "Chemical Microbiology." Butterworth, London and Washington, D.C.
164. Schatz, A., and Borell, C., Jr. (1952). Growth and hydrogenase activity of a new bacterium, *Hydrogenomonas facilis*. *J. Bacteriol.* **63**, 87.
165. Schindler, J. (1964). Die Synthese von Poly-β-hydroxy-buttersäure durch *Hydrogenomonas H* 16: Die zu β-Hydroxy-butyryl-CoA führenden Reaktionsschritte. *Arch. Mikrobiol.* **49**, 236.
166. Schlegel, H. G. (1960). *In* "Handbuch der Pflanzenphysiologie" (W. Ruhland, ed.), Vol. 5, Part 2, p. 649. Springer, Berlin; as cited by Lees (120).
167. Schlegel, H. G. (1966). Physiology and biochemistry of Knallgasbacteria. *Advan. Comp. Physiol. Biochem.* **2**, 185.
168. Schlegel H. G., and Gottschalk, G. (1962). Poly-β-hydroxybuttersäure, ihre Verbreitung, Funktion und Biosynthese. *Angew Chem.* **74**, 342.
169. Schlegel, H. G., Gottschalk, G., and von Bartha, R. (1961). Formation and utilization of poly-β-hydroxy-butyric acid by Knallgas bacteria (*Hydrogenomonas*). *Nature* **191**, 463.
170. Schöberl, P., and Engel, H. (1964). Das Verhalten der nitrifizierenden Bakterien gegenüber gelöstem Sauerstoff. *Arch. Mikrobiol.* **48**, 393.
171. Schön, G. (1965). Untersuchungen über den Nutzeffekt von *Nitrobacter winogradskyi* Buch. *Arch. Mikrobiol.* **50**, 111.

172. Senez, J. C. (1962). Some considerations on the energetics of bacterial growth. *Bacteriol. Rev.* **26**, 96.
173. Skarzynski, B., Ostrowski, W., and Krawczyk, A. (1957). *Bull. Acad. Polon. Sci., Classe (II)* **5**, 159; as cited by Lees (119).
174. Skerman, V. B. D. (1959). "A Guide to the Identification of the Genera of Bacteria," 2nd ed. Williams & Wilkins, Baltimore, Maryland.
175. Smith, A. J., London, J., and Stanier, R. Y. (1967). Biochemical basis of obligate autotrophy in blue green algae and thiobacilli. *J. Bacteriol.* **94**, 972.
176. Speyer, J. F., and Dickman, S. R. (1956). On the mechanism of action of aconitase. *J. Biol. Chem.* **220**, 193.
177. Stanier, R. Y., Gunsalus, I. C., and Gunsalus, C. F. (1953). The enzymatic conversion of mandelic acid to benzoic acid. II. Properties of the particulate fractions. *J. Bacteriol.* **66**, 543.
178. Stanier, R. Y., Doudoroff, M., and Adelberg, E. (1961). "General Microbiology." Macmillan, New York.
179. Starkey, R. L. (1934). Isolation of some bacteria which oxidize thiosulfate. *Soil Sci.* **39**, 197.
180. Starkey, R. L. (1934). The production of polythionate from thiosulphate by microorganisms. *J. Bacteriol.* **28**, 387.
181. Straat, P. A., and Nason, A. (1965). Characterisation of a nitrate reductase from the chemoautotroph *Nitrobacter agilis. J. Biol. Chem.* **240**, 1412.
182. Suzuki, I. (1965). Oxidation of elemental sulfur by an enzyme system of *Thiobacillus thiooxidans. Biochim. Biophys. Acta* **104**, 359.
183. Suzuki, I., and Silver, M. (1966). The initial product and properties of the sulfur-oxidizing enzyme of thiobacilli. *Biochim. Biophys. Acta* **122**, 22.
184. Suzuki, I., and Werkman, C. H. (1958). Glutathione and sulfur oxidation by *Thiobacillus thiooxidans. Proc. Natl. Acad. Sci. U.S.* **45**, 239.
185. Suzuki, I., and Werkman, C. H. (1958). Chemoautotrophic carbon dioxide fixation by extracts of *Thiobacillus thiooxidans.* II. Formation of phosphoglyceric acid. *Arch. Biochem. Biophys.* **77**, 112.
186. Tang, P. S. (1933). The rate of oxygen consumption by tissues and lower organisms as a function of oxygen tension. *Quart. Rev. Biol.* **8**, 1260.
187. Tate, S. S., and Datta, S. P. (1965). The equilibrium of the reaction catalyzed by citrate oxaloacetatelyase. *Biochem. J.* **94**, 470.
188. Trudinger, P. A. (1961). Thiosulphate oxidation and cytochromes in *Thiobacillus X (neapolitanus). Biochem. J.* **78**, 673.
189. Trudinger, P. A. (1961). Thiosulphate oxidation and cytochromes in *Thiobacillus X.* 2. Thiosulphate-oxidizing enzyme. *Biochem. J.* **78**, 680.
190. Trudinger, P. A. (1964). Oxidation of thiosulphate by intact cells of *Thiobacillus X.* Effects of some experimental conditions. *Australian J. Biol. Sci.* **17**, 738.
191. Trudinger, P. A. (1964). The effects of thiosulfate and oxygen concentration on tetrathionate oxidation by *Thiobacillus X* and *Thiobacillus thioparus. Biochem. J.* **90**, 640.
192. Trudinger, P. A. (1965). Effect of thiol-binding reagents on metabolism of thiosulphate and tetrathionate by *Thiobacillus neapolitanus. J. Bacteriol.* **89**, 617.
193. Trudinger, P. A. (1965). Effect of thiol-binding reagents on the metabolism of thiosulphate and tetrathionate by *Thiobacillus neapolitanus. J. Bacteriol.* **89**, 622.
194. Trudinger, P. A. (1965). Permeability of *Thiobacillus neapolitanus* ("*Thiobacillus X*") to thiosulphate. *Australian J. Biol. Sci.* **18**, 563.
195. Trudinger, P. A. (1967). The metabolism of inorganic sulphur compounds by Thiobacilli. *Rev. Pure Appl. Chem.* **17**, 1.

196. Trudinger, P. A. (1967). Metabolism of thiosulfate and tetrathionate by heterotrophic bacteria from soil. *J. Bacteriol.* **93**, 550.
197. Trüper, H. G. (1965). Tricarboxylic acid cycle and related enzymes in *Hydrogenomonas strain H 16 G*, grown on various carbon sources. *Biochim. Biophys. Acta* **111**, 565.
198. Umbreit, W. W. (1962). Comparative physiology of autotrophic bacteria. *Bacteriol. Rev.* **26**, 145.
199. Van Demark, P. J., and Smith, P. F. (1964). Evidence for a tricarboxylic acid cycle in *Mycoplasma hominis. J. Bacteriol.* **88**, 1602.
200. van Gool, A., and Laudelout, H. (1966). The mechanism of nitrite oxidation by *Nitrobacter winogradskyi. Biochim. Biophys. Acta* **113**, 41.
201. van Gool, A., and Laudelout, H. (1967). Spectrophotometric and kinetic study of nitrite and formate oxidation in *Nitrobacter winogradskyi. J. Bacteriol.* **93**, 215.
202. Vishniac, W., and Santer, M. (1957). The Thiobacilli. *Bacteriol. Rev.* **21**, 195.
203. White, A., Handler, P., and Smith, E. L. (1964). "Principles of Biochemistry," 3rd ed. McGraw-Hill, New York.
204. White, D. C. (1966). The obligatory involvement of the electron transport system in the catabolic metabolism of *Haemophilus parainfluenzae. Antonie van Leeuwenhoek, J. Microbiol. Serol.* **32**, 139.
205. White, D. C., and Smith, L. (1964). Localization of the enzymes that catalyze hydrogen and electron transport in *Haemophilus parainfluenzae* and the nature of the respiratory chain system. *J. Biol. Chem.* **239**, 3956.
206. Wimpenny, J. W. T. (1966). The regulation of Krebs cycle enzymes in *Escherichia coli. Biochem. J.* **100**, 59P.
207. Wise, W. S. (1951). The measurement of the aeration of culture media. *J. Gen. Microbiol.* **5**, 167.
208. Yates, M. G., and Nason, A. (1966). Electron transport systems of the chemoautotroph *Ferrobacillus ferrooxidans.* II. Purification and properties of a heat-labile iron-cytochrome c reductase. *J. Biol. Chem.* **241**, 4872.
209. Yoshida, T., and Alexander, M. (1964). Hydroxylamine formation by *Nitrosomonas europaea. Can. J. Microbiol.* **10**, 923.

SUPPLEMENTARY READINGS

Allen, S. H. G. (1966). The isolation and characterization of malate-lactate transhydrogenase from *Micrococcu lactilyticus. J. Biol. Chem.* **241**, 5266.
Ammann, E. C. B., and Reed, L. L. (1967). Metabolism of nitrogen compounds by *Hydrogenomonas eutropha.* I. Utilization of uric acid, allantoin, hippuric acid, and creatinine. *Biochim. Biophys. Acta* **141**, 135.
Bartha, R., and Ordal, Z. J. (1965). Nickel-dependent chemolithotrophic growth of two *Hydrogenomonas* strains. *J. Bacteriol.* **89**, 1015.
Barton, L. L., and Shively, J. M. (1968). Thiosulfate utilization by *Thiobacillus thiooxidans. J. Bacteriol.* **95**, 720.
Blaylock, B. A. (1968). Cobamide-dependent methanol-cyanocob(I)-alamin methyltransferase of *Methanosarcina barkeri. Arch. Biochem. Biophys.* **124**, 314.
Bryant, M. P., McBride, B. C., and Wolfe, R. S. (1968). Hydrogen-oxidizing methane bacteria. I. Cultivation and methanogenesis. *J. Bacteriol.* **95**, 1118.
Cazzulo, J. J., and Stoppani, A. O. M. (1967). Purification and properties of pyruvate carboxylase from Baker's yeast. *Arch. Biochem. Biophys.* **121**, 596.
DeSicco, B. T., and Stukus, P. E. (1968). Autotrophic and heterotrophic metabolism of *Hydrogenomonas.* I. Growth yields and patterns under dual substrate conditions. *J. Bacteriol.* **95**, 1469.

Din, G. A., Suzuki, I., and Lees, H. (1967). Carbon dioxide fixation and phosphoenolpyruvate carboxylase in *Ferrobacillus ferrooxidans*. *Canad. J. Microbiol.* **13**, 1413.

Eady, R. R., and Large, P. J. (1968). Purification and properties of an amine dehydrogenase from *Pseudomonas* AM 1 and its role in growth on methylamine. *Biochem. J.* **106**, 245.

Gale, N. L., and Beck, J. V. (1967). Evidence for the Calvin cycle and hexose monophosphate pathway in *Thiobacillus ferrooxidans*. *J. Bacteriol.* **94**, 1052.

Gupta, N. K., and Vennesland, B. (1966). Glyoxylate carboligase of *E. coli*. Some properties of the enzyme. *Arch. Biochem. Biophys.* **113**, 255.

Harder, W., and Veldkamp, H. (1967). A continuous culture study of an obligately psychrophilic *Pseudomonas* species. *Arch. Mikrobiol.* **59**, 123.

Hardy, R. W. F., and Knight, E., Jr. (1966). Reductant-dependent adenosine triphosphatase of nitrogen-fixing extracts of *Azotobacter vinelandii*. *Biochim. Biophys. Acta* **122**, 520.

Hardy, R. W. F., and Knight, E. Jr. (1967). ATP-dependent reduction of azide and HCN by N_2-fixing enzymes of *Azotobacter vinelandii* and *Clostridium pasteurianum*. *Biochim. Biophys. Acta* **139**, 69.

Hempfling, W. P., Trudinger, P. A., and Vishniac, W. (1967). Purification and some properties of sulfite oxidase from *Thiobacillus neapolitanus*. *Arch. Mikrobiol.* **59**, 149.

Hollinshead, J. A. (1965). Microbial growth on C_1-compounds: The role of folate in the metabolism of *Pseudomonas* AM 1. *Biochem. J.* **96**, 49P.

Hollinshead, J. A. (1966). Microbial growth on C_1-compounds. The role of folate in the metabolism of *Pseudomonas* AM 1. *Biochem. J.* **99**, 389.

Holmström, B. (1967). Studies on the cultivation of *Listeria monocytogenes* in batch and continuous cultures. *Canad. J. Microbiol.* **13**, 1551.

Jannasch, H. W. (1967). Enrichments of aquatic bacteria in continuous culture. *Arch. Mikrobiol.* **59**, 165.

Itagaki, E., Palmer, G., and Hager, L. P. (1967). Studies on cytochrome b_{562} of *Escherichia coli*. II. Reconstitution of cytochrome b_{562} from apoprotein and hemin. *J. Biol. Chem.* **242**, 2272.

Johnson, M. J. (1967). Aerobic microbial growth at low oxygen concentrations. *J. Bacteriol.* **94**, 201.

Kaltwasser, H. (1968). Induktive Bildung partikelgebundener Uricase bei *Hydrogenomonas H 16* und anderen aeroben Bakterien. *Arch. Mikrobiol.* **60**, 10.

Kaltwasser, H., and Krämer, J. (1968). Verwertung von Cytosin und Uracil durch *Hydrogenomonas facilis* und *Hydrogenomonas H 16*. *Arch. Mikrobiol.* **60**, 172.

Katsuki, H., Takeo, K., Kameda, K., and Tanaka, S. (1967). Existence of two malic enzymes in *Escherichia coli*. *Biochem. Biophys. Res. Commun.* **27**, 331.

Kelly, D. P. (1968). Fluoroacetate toxicity in *Thiobacillus neapolitanus* and its relevance to the problem of obligate chemoautotrophy. *Arch. Mikrobiol.* **61**, 59.

Kuehn, G. D., and McFadden, B. A. (1968). Factors affecting the synthesis and degradation of ribulose-1,5-diphosphate carboxylase in *Hydrogenomonas eutropha*. *J. Bacteriol.* **95**, 937.

Kufe, D. W., and Howland, J. L. (1968). Oxidative phosphorylation in *Corynebacterium diphtheriae*. *Biochim. Biophys. Acta* **153**, 291.

Kurup, C. K. R., and Brodie, A. F. (1967). Nonheme iron: A functional component of malate-vitamin K reductase. *Biochem. Biophys. Res. Commun.* **28**, 862.

Leininger, K. R., and Westley, J. (1968). The mechanism of the rhodanese-catalyzed thiosulfate-cyanide reaction. Thermodynamic and activation parameters. *J. Biol. Chem.* **243**, 1892.

LeJohn, H. B., van Caeseele, L., and Lees, H. (1967). Catabolic repression in the facultative chemoautotroph *Thiobacillus novellus*. *J. Bacteriol.* **94**, 1484.

LeJohn, H. B., Suzuki, I., and Wright, J. A. (1968). Glutamate dehydrogenases of *Thiobacillus novellus*. Kinetic properties and a possible control mechanism. *J. Biol. Chem.* **243**, 118.

Marunouchi, T., and Moris, T. (1967). Studies on the sulfite-dependent ATPase of a sulfur oxidizing bacterium, *Thiobacillus thiooxidans*. *J. Biochem. (Tokyo)* **62**, 401.

Mayberry, W. R., Prochazka, G. J., and Payne, W. J. (1967). Growth yields of bacteria on selected organic compounds. *Appl. Microbiol.* **15**, 1332.

Mayeux, J. V., and Johnson, E. J. (1967). Effect of adenosine monophosphate, adenosine diphosphate, and reduced nicotin-amide adenine nucleotide on adenosine triphosphate-dependent carbon dioxide fixation in the autotroph *Thiobacillus neapolitanus*. *J. Bacteriol.* **94**, 409.

Moyer, R. W., Ramaby, R. F., Butler, L. G., and Boyer, P. D. (1967). The formation and reactions of a non-phosphorylated high energy form of succinyl-coenzyme A synthetase. *J. Biol. Chem.* **242**, 4299.

Murphy, W. H., Barnaby, C., Lin, F.-J., and Kaplan, N. O. (1967). Malate dehydrogenases. II. Purification and properties of *Bacillus subtilis*, *B. stearothermophilus* and *Escherichia coli* malate dehydrogenases. *J. Biol. Chem.* **242**, 1548.

Murphy, W. H., and Kaplan, N. O. (1967). Malate dehydrogenases. III. Alteration of catalytic properties during purification of *Bacillus subtilis* malate dehydrogenases. *J. Biol. Chem.* **242**, 1560.

Ramaby, R. F., Bridger, W. A., Moyer, R. W., and Boyer, P. D. (1967). The preparation, properties, and reactions of succinyl coenzyme A synthetase and its phosphorylated form. *J. Biol. Chem.* **242**, 4287.

Repaske, R., and Dans, C. C. (1968). A factor for coupling NAD to hydrogenase in *Hydrogenomonas eutropha*. *Biochem. Biophys. Res. Commun.* **30**, 136.

Robertson, R. N. (1967). The separation of protons and electrons as a fundamental biological process. *Endeavour* **XXVI**, 134.

Schuster, E., and Schlegel, H. G. (1967). Chemolithotrophes Wachstum von *Hydrogenomonas H 16* im Chemostaten mit elektrolytischer Knallgaserzeugung. *Arch. f. Mikrobiol.* **58**, 380.

Silverman, M. P. (1967). Mechanism of bacterial pyrite oxidation. *J. Bacteriol.* **94**, 1046.

Sinha, D. B., and Walden, C. C. (1967). Formation of polythionates and their interrelationships during oxidation of thiosulfate by *Thiobacillus ferrooxidans*. *Can. J. Microbiol.* **12**, 1041.

Smith, A. J., and Hoare, D. S. (1968). Acetate assimilation by *Nitrobacter agilis* in relation to its "obligate autotrophy". *J. Bacteriol.* **95**, 844.

Smith, A. J., and Hoare, D. S. (1968). *Nitrobacter agilis*—an obligate or a facultative autotroph. *Biochem. J.* **106**, 40P.

Smith, A. J., London, J., and Stanier, R. Y. (1967). Biochemical basis of obligate autotrophy in blue-green algae and thiobacilli. *J. Bacteriol.* **94**, 972.

Stern, J. R., and Bambers, G. (1966). Glutamate biosynthesis in anaerobic bacteria. I. The citrate pathways of glutamate synthesis in *Clostridium kluyveri*. *Biochemistry* **5**, 1113.

Stern, J. R., Hagre, C. S., and Bambers, G. (1966). Glutamate biosynthesis in anaerobic bacteria. II. Stereospecificity of aconitase and citrate synthetase of *Clostridium kluyveri*. *Biochemistry* **5**, 1119.

Stokes, J. L., and Powers, M. T. (1967). Stimulation of poly-β-hydroxybutyrate oxidation in *Sphaerotilus discophorus* by manganese and magnesium. *Arch. Mikrobiol.* **59**, 295.

Syrett, P. J., and John, P. C. L. (1968). Isocitrate lyase: Determination of K_m values and inhibition by phosphoenol pyruvate. *Biochim. Biophys. Acta* **151**, 295.

Tigerstrom, M. van, and Campbell, J. J. R. (1966). The accumulation of α-ketoglutarate by suspensions of *Pseudomonas aeruginosa*. *Canad. J. Microbiol.* **12**, 1005.

Trudinger, P. A., and Kelly, D. P. (1968). Reduced nicotinamide adenine dinucleotide oxidation by *Thiobacillus neapolitanus* and *Thiobacillus strain C*. *J. Bacteriol.* **95**, 1962.

Uden, N. van (1967). Transport-limited growth in the chemostat and its competitive inhibition; a theoretical treatment. *Arch. Mikrobiol.* **58**, 145.

Uden, N. van (1967). Transport-limited fermentation and growth of *Saccharomyces cerevisiae* and its competitive inhibition. *Arch. Mikrobiol.* **58**, 155.

Wang, W. S., and Lundgren, D. G. (1968). Peptidoglycan of a chemolithotrophic bacterium, *Ferrobacillus ferrooxidans*. *J. Bacteriol.* **95**, 1851.

Weitzman, P. D. J. (1967). Allosteric fine control of citrate synthase in *Escherichia coli*. *Biochim. Biophys. Acta* **139**, 526.

Whiteley, H. R. (1967). Induced synthesis of formyltetrahydrofolate synthetase in *Micrococcus aerogenes*. *Arch. Mikrobiol.* **59**, 315.

Williams, C. H., Zanetti, G., Arscott, L. D., and McAllister, J. K. (1967). Lipoamide dehydrogenase, glutathione reductase, thioredoxin reductase, and thioredoxin. A simultaneous purification and characterization of the four proteins from *Escherichia coli B*. *J. Biol. Chem.* **242**, 5226.

Wimpenny, J. W. T., and Warmsley, A. M. H. (1968). The effect of nitrate on Krebs cycle enzymes in various bacteria. *Biochim. Biophys. Acta* **156**, 297.

Witz, D. F., Detroy, R. W., and Wilson, P. W. (1967). Nitrogen fixation by growing cells and cell-free extracts of the *Bacillaceae*. *Arch. Mikrobiol.* **55**, 369.

Wright, J. A., Maeba, P., and Sanwal, B. D. (1967). Allosteric regulation of the activity of citrate synthetase of *Escherichia coli* by α-ketoglutarate. *Biochem. Biophys. Res. Commun.* **29**, 34.

Yagi, T., Honya, M., and Tamija, T. (1968). Purification and properties of hydrogenases of different origins. *Biochim. Biophys. Acta* **153**, 699.

Zagorski, W., Michalska-Trenkner, E., Suchanek, B., and Kaniuga, Z. (1965). Oxidation of malate by *Mycobacterium phlei* extracts. *Bull. Acad. Polon. Sci., Ser. Sci. Biol.* **13**, 495; *Chem. Abstr.* **64**, 8521 (1966).

ZoBell, C. E., and Hittle, L. L. (1967). Some effects of hyperbaric oxygenation on bacteria at increased hydrostatic pressure. *Canad. J. Microbiol.* **13**, 1311.

6

CHEMOSYNTHESIS—FERMENTATION

FERMENTATION

The word "fermentation" has undergone numerous changes in meaning during the past hundred years. According to the derivation of the term it signifies merely a gentle bubbling or boiling condition. The term was first applied when the only known reaction of this kind was the production of wine, the bubbling, of course, being caused by the production of carbon dioxide.

It was not until Gay-Lussac studied the chemical aspects of the process that the meaning was changed to signify the breakdown of sugar into ethanol and carbon dioxide (41). It was, however, Pasteur who marked the birth of chemical microbiology with his association of microbes with the fermentation in 1857. He used the terms "cell" and "ferment" interchangeably in referring to the microbe.

The term "fermentation" thus became associated with the idea of cells, gas production, and the production of organic by-products.

The evolution of gas and the presence of whole cells were invalidated as criteria for defining fermentation when it was discovered that in some fermentations such as the production of lactic acid no gas is liberated, while other fermentation processes could be obtained with cell-free extracts, indicating that the whole cell may not be necessary.

The position was further complicated by the discovery that the ancient process of vinegar production, generally referred to as the acetic acid fermentation, which yielded considerable quantities of organic by-products, was a strictly aerobic process.

Fermentation clearly needed to be redefined.

Although carbohydrates are often regarded as being essential materials for fermentations, organic acids (including amino acids) and proteins, fats and other organic compounds are fermentable substrates for selected microorganisms. It was soon realized that these substances play a dual role as a source of food and as a source of energy for the microorganisms. The energy produced by total combustion (oxidation) of the substance in a calorimeter is its potential energy. The nearest approach to complete oxidation biologically occurs with acidic oxidations, which, with glucose, yield carbon dioxide and water and result in the liberation of a considerable quantity of energy.

Under anaerobic conditions only a fraction of the potential energy is liberated because oxidation is incomplete. In order to obtain an amount of energy equivalent to that obtained under aerobic conditions, several times as much glucose must be broken down under anaerobic conditions. There is, in consequence, a high yield of unoxidized organic by-products.

Fermentation came to be regarded then as the anaerobic decomposition of organic compounds to organic products, which could not be further metabolized by the enzyme systems of the cells without the intervention of oxygen. The fermentation products differed with different microorganisms, being governed in the main by the enzyme complex of the cells and the environmental conditions.

The economic value of these by-products led to the development of industrial microbiology.

With the recognition of fermentation as an anaerobic process, parallels were drawn between the biochemistry of microorganisms and mammalian tissues. Since the intermediates of the metabolism of glucose were found to be the same, it was postulated that all fermentation processes must follow a similar path. Consequently, the microbial fermentation of carbohydrates was considered to be similar to mammalian glycolysis. This is the reason why many authors use the terms "glycolysis" or "glycolytic pathway" to describe one method of anaerobic breakdown of carbohydrates by microorganisms and why "fermentation" became synonymous with "glycolysis." The two processes differ however in two significant ways.

(1) There is no storage of glycogen in bacteria.
(2) Lactate is not always an end product or intermediate in the bacterial anaerobic carbohydrate breakdown.

In addition, during the last decade it was discovered that various bacteria are able to use pathways other than the Embden-Meyerhof-Parnas pathway for anaerobic breakdown of carbohydrates.

The application of fermentation to all of these processes required some other form of definition.

The intensive research into electron transport systems of microbial metabolism has partly clarified the position, although a number of aspects await attention. Based on the electron donor and acceptor systems, it is now clearly understood that all processes which have as a terminal electron acceptor an organic compound are called "fermentations." With this definition, it is possible to state that acetic acid bacteria are not fermentative but respire

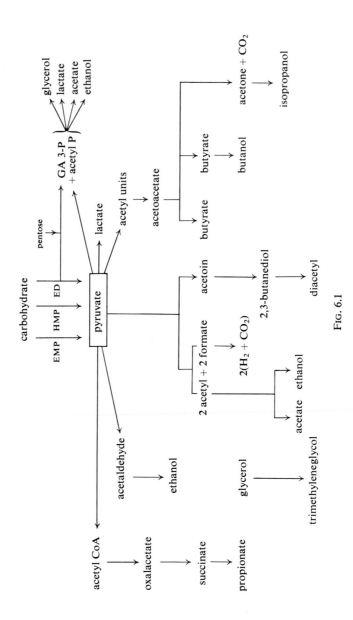

Fig. 6.1

aerobically while for other bacteria the definition is not restricted to the use of any particular pathway in the fermentative process. It was also found that fermentative bacteria may dispense with the use of their cytochromes under anaerobic conditions since their phosphorylation processes are substrate phosphorylations in which the electron donor is an organic substrate that transfers its electron to an NAD^+ or $NADP^+$ system. The amount of NAD^+ in microorganisms is, however, limited and must therefore be regenerated if metabolism is to continue. Under anaerobic conditions this regeneration can be accomplished by an oxidation–reduction mechanism involving pyruvate or other compounds derived from pyruvate. These reactions from pyruvate can vary considerably among different microorganisms and therefore lead to the formation of characteristic end products, which are used in bacterial classification. A short summary of the various end products formed from pyruvate is given in Table 6.1 and Fig. 6.1. Since these end products and their formation are used in classification, the various bacterial groups will be considered in more detail later.

CARBON, ENERGY AND BALANCE

In addition to the identification of initial and final products and the production of carbon and oxidation balance, more concerted efforts have been made during the past decade to separate the processes of energy production and storage from those of synthesis. The mass of cells formed is related to the amount of energy-producing substrate used and also to the number of moles of ATP formed during the utilization of that substrate. This applies, however, for conditions where the substrate is used only for production, and an alternate supply of amino acids and other monomers is provided for growth. This relationship can now be expressed in two ways:

$$\text{Yield}_{\text{energy substrate (e.g., glucose)}} = Y_G = \frac{\text{dry weight of cells (gm)}}{\text{moles glucose fermented}}$$

$$\text{Yield}_{\text{ATP}} = Y_{\text{ATP}} = \frac{\text{dry weight of cells (gm) moles ATP formed}}{\text{moles substrate fermented}}$$

As stated earlier, the number of moles of ATP varies with the pathways used. The difficulties of obtaining this information was discussed earlier, and it is therefore not surprising that only very few microorganisms have been investigated, i.e., *Streptococcus faecalis* ($Y_G = 20$; $Y_{\text{ATP}} = 10$) and *Zymomonas mobilis* ($Y_G = 8.3$; $Y_{\text{ATP}} = 8.3$)(3).

The present methods for end product detection are based upon methods originated from diagnostic methods used in medical microbiology. These methods have been refined and improved, but they still give only a qualitative measurement of the major end product. Our present state of knowledge in carbohydrate fermentation is confined to the main end products formed from hexoses and some of the organisms responsible for these transformations are listed in Table 6.1 (53).

TABLE 6.1

PRINCIPAL CLASSES OF CARBOHYDRATE FERMENTATION[a]

Class	End products	Organisms
(1) Alcohol	Ethanol	Yeasts
	CO_2	Zymomonas mobilis
(2) Lactic acid (homofermenter)	Lactic acid	Streptococcus Lactobacillus
(3) Mixed lactic acid (heterofermenter)	Lactic acid	Leuconostoc
	Ethanol	
	Acetic acid	
	CO_2	
(4) Mixed acid	Lactic acid	Escherichia Pseudomonas
	Ethanol	
	Acetic acid	
	$H_2 + CO_2$	
	Formic acid	
	Trimethylene glycol	
(5) Butylene glycol (2,3-butanediol)	As for (4) but also 2,3-butanediol	Aerobacter Bacillus polymyxa Pseudomonas
(6) Butyric acid butanol acetone	Butyric acid	Clostridia
	Acetic acid	Bacillus marcerans
	H_2, CO_2	
	Butanol	
	Ethanol	
	Acetone	
	Isopropanol	
(7) Propionic acid	Propionic acid	Propionibacterium
	Acetic acid	
	CO_2	

[a] From Stanier et al. (53). Reprinted with permission of Prentice-Hall.

It has, however, to be mentioned that environmental conditions play a most important role in end product formation. Investigations of end products formed during the growth of *Escherichia coli* ML 30(20) have shown that glucose degradation, which normally leads to the formation of acetate and carbon dioxide, can be altered by an anaerobic shock of the organism. Under the altered conditions, ethanol accumulates in addition to acetate and carbon dioxide. This change can be readily made by appropriate transition from aerobic to anaerobic environmental conditions. This anaerobic mode of growth poses special problems in a great number of heterotrophic organisms since their over-all ATP requirement for biosynthesis can be satisfied only by degradation of a relatively large quantity of an organic compound that serves as the energy source. Because of this, a number of various specific control mechanisms are necessary to regulate the electron flow in the metabolism of strict and facultative anaerobes. One of these controls is the ability of many such microorganisms to dispose of "excess" electrons (e) in the form of molecular hydrogen (H_2) (24) through the activity of hydrogenases

$$2e + 2H^+ \rightarrow H_2$$

In the case of NAD-dependent hydrogenase, the coenzyme NAD^+ is bound to the enzyme and is reduced to $NADH + H^+$ in the presence of hydrogen (2). The velocity of this reduction again is related to the concentration of reduced NAD and the redox ratio $NADH + H^+/NAD^+$. This allosteric type of inhibition is also a control of the hydrogen transport exhibited by consecutive hydrogen-requiring reactions.

The ability to produce molecular hydrogen is very widespread (24) over entirely different taxonomic and physiological types of microorganisms which could be categorized into four groups:

(1) photosynthetic microorganisms;
(2) heterotrophic anaerobes, whose growth is inhibited by molecular oxygen;
(3) heterotrophic anaerobes that typically contain cytochromes and evolve hydrogen from formate; and
(4) heterotrophic anaerobes that contain cytochromes as electron carriers.

Very little is known about the control of anaerobic electron flow, except that there is no hydrogen production on iron-deficient media. In typical saccharolytic clostridia, the absence of such a hydrogen-evolving system leads to a marked shift from the usual metabolic pattern (see section entitled "Lactate Production") to lactate production. The loss of the hydrogen production [or "hydrogen valve" (24)] restricts these organisms to more conventional fermentations, which can be observed in those organisms which are not able to produce molecular hydrogen through lack of the hydrogenases. This type of depression can come from oxygen in the case of facultative anaerobes. In general, it could be said that the yield of molecular hydrogen is directly related to the state of reduction of the fermented energy source. Thus microorganisms must cope with special problems in controlling their energy metabolism. This is probably necessitated by the variation in the ATP content in such organisms which makes it necessary to disperse a variable number of electrons (24).

THE FORMATION OF PROPIONATE

Propionic acid is a product of carbohydrate fermentation by species of the genus *Propionibacterium* and some other related species. These bacteria are

unicellular, nonphotosynthetic, nonsporing organisms, which ferment glucose
or lactate to propionic acid under anaerobic conditions. Anaerobically they
occur as chains of cocci, but they can also grow quite well under aerobic
conditions where they appear as rods. Pleomorphic forms are quite common.

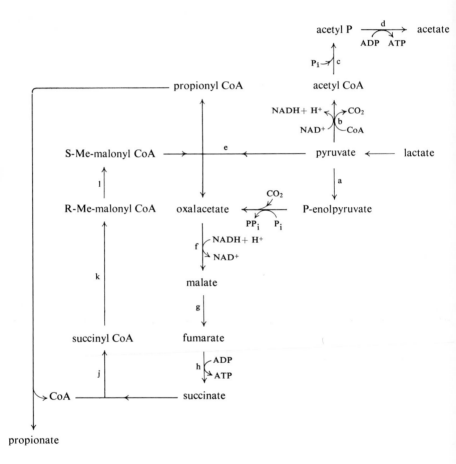

FIG. 6.2. The formation of propionate by species of the genus *Propionibacterium*.

Investigations of the propionic acid formation with *Propionibacterium pentosaceum* and *Propionibacterium shermanii* 52 W(6) lead to the proposal of the
pathway shown in Fig. 6.2.

The first work of importance on the chemistry of the propionic acid bacteria
was that of Fitz(22) who suggested that a dissimilation of lactic acid occurs

$$3\,CH_3CHOHCOOH \rightarrow CH_3CH_2COOH + CH_3COOH + CO_2 + H_2O$$

The detection of succinic acid(62) and the suggestion by van Niel(61) that pyruvate is an intermediate and his proposition that one molecule of this C-3 compound was oxidized to acetic acid and carbon dioxide and two other reduced to propionic acid made it clear that a complex pathway must be involved in the formation of propionic acid.

The greatest problem was the high molecular ratio of propionic to acetic acid:

$$3 \text{ glucose} \rightarrow 4 \text{ propionate} + 2 \text{ acetate} + 2 CO_2 + 2 H_2O$$

and the role of succinic acid. The propionic/acetic acid ratio of 2:1 had never been observed before. With the discovery of the existence of part of the TCA cycle in these organisms(31,68) at least the formation of succinic acid was solved. Using labeled C^{11} and C^{13} the pathway for succinic acid(17,70,71) was postulated and confirmed to be as follows:

$$\text{oxalacetate} \rightleftharpoons \text{malate} \rightleftharpoons \text{fumarate} \rightleftharpoons \text{succinate}$$

The steps in the conversion of succinic acid to propionic acid were still unknown. The assumption that lactate was an intermediate(29) in the pathway of pyruvate to propionate was opposed by Barker and Lipmann(11). The discovery of the succinate decarboxylation system in *Propionibacterium pentosaceum*(19) supported the evidence that propionate must be formed via succinate. This decarboxylation system was found to be ATP- and CoA-dependent(65). The dependency suggested that succinyl CoA might be the activated substrate for the decarboxylase with the possible involvement of propionyl CoA.

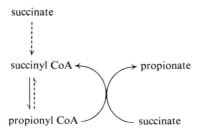

A parallel was drawn at this time to the metabolism of propionic acid in animal tissues(12), whereby the isomerization of methylmalonyl CoA drew the particular interest of the investigators. Methylmalonyl CoA has an asymmetric carbon atom and the corresponding isomerase was found to be stereospecific. The transcarboxylation reaction also was reversible. In other words, the carboxyl group of methylmalonyl (or succinyl) CoA would be transferred to an acceptor molecule of propionyl CoA, which would thereby be converted to succinyl (or methylmalonyl) CoA with the release of one molecule of propionyl CoA (21):

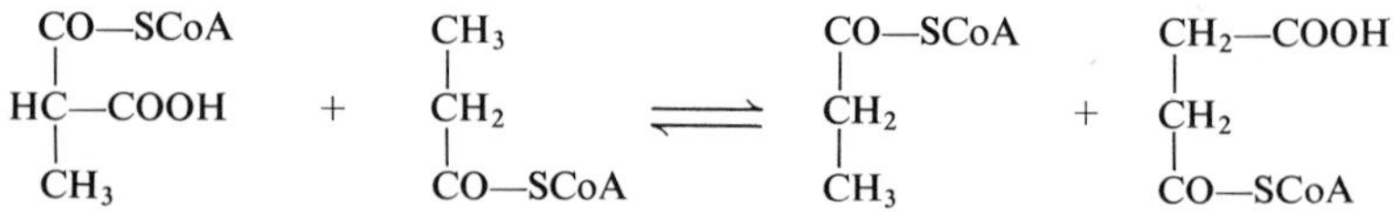

$$
\begin{array}{ccccc}
\text{CO—SCoA} & & \text{CH}_3 & & \text{CO—SCoA} & & \text{CH}_2\text{—COOH} \\
| & & | & & | & & | \\
\text{HC—COOH} & + & \text{CH}_2 & \rightleftharpoons & \text{CH}_2 & + & \text{CH}_2 \\
| & & | & & | & & | \\
\text{CH}_3 & & \text{CO—SCoA} & & \text{CH}_3 & & \text{CO—SCoA}
\end{array}
$$

methylmalonyl CoA   propionyl CoA   propionyl CoA   succinyl CoA

This enzymatic carboxylation of propionyl CoA yields only one of the two isomers of methylmalonyl CoA. The final solution to the problem came in 1960, when Swick and Wood (56) demonstrated this new type of biochemical reaction in the propionic acid fermentation. This reaction permitted a direct carboxylation of pyruvate without the intervention of carbon dioxide:

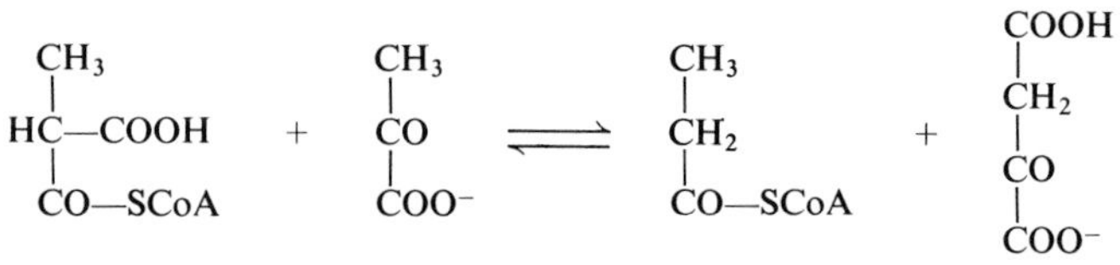

$$
\begin{array}{ccccc}
\text{CH}_3 & & \text{CH}_3 & & \text{CH}_3 & & \text{COOH} \\
| & & | & & | & & | \\
\text{HC—COOH} & + & \text{CO} & \rightleftharpoons & \text{CH}_2 & + & \text{CH}_2 \\
| & & | & & | & & | \\
\text{CO—SCoA} & & \text{COO}^- & & \text{CO—SCoA} & & \text{CO} \\
& & & & & & | \\
& & & & & & \text{COO}^-
\end{array}
$$

methylmalonyl CoA   pyruvate   propionyl CoA   oxalacetate

The reaction is catalyzed by a methylmalonyl-oxalacetate transcarboxylase (67). This enzyme appears to have a broad specificity for the CoA esters, which is a very interesting characteristic because it permits the carboxyl group of oxalacetate arising in the TCA cycle or elsewhere to be utilized in fatty acid synthesis and vice versa. From the point of view of economy and control of cellular reactions, it would seem advantageous to transfer carboxyl groups just as ester phosphates are transferred. Oxalacetate is also the only keto acid that has been found to serve as a carboxyl donor. There is no cofactor required, but the enzyme contains biotin (52).

The two methylmalonyl CoA compounds performing the described reactions were, however, in two different isomeric forms. The enzyme which converted one isomeric form into the other was found to be methylmalonyl racemase (4). This enzyme did not function by transfer of the CoA moiety between carboxyl groups.

The pathways which can be followed by these bacteria to produce pyruvate from glucose will be disregarded except to state that phosphoenol pyruvate is formed as an intermediate. The first reaction of this intermediate, under normal conditions, is

$$
\begin{array}{ccc}
\underset{|}{\text{CH}_2} & & \underset{|}{\text{CH}_3} \\[-2pt]
\text{C}-\text{OPO}_3^{2-} + \text{ADP} & \longrightarrow & \text{C}{=}\text{O} + \text{ATP} \\[-2pt]
\underset{|}{\text{COO}^-} & & \underset{|}{\text{COO}^-}
\end{array}
$$

phosphoenolpyruvate   pyruvate

which is catalyzed by pyruvate kinase (ATP:pyruvate phosphotransferase, E.C. 2.7.1.40). In this reaction not only ADP, but also UDP, GDP, CDP, IDP, and deoxy-ADP can act as acceptor.

Once pyruvate has been formed, the pathway splits into two, one terminating in the formation of acetate and carbon dioxide, and the second in the formation of propionate. The step toward acetate formation is the conversion of pyruvate to acetyl CoA catalyzed by a pyruvate dehydrogenase, which is very likely

$$
\begin{array}{ccc}
\underset{|}{\text{CH}_3} & & \underset{|}{\text{CH}_3} \\[-2pt]
\text{C}{=}\text{O} + \text{NAD}^+ + \text{CoA} & \longrightarrow & \text{C}{=}\text{O} + \text{CO}_2 + \text{NADH} + \text{H}^+ \\[-2pt]
\underset{|}{\text{COO}^-} & & \underset{|}{\text{SCoA}}
\end{array}
$$

pyruvate   acetyl CoA

pyruvate:cytochrome b_1 oxidoreductase (E.C. 1.2.2.2) since there is no report of a lipoate requirement as found in aerobic bacteria. This enzyme should not be confused with the other pyruvate dehydrogenase (pyruvate:lipoate oxidoreductase (acceptor-acetylating), E.C. 1.2.4.1), which also forms acetyl CoA in its reaction but involves a system of four other enzymes as described for the TCA cycle in aerobic respiration (see Chapter 5).

A phosphotransacetylase (acetyl CoA:orthophosphate acetyltransferase, E.C. 2.3.1.8)(50) catalyzes the reaction before acetate is formed by transferring

$$
\begin{array}{ccc}
\underset{|}{\text{CH}_3} & & \underset{|}{\text{CH}_3} \\[-2pt]
\text{C}{=}\text{O} + \text{H}_3\text{PO}_4 & \longrightarrow & \text{C}-\text{OPO}_3^{2-} + \text{CoA} \\[-2pt]
\underset{|}{\text{SCoA}} & &
\end{array}
$$

acetyl CoA   acetyl phosphate

the phosphate group to ADP with the help of acetylkinase (ATP:acetate phosphotransferase, E.C. 2.7.2.1)(43). The other branch-off to propionate is a double cycling pathway which can start either from pyruvate or from phosphoenol pyruvate. Methylmalonyl CoA reacts with pyruvate to form propionyl

$$
\begin{array}{ccc}
\underset{|}{\text{CH}_3} & & \underset{|}{\text{CH}_3} \\[-2pt]
\text{C}-\text{OPO}_3^{2-} + \text{ADP} & \longrightarrow & \text{COO}^- + \text{ATP} \\[-2pt]
\end{array}
$$

acetyl phosphate   acetate

CoA and oxalacetate. The reaction with pyruvate occurs only with S-methyl-malonyl CoA. The R-methylmalonyl CoA(20,42) is initially formed from succinyl CoA by the enzyme methylmalonyl isomerase(18,26,38,52,55,56), which is possibly identical with methylmalonyl CoA:carbonylmutase (E.C. 5.4.99.2). It is converted to S-methylmalonyl CoA by a methylmalonyl racemase(4,38), now called "methylmalonyl CoA racemase" (E.C. 5.1.99.1).

Methylmalonyl-oxalacetate transcarboxylase(56,67,69) (methylmalonyl CoA:pyruvate carboxyltransferase, E.C. 2.1.3.1), which requires biotin(5), catalyzes the reaction:

$$
\begin{array}{cccc}
\underset{\text{methylmalonyl CoA}}{\overset{\displaystyle \text{COOH}}{\underset{\displaystyle \text{CO—SCoA}}{CH_3\!-\!\overset{|}{\underset{|}{CH}}}}}
& + \;
\underset{\text{pyruvate}}{\overset{\displaystyle CH_3}{\underset{\displaystyle COO^-}{\overset{|}{\underset{|}{CO}}}}}
& \longrightarrow \;
\underset{\text{propionyl CoA}}{\overset{\displaystyle CH_3}{\underset{\displaystyle CO\!-\!SCoA}{\overset{|}{\underset{|}{CH_2}}}}}
& + \;
\underset{\text{oxalacetate}}{\overset{\displaystyle COO^-}{\underset{\displaystyle COO^-}{\overset{|}{\underset{|}{\overset{\displaystyle CH_2}{\underset{\displaystyle C=O}{\overset{|}{|}}}}}}}}
\end{array}
$$

Malate and finally succinate are produced from the formed oxalacetate via the TCA cycle acting in reverse: The enzymes involved in the first two reactions are L-malate:NAD oxidoreductase (E.C. 1.1.1.37) and L-malate hydrolyase (E.C. 4.2.1.2). A fumarate reductase, which does not occur in the TCA cycle,

$$
\underset{\text{oxalacetate}}{\overset{\displaystyle COO^-}{\underset{\displaystyle COO^-}{\overset{|}{\underset{|}{\overset{\displaystyle CH_2}{\underset{\displaystyle C=O}{\overset{|}{|}}}}}}}}
\; + NADH + H^+ \; \longrightarrow \;
\underset{\text{malate}}{\overset{\displaystyle COO^-}{\underset{\displaystyle COO^-}{\overset{|}{\underset{|}{\overset{\displaystyle CH_2}{\underset{\displaystyle CHOH}{\overset{|}{|}}}}}}}}
$$

$$
\underset{\text{malate}}{\overset{\displaystyle COO^-}{\underset{\displaystyle COO^-}{\overset{|}{\underset{|}{\overset{\displaystyle CH_2}{\underset{\displaystyle CHOH}{\overset{|}{|}}}}}}}}
\; \longrightarrow \;
\underset{\text{fumarate}}{\overset{\displaystyle COO^-}{\underset{\displaystyle COO^-}{\overset{|}{\underset{\|}{\overset{\displaystyle CH}{\underset{\displaystyle CH}{\overset{\|}{|}}}}}}}}
$$

$$
\underset{\text{fumarate}}{\overset{\displaystyle COO^-}{\underset{\displaystyle COO^-}{\overset{|}{\underset{\|}{\overset{\displaystyle CH}{\underset{\displaystyle CH}{\overset{\|}{|}}}}}}}}
\; + H_2O \; \longrightarrow \;
\underset{\text{succinic acid}}{\overset{\displaystyle COOH}{\underset{\displaystyle COOH}{\overset{|}{\underset{|}{\overset{\displaystyle CH_2}{\underset{\displaystyle CH_2}{\overset{|}{|}}}}}}}}
$$

reduces fumarate to succinate, whereby ATP and FP are formed. Considering the steps from oxalacetate to succinate the following energy-yielding process occurs:

$$NADH + H^+ + P_i + ADP + FP \rightarrow NAD^+ + ATP + FPH + H^+$$

Propionyl CoA, which was formed earlier in the reaction of pyruvate and methylmalonyl CoA, transfers its coenzyme to succinate with the enzyme succinyl CoA:3-oxoacid CoA transferase (E.C. 2.8.3.6)(51) as catalyst:

$$
\begin{array}{cccc}
\text{COO}^- & \text{CH}_3 & \text{COOH} & \text{CH}_3 \\
| & | & | & | \\
\text{CH}_2 & \text{CH}_2 & \text{CH}_2 & \text{CH}_2 \\
| \quad + \quad | & & | \quad + \quad | \\
\text{CH}_2 & \text{CO—SCoA} & \text{CH}_2 & \text{COO}^- \\
| & & | & \\
\text{COO}^- & & \text{CO—SCoA} & \\
\end{array}
$$

$$\text{succinate} \quad \text{propionyl CoA} \qquad\qquad \text{succinyl CoA} \quad \text{propionate}$$

With this reaction the actual accumulating end product, propionate, is formed.

The C_1 compound, which is released from S-methylmalonyl CoA and cleaves with pyruvate to form oxalacetate, is suggested as almost certainly representing carbon dioxide(5), but this requires further investigation.

An interesting feature of this pathway is the apparent high yield of ATP. On the basis of cell yields it was found that approximately 6 moles of ATP are formed per 1.5 moles of glucose(9). Reactions a and d together would yield 4 moles of the 6 moles of ATP, and 2 moles must therefore arise from the reaction-yielding propionate. This is possible because of the unique feature of propionate formation, which involves a complete reduction of fumarate to succinate and oxidation of pyruvate to acetate and carbon dioxide. An electron transport–coupled phosphorylation may occur during this step through the reduction of a flavoprotein by $NADH + H^+$.

SUCCINIC ACID PRODUCTION BY *PROPIONIBACTERIUM*

Succinate occasionally accumulates in the fermentation of glucose by propionibacteria. In this case the cycle is broken and the oxalacetate must be generated by fixation of carbon dioxide. This fixation is catalyzed by the enzyme phosphoenol pyruvate carboxytransphosphorylase(46,47):

$$
\begin{array}{cc}
\text{CH}_2 & \text{COO}^- \\
| & | \\
\text{CO—PO}_3^{2-} + CO_2 \longrightarrow & \text{CH}_2 + PP_i \\
| & | \\
\text{COO}^- & \text{C=O} \\
& | \\
& \text{COO}^- \\
\end{array}
$$

$$\text{phosphoenol} \qquad\qquad\qquad \text{oxalacetate}$$
$$\text{pyruvate}$$

The yield of ATP, of course, would decrease, since phosphoenol pyruvate would only partly be available to form pyruvate.

Under many conditions succinate has been found as a minor product of the fermentation which may account for the finding of less than 6 moles of ATP in propionibacteria.

There are other bacteria which produce succinic acid via methylmalonyl CoA esters(10,27), and it is likely that their intermediary metabolism might be closely related to the propionibacteria. These organisms, which occur in the rumen(27), are as follows:

(a) *Bacteroides* sp.(16)
(b) *Ruminococcus flavefaciens*(45)
(c) *Succinomonas amylolytica*(16)
(d) *Succinovibrio dextrinosolvens*(15)
(e) *Borrelia* sp.(14)
(f) *Cytophage succinicans*(7)

Apart from propionibacteria there are two bacterial taxa which are able to produce propionic acid from lactate, viz., *Veillonella gazogenes* and *Clostridium propionicum*. *Veillonella* and *Propionibacterium* are very similar or even identical from pyruvate onward. *Veillonella*, however, does not ferment glucose, but only lactate.

Clostridium propionicum possesses an entirely different mechanism. It is known that the route from lactate is

lactate → acrylate → propionate

but other intermediates have not been elucidated. It appears that this pathway, which also occurs in *Bacteroides ruminicola*(63), involves acrylyl CoA as an intermediate.

Although *Peptostreptococcus elsdenii* is not an organism normally classified with the propionic acid producers, its lactate metabolism(8) certainly looks very similar to the anticipated pathway in *Clostridium propionicum* and *Bacteroides ruminicola*. *Peptostreptococcus elsdenii* is strictly anaerobic and metabolizes lactate to propionate according to the pattern given in Scheme 6.1. Lactate can be metabolized to pyruvate since this organism possesses the enzymes lactate dehydrogenase (E.C. 1.1.1.27) and a diaphorase. It is suggested that the conversion of lactate to propionate occurs via the CoA esters of lactate, acrylate, and propionate. Lactate can be converted to lactyl CoA under the action of CoA transphorase [acetyl CoA:acetyl CoA required for this step is formed via the phosphoroclastic split (see Section entitled "The Formation of Acetate")] using the enzyme phosphotransacetylase (E.C. 2.3.1.8). Lactyl CoA dehydrase catalyzes the reaction between lactyl CoA and acrylyl CoA. The conversion of acrylyl CoA to propionyl CoA is mediated by acyl CoA dehydrogenase and the final product, propionate, is arrived at in a similar way to that of lactyl CoA or acrylyl CoA by reacting with acetate and a CoA transferase (E.C. 2.8.3.1). Whether or not this pathway is applicable to *Clostridium propionicum* and *Bacteroides ruminicola* is not known.

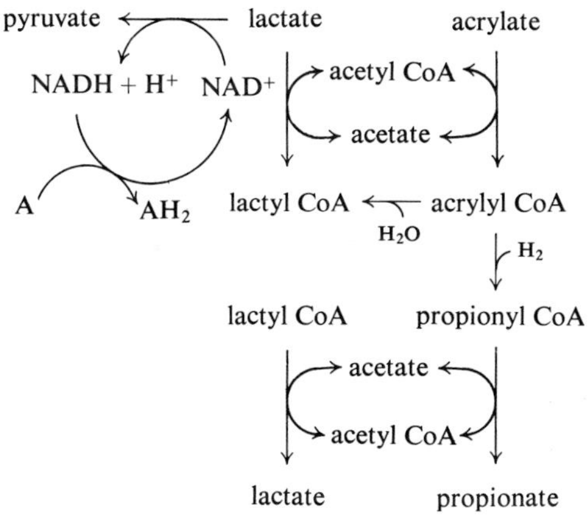

SCHEME 6.1

THE PRODUCTION OF BUTYRIC ACID, BUTANOL, AND ACETONE

The group of bacteria which carry out a fermentation with end products such as acetate, butyrate, butanol, acetone, and isopropanol belong to the genus *Clostridium* and the genus *Butyribacterium*. The species of the genus *Clostridium* are commonly divided into a number of groups, depending upon their carbon-source metabolism. Those which ferment carbohydrates and have limited proteolytic properties are called "saccharolytic clostridia" and these are the ones dealt with here. The great variety of end products formed are shown in the fermentation balance sheet for clostridia (72) in Table 6.2.

The balance sheet indicates that all studied strains produce butyric acid and acetic acid. *Clostridium butyricum* and *C. lactoacetophilum* produce butyric acid as their major end product together with carbon dioxide and hydrogen. Other strains produce mostly butanol and acetone (*Clostridium acetobutylicum*) or butanol alone (*Clostridium butylicum*) together with carbon dioxide and hydrogen. There are only a few which can produce appreciable amounts of acetoin (*Clostridium acetobutylicum*) or isopropanol (*Clostridium butylicum*). Studies on *Clostridium perfringens* reveal significant differences in the metabolic activities between iron-deficient strains and the normal strains. The over-all pathways in the fermentation of glucose by species of *Clostridium* and *Butyribacterium* are demonstrated in Fig. 6.3.

TABLE 6.2

METABOLIC ACTIVITIES OF VARIOUS SPECIES OF CLOSTRIDIA[a]

End products		Moles/100 moles glucose fermented					
	C. butyricum	C. lactoacidophilum (C. tyrobutyricum)	C. perfringens	C. acetobutylicum	C. butylicum	B. rettgeri
Butyric acid	76	73	9	34	4	17	29
Acetic acid	42	28	15	60	14	17	88
Lactic acid			160	33			107
CO_2	188	190	24	176	221	203	48
H_2	235	182	21	214	135	77	74
Ethanol			10 ←Fe deficient→	26	7		
Butanol					56	58	
Acetone					22	—	
Acetoin					6	—	
Isopropanol						12	
% C recovered	96	91	98	97	99	96	110
O/R Balance	0.97	1.16	0.81	1.05	1.01	1.06	0.74

[a] From W. A. Wood(72).

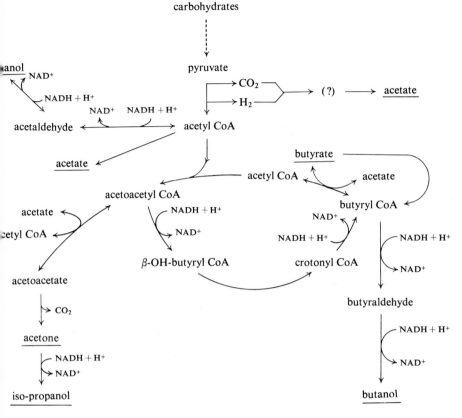

FIG. 6.3. The formation of acetate, acetone, butanol, and butyric acid by species of the genus *Clostridium*.

The Formation of Acetate

The first step in acetate formation is the breakdown of pyruvate to acetyl CoA. This step has been described already for aerobic conditions. It requires, apart from pyruvate dehydrogenase, lipoate and thiamine pyrophosphate (TPP). Under anaerobic conditions there are three systems in operation(72), two of which are similar:

(1) Pyruvate is converted into acetyl CoA or acetyl phosphate with the formation of hydrogen and carbon dioxide by a mechanism which does not involve formate as the precursor for hydrogen and carbon dioxide.

(2) Pyruvate is converted into acetyl CoA or acetyl phosphate with the formation of formate which may be converted to hydrogen and carbon dioxide by the hydrogenlyase system.

(3) Pyruvate is decarboxylated directly to acetaldehyde and carbon dioxide.

Whereas system (3) occurs mainly in yeasts and higher plants, system (1) is characteristic for clostridia and system (2) for the *Enterobacteriaceae*. Systems (1) and (2) require CoA and TPP. It is well known that in the enterobacteria, the energy available in the thiol ester bond of acetyl CoA enters the high-energy phosphate pool by means of two reactions. Reaction (1) is catalyzed by phosphotransacetylase (acetyl CoA:orthophosphate acetyltransferase, E.C. 2.3.1.8) and reaction (2) by acetokinase (ATP:acetate phosphotransferase, E.C. 2.7.2.1), which forms the end product acetate:

(1) acetyl CoA + orthophosphate $\rightarrow$ CoA + acetyl phosphate

(2) acetyl phosphate + ADP $\rightarrow$ acetate + ATP

For each mole of acetate formed, one mole of ATP is generated. This metabolic system is a simple degradation of pyruvate to acetate, with the over-all production of 2 moles of acetic acid from 1 mole of glucose. Barker(10), however, found that in *Clostridium thermoaceticum* not two, but three, moles of acetate are formed from 1 mole of glucose, suggesting a more complicated system. The breakdown of pyruvate was therefore reinvestigated, and it was found that carbon dioxide must be reduced in some manner in order to form the additional mole of acetate. To carry out this reduction, a hydrogen acceptor had to be found. It had been known for quite some time that in clostridia the degradation of pyruvate to acetyl CoA involved the release of carbon dioxide and hydrogen. Wood, in his review(72), noted that it was assumed from experience in studies on enterobacteria that formate must be an intermediate in clostridia being decomposed in the following reaction with formic hydrogenlyase as catalyst. This reaction was found to occur in the enterobacteria in two steps:

$$HCOOH + A \rightarrow H_2A + CO_2$$
$$H_2A \rightarrow A + H_2$$

The compound A is now known to be ferredoxin and the enzymes involved in the above reactions are formate dehydrogenase (formate:cytochrome b_1 oxidoreductase, E.C. 1.2.2.1) and hydrogenase (hydrogen:ferredoxin oxidoreductase, E.C. 1.12.1.1). Formate, however, could not be detected in clostridia. Valentine(58) tried to solve this problem in another way, without considering formate as intermediate and assumed that a ferredoxin-linked cleavage may occur generally in clostridia. It was found present in *Clostridium pasteurianum* (37, 59, 64), *C. lactoacetophilum*(58), *C. acidi-urici*(58), *C. thermosaccharolyticum*. (*C. nigrificans*)(66, 68), *Micrococcus lactilyticus*(58), *Peptostreptococcus elsdenii*(58), *Butyribacterium rettgeri*(58), *Diplococcus glycinophilus*(58), and *C. kluyveri*(23). He states that pyruvate is first decarboxylated by pyruvic dehydrogenase (which could be pyruvate:cytochrome b_1 oxidoreductase, E.C. 1.2.2.2) with the formation of a thiamine pyrophosphate enzyme complex, from where electrons are transferred to ferredoxin. The reduced ferredoxin is then reoxidized by hydrogenase (E.C. 1.12.1.1) and forms molecular hydrogen. The enzyme-TPP complex is attacked by a phosphotransacetylase (E.C. 2.3.1.8) and forms acetyl CoA (see Scheme 6.2). This mechanism would fulfill all the discovered requirements in the form of TPP, CoA, and also 2 acetyl CoA and $2 CO_2$. This requires the production of a further acetate. Having arrived at carbon dioxide and hydrogen, the question then arises: Can clostridia produce acetate from these two products as suggested by Lamanna and Mallett(33)?

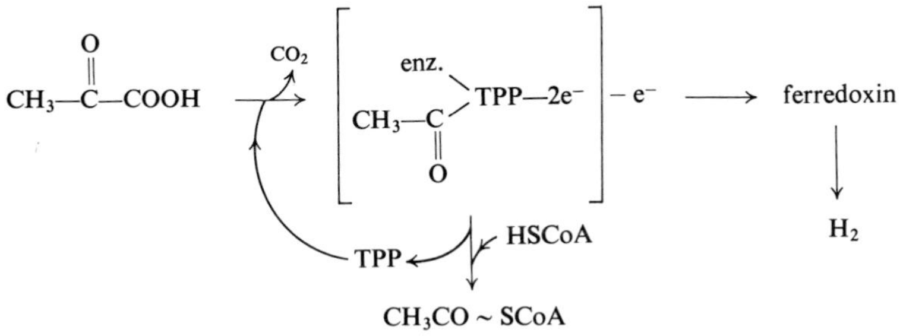

SCHEME 6.2.(Reprinted with the permission of the American Society of Microbiologists.)

Tracer element work(34) showed the existence of an interaction between $C^{14}O_2$ and molecular hydrogen to form formate and led also to the isolation of a NADP-linked formate dehydrogenase (E.C. 1.2.2.1 or 1.2.1.2) from *Clostridium thermoaceticum*. This observation indicated then that formate must be an intermediate in the reduction of CO_2 to the methyl group of acetate, which was proved when C^{14}-formate was found to be preferentially incorporated into this methyl group. The oxidation of reduced NADP and net synthesis of formate from carbon dioxide has not yet been demonstrated and from the redox potentials of both systems it would not seem possible for this to occur:

$$NADPH + H^+/NADP^+ \quad -0.324$$

$$formate/CO_2 \quad\quad\quad -0.440$$

This reduction of carbon dioxide must certainly go via some carrier system. The mechanism used by *Methanobacterium* may offer a solution (see Chapter 3). It is also possible that the NADP-formic dehydrogenase is responsible for the formation of carbon dioxide from formate and that another electron carrier is involved in the reduction of carbon dioxide to formate. Studies with *Clostridium thermoaceticum*, which does not produce hydrogen, showed that ferredoxin is very unlikely to play such a role. The mechanism for the formation of this third molecule of acetate is therefore still obscure.

Two mechanisms have been proposed for the conversion of carbon dioxide to the third molecule of acetate during investigations with *Clostridium thermoaceticum*:

(1) the direct conversion of carbon dioxide to acetate with cobalt-methyl-cobalamine as methyl group donor(40), and
(2) an indirect conversion of carbon dioxide to acetate via α-ketoisovalerate (32).

The direct conversion of carbon dioxide to acetate with cobalt-methylcobal-amine was suggested as a parallel methyl group transfer mechanism to the methane-oxidizing bacteria (see Chapter 5), particularly when it was observed that *Clostridium thermoaceticum* is able to catalyze the synthesis of this compound from carbon dioxide and reduced vitamin B_{12} (39). This direct conversion requires pyruvate, CoA, and ferredoxin. Pyruvate is thought to act either as a source of acetate carboxyl group, which is involved in the transcarboxylation, or as a source of electrons needed for the reductive cleavage of cobalt-carboxyl-methylcobalamine to acetate, or as a source of energy in producing acetyl CoA, acetyl phosphate, and ATP, which would be needed for the synthesis of cobalt-carboxymethylcobalamine from cobalt-methylcobalamine.

The indirect conversion of carbon dioxide into acetate originates in the observations(32) that $^{14}CO_2$ was extensively incorporated into a compound which was found to be α-ketoisovalerate. The possibility of being able to synthesize this keto acid from pyruvate via acetolactate, acetate, and acetyl CoA could be visualized and formed the basis of this hypothesis (see pathway on page 275).

Pyruvate is able to undergo condensation and decarboxylation (see Section entitled "The Butanediol Producer") to form α-acetolactate, which in turn is metabolized to α-ketoisovalerate. The fixation of carbon dioxide together with CoASH converts α-ketoisovalerate to β-methylcrotonyl CoA. The latter is then broken down to acetoacetate, acetyl CoA, and finally to acetate. The breakdown of acetoacetate may go via acetoacetyl CoA as described for *Clostridium kluyveri* (see Section entitled "Acetone Production"). The described mechanism would explain the formation of 3 moles of acetate from 1 mole of glucose and might also explain the unique stoichiometry which is associated with the fermentation of glucose by *C. thermoaceticum*(32). Both theories could apply independently.

Whereas no formate was found in the metabolism of glucose by *Clostridium thermoaceticum*, *C. kluyveri* possesses a formyl CoA hydrolase(49) apart

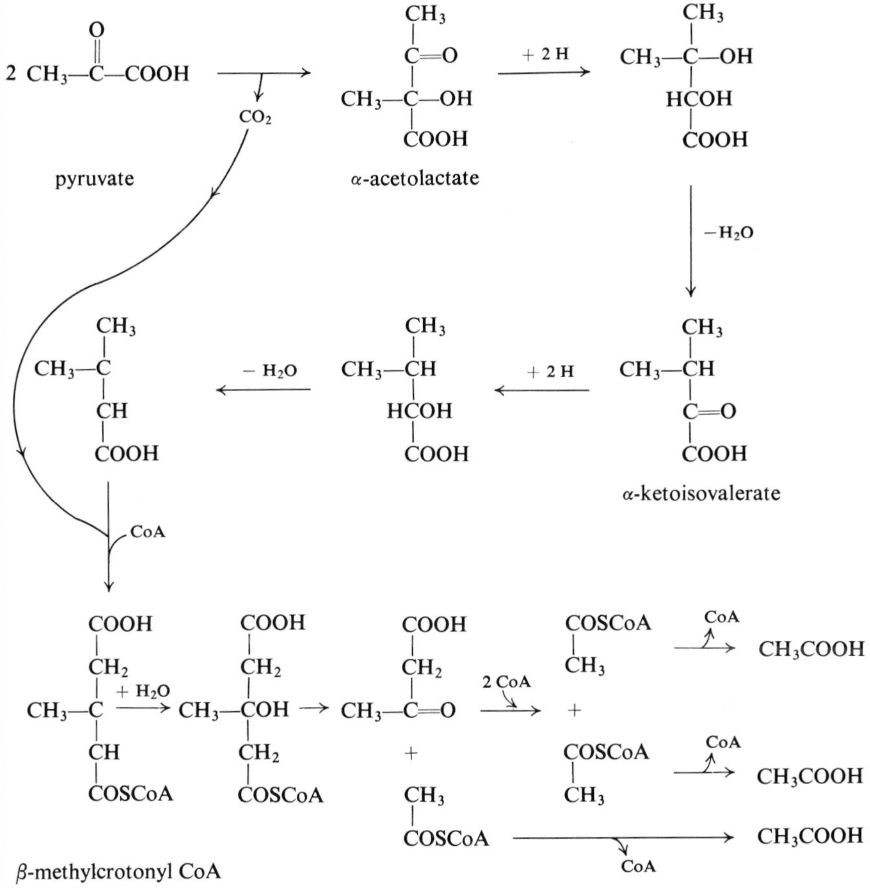

β-methylcrotonyl CoA

from the phosphoacetyltransferase and a CoA transferase. Thus, *C. kluyveri* appears to be able to form acetate in the following way:

$$\text{acetyl P} + \text{CoASH} \xrightarrow{\text{E.C. 2.3.1.8}} \text{acetyl CoA} + P_i$$

$$\text{acetyl CoA} + \text{formate} \xrightarrow{\text{CoA transferase}} \text{formyl CoA} + \text{acetate}$$

$$\text{formyl CoA} + H_2O \xrightarrow{\text{E.C. 3.1.2.10}} \text{formate} + \text{CoASH}$$

net: $\text{acetyl P} + H_2O \rightarrow \text{acetate} + P_i$

These differences in pathways may be very important in the further classification of clostridia.

The Formation of Butyrate

Saccharolytic clostridia ferment glucose to butyrate. The intermediate acetyl CoA will be taken as the starting point. From the point of view of energetics the production of acetate as sole end product would not be satisfactory since it becomes more and more difficult to reoxidize $NADH + H^+$ with the dropping of the pH into the acid region(10). It is therefore not surprising to find in the clostridia a similar cyclic mechanism to that in the propionibacteria. This cyclic mechanism brings about the formation of butyric acid, which is a much less acid end product than acetate (see Scheme 6.3).

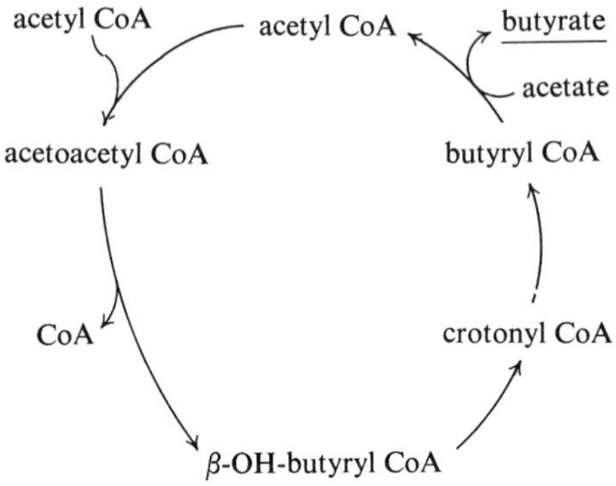

SCHEME 6.3

Two acetyl CoA molecules undergo a condensation to form acetoacetyl CoA with acetoacetyl CoA thiolase (acetyl CoA : acetyl CoA : C-acetyltransferase, E.C. 2.3.1.9) as the catalyzing enzyme, liberating 1 mole of CoA:

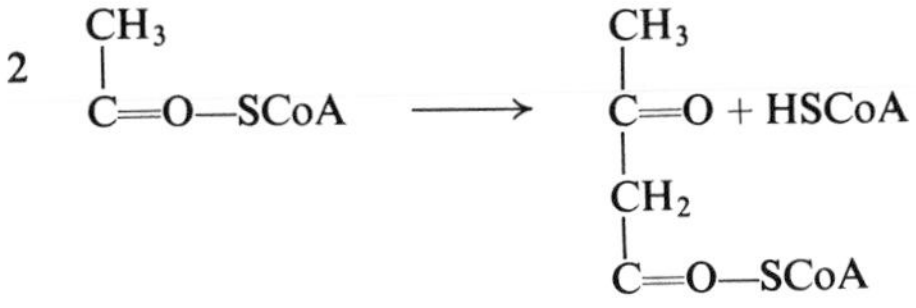

acetyl CoA   acetoacetyl CoA

The next step in the cycle is a reductive step, whereby acetoacetyl CoA is reduced to β-hydroxybutyryl CoA and reduced NAD is oxidized to NAD^+:

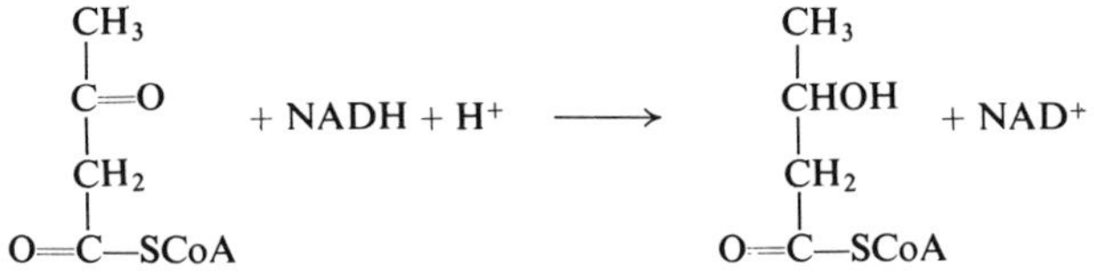

acetoacetyl CoA β-hydroxybutyryl CoA

This reaction is catalyzed by the action of 3-hydroxybutyrate dehydrogenase (D-3-hydroxybutyrate:NAD oxidoreductase, E.C. 1.1.1.30). The dehydration of β-hydroxybutyryl CoA is caused by a crotonase (L-3-hydroxyacyl CoA hydrolyase, E.C. 4.2.1.17) forming crotonyl CoA and water:

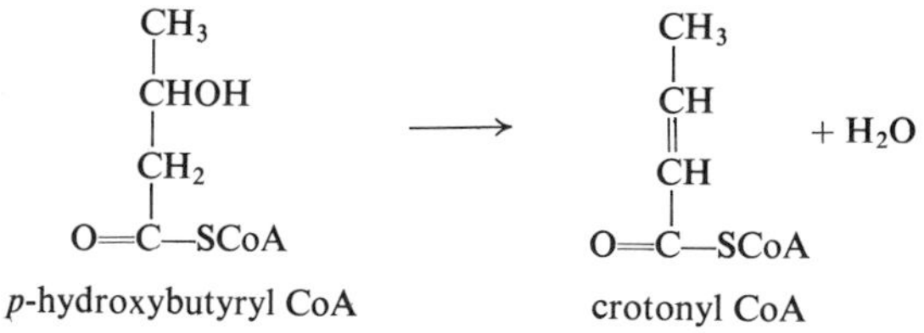

$$
\begin{array}{c}
CH_3 \\
| \\
CHOH \\
| \\
CH_2 \\
| \\
O{=}C{-}SCoA
\end{array}
\longrightarrow
\begin{array}{c}
CH_3 \\
| \\
CH \\
\| \\
CH \\
| \\
O{=}C{-}SCoA
\end{array}
+ H_2O
$$

p-hydroxybutyryl CoA   crotonyl CoA

A NAD-linked dehydrogenase (butyryl CoA:(acceptor) oxidoreductase, E.C. 1.3.99.2) is then responsible for the further reduction to butyryl CoA:

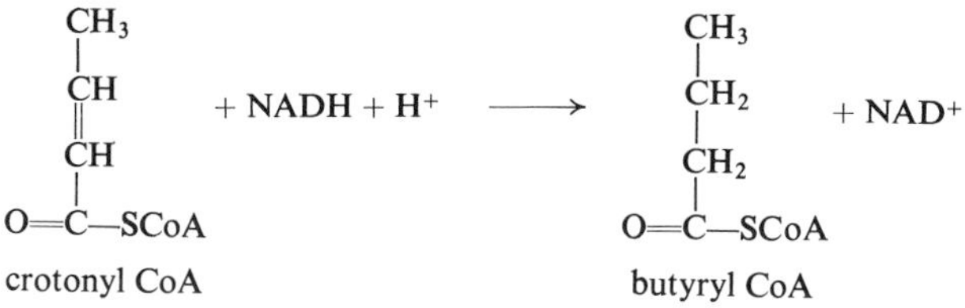

$$
\begin{array}{c}
CH_3 \\
| \\
CH \\
\| \\
CH \\
| \\
O{=}C{-}SCoA
\end{array}
+ NADH + H^+
\longrightarrow
\begin{array}{c}
CH_3 \\
| \\
CH_2 \\
| \\
CH_2 \\
| \\
O{=}C{-}SCoA
\end{array}
+ NAD^+
$$

crotonyl CoA   butyryl CoA

The last step in the cyclic mechanism is a transfer reaction, whereby acetate and butyryl CoA act together with a fatty acid-SCoA transferase (butyryl CoA:acetatetransferase?) to produce acetyl CoA and butyrate. Acetyl CoA is now available again to reenter the reaction sequence.

Formation of Acetone, Isopropanol, Butanol, and Ethanol

A number of the saccharolytic clostridia, which normally ferment carbohydrates to butyric acid, are able to change their system, favoring the production of acetone, and concurrently convert the butyrate already produced to butanol. This new system comes into operation as soon as the butyrate production has lowered the pH of the medium to about 4.0.

Acetone Production. Clostridium acetobutylicum possesses a transferase system which diverts acetoacetyl CoA from the normal cyclic mechanism to produce acetoacetate:

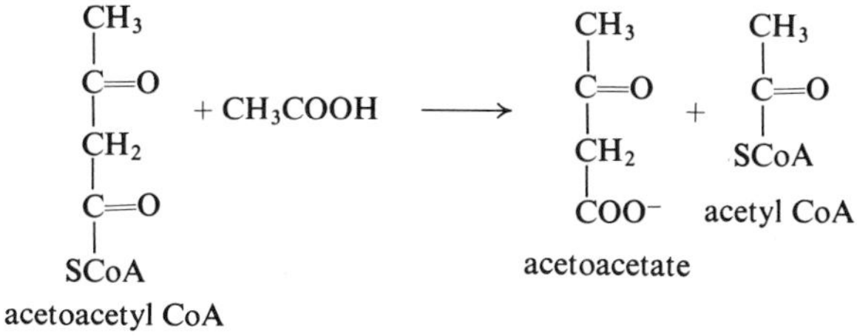

$$
\begin{array}{c}
CH_3 \\
| \\
C{=}O \\
| \\
CH_2 \\
| \\
C{=}O \\
| \\
SCoA
\end{array}
+ CH_3COOH
\longrightarrow
\begin{array}{c}
CH_3 \\
| \\
C{=}O \\
| \\
CH_2 \\
| \\
COO^-
\end{array}
+
\begin{array}{c}
CH_3 \\
| \\
C{=}O \\
| \\
SCoA
\end{array}
$$

acetoacetyl CoA   acetoacetate   acetyl CoA

This transferase is different from the fatty acid-SCoA transferase since *Clostridium kluyveri* does not possess the latter enzyme but is able to form acetoacetate from acetoacetyl CoA. The decarboxylation of acetoacetate to acetone is an irreversible step:

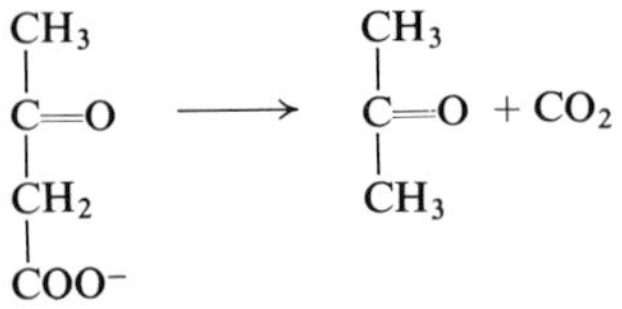

$$
\begin{array}{ccc}
\text{CH}_3 & & \text{CH}_3 \\
| & & | \\
\text{C}=\text{O} & \longrightarrow & \text{C}=\text{O} + \text{CO}_2 \\
| & & | \\
\text{CH}_2 & & \text{CH}_3 \\
| & & \\
\text{COO}^- & & \\
\end{array}
$$

acetoacetate   acetone

The enzyme responsible for this reaction is acetoacetate decarboxylase (aceto-acetate carboxylyase, E.C. 4.1.1.4).

Isopropanol Production. Clostridium butylicum is to our present knowledge the only bacterium which can carry the reaction sequence one step further by reducing all the acetone produced to isopropanol by means of isopropanol

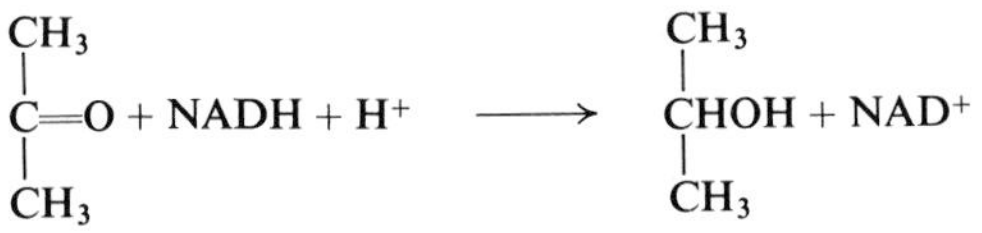

$$
\begin{array}{ccc}
\text{CH}_3 & & \text{CH}_3 \\
| & & | \\
\text{C}=\text{O} + \text{NADH} + \text{H}^+ & \longrightarrow & \text{CHOH} + \text{NAD}^+ \\
| & & | \\
\text{CH}_3 & & \text{CH}_3 \\
\end{array}
$$

acetone   isopropanol

dehydrogenase (E.C. 1.1.1 group). *Clostridium butylicum*, on the other hand, does not produce ethanol.

Ethanol Production. It was mentioned earlier that the production of ethanol occurs normally together with the acetone-butanol formation in *Clostridium acetobutylicum.* The mode of ethanol production is different from yeast since it branches off from acetyl CoA, whereby an aldehyde dehydrogenase (aldehyde: NAD oxidoreductase (acylating CoA), E.C. 1.2.1.10) produces acetaldehyde and NAD^+. The NAD-dependent alcohol dehydrogenase (alcohol:NAD oxidoreductase, E.C. 1.1.1.1) finally produces the end product ethanol.

Butanol Production. The diversion of the original cyclic system to form acetone stops further production of butyrate. Apart from the interruption of the cycle, two steps which generate NAD^+ are also eliminated, which means that some

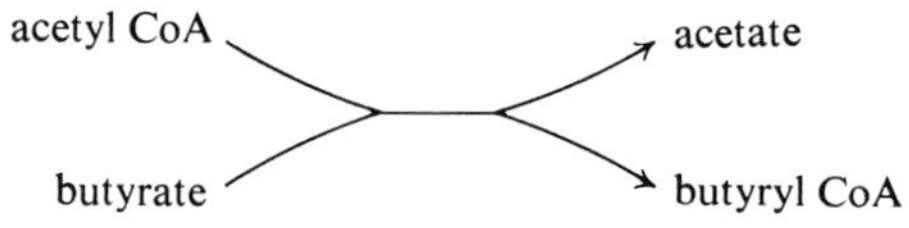

acetyl CoA ⟶ acetate
butyrate ⟶ butyryl CoA

other reduction process must be found. The reduction of butyrate to butanol is carried out in three consecutive reactions. The first step is virtually a reverse of the last reaction in the cycle whereby a CoA transferase transfers the coenzyme from an acetyl group to the butyryl group. The acetate formed is used for the generation of acetyl CoA in the acetone production.

Butyryl CoA may be formed in another way if there is a deficiency in the amount of acetyl CoA available. Adenosine triphosphate and CoA are required. The reduction of butyryl CoA to butyraldehyde is NAD-linked

$$\text{butyrate} \quad \xrightarrow[\text{ATP} \qquad \text{AMP} + \text{PP}_i]{\text{HSCoA}} \quad \text{butyryl CoA}$$

and catalyzed by the same aldehyde dehydrogenase (E.C. 1.2.1.10) which reduces acetyl CoA to acetaldehyde:

$$\text{butryl CoA} + \text{NADH} + \text{H}^+ \rightarrow \text{butyraldehyde} + \text{NAD}^+ + \text{HSCoA}$$

The final reduction to butanol is also carried out with a well-known enzyme, NAD-linked alcohol dehydrogenase (E.C. 1.1.1.1);

$$\text{butyraldehyde} + \text{NADH} + \text{H}^+ \rightarrow n\text{-butanol} + \text{NAD}^+$$

This production of butanol occurs after the change to the production of acetone has taken place.

The metabolic pathway of *Clostridium acetobutylicum* is therefore first from glucose via pyruvate to butyrate until so much butyrate has been accumulated together with some acetate that the pH of the medium drops to 4.0. At this point the cyclic mechanism is interrupted and acetone production starts. As a consequence of this change, the accumulated butyrate is further reduced to butanol. For the reduction of butyrate to butanol, the organism uses the same enzymes as for the ethanol production.

Lactate Production

Some of the saccharolytic clostridia and other butyrate producers such as *Butyribacterium* and *Clostridium perfringens* are able to reduce pyruvate to lactic acid since they possess a lactic acid dehydrogenase. This reduction, however, occurs only if the bacteria are grown under iron-deficient conditions (72).

Formation of Butanol from Ethanol and Acetate

Clostridium kluyveri can grow on an ethanol-acetate medium, producing butyrate by the mechanism already described. The ethanol is oxidized to

acetyl CoA in two reversible steps, whereby NADP-linked alcohol dehydrogenase (E.C. 1.1.1.1) first converts ethanol into acetaldehyde and subsequently
a NAD-linked acetaldehyde dehydrogenase converts acetaldehyde into acetyl
CoA with the help of CoA. If phosphate is added to the medium, a transfer
reaction occurs forming acetyl phosphate and regenerating CoA for further
oxidation of aldehyde. In general this does not occur and acetyl CoA joins
the cycle in order to produce butanol, provided acetate predominates in the
medium (30).

When ethanol is in excess in the medium, *Clostridium kluyveri* produces not
butyrate but caproate as the main product of the fermentation:

$$\text{acetyl CoA} \longleftarrow \qquad \longrightarrow \text{caproate}$$
$$\text{butyrate}$$
$$\text{butyryl CoA}$$
$$\uparrow$$

The production of caproate is via the same cyclic mechanism as for butyrate
until the last step where, instead of acetate, butyrate takes the place in the
transferase reaction, forming caproate and acetyl CoA.

Formation of Succinate from Pyruvate

There exists another fermentative pathway for *Clostridium kluyveri* which
produces succinate as the major end product. The appearance of succinate is
matched quantitatively with the disappearance of carbon dioxide. The proposed scheme is outlined in Fig. 6.4(33).

The formation of acetyl CoA from pyruvate was outlined earlier. Acetyl
CoA carboxylase (acetyl CoA:carbon dioxide ligase (ADP), E.C. 6.4.1.2)
incorporated CO_2 and water into acetyl CoA, forming malonyl CoA:

$$
\begin{array}{c}
CH_3 \\
| \\
C{=}O + CO_2 + H_2O + ATP \\
| \\
SCoA
\end{array}
\longrightarrow
\begin{array}{c}
COOH \\
| \\
CH_2 \quad + ADP \\
| \\
C{=}O \\
| \\
SCoA
\end{array}
$$

acetyl CoA   malonyl CoA

This reaction is ATP-dependent and requires biotin and Mn^{2+} like most of the
CO_2 fixation reactions. Malonyl CoA is then reduced by a NAD-dependent
malonate′ semialdehyde dehydrogenase (malonate semialdehyde:NAD(P)

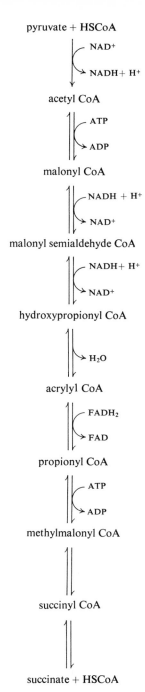

pyruvate + HSCoA

NAD^+

$NADH + H^+$

acetyl CoA

ATP

ADP

malonyl CoA

$NADH + H^+$

NAD^+

malonyl semialdehyde CoA

$NADH + H^+$

NAD^+

hydroxypropionyl CoA

H_2O

acrylyl CoA

$FADH_2$

FAD

propionyl CoA

ATP

ADP

methylmalonyl CoA

succinyl CoA

succinate + HSCoA

FIG. 6.4. The formation of succinate from pyruvate by *Clostridium kluyveri* (33) (reprinted with permission of Williams & Wilkins).

oxidoreductase, E.C. 1.2.1.15) to malonyl semialdehyde CoA and $NADH + H^+$:

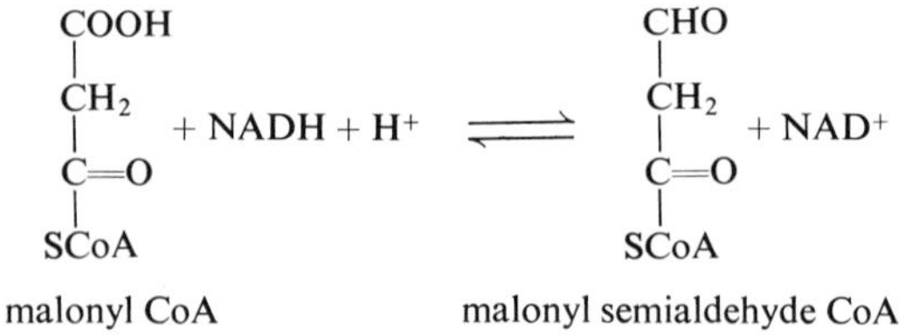

$$
\begin{array}{c}
\text{COOH} \\
| \\
\text{CH}_2 \\
| \\
\text{C}=\text{O} \\
| \\
\text{SCoA}
\end{array}
+ NADH + H^+ \ \rightleftharpoons \
\begin{array}{c}
\text{CHO} \\
| \\
\text{CH}_2 \\
| \\
\text{C}=\text{O} \\
| \\
\text{SCoA}
\end{array}
+ NAD^+
$$

malonyl CoA   malonyl semialdehyde CoA

A second reduction step follows immediately thereafter under the action of β-hydroxypropionate dehydrogenase (3-hydroxypropionate:NAD oxidoreductase, E.C. 1.1.1.59) forming hydroxypropionyl CoA and NAD^+. The

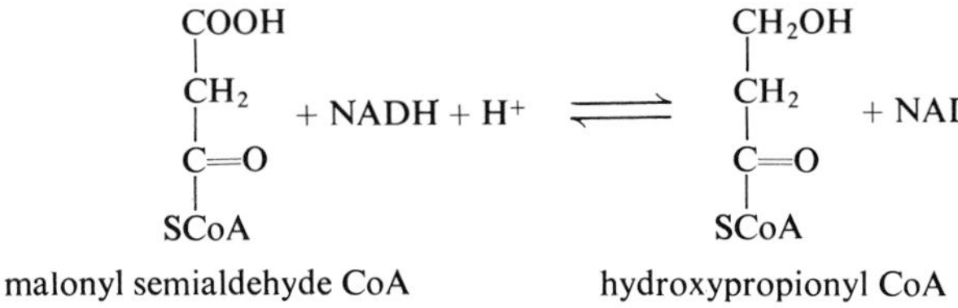

$$
\begin{array}{c}
\text{COOH} \\
| \\
\text{CH}_2 \\
| \\
\text{C}=\text{O} \\
| \\
\text{SCoA}
\end{array}
+ NADH + H^+ \ \rightleftharpoons \
\begin{array}{c}
\text{CH}_2\text{OH} \\
| \\
\text{CH}_2 \\
| \\
\text{C}=\text{O} \\
| \\
\text{SCoA}
\end{array}
+ NAD^+
$$

malonyl semialdehyde CoA   hydroxypropionyl CoA

release of 1 mole of H_2O during the next reaction with enoyl CoA hydratase (L-3-hydroxyacyl CoA hydrolyase, E.C. 4.2.1.17) leads to the formation of acrylyl CoA:

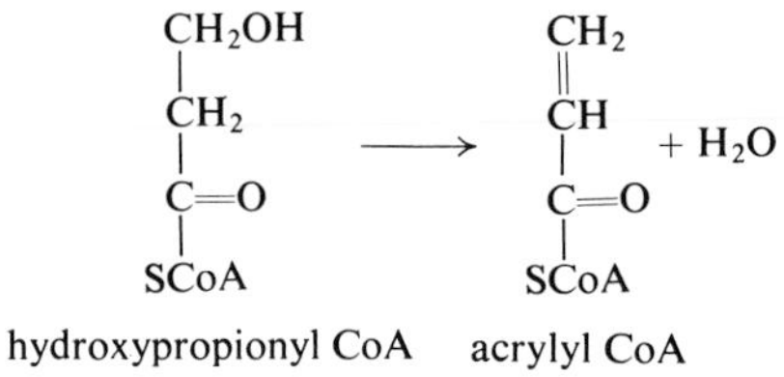

$$
\begin{array}{c}
\text{CH}_2\text{OH} \\
| \\
\text{CH}_2 \\
| \\
\text{C}=\text{O} \\
| \\
\text{SCoA}
\end{array}
\longrightarrow \
\begin{array}{c}
\text{CH}_2 \\
\| \\
\text{CH} \\
| \\
\text{C}=\text{O} \\
| \\
\text{SCoA}
\end{array}
+ H_2O
$$

hydroxypropionyl CoA   acrylyl CoA

With $FADH + H^+$ as hydrogen donor, acrylyl CoA receives 1 molecule of H_2 and is reduced to propionyl CoA, whereby $FADH + H^+$ is simultaneously oxidized to FAD^+:

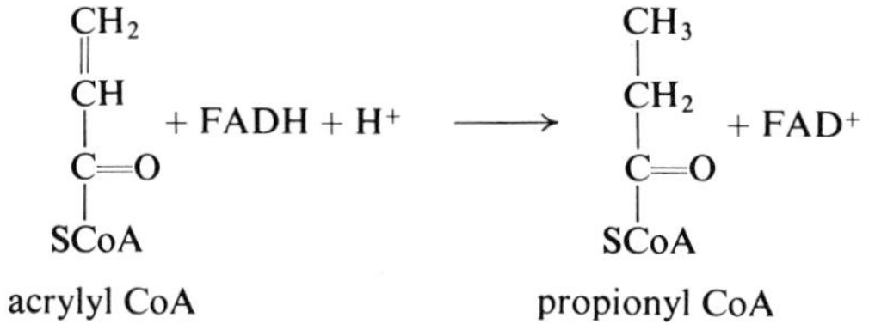

$$
\begin{array}{c}
\text{CH}_2 \\
\| \\
\text{CH} \\
| \\
\text{C}=\text{O} \\
| \\
\text{SCoA}
\end{array}
+ FADH + H^+ \longrightarrow \
\begin{array}{c}
\text{CH}_3 \\
| \\
\text{CH}_2 \\
| \\
\text{C}=\text{O} \\
| \\
\text{SCoA}
\end{array}
+ FAD^+
$$

acrylyl CoA   propionyl CoA

A second molecule of carbon dioxide is now fixed in the presence of biotin, Mn^{2+} and ATP which results in the formation of methylmalonyl CoA:

$$
\begin{array}{c}
CH_3 \\
|\\
CH_2 \\
|\\
C{=}O \\
|\\
SCoA
\end{array}
\;+\;ATP+CO_2 \quad\longrightarrow\quad
\begin{array}{c}
CH_3 \\
|\\
CH{-}COOH \\
|\\
C{=}O \\
|\\
SCoA
\end{array}
\;+\;ADP
$$

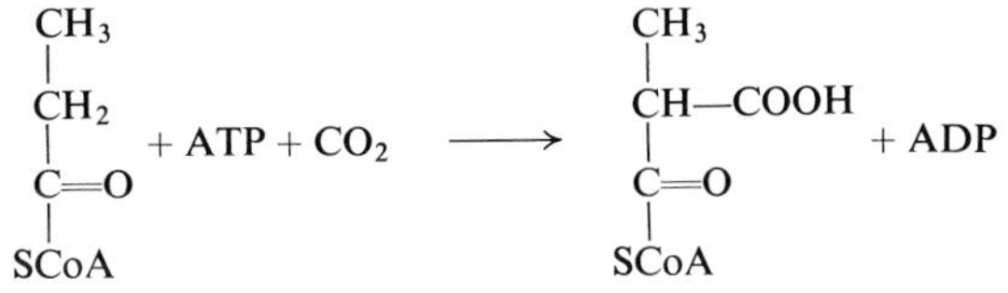

propionyl CoA   methylmalonyl CoA

The enzyme catalyzing this reaction is a propionyl CoA carboxylase (propionyl CoA: carbon dioxide ligase (ADP), E.C. 6.4.1.3). The conversion of methylmalonyl CoA to succinyl CoA requires a coenzyme of the vitamin B_{12} group and methylmalonyl CoA mutase (methylmalonyl CoA: CoA carbonyl mutase, E.C. 5.4.99.2):

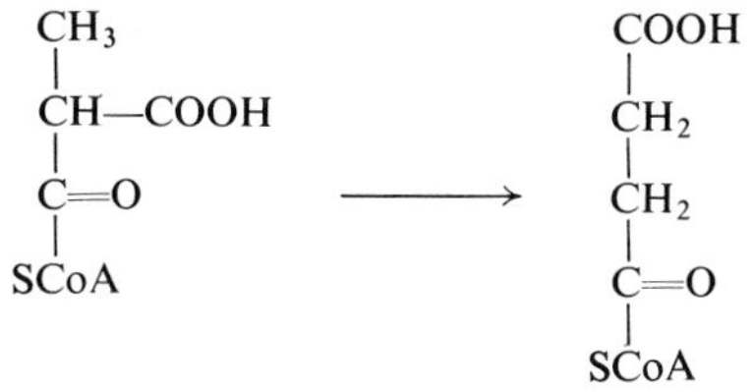

$$
\begin{array}{c}
CH_3 \\
|\\
CH{-}COOH \\
|\\
C{=}O \\
|\\
SCoA
\end{array}
\quad\longrightarrow\quad
\begin{array}{c}
COOH \\
|\\
CH_2 \\
|\\
CH_2 \\
|\\
C{=}O \\
|\\
SCoA
\end{array}
$$

methylmalonyl CoA   succinyl CoA

The final end product succinate is formed with the production of 1 mole of ATP from the interaction of succinyl CoA and succinyl CoA synthetase (succinate: CoA ligase (ADP), E.C. 6.2.1.5):

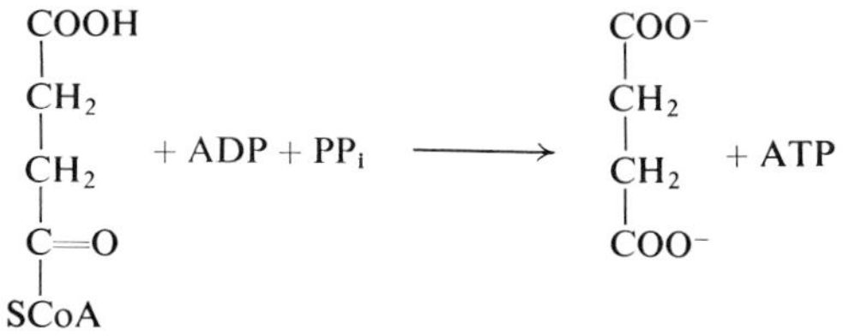

$$
\begin{array}{c}
COOH \\
|\\
CH_2 \\
|\\
CH_2 \\
|\\
C{=}O \\
|\\
SCoA
\end{array}
\;+\;ADP+PP_i \quad\longrightarrow\quad
\begin{array}{c}
COO^- \\
|\\
CH_2 \\
|\\
CH_2 \\
|\\
COO^-
\end{array}
\;+\;ATP
$$

succinyl CoA   succinate

Most of the other bacterial species which form succinate from pyruvate do so via the glyoxylate cycle.

THE PRODUCTION OF ETHANOL, FORMATE, CARBON DIOXIDE, HYDROGEN, SUCCINATE, LACTATE, 2,3-BUTANEDIOL, AND TRIMETHYLENE GLYCOL BY ENTEROBACTERIA

A great number of strains of the family *Enterobacteriaceae* have been isolated and their classification is still in a constant state of flux(13). Metabolically one could split them into three large groups as follows:

(1) the mixed acid producer (methyl red positive; Voges-Proskauer negative),
(2) the butanediol producers (methyl red negative; Voges-Proskauer positive),
(3) the trimethylene glycol producers.

Table 6.3. demonstrates the differences in the ratio and combination of end products formed with the first two groups(72). While these two groups are usually exclusive, some organisms [e.g., *Klebsiella edwardsii* var. *atlantae* and the "Oxytoca" group(48)] fail to convert the acids completely and are methyl red positive and Voges-Proskauer positive. The catabolism of sugars occurs both by the EMP and HMP pathways, at least in all strains which have been investigated so far. Their physiological behavior and the end products of their glucose fermentation, however, suggests a common mechanism. There is no doubt that all the enzymes of the EMP pathway are present in *Escherichia coli* and in species of *Aerobacter*. Several of these enzymes have been detected in the following genera—*Serratia, Erwinia, Salmonella, Klebsiella*, and *Paracolobacterium*. The enzymes of the HMP pathway were first detected in *Escherichia coli* and later in species of *Aerobacter, Paracolobactrum, Serratia, Klebsiella, Salmonella, Erwinia*, and *Proteus*.

Assuming that the intermediary metabolism of sugars is the same for all the *Enterobacteriaceae*, the difference in their fermentation pattern is owing to the variations in the enzymes concerned with the decomposition of pyruvate.

The Mixed Acid Producers

The most characteristic representative of this group is undoubtedly *Escherichia coli* which metabolizes pyruvate in the following way:

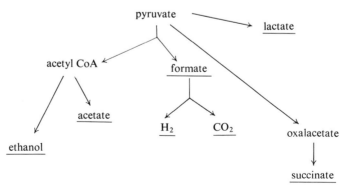

TABLE 6.3

DIFFERENCES IN RATIO AND COMBINATION OF END PRODUCTS BETWEEN MIXED ACID AND BUTANEDIOL PRODUCERS

	Mixed Acid Producer							Butanediol Producer				
	Escherichia coli			E. aurescens	A. aerogenes	Enterobacter indologenes		Serratia marcescens		S. plymuthicum	S. kielensis	E. carotovora
End products	pH 6.2	pH 7.8	Resting cells aerobic			47 hr	209 hr	Anaerobic	Aerobic			
	(mM/100 mmoles glucose fermented)											
2,3-Butanediol	0.3	0.3	—	—	19	58	66	64	53	47	—	75
Acetoin	0.06	0.2	—	—	—	2	0	2	8	4	2	—
Glycerol	1.4	0.3	—	—	4	—	0	1	1	2	2	—
Ethanol	50	50	77	40	52	70	69	46	29	51	46	66
Formate	2	86	121	70	68	54	17	48	3	3	2	134
Acetate	36	39	78	40	52	8	0.5	4	9	5	50	64
Lactate	80	70	20	80	10	6	3	10	21	34	104	23
Succinate	11	15	39	10	13	—	—	8	9	7	2	11
CO$_2$	88	2	—	2	80	140	172	117	159	145	100	13
H$_2$	75	26	—	—	—	11	35	—	0.2	59	91	—
O/R balance	1.06	0.91	1.04			1.01	0.99	1.02	—	0.98	1.07	0.97

Any of the underlined compounds can be major end products. If this system were operating alone, the following ratios should hold:

moles (ethanol + acetate) = moles (H_2 + formate)   and H_2 = (CO_2 + succinate)

These ratios hold only for the mixed acid fermenters since pyruvate is broken down in the phosphoroclastic split (see Section entitled "Formation of Acetaldehyde") to equimolar quantities of acetyl CoA and formate:

1 mole of pyruvate → 1 mole of acetyl CoA + 1 mole of formate

Hence,

moles pyruvate = moles acetyl CoA = moles formate   (a)

The acetyl CoA is then converted entirely into ethanol, acetate, or both, but in any case

moles pyruvate = moles ethanol + moles acetate   (b)

From Eqs. (a) and (b) then follows:

moles (ethanol + acetate) ≡ moles formate   (c)

The produced formate may be split into H_2 and CO_2 in equimolar quantities, whereby

1 mole of H_2 or 1 mole of CO_2 represents 1 mole of formate decomposed   (d)

Since it may well be that not all formate is decomposed, the following relation may exist:

moles total formate = moles residual formate + moles decomposed formate

Taking Eq. (d) into consideration,

moles total formate = moles formate + moles H_2 (e)

the final equation is derived by introducing Eq. (e) into (c):

moles (ethanol + acetate) ≡ moles formate + moles H_2

The end product hydrogen was chosen since all H_2 formed comes from formate, whereas in the case of carbon dioxide this need not necessarily be the case. Carbon dioxide is also very likely to be again consumed. If the requirements of this equation have been fulfilled, a phosphoroclastic split occurs.

If CO_2 is taken into consideration, there exists the possibility that some CO_2 (which has been solely derived from formate) is consumed in the production of succinate at the rate of 1 mole of CO_2 per mole succinate:

moles CO_2 (from formate) = moles CO_2 + moles CO_2 consumed in succinate production

Since the total moles CO_2 formed from formate equal the total moles H_2 formed from formate:

moles H_2 = moles CO_2 + moles succinate

This reaction should hold if the CO_2 and succinate are not involved in any further reactions, and if no other CO_2 is produced. This does not apply to the butanediol fermenters which produce additional CO_2 in the course of butanediol production. From the fermentation balances the observations given in Table 6.4 can be made.

TABLE 6.4

OBSERVATIONS FROM FERMENTATION BALANCES

	mM per 100 moles glucose			
Organism	Ethanol + acetate	H_2 + formate	H_2	CO_2 + succinate
E. coli	90	90	0	15
E. coli (pH 6.2)	86	77	75	99
E. coli (pH 7.8)	89	112	26	17
E. aurescens	80	70	0	10
E. carotovora	120	130	0	10
Serratia plymuthicum	56	62	60	156
S. kielensis	100	102	100	102
S. kielensis	96	93	91	102

Formation of Acetaldehyde and Ethanol. (1) *Formation of acetaldehyde.* Pyruvic acid can be decarboxylated to acetaldehyde and carbon dioxide with pyruvic decarboxylase (2-oxoacid carboxylase, E.C. 4.1.1.1). This reaction requires Mn^{2+} and TPP as cofactor. It is assumed that (a) an "activated acetaldehyde" in the form of the carbanion CH_3CO^- linked to TPP occurs as an intermediate, and that this hypothetical acetaldehyde-TPP compound reacts with H^+ to give free acetaldehyde and to regenerate TPP

$$CH_3{-}CO{-}COOH \xrightarrow{TPP} CH_3{-}CHO + CO_2$$

or (b) a phosphoroclastic split occurs(33), whereby inorganic phosphate, TPP, CoA, lipoate, Mn^{2+} or Fe^{2+} are required for the reaction. The latter would be a similar process to that of the clostridia, only with the formation of formate instead of carbon dioxide and hydrogen (see Section entitled "The Production of Butyric Acid, Butanol and Acetone").

This phosphoroclastic split is also referred to as "thioclastic split"(18) because of the involvement of lipoate in contrast to the yeast system described under (a), which also involves a phosphate compound as cofactor. McCormick et al.(35), however, distinguished between the phosphoroclastic split and the thioclastic split. They considered the formation of acetyl phosphate, carbon dioxide, and hydrogen as the thioclastic split, whereas the formation of acetyl phosphate and formate is referred to as the "phosphoroclastic split." It is difficult to decide whether or not these two terms should continue to be used in order to express either the formation of formate or of $CO_2 + H_2$, since acetyl phosphate is obtained in both cases and the phosphotransacetylase is also present. There may be justification if acetyl CoA is the first product in one case (e.g., *Enterobacteriaceae*) and acetyl phosphate in the other (e.g., *Clostridia*). Because of the different opinions, thioclastic and phosphoroclastic will be considered as being synonymous.

The phosphoroclastic split can form either acetyl CoA or acetyl phosphate which are held in equilibrium by a phosphotransacetylase (E.C. 2.3.1.8):

$$
\begin{array}{ccc}
\mathrm{CH_3} & & \mathrm{CH_3} \\
| & & | \\
\mathrm{C{=}O} & \longrightarrow \quad \mathrm{HCOOH} \; + & \mathrm{C{=}O} \\
| & & | \\
\mathrm{COO^-} & & \mathrm{SCoA} \\
\text{pyruvate} & & \text{acetyl CoA}
\end{array}
$$

$$
\begin{array}{c}
\mathrm{CH_3} \\
| \\
\mathrm{C{=}O} \\
| \\
\text{Ⓟ} \\
\text{acetyl phosphate}
\end{array}
$$

It is assumed (35,44) that acetyl CoA is the first product. The formation of acetaldehyde from acetyl CoA requires a NAD-linked aldehyde dehydrogenase (aldehyde: NAD oxidoreductase (acylating CoA) E.C. 1.2.1.10):

$$
\begin{array}{cc}
\mathrm{CH_3} & \mathrm{CH_3} \\
| & | \\
\mathrm{C{=}O} + \mathrm{NADH} + \mathrm{H^+} \longrightarrow & \mathrm{CHO} + \mathrm{HSCoA} + \mathrm{NAD^+} \\
| & \\
\mathrm{SCoA} & \\
\text{acetyl CoA} & \text{acetaldehyde}
\end{array}
$$

This is not the only way in which acetaldehyde is formed by the *Enterobacteriaceae*. If the species is producing acetate as well, acetaldehyde can be produced from acetate with a different aldehyde dehydrogenase. The aldehyde dehydrogenase catalyzing this reaction is very likely aldehyde: NAD oxidoreductase

$$
\begin{array}{cc}
\mathrm{CH_3} & \mathrm{CH_3} \\
| \quad + \mathrm{NADH} + \mathrm{H^+} \longrightarrow & | \quad + \mathrm{NAD^+} + \mathrm{H_2O} \\
\mathrm{COO^-} & \mathrm{CHO} \\
\text{acetate} & \text{acetaldehyde}
\end{array}
$$

(E.C. 1.2.1.3) which has a wide specificity. The second possibility, which has not been reported, would be aldehyde: NAD(P) oxidoreductase (E.C. 1.2.1.5), which catalyzes the same reaction but can in addition be linked with $NADP^+$.

(2) *Formation of ethanol.* The formation of ethanol from acetaldehyde requires alcohol dehydrogenase (alcohol: NAD oxidoreductase, E.C. 1.1.1.1), which acts on primary and secondary alcohols in general, and Zn^{2+}. During this formation of ethanol from pyruvate, 2 moles of reduced NAD are regenerated per mole of ethanol and the product is neutral.

$$\begin{array}{c} CH_3 \\ | \\ CHO \end{array} + NADH + H^+ \xrightarrow{Zn^{2+}} \begin{array}{c} CH_3 \\ | \\ CH_2OH \end{array} + NAD^+$$

$$\text{acetaldehyde} \qquad\qquad \text{ethanol}$$

Formation of Acetate. Acetate can be formed from acetyl CoA via three alternative ways(33) which is a rather wasteful system with an acetyl CoA hydrolase (E.C. 3.1.2.1) as catalyst. This degradation of acetyl CoA produces

$$(1) \qquad \begin{array}{c} CH_3 \\ | \\ C{=}O \\ | \\ SCoA \end{array} + H_2O \longrightarrow \begin{array}{c} CH_3 \\ | \\ COO^- \end{array} + HSCoA$$

$$\text{acetyl CoA} \qquad\qquad \text{acetate}$$

1 mole of ATP but requires AMP and pyrophosphate in addition to the enzyme acetyl CoA synthetase (acetate: CoA ligase (AMP), E.C. 6.2.1.1), which also acts on propionate and acrylate. The last sequence, however,

$$(2) \qquad \begin{array}{c} CH_3 \\ | \\ C{=}O \\ | \\ SCoA \end{array} + AMP + PP_i \longrightarrow \begin{array}{c} CH_3 \\ | \\ COO^- \end{array} + ATP$$

$$\text{acetyl CoA} \qquad\qquad \text{acetate}$$

seems to be more likely in the case of *Escherichia coli*. This breakdown requires inorganic phosphate and phosphate acetyltransferase (E.C. 2.3.1.8) and acetokinase (ATP: acetate phosphotransferase, E.C. 2.7.2.1) to form the end product acetate. The presence of phosphate acetyltransferase in the genus *Escherichia* is indicated by the existence of the equilibrium between acetyl CoA and acetyl phosphate. The acetate can then be converted to acetaldehyde and ethanol as described above.

Whether or not the similarity of the phosphoroclastic split of the clostridial and the coli type is so close is still under dispute. The most important fact is the consistent failure of components isolated from strict anaerobes to interact

(3)
$$
\begin{array}{ccc}
\text{CH}_3 & & \text{CH}_3 \\
| & & | \\
\text{C}{=}\text{O} + \text{P}_i & \longrightarrow & \text{C}{=}\text{O} \\
| & & | \\
\text{SCoA} & & \text{\textcircled{P}}
\end{array}
$$

acetyl CoA   acetyl phosphate

$$
\begin{array}{c}
\nearrow \text{ADP} \\
\searrow \text{ATP} \\
\downarrow
\end{array}
$$

$$\text{CH}_3{-}\text{COO}^-$$
acetate

with those from facultative anaerobes. For example, the formic dehydrogenase of the coliform bacteria will not couple with the hydrogenase of crude clostridial extracts to give active hydrogenlyase.

The formation of carbon dioxide and hydrogen from formate by the formic hydrogenlyase system is therefore thought(24) to comprise two enzymatic reactions, a soluble formic dehydrogenase and a membrane-bound hydrogenase with two unidentified intermediate electron carriers X_1 and X_2. There exists evidence for the identity of X_2 as a c-type cytochrome of low redox potential ($E_m = -225$ mV). Such low potential cytochromes are only produced by coliform bacteria during anaerobic growth. Accordingly, X_1 may well have the function of a cytochrome c reductase. Many efforts were undertaken to detect ferredoxin in the facultative anaerobes after this compound had been

$$
\text{HCOOH} \xrightarrow[\text{CO}_2]{} \left[\begin{array}{c} X_1 \\ \text{cyt. reductase} \end{array} \right] \longrightarrow \left[\begin{array}{c} X_2 \\ \text{cyt. c} \end{array} \right] \xrightarrow[2\text{H}^+]{} \text{H}_2
$$

found in clostridia. It was hoped that the above-mentioned ferredoxin system could also be applied to the hydrogenlyase system, but the results were negative. These results led to the assumption that there were many qualitative differences in the hydrogen-evolving system of strict and facultative anaerobes. This coincides with the findings outlined in Chapter 5 in regard to the electron carrier system of *Escherichia coli*.

Aeromonas hydrophilia, which has a coli-type metabolism, also produces cytochrome c of a low potential and can show formate hydrogenlyase activity when grown anaerobically. The possible absence of ferredoxin would also be consonant with studies on *Clostridium thermoaceticum*(34), which does not have a ferredoxin, except for the NAD-linked formate dehydrogenase. The latter catalyzes an exchange between carbon dioxide and formate. No other electron carrier has, however, been isolated. *Clostridium thermoaceticum* appears to behave differently from all other clostridia since it also produces formate.

The present state of knowledge is therefore that formate is reacted upon by a NAD-linked formate dehydrogenase (E.C. 1.2.1.2), which liberates carbon dioxide and reduces NAD. The latter is reoxidized either by ferredoxin or by a cytochrome c reductase which in turn is oxidized by a low potential cytochrome c. This low potential cytochrome c exchanges its electrons with hydrogenase

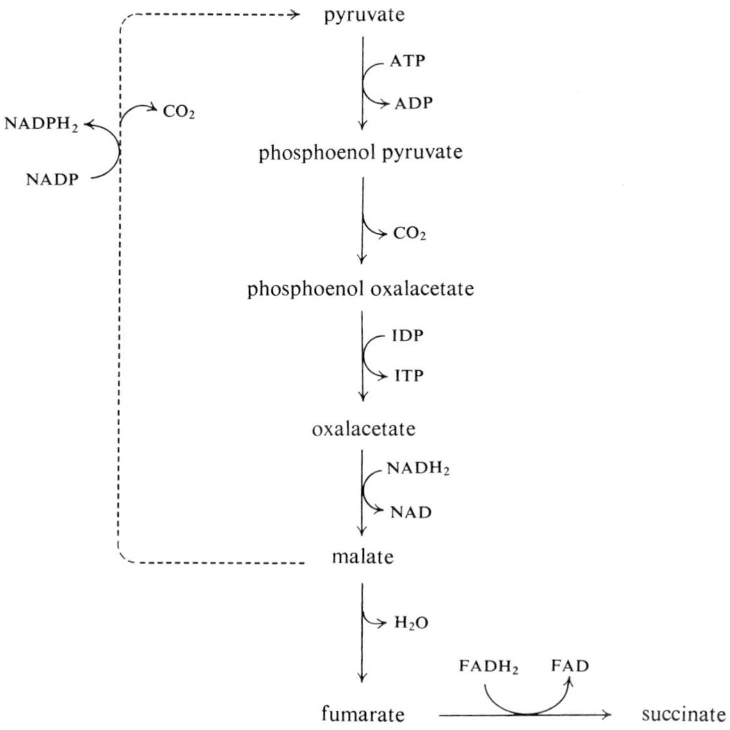

pyruvate

ATP → ADP

NADPH$_2$ ← CO$_2$

NADP

phosphoenol pyruvate

CO$_2$

phosphoenol oxalacetate

IDP → ITP

oxalacetate

NADH$_2$ → NAD

malate

H$_2$O

FADH$_2$ → FAD

fumarate ──────→ succinate

specific for coli-type bacteria and forms hydrogen. Whether this low potential cytochrome c is identical or not with ferredoxin has not been elucidated (36), although the potentials would suggest this possibility.

The importance in this reaction sequence is the breakdown of formate to an equal amount of CO$_2$ and H$_2$.

There are, however, a number of bacteria which have completely lost the ability to break down formate and therefore accumulate this compound as a major end product, e.g., *Salmonella typhi*, *Shigella* spp., *Proteus rettgeri*, and *Serratia marcescens*. It may be significant that these organisms normally live in alkaline solutions in the intestine.

Formation of Succinate. The aerobic formation of succinate during the TCA cycle was dealt with under aerobic respiration. It was also demonstrated that clostridia are able to form succinate under anaerobic conditions. The *Enterobacteriaceae* in general use a third pathway (18, 33) which contains a few TCA enzymes (see page 291). Pyruvate is phosphorylated to phosphoenol pyruvate, requiring Mg^{2+}, K^+, ATP, and a pyruvate kinase (ATP:pyruvate phosphotransferase, E.C. 2.7.1.40):

$$
\begin{array}{ccc}
\begin{array}{l}
CH_3 \\
| \\
C{=}O + ATP + Mg^{2+} + K^+ \\
| \\
COO^-
\end{array}
& \longrightarrow &
\begin{array}{l}
CH_2 \\
| \\
C{-}O \sim \circled{P} + ADP \\
| \\
COO^-
\end{array}
\\
\text{pyruvate} & & \text{phosphoenol pyruvate}
\end{array}
$$

The incorporation of 1 mole of carbon dioxide and the functioning of a phosphoenol pyruvate carboxylase leads to phosphoenol oxalacetate:

$$
\begin{array}{ccc}
\begin{array}{l}
CH_2 \\
| \\
C{-}O \sim \circled{P} + CO_2 \\
| \\
COO^-
\end{array}
& \longrightarrow &
\begin{array}{l}
COOH \\
| \\
CH_2 \\
| \\
C{-}O \sim \circled{P} \\
| \\
COO^-
\end{array}
\\
\text{phosphoenol pyruvate} & & \text{phosphoenol oxalacetate}
\end{array}
$$

The next step in the sequence is an energy-yielding reaction, whereby the phosphate group is transferred to IDP resulting in the formation of ITP and oxalacetate. No one has reported whether an enzyme catalyzes this reaction, but it can be assumed that a phosphatetransferase is acting since the reaction requires Mg^{2+}. The further conversion of oxalacetate to succinate via malate and fumarate is identical with the steps in the TCA cycle. The *Enterobacteriaceae* may also be able to close the cycle by employing malate dehydrogenase [L-malate:NADP oxidoreductase (decarboxylating), E.C. 1.1.1.40] for the formation of pyruvate from malate. With this cycle, the organisms can fix the CO_2 evolved during the decarboxylation step from malate to pyruvate in the conversion of phosphoenol pyruvate to phosphoenol oxalacetate, but they are not able to regenerate reduced NADP. It seems therefore more likely that the reaction from malate to pyruvate takes place at an insignificant rate.

Escherichia coli and *Aerobacter aerogenes* are also able to use the same pathway as described in detail for *Clostridium kluyveri*. Whether this pathway is significant for use in classification is not clear yet and more research has to be done. If, however, only a selected group of organisms among the *Enterobacteriaceae* is able to form succinate via the second pathway, this could become a significant characteristic. The overall effect in regard to energy

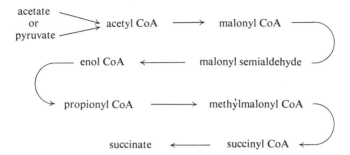

and reduced NAD and FAD regeneration is much the same in either of the two pathways.

Formation of Lactate. The production of lactate by a reaction of lactate dehydrogenase (L-lactate:NAD oxidoreductase, E.C. 1.1.1.27 or D-lactate: NAD oxidoreductase, E.C. 1.1.1.28) on pyruvate results in regeneration of reduced NAD:

$$\begin{array}{ccc} CH_3 & & CH_3 \\ | & & | \\ C{=}O + NADH + H^+ & \longrightarrow & CHOH + NAD^+ \\ | & & | \\ COO^- & & COO^- \\ \text{pyruvate} & & \text{lactate} \end{array}$$

It is assumed that both enzymes are present, although not very much emphasis has been given to the lactate isomer being formed. The amount of lactate varies greatly (72). It may account for as much as half of the pyruvate (*Serratia kielensis*) or may not be produced at all (*Aerobacter aerogenes*). Apart from this variation, lactate production also varies with the conditions under which any one organism is grown.

The Butanediol Producers

The Voges-Proskauer reaction used in studies on the taxonomy of entero-bacteria is based on a reaction between diacetyl and the guanidine nucleus found in creatine and in the peptone of the medium (in an alkaline solution). The butanediol producers also produce acetoin, and these two substances when oxidized by air in alkaline solutions to diacetyl give the positive Voges-Proskauer reaction.

Formation of 2,3-Butanediol (2,3-Butylene Glycol). In addition to the mixed acid products, a number of bacteria are able to produce 2,3-butanediol which is a neutral compound produced from acetoin (acetylmethylcarbinol) that serves as hydrogen acceptor for reduced NAD regeneration. There are, however, three postulated pathways, which lead from pyruvate to acetoin(33, 72) found in microorganisms (see Schemes 6.4–6.6).

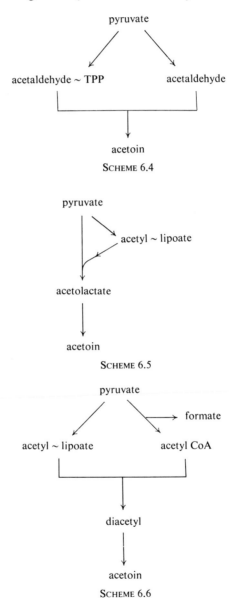

pyruvate

acetaldehyde ~ TPP   acetaldehyde

acetoin

SCHEME 6.4

pyruvate

acetyl ~ lipoate

acetolactate

acetoin

SCHEME 6.5

pyruvate

                              → formate

acetyl ~ lipoate   acetyl CoA

diacetyl

acetoin

SCHEME 6.6

The first postulated reaction sequence has only been found in yeasts and depends on the direct formation of acetaldehyde from pyruvate with a subsequent carboligase reaction forming acetoin. This scheme is not likely to be present in bacteria which without exception form acetyl CoA from pyruvate. This restricts the discussion to the second and third pathway. The significant difference between the two is that the second mechanism forms acetoin from acetolactate, whereas in the third mechanism diacetyl is the precursor of acetoin.

The formation of acetoin from acetolactate. *Aerobacter aerogenes*, *Bacillus subtilis*, *Clostridium acetobutylicum*, and *Streptococcus faecalis* do not contain a decarboxylase system and are not able to produce appreciable amounts of aldehyde(72). Therefore, a single enzyme presumably must be responsible for the pyruvate decarboxylation and aldehyde transfer and formation of the stable intermediate α-(+)acetolactate and carbon dioxide:

$$2 \text{ pyruvate} \quad \xrightarrow[\text{Mn}^{2+}]{\text{TPP}} \quad \alpha\text{-}(+)\text{acetolactate} + CO_2$$

The acetyl lipoate complex can be formed and CO_2 released from pyruvate by part of the pyruvate dehydrogenase system (pyruvate:lipoate oxidoreductase (acceptor acetylating), E.C. 1.2.4.1, requiring TPP). This "activated acetate" combines with a second molecule of pyruvate to form acetolactate:

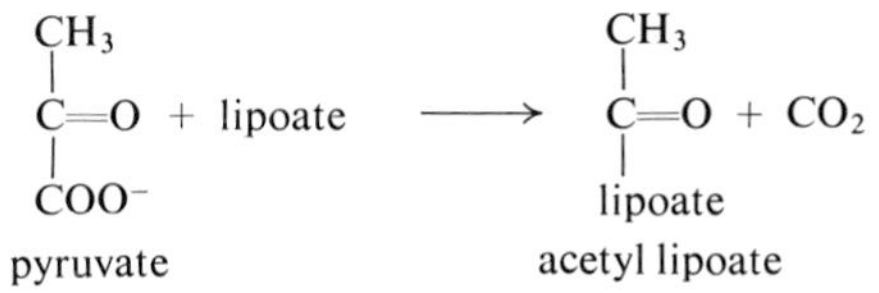

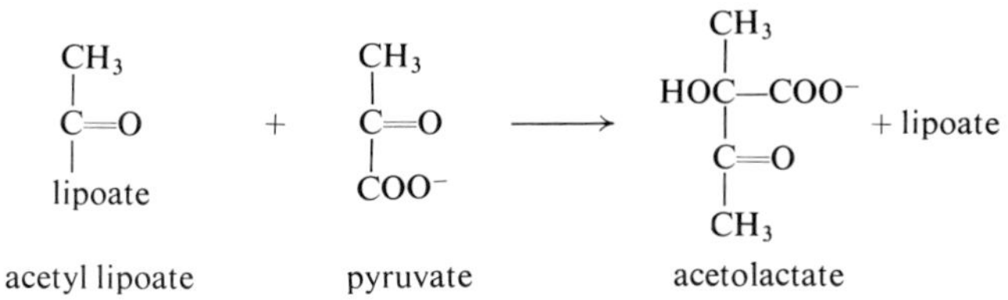

$$\begin{array}{l} CH_3 \\ | \\ C{=}O + \text{lipoate} \\ | \\ COO^- \\ \text{pyruvate} \end{array} \longrightarrow \begin{array}{l} CH_3 \\ | \\ C{=}O + CO_2 \\ | \\ \text{lipoate} \\ \text{acetyl lipoate} \end{array}$$

$$\begin{array}{l} CH_3 \\ | \\ C{=}O \\ | \\ \text{lipoate} \\ \text{acetyl lipoate} \end{array} + \begin{array}{l} CH_3 \\ | \\ C{=}O \\ | \\ COO^- \\ \text{pyruvate} \end{array} \longrightarrow \begin{array}{l} CH_3 \\ | \\ HOC{-}COO^- \\ | \\ C{=}O \\ | \\ CH_3 \\ \text{acetolactate} \end{array} + \text{lipoate}$$

Acetolactate decarboxylase (2-hydroxy-4-oxopentanoate carboxylyase, E.C. 4.1.1.5) decarboxylates acetolactate to acetoin:

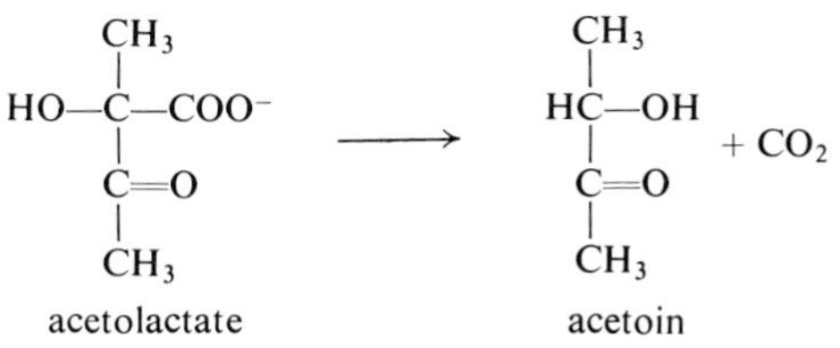

$$\begin{array}{l} CH_3 \\ | \\ HO{-}C{-}COO^- \\ | \\ C{=}O \\ | \\ CH_3 \\ \text{acetolactate} \end{array} \longrightarrow \begin{array}{l} CH_3 \\ | \\ HC{-}OH \\ | \\ C{=}O \\ | \\ CH_3 \\ \text{acetoin} \end{array} + CO_2$$

The formation of acetoin from diacetyl. The third mechanism is a combination of the mixed acid type of degradation of pyruvate and the second mechanism. The organisms are able to form acetyl lipoate with pyruvate dehydrogenase (E.C. 1.2.4.1) and at the same time also form acetyl CoA in the phosphoroclastic (or thioclastic) split. Both "active acetates" now undergo a condensation reaction and form diacetyl:

$$
\begin{array}{ccccc}
\text{CH}_3 & & \text{CH}_3 & & \text{CH}_3 \\
| & & | & & | \\
\text{C}{=}\text{O} & + & \text{C}{=}\text{O} & \longrightarrow & \text{C}{=}\text{O} \quad + \text{ lipoate} + \text{HSCoA} \\
| & & | & & | \\
\text{lipoate} & & \text{SCoA} & & \text{C}{=}\text{O} \\
& & & & | \\
& & & & \text{CH}_3 \\
\text{acetyl lipoate} & & \text{acetyl CoA} & & \text{diacetyl}
\end{array}
$$

The presence of acetoin dehydrogenase (acetoin: NAD oxidoreductase, E.C. 1.1.1.5) reduces diacetyl to acetoin:

$$
\begin{array}{ccccc}
\text{CH}_3 & & & & \text{CH}_3 \\
| & & & & | \\
\text{C}{=}\text{O} & & & & \text{CHOH} \\
| & + \text{ NADH} + \text{H}^+ & \longrightarrow & & | \quad + \text{ NAD}^+ \\
\text{C}{=}\text{O} & & & & \text{C}{=}\text{O} \\
| & & & & | \\
\text{CH}_3 & & & & \text{CH}_3 \\
\text{diacetyl} & & & & \text{acetoin}
\end{array}
$$

Acetoin from the second mechanism can also be oxidized to diacetyl by acetoin dehydrogenase (E.C. 1.1.1.5). The latter reaction has not been reported as being present in enterobacteria. The over-all reactions of both mechanisms are very similar, although the last scheme may be more economical since the organisms are using existing enzymes for the formation of acetyl CoA. Having the enzymatic complex of the mixed acid fermenters, these organisms produce acetyl CoA but because of the presence of an additional enzyme they form butanediol in such a way that virtually no other by-product can be formed.

It has been found that all bacteria producing 2,3-butanediol as their end product form D(−)-acetoin from pyruvate. The formation of 2,3-butanediol was for a long time thought to be a simple reduction process involving a butanediol dehydrogenase (2,3-butanediol: NAD oxidoreductase, E.C. 1.1.1.4) with NADH + H$^+$ being oxidized to NAD$^+$. Taylor and Juni(57), however, stressed that there exist a number of butanediol dehydrogenases which are all stereoisomerically specific. *Bacillus polymyxa*, for example, contains D(−)-2,3-butanediol dehydrogenase, *Aerobacter aerogenes* and *Pseudomonas hydrophila* contain the L(+)-, and *Bacillus subtilis* contains both the D(−)- and the L(+)-butanediol dehydrogenases. *Pseudomonas hydrophila* also possesses an acetoin racemase. The presence of all these combinations of enzymes can explain the occurrence of various combinations of the three isomers in carbohydrate fermentation. Taylor and Juni(57) therefore postulated the following mechanisms which may occur in the reduction of acetoin to butanediol (reprinted with the permission of Elsevier, Amsterdam):

$$
\begin{array}{ccc}
\mathrm{CH_3} & & \mathrm{CH_3} \\
| & & | \\
\mathrm{C{=}O} & \rightleftharpoons & \mathrm{C{=}O} \\
| & & | \\
\mathrm{HOC{-}H} & & \mathrm{HCOH} \\
| & & | \\
\mathrm{CH_3} & & \mathrm{CH_3}
\end{array}
$$

L(+)-acetoin   D(−)-acetoin

$+2\mathrm{H} \big\| -2\mathrm{H}$ $-2\mathrm{H}$ $+2\mathrm{H}$ $+2\mathrm{H} \big\| -2\mathrm{H}$
$+2\mathrm{H}$ $-2\mathrm{H}$

$$
\begin{array}{ccc}
\mathrm{CH_3} & \mathrm{CH_3} & \mathrm{CH_3} \\
| & | & | \\
\mathrm{HCOH} & \mathrm{HCOH} & \mathrm{HOCH} \\
| & | & | \\
\mathrm{HOCH} & \mathrm{HCOH} & \mathrm{HC{-}OH} \\
| & | & | \\
\mathrm{CH_3} & \mathrm{CH_3} & \mathrm{CH_3}
\end{array}
$$

L(+)-2,3-butanediol   meso-2,3-butanediol   D(−)2,3-butanediol

Almost all bacteria form D(−)-acetoin. The type of butanediol produced depends on whether the organism

(1) has an acetoin racemase which converts D(−)-acetoin to L(+)-acetoin—the presence of D(−)-butanediol dehydrogenase would produce *meso*-2,3-butanediol, whereas a L(+)-butanediol dehydrogenase forms L(+)-2,3-butanediol, and

(2) has no acetoin racemase, in which case D(−)-butanediol dehydrogenase converts D(−)-acetoin into D(−)-2,3-butanediol and L(+)-butanediol dehydrogenase would produce *meso*-2,3-butanediol.

Since all these reactions are reversible and the dehydrogenases NAD-linked, the presence of an acetoin racemase would undoubtedly lead to the formation of either L(+)-2,3-butanediol or *meso*-2,3-butanediol with the regeneration of $\mathrm{NADH} + \mathrm{H^+}$. If there is no acetoin racemase available, D(−)- and *meso*-2,3-butanediol would be the end products. In each case the final end product depends on the action of one or the other stereospecific dehydrogenase.

Whatever way butanediol is formed, the overall reaction is the same

$$2 \text{ pyruvate} \rightarrow 2\mathrm{CO_2} + 2,3\text{-butanediol}$$

This formation of butanediol seems to be strictly pH-dependent(72). If the pH rises above 6.3, acetic acid and formic acid accumulate and the production of CO_2, H_2, acetoin, and 2,3-butanediol is prevented. Below pH 6.3, however, the system switches over to acetoin and 2,3-butanediol production. A number of bacteria are known for their butanediol production: *Aerobacter aerogenes*, *Pseudomonas hydrophila*, *Erwinia carotovora*, *Serratia marcescens*, *Bacillus subtilis*, and others. Some microorganisms such as *Bacillus polymyxa* are used for industrial applications and 2,3-butanediol production(1). The production of acetoin is also used for the biochemical diagnosis of *Neisseria* since *N. intracellularis*, *N. mucosa*, *N. perflava*, *N. sicca*, *N. flava*, *N. subflava*, *N. denitrificans*, *N. flavescens*, *N. ovis*, and *N. cuniculi* are positive and *N. animalis*, *N. cinerea*, *N. catarrhalis*, and *N. canis* are negative(60).

Whether or not the stereospecific reaction of butanediol formation could play a similar role in classification as lactic acid does for the homofermentative lactobacilli has to be further investigated.

Formation of Trimethylene Glycol

The formation of trimethylene glycol appears to bear no relationship to any other fermentation product or intermediate. *Citrobacter freundii* and *Aerobacter aerogenes* have the mechanisms to reduce glycerol to trimethylene glycol:

$$
\begin{array}{ccc}
CH_2OH & & CH_2OH \\
| & & | \\
CHOH & \longrightarrow & CH_2 \\
| & & | \\
CH_2OH & & CH_2OH
\end{array}
$$

This process apparently is only possible on a glycerol-glucose medium(72) since the organisms responsible are not able to utilize glycerol alone. Glycerol also seems to compete with ethanol production. In the presence of glycerol, ethanol formation almost ceases and acetate is formed instead. This led to the assumption that the reoxidation of $NADH + H^+$ must occur in the last step of trimethylene glycol production. With *Citrobacter freundii* it was found that glycerol is converted first to β-hydroxypropionaldehyde, which is then reduced to trimethylene glycol:

$$
\begin{array}{ccccc}
CH_2OH & \overset{H_2O}{\underset{\curvearrowright}{\longrightarrow}} & CH_3 & & CH_2OH \\
| & & | & & | \\
CHOH & & CHOH & \longrightarrow & CH_2 \\
| & & | & & | \\
CH_2OH & & CHO & & CH_2OH
\end{array}
$$

This process is assumed to be independent from the carbohydrate metabolism, occurring only if glycerol is supplied. There are, however, two processes known amongst microorganisms whereby glycerol formation can be regarded as a branch-off pathway from dihydroxyacetone phosphate:

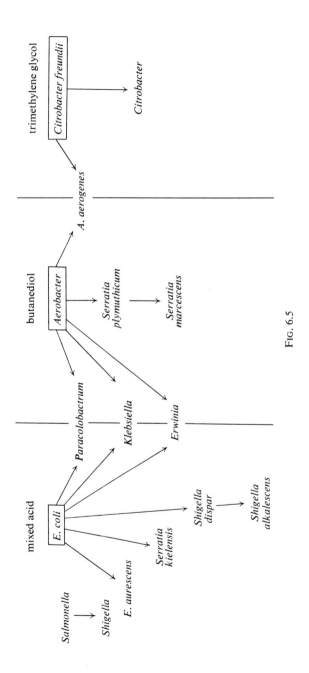

FIG. 6.5

(1) Under alkaline conditions yeasts are able to produce glycerol from dihydroxyacetone phosphate and acetaldehyde (41). This is known as the Eoff process in industrial microbiology. Sodium or potassium carbonate are used for making the reaction alkaline. Having done so, the organism is still able to produce acetaldehyde, but the alcohol dehydrogenase becomes inactive.

(2) *Acetobacter suboxydans* is able to oxidize glycerol to dihydroxyacetone phosphate via two pathways as will be outlined later in detail. One pathway proceeds

glycerol → glycerol α-phosphate → dihydroxyacetone phosphate

and the second pathway

glycerol → dihydroxyacetone → dihydroxyacetone phosphate

This organism possesses therefore a glycerokinase, glycerol dehydrogenase, and a glycerol α-phosphate dehydrogenase (25).

Whether the enterobacteria which produce trimethylene glycol possess a glycerophosphate dehydrogenase (L-glycerol 3-phosphate:(acceptor) oxidoreductase, E.C. 1.1.99.5) which would convert dihydroxyacetone phosphate to glycerol 3-phosphate is not known as yet. The presence of this enzyme together with glycerol kinase (ATP:glycerol phosphotransferase, E.C. 2.7.1.30) would produce glycerol from dihydroxyacetone phosphate.

Should it be proved that the *Enterobacteriaceae* possess either of the two pathways for the production of glycerol from triose phosphate it would suggest a possible overlap with the acetic acid bacteria (see Fig. 6.5).

REFERENCES

1. Adams, G. A., and Stanier, R. Y. (1945). Production and properties of 2,3-butanediol. III. Studies on the biochemistry of carbohydrate fermentation by *Aerobacillus polymyxa*. *Can. J. Res.* **B23**, 1.
2. Ahrens, J., and Schlegel, H. (1966). Zur Regulation der NAD-abhängigen Hydrogenase-Aktivität. *Arch. Mikrobiol.* **55**, 257.
3. Aiba, S., Humphrey, A. E., and Millis, N. F. (1965). "Biochemical Engineering." Univ. of Tokyo Press, Tokyo, Japan.
4. Allen, S. H. G., Kellermeyer, R. W., Stjernholm, R. C., Jacobson, B. E., and Wood, H. G. (1963). The isolation, purification and properties of methylmalonyl racemase. *J. Biol. Chem.* **238**, 1637.
5. Allen, S. H. G., Jacobson, B. E., and Stjernholm, R. (1964). Biocytin as a constituent of methylmalonyl-oxaloacetic transcarboxylase and propionyl CoA carboxylase of bacterial origin. *Arch. Biochem. Biophys.* **105**, 494.
6. Allen, S. H. G., Kellermeyer, R. W., Stjernholm, R. L., and Wood, H. G. (1964). Purification and properties of enzymes involved in the propionic acid fermentation. *J. Bacteriol.* **87**, 171.
7. Anderson, R. L., and Ordal, Z. J. (1961). *Cytophaga succinicans* sp.n., a facultatively anaerobic, aquatic myxobacterium. *J. Bacteriol.* **81**, 130.

8. Baldwin, R. L., Wood, W. A., and Emergy, R. S. (1965). Lactate metabolism by *Peptostreptococcus elsdenii*. Evidence for lactyl coenzyme A dehydrase. *Biochim. Biophys. Acta* **97**, 202.
9. Banchop, T., and Elsden, S. R. (1960). The growth of microorganisms in relation to their energy supply. *J. Gen. Microbiol.* **23**, 457.
10. Barker, H. A. (1956). "Bacterial Fermentations. CIBA Lectures in Microbial Chemistry." Wiley, New York.
11. Barker, H. A., and Lipmann, F. (1944). On lactic acid metabolism in propionic acid bacteria and the problem of oxidoreduction in the system fatty hydroxy-keto acid. *Arch. Biochem.* **4**, 361; as cited by Johns (28).
12. Beck, W. S., and Ochoa, S. (1958). Metabolism of propionic acid in animal tissues. *J. Biol. Chem.* **232**, 931.
13. Breed, R. S. (1957). "Bergey's Manual of Determinative Bacteriology," 7th ed. Williams & Wilkins, Baltimore, Maryland.
14. Bryant, M. P. (1952). The isolation and characteristics of a spirochaete from the bovine rumen. *J. Bacteriol.* **64**, 325.
15. Bryant, M. P., and Small, N. (1956). Characteristics of two new genera of anaerobic curved rods isolated from the rumen of cattle. *J. Bacteriol.* **72**, 22.
16. Bryant, M. P., Small, N., Bouma, C., and Chum, H. (1958). *Bacteroides ruminicola* msp. and *Succinomonas amylolytica* the new genus and species. *J. Bacteriol.* **76**, 15.
17. Carson, S. F., and Ruben, S. (1940). CO_2 assimilation by propionic acid bacteria studied by the use of radioactive carbon. *Proc. Natl. Acad. Sci. U.S.* **26**, 418; as cited by Johns (28).
18. DeLey, J. (1962). Comparative biochemistry and enzymology in bacterial classification. *Symp. Soc. Gen. Microbiol.* **12**, 190.
19. Delwiche, E. A., Phares, E. F., and Carson, S. F. (1956). Succinic acid decarboxylation system in *Propionibacterium pentosaceum* and *Veillonella gazogenes*. I. Activation, decarboxylation and related reactions. *J. Bacteriol.* **71**, 589.
20. Dobrogosz, W. J. (1966). Altered endproduct patterns and catabolic repression in *Escherichia coli*. *J. Bacteriol.* **91**, 2263.
21. Eggerer, H., Stadtman, E. R., Overath, P., and Lynen, F. (1960). Zum Mechanismus der durch Cobalamin-Coenzym katalysierten Umlagerung von Methylmalonyl-CoA in Succinyl-CoA. *Biochem. Z.* **333**, 1.
22. Fitz, R. (1878). *Ber Deut. Chem. Ges.* **11**, 1896; as cited by Wood and Werkman (68).
23. Fredericks, W. W., and Stadtman, E. R. (1965). The role of ferredoxin in the hydrogenase system from *Clostridium kluyveri*. *J. Biol. Chem.* **240**, 4065.
24. Gray, C. T., and Gest, H. (1965). Biological formation of molecular hydrogen. A "hydrogen valve" facilitates regulation of anaerobic energy metabolism in many microorganisms. *Science* **148**, 186.
25. Hauge, J. G., King, T. E., and Cheldelin, V. H. (1955). Alternative conversion of glycerol to dihydroxyacetone in *Acetobacter suboxydans*. *J. Biol. Chem.* **214**, 1.
26. Hegre, C. S., Miller, S. J., and Lane, M. D. (1962). Studies on methylmalonyl isomerase. *Biochim. Biophys. Acta* **56**, 538.
27. Hungate, R. E. (1966). "The Rumen and its Microbes." Academic Press, New York.
28. Johns, A. T. (1951). The mechanism of propionic acid formation by propionibacteria. *J. Gen. Microbiol.* **5**, 337.
29. Kluyver, A. J. (1931). "The Chemical Activities of Microorganisms." Oxford Univ. Press (Univ. London), London and New York.
30. Kornberg, H. L., and Elsden, S. R. (1961). The metabolism of 2-carbon compounds by microorganisms. *Advan. Enzymol.* **23**, 401.

31. Krebs, H. A., and Eggleston, L. V. (1941). Biological synthesis of oxaloacetate from pyruvic acid and carbon dioxide. 2. The mechanism of CO_2-fixation in propionic acid bacteria. *Biochem. J.* **35**, 676.
32. Kuratomi, K., and Stadtman, E. R. (1966). The conversion of carbon dioxide to acetate. II. The role of α-ketoisovalerate in the synthesis of acetate by *Clostridium thermoaceticum. J. Biol. Chem.* **241**, 4217.
33. Lamanna, C., and Mallette, M. F. (1965). "Basic Bacteriology—its Biological and Chemical Background." Williams & Wilkins, Baltimore, Maryland.
34. Li, L.-F., Jungdahl, L. L., and Wood, H. G. (1966). Properties of NAD-dependent formate dehydrogenase from *Clostridium thermoaceticum. J. Bacteriol.* **92**, 405.
35. McCormick, N. G., Ordal, Z. J., and Whiteley, H. R. (1962). Degradation of pyruvate by *Micrococcus lactilyticus. J. Bacteriol.* **83**, 887.
36. Mahler, H. R., and Cordes, E. H. (1966). "Biological Chemistry." Harper, New York.
37. Mortensen, L. E., Valentine, R. C., and Carnahan, J. E. (1963). Ferredoxin in the phosphoroclastic reaction of pyruvic acid and its relation to nitrogen fixation in *Clostridium pasteurianum. J. Biol. Chem.* **238**, 794.
38. Overath, P. E., Stadtman, E. R., Kellerman, G. M., and Lynen, F. (1962). Zum Mechanismus der Umlagerung von Methylmalonyl-CoA in Succinyl-CoA. III. Reinigung und Eigenschaften der Methylmalonyl-CoA Isomerase. *Biochem. Z.* **336**, 77.
39. Poston, J. M., and Kuratomi, K. (1965). *Federation Proc.* **24**, 421; as cited in Poston *et al.* (40).
40. Poston, J. M., Kuratomi, K., and Stadtman, E. R. (1966). The conversion of carbon dioxide to acetate. I. The use of cobalt-methylcobalamin as a source of methyl groups for the synthesis of acetate by cell-free extracts of *Clostridium thermoaceticum. J. Biol. Chem.* **241**, 4209.
41. Prescott, S. C., and Dunn, C. G. (1959). "Industrial Microbiology," 3rd ed. McGraw-Hill, New York.
42. Rety, J., and Lynen, F. (1964). The absolute configuration of methyl malonyl-CoA. *Biochem. Biophys. Res. Commun.* **16**, 358.
43. Rose, I. A., Grunberg-Manago, M., Korey, S. R., and Ochoa, S. (1954). Enzymatic phosphorylation of acetate. *J. Biol. Chem.* **211**, 737.
44. Sagers, R. D., Benziman, M., and Klein, S. M. (1963). Failure of arsenate to uncouple the phosphotransacetylase system in *Clostridium acidi-urici. J. Bacteriol.* **86**, 978.
45. Sijpesteyn, A. (1951). On *Ruminococcus flavefaciens*, a cellulose-decomposing bacterium from the rumen of sheep and cattle. *J. Gen. Microbiol.* **5**, 869.
46. Sin, P. M. L., and Wood, H. G. (1962). Phosphoenolpyruvic carboxytransphosphorylase, a CO_2 fixation enzyme from propionic acid bacteria. *J. Biol. Chem.* **237**, 3044.
47. Sin, P. M. L., Wood, H. G., and Stjernholm, R. L. (1961). Fixation of CO_2 by phosphoenolpyruvic carboxy transphosphorylase. *J. Biol. Chem.* **236**, PC21.
48. Skerman, V. B. D. (1967). "A Guide to the Identification of the Genera of Bacteria," 2nd ed. Williams & Wilkins, Baltimore, Maryland.
49. Sly, W. S., and Stadtman, E. R. (1963). Formate metabolism. I. Formyl-coenzyme A, an intermediate in the formate-dependent decomposition of acetylphosphate in *Clostridium kluyveri. J. Biol. Chem.* **238**, 2632.
50. Stadtman, E. R. (1952). The purification and properties of phosphotransacetylase. *J. Biol. Chem.* **196**, 527.
51. Stadtman, E. R. (1953). The CoA-transphorase system in *Clostridium kluyveri. J. Biol. Chem.* **203**, 501.
52. Stadtman, E. R., Overath, P., Eggerer, H., and Lynen, F. (1960). The role of biotin and vitamin B_{12} coenzyme in propionate metabolism. *Biochem. Biophys. Res. Commun.* **2**, 1.

53. Stanier, R. Y., Doudoroff, M., and Adelberg, E. A. (1965). "The Microbial World," 2nd ed. Prentice-Hall, Englewood Cliffs, New Jersey.
54. Stephenson, M. (1949). "Bacterial Metabolism," 3rd ed. Longmans, Green, New York.
55. Stjernholm, R., and Wood, H. G. (1961). Methylmalonyl isomerase. II. Purification and properties of the enzyme from *Propionibacteria*. *Proc. Natl. Acad. Sci. U.S.* **47**, 303.
56. Swick, R. W., and Wood, H. G. (1960). The role of transcarboxylation in propionic acid fermentation. *Proc. Natl. Acad. Sci. U.S.* **46**, 28.
57. Taylor, M. B., and Juni, E. (1960). Stereoisomeric specificities of 2,3-butanediol dehydrogenases. *Biochim. Biophys. Acta* **39**, 448.
58. Valentine, R. C. (1964). Bacterial Ferredoxin. *Bacteriol. Rev.* **28**, 497.
59. Valentine, R. C., Mortensen, L. E., and Carnahan, J. E. (1963). The hydrogenase system of *Clostridium pasteurianum*. *J. Biol. Chem.* **238**, 1141.
60. Vandekarkove, M., Fancon, R., Andiffren, P., and Oddon, A. (1965). Metabolism of carbohydrates by *Neisseria intracellularis*. V. Evidence of acetylmethylcarbinol produced from glucose. *Med. Trop.* **25**, 457; *Chem. Abstr.* **64**, 5483 (1966)
61. van Niel, C. B. (1928). Dissertation, Delft; as cited by Wood and Werkman (68).
62. Virtanen, A. I. (1923). *Soc. Sci. Fennica, Commentationes Phys.-Math.* **1**, 36; as cited by Wood and Werkman (68).
63. Wallhöfer, P., and Baldwin, R. L. (1967). Pathway of propionate formation in *Bacteroides ruminicola*. *J. Bacteriol.* **93**, 504.
64. Westlake, D. W. S., Shug, A. L., and Wilson, P. W. (1961). The pyruvic dehydrogenase system of *Clostridium pasteurianum*. *Can. J. Microbiol.* **7**, 515.
65. Whiteley, H. R. (1953). Mechanism of propionic acid fermentation by succinate decarboxylation. *Proc. Natl. Acad. Sci. U.S.* **39**, 772.
66. Wilder, M., Valentine, R. C., and Akagi, J. M. (1963). Ferredoxin of *Clostridium thermosaccharolyticum*. *J. Bacteriol.* **86**, 861.
67. Wood, H. G., and Stjernholm, R. (1961). Transcarboxylase. II. Purification and properties of methylmalonyl-oxaloacetic transcarboxylase. *Proc. Natl. Acad. Sci. U.S.* **47**, 289.
68. Wood, H. G., and Werkman, C. H. (1936). Mechanisms of glucose dissimilation by the propionic acid bacteria. *Biochem. J.* **30**, 618.
69. Wood, H. G., Allen, S. H. G., Stjernholm, R., and Jacobson, B. (1963). Transcarboxylase. III. Purification and properties of methylmalonyl-oxaloacetic transcarboxylase containing tritiated biotin. *J. Biol. Chem.* **238**, 547.
70. Wood, H. G., Werkman, C. H., Hemingway, A., and Nier, A. O. (1940). Heavy carbon as a tracer in bacterial fixation of carbon dioxide. *J. Biol. Chem.* **135**, 789.
71. Wood, H. G., Werkman, C. H., Hemingway, A., and Nier, A. O. (1940). Heavy carbon as a tracer in heterotrophic carbon dioxide assimilation. *J. Biol. Chem.* **139**, 365.
72. Wood, W. A. (1961). Fermentation of carbohydrates and related compounds. *In* "The Bacteria" (I. C. Gunsalus and R. Y. Stanier, eds.), Vol. 2, p. 59. Academic Press, New York.

SUPPLEMENTARY READINGS

Ailhaud, G. P., Vagelos, P. R., and Goldfine, H. (1967). Involvement of acyl carrier protein in acylation of glycerol-3-phosphate in *Clostridium butyricum*. I. Purification of *Clostridium butyricum* acyl carrier protein and synthesis of long chain acyl derivatives of acyl carrier protein. *J. Biol. Chem.* **242**, 4459.

Azova, L. G., and Gorobtsova, T. A. (1966). Utilization of lactic acid by butyric acid bacteria. *Nauchen. Dokl. Vysshei Shkoly, Biol. Nauki* **1966**, 187; *Chem. Abstr.* **65**, 5907 (1966).

Bachmayer, H., Yasunobu, K. T., Peel, J. L., and Mayhew, S. (1968). Non-heme iron protein. V. The amino acid sequence of rubredoxin from *Peptostreptococcus elsdenii. J. Biol. Chem.* **243**, 1022.

Barker, H. A. (1967). Citramalate lyase of *Clostridium tetanomorphum. Arch. Mikrobiol.* **59**, 4.

Bennett, R., Taylor, D. R., and Hurst, A. (1966). D- and L-lactate dehydrogenase in *Escherichia coli. Biochim. Biophys. Acta* **118**, 512.

Benson, A. M., Mower, H. F., and Yasunobu, K. T. (1967). The amino acid sequence of *Clostridium butyricum* ferredoxin. *Arch. Biochem. Biophys.* **121**, 563.

Biggins, D. R., and Dilworth, M. J. (1968). Control of pyruvate phosphoroclastic activity in extracts of *Clostridium pasteurianum* by ADP and acetylphosphate. *Biochim. Biophys. Acta* **156**, 285.

Cazzulo, J. J., and Stoppani, A. O. M. (1967). Purification and properties of pyruvate carboxylase from Baker's yeast. *Arch. Biochim. Biophys.* **121**, 596.

Crawford, I. P., Sikes, S., and Melhorn, D. K. (1967). The natural relationship of *Aeromonas formicans. Arch. Mikrobiol.* **59**, 72.

Druskeit, W., Gersonde, K., and Netter, H. (1967). pH-abhängige magnetostatische und spektrale Eigenschaften des oxydierten Ferredoxins aus *Clostridium pasteurianum. European J. Biochem.* **2**, 176.

Feigenblum, E., and Krasna, A. I. (1967). Evolution of hydrogen gas from nicotinamide nucleotides by *Proteus vulgaris. Biochim. Biophys. Acta* **141**, 250.

Forrest, W. W. (1967). Energies of activation and uncoupled growth in *Streptococcus faecalis* and *Zymomonas mobilis. J. Bacteriol.* **94**, 1459.

Fukuyama, T., and Ordal, Z. J. (1965). Induced biosynthesis of formic hydrogenlyase in iron-deficient cells of *Escherichia coli. J. Bacteriol.* **90**, 673.

Galivan, J. H., and Allen, S. H. G. (1968). Methylmalonyl coenzyme A decarboxylase. Its role in succinate decarboxylation by *Micrococcus lactilyticus. J. Biol. Chem.* **243**, 1253.

Gersonde, K., and Druskeit, W. (1968). Zur Frage des "labilen" Schwefels in Ferredoxin aus *Clostridium pasteurianum. European J. Biochem.* **4**, 391.

Goldfine, H., Ailhaud, G. P., and Vagelos, P. R. (1967). Involvement of acyl carrier protein in acylation of glycerol-3-phosphate in *Clostridium butyricum*. II. Evidence for the participation of acyl thioesters of acyl carrier protein. *J. Biol. Chem.* **242**, 4466.

Harvey, R. J., Marr, A. G., and Painter, P. R. (1967). Kinetics of growth of individual cells of *Escherichia coli* and *Azotobacter agilis. J. Bacteriol.* **93**, 605.

Hayaishi, S., and Lin, E. C. C. (1967). Purification and properties of glycerol kinase from *Escherichia coli. J. Biol. Chem.* **242**, 1030.

Halpern, Y. S., and Even-Shoshan, A. (1967). Further evidence for two distinct acetolactate synthetases in *Aerobacter aerogenes. Biochim. Biophys. Acta* **139**, 502.

Heer, E., and Bachofen, R. (1966). Pyruvatstoffwechsel von *Clostridium butyricum. Arch. Mikrobiol.* **54**, 1.

Hernandez, E., and Johnson, M. J. (1967). Anaerobic growth yields of *Aerobacter cloacae* and *Escherichia coli. J. Bacteriol.* **94**, 991.

Hernandez, E., and Johnson, M. J. (1967). Energy supply and cell yields in aerobically grown microorganisms. *J. Bacteriol.* **94**, 996.

Hodgson, B., and McGarry, J. D. (1968). A direct pathway for the conversion of propionate into pyruvate in *Moraxella lwoffi. Biochem. J.* **107**, 7.

Hodgson, B., and McGarry, J. D. (1968). A direct pathway for the metabolism of propionate in cell free extracts from *Moraxella lwoffi. Biochem. J.* **107**, 19.

Jungermann, K., Thaver, R. K., and Decker, K. (1968). The synthesis of one-carbon units from CO_2 in *Clostridium kluyveri. European J. Biochem.* **3**, 351.

Kidman, A. D., Ackrell, B. A. C., and Asato, R. N. (1968). Properties of three isoenzymes of *Clostridium pasteurianum* hydrogenase. *Biochim. Biophys. Acta* **159**, 185.

Knight, E. Jr., D'Eustachio, A. J., and Hardy, R. W. F. (1966). Flavodoxin: A flavoprotein with ferredoxin activity from *Clostridium pasteurianum. Biochim. Biophys. Acta* **113**, 626.

Knight, E. Jr., and Hardy, R. W. F. (1966). Isolation and characteristics of flavodoxin from nitrogen-fixing *Clostridium pasteurianum. J. Biol. Chem.* **241**, 2752.

Kolodziej, B. J., Wegener, W. S., and Ajl, S. J. (1968). Propionate metabolism. IV. Significance of carboxylation reactions during adaptation to propionate. *Arch. Biochem. Biophys.* **123**, 66.

Kupfer, D. G., and Canale-Parola, E. (1967). Pyruvate metabolism in *Sarcina maxima. J. Bacteriol.* **94**, 984.

Moyer, R. W., Ramaley, R. F., Butler, L. G., and Boyer, P. D. (1967). The formation and reactions of a nonphosphorylated high energy form of succinyl coenzyme A synthetase. *J. Biol. Chem.* **242**, 4299.

Murphey, W. H., Barnaby, C., Lin, F.-J., and Kaplan, N. O. (1967). Malate dehydrogenase. II. Purification and properties of *Bacillus subtilis, B. stearothermophilus* and *Escherichia coli* malate dehydrogenases. *J. Biol. Chem.* **242**, 1548.

Murphey, W. H., and Kaplan, N. O. (1967). Malate dehydrogenase. III. Alteration of catalytic properties during purification of *Bacillus subtilis* malate dehydrogenases. *J. Biol. Chem.* **242**, 1560.

O'Hara, J., Gray, C. T., Puig, J., and Pichinoty, F. (1967). Defects in formate hydrogenlyase in nitrate-negative mutants of *E. coli. Biochem. Biophys. Res. Commun.* **28**, 951.

Peters, D. S., and Matrone, G. (1967). The propionate-activating system of rumen bacteria. *Biochim. Biophys. Acta* **137**, 478.

Prescott, D. J., and Rabinowitz, J. L. (1968). The enzymatic carboxylation of propionyl coenzyme A. Studies involving deuterated and tritiated substrates. *J. Biol. Chem.* **243**, 1551.

Ramaley, R. F., Bridger, W. A., Moyer, R. W., and Boyer, P. D. (1967). The preparation, properties, and reactions of succinyl coenzyme A synthetase and its phosphorylated form. *J. Biol. Chem.* **242**, 4287.

Rasmussen, R. K., and Klein, H. P. (1968). Effects of metals on acetyl coenzyme A carboxylase activity of *Saccharomyces cerevisiae. J. Bacteriol.* **95**, 727.

Renz, P. (1968). Enzymic synthesis of cobinamide phosphate from cobinamide by extracts of *Propionibacterium shermanii. Biochim. Biophys. Res. Commun.* **30**, 373.

Stormer, F. C. (1967). Isolation of crystalline pH 6 acetolactate-forming enzyme from *Aerobacter aerogenes. J. Biol. Chem.* **242**, 1756.

Thauer, R. K., Jungermann, K., Henninger, H., Wenning, J., and Decker, K. (1968). The energy metabolism of *Clostridium kluyveri. European J. Biochem.* **4**, 173.

Thayer, D. W., and Ogg, J. E. (1967). Aldehydes and ketones produced during fermentation by *Escherichia coli. J. Bacteriol.* **94**, 488.

Uyeda, K., and Rabinowitz, J. C. (1967). Enzymes of clostridial purine fermentation. *J. Biol. Chem.* **242**, 4378.

Wegener, W. S., Reeves, H. C., and Ajl, S. J. (1968). Propionate metabolism. II. Factors regulating adaptation of *Escherichia coli* to propionate. *Arch. Biochem. Biophys.* **123**, 55.

Wegener, W. S., Reeves, H. C., and Ajl, S. J. (1968). Propionate metabolism. III. Studies on the significance of the α-hydroxyglutarate pathway. *Arch. Biochem. Biophys.* **123**, 62.

Wimpenny, J. W. T. (1968). Regulation of enzyme profiles in *Escherichia coli*: the effects of oxygen, nitrate or nitrite. *Biochem. J.* **106**, 34P.

Winter, H. C., and Burris, R. H. (1968). Stoichiometry of the adenosine triphosphate requirement for N_2 fixation and H_2 evolution by a partially purified preparation of *Clostridium pasteurianum. J. Biol. Chem.* **243**, 940.

Wittenberger, C. L., and J. G. Fulco (1967). Purification and allosteric properties of a nicotinamide adenine dinucleotide-linked D(−)-specific lactate dehydrogenase from *Butyribacterium rettgeri. J. Biol. Chem.* **242**, 2917.

Blair, A. H., and Barker, H. A. (1966). Assay and purification of (+)-citramalate hydro-lyase components from *Clostridium tetanomorphum. J. Biol. Chem.* **241**, 400.

7

ACETIC ACID BACTERIA

The acetic acid bacteria are divided(14,46a) into the polarly flagellated *Acetomonas* Leifson 1954 (syn. *Gluconobacter* Asai 1935) and the peritrichous *Acetobacter* Beijerinck 1898. The physiology and biochemistry are very similar except that *Acetobacter* oxidizes ethanol to carbon dioxide and water via acetate and the TCA cycle, whereas *Acetomonas* oxidizes ethanol to acetate only(59, 60).

This separation into two genera is further supported by a comparison of the infrared spectra of some 22 strains of the acetic acid bacteria(57) and emphasized by the distinction between the various strains as lactophilic and glycophilic (11,66). These terms signify a preference for metabolism of lactate (*Acetobacter*) or glycols (*Acetomonas*)(53). In older literature species of *Acetomonas* appear under the name of "*Acetobacter*." Frateur(23) classified the acetic

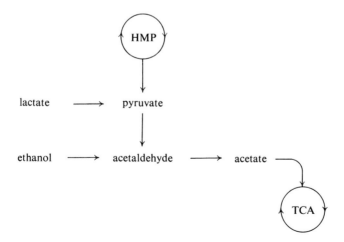

FIG. 7.1. Carbohydrate metabolism of the *Acetobacter peroxydans* group.

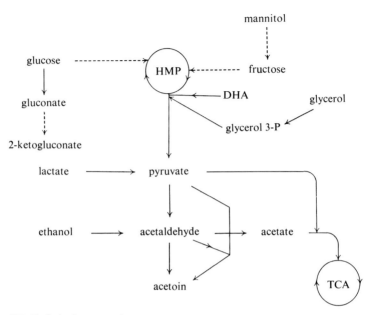

FIG. 7.2. Carbohydrate metabolism of the *Acetobacter oxydans* group (62) (reprinted with permission of the *Antonie van Leeuwenhoek J. for Microbiology and Serology*).

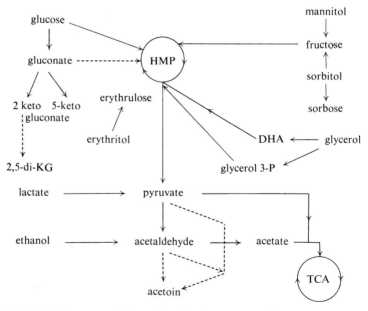

FIG. 7.3. Carbohydrate metabolism of the *Acetobacter mesoxydans* group (62) (reprinted with permission of the *Antonie van Leeuwenhoek J. for Microbiology and Serology*).

acid bacteria into only one genus *Acetobacter*, which he divided into four different groups: *peroxydans*, *oxydans*, *mesoxydans*, and *suboxydans*. Stout-hamer(62) summarized the carbohydrate metabolism of the last three and DeLey(14) of the *peroxydans* group in Figs. 7.1–7.4.

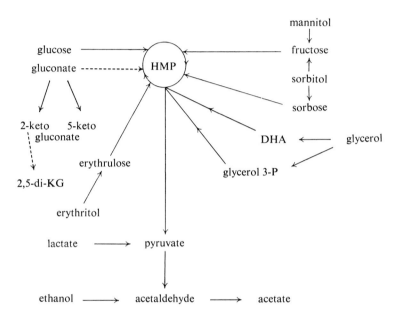

Fig. 7.4. Carbohydrate metabolism of *Acetomonas* (*Gluconobacter*)(62) (reprinted with permission of the *Antonie van Leeuwenhoek J. for Microbiology and Serology*).

The classification scheme of Frateur(23) was modified by DeLey(14) who placed the three groups *peroxydans*, *oxydans*, and *mesoxydans* into the genus *Acetobacter* and the *suboxydans* group into *Gluconobacter*.

In dealing with the metabolic activities of the acetic acid bacteria it was thought best to start with those compounds which require partly or wholly systems dealt with during the previous chapters. Special attention is given to those systems which are known to be characteristic for these bacteria.

Lactate Metabolism

The enzymatic mechanism for lactate breakdown by growing cells is essentially identical in *Acetobacter* and *Acetomonas*(18). Both isomers of the lactate are metabolized by two sets of enzymes which do not require any co-factor and which are located in the particulate fraction of the cell. Resting cells of *Acetobacter peroxydans* are able to metabolize D-lactate about four times as fast as L-lactate, and the activity is located in the soluble fraction(17). In the particulate fraction no NAD- and NADP-linked lactate dehydrogenase or lactate racemase was found, but instead, a D-lactate oxidase (D-lactate: oxygen oxidoreductase, E.C. 1.1.3 group) was found to be present:

$$\text{D-lactate} + O_2 \rightarrow \text{acetate} + CO_2 + H_2O_2$$

Acetobacter therefore can oxidize lactate to acetate and also lactate to pyruvate. Pyruvate itself is metabolized in three different ways by acetic acid bacteria:

(1) A pyruvate decarboxylase (2-oxoacid carboxylyase, E.C. 4.1.1.1) acts on pyruvate and forms acetaldehyde and carbon dioxide. This mechanism has been observed in *Acetomonas suboxydans*(38) and *Acetobacter peroxydans*(17).

(2) A pyruvate oxidase system, which was found to be a joint action of pyruvate decarboxylase (E.C. 4.1.1.1), which forms acetaldehyde and carbon dioxide, and an NAD- or NADP-linked aldehyde dehydrogenase(18). This system requires thiamine pyrophosphate and was found in *Acetobacter pasteurianum*(41) and *A. liquefaciens*. This system seems to be semi-inducible, since no or doubtful activities were found in lactate-grown cells. The aldehyde dehydrogenase is not activated by CoA or glutathion and could therefore be any of the three pyridine nucleotide-linked dehydrogenases (E.C. 1.2.1.3, E.C. 1.2.1.4, or E.C. 1.2.1.5).

(3) A combination of a pyruvate decarboxylase, a cytochrome system which does not require cofactors, and molecular oxygen as hydrogen acceptor(17). This combination appears to be similar to the function of pyruvate dehydrogenase (pyruvate:cytochrome b_1 oxidoreductase, E.C. 1.2.2.2) which requires TPP. In this pyruvate dehydrogenase system one certainly finds the combination of pyruvate decarboxylase (E.C. 4.1.1.1), which is a thiamine pyrophosphate flavoprotein and a cytochrome. There is, however, no conclusive evidence for the latter statement available as yet. The product of this reaction is, in either case, acetate.

The presence of a pyruvate decarboxylase indicates that *Acetomonas suboxydans* must have a yeast-type system of pyruvate decarboxylation which leads directly to acetaldehyde. It is one of the few bacteria which can use this system, and this fact can certainly be associated with the failure of this organism to form acetyl phosphate or acetyl CoA. It may also be a reason why acetate is not further metabolized. It would be of interest to see whether this applies to all species of *Acetomonas*. In the case of *Acetobacter peroxydans*, on the other hand, the further breakdown of acetate does not seem to be interrupted. The role of the marked peroxidase activity exhibited for lactate and alcohol metabolism(20) is still obscure.

The electron transport system in *A. peroxydans*(17) from the dehydrogenases to oxygen certainly involves cytochromes and cytochrome oxidase. This is in contrast to *Acetomonas suboxydans* where only a cytochrome a_1 (590 mμ), which must function as an oxygen-transferring enzyme(32), was found. Lactate dehydrogenase is almost certainly associated with cytochrome c_1 (554 mμ).

ETHANOL METABOLISM

It is still questionable whether acetaldehyde is an intermediate in ethanol oxidation in the case of *Acetobacter peroxydans*(1) since this species oxidizes ethanol, pyruvate, and a number of TCA cycle intermediate(5) to carbon dioxide and water, but hardly oxidizes acetate at all. Crude cell-free extracts were found to only weakly oxidize ethanol, by means of an NAD-linked alcohol dehydrogenase, to acetate and intermediates of the TCA cycle beyond oxalacetate. This enzyme of *Acetobacter peroxydans* resembles the corresponding alcohol dehydrogenase of higher organisms (39).

Acetomonas suboxydans was shown to have a powerful acetaldehyde dehydrogenase, which reduces $NADP^+$ at four times the rate of NAD^+ reduction(40). It is not certain, however, whether the number of dehydrogenases involved is one or two. It is also possible that two alcohol-cytochrome reductases are present(47). The pH optimum of the alcohol dehydrogenase in the *Acetobacter oxydans* and *Acetobacter mesoxydans* groups was 3.7–4.7, whereas it was 5.7–6.2 in *Acetomonas*. Since the cytochrome a_1 (590 mμ), b (565 mμ), and cytochrome 553 were found, it has been postulated that the alcohol–cytochrome 553 reductase is one of the important components responsible for acetic acid production. In contrast to this, *Acetobacter* seemed to have cytochrome o as terminal oxidase(8,9). *Acetomonas* therefore seems to have two different terminal oxidases for lactate and for ethanol oxidation.

In *Acetobacter peroxydans* a NAD-linked ethanol dehydrogenase (E.C. 1.1.1.1) as well as a NAD-linked aldehyde dehydrogenase (E.C. 1.2.1.3 or E.C. 1.2.1.10) are present(3) if the organism is grown with ethanol as the carbon source.

Both lactate and ethanol metabolism can therefore be summarized as follows(17):

(1) If the organism is grown on lactate and tested on lactate

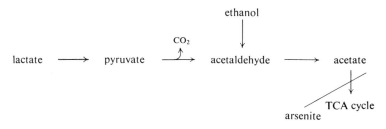

(2) If the organism is grown on ethanol or glucose and tested on lactate and ethanol

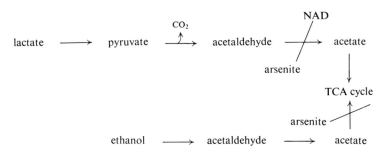

Acetobacter xylinum was found to accumulate oxalacetate if grown on malate. The malate oxidation must be accomplished by a mechanism other than the NAD-linked malic dehydrogenase (L-malate:NAD oxidoreductase (decarboxylating), E.C. 1.1.1.39 or E.C. 1.1.1.38), since whenever this enzyme is present, oxalacetate cannot accumulate(55). It appears that in the case of *Acetobacter xylinum* malate dehydrogenase (L-malate:NAD oxidoreductase, E.C. 1.1.1.37)(6a) functions to form oxalacetate from L-malate with the reduction of NAD and the coupled formation of ATP. Kornberg and Phizackerley(44) first noted this reaction with *Pseudomonas* in which the malate-oxidizing system oxidizes malate with oxygen or dichlorophenolindophenol (DPI) as the acceptor. Investigations on cell-free extracts of *Acetobacter*

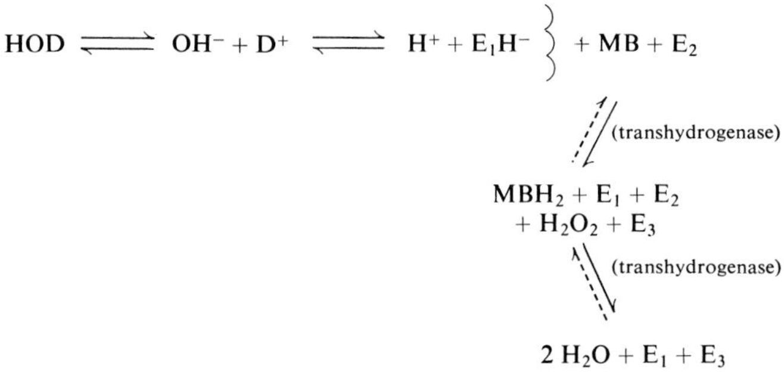

$$HOD \rightleftharpoons OH^- + D^+ \rightleftharpoons H^+ + E_1H^- \left.\right\} + MB + E_2$$

(transhydrogenase)

$$MBH_2 + E_1 + E_2 \\ + H_2O_2 + E_3$$

(transhydrogenase)

$$2 H_2O + E_1 + E_3$$

xylinum revealed that oxalacetate is decarboxylated to pyruvate and carbon dioxide(6). It appears therefore that *Acetobacter xylinum* oxidizes malate not in one step, but requires two steps with malate dehydrogenase (E.C. 1.1.1.37) and oxalacetate decarboxylase (oxalacetate carboxylyase, E.C. 4.1.1.3) as catalyzing enzymes. Adenosine triphosphate, ADP, GTP, GDP, and inorganic phosphate do not promote the decarboxylation.

Acetobacter peroxydans differs from all the other *Acetobacter* species in lacking catalase. Hydrogen peroxide can be reduced at the expense of hydrogen which is also utilized for the reductions of quinone, oxygen, and methylene blue, but not of acetaldehyde or fumarate(2). It was found that NAD^+ is not involved at the expense of molecular hydrogen in the electron transfer. Ethanol and hydrogen (from H_2O_2) must therefore compete for an electron acceptor. It is probable that a cytochrome c type of respiration takes place in this organism in contrast to the flavoprotein oxygen pathway(63), particularly since it has been confirmed that H_2O_2 is reduced and H_2O formed(64).

GLUCOSE METABOLISM

In the early stages of investigation it was thought that the EMP pathway was present in acetic acid bacteria. This was challenged by DeLey(14) and present indications are that the EMP pathway is completely absent(53). The main metabolic pathway of glucose metabolism is therefore the HMP pathway as shown in Figs. 7.1–7.4.

Acetobacter and *Acetomonas* are well known for their oxidative versatility, substrates ranging from carbohydrates to a great number of straight chain polyols(52). The oxidation of polyols and reduction of ketones are carried out by specific dehydrogenases which follow the Bertrand-Hudson rule. Bertrand(7) found with *Acetobacter xylinum* that a generalization could be made concerning the structure of polyols susceptible to oxidation. According to his established rule, a secondary group of a polyol was oxidized to ketone if it has the cis configuration with respect to the primary alcohol group:

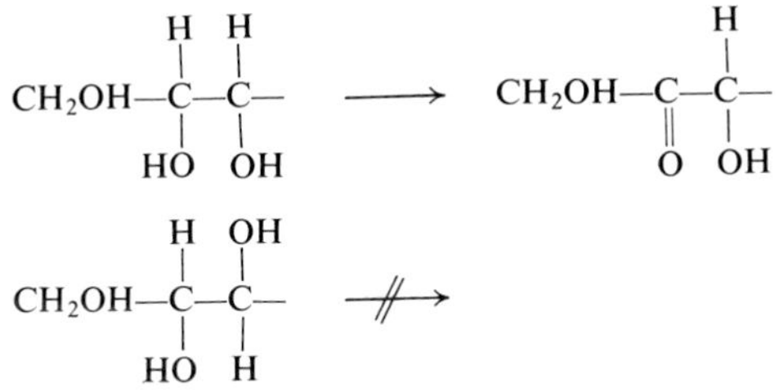

$$
\begin{array}{ccc}
\overset{\text{H}}{\underset{\text{HO}}{\text{CH}_2\text{OH}-\text{C}}}\overset{\text{H}}{\underset{\text{OH}}{\text{C}}}- & \longrightarrow & \overset{\text{}}{\underset{\text{O}}{\text{CH}_2\text{OH}-\text{C}}}\overset{\text{H}}{\underset{\text{OH}}{\text{C}}}-
\end{array}
$$

$$
\overset{\text{H}}{\underset{\text{HO}}{\text{CH}_2\text{OH}-\text{C}}}\overset{\text{OH}}{\underset{\text{H}}{\text{C}}}- \quad \not\longrightarrow
$$

With glucose the terminal aldehyde group is oxidized to a carboxyl group. This was explained by considering glucose as a cyclic polyol to which the Bertrand rule may not apply.

The most versatile microorganism as far as carbohydrate metabolism is concerned is undoubtedly *Acetomonas suboxydans*. It oxidizes a great number of polyols in one- or two-step oxidations. It has been suggested that *A. suboxydans* is a "metabolic cripple"(10) since in numerous instances, it is unable to oxidize the compounds beyond the first or second step. Cell-free extracts of *Acetomonas suboxydans* were shown to possess two kinds of glucose dehydrogenases(24), one DPI (2,6-dichlorophenolindophenol)-linked and a second NADP-linked. It is very likely that the DPI-linked dehydrogenase is identical with the glucose oxidase (β-D-glucose:oxygen oxidoreductase, E.C. 1.1.3.4) which is a flavoprotein. The NADP-linked one is identical with the glucose dehydrogenase (β-D-glucose:NAD(P) oxidoreductase, E.C. 1.1.1.47) which catalyzes the reaction:

$$\text{glucose} + O_2 \rightarrow \text{D-glucono-}\delta\text{-lactone} + H_2O_2$$

$$\text{glucose} + NADP^+ \rightarrow \text{D-glucono-}\delta\text{-lactone} + NADPH + H^+$$

Phosphate does not participate in this glucose oxidation, although the reaction is strictly $NADP^+$-dependent in *Acetomonas suboxydans*(48). A 5-ketogluconate reductase (D-gluconate:NADP oxidoreductase, E.C. 1.1.1 group) metabolizes the gluconate further to 5-ketogluconate:

$$\text{gluconate} + NADP^+ \rightleftharpoons \text{5-ketogluconate} + NADPH + H^+$$

A pH optimum of 7.5 favors the forward reaction, while one of 9.5 favors the reverse reaction(49).

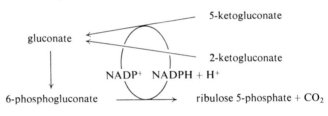

SCHEME 7.1

Investigations into the dissimilation of glucose with the radiorespirometric method(42) revealed that in the presence of oxygen, the HMP pathway accounts for all the glucose metabolized (to CO_2 and water) the remainder being directly oxidized to 2-ketogluconate. This exclusive use of the HMP pathway by all acetic acid bacteria gives the clear-cut difference between them and the related genera of the family *Pseudomonadaceae*.

The connection between the glucose $\rightarrow$ 5-ketogluconate reaction and the HMP pathway was established by DeLey and Stouthamer(19) when they discovered the following three enzymes:

(1) a soluble NADP-specific dehydrogenase yielding 2-ketogluconate, which could be a 2-ketogluconate reductase (D-gluconate:NAD(P) oxidoreductase, E.C. 1.1.1 group);

(2) a soluble NADP-specific dehydrogenase yielding 5-ketogluconate, which is possibly 5-ketogluconate reductase (D-gluconate:NAD(P) oxidoreductase, E.C. 1.1.1.69); and

(3) a particulate, possibly cytochrome-linked, gluconate oxidase yielding 2-ketogluconate (E.C. 1.2. group).

Since there was no 5-ketogluconokinase detectable, both 2- and 5-ketogluconate are metabolized by a reductase to gluconate. This was followed by a gluconokinase (ATP:D-gluconate 6-phosphotransferase, E.C. 2.7.1.12) and 6-phosphogluconate dehydrogenase (6-phospho-D-gluconate:NADP oxidoreductase (decarboxylating), E.C. 1.1.1.44) which catalyzed the same reactions as described in the HMP pathway (see Chapter 4 and Scheme 7.1).

Acetobacter melanogenum, however, does not possess a gluconokinase (E.C. 2.7.1.12) and therefore oxidizes 2-ketogluconate further to 2,5-diketogluconate by means of a ketogluconate dehydrogenase (2-keto-D-gluconate: (acceptor) oxidoreductase, E.C. 1.1.99.4). The end product of this reaction is

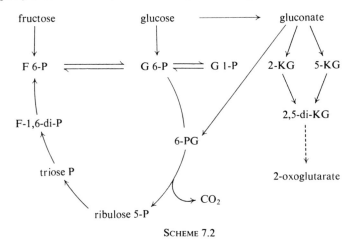

SCHEME 7.2

very unstable (34), especially above pH 4.5, and gives rise to brown-colored decomposition products. It seems therefore that *Acetobacter melanogenum* possesses two completely separate systems for the oxidation of glucose and hexose phosphates (33). Probably because of this, *A. melanogenum* is able to oxidize 2-ketogluconate further to 2,5-diketogluconate and through a series of unknown intermediates to α-oxoglutarate (12). This organism has no phosphohexokinase activity.

Acetobacter xylinum combines the activities of *A. melanogenum* and *Acetomonas suboxydans* in being able (25, 56) to

(1)   phosphorylate glucose → glucose 6-phosphate

(2)   oxidize glucose → gluconate → 2-keto- and 5-ketogluconate →
                                                    α-oxoglutarate + CO_2

Only a minor fraction of glucose undergoes phosphorylation as such, and the bulk of glucose carbon can be introduced into the hexose phosphate pool indirectly via gluconate which is phosphorylated to 6-phosphogluconate. Pyruvate and acetate may also originate from 5-oxogluconate in *Acetomonas suboxydans* (see Scheme 7.2).

Inhibition studies with iodoacetate have revealed that a further pathway must exist in *A. xylinum* which does not involve glyceraldehyde 3-phosphate dehydrogenase(55a). *Acetobacter xylinum* is still able to synthesize cellulose after the addition of the inhibitor. It was also observed that inorganic phosphate was converted to acyl phosphate which could be linked to a hexose phosphorylation system

$$\text{fructose 6-P} + \text{P}_i \;\rightarrow\; \text{acetyl P} + \text{erythrose 4-P}$$

$$\text{erythrose 4-P} + \text{fructose 6-P} \;\rightarrow\; \text{sedoheptulose 7-P} + \text{glyceraldehyde 3-P}$$

$$\text{sedoheptulose 7-P} + \text{glyceraldehyde 3-P} \;\rightarrow\; \text{ribose 5-P} + \text{xylulose 5-P}$$

$$\text{ribose 5-P} \;\rightarrow\; \text{xylulose 5-P}$$

$$\text{2 xylulose 5-P} + \text{2 P}_i \;\rightarrow\; \text{2 acetyl P} + \text{glyceraldehyde 3-P}$$

$$\text{net: fructose 6-P} + \text{2 P}_i \;\rightarrow\; \text{2 acetyl P}$$

$$\text{3 acetyl P} + \text{3 ADP} \;\rightarrow\; \text{3 ATP} + \text{3 acetate}$$

The enzyme catalyzing the initial step was called "fructose 6-phosphate phosphoketolase," (56a) which is different from the xylulose 5-phosphate phosphoketolase. The presence of this enzyme can be evaluated as a "short circuit" pathway (58a) for the case that no phosphofructokinase or no glucose 6-phosphate dehydrogenase is present. The detailed description of this pathway was given earlier (see Chapter 4). It is interesting to note that apart from *Acetobacter xylinum* only species of the genus *Bifidobacterium* possess this pathway to our present knowledge.

A similar system exists with fructose as carbon source in the case of *Acetobacter cerinus*(3a, 21). The oxidation of

$$\text{D-fructose} \;\rightarrow\; \text{5-keto-D-fructose}$$

conforms to Bertrand's rules. A very active reduction of 5-keto-D-fructose by $NADPH_2$ could be observed. This reaction, leading to the formation of D-fructose, strongly favors the reduction of 5-keto-D-fructose at equilibrium. The enzyme which catalyzes this reaction is NADPH-dicarbonyl-hexose reductase(22) and is extremely substrate specific(4).

The reversible oxidation of

$$\text{D-mannitol} \;\rightleftharpoons\; \text{D-fructose}$$

is catalyzed by an NAD(P)-mannitol dehydrogenase. This enzyme is mannitol: NAD(P) oxidoreductase (E.C. 1.1.1.67). In the case of a cytochrome-linked dehydrogenase (D-mannitol:cytochrome oxidoreductase, E.C. 1.1.2.2) not only is D-mannitol converted to D-fructose, but also this enzyme oxidizes erythritol, D-glucitol, D-arabinitol, and ribitol.

The possibility of manufacturing D-fructose commercially from mannitol under aerobic conditions was first considered with *Acetomonas suboxydans* (50). The NAD$^+$- or NADP$^+$-linked dehydrogenase seems to be a constitutive enzyme of *Acetomonas suboxydans* (58). Apart from a mannose isomerase (D-mannose ketol isomerase, E.C. 5.3.1.7) which converts

$$\text{D-mannose} \rightleftharpoons \text{D-fructose}$$

there was also a NADPH-aldohexose dehydrogenase which oxidizes D-mannose, D-glucose, or 2-deoxy-D-glucose. This enzyme could be of the general type E.C. 1.6.99.1 (reduced NADP:(acceptor) oxidoreductase).

Investigations into the polyol oxidation of *Acetomonas suboxydans* showed (37) that this organism is able to oxidize a great number of acyclic polyols and related substances according to the rules of Bertrand. The secondary OH group involved in the oxidation must have a D-configuration with respect to the primary alcohol group adjacent to the site of oxidation. *Acetomonas suboxydans* therefore contains six different polyol dehydrogenases and each of these has a unique structural specificity:

(1) NADP$^+$-xylitol dehydrogenase (xylitol: NADP oxidoreductase, E.C. 1.1.1.10)
(2) NAD$^+$-D-mannitol dehydrogenase
(3) NAD$^+$-D-erythro dehydrogenase
(4) NAD$^+$-D-xylo (D-sorbitol) dehydrogenase (67)
(5) NADP$^+$-D-xylo dehydrogenase
(6) NADP$^+$-D-lyxo-(D-mannitol) dehydrogenase

Acetic acid bacteria which do not utilize glucose via glucose 6-phosphate and the HMP pathway are able to enter the cycle via phosphogluconate because of their highly active system of splitting this compound. Hexose phosphate can be resynthesized from triose phosphates which can enter a common pool after being formed through the simultaneous action of the HMP and ED pathways (65) via fructose 1,6-diphosphate by aldolase (E.C. 4.1.2.13) activity. Hochster (29) reported that the C-1-keto sugar diphosphatase (FDPase) hydrolyzes the 1-phosphate group to yield fructose 1-phosphate and inorganic phosphate and that after isomerization to glucose 6-phosphate, the latter joins the hexose phosphate pool together with the hexose phosphate from the glucose phosphorylation. This proposal lacks support. The correct sequence is as follows:

(1) Hexose diphosphatase (D-fructose-1,6-diphosphate 1-phosphohydrolase, E.C. 3.1.3.11) catalyzes the reaction

$$\text{D-fructose 1,6-diphosphate} + H_2O \rightarrow \text{D-fructose 6-phosphate} + P_i$$

forming fructose 6-phosphate(10) and not fructose 1-phosphate as reported by Hochster(29).

(2) The isomerization to glucose 6-phosphate is certainly carried out by a glucose phosphate isomerase (D-glucose 6-phosphate ketol isomerase, E.C. 5.3.1.9) in the following way,

$$\text{glucose 6-phosphate} \rightarrow \text{D-fructose 6-phosphate}$$

The phosphofructokinase (ATP:D-fructose 6-phosphate 1-phosphotrans-ferase, E.C. 2.7.1.11) activity is very weak and glucose 6-phosphate therefore enters the HMP pathway as mentioned earlier.

Evidence for the presence of oxidative phosphorylation indicated(43) that the P/O ratios during the oxidation of glucose and glycerol are less than one. The phosphorylated products soon reach a maximum since there are no acceptors available. Inorganic phosphate is therefore present in large amounts and this explains the presence of high molecular weight polymer metaphos-phate, which is approximately 5–10 times the phosphate equivalent found in ATP. The rapid turnover of inorganic pyrophosphate and the fact that the specific activities of the labile phosphates in ADP and ATP approaches the specific activity of pyrophosphate point strongly to inorganic pyrophosphate as an intermediate in oxidative phosphorylation(43).

Oxydograms on i-erythritol were developed to assay for the function of erythrulose by strains of acetic acid bacteria. Within the genus *Acetobacter* a distinction can be made between the *mesoxydans* group, which forms ery-thritol and the *oxydans* and *peroxydans* group, which are not able to convert erythritol to erythrulose(15).

GLYCEROL METABOLISM

Acetomonas suboxydans which does not possess a TCA cycle is also able to grow and utilize glycerol(26). This glycerol metabolism proceeds along two pathways(27):

(1) Glycerol is oxidized to dihydroxyacetone, which proceeds at pH 6.0 and is independent of ATP. This reaction is catalyzed by a glycerol dehydro-genase (glycerol: NAD oxidoreductase, E.C. 1.1.1.6). A kinase reaction would then phosphorylate dihydroxyacetone since this reaction has been found to be ATP-dependent and also requires Mg^{2+}

$$\text{glycerol} \longrightarrow \text{dihydroxyacetone} \xrightarrow[\text{Mg}^{2+}]{\text{ATP}} \text{dihydroxyacetone phosphate}$$

(2) Glycerol is first phosphorylated by glycerol kinase (ATP:glycerol phosphotransferase, E.C. 2.7.1.30) to L-glycerol 3-phosphate. Glycerol

phosphate dehydrogenase (L-glycerol 3-phosphate (acceptor) oxidoreductase, E.C. 1.1.99.5) finally converts glycerol 3-phosphate to dihydroxyacetone phosphate.

The over-all scheme for glycerol metabolism is therefore

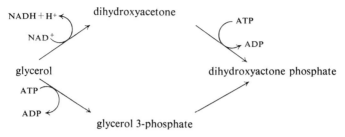

Dihydroxyacetone phosphate is then isomerized by the triose phosphate isomerase (D-glyceraldehyde 3-phosphate ketol isomerase, E.C. 5.3.1.1) to glyceraldehyde 3-phosphate and the fructose diphosphate aldolase (E.C. 4.1.2.13) equilibria forms fructose 1,6-diphosphate(28). The actions of hexose diphosphatase (E.C. 3.1.3.11) and glucose 6-phosphate isomerase (E.C. 5.3.1.9) produce glucose 6-phosphate. The oxidation of glucose 6-phosphate to 6-phosphogluconate and further to ribose 5-phosphate is the only way for the glycerol metabolism to function. The amount of phosphate present in the medium appears to be important(58a).

The activities of *Acetomonas suboxydans* could therefore be summarized as shown in Fig. 7.5.

ACETOIN FORMATION

A number of *Acetobacter* strains are further able to convert pyruvate into acetoin(13). *Acetobacter rancens, A. pasteurianum,* and *A. ascendens* have two possible pathways to form acetoin:

(1) A yeast-type degradation of pyruvate with TPP as cofactor

$$2 \text{ pyruvate} + 2 \text{ TPP} \rightarrow [2 \text{ aldehyde-TPP}] + CO_2$$

$$[\text{aldehyde-TPP}] \rightarrow CH_3CHO + TPP$$

$$[\text{aldehyde-TPP}] + CH_3CHO \rightarrow \text{acetoin} + TPP$$

This pathway seems also to be favored by *Acetomonas suboxydans*(54).

(2) A pathway described earlier (see Chapter 6), whereby aldehyde-TPP is converted to α-acetolactate first and then to the end product acetoin.

The acetic acid bacteria are unique in being able to use both pathways, whereas microorganisms such as *Streptococcus faecalis* and *Aerobacter aerogenes* can use only one of the pathways.

There seems to be no pathway which involves acetyl phosphate or acetyl CoA in the acetic acid bacteria. The formation of either diacetyl or 2,3-butane-diol from acetoin is very unlikely since an NADH-linked reduction could not

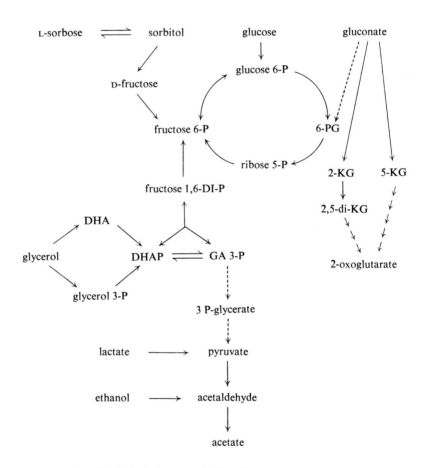

FIG. 7.5. Carbohydrate metabolism of *Acetomonas suboxydans*.

be observed and also because of the highly oxidizing conditions existing throughout the growth.

The low efficiency of energy transfer in *Acetomonas suboxydans* is partly explained by the presence of only one cytochrome. The ATP production per mole of hexose oxidized is only slightly higher than that in the anaerobic microorganisms(62a). This organism must therefore obtain its energy from the lactate and ethanol oxidation.

GLYCOL OXIDATION

Glycerol is not only metabolized in the HMP cycle but also can function as an inducer for glycol dehydrogenases in cells which were originally grown on glucose or lactate medium (45). The formation of these enzymes seems to be especially dependent on glycerol although a nitrogen source as well as an energy source such as glucose is required (46). The glycol oxidation of the *Acetobacter* and *Acetomonas* groups appears to involve three basic enzymes (36):

(1) A soluble NAD-linked primary alcohol dehydrogenase which does not react with NADP (16) but seems to require the

$$>CH—CH_2OH \text{ group}$$

because methanol is not oxidized and the presence of an OH group or a second CH_2OH group at carbon-2 decreases or inhibits enzymatic action. The further the second CH_2OH group is removed from the one to be attacked, the greater is its susceptibility to enzymatic action. The end products are most likely to be the corresponding aldehydes since strong NAD- and NADP-linked dehydrogenases were found to be present (40) in *Acetomonas suboxydans*.

(2) A soluble NAD secondary alcohol dehydrogenase which attacks glycols with a secondary OH group. This enzyme seems to be less specific. The presence of an adjacent OH group improves the enzymatic activity and the end products appear to be the corresponding ketones. The presence of a third OH group, a C=O or a COOH group in the molecule decreases the enzymatic activity.

(3) A particulate oxidative system by which the oxidation of glycols proceeds with the uptake of oxygen. It is very likely that an electron transport system via cytochromes occurs. This oxidative system not only oxidizes all primary and secondary alcohols but many other compounds as well, e.g., hexoses, pentoses, polyols, and aldehydes. The oxidation of ω-diols depends upon the distance between the terminal CH_2OH groups (36). In short-chain diols, i.e., where these groups are situated closely together as in 1,2-ethanediol, only one of them can be oxidized. The resulting carboxyl group apparently prevents further enzymatic action. With larger molecules the negative influence of the carboxyl group decreases, and the oxidation proceeds with both types of molecules at once to the dicarboxylic acids. It appears that cytochrome 553 is tightly bonded to the enzyme aggregate. There is no evidence for the participation of NAD, NADP, flavins, ubiquinones, or free heavy metals in this system.

Further details of glycol oxidations in acetic acid bacteria are presented in a review article by DeLey and Kersters (16).

Oxidation of the Primary Alcohol Group

Acetobacter xylinum, A. aceti, A. acetosus, A. kuetzingianus, A. pasteurianus, A. acetigenus, A. ascendens, Acetomonas suboxydans (*oxydans*), and *Acetomonas industrium* are able to oxidize ethylene glycol to glycolic acid, with glycolic acetaldehyde as a possible intermediate:

$$
\begin{array}{ccc}
\begin{array}{l} CH_2OH \\ | \\ CH_2OH \end{array} & \longrightarrow & \begin{array}{l} COOH \\ | \\ CH_2OH \end{array} \\
\text{ethylene glycol} & & \text{glycolic acid}
\end{array}
$$

The mechanism by which this C-2 substrate is converted into cell material, however, is still unknown. Ethylene glycol monomethyl ether (methylcellosolve) is quickly oxidized by resting cells of *Acetomonas suboxydans* with the uptake of 1 mole of O_2 per mole substrate with the possible formation of

$$
\begin{array}{ccc}
\begin{array}{l} CH_2OH \\ | \\ CH_2OCH_3 \end{array} & \longrightarrow & \left[\begin{array}{l} COOH \\ | \\ CH_2OCH_3 \end{array} \right] \\
\text{monomethyl ether} & & \alpha\text{-methoxy acetic acid}
\end{array}
$$

α-methoxy acetic acid. The monoethyl ether of ethylene glycol (cellosolve) is oxidized very slowly, and therefore this oxidation never comes to completion with submerged cultures of *Acetomonas suboxydans* (31,51). The α-ethoxy

$$
\begin{array}{ccc}
\begin{array}{l} CH_2OH \\ | \\ CH_2OCH_2CH_3 \end{array} & \longrightarrow & \begin{array}{l} COOH \\ | \\ CH_2OCH_2CH_3 \end{array} \\
\text{cellosolve} & &
\end{array}
$$

acetic acid is formed. An incomplete oxidation occurs also with diethylene glycol in aerated submerged cultures of *Acetomonas suboxydans* with the formation of β-hydroxy-ethoxy acetic acid as an intermediate and the corresponding dicarboxylic acid as end product:

$$
\begin{array}{ccccc}
\begin{array}{l} CH_2OH \\ | \\ CH_2 \\ | \\ O \\ | \\ CH_2 \\ | \\ CHOH \end{array} & \longrightarrow & \begin{array}{l} COOH \\ | \\ CH_2 \\ | \\ O \\ | \\ CH_2 \\ | \\ CH_2OH \end{array} & \longrightarrow & \begin{array}{l} COOH \\ | \\ CH_2 \\ | \\ O \\ | \\ CH_2 \\ | \\ COOH \end{array}
\end{array}
$$

The monomethyl ether of diethylene glycol can be oxidized by *Acetomonas suboxydans* as well, but the yield of 2-(2-methoxy)ethoxy acetic acid is only 36 %.

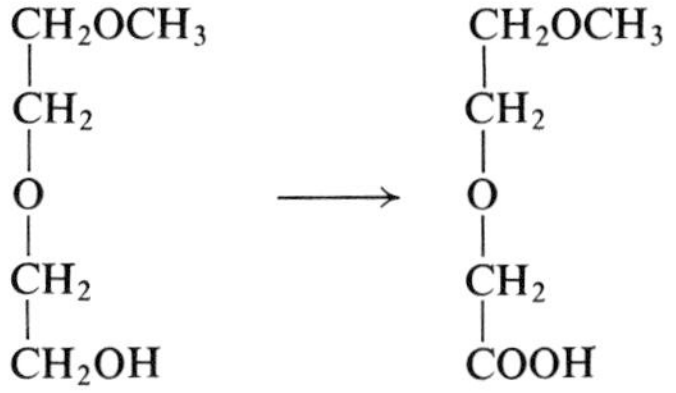

$$
\begin{array}{ccc}
CH_2OCH_3 & & CH_2OCH_3 \\
| & & | \\
CH_2 & & CH_2 \\
| & & | \\
O & \longrightarrow & O \\
| & & | \\
CH_2 & & CH_2 \\
| & & | \\
CH_2OH & & COOH
\end{array}
$$

Triethylene glycol is oxidized very rapidly with resting cells of *Acetomonas suboxydans* with an uptake of 1 mole of O_2 per mole substrate, probably to a carboxyl group on one end of the molecule, followed by a slower oxidation to another carboxyl group at the other end (35).

Acetomonas melanogenus grows rapidly on trimethylene glycol (1,3-propanediol) and oxidizes this compound to malonic acid with hydracrylic acid (β-hydroxypropionic acid) as an intermediate:

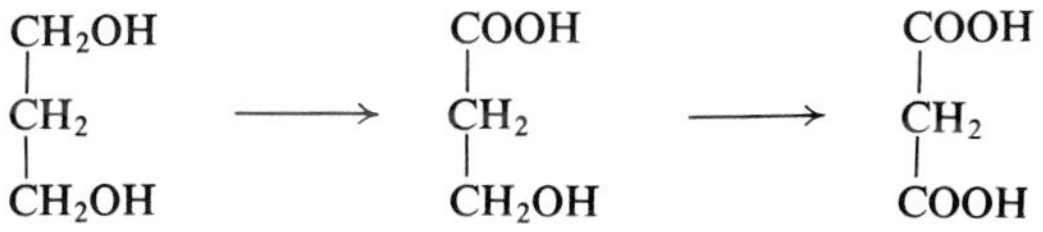

$$
\begin{array}{ccccc}
CH_2OH & & COOH & & COOH \\
| & & | & & | \\
CH_2 & \longrightarrow & CH_2 & \longrightarrow & CH_2 \\
| & & | & & | \\
CH_2OH & & CH_2OH & & COOH
\end{array}
$$

Acetomonas suboxydans is only able to grow on and utilize this compound very slowly.

D,L-1,3-Butanediol seems to be a good substrate for all acetic acid bacteria since all strains studied to date are able to oxidize it to D,L-β-hydroxybutyric acid:

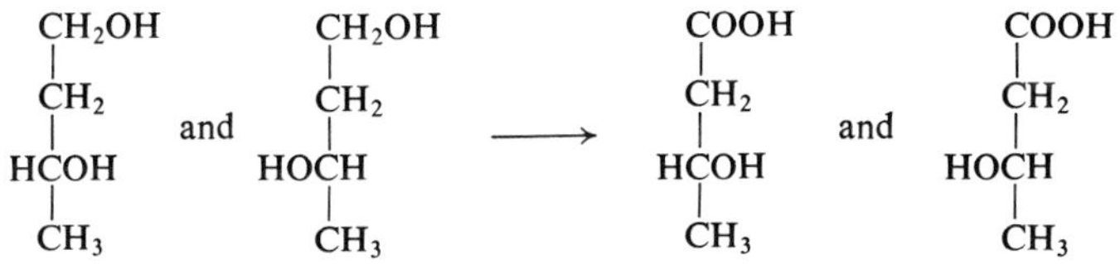

$$
\begin{array}{ccccccc}
CH_2OH & & CH_2OH & & COOH & & COOH \\
| & & | & & | & & | \\
CH_2 & \text{and} & CH_2 & \longrightarrow & CH_2 & \text{and} & CH_2 \\
| & & | & & | & & | \\
HCOH & & HOCH & & HCOH & & HOCH \\
| & & | & & | & & | \\
CH_3 & & CH_3 & & CH_3 & & CH_3
\end{array}
$$

Acetomonas strains are able to oxidize 1,4-butanediol to succinate with γ-hydroxybutyric acid as intermediate:

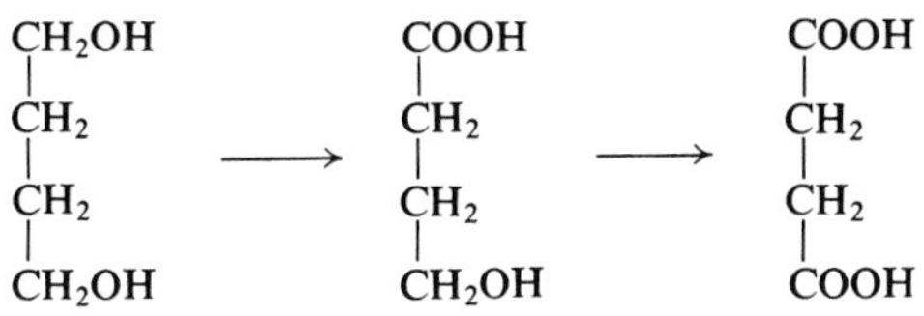

$$
\begin{array}{ccccc}
CH_2OH & & COOH & & COOH \\
| & & | & & | \\
CH_2 & & CH_2 & & CH_2 \\
| & \longrightarrow & | & \longrightarrow & | \\
CH_2 & & CH_2 & & CH_2 \\
| & & | & & | \\
CH_2OH & & CH_2OH & & COOH
\end{array}
$$

Acetobacter strains of the *mesoxydans, oxydans,* and *peroxydans* group can oxidize succinate even further through the TCA cycle.

Glutaric acid is produced in two steps from 1,5-pentanediol by *Acetomonas suboxydans* forming α-hydroxyvaleric acid as intermediate. The same oxidation

$$
\begin{array}{ccccc}
\text{CH}_2\text{OH} & & \text{COOH} & & \text{COOH} \\
| & & | & & | \\
(\text{CH}_2)_3 & \longrightarrow & (\text{CH}_2)_3 & \longrightarrow & (\text{CH}_2)_3 \\
| & & | & & | \\
\text{CH}_2\text{OH} & & \text{CH}_2\text{OH} & & \text{COOH}
\end{array}
$$

system applies for 1,6-hexanediol, which oxidizes to adipic acid via a hydroxy-caproic acid and for 1,7-heptanediol, which forms pimelic acid with 7-hydroxy-heptylic acid as intermediate.

$$
\begin{array}{ccccc}
\text{CH}_2\text{OH} & & \text{COOH} & & \text{COOH} \\
| & & | & & | \\
(\text{CH}_2)_4 & \longrightarrow & (\text{CH}_2)_4 & \longrightarrow & (\text{CH}_2)_4 \\
| & & | & & | \\
\text{CH}_2\text{OH} & & \text{CH}_2\text{OH} & & \text{COOH}
\end{array}
$$

$$
\begin{array}{ccccc}
\text{CH}_2\text{OH} & & \text{COOH} & & \text{COOH} \\
| & & | & & | \\
(\text{CH}_2)_5 & \longrightarrow & (\text{CH}_2)_5 & \longrightarrow & (\text{CH}_2)_5 \\
| & & | & & | \\
\text{CH}_2\text{OH} & & \text{CH}_2\text{OH} & & \text{COOH}
\end{array}
$$

Oxidation of Secondary Alcohol Groups

Experiments have shown that the mode of attack on secondary alcohol groups depends upon the distance between both groups in the molecules. When groups are adjacent as in 1,2-propanediol, only secondary alcohol groups are oxidized.

$$
\begin{array}{ccccc}
\text{CH}_3 & & \text{CH}_3 & & \text{CH}_3 \\
| & & | & & | \\
\text{HCOH} & \rightleftharpoons & \text{C}{=}\text{O} & \longleftarrow & \text{HOCH} \\
| & & | & & | \\
\text{CH}_2\text{OH} & & \text{CH}_2\text{OH} & & \text{CH}_2\text{OH} \\
\text{D}(-) & & \text{acetol} & & \text{L}(+)
\end{array}
$$

When both groups are separated by a CH_2 group as in 1,3-butanediol the opposite happens; The primary alcohol group is oxidized but the secondary CHOH group is not attacked at all.

Acetobacter rancens(30) is able to oxidize acetol further:

$$
\text{acetol} \dashrightarrow \text{pyruvate} \xrightarrow{\;\;\text{CO}_2\uparrow\;\;} \text{acetaldehyde} \dashrightarrow \text{acetate}
$$
$$
\downarrow
$$
$$
\text{acetoin}
$$

The mechanisms of oxidation of 2,3-butanediol and acetoin are not clear as yet, although it appears that *meso*-2,3-butanediol is oxidized to L(+)-acetoin, D(−)-, and L(+)-2,3-butanediol to D(−)-acetoin. The oxidation of acetoin may be possible for all strains of the *mesoxydans* and *oxydans* group.

QUINATE METABOLISM

Little attention has been given so far to the cyclohexane-diols, -triols, and -tetrols. Quinate oxidase was found in five out of sixty-six strains of *Acetomonas oxidans* tested (65a). The three acids studied are closely related with regard to the relative position of the secondary OH group in the molecule. Quinic acid and dihydroshikimic acid have an axial OH group at C-5, whereas shikimic acid has a "quasi-axial" group at C-3 (see Scheme 7.3). The oxidation of

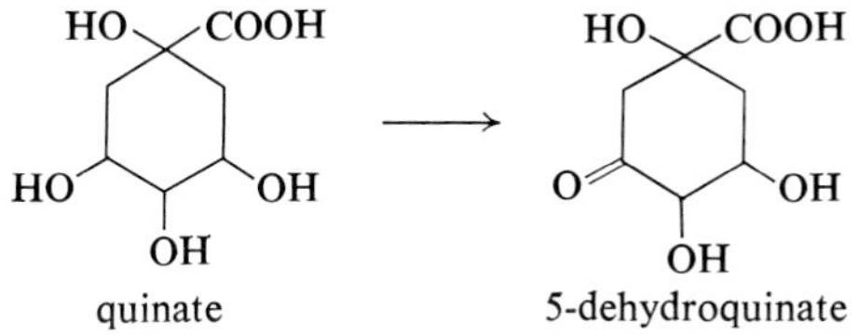

quinate   5-dehydroquinate

SCHEME 7.3

quinate does not go further than 5-dehydroquinate. The oxidase involved in this reaction is not stimulated by addition of NAD^+, $NADP^+$, FAD, FMN, or riboflavin, but all indications lead to the involvement of cytochrome 555 (= cytochrome o). It was therefore suggested to name the enzyme "quinate–cytochrome 555" (*Acetomonas oxydans*) oxidoreductase (65a).

Both strains of *Acetomonas oxydans* CR 49 and X 1/1 showed a shikimate dehydrogenase activity. Since the activity of NADPH oxidase (4a), which is

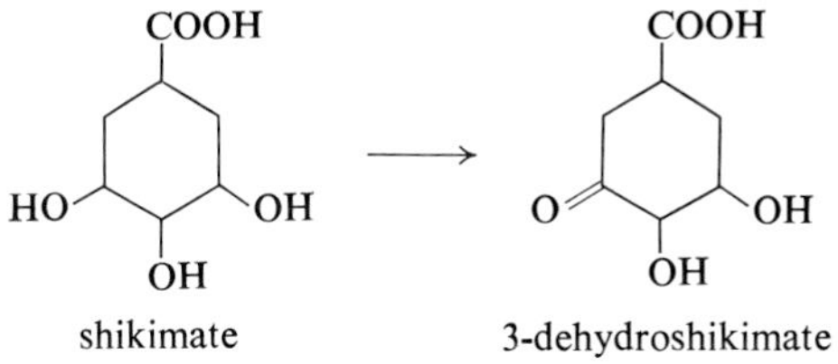

shikimate   3-dehydroshikimate

SCHEME 7.4

part of the shikimate oxidase system, was very weak in strain CR 49, it is thought (65a) that a primary dehydrogenase probably tightly bound to cytochrome 555 (*A. oxydans*) may be involved (see Scheme 7.4).

Although a good yield was observed from the oxidation of dihydroshikimate (65a) the enzyme catalyzing the reaction is not known. It is assumed that a flavoprotein together with cytochrome 555 may also be involved here.

These three examples of oxidations of acidic cyclohexane derivatives by *Acetomonas oxydans* give a good indication that it follows the same rules as those for nonacidic derivatives, namely, that only axial hydroxyl groups are oxidized.

REFERENCES

1. Atkinson, D. E. (1956). The oxidation of ethanol and tricarboxylic acid cycle intermediates by *Acetobacter peroxydans*. *J. Bacteriol.* **72**, 195.
2. Atkinson, D. E. (1956). Hydrogen metabolism in *Acetobacter peroxydans*. *J. Bacteriol.* **72**, 189.
3. Atkinson, D. E., and Serat, W. F. (1960). The cofactor specificity of ethanol dehydrogenase from *Acetobacter peroxydans*. *Biochim. Biophys. Acta* **39**, 154.
3a. Avigad, G., and England, S. (1965). 5-Keto-D-fructose. I. Chemical characterization and analytical determination of the dicarboxylhexose produced by *Gluconobacter cerinus*. *J. Biol. Chem.* **240**, 2290.
4. Avigad, G., England, S., and Pifko, S. (1966). 5-Keto-D-fructose. IV. A specific nicotinamide adenine dinucleotide phosphate-linked reductase from *Gluconobacter cerinus*. *J. Biol. Chem.* **241**, 373.
4a. Balinsky, D., and Davies, D. D. (1961). Aromatic biosynthesis in higher plants. I. Preparation and properties of dehydroshikimic reductase. *Biochem. J.* **80**, 292.
5. Benziman, M., and Abeliovitz, A. (1964). Metabolism of dicarboxylic acids in *Acetobacter xylinum*. *J. Bacteriol.* **87**, 270.
6. Benziman, M., and Heller, N. (1964). Oxalacetate decarboxylation and oxalacetate-CO_2 exchange in *Acetobacter xylinum*. *J. Bacteriol.* **88**, 1678.
6a. Benziman, M., and Levy, L. (1966). Phosphorylation coupled to malate oxidation in *Acetobacter xylinum*. *Biochem. Biophys. Res. Commun.* **24**, 214.
7. Bertrand, G. (1904). *Ann. Chim. Phys.* **8**, 181; cited by Rainbow (52).
8. Castor, L. N., and Chance, B. (1955). Photochemical action spectra of carbon monoxide-inhibited respiration. *J. Biol. Chem.* **217**, 453.
9. Castor, L. N., and Chance, B. (1959). Photochemical determination of the oxidases of bacteria. *J. Biol. Chem.* **234**, 1589.
10. Cheldelin, V. H. (1961). The acetic acid bacteria. *In* "Metabolic Pathways in Microorganisms." E. R. Squibb lectures on chemistry of microbial products. Wiley, New York.
11. Cooksey, K. E., and Rainbow, C. (1962). Metabolic patterns in acetic acid bacteria. *J. Gen. Microbiol.* **27**, 135.
12. Datta, A. G., and Katznelson, H. (1957). Oxidation of 2,5-diketo-gluconate by a cell-free extract from *Acetobacter melanogenum*. *Nature* **179**, 153.
13. DeLey, J. (1959). On the formation of acetoin by *Acetobacter*. *J. Gen. Microbiol.* **21**, 352.
14. DeLey, J. (1961). Comparative carbohydrate metabolism and a proposal for a phylogenetic relationship of the acetic acid bacteria. *J. Gen. Microbiol.* **24**, 31.
15. DeLey, J. (1963). The use of *i*-erythritol for the classification of acetic acid bacteria. *Antonie van Leeuwenhoek J. Microbiol. Serol.* **29**, 177.
16. DeLey, J., and Kersters, K. (1964). Oxidation of aliphatic glycols by acetic acid bacteria. *Bacteriol. Rev.* **28**, 164.
17. DeLey, J., and Schell, J. (1959). Studies on the metabolism of *Acetobacter peroxydans*. II. The enzymic mechanism of lactate metabolism. *Biochim. Biophys. Acta* **35**, 154.
18. DeLey, J., and Schell, J. (1962). Lactate and pyruvate catabolism in acetic acid bacteria. *J. Gen. Microbiol.* **29**, 589.

19. DeLey, J., and Stouthamer, A. J. (1959). The mechanism and localization of hexonate metabolism in *Acetobacter suboxydans* and *Acetobacter melanogenum*. *Biochim. Biophys. Acta* **34**, 171.

20. DeLey, J., and Vervloet, V. (1961). Studies on the metabolism of *Acetobacter peroxydans*. III. Some properties and localization of peroxidases. *Biochim. Biophys. Acta* **50**, 1.

21. Englard, S., and Avigad, G. (1965). 5-Keto-D-fructose. II. Patterns of formation and of associated dehydrogenase activities in *Gluconobacter cerinus*. *J. Biol. Chem.* **240**, 2297.

22. Englard, S., Avigad, G., and Prosky, L. (1965). 5-Keto-D-fructose. III. Proof of structure based on stereospecific patterns of enzymatic reduction. *J. Biol. Chem.* **240**, 2302.

23. Frateur, J. (1950). Essai sur la systematique des Acetobacters. *Cellule Rec. Cytol. Histol.* **53**, 297; cited by DeLey (14).

24. Galante, E., Scalaffa, P., and Lanzani, G. A. (1963). Attivita Enzymatiche di *Acetobacter suboxydans*. I. Glucosiodeidrogenasi. *Enzymologia* **26**, 23.

25. Gromet, Z., Schramm, M., and Hestrin, S. (1957). Synthesis of cellulose by *Acetobacter xylinum*. IV. Enzyme systems present in a crude extract of glucose-grown cells. *Biochem. J.* **67**, 679.

26. Hauge, J. G., King, T. E., and Cheldelin, V. H. (1954). Alternate pathways of glycerol oxidation in *Acetobacter suboxydans*. *Nature* **174**, 1104.

27. Hauge, J. G., King, T. E., and Cheldelin, V. H. (1955). Alternate conversions of glycerol to dihydroxyacetone in *Acetobacter suboxydans*. *J. Biol. Chem.* **214**, 1.

28. Hauge, J. G., King, T. E., and Cheldelin, V. H. (1955). Oxidation of dihydroxyacetone via the pentose cycle in *Acetobacter suboxydans*. *J. Biol. Chem.* **214**, 11.

29. Hochster, R. M. (1962). Specificity of the C-1 keto sugar diphosphatase of *Xanthomonas phaseoli*. *Nature* **193**, 71.

30. Hooft Visser't, F. (1925). Biochemische onderzoekingen over het geslacht *Acetobacter*. Ph.D. Thesis, Technische Univ. Delft; cited by DeLey and Kersters (16).

31. Hromatka, O., and Polesovsky, W. (1962). Untersuchungen über die Essiggärung. VII. Über die Oxydation verschiedener primärer Alkohole und Glykole. *Enzymologia* **24**, 372.

32. Iwasaki, Y. (1960). Components of the electron-transferring system in *Acetobacter suboxydans* and reconstruction of the lactate oxidation system. *J. Plant Cell Physiol. (Tokyo)* **1**, 207.

33. Katznelson, H. (1958). Hexose phosphate metabolism by *Acetobacter melanogenum*. *Can. J. Microbiol.* **4**, 25.

34. Katznelson, H., Tanenbaum, S. W., and Tatum, E. L. (1953). Glucose, gluconate, and 2-ketogluconate oxidation by *Acetobacter melanogenum*. *J. Biol. Chem.* **204**, 43.

35. Kersters, K., and DeLey, J. (1963). The oxidation of glycols by acetic acid bacteria. *Biochim. Biophys. Acta* **71**, 311.

36. Kersters, K., and DeLey, J. (1963). The oxidation of glycols by acetic acid bacteria. *Biochim. Biophys. Acta* **71**, 311.

37. Kersters, K., Wood, W. A., and DeLey, J. (1965). Polyol dehydrogenases of *Gluconobacter oxydans*. *J. Biol. Chem.* **240**, 965.

38. King, T. E., and Cheldelin, V. H. (1954). Oxidations in *Acetobacter suboxydans*. *Biochim. Biophys. Acta* **14**, 108.

39. King, T. E., and Cheldelin, V. H. (1954). Pyruvic carboxylase in *Acetobacter suboxydans*. *J. Biol. Chem.* **208**, 821.

40. King, T. E., and Cheldelin, V. H. (1956). Oxidation of acetaldehyde by *Acetobacter suboxydans*. *J. Biol. Chem.* **220**, 177.

328   7. ACETIC ACID BACTERIA

41. King, T. E., Kawasaki, E. H., and Cheldelin, V. H. (1956). Tricarboxylic acid cycle activity in *Acetobacter pasteurianum. J. Bacteriol.* **72**, 418.
42. Kitos, P. A., Wang, C. H., Mohler, B. A., King, T. E., and Cheldelin, V. H. (1958), Glucose and gluconate dissimilation in *Acetobacter suboxydans. J. Biol. Chem.* **233**, 1295.
43. Klungsöyr, L., King, T. E., and Cheldelin, V. H. (1957). Oxidative phosphorylation in *Acetobacter suboxydans. J. Biol. Chem.* **227**, 135.
44. Kornberg, H. L., and Phizackerley, P. J. R. (1961). Malate oxidation by *Pseudomonas* spp. *Biochem. J.* **79**, 10P.
45. Lamborg, M., and Kaplan, N. O. (1960). Adaptive formation of a vic glycol dehydrogenase in *Aerobacter aerogenes. Biochim. Biophys. Acta* **38**, 284.
46. Lamborg, M., and Kaplan, N. O. (1960). A comparison of some vic glycol dehydrogenase systems found in *Aerobacter aerogenes. Biochim. Biophys. Acta* **38**, 272.
46a. Leifson, E. (1954). The flagellation and taxonomy of species of *Acetobacter. Antonie van Leeuwenhoek, J. Microbiol. Serol.* **20**, 102.
47. Nakayama, T., and DeLey, J. (1965). Localization and distribution of alcohol-cytochrome 553 reductase in acetic acid bacteria. *Antonie van Leeuwenhoek, J. Microbiol. Serol.* **31**, 205.
48. Okamoto, K. (1963). Enzymatic studies on the formation of 5-ketogluconic acid. I. Glucose dehydrogenase. *J. Biochem. (Tokyo)* **53**, 348.
49. Okamoto, K. (1963). Enzymatic studies on the formation of 5-ketogluconic acid. II. 5-Ketogluconate reductase. *J. Biochem. (Tokyo)* **53**, 448.
50. Peterson, M. H., Friedland, W. C., Denison, F. W., Jr., and Sylvester, J. C. (1956). The conversion of mannitol to fructose by *Acetobacter suboxydans. Appl. Microbiol.* **4**, 316.
51. Polesovsky, W. (1951). Untersuchungen über die Bildung von Carbonsäuren durch submerse Vergärung primärer Alkohole. Ph.D. Thesis, Univ. Wien, Vienna, Austria; cited by DeLey and Kersters (16).
52. Rainbow, C. (1961). The biochemistry of the acetobacters. *Progr. Ind. Microbiol.* **3**, 43.
53. Rainbow, C. (1966). Nutrition and metabolism of acetic acid bacteria. *Wallerstein Lab. Commun.* **29**, 5.
54. Rao, M. R. R. (1955). Pyruvate and acetate metabolism in *Acetobacter suboxydans* and *Acetobacter aceti*. Thesis, Urbana, Illinois, cited by DeLey (13).
55. Ravel, D. N., and Wolfe, R. G. (1963). Malic dehydrogenase. V. Kinetic studies of substrate inhibition by oxalacetate. *Biochemistry* **2**, 220.
55a. Schramm, M., and Racker, E. (1957). Formation of erythrose-4-phosphate and acetyl-phosphate by a phosphoroclastic cleavage of fructose-6-phosphate. *Nature* **179**, 1349.
56. Schramm, M., Gromet, Z., and Hestrin, S. (1957). Role of hexose phosphate in synthesis of cellulose by *Acetobacter xylinum. Nature* **179**, 28.
56a. Schramm, M., Klybas, V., and Racker, E. (1958). Phosphorolytic cleavage of fructose-6-phosphate by fructose-6-phosphate phosphoketolase from *Acetobacter xylinum. J. Biol. Chem.* **233**, 1283.
57. Scopes, A. W. (1962). The infrared spectra of some acetic acid bacteria. *J. Gen. Microbiol.* **28**, 69.
58. Shaw, D. R. D., and Bygrave, F. L. (1966). NAD⁺-linked D-mannitol dehydrogenase in *Acetobacter suboxydans. Biochim. Biophys. Acta* **113**, 608.
58a. Shchalkunova, S. A. (1966). The effect of phosphates on the growth of acetic acid bacteria and the oxidation of glycerol by them. *Tr. Petergofsk. Biol. Inst., Leningr. Gós. Univ.* **19**, 57; *Chem. Abstr.* **65**, 19024 (1966).

59. Shimwell, J. C., and Carr, J. G. (1960). Support for differentiation of *Acetobacter* and *Acetomonas*. *Antonie van Leeuwenhoek, J. Microbiol. Serol.* **26**, 430.
60. Shimwell, J. L. (1958). Flagellation and taxonomy of *Acetobacter* and *Acetomonas*. *Antonie van Leeuwenhoek, J. Microbiol. Serol.* **24**, 187.
61. Skerman, V. B. D. (1967). "A Guide to the Identification of the Genera of Bacteria," 2nd ed. Williams & Wilkins, Baltimore, Maryland.
62. Stouthamer, A. H. (1959). Oxidative possibilities in the catalase positive *Acetobacter* species. *Antonie van Leeuwenhoek, J. Microbiol. Serol.* **25**, 242.
62a. Stouthamer, A. H. (1962). Energy production in *Gluconobacter liquefaciens*. *Biochim. Biophys. Acta* **56**, 19.
63. Tanenbaum, S. W. (1956). The metabolism of *Acetobacter peroxidans*. I. Oxidative enzymes. *Biochim. Biophys. Acta* **21**, 335.
64. Tanenbaum, S. W. (1956). The metabolism of *Acetobacter peroxydans*. II. Hydrogen-activating and related enzymes. *Biochim. Biophys. Acta* **21**, 343.
65. White, G. A., and Wang, C. H. (1964). The dissimilation of glucose and gluconate by *Acetobacter xylinum*. 1. The origin and the fate of triose phosphate. *Biochem. J.* **90**, 408.
65a. Whiting, G. C., and Coggins, R. A. (1967). The oxidation of D-quinate and related acids by *Acetomonas oxydans*. *Biochem. J.* **102**, 283.
66. Williams, P. J. deB., and Rainbow, C. (1964). Enzymes of the tricarboxylic acid cycle in acetic acid bacteria. *J. Gen. Microbiol.* **35**, 237.
67. Zhdan-Pushkina, S. M., and Kreneva, R. A. (1963). Sorbitol oxidation with reference to intensive and delayed reproduction of *Acetobacter suboxydans*. *Mikrobiologiya* **32**, 711.

SUPPLEMENTARY READINGS

Daniel, R. M., and Redfearn, E. R. (1968). The reduced nicotinamide adenine dinucleotide oxidase system of *Acetobacter suboxydans*. *Biochem. J.* **106**, 49P.
Ramamurti, K., and Jackson, C. P. (1966). Utilization of glycerol by *Acetobacter acetigenum* under different cultural conditions. *Canad. J. Microbiol.* **12**, 795.

8
LACTIC ACID BACTERIA

The lactic acid bacteria are represented by species of the *Lactobacillaceae* which are well-known spoilage organisms in food such as dairy products. They are morphologically a heterogeneous group and are biochemically characterized by their main end product, lactic acid. These organisms are gram-positive, nonsporulating cocci or rods. Some are catalase positive and some catalase negative. All species of this family are obligate fermenters and are roughly subdivided into five different groups(65) as shown in Table 8.1.

TABLE 8.1

FIVE GROUPS OF LACTIC ACID SPECIES[a]

Cell form	Nature of fermentation	Name of genus
Cocci in chains	Homofermentative	*Streptococcus*
Cocci in chains	Heterofermentative	*Leuconostoc*
Cocci in tetrads	Homofermentative	*Pediococcus*
Rods, usually in chains	Homofermentative	*Lactobacillus*
Rods, usually in chains	Heterofermentative	

[a] From Stanier *et al.*(65). Reprinted with permission of Prentice-Hall.

There is now general acceptance of two broad divisions of the lactobacilli into homofermentative and heterofermentative strains(7), based obviously on the percentage of by-products other than lactic acid formed during fermentation. If all strains would either produce less than 10% or more than 40% by-products, this division would be easy, but in practice this is not so. Therefore an indefinite demarcation line exists between homo- and heterofermentative types. Davis and Hayward(15,16,43) claim that the main characteristic of taxonomic importance, the proportion of end product formed in fermentation, is reasonably constant, and that borderline cases or apparent changes from the homofermentative character result from inadequate initial purification. There is, however, insufficient evidence presented to support this claim that the by-products of homofermentation are constant. The heterofermentation end

TABLE 8.2

CONFIGURATION OF LACTIC ACID PRODUCED BY
VARIOUS MICROORGANISMS[a]

Organisms	Configuration
(I) Homofermenter	
Streptococcus sp.	L(+)[b]
Lactobacillus caucascus and L. lactis	D(−)[c]
L. leichmanii	D(−)
L. helveticus and *L. bifidus*	D,L[d]
L. plantarum	D,L
L. thermophilus and *L. delbrückii*	L(+)
L. bulgaricus	D,L or D(−)
L. casei	L(+), L(+) and D(−)
Pediococcus sp.	D,L
Bacillus sp.	L(+)
Clostridium sp.	D,L
Butyribacterium rettgeri	D,L
(II) Heterofermenter	
Lactobacillus brevis, L. buchneri,	
L. pasteurianus, and *L. fermenti*	D,L
Leuconostoc sp.	D(−)
Microbacterium sp.	L(+)
Rhizopus sp.	L(+)
(III) Mixed Fermenter	
Serratia sp.	D(−)

[a] From Wood(71).
[b] L(+)—2 μ salt × 2H$_2$O α D = −8.25° (4%; 25°C); H$_2$O = 12.89%.
[c] D(−)—2 μ salt × 2H$_2$O α D = +8.25° (4%; 25°C); H$_2$O = 12.89%.
[d] D,L—2 μ salt × 3H$_2$O α D = ±0; H$_2$O = 18.18%.

products increase as sugar concentration increases(12). These and other observations(16a, 22, 59, 62) support far more the thesis that adverse conditions favor the production of by-products.

A characteristic feature of the lactic acid produced by the *Lactobacillaceae* is that the optical activity of the acid depends upon the strain of organism (53). Two factors appear to be responsible for this final activity:

(1) The stereospecificity of the lactate dehydrogenase involved. Organisms producing D,L-lactic acid may contain the enzyme for the D-isomer as well as that for the L-isomer. These two different enzymes may or may not be NAD-linked. The organism could also contain either or both of the isomeric dehydrogenases and form D- or L-lactic acid or *meso*-lactic acid.

(2) The presence or absence of a lactate racemase. In some cases, strains of the *Lactobacillaceae* produce racemic mixtures irrespective of the specificity of the lactic dehydrogenase present, which can only be attributed to a racemase.

In *Lactobacillus plantarum*, for example, both L- and D-stereospecific NAD-linked dehydrogenases are operating with equal activity in glucose-metabolizing cells(21,57). However, Kitahara(52) suggested that the production of D,L-lactic acid may result from the joint action of D-lactate dehydrogenase (D-lactate:NAD oxidoreductase, E.C. 1.1.1.28) and a lactate racemase (E.C. 5.1.2.1). Table 8.2 gives some idea on the distribution of lactic acid configuration produced by various microorganisms.

HOMOFERMENTATION

All strains of the *Lactobacillaceae* which produce as much as 1.8 moles of lactic acid per mole of glucose with minor amounts of acetic acid, ethanol, and carbon dioxide are grouped as the homofermenters. The genera represented are *Diplococcus*, *Streptococcus*, *Pediococcus*, *Lactobacillus*, and *Microbacterium*, which range from facultative anaerobic to aerobic microorganisms.

Existence of the EMP Pathway in the Lactic Acid Bacteria

The best evidence for the operation of the EMP pathway comes from experiments using labeled glucose(18). Although it is thought that *Streptococcus faecalis* ferments glucose by a combination of EMP, HMP, and ED pathways, transaldolase and 2-keto-3-deoxy phosphogluconate aldolase are considered to be inducible enzymes(64). In *Streptococcus faecalis*, the nature of the end products of fermentation is very much dependent on cultural conditions. At the pH value of 5.0 to 6.0 at which the fermentation occurs pyruvate is reduced by a stereospecific lactate dehydrogenase to D-, L-, or D,L-lactic acid. At neutral or slightly alkaline pH, however, pyruvate metabolism leads to the production of formic and acetic acid and ethanol in the ratio 2:1:1, a typical heterolactic fermentation(39).

As well as fermenting glucose, homofermentative microorganisms also use fructose, mannose, galactose, and disaccharides such as lactose, maltose, and sucrose as substrates. These sugars are presumably converted into intermediates of the EMP pathway by inducible enzymes. In *Streptococcus pyogenes* the fermentation of galactose accounts for 50% of the galactose-carbon, whereas the remainder is found in acetate, formate, and ethanol (2:1:1). This metabolism is very similar to the gluconate metabolism (63, 64) of *Strepto-coccus faecalis* at high pH. It is possible that another independent pathway may be involved (18).

The enzymology of the homofermentative bacteria has been studied most completely with *Microbacterium lacticum* (56, 66) and shows quite clearly the sole use of the EMP pathway. Since, however, a great number of homolactic organisms can form products other than lactic acid in major amounts under certain conditions, it has been proposed that "homolactic" should refer only to those lactic acid bacteria which contain fructose diphosphate aldolase (E.C. 4.1.2.13), but not dehydrogenases for glucose 6-phosphate and 6-phos-phogluconate, whereas "fermentative homofermenters" contain both the fructose diphosphate aldolase and the glucose 6-phosphate dehydrogenase (9). Isotope-labeled experiments with homofermenters leave no doubt that the EMP pathway is the quantitatively significant mechanism (32). However, further evidence is needed to justify this proposal. There is also no doubt that the present definition for homofermenters is not precise and needs modification.

HETEROFERMENTATION

Organisms which ferment hexoses with the production of less than 1.8 moles of lactic acid per mole of glucose and in addition ethanol, acetate, glycerol, mannitol, and carbon dioxide are called "heterofermenters." The main group of organisms are strains of *Leuconostoc*, some strains of *Lacto-bacillus*, the anaerobic peptostreptococci and the anaerobic species of *Eubacterium*, *Catenabacterium*, *Ramibacterium*, and *Bifidobacterium*. There exist several types of heterofermentative mechanisms (18):

(1) Leuconostoc-type heterofermentation, which results in the formation of 0.8 mole of lactic acid, 0.1–0.2 mole of acetate, 0.9 mole of CO_2, 0.8 mole of ethanol, and 0.2–0.4 mole of glycerol. Glycerol is not formed in all cases.

(2) Peptostreptococcus-type heterofermentation, whereby lactic and pro-pionic acids are the end products of glucose fermentation.

(3) A third type of heterofermentation which is characteristic of all those bacteria which produce lactic and butyric acids as the end products of glucose metabolism.

It is, of course, possible that two of these patterns may be superimposed to varying degrees. *Lactobacillus brevis*, for example, metabolizes glucose if grown at 24°C heterofermentatively but requires an external hydrogen acceptor if grown at 37°C:

$$\text{glucose} + H_2O \rightarrow \text{lactic acid} + \text{acetate} + CO_2 + 4H^+$$

It has also been observed that fermentation of fructose occurs at 37°C with the formation of mannitol:

$$3 \text{ fructose } \rightarrow 1 \text{ lactate} + 1 \text{ acetate} + 2 \text{ mannitol} + 1 CO_2$$
$$1 \text{ glucose} + 2 \text{ fructose } \rightarrow 1 \text{ lactate} + 1 \text{ acetate} + 2 \text{ mannitol} + 1 CO_2$$

Under these conditions fructose acts as the hydrogen acceptor. Unlike the clostridia, the heterofermentive lactobacilli are unable to eliminate hydrogen as hydrogen gas. The more common internal electron acceptors of hetero-fermentation are pyruvate, dihydroxyacetone phosphate, or acetaldehyde. Acetyl CoA can also serve as electron acceptor but only in a limited number of genera. Stoichiometry is adhered to in some organisms such as *Lactobacillus brevis*, but less so in others, and it is never as significant as in the homo-fermenters.

Leuconostoc species and *Lactobacillus plantarum* possess the so-called phosphoketolase pathway (see Chapter 4). All three other pathways EMP, HMP, and ED were found to be absent. In the over-all reaction glucose is fermented to CO_2, ethanol, and lactate with the production of one mole of ATP per mole of glucose (61), which is only half the energy produced by the homofermenters.

Investigations into the presence of enzymes in heterofermentative micro-organisms have revealed the presence of hexokinase (ATP:D-hexose 6-phos-photransferase, E.C. 2.7.1.1), phosphoglycerate kinase (ATP:3-phospho-D-glycerate 1-phosphotransferase, E.C. 2.7.2.3), glycerophosphate dehydrogenase (L-glycerol-3-phosphate:(acceptor) oxidoreductase, E.C. 1.1.99.5), D-lactate dehydrogenase (D-lactate:NAD oxidoreductase, E.C. 1.1.1.28), ethanol dehydrogenase (alcohol:NAD oxidoreductase, E.C. 1.1.1.1)(20), acetaldehyde dehydrogenase, and acetoin dehydrogenase (acetoin:NAD oxidoreductase, E.C. 1.1.1.5). Fructose diphosphate aldolase (E.C. 4.1.2.13) and triose phosphate isomerase (D-glyceraldehyde 3-phosphate ketol isomerase, E.C. 5.3.1.1) were absent. The lack of the latter two enzymes makes it impossible for the EMP pathway to function. Enzymes of the HMP pathway present were a glucose 6-phosphate dehydrogenase (E.C. 1.1.1.49) and the 6-phospho-gluconate dehydrogenase (E.C. 1.1.1.43)(47,71).

On the basis of enzymatic studies, Buyze *et al.*(9) concluded that three types of lactic acid bacteria exist:

(1) obligate homofermenters, containing fructose diphosphate aldolase (E.C. 4.1.2.13) but no glucose 6-phosphate dehydrogenase (E.C. 1.1.1.49) and no 6-phosphogluconate dehydrogenase (E.C. 1.1.1.43);

(2) obligate heterofermenters, containing the dehydrogenases mentioned under (1) but no fructose diphosphate aldolase; and

(3) facultative homofermenters, containing all three enzymes and able to use either of the pathways.

A different approach was taken in using infrared spectra (34) for grouping the different species of lactobacilli. With only a few exceptions, the spectra could be grouped into five distinct spectral types, each of which appeared to correspond to a species of lactobacilli or a group of related species.

CITRATE METABOLISM

Although the lactic acid was always considered to be the sole end product of homofermentative bacteria it was noted that *Streptococcus lactis, Streptococcus citrovorum*, and *Streptococcus paracitrovorum* play an important role in flavor development in milk, butter, and cheese (41). This production of flavor was found to be owing to the production of acetoin and diacetyl from citrate

$$\text{citrate} \rightarrow \text{oxalacetate} + \text{acetate}$$

$$\text{oxalacetate} \rightarrow \text{pyruvate} + CO_2$$

$$2 \text{ pyruvate} \rightarrow \text{acetoin} + 2 CO_2 (28)$$

In the lactic acid bacteria, therefore, energy can also be derived by citrate metabolism (10, 37, 42) in the absence of carbohydrate fermentation or lactate production. The balance of products is markedly dependent upon pH. If the pH increases, more acetate and formate are obtained at the expense of lactate and carbon dioxide (16b). Above pH 7.0 virtually no lactate is produced at all (71)

$$\text{citrate} \rightarrow CO_2 + \text{formate} + 2 \text{ acetate}$$

Whichever end products are formed, the first steps of citrate fermentation will always be the formation of pyruvate. The degradation of pyruvate is markedly pH-dependent:

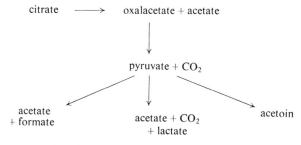

Streptococcus faecalis, when grown on citrate, produces the citrate-cleaving enzyme citratelyase (citrate oxalacetatelyase, E.C. 4.1.3.6) which is, in contrast to citrate synthase [citrate oxalacetatelyase (CoA acetylating), E.C. 4.1.3.7], independent of any cofactor and catalyzes the reaction:

$$\text{citrate} \rightarrow \text{oxalacetate} + \text{acetate}$$

Citric acid is also essential for the production of diacetyl(11).

HEXONIC ACID METABOLISM

In the lactic acid bacteria, the fermentation of hexonic acids resembles the fermentation of glucose:

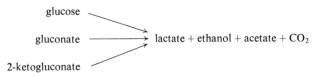

glucose

gluconate $\longrightarrow$ lactate + ethanol + acetate + CO_2

2-ketogluconate

Cells of *Streptococcus faecalis*, however, grown on gluconate ferment glucose, gluconate, and 2-ketogluconate, but glucose-grown cells were unable to attack gluconate. It was therefore assumed that a multiple pathway for gluconate fermentation must exist(64) and it was therefore postulated that after the phosphorylation of gluconate to 6-phosphogluconate had taken place, two pathways function equally for the further dissimilation of 6-phosphogluconate:

(1) oxidation of 6-phosphogluconate via the HMP and EMP pathways

$$3 \text{ 6-PG} \rightarrow 3 \text{ pentose phosphate} + 3 CO_2 + 6 H^+ \quad \text{(HMP)}$$

$$3 \text{ pentose phosphate} \rightarrow 2 \text{ F 6-P} + \text{glyceraldehyde 3-P} \quad \text{(HMP)}$$

$$2 \text{ F 6-P} + \text{glyceraldehyde 3-P} \rightarrow 5 \text{ lactate} \quad \text{(EMP)}$$

(2) oxidation of 6-phosphogluconate via the ED and EMP pathways

$$3 \text{ 6-PG} \rightarrow 3 \text{ pyruvate} + 3 \text{ glyceraldehyde 3-P} \quad \text{(ED)}$$

$$3 \text{ pyruvate} + 6 H^+ \rightarrow 3 \text{ lactate} \quad \text{(EMP)}$$

$$3 \text{ glyceraldehyde 3-P} \rightarrow 3 \text{ lactate} \quad \text{(EMP)}$$

The overall stoichiometry of these pathways would therefore be

$$\text{6-phosphogluconate} \rightarrow 1.83 \text{ lactate} + 0.5 CO_2$$

This has been worked out only for *Streptococcus faecalis*, which is considered a homofermentative organism. The details of the 2-ketogluconate metabolism have not been elucidated. By analogy to *Enterobacter cloacae*(17) and *Pseudomonas fluorescens*(58) it would be expected that 2-ketogluconate is first phosphorylated to 2-keto-6-phosphogluconate, followed by a reduction to 6-phosphogluconate. Whether the 6-phosphogluconate is metabolized as above or heterofermentatively is still obscure.

MANNITOL FORMATION

Lactobacillus plantarum and *Lactobacillus pentoaceticum* utilize identical pathways for the fermentation of pentoses and glucose but different pathways if fructose is the main carbon source (46). *Lactobacillus pentoaceticum* produces D-mannitol in addition to lactic and acetic acids, whereas *L. plantarum* produces lactic and acetic acid only:

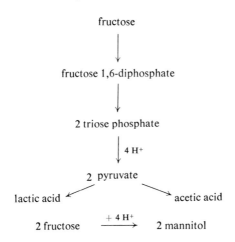

fructose

↓

fructose 1,6-diphosphate

↓

2 triose phosphate

↓ 4 H⁺

2 pyruvate

lactic acid ← → acetic acid

2 fructose $\xrightarrow{+\ 4\ H^+}$ 2 mannitol

Since the *Lactobacillaceae* have a cytochrome-independent electron transport system, the mannitol dehydrogenase is most probably mannitol: NAD oxidoreductase (E.C. 1.1.1.67). This enzyme must therefore be absent in *Lactobacillus plantarum*. Instead of having 3 moles of fructose as sole carbon source, glucose and fructose could also be present in the ratio of 1:2 in favor of fructose in order to form mannitol. The reaction is NAD-dependent and could therefore be used as a distinct characteristic for the identification and separation of these two species.

DEOXYRIBOSE METABOLISM

The metabolism of deoxyriboses does not occur in cells grown on glucose, arabinose, or xylose (46), but it can be induced in *Lactobacillus plantarum* and possibly in other species of the *Lactobacillaceae*. In the presence of a mixture of glucose and deoxyribose the metabolic breakdown of the latter begins only after full growth is reached. It is therefore very probable that growth occurs at the expense of glucose and that deoxyribose metabolism has no connection with growth and is also relatively independent of the quantity added or present. It is significant that no growth occurs during deoxyribose utilization. The inducible enzyme for this breakdown of deoxyribose has been shown to be deoxyribose phosphate aldolase (2-deoxy-D-ribose 5-phosphate acetaldehydelyase, E.C. 4.1.2.1), which catalyzes the reaction

2-deoxy-D-ribose phosphate → D-glyceraldehyde 3-P + acetaldehyde

D-Glyceraldehyde 3-phosphate, of course, can be broken down to lactic acid since *L. plantarum* possesses all enzymes of the EMP pathway, and acetaldehyde is converted to acetate. The end products of this metabolism are therefore lactic acid and acetate. The net energy yield is 1 mole of ATP per mole deoxyribose fermented (29).

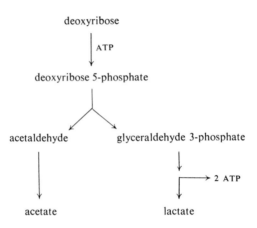

The first phosphorylation step requires ATP and deoxyribose kinase.

POLYSACCHARIDE FORMATION

The production of large mucoid colonies is a well-established feature of *Leuconostoc*, a heterofermentative chain-forming coccus grown in high sucrose plant extracts. It is also known that a number of strains of heterofermentative lactobacilli produce dextran following prolonged cultivation in acid media. The production of high molecular weight compounds is only mentioned here since their formation is a biosynthetic feature and not a catabolic one, but nonetheless characteristic for some species in the *Lactobacillaceae*.

BIOTIN DEGRADATION

Lactobacillus plantarum was found to metabolize D-biotin (3), which was converted to biotin vitamers. The biotin vitamers could be distinguished as being combinable and noncombinable with avidin (4). There is some evidence available (5) which suggests that *L. plantarum* may possess an enzyme system which not only converts biotin into vitamers but also metabolizes oxybiotin and desthiobiotin to products which are not utilizable by *Saccharomyces cerevisiae* and are still unknown. *Lactobacillus plantarum* is not unique in its biotin metabolism since *L. casei* (6) appears to have a similar system.

Lactate Metabolism by Group N Streptococci

A new pathway has recently been reported by Lees and Jago (56a) for group N streptococci. These bacteria, namely, *Streptococcus diacetilactis*, *S. lactis*, and *S. cremoris* grow on lactose and casein hydrolysate, whereby they utilize threonine with the formation of glycine and acetaldehyde:

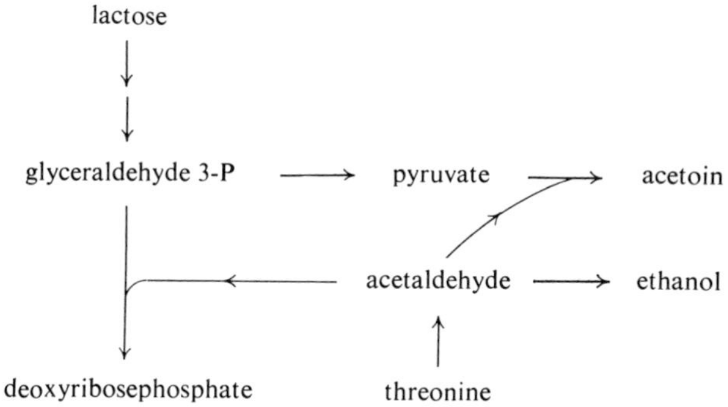

The enzyme catalyzing the utilization of threonine is threonine aldolase (L-threonine acetaldehydelyase, E.C. 4.1.2.5) whereby pyridoxal phosphate is

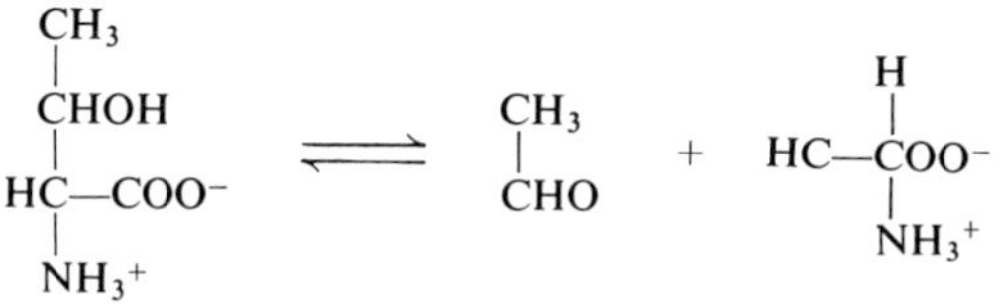

L-threonine glycine

required as cofactor. Acetaldehyde itself can be metabolized further via three different ways depending upon the availability of three enzymes as well as the utilization of lactose via the EMP pathway:

(1) Acetaldehyde and glyceraldehyde 3-phosphate are cleaved under the catalytic action of deoxyriboaldolase (2-deoxy-D-ribose 5-phosphate acetaldehydelyase, E.C. 4.1.2.4) to form deoxyribose phosphate:

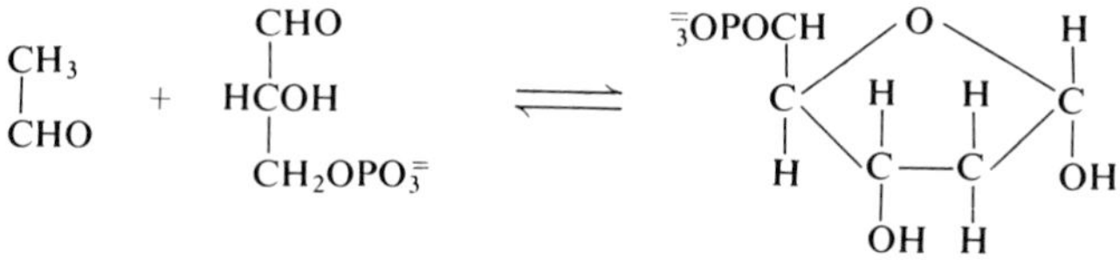

D-glyceraldehyde 3-phosphate 2-deoxyribose 5-P

(2) The group N streptococci also possess an enzyme, which cleaves pyruvate with acetaldehyde with the formation of acetoin:

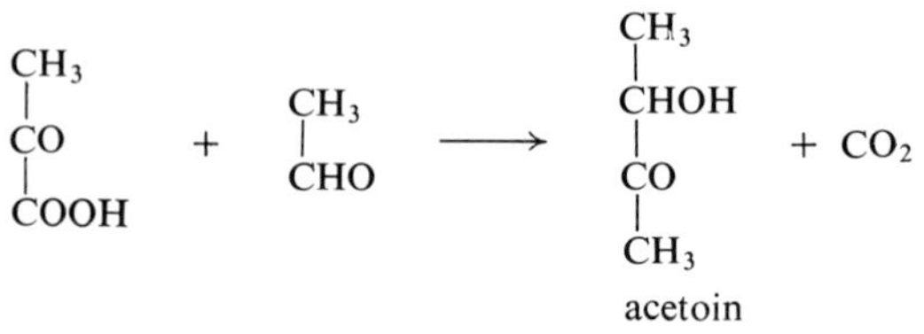

$$
\begin{array}{c}
CH_3 \\
| \\
CO \\
| \\
COOH
\end{array}
\quad + \quad
\begin{array}{c}
CH_3 \\
| \\
CHO
\end{array}
\quad \longrightarrow \quad
\begin{array}{c}
CH_3 \\
| \\
CHOH \\
| \\
CO \\
| \\
CH_3
\end{array}
\quad + \quad CO_2
$$

acetoin

The action of this enzyme has been called a synthetase reaction by Lees and Jago, who gave the enzyme the name "acetoin synthetase."

(3) The third possible acetaldehyde metabolism is directed by an active alcohol dehydrogenase (alcohol: NAD oxidoreductase, E.C. 1.1.1.1) which converts acetaldehyde to ethanol:

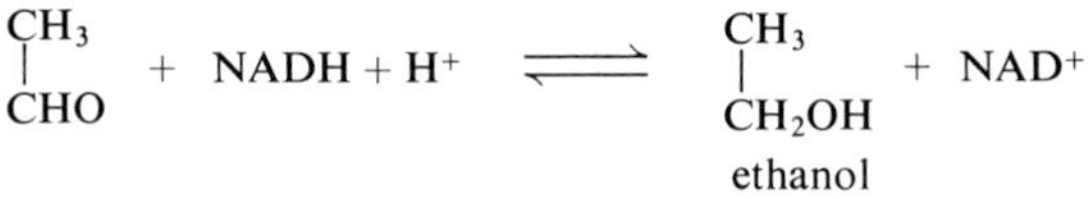

$$
\begin{array}{c}
CH_3 \\
| \\
CHO
\end{array}
\quad + \quad NADH + H^+ \quad \rightleftharpoons \quad
\begin{array}{c}
CH_3 \\
| \\
CH_2OH
\end{array}
\quad + \quad NAD^+
$$

ethanol

There may be, of course, a number of group N streptococci which do not follow this metabolism as was shown with the glycine requiring *Streptococcus cremoris* Z 8. This strain lacked the threonine aldolase.

ELECTRON TRANSPORT SYSTEMS

The *Lactobacillaceae* have powerful fermentative properties. They may contain cytochromes but do not use them. Their respiratory system depends upon a flavoprotein(26):

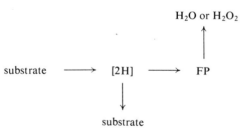

Under aerobic conditions the electrons are passed from the substrate to a flavoprotein which reacts with oxygen to produce H_2O or hydrogen peroxide. Under anaerobic conditions a second substrate serves as a hydrogen acceptor (27):

$$FPH + H^+ + O_2 \rightarrow FP^+ + H_2O_2 \qquad \text{2-electron transfer}$$

$$2(FPH + H^+) + O_2 \rightarrow 2FP^+ + 2H_2O \qquad \text{4-electron transfer}$$

In addition to these flavoproteins which react directly with oxygen there are a number of additional enzymes, diaphorases, in bacteria, yeasts, animals, and plants which may be reoxidized by artificial acceptors. There is now enough evidence to indicate that flavoprotein systems are the major link between substrate and oxygen in the lactic acid bacteria.

During the oxidation of glucose by cell suspensions of *Lactobacillus delbrückii* or *L. acidophilus* a 1:1 equivalence between oxygen uptake and hydrogen peroxide production was observed(1).

$$H_2A + O_2 \rightarrow A + H_2O_2$$

Since this observation was reported also with *L. bulgaricus*, it was postulated that these bacteria contain a flavoprotein which accounts for the entire respiration. However, *Streptococcus faecalis* exhibits rapid oxidation without the need for high oxygen concentrations, and peroxide was not always the end product but was broken down by flavoprotein NAD peroxidase (reduced NAD:hydrogen peroxide oxidoreductase, E.C. 1.11.1.1):

$$NADH + H^+ + H_2O_2 \rightarrow NAD^+ + 2H_2O$$

Other streptococci and lactobacilli were able to reduce peroxide in the presence of oxidizable substrate with enzymes which did not involve any heavy metal catalysts and were therefore called "atypical peroxidases."

The combined action of these two enzymes, FP-linked NAD oxidase(25) and FP-linked NAD peroxidase, provides the required 4-electron step of oxygen reduction to water(24):

$$NADH + H^+ + O_2 \rightarrow NAD^+ + H_2O_2$$
$$NADH + H^+ + H_2O_2 \rightarrow NAD^+ + H_2O$$
$$\overline{2NADH + H^+ + O_2 \rightarrow 2NAD^+ + 2H_2O}$$

Flavoprotein-linked Oxidases

At least five distinct flavoproteins which catalyze $NADH_2$ oxidation have been isolated from *Streptococcus faecalis*. Apart from the two mentioned above these are:

(a) cytochrome c reductase (reduced NAD:(acceptor) oxidoreductase, E.C. 1.6.99.3);
(b) diaphorase that uses 2,6-dichlorophenolindophenol, ferricyanide, and a series of quinones as oxidants; and
(c) a menadione reductase (reduced NAD(P):(acceptor) oxidoreductase, E.C. 1.6.99.2).

These five enzymes can be separated from each other(67) thus suggesting that all $NADH_2$ oxidase activity in a crude cell-free extract cannot be attributed to a single "NADH$_2$-oxidase." These oxidases are very unstable during isolation, but can be reactivated with thiol groups(68)

Flavoprotein-linked Peroxidases

Flavoprotein-linked peroxidases of lactic acid bacteria are divided into atypical and typical peroxidases:

(1) Atypical peroxidases—*Streptococcus mastitidis*, *Streptococcus faecalis* strain B 33 a, *Streptococcus mitis*, *Lactobacillus brevis*, and *Leuconostoc mesenteroides* strain 548 are catalase- and cytochrome-free organisms(30, 35, 51, 62) which can catalyze the reduction of hydrogen peroxide to water with oxidizable substrates as electron donors. The oxygen uptake therefore does not result in a peroxide accumulation. The oxidizable substrates can be alcohol, glucose, glycerol, lactate, or fructose.

(2) Typical peroxidase(27)—The flavoprotein-linked NAD peroxidase (E.C. 1.11.1.1) has been isolated from *Streptococcus faecalis* 10C1. The prosthetic group of this enzyme contains FAD but no heme or metal group and the enzyme is specific only for NADH$_2$. Apart from *Leuconostoc mesenteroides* and *L. delbrückii*, this enzyme has been detected in three streptococcal strains, *S. faecalis* 10C1, *S. faecalis* B 33 a, and *S. mastitidis*. The survey of this enzyme is difficult and has not been as extensive as that of atypical peroxidases since catalase and possibly cytochrome c peroxidase offer serious interferences.

Diaphorases

Diaphorases are enzymes that may couple oxidation of reduced NAD to the reduction of artificial electron acceptors:

$$NAD(P)H + H^+ + A \rightarrow NAD(P)^+ + AH_2$$

Many of these enzymes are flavoproteins (Table 8.3). Since the cell apparently does not use them as physiological oxidants, their significance in the cell is questionable.

It is known that the velocity constants for the reaction between reduced diaphorase from *Streptococcus faecalis* and various oxidized quinones are very high. Low concentrations of these quinones can act readily as efficient electron carriers by accepting them from reduced NAD. When the quinones involved are autoxidizable, a direct path from reduced NAD $\rightarrow$ O$_2$ would be established. There is some evidence available that supports the view that quinones may play an important role in the metabolism of lactic acid bacteria (33, 60).

Direct Flavoprotein Oxidases

The absence of oxidases for $NADH_2$ in extracts of *L. delbrückii* suggests that this organism does use direct substrate oxidases in its oxidative metabolism (40).

TABLE 8.3

PURIFIED DIAPHORASES[a]

Enzymes	Substrate	Oxidant	Prosthetic group	Molecular weight	Turnover No.
Straub's soluble diaphorase (pig heart)	$NADH_2$	Methylene blue	FAD	67,000	8,500
New yellow enzyme (yeast)	$NADPH_2$	Methylene blue	FAD	60,000	130
S. faecalis	$NADH_2$	$(FeCN_6)^{2-}$ 2,6-DCIP *p*-Benzoquinone	FMN	53,000	6,000 29,000 88,000
E. coli	$NADH_2$	Menadione Quinones	— —	— —	50 —
P. fluorescens	$NADH_2$	2,6-DCIP	FMN	—	80
L. mesenteroides	$NADH_2$	Menadione	—	—	80
S. faecalis	$NADH_2$	Menadione	FAD, FMN	—	40–100
L. debrückii	$NADH_2$	Menadione 2,6-DCIP	—	—	30 30

[a] From Dolin (26).

(a) Pyruvate oxidation—The oxidation of pyruvate in *L. delbrückii* follows the pattern:

$$pyruvate + P_i + O_2 \xrightarrow[TPP]{FAD} acetyl\ P + CO_2 + H_2O_2$$

$$pyruvate + H_2O_2 \xrightarrow{spontaneous} acetate + CO_2 + H_2O$$

$$2\ pyruvate + P_i + O_2 \rightarrow acetyl\ P + acetate + 2\ CO_2 + H_2O$$

The feature of this reaction is the generation of acetyl P with either oxygen or ferricyanide as electron acceptor. The detailed mechanism of this acetyl P formation is not yet established but is probably different from that of the NAD-linked systems (36). It may well be that this system could provide a mechanism whereby energy-rich compounds can be generated at the flavoprotein level.

(b) Pyruvate dismutation—The dismutation to pyruvate to lactate, acetate, and carbon dioxide also occurs in *L. delbrückii*. Two enzymes are involved in this process, pyruvate oxidase (pyruvate:oxygen oxidoreductase (phosphorylating), E.C. 1.2.3.3), which is a thiamine pyrophosphate requiring flavoprotein and lactate oxidase (L-lactate:oxygen oxidoreductase, E.C. 1.1.3.2), which catalyzes the following sequence(40):

$$\text{pyruvate} + P_i + FAD \rightarrow \text{acetyl P} + CO_2 + FADH + H^+ \qquad (1)$$

$$FADH + H^+ + \text{riboflavin} \rightarrow FAD^+ + \text{riboflavin} \cdot H_2 \qquad (2)$$

$$\text{riboflavin} \cdot H_2 + FAD^+ \rightarrow \text{riboflavin} + FADH + H^+ \qquad (3)$$

$$FADH + H^+ + \text{pyruvate} \rightarrow FAD^+ + \text{lactate} \qquad (4)$$

$$2 \text{ pyruvate} + P_i \rightarrow \text{lactate} + \text{acetyl P} + CO_2$$

In reactions (1) and (2) pyruvate oxidase is linked to FAD or reduced FAD, whereas in reactions (3) and (4) lactate oxidase is linked to the flavoprotein. This reaction sequence, in which high concentrations of riboflavin serve to link two FAD oxidases, may be a model for anaerobic electron transport between flavoproteins.

Dehydrogenase Activity

Leuconostoc mesenteroides 39 is able to use part of the pyruvate oxidase system or pyruvate dehydrogenase complex since it possesses the lipoamide dehydrogenase (reduced NAD:lipoamide oxidoreductase, E.C. 1.6.4.3) which catalyzes the reversible reaction

$$\text{lipoate-SH}_2 + NAD^+ \rightleftharpoons \text{lipoate} + NADH + H^+$$

This enzyme is a flavoprotein. It is also assumed that *L. mesenteroides* has a second type of lipoamide dehydrogenase which must be similar to that of *Escherichia coli*. This enzyme, however, is difficult to demonstrate.

Flavoprotein Respiration

An electron transport system as such need not be coupled with phosphorylation in order to be useful. A variety of substrates that would not otherwise be used because of lack of hydrogen acceptors could be made available to fermentative organisms in alternate transport mechanisms to oxygen. In these reactions, energy becomes available through substrate-linked phosphorylation, as we have seen in fermentation processes.

Many lactic acid bacteria, for example, are able to metabolize glycerol only under aerobic conditions(38), whereas under anaerobic conditions this cannot happen without an exogenous hydrogen acceptor. In *Streptococcus faecalis* it is assumed that a direct flavoprotein glycerophosphate oxidase may be used for the transfer of electrons to oxygen. Other strains of a more aerobic character possess a reduced NAD oxidase which allows the coupling between triose phosphate dehydrogenation and oxygen reduction. Even if the reoxidation of NADH + H$^+$ is not energetically coupled, the oxidation of glucose with oxygen as electron acceptor furnishes more energy for growth than the lactic acid fermentation, since, aerobically, pyruvate is removed from its role as the obligatory hydrogen acceptor and can be oxidized to acetyl CoA, yielding one more energy-rich bond per triose.

Such oxidative reactions become useful only if an enzyme is present to dispose of hydrogen peroxide. The accumulation of hydrogen peroxide eventually would inhibit the oxidation. But organisms such as *Streptococcus faecalis* that do not possess a peroxidase appear to use this pathway and seem to be more resistant toward hydrogen peroxide. In the case of species of *Pediococcus* the use of the above-mentioned system of glycerol oxidation is dependent upon catalase production. There appears to exist a relationship between catalase production and glycerol utilization, namely, the higher the catalase content of cells, the better the growth on glycerol.

At least two types of catalase are observed in lactic acid bacteria(69):

(1) The "classical" catalase (H$_2$O$_2$:H$_2$O$_2$ oxidoreductase, E.C. 1.11.1.6) (23) which vigorously destroys hydrogen peroxide and is not sensitive to acid pH. This catalase was observed in certain strains of homo- and heterofermentative lactobacilli, *Pediococcus* and *Leuconostoc* only when grown on a heme-containing medium. Unlike most catalase-producing bacteria these organisms cannot synthesize the heme component of the catalase.

(2) A pseudocatalase which has no heme prosthetic group and is often acid sensitive can be found in strains of *Leuconostoc*, *Pediococcus*, and *L. plantarum* (one strain only).

It has been suggested by Whittenbury(69) that lactic acid bacteria may have a rudimentary respiratory system and that only some of them have the ability to form heme proteins if provided with a source of iron porphyrins. Both types of catalases have been found in the same organism(50) which would support Whittenbury's suggestion.

The addition of hemin to anaerobic cultures of *Staphylococcus*(44) caused an increase in nitrate reductase activity (see Chapter 3) and an increase in catalase to the level found in cultures grown under oxygen. This suggests that the primary part which oxygen plays in the formation of staphylococcal catalase could be associated with heme biosynthesis. This theory is supported by earlier findings with *Rhodopseudomonas spheroides*(13) and *Staphylococcus aureus*(48, 55) that oxygen induces catalase activity. Large parts of the protein moiety of catalase are formed in catalase-negative staphylococci(49). The proof for the suggestion that the heme biosynthesis is interrupted by lack of oxygen was provided by quantitative catalase tests, carried out on 14 strains of *Haemophilus* species cultured with graded amounts of hemin, which revealed that the catalase activity increased in proportion to the hemin concentration in the medium(2). This behavior of the catalase is reflected in the division of the heterofermentative bacteria into two groups(69). The first group comprises those heterofermenters which show a positive catalase test on normal agar and on blood agar, and the second group contains those which show a positive catalase test only on blood agar. In the *Lactobacillaceae* a parallel could be drawn to the cytochrome system which leads to nitrate reductase. Apart from the catalase, which depends upon heme biosynthesis and therefore oxygen in

TABLE 8.4

CYTOCHROME FORMATION IN LACTIC ACID BACTERIA[a]

H_2O_2 splitting characteristics and organisms	Medium used[b]	Cytochromes detected after $Na_2S_2O_4$ addition
Catalase positive; pseudocatalase negative		
L. plantarum NCIB 5914	A	None
	B	a_2; b_1
L. brevis NCIB 947	A	None
	B	b_1
Leuconostoc mesenteroides NCIB 8018	A	None
	B	None
S. faecalis H 69 D5	A	None
	B	a_1; a_2; b_1
Catalase negative; pseudocatalase negative		
L. plantarum NCIB 6105	A	b_1 (very weak)
	B	b_1 (very weak)
Catalase negative; pseudocatalase positive		
Leuconostoc citrovorum NCIB 7837	C	None
Leuconostoc mesenteroides RW 66	C	None

[a] From Whittenbury(69). Reprinted with permission of Cambridge University Press.
[b] Here, A = 1.0% (w/v) glucose agar; B = 1.0% glucose agar plus heated blood; and C = 0.05% glucose.

the medium and is possibly affected also by glucose concentrations(14), there exists a second hydrogen peroxide enzyme, which is provisionally named "pseudocatalase(70)." The latter appears to be an acid-sensitive non-heme-containing enzyme, which is mostly found in *Leuconostoc* and *Pediococcus* (19,31). When these organisms are grown under anaerobic conditions and fail to split H_2O_2 in a "normal" catalase test it is absolutely necessary to add heme before the conclusion can be drawn as to whether the organism has the ability to produce catalase or not. Catalase-negative organisms can therefore become catalase-positive with changes in nutrition. This change would not result from the formation of an adaptive or constitutive enzyme but from the synthesis of the prosthetic group of catalase, heme.

Four organisms (Table 8.4) which formed catalase also possessed cytochromes when grown in the presence of heated blood but not in its absence. Heavier suspensions of these strains may probably have given the same result as *Streptococcus faecalis* H 69 D5. Whether these cytochromes are functional and why they are formed remains to be determined. Anticipating the difficulties of measuring and finding cytochromes in anaerobic organisms, the question remains whether there are more cytochromes present which one is still unable to detect and whether they play a similar function than in anaerobic microorganisms mentioned in an earlier chapter.

REFERENCES

1. Bertho, A., and Gluck, H. (1931). *Naturwissenschaften* **19**, 88 as cited by Dolin (27).
2. Bieberstein, E. L., and Gills, M. (1961). Catalase activity of *Haemophilus* species grown with graded amounts of hemin. *J. Bacteriol.* **81**, 380.
3. Birnbaum, J., and Lichstein, H. C. (1965). Conversion of D-biotin to biotin vitamers by *Lactobacillus arabinosus. J. Bacteriol.* **89**, 1035.
4. Birnbaum, J., and Lichstein, H. C. (1966). Metabolism of biotin and analogues of biotin by microorganisms. II. Further studies on the conversion of D-biotin to biotin vitamers by *Lactobacillus plantarum. J. Bacteriol.* **92**, 913.
5. Birnbaum, J., and Lichstein, H. C. (1966). Metabolism of biotin and analogues of biotin by microorganisms. III. Degradation of oxybiotin and desthiobiotin by *Lactobacillus plantarum. J. Bacteriol.* **92**, 920.
6. Birnbaum, J., and Lichstein, H. C. (1966). Metabolism of biotin and analogues of biotin by microorganisms. IV. Degradation of biotin, oxybiotin and desthiobiotin by *Lactobacillus casei. J. Bacteriol.* **92**, 925.
7. Breed, R. S., Murray, E. G. D., and Smith, N. R. (1957). "Bergey's Manual of Determinative Bacteriology," 7th ed. Williams & Wilkins, Baltimore, Maryland.
8. Breslow, R. (1959). Discussion section in "Aldol and Ketol Condensations" by B. L. Horecker. *J. Cellular Comp. Physiol.* **54**, Suppl. 1, 100.
9. Buyze, G., van der Hamer, C. J. A., and deHaan, P. G. (1957). Correlation between hexose monophosphate-shunt, glycolytic system and fermentation-type in Lactobacilli. *Antonie van Leeuwenhoek, J. Microbiol. Serol.* **23**, 345.
10. Campbell, J. J. R., and Gunsalus, I. C. (1944). Citric acid fermentation by Streptococci and Lactobacilli. *J. Bacteriol.* **48**, 71.
11. Christensen, M. D., and Pedersαn, C. S. (1958). Factors affecting diacetyl production by lactic acid bacteria. *Appl. Microbiol.* **6**, 319.
12. Christensen, M. D., Albury, M. N., and Pederson, C. S. (1958). Variation in the acetic acid-lactic acid ratio among the lactic acid bacteria. *Appl. Microbiol.* **6**, 316.
13. Clayton, R. K. (1960). Protein synthesis in the induced formation of catalase in *Rhodopseudomonas spheroides. J. Biol. Chem.* **235**, 405.
14. Dacre, J. C., and Sharpe, M. E. (1956). Catalase production by lactobacilli. *Nature* **178**, 700.
15. Davis, G. H. G., and Hayward, A. C. (1955). The stability of *Lactobacillus strains. J. Gen. Microbiol.* **13**, 533.
16. Davis, J. G. (1960). The Lactobacilli. *Progr. Ind. Microbiol.* **2**, 3.
16a. Deibel, R. H., and Kvetkas, M. J. (1964). Fumarate reduction and its role in the diversion of glucose fermentation by *Streptococcus faecalis. J. Bacteriol.* **88**, 858.

16b. Deibel, R. H., and Niven, C. F., Jr. (1964). Pyruvate fermentation by *Streptococcus faecalis. J. Bacteriol.* **88**, 4.

17. DeLey, J. (1954). Phospho-2-keto-D-gluconate, an intermediate in the carbohydrate metabolism of *Aerobacter cloacae. Biochim. Biophys. Acta* **13**, 302.

18. DeLey, J. (1962). Comparative biochemistry and enzymology in bacterial classification. *Symp. Soc. Gen. Microbiol.* **12**, 164.

19. Delwiche, E. A. (1961). Catalase of *Pediococcus cerevisiae. J. Bacteriol.* **81**, 416.

20. DeMoss, R. D. (1954). A triphosphopyridine nucleotide dependent alcohol dehydrogenase from *Leuconostoc mesenteroides. J. Bacteriol.* **68**, 252.

21. Dennis, D., and Kaplan, N. O. (1960). D- and L-lactic acid dehydrogenases in *Lactobacillus plantarum. J. Biol. Chem.* **235**, 810.

22. de Vleeschanwer, A., deGrotte, J., and Wilsens, A. (1961). Fermentation of glucose-^{14}C by *Lactobacillus brevis. Mededel. Landbouwhogeschool Opzoekingssta. Staat Gent* **26**, 165; *Chem. Abstr.* **60**, 4487 (1962).

23. Dixon, M., and Webb, E. C. (1964). "Enzymes," 2nd ed. Longmans, Green, New York.

24. Dolin, M. I. (1955). The DPNH-oxidizing enzymes of *Streptococcus faecalis*. II. The enzymes utilizing oxygen, cytochrome c, peroxide and 2,6-dichlorophenol-indophenol or ferricyanide as oxidants. *Arch. Biochem. Biophys.* **55**, 415.

25. Dolin, M. I. (1957). The *Streptococcus faecalis* oxidase for reduced pyridine nucleotide. III. Isolation and properties of a flavin peroxidase for reduced diphosphopyridine nucleotide. *J. Biol. Chem.* **225**, 557.

26. Dolin, M. I. (1961). Survey of microbial electron transport mechanisms. *In* "The Bacteria" (I. C. Gunsalus and R. Y. Stanier, eds.), Vol. 2, p. 319, Academic Press, New York.

27. Dolin, M. I. (1961). Cytochrome-independent electron transport enzymes of bacteria. *In* "The Bacteria" (by I. C. Gunsalus and R. Y. Stanier, eds.), Vol. 2, p. 425. Academic Press, New York.

28. Dolin, M. I., and Gunsalus, I. C. (1951). Pyruvic acid metabolism. II. An acetoin-forming enzyme system in *Streptococcus faecalis. J. Bacteriol.* **62**, 199.

29. Domagk, G. F., and Horecker, B. L. (1958). Pentose fermentation by *Lactobacillus plantarum. J. Biol. Chem.* **233**, 283.

30. Douglas, H. C. (1947). Hydrogen peroxide and the metabolism of *Lactobacillus brevis. J. Bacteriol.* **54**, 272.

31. Felton, E. A., Evans, J. B., and Niven, C. F. (1953). Production of catalase by the pediococci. *J. Bacteriol.* **65**, 481.

32. Gibbs, M., Damrose, R., Bennett, F. A., and Bubeck, M. R. (1950). On the mechanism of bacterial fermentation of glucose to lactic acid studied with C[14]-glucose. *J. Biol. Chem.* **184**, 545.

33. Glick, M. C., Zillikar, F., and György, P. (1959). Supplementary growth promoting effect of 2-methyl-1,4-naphthoquinone on *Lactobacillus bifidus* var. *J. Bacteriol.* **77**, 230.

34. Goulden, J. D. S., and Sharpe, M. E. (1958). The infra-red absorption spectra of lactobacilli. *J. Gen. Microbiol.* **19**, 76.

35. Greisen, E. C., and Gunsalus, I. C. (1943). Hydrogen peroxide destruction by *Streptococci. J. Bacteriol.* **45**, 16.

36. Gunsalus, I. C. (1954). *In* "The Mechanism of Enzyme Action" (W. D. McElroy and B. Glass, eds.), p. 545. Johns Hopkins Press, Baltimore, Maryland.

37. Gunsalus, I. C., and Campbell, J. J. R. (1944). Diversion of the lactic acid fermentation with oxidized substrates. *J. Bacteriol.* **48**, 455.

38. Gunsalus, I. C., and Sherman, G. M. (1943). The fermentation of glycerol by *Streptococci. J. Bacteriol.* **45**, 155.

39. Gunsalus, I. C., Horecker, B. L., and Wood, W. A. (1955). Pathways of carbohydrate metabolism in microorganisms. *Bacteriol. Rev.* **19**, 79.
40. Hager, L-P., Geller, D. M., and Lipmann, F. (1954). Flavoprotein-catalyzed pyruvate oxidation in *Lactobacillus delbrückii*. *Federation Proc.* **13**, 734.
41. Harvey, R. J. (1960). Production of acetone and acetaldehyde by lactic acid streptococci. *J. Dairy Res.* **27**, 41.
42. Harvey, R. J., and Collins, E. B. (1963). Roles of citrate and acetoin in the metabolism of *Streptococcus diacetilactis*. *J. Bacteriol.* **86**, 1301.
43. Hayward, A. C. (1957). Detection of gas production from glucose by heterofermentative lactic acid bacteria. *J. Gen. Microbiol.* **16**, 9.
44. Heady, R. E., Jacobs, N. J., and Deibel, R. H. (1964). Effect of haemin supplementation on porphyrin accumulation and catalase synthesis during anaerobic growth of *Staphyloccus*. *Nature* **203**, 1285.
45. Heath, E. C., Hurnitz, J., Horecker, B. L., and Ginsburg, A. G. (1958). Pentose fermentation by *Lactobacillus plantarum*. I. The cleavage of xylulose-5-phosphate by phosphoketolase. *J. Biol. Chem.* **231**, 1009.
46. Horecker, B. L. (1962). "Pentose Metabolism in Bacteria. CIBA Lectures in Microbial Biochemistry." Wiley, New York.
47. Hurnitz, J. (1958). Pentose phosphate cleavage by *Leuconostoc mesenteroides*. *Biochim. Biophys. Acta* **28**, 599.
48. Jensen, J. (1957). Biosynthesis of hematin compounds in a hemin requiring strain of *Micrococcus pyogenes* var. *aureus*. I. The significance of coenzyme A for the terminal synthesis of catalase. *J. Bacteriol.* **73**, 324.
49. Jensen, J., and Hyde, M. O. (1963). "Apocatalase" of catalase-negative staphylococci. *Science* **141**, 45.
50. Johnston, M. A., and Delwiche, E. A. (1965). Distribution and characteristics of the catalases of Lactobacillaceae. *J. Bacteriol.* **90**, 347.
51. Johnston, M. A., and McCleskey, C. S. (1958). Further studies on the aerobic metabolism of *Leuconostoc mesenteroides*. *J. Bacteriol.* **75**, 98.
52. Kitahara, K. (1952). *J. Agr. Chem. Soc. Japan* **26**, 162; cited by Mizushi *et al.* (57).
53. Kopeloff, L. M., Kopeloff, N., Etchells, J. L., and Posselt, E. (1937). Optical activity of lactic acid produced by *Lactobacillus acidophilus* and Lactobacillus bulgaricus. *J. Bacteriol.* **33**, 89.
54. Koser, S., and Staedell, J. T. (1959). Glucosamine utilization by Lactobacilli. *Proc. Soc. Am. Bacteriol.* p. 41.
55. Kovacs, E., Mazarean, H. H., and Jaki, A. (1965). Relation between the synthesis of catalase and the intensity of respiration in cultures of *Staphylococcus aureus*. *Enzymologia* **28**, 316; *Chem. Abstr.* **63**, 8761 (1965).
56. Krichevsky, M. I., and Wood, W. A. (1961). Pathway of ribose-5-phosphate utilization in *Microbacterium lacticum*. *J. Bacteriol.* **81**, 246.
56a. Lees, G. J., and Jago, G. R. (1967). Personal communication.
57. Mizushi, S., Machida, Y., and Kitahara, K. (1964). Quantitative studies on glycolytic enzymes in *Lactobacillus plantarum*. *J. Gen. Appl. Microbiol.* (*Tokyo*) **10**, 33.
58. Narrod, S. A., and Wood, W. A. (1956). Carbohydrate oxidation by *Pseudomonas fluorescens*: Evidence for glucokinase and 2-ketoglucokinase. *J. Biol. Chem.* **220**, 45
59. O'Kane, D. J. (1950). Influence of the pyruvate oxidation factor on the oxidative metabolism of glucose by *Streptococcus faecalis*. *J. Bacteriol.* **60**, 449.
60. Peterson, W. H., and Peterson, M. S. (1945). Relation of bacteria to vitamin and other growth factors. *Bacteriol. Rev.* **9**, 49.
61. Rainbow, C., and Rose, A. H., eds. (1963). "Biochemistry of Industrial Microorganisms." Academic Press, New York.

62. Seeley, H. W., and Vandemark, P. J. (1951). An adaptive peroxidation of *Streptococcus faecalis. J. Bacteriol.* **61**, 27.
63. Sokatch, J. T., and Gunsalus, I. C. (1954). The enzymes of an adaptive gluconate fermentation pathway in *Streptococcus faecalis. Bacteriol. Proc.* p. 109.
64. Sokatch, J. T., and Gunsalus, I. C. (1957). Aldonic acid metabolism. I. Pathway of carbon in an inducible gluconate fermentation by *Streptococcus faecalis. J. Bacteriol.* **73**, 452.
65. Stanier, R. Y., Doudoroff, M., and Adelberg, E. A. (1965). "The Microbial World," 2nd ed. Prentice-Hall, Englewood Cliffs, New Jersey.
66. Vandemark, P. J., and Wood, W. A. (1956). The pathways of glucose dissimilation by *Microbacterium lacticum. J. Bacteriol.* **71**, 385.
67. Walker, G. A., and Kilgour, G. L. (1965). Pyridine nucleotide oxidizing enzymes of *Lactobacillus casei.* I. Diaphorase. *Arch. Biochem. Biophys.* **111**, 529.
68. Walker, G. A., and Kilgour, G. L. (1965). Pyridine nucleotide oxidizing enzymes of *Lactobacillus casei.* II. Oxidase and Peroxidase. *Arch. Biochem. Biophys.* **111**, 534.
69. Whittenbury, R. (1960). Two types of catalase-like activity. *Nature* **187**, 433.
70. Whittenbury, R. (1964). Hydrogen peroxide formation and catalase activity in the lactic acid bacteria. *J. Gen. Microbiol.* **35**, 13.
71. Wood, W. A. (1961). Fermentation of carbohydrates and related compounds. *In* "The Bacteria" (I. C. Gunsalus and R. Y. Stanier, eds.), Vol. 2, p. 59. Academic Press, New York.

SUPPLEMENTARY READINGS

Avigad, G., and Levin, N. (1967). Reduced nicotinamide dinucleotide phosphate diaphorase from *Bacillus subtilis. European J. Biochem.* **1**, 102.
Bernofsky, C., and Mills, R. C. (1966). Diaphorase from *Aerobacter aerogenes. J. Bacteriol.* **92**, 1404.
DeMoss, R. D. (1968). Kinases in *Leuconostoc mesenteroides. J. Bacteriol.* **95**, 1692.
Egan, B., and Morse, M. L. (1966). Carbohydrate transport in *Staphylococcus aureus.* III. Studies of the transport process. *Biochim. Biophys. Acta* **112**, 63.
Gandy, T., and Wolfe, R. S. (1965). Ureidoglycolate synthetase of *Streptococcus allantoicus.* II. Properties of the enzyme and reaction equilibrium. *J. Bacteriol.* **90**, 1531.
Hillcoat, B. L., and Blackley, R. L. (1966). Dihydrofolate reductase of *Streptococcus faecalis.* I. Purification and some properties of reductase from the wild strain and from strain A. *J. Biol. Chem.* **241**, 2995.
Jones, D., Deibel, R. H., and Niven, C. F. (1964). Catalase activity of two *Streptococcus faecalis* strains and its enhancement by aerobiosis and added cations. *J. Bacteriol.* **88**, 602.
London, J. (1968). Regulation and function of lactate oxidation in *Streptococcus faecium. J. Bacteriol.* **95**, 1380.
Low, I. E., Eaton, M. D., and Proctor, P. (1968). Relation of catalase to substrate utilization by *Mycoplasma pneumoniae. J. Bacteriol.* **95**, 1425.
Mickelson, M. N. (1967). Aerobic metabolism of *Streptococcus agalactiae. J. Bacteriol.* **94**, 184.
Naik, V. R., and Nadkarni, G. B. (1968). Adaptive alterations in the fermentative sequence of *Lactobacillus casei. Arch. Biochem. Biophys.* **123**, 431.
Sakai, S., and Yamanaka, K. (1968). Crystalline D-mannitol ÷ NAD oxidoreductase from *Leuconostoc mesenteroides. Biochim. Biophys. Acta* **151**, 684.

Sapico, V., and Anderson, R. L. (1967). An adenosine-5'-triphosphate:hexose-6-phospho-transferase specific for D-mannose and D-frucrose from *Leuconostoc mesenteroides*. Purification, properties, and evidence for a single enzyme. *J. Biol. Chem.* **242**, 5086.

Yamanaka, K. (1968). Purification, crystallization and properties of the D-xylose isomerase from *Lactobacillus brevis*. *Biochim. Biophys. Acta* **151**, 670.

9

PSEUDOMONADACEAE

The genus *Pseudomonas* is a group of heterotrophic, gram-negative, rodlike bacteria which do not form spores and possess, if motile, polar flagellation.

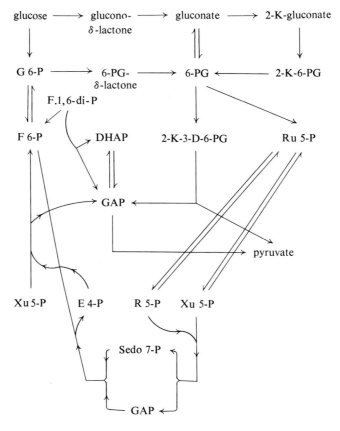

SCHEME 9.1. A general map of carbohydrate metabolism in pseudomonads.

They are strict aerobes(10, 131). They are known for their very active oxidation of carbohydrates and breakdown of aromatic rings(28) and their formation of poly-β-hydroxybutyric acid. Thorough studies on the intermediary metabolism of this genus has only been done in a relatively small number of species: *Pseudomonas fluorescens, Pseudomonas aeruginosa, Pseudomonas ovalis,* and *Pseudomonas saccharophila.* Very little is known on the carbohydrate metabolism of other genera which appear to be closely related to *Pseudomonas,* namely, *Xanthomonas, Vibrio, Agrobacterium, Chromobacterium,* and *Protaminobacter.* The general map of carbohydrate metabolism in several pseudomonads(4a, 13–15, 20, 31, 33–38, 42, 43, 45, 49, 64, 71–74, 84, 85, 90, 91, 100, 105, 106, 115, 122, 138, 140, 142, 154, 157, 162, 163, 165–167) is summarized in Scheme 9.1.

Pseudomonads use mainly the HMP and ED pathways(164), but not the EMP pathway. *Pseudomonas saccharophila* in fact was the organism with which Entner and Doudoroff discovered the pathway which now bears their name. All three pathways have been discussed at length in an earlier chapter and the nonphosphorylation steps were also discussed with the acetic acid bacteria.

METABOLISM OF L-ARABINOSE, D-ARABINOSE, AND D-GALACTOSE

The breakdown of L-arabinose follows very closely glucose metabolism via the ED pathway:

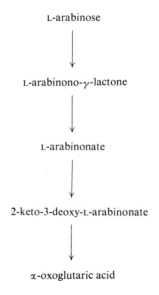

L-arabinose

↓

L-arabinono-γ-lactone

↓

L-arabinonate

↓

2-keto-3-deoxy-L-arabinonate

↓

α-oxoglutaric acid

L-Arabinose is first attacked by a dehydrogenase (L-arabinose: NAD oxido-reductase, E.C. 1.1.1.47) forming the corresponding lactone. This reaction is

```
   ┌──CHOH              ┌──C=O                    COOH
   │  HCOH              │  HCOH                    HCOH
 O │  HOCH      ──→   O │  HOCH        ──→         HOCH
   │  CH                │  CH                      HOCH
   └──HCOH             └──HCOH                     HCOH
      CH₂OH               CH₂OH                    CH₂OH
```

D-galactofuranose   D-galactono-   D-galactonic acid
                 δ-lactone

```
       COOH
       C=O
       CH₃

       CHO                        COOH
       HCOH                       C=O
       CH₂OPO₃H₂                  CH₂
                                  HOCH
                                  CH₂OH
```

glyceraldehyde 3-P   2-keto-3-deoxy-
                    D-galactonic acid

```
   ┌──CHOH              ┌──C=O                    COOH
   │  ‖HCOH             │  HCOH                    HCOH
 O │  HOCH      ──→   O │  HOCH        ──→         HOCH
   └──CH               └──CH                       HOCH
      CH₂OH               CH₂OH                    CH₂OH
```

D-arabinofuranose   D-arabono-   D-arabonic acid
                 γ-lactone

```
       COOH
       C=O
       CH₃

       COOH                       COOH
       CH₂OH                      C=O
                                  CH₂
                                  HOCH
                                  CH₂OH
```

glycolic acid   2-keto-3-deoxy-
                  D-arabonic acid

NAD-linked and produces 1 mole of reduced NAD. Arabinonolactonase (L-arabinono-γ-lactone hydrolase, E.C. 3.1.1.15) hydrolyzes the lactone to L-arabinonate, which undergoes a reaction together with L-arabinonate dehydratase (L-arabinonate hydrolyase, E.C. 4.2.1.25) producing 2-keto-3-deoxy-L-arabinonate. Whereas in the ED pathway a split of the molecule occurs, this is not the case here. 2-Keto-3-deoxy-L-arabinonate forms, with the addition of $2H^+$, α-oxoglutarate. *Pseudomonas* species are therefore able to produce this dicarboxylic acid straight from L-arabinose without the formation of pyruvate.

In the metabolism of D-arabinose(114) and D-galactose(30), the last step is a completely different one, and it follows more closely the ED pathway:

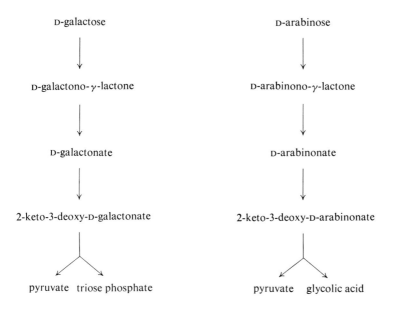

D-galactose   D-arabinose

D-galactono-γ-lactone   D-arabinono-γ-lactone

D-galactonate   D-arabinonate

2-keto-3-deoxy-D-galactonate   2-keto-3-deoxy-D-arabinonate

pyruvate   triose phosphate   pyruvate   glycolic acid

The enzymes involved in the D-galactose metabolism are galactose dehydrogenase(22) (D-galactose:NAD oxidoreductase, E.C. 1.1.1.48), a lactonase (E.C. 3.1 group), and a galactonate dehydratase (D-galactonate hydrolyase, E.C. 4.2.1.6). The 2-keto-3-deoxygalactonate is then phosphorylated with a kinase (E.C. 2.7 group) to 2-keto-3-deoxygalactonate 6-phosphate and an aldolase-type enzyme splits the molecule to form pyruvate and triose phosphate. A slightly different, but similar, breakdown occurs with D-arabinose, whereby the enzymes arabinose dehydrogenase(22) (E.C. 1.1 group), lactonase (E.C. 3.1 group), and an arabinonate dehydratase (D-arabinonate hydrolyase, E.C. 4.2.1.5) form 2-keto-3-deoxyarabinonate. A NAD-linked dehydrogenase-type reaction forms a 2,4-ketoarabinonate ($COOH–CO–CH_2CO–CH_2OH$)

followed by a hydrolysis, which leads to the formation of pyruvate and glycolic acid. Although in the cases of D-galactose and D-arabinose metabolism, no 2-oxoglutarate is formed directly, it is assumed that this dicarboxylic acid is produced from pyruvate via the TCA cycle (29) by *Pseudomonas fluorescens*.

Bionic Acids

A number of *Pseudomonas* strains are able to convert sugars into their bionic acids. *Pseudomonas graveolus*, for example, converts maltose → maltobionic acid. *Pseudomonas quercito-pyrogallica* oxidizes lactose and maltose to lacto- and maltobionic acids (142), respectively. As the culture ages the bionates are hydrolyzed by β-galactosidase (β-D-galactoside galactohydrolase, E.C. 3.2.1.23). *Pseudomonas fragi*, *P. graveolus*, *P. synxantha*, and *P. vendrelli* oxidize D-arabinose to D-arabonic acid; *P. fluorescens*, *P. fragi*, *P. mildenbergii*, *P. putida*, *P. synxantha*, and *P. vendrelli* oxidize L-arabinose to L-arabonic acid; *P. fluorescens*, *P. fragi*, *P. graveolens*, *P. mildenbergii*, *P. ovalis*, and *P. putida* oxidize D-xylose to D-xylonic acid and *P. fluorescens*, *P. fragi*, *P. graveolens*, *P. mildenbergii*, *P. ovalis*, *P. putrefaciens*, *P. synxantha*, and *P. vendrelli* oxidize D-ribose to D-ribonic acid (91).

Polygalacturonate Metabolism

One *Pseudomonas* strain metabolizes polygalacturonate via the ED pathway (29):

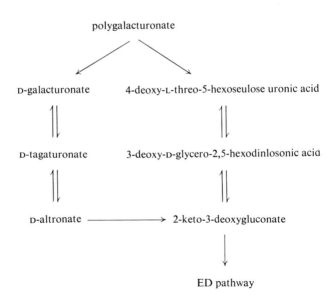

ED pathway

METABOLISM OF KREBS CYCLE INTERMEDIATES

Pseudomonas aeruginosa, P. fluorescens, P. nigrificans, and *Xanthomonas phaseoli* are named as having the TCA cycle and the inducible glyoxylate shunt enzymes(70a, 94, 127, 152). However, permeability(21) seems to pose some problems. Although cell-free extracts readily use all TCA intermediates, whole cells show a lag phase of varying times as a permease system is induced.

The Glyoxylate Cycle

It was outlined in the chapter on aerobic respiration that the TCA cycle was responsible for terminal respiration and was also the only one for the complete oxidation of acetate(83). The cycle therefore is unable to produce

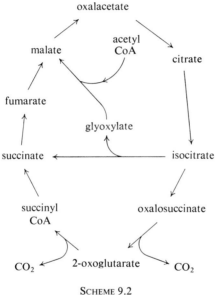

SCHEME 9.2

compounds more oxidized than acetate. In addition to its role in terminal respiration, the TCA cycle also plays an important role in synthesis of cell material(50, 125). It provides α-oxoglutarate which is the precursor of glutamic acid, one of the key compounds in amino acid and protein biosynthesis or oxalacetate, which supplies aspartate and other amino acids(80). If the cycle operates only for the oxidation of acetate, then all that is required is a supply of acetate and a catalytic amount of oxalacetate, which is regenerated in the cycle. If, however, synthetic processes are going on at the same time there is a continual tapping off of both α-oxoglutarate and of the 4-carbon dicarboxylic acids which also serve as important precursors for biosynthetic processes. Such a draining off of intermediates will only continue to operate if the resulting deficit of 4-carbon dicarboxylic acids is made up. This problem is even stronger when microorganisms use acetate as both carbon and energy source. The cell must be able to synthesize the 4-carbon dicarboxylic acids from acetate. The organisms therefore use a second system by which they make use of six of the eight reactions of the TCA cycle, and bypass those steps which result in the evolution of carbon dioxide (isocitrate $\rightarrow$ α-oxoglutarate $\rightarrow$ succinate + CO_2). They replace these with reactions the net effect of which leads to an increase in the organic acid carbon of the system(79). This new reaction sequence is called the "glyoxylate bypass of the TCA cycle" or simply the "glyoxylate cycle"(76,81,82) (see Scheme 9.2).

The formation of L-isocitrate from acetyl CoA and oxalacetate is the same as in the TCA cycle, involving the two enzymes citrate synthase (E.C. 4.1.3.7) and aconitate hydratase (E.C. 4.2.1.3). Instead of metabolizing isocitrate to oxalosuccinate, isocitrate undergoes an aldo cleavage to succinate and glyoxylate(109). This reaction is catalyzed by isocitratelyase(132) (threo-D-

$$
\begin{array}{c}
\text{COOH} \\
| \\
\text{CH}_2 \\
| \\
\text{CH--COOH} \\
| \\
\text{CHOH} \\
| \\
\text{COOH} \\
\text{isocitrate}
\end{array}
\rightleftharpoons
\begin{array}{c}
\text{COOH} \\
| \\
\text{CH}_2 \\
| \\
\text{CH}_2 \\
| \\
\text{COOH} \\
\text{succinate}
\end{array}
\quad + \quad
\begin{array}{c}
\text{CHO} \\
| \\
\text{COOH} \\
\text{glyoxylate}
\end{array}
$$

isocitrate glyoxylatelyase, E.C. 4.1.3.1). The second step of this bypass involves the condensation of acetyl CoA with glyoxylate to form malate with malate synthase [L-malate glyoxylatelyase (CoA acetylating), E.C. 4.1.3.2]

$$
\begin{array}{c}
\text{CH}_3 \\
| \\
\text{CO--SCoA}
\end{array}
\quad + \quad
\begin{array}{c}
\text{CHO} \\
| \\
\text{COOH}
\end{array}
\longrightarrow
\begin{array}{c}
\text{COOH} \\
| \\
\text{CH}_2 \\
| \\
\text{CHOH} \\
| \\
\text{COOH} \\
\text{malate}
\end{array}
\quad + \quad \text{COA--SH}
$$

as catalyst. There is no combustion of acetate with energy release, but a net provision of 4-carbon dicarboxylic acids. The subsequent metabolism of these acids therefore provides the precursors of most cell constituents and allows the organism to grow on acetate as the sole carbon source. It is assumed that isocitratelyase (E.C. 4.1.3.1) controls or regulates the simultaneous operations of the TCA and glyoxylate cycle. The possibility of regulation of isocitratelyase by pyruvate and phosphoenol pyruvate has also been taken into consideration (78).

Whether or not the presence of "malic enzyme" (E.C. 1.1.1.38, E.C. 1.1.1.39, and E.C. 1.1.1.40), which converts malate directly to pyruvate, plays a control function (65) is not known, although its presence in *Pseudomonas putida* would give such indication.

METABOLISM OF GLYCOLLATE

The growth of microorganisms on C-2 compounds as the sole source of carbon necessitates reactions whereby the C-2 substrates provide both metabolic energy and the carbon skeleton for cellular constituents. In the case of acetate both these functions are fulfilled with the operation of the TCA cycle and glyoxylate cycle. These cycles are, however, not sufficient for C-2 compounds at "higher oxidation levels than acetate" (83). The metabolism of glycollate therefore must undergo some preliminary reactions to form a key intermediate which could connect with the TCA cycle or the glyoxylate cycle and also which could be able to build cell constituents.

The sequence in Scheme 9.3 has therefore been postulated (80). Glycollate

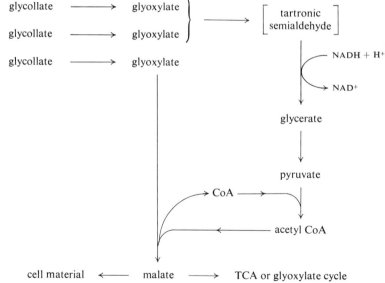

SCHEME 9.3. Postulated route for the formation of cell constituents from glycollate by *Pseudomonas* (B$_2$ aba) (reprinted with the permission of *The Biochemical Journal*, London).

is oxidized to glyoxylate by a still unidentified enzyme, which could be similar to the flavoprotein glycollic acid oxidase found in plants (19, 171) (glycollate:

oxygen oxidoreductase, E.C. 1.1.3.1). This reaction requires molecular oxygen and is exergonic with $\Delta F = -41$ kcal/mole at pH 8.0(17).

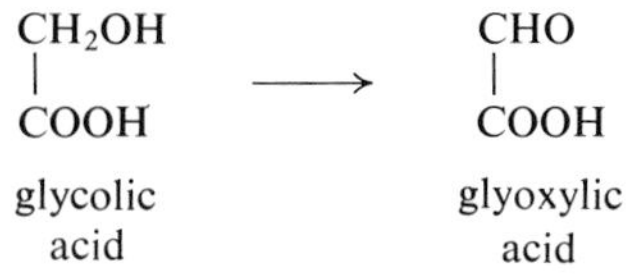

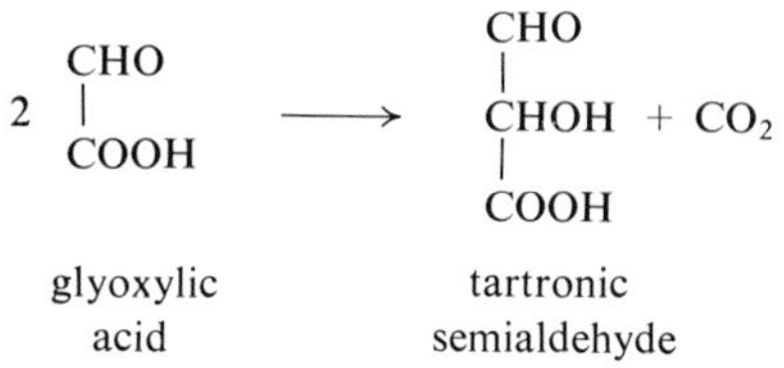

$$
\begin{array}{ccc}
\text{CH}_2\text{OH} & & \text{CHO} \\
| & \longrightarrow & | \\
\text{COOH} & & \text{COOH} \\
\text{glycolic} & & \text{glyoxylic} \\
\text{acid} & & \text{acid}
\end{array}
$$

$$
2\;
\begin{array}{c}
\text{CHO} \\
| \\
\text{COOH}
\end{array}
\longrightarrow
\begin{array}{c}
\text{CHO} \\
| \\
\text{CHOH} \;+\; \text{CO}_2 \\
| \\
\text{COOH}
\end{array}
$$
$$
\begin{array}{ccc}
\text{glyoxylic} & & \text{tartronic} \\
\text{acid} & & \text{semialdehyde}
\end{array}
$$

Two glyoxylate molecules condense now under the function of a carboligase (80) to an intermediate called "tartronic semialdehyde." Tartronic semialdehyde reductase (D-glycerate:NAD(P) oxidoreductase, E.C. 1.1.1.60) reduces this semialdehyde to glycerate in a NAD-linked reaction. It is now

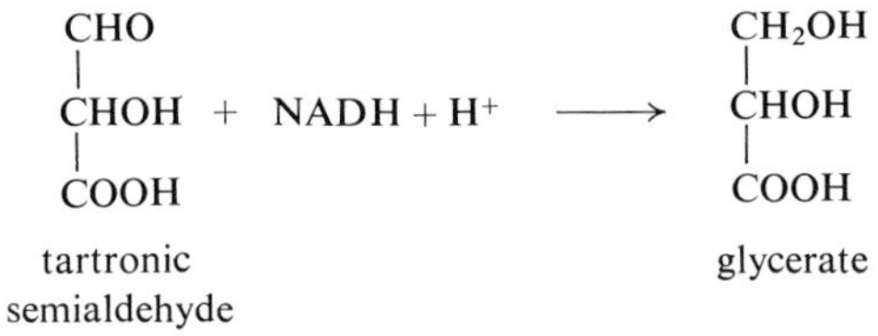

$$
\begin{array}{c}
\text{CHO} \\
| \\
\text{CHOH} \;+\; \text{NADH} + \text{H}^+ \\
| \\
\text{COOH}
\end{array}
\longrightarrow
\begin{array}{c}
\text{CH}_2\text{OH} \\
| \\
\text{CHOH} \\
| \\
\text{COOH}
\end{array}
$$
$$
\begin{array}{cc}
\text{tartronic} & \qquad\qquad \text{glycerate} \\
\text{semialdehyde} &
\end{array}
$$

assumed that glycerate itself is phosphorylated in a kinase reaction which almost certainly would involve glycerate kinase (ATP:glycerate 3-phosphotransferase, E.C. 2.7.1.31) and the formation of 3-phosphoglycerate. The latter product is further metabolized to pyruvate via phosphoenol pyruvate. High activities of isocitratelyase (E.C. 4.1.3.1) and malate synthase (E.C. 4.1.3.2) suggest that acetyl CoA and malate are the two key intermediates for the complete oxidation of glycollate to carbon dioxide and for cell material. The presence of malate synthase, however, could also suggest a direct conversion of glyoxylate to malate with the formation of acetyl CoA.

Some *Pseudomonas* species are also able to reduce glyoxylate to glycollate, which is catalyzed by glyoxylate reductase (glycollate:NAD oxidoreductase, E.C. 1.1.1.26)(4).

OXIDATION OF MALONATE

The well-known inhibitor of succinate dehydrogenase (E.C. 1.3.99.1), malonate, can be oxidized by several strains of *Pseudomonas* nearly to completion. Malonate is first oxidized to malonate semialdehyde by a malonate semialdehyde dehydrogenase (malonate semialdehyde: NAD(P) oxidoreductase, E.C. 1.2.1.15). Malonic semialdehyde is also a hydration product of acetylene monocarboxylic acid in *Pseudomonas fluorescens*. The hydration is catalyzed by malonate semialdehyde dehydratase (malonate semialdehyde hydrolyase, E.C. 4.2.1.27).

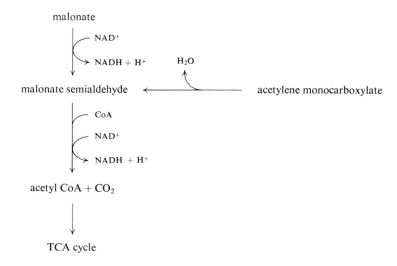

A decarboxylation of malonate semialdehyde, which requires ATP, CoA, and Mg^{2+}(159–161, 168, 169), produces acetyl CoA, which can then enter the TCA cycle. The enzyme responsible for this last step is malonate semialdehyde dehydrogenase (malonate semialdehyde: NAD(P) oxidoreductase (acylating CoA), E.C. 1.2.1.18), and could well be a dehydrogenase complex.

Oxidation of Oxalate and Formate

Pseudomonas oxalaticus is able to grow on formate or oxalate as sole carbon source. In the case of formate, an oxidation with formate dehydrogenase (formate: cytochrome b_1 oxidoreductase, E.C. 1.2.2.1) produces CO_2, which is fixed by a mechanism similar to the Calvin cycle. Carbon dioxide enters at the level of phosphoglyceric acid or malic acid. Carbon dioxide can, however, also be fixed into pyruvate or phosphoenol pyruvate:

$$\text{pyruvate} + CO_2 \xrightarrow[\text{NADPH} + H^+]{\quad\quad} \text{NADP}^+ \quad\text{malate}$$

$$\text{phosphoenol pyruvate} + CO_2 \xrightarrow[\text{IDP}]{\quad\text{ITP}\quad} \text{oxalacetate}$$

Grown on oxalate, ribulose diphosphate carboxylase [3-phospho-D-glycerate carboxylyase (dimerizing), E.C. 4.1.1.39] or carboxydismutase is absent(119–121) and the Calvin cycle therefore is inoperative. Kornberg(77) suggested the scheme given in Scheme 9.4.

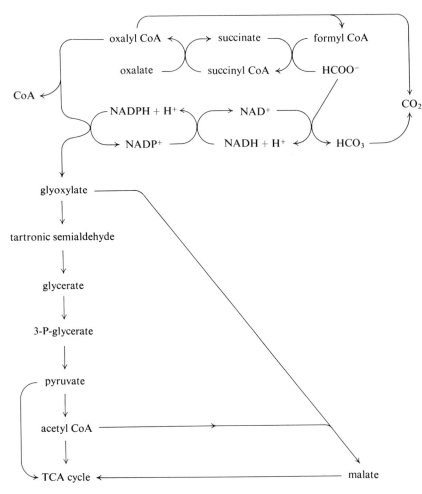

SCHEME 9.4

Oxalate is oxidized to glyoxylate. In order to be able to join either the TCA or the glyoxylate cycle, acetyl CoA has to be formed, which is done via several intermediates and pyruvate. Acetyl CoA and glyoxylate are then able to form malate with the help of malate synthase (L-malate glyoxylatelyase (CoA acetylating), E.C. 4.1.3.2). Malate itself as well as acetyl CoA and pyruvate are able to carry out the oxidation of oxalate to completion. It is assumed that the use of the glyoxylate cycle is mainly for building up cell material of poly-β-hydroxybutyric acid, whereas the TCA cycle provides the energy. With *Pseudomonas ovalis*, Kornberg(77) and Morris(103) clarified the pathway from glyoxylate to glycerate. They demonstrated that the conversion of glyoxylate to tartronic semialdehyde is carried out by a glyoxylate carboligase with the tartronate semialdehyde reductase(148) (D-glycerate:NAD(P) oxidoreductase, E.C. 1.1.1.60) being responsible for the formation of glycerate. Glycerate kinase (ATP:D-glycerate 3-phosphotransferase, E.C. 2.7.1.31) phosphorylates glycerate and forms 3-phosphoglycerate. The continuation of the scheme is identical with the EMP pathway.

The decarboxylation of oxalyl CoA to formyl CoA + CO_2 is catalyzed by oxalyl CoA decarboxylase (oxalyl CoA carboxylyase, E.C. 4.1.1.8)(118). This reaction requires thiamine pyrophosphate as cofactor and is stimulated by the presence of Mg^{2+} or Mn^{2+} ions.

ITACONATE METABOLISM

Pseudomonas sp. "B_2s abo" and *P. fluorescens* are able to metabolize itaconate and *P. fluorescens* in addition methyl succinate almost to completion.

$$
\begin{array}{ccc}
\text{CH—COOH} & & \text{COOH} \\
\parallel & & \mid \\
\text{C—COOH} & \longrightarrow & \text{C}{=}\text{CH}_2 \quad + \text{ CO}_2 \\
\mid & & \mid \\
\text{CH}_2\text{—COOH} & & \text{CH}_2\text{—COOH}
\end{array}
$$

Itaconate can be derived from the TCA cycle via aconitate. Aconitate decarboxylase (*cis*-aconitate carboxylyase, E.C. 4.1.1.6) is the catalyst for this reaction. The over-all mechanism for itaconate metabolism has been elucidated by

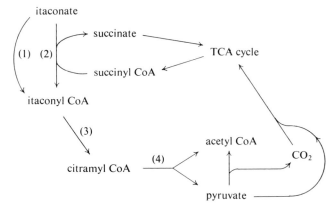

SCHEME 9.5. (Reprinted with permission of Cambridge University Press.)

Cooper and Kornberg(23) and diagramed by DeLey(29) (see Scheme 9.5). Enzymes involved are:

  (1) succinyl CoA synthetase,
  (2) itaconate CoA transferase,
  (3) itaconyl CoA hydratase, and
  (4) citramyl CoA lyase.

Itaconate can be converted directly to itaconyl CoA with a succinyl CoA synthetase (E.C. 6.2.1.4) or in conjunction with succinyl CoA and an itaconate CoA transferase. In addition to itaconyl CoA, the latter reaction produces

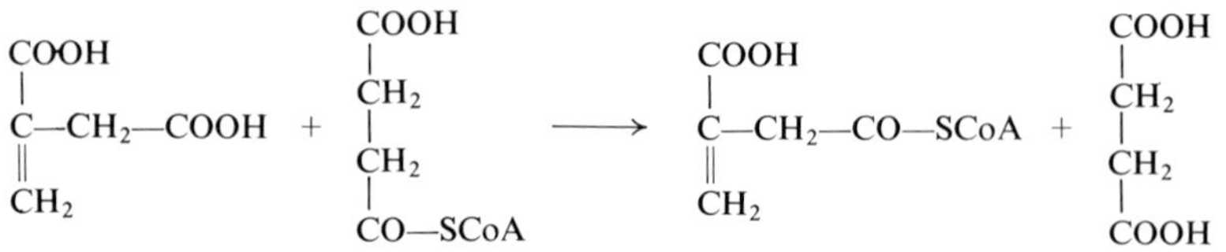

$$
\underset{\text{itaconate}}{\overset{\displaystyle \text{COOH}}{\underset{\displaystyle \text{CH}_2}{\overset{\displaystyle |}{\underset{\displaystyle \|}{\text{C}-\text{CH}_2-\text{COOH}}}}}} \quad + \quad \underset{\text{succinyl CoA}}{\overset{\text{COOH}}{\underset{\text{CO}-\text{SCoA}}{\text{CH}_2\ \text{CH}_2}}} \quad \longrightarrow \quad \underset{\text{itaconyl CoA}}{\overset{\displaystyle \text{COOH}}{\underset{\displaystyle \text{CH}_2}{\text{C}-\text{CH}_2-\text{CO}-\text{SCoA}}}} \quad + \quad \underset{\text{succinate}}{\overset{\text{COOH}}{\underset{\text{COOH}}{\text{CH}_2\ \text{CH}_2}}}
$$

COOH
|
C—CH₂—COOH   +
‖
CH₂

itaconate

COOH
|
CH₂
|
CH₂
|
CO—SCoA

succinyl CoA

⟶

COOH
|
C—CH₂—CO—SCoA
‖
CH₂

itaconyl CoA

+

COOH
|
CH₂
|
CH₂
|
COOH

succinate

succinic acid, which immediately reenters the TCA cycle. Itaconyl CoA hydratase converts itaconyl CoA to citramyl CoA:

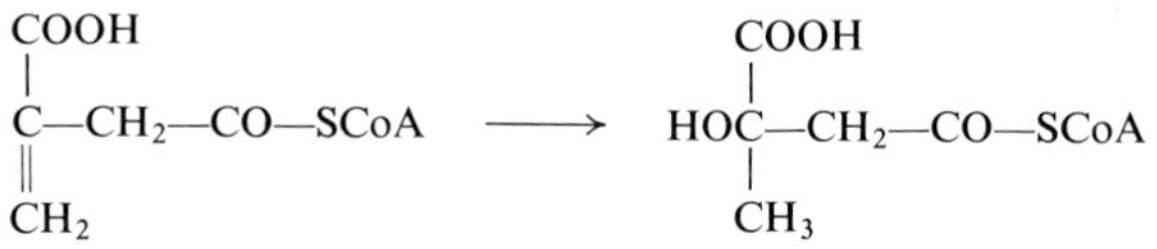

COOH
|
C—CH₂—CO—SCoA   ⟶
‖
CH₂

itaconyl CoA

COOH
|
HOC—CH₂—CO—SCoA
|
CH₃

citramyl CoA

The split of the carbon chain into pyruvate and acetyl CoA is caused by citramyl CoA lyase:

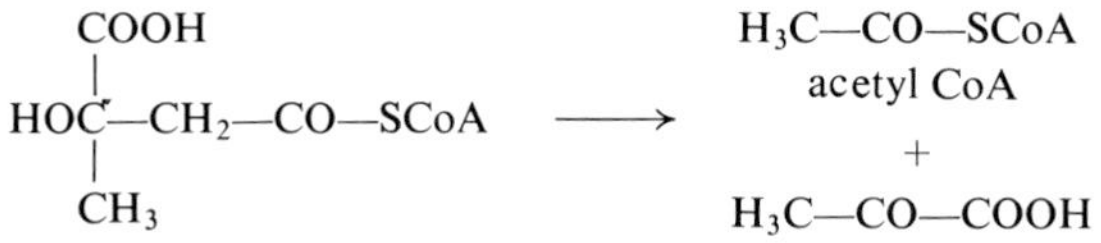

COOH
|
HOC—CH₂—CO—SCoA   ⟶
|
CH₃

citramyl CoA

H₃C—CO—SCoA
acetyl CoA
+
H₃C—CO—COOH
pyruvate

Both end products enter the TCA cycle for further metabolism. This itaconate degradation was also found in *Micrococcus* sp.(24).

TARTRATE METABOLISM

  The breakdown of tartrate is marked by its stereospecific behavior. Stereo-specific dehydrases attack (+), (−), or mesotartrate and form oxalacetic acid. These reactions depend also on the availability of tartrate permeases which bring the product to be metabolized across the cell membrane.

Other *Pseudomonas* species seem to have different pathways. Dagley and Trudgill(25) found a (+)-tartrate decarboxylase and the following reaction sequence:

$$\text{tartrate} \longrightarrow \text{glycerate} \longrightarrow \text{3-phosphoglycerate}$$
$$\downarrow$$
$$\text{pyruvate}$$

This pathway joins the EMP pathway at the 3-phosphoglycerate level similar to that found with species metabolizing oxalate.

Whichever way acids are metabolized, in most instances they join one of the three pathways, TCA, glyoxylate, or dicarboxylic acid cycle.

GLUCARATE METABOLISM

Glucarate can be metabolized as the sole source of carbon and energy by enterobacteria and *Pseudomonas*(148). However, they use distinctly different pathways:

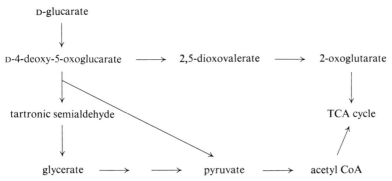

The pathway taken by the *Pseudomonas* strains branches off at the D-4-deoxy-5-oxoglutarate level, since this compound undergoes a dehydration coupled with a decarboxylation to form 2,5-dioxovalerate:

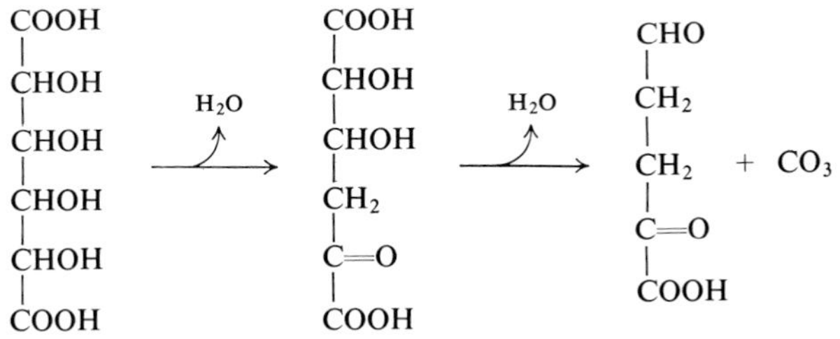

COOH   COOH   CHO
|
CHOH H_2O CHOH H_2O CH_2
|
CHOH $\longrightarrow$ CHOH $\longrightarrow$ CH_2 + CO_3
|
CHOH CH_2 C=O
|
CHOH   C=O   COOH
|
COOH   COOH

D-glucarate   D-4-deoxy-5-   2,5-dioxovalerate
         oxoglucarate

This 2,5-dioxovalerate is now oxidized by NAD-linked dehydrogenase and produces the key intermediate of the TCA cycle, 2-oxoglutarate:

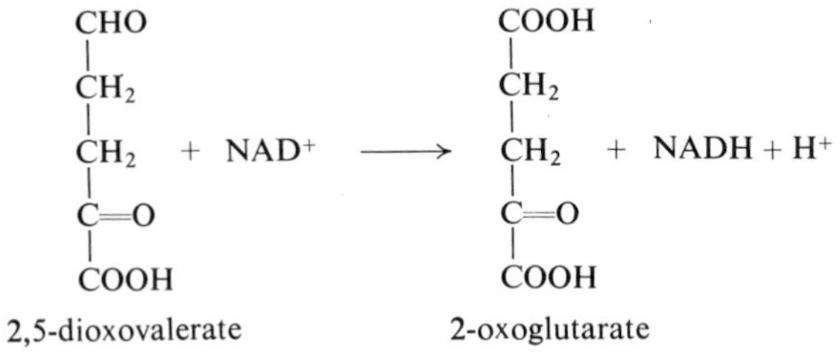

$$
\begin{array}{ccc}
\text{CHO} & & \text{COOH} \\
| & & | \\
\text{CH}_2 & & \text{CH}_2 \\
| & & | \\
\text{CH}_2 & + \text{NAD}^+ \longrightarrow & \text{CH}_2 & + \text{NADH} + \text{H}^+ \\
| & & | \\
\text{C}=\text{O} & & \text{C}=\text{O} \\
| & & | \\
\text{COOH} & & \text{COOH} \\
\text{2,5-dioxovalerate} & & \text{2-oxoglutarate}
\end{array}
$$

The enterobacteria are not able to carry out the dehydration step from D-4-deoxy-5-oxoglucarate to 2,5-dioxovalerate, but form tartronic semi-aldehyde, which in turn is metabolized in a manner similar to that described for the glycollate metabolism.

GLUTARATE METABOLISM

The metabolism by *Pseudomonas fluorescens* of glutarate to carbon dioxide and acetyl CoA(108) is similar to that of animal tissue(149):

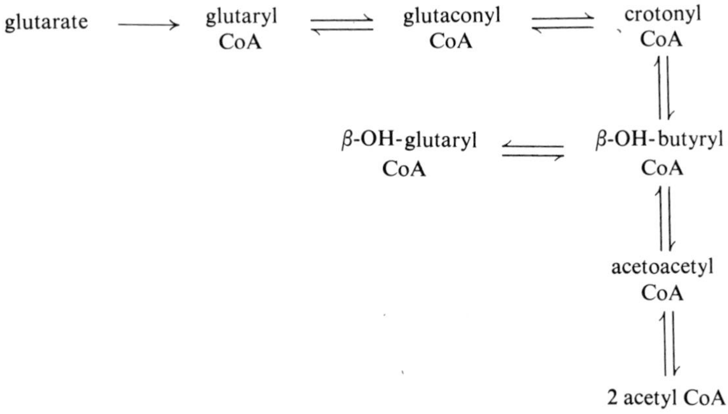

$$
\begin{array}{ccc}
\text{glutarate} \longrightarrow & \underset{\text{CoA}}{\text{glutaryl}} \rightleftharpoons & \underset{\text{CoA}}{\text{glutaconyl}} \rightleftharpoons & \underset{\text{CoA}}{\text{crotonyl}}
\end{array}
$$

$$
\begin{array}{cc}
\underset{\text{CoA}}{\beta\text{-OH-glutaryl}} \longleftarrow & \underset{\text{CoA}}{\beta\text{-OH-butyryl}} \\
& \updownarrow \\
& \underset{\text{CoA}}{\text{acetoacetyl}} \\
& \updownarrow \\
& \text{2 acetyl CoA}
\end{array}
$$

Glutarate must first be activated(102), or a CoA transferase reaction must take place to form the CoA derivative glutaryl CoA:

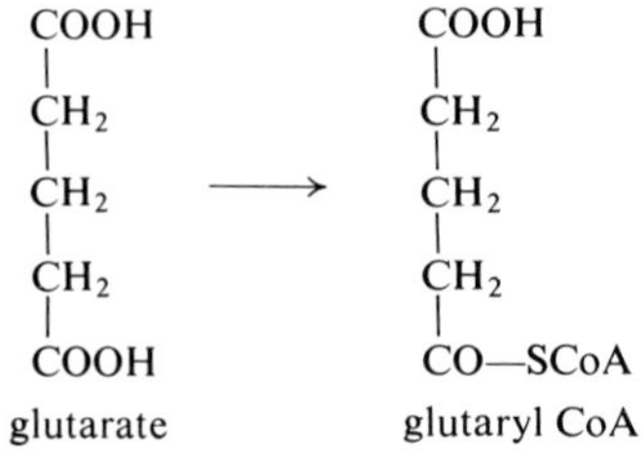

$$
\begin{array}{ccc}
\text{COOH} & & \text{COOH} \\
| & & | \\
\text{CH}_2 & & \text{CH}_2 \\
| & & | \\
\text{CH}_2 & \longrightarrow & \text{CH}_2 \\
| & & | \\
\text{CH}_2 & & \text{CH}_2 \\
| & & | \\
\text{COOH} & & \text{CO}-\text{SCoA} \\
\text{glutarate} & & \text{glutaryl CoA}
\end{array}
$$

Glutarate cannot be metabolized as a free acid but must be converted to its CoA derivative(149,150). This would parallel the findings of Gholson and co-workers(48) who found that not glutarate, but glutaryl CoA was formed from α-ketoadipate during the metabolism of tryptophan in animal tissue. The first product in the oxydation of glutaryl CoA by a dehydrogenase was glutaconyl CoA which was immediately followed by a decarboxylation to

$$
\begin{array}{ccc}
\begin{array}{c}
\text{COOH} \\
| \\
\text{CH}_2 \\
| \\
\text{CH}_2 \\
| \\
\text{CH}_2 \\
| \\
\text{CO—SCoA}
\end{array}
\xrightarrow{}
\begin{array}{c}
\text{COOH} \\
| \\
\text{CH}_2 \\
| \\
\text{CH} \\
\| \\
\text{CH} \\
| \\
\text{CO—SCoA}
\end{array}
\xrightarrow{}
\begin{array}{c}
\text{CH}_3 \\
| \\
\text{CH} \\
\| \\
\text{CH} \\
| \\
\text{CO—SCoA}
\end{array}
\\[1em]
\text{glutaryl CoA} & \text{glutaconyl CoA} & \text{crotonyl CoA}
\end{array}
$$

crotonyl CoA. The enzyme "glutaryl CoA dehydrogenase" catalyzes both reactions, the dehydrogenation as well as the decarboxylation and is a flavoprotein.

Crotonyl CoA can now undergo a hydration by the action of crotonase (L-3-hydroxyacyl CoA hydrolyase, E.C. 4.2.1.17) and forms β-hydroxybutyryl CoA(107):

$$
\begin{array}{cc}
\begin{array}{c}
\text{CH}_3 \\
| \\
\text{CH} \\
\| \\
\text{CH} \\
| \\
\text{CO—SCoA}
\end{array}
\xrightarrow{}
\begin{array}{c}
\text{CH}_3 \\
| \\
\text{CHOH} \\
| \\
\text{CH}_2 \\
| \\
\text{CO—SCoA}
\end{array}
\\[1em]
\text{crotonyl CoA} & \text{β-hydroxybutyryl} \\
& \text{CoA}
\end{array}
$$

Crotonyl CoA itself can also enter the fatty acid oxidation pathway, where it is converted to acetoacetyl CoA and to 2 acetyl CoA. Whether or not *Pseudomonas* can take the alternate route via β-hydroxyglutarate to β-hydroxybutyryl CoA or even metabolize β-hydroxyglutarate via acetone dicarboxylate, acetoacetate to acetate(61) is not confirmed.

METHANOL METABOLISM

Pseudomonas oxalaticus is also able to grow as *Pseudomonas* AM 1 (66) does (see Chapter 5) and derives its energy from the oxidation of formate(29):

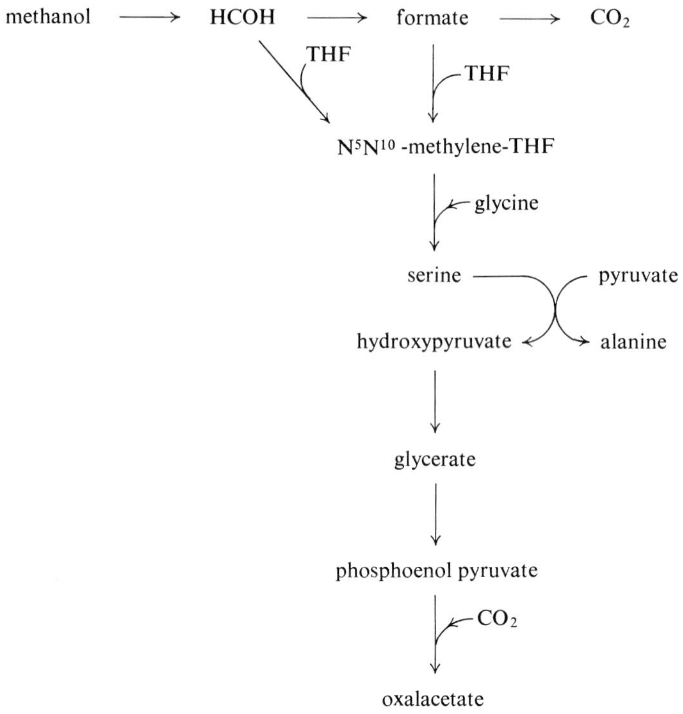

methanol $\longrightarrow$ HCOH $\longrightarrow$ formate $\longrightarrow$ CO_2

THF

THF

N^5N^{10}-methylene-THF

glycine

serine — pyruvate

hydroxypyruvate — alanine

glycerate

phosphoenol pyruvate

CO_2

oxalacetate

When grown on methanol, the metabolism of *Pseudomonas oxalaticus* is heterotrophic and serine is among the first formed intermediates. Because of its great similarities to the metabolism of *Pseudomonas methanica, P. oxalaticus* may possibly be identical with *Pseudomonas methanica*(117).

The isolation of an *Achromobacter* MS has been reported(153) which is capable of growing on trimethylsulfonium chloride as its sole source of carbon. During growth dimethylsulfide is formed while the remaining methyl group is incorporated into cell material with the help of folic acid.

METABOLISM OF 2,3-BUTANEDIOL

It was shown earlier that 2,3-butanediol is a major end product of carbohydrate metabolism of *Aerobacter* and *Bacillus*. Pseudomonads break down 2,3-butanediol aerobically. Almost all other oxidation reactions involving 2,3-butanediol can also take place anaerobically(67).

Butanediol dehydrogenase (2,3-butanediol:NAD oxidoreductase, E.C. 1.1.1.4) oxidizes 2,3-butanediol to acetoin. This is followed by a second oxidation step, catalyzed by acetoin dehydrogenase (acetoin:NAD oxidoreductase, E.C. 1.1.1.5):

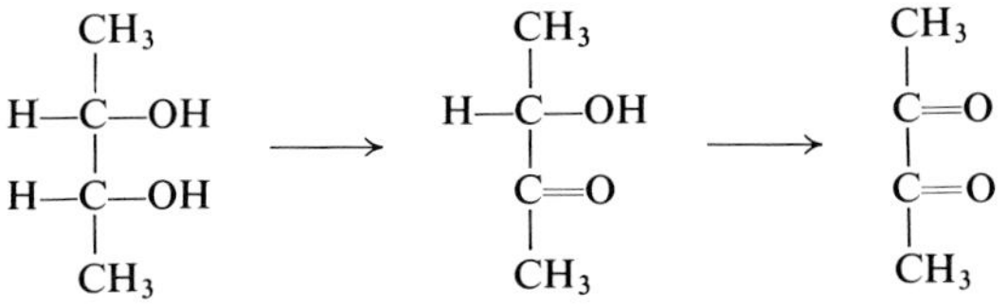

$$
\begin{array}{ccc}
\mathrm{CH_3} & \mathrm{CH_3} & \mathrm{CH_3} \\
| & | & | \\
\mathrm{H\!-\!C\!-\!OH} & \mathrm{H\!-\!C\!-\!OH} & \mathrm{C\!=\!O} \\
| & | & | \\
\mathrm{H\!-\!C\!-\!OH} & \mathrm{C\!=\!O} & \mathrm{C\!=\!O} \\
| & | & | \\
\mathrm{CH_3} & \mathrm{CH_3} & \mathrm{CH_3} \\
\text{2.3-butanediol} & \text{acetoin} & \text{diacetyl}
\end{array}
$$

The formation of acetate and acetaldehyde-TPP complex and the combination of a second molecule of diacetyl with this complex are analogous to the synthesis of α-acetolactate from pyruvate, but the enzymes are specific and

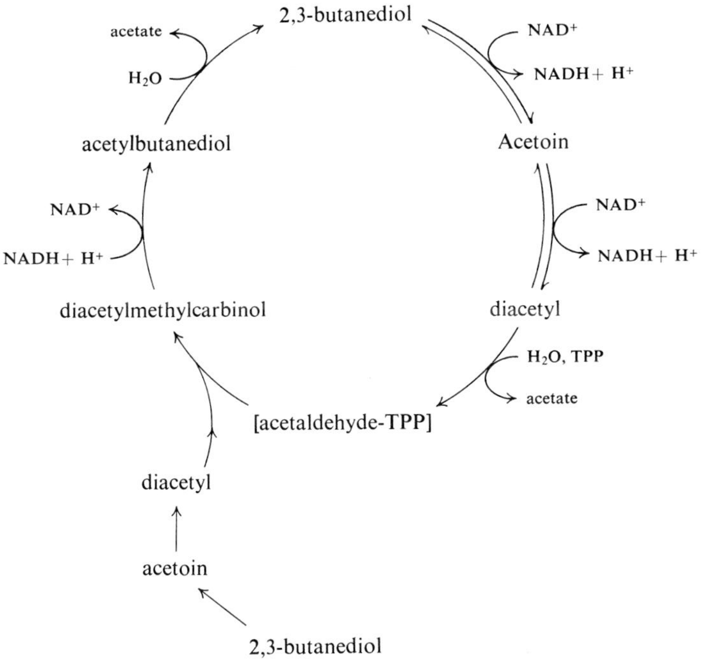

SCHEME 9.6

are not interchangeable with the pyruvate enzyme system of *Aerobacter* (see Scheme 9.6). Diacetyl together with acetaldehyde-TPP form diacetylmethylcarbinol:

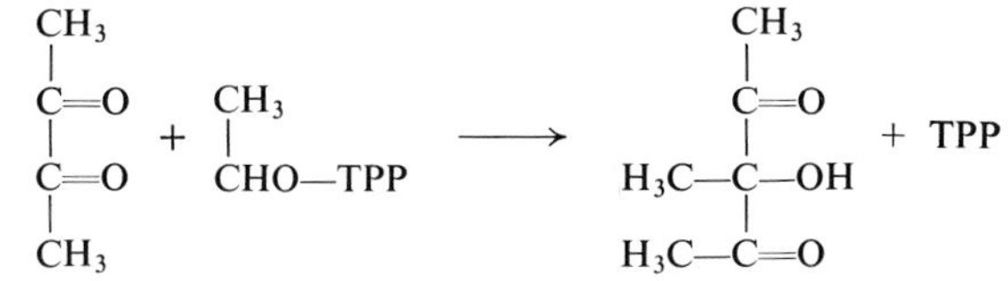

$$
\begin{array}{ccc}
\mathrm{CH_3} & & \mathrm{CH_3} \\
| & & | \\
\mathrm{C\!=\!O} & \mathrm{CH_3} & \mathrm{C\!=\!O} \\
| & + \ | & \longrightarrow \quad | \qquad + \ \mathrm{TPP} \\
\mathrm{C\!=\!O} & \mathrm{CHO\!-\!TPP} & \mathrm{H_3C\!-\!C\!-\!OH} \\
| & & | \\
\mathrm{CH_3} & & \mathrm{H_3C\!-\!C\!=\!O} \\
\text{diacetyl} & & \text{diacetylmethylcarbinol}
\end{array}
$$

A diacetylmethylcarbinol reductase, which is probably very similar to butanediol dehydrogenase (E.C. 1.1.1.4) since it is NAD-linked(68), reduces diacetylmethylcarbinol to acetylbutanediol:

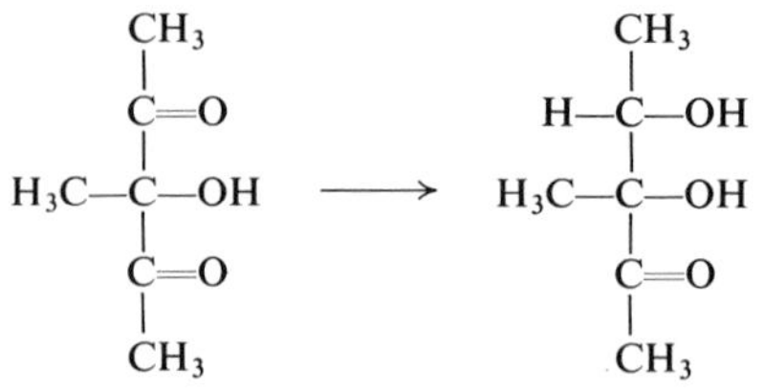

$$
\begin{array}{ccc}
\begin{array}{c}
CH_3 \\
| \\
C{=}O \\
| \\
H_3C{-}C{-}OH \\
| \\
C{=}O \\
| \\
CH_3
\end{array}
&
\longrightarrow
&
\begin{array}{c}
CH_3 \\
| \\
H{-}C{-}OH \\
| \\
H_3C{-}C{-}OH \\
| \\
C{=}O \\
| \\
CH_3
\end{array}
\\
\text{diacetylmethylcarbinol} & & \text{acetyl butanediol}
\end{array}
$$

Hydrolysis now occurs, and in a step similar to that of acetaldehyde-TPP formation, a further molecule of acetate is formed together with butanediol. In this cyclic process, 2 molecules of acetate are formed from 2 molecules of 2,3-butanediol. It seems probable that the same cycle operates for acetoin or diacetyl metabolism. This cycle was shown to be operative in *Pseudomonas fluorescens*(67) and *Pseudomonas* sp.(63). The acetate produced is used for synthesizing cell material in processes involving the TCA and glyoxylate cycle.

ETHANOL FORMATION BY *ZYMOMONAS MOBILIS*

It seems to be worthwhile to say a few words on *Zymomonas mobilis* since this organism is a member of the family *Pseudomonadaceae*. All available evidence, enzymatic and otherwise, reveals that *Zymomonas mobilis* has a yeast-type fermentation of carbohydrates to ethanol. It is an anaerobic organism, and one would expect it to use the EMP pathway to produce pyruvate. This, however, is not so, since *Zymomonas mobilis* is the only bacterium known which uses the ED pathway in order to form pyruvate and finally ethanol. Its fermentation balance is(27)

1 mole of glucose $\rightarrow$ 1.8 moles of ethanol + 0.8 mole of CO_2 + 0.2 mole of lactate

The enzyme fructose diphosphate aldolase (E.C. 4.1.2.13) as well as 6-phosphogluconate dehydrogenase are absent. It is suggested that NAD is the physiological electron carrier in the balanced oxidation–reduction reactions, although no NAD-NADP transhydrogenase (reduced NADP:NAD oxidoreductase, E.C. 1.6.1.1) has been detected.

METABOLISM OF HIGHER MOLECULAR WEIGHT COMPOUNDS

Pseudomonas species with their great number of oxygenases(53) are able to metabolize a variety of higher molecular compounds such as hydrocarbons and mandelate.

Hydrocarbon Metabolism

Since it was discovered that hydrocarbons can be metabolized by microorganisms(95), possible industrial applications have been considered(11), because three classes of products could be accounted for(44):

(1) a conversion to products which consist of oxygenated molecules with no change in the carbon skeleton;
(2) oxygenated products with shorter chains, produced by oxidative degradation; and
(3) biosynthetic products such as amino acid, vitamins, and lipids.

Any metabolism of hydrocarbons must, of course, be oxidative. A number of strains of *Pseudomonas* are able to adapt very quickly to use hydrocarbons as sole carbon sources and can revert to grow on nonhydrocarbon media as rapidly(47).

Alkanes and Alkene Oxidation. Some of the alkanes and alkenes are oxidized by the incorporation of oxygen in the molecules(44).

Monoterminal oxidation. The most common type of oxidation for hydrocarbon chains is the monoterminal oxidation in combination with a β-oxidation. The β-oxidation of fatty acids can lead to a great number of biosynthetic

$$R-CH_2 \cdot CH_2 \cdot CH_3 \xrightarrow{O_2} R-CH_2-CH_2-\underset{\underset{OH}{|}}{CH_2} \xrightarrow{-2H} R-CH_2-CH_2-\underset{\underset{O}{\|}}{CH}$$

$$\downarrow \begin{array}{l} +H_2O \\ -2H \end{array}$$

$$R-COOH + CH_3-COOH \xleftarrow{\beta\text{-oxidation}} R-CH_2-CH_2-\underset{\underset{O}{\|}}{COH}$$

materials which will not be considered here, but the principle involved is best demonstrated in wax synthesis(141).

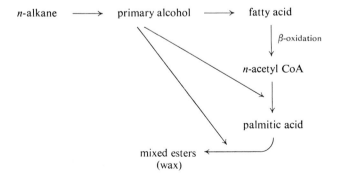

Diterminal oxidation. Most bacteria attack only one end of the chain. *Pseudomonas aeruginosa* grows on 2-methylhexane and produces a mixture of acids:

$$\text{2-methylhexane} \rightarrow \begin{array}{l} \text{5-methylhexanoic acid} \\ \text{2-methylhexanoic acid} \end{array}$$

It is assumed that this bacterium still attacks only one end at a time (44). Other acids which have been identified by similar oxidation steps are from decane or dodecane: 11-formyl undecanoic acid, 12-hydroxy dodecanoic acid, and 3-hydroxy dodecanoic acid.

In addition to the β-oxidation, a ω-oxidation can take place which was originally thought to be present only in mammalian tissue (124) and may be more widespread than anticipated at the moment (86):

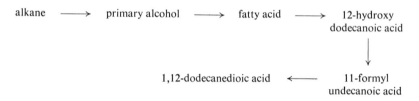

Peterson *et al.* (116) were able to extract the soluble CO–hydroxylation system from *Pseudomonas oleovorans* and separated this soluble system into three compounds: rubredoxin, NAD(P)-rubredoxin reductase, and the ω-hydroxylase. All three components are involved in the octane metabolism to *n*-octanol, which is a similar system to the metabolism of alkane. In *Pseudomonas desmolytica* three similar proteins, namely, hydrocarbon hydroxylase, NADH$_2$-rubredoxin reductase, and a rubredoxin-like protein, have been found (87) in the hydrocarbon oxidation system. These three proteins may well be identical with the one from *P. oleovorans* and play a similar, if not identical, role. The simultaneous use by *Pseudomonas* species of β-oxidation and ω-oxidation connects alkanes to fatty acids and finally dicarboxylic acids (see Scheme 9.7). Where no β-oxidation occurs, higher molecular esters such

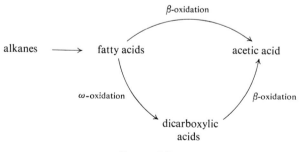

Scheme 9.7

as wax are formed. Similar reaction sequences have been found to exist in mycobacteria (92).

Petroleum Hydrocarbon Oxidation. This field of microbial activity is relatively unexplored in regard to metabolic activity studies. A recent review (151) gives a concise account of the present state of knowledge of the organisms involved as well as their activities, and it should be consulted for detailed information.

Aliphatic Hydrocarbons. The degradation of paraffinic hydrocarbon occurs by an initial oxidative attack on one methyl group, which is followed by the formation of the corresponding alcohol, aldehyde, and fatty acid. The latter is then further degraded by β-oxidation. The importance of primary and secondary alcohols as intermediates in these pathways is still obscure.

It seems that hydrocarbons with eight or more carbon atoms in the chain undergo exclusively a α,ω-oxidation first. This could be regarded as an alternative pathway to that of the formation of fatty acids.

Asymmetric branched hydrocarbons such as 2-methylhexane undergo oxidation on all terminal groups. As far as α-olefins are concerned, bacteria prefer to attack the saturated end of the molecule, but it was also demonstrated that the terminal double bond can be oxidized as well. This oxidation is carried out by enzymes which are associated with the oxidation of the saturated end of the molecule. These enzymes are therefore not very specific with respect to molecular configuration.

Oxidation of C_2–C_5 paraffins (151). The oxidation of propane to propionic

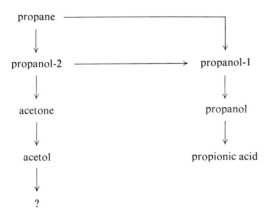

acid is assumed to be the major route since it is a terminal oxidation pathway. The alternative pathway occurs only in short chain paraffin oxidation and is called the "2-keto pathway."

Oxidation of C_6–C_{12} paraffins. The major route would be the one with a monoterminal oxidation, which is followed by a β-oxidation. *n*-Decane is oxidized by an oxygenase system to *n*-decanol, which is degraded further under the influence of an alcohol and an aldehyde dehydrogenase to *n*-decanoic acid. β-Oxidation is responsible then for the production of acetic acid. The alternate pathway shows first α,ω-oxidation of *n*-decane which followed by β-oxidation after *n*-octane-1:8-dicarboxylic acid is formed. Both pathways can be linked together by ω-oxidation of *n*-decanal, producing *n*-octane-1:8-dicarboxylic acid. The nature of the end product formed depends on whether

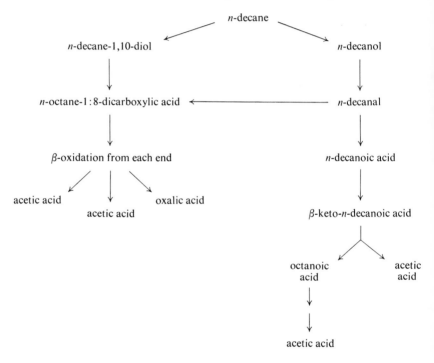

the alkane has an odd or even number of carbon atoms in the chain(158). β-Oxidation of an odd-numbered alkane after oxidation to acid would give the following:

(1) in a monoterminal attack—acetic and propionic acid
(2) in a diterminal attack—acetic and malonic acid

It seems therefore that the oxidation of straight chain hydrocarbons follows a similar pattern.

    Some species of *Pseudomonas* appear unable to form *n*-decanal. *Pseudomonas æruginosa*, for example, metabolizes decane to 1-, 2-, 3-, 4-, and sometimes 5-decanol and the corresponding ketones(46). These products are further metabolized to decanoic, nonanoic, octanoic, and heptanoic acids, thus producing the acids direct from the corresponding alcohol. A similar pattern was found during the investigations into the metabolism of long chain methyl ketones(41). The proposed pathway in *Pseudomonas* is:

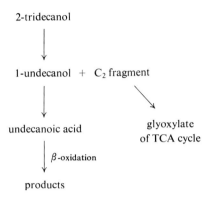

It is suggested(41) that a subterminal oxidative cleavage of a ketone molecule may be favored as a general principle over the monoterminal oxidation principle.

Aromatic Hydrocarbons. The oxidation and degradation of aromatic hydrocarbons in pseudomonads is very rare. Most of the studies done so far have been carried out with *Pseudomonas fluorescens* and *Pseudomonas aeruginosa*. Catechol appears to play a major role in this metabolism(151) (see Scheme 9.8).

Naphthalene metabolism. Further investigations on naphthalene metabolism (99) revealed that there are more steps between naphthalene and catechol than indicated in the general scheme on page 378.

Mandelate pathway. One of the best studied pathways of a cycloparaffin degradation by *Pseudomonas fluorescens* is undoubtedly the mandelate pathway(58–60, 139). The pattern is very similar to the proposed over-all mechanism as catechol is an intermediate (see Scheme 9.9). This mandelate pathway can be separated into two sections:

(1) the mandelate group, which contains all the compounds listed in Scheme 9.9 including benzoate, and
(2) the catechol group, which contains the compounds from catechol to α-ketoadipic acid.

Both sections are joined by an oxygenase system. D-Mandelate has first to be isomerized to its L-isomer, which is carried out by a mandelate racemase (E.C. 5.1.2.2)(156). The L-isomer of mandelate is then oxidized by a L-mandelate dehydrogenase (E.C. 1.1 group), which produces benzoyl formate.

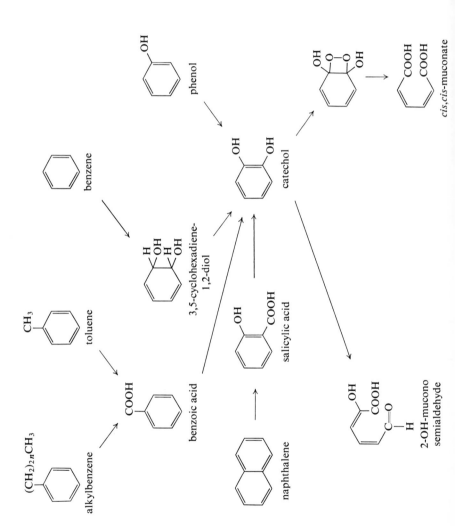

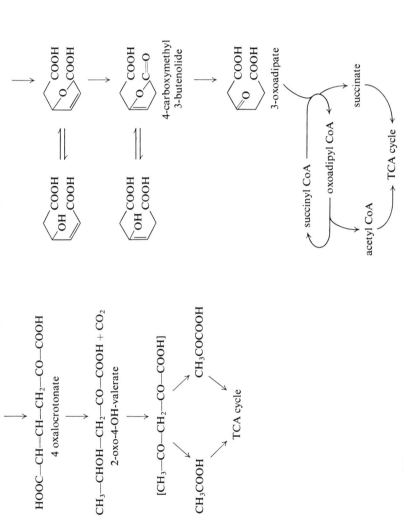

SCHEME 9.8. Degradation of aromatic hydrocarbons by pseudomonads (reprinted with permission of John Wiley and Sons).

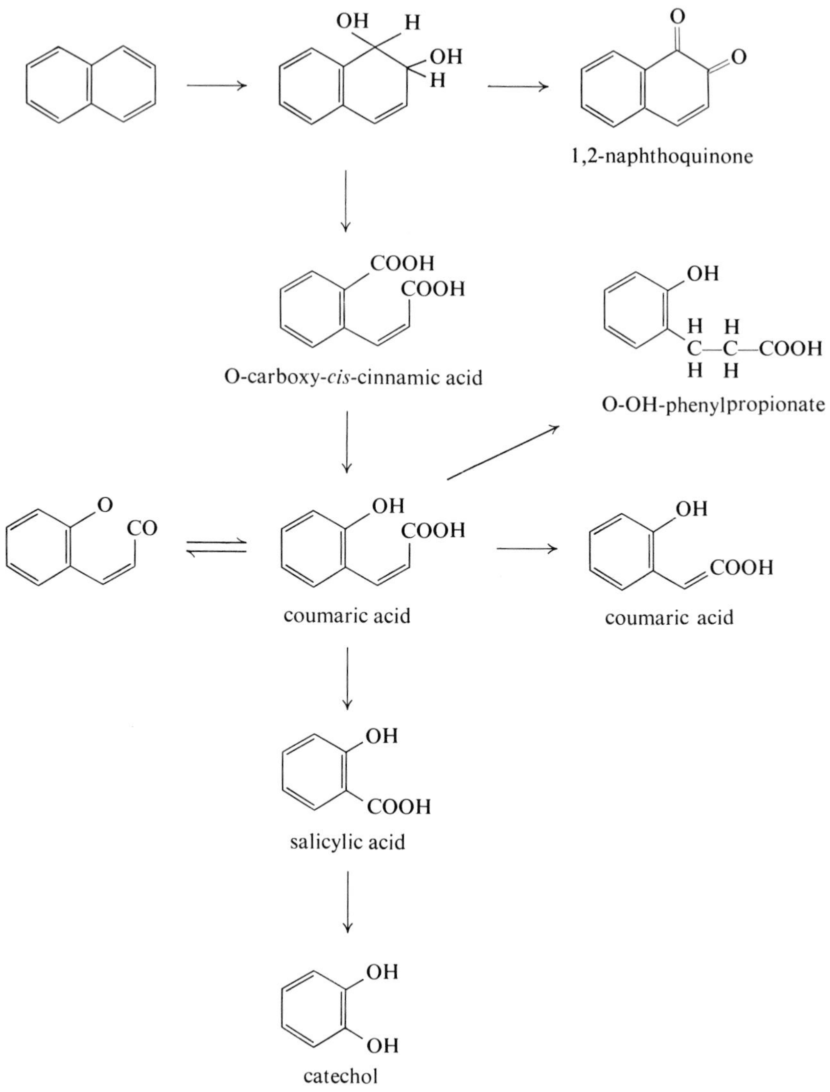

1,2-naphthoquinone

O-carboxy-*cis*-cinnamic acid

O-OH-phenylpropionate

coumaric acid

coumaric acid

salicylic acid

catechol

A decarboxylase (benzoylformate carboxylyase, E.C. 4.1.1.7) forms benzaldehyde and carbon dioxide, and the following oxidation is NADP-linked benzaldehyde:NADP oxidoreductase, E.C. 1.2.1.7) forming benzoate. This intermediate can also be formed if benzyl alcohol serves as carbon source (70). A benzyl alcohol dehydrogenase converts this alcohol into benzaldehyde, which in turn is metabolized to benzoate as already described. A benzoate oxidase system, which has not been fully elucidated, transforms benzoate into catechol.

379

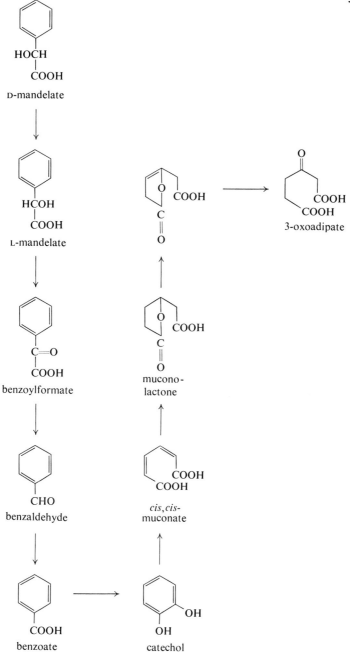

SCHEME 9.9. Degradation of mandelate by Pseudomonas fluorescens (reprinted with permission of the American Society of Microbiologists).

Protocatechase (catechol:oxygen 1,2-oxidoreductase, E.C. 1.13.1.1) splits the benzene ring open and converts catechol to *cis,cis*-muconate. The next enzymes involved in this degradation are a lactonizing enzyme, a muconolactone isomerase, and finally an enol lactone hydrolase. The latter three enzymes have also been found in *P. putida*(111). β-Ketoadipate undergoes the same reactions as shown in the general over-all mechanism and finally produces acetate or acetyl phosphate. The discovery that nonfluorescent species of *Pseudomonas* produced protocatechuate instead of catechol from *p*-cresol(6) renewed interest in the oxidative attack of benzoid substrates. This finding supported an earlier suggestion(112) that both catechol or protocatechuate could serve as the last intermediate possessing an aromatic structure toward β-ketoadipate formation(130). The identification of the two intermediates in the protocatechuate pathway of *Pseudomonas putida*, β-carboxy *cis,cis*-muconate and γ-carboxy muconolactone (γ-carboxy-γ-carboxymethyl-Δ^{α}-butenolide)(113), together with the enzymes catalyzing these reactions(110), firmly established this pathway (see Scheme 9.10).

The oxidation of protocatechuate to β-carboxy *cis,cis*-muconate(93) is catalyzed by an oxygenase (protocatechuate: oxygen 3,4-oxidoreductase, E.C. 1.13.1.3). The product of this oxidation undergoes a lactonization, whereby γ-carboxy muconolactone is formed. This reaction requires the β-carboxy *cis,cis*-muconate lactonizing enzyme. A decarboxylation step converts γ-carboxy muconlactone into β-ketoadipate enol lactone with the help of γ-carboxy muconolactone decarboxylase. The transformation into β-keto-adipate is the same as described under the catechol pathway, whereby β-keto-adipate enol lactone hydrolase is required. β-Ketoadipate enol lactone(113) is identical with 4-carboxymethyl-3-butenolide(151). The formation of acetyl CoA and succinyl CoA from β-ketoadipate is carried out in two steps with the involvement of the enzymes succinyl CoA:β-ketoadipate CoA transferase, which forms oxoadipyl CoA and β-ketoadipyl CoA thiolase. This finally breaks the chain into two end products. It seems that two completely separate pathways are involved in the metabolism of benzoid substrates—the catechol and protocatechuate pathway. *Pseudomonas putida* was found to possess the enzymes of both but used only one of them(111).

A number of bacteria are known to use *p*-hydroxybenzoate as carbon source(26) for their energy metabolism. *p*-Hydroxybenzoate is initially attacked by the hydroxylation in position 3 to yield protocatechuate (3,4-di-hydroxybenzoate), which is catalyzed by the enzyme *p*-hydroxybenzoate hydroxylase(62). Apart from the attack of protocatechuate by ortho cleavage, yielding β-carboxy *cis,cis*-muconate, there is also a report about a meta cleavage attack of protocatechuate by *Pseudomonas desmolytica*(147), which yields γ-carboxy *cis,cis*-muconic semialdehyde. The enzyme involved in this reaction must be protocatechuate 4,5-oxygenase (protocatechuate: oxygen

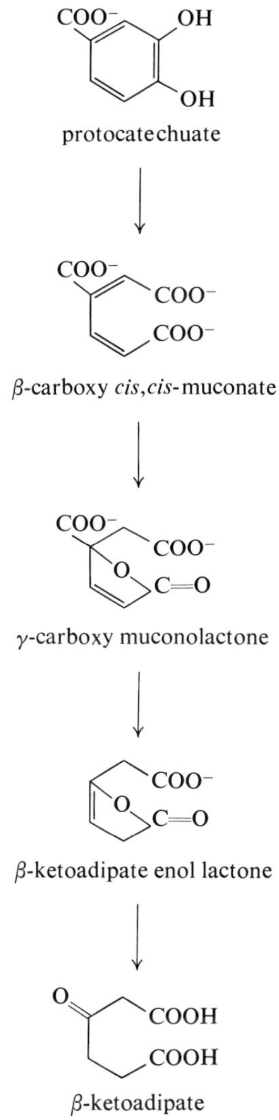
COO⁻
OH
OH
protocatechuate
COO⁻
COO⁻
COO⁻
β-carboxy *cis,cis*-muconate
COO⁻
COO⁻
O
C=O
γ-carboxy muconolactone
COO⁻
O
C=O
β-ketoadipate enol lactone
O
COOH
COOH
β-ketoadipate

SCHEME 9.10

4,5-oxidoreductase, E.C. 1.13.1.8). Despite the different attack on protocatechuate, the *p*-hydroxybenzoate hydroxylase of *Pseudomonas putida* and of *Pseudomonas desmolytica* appear to be similar in their properties since both contain bound FAD and are specific for reduced $NADP^+$ (62, 170). An almost identical pathway of benzoate and *p*-hydroxybenzoate degradation exists in *Moraxella calcoacetica*. However, the regulation of the enzymes appears to be distinctively different from that of *Pseudomonas* (16).

An oxidative demethylation reaction was observed with *Pseudomonas fluorescens* and vanillate as substrate(18). Incomplete evidence suggests that the aromatic ring opens via the protocatechuate pathway. The demethylation reaction involved the absorption of 0.5 mole of O_2/mole substrate and required reduced glutathion and nucleotide, possibly reduced $NADP^+$. The methyl group was removed sequentially as formaldehyde, formate, and CO_2, whereby formaldehyde dehydrogenase (E.C. 1.2.1.1) and formate dehydrogenase (E.C. 1.2.2.1) were involved.

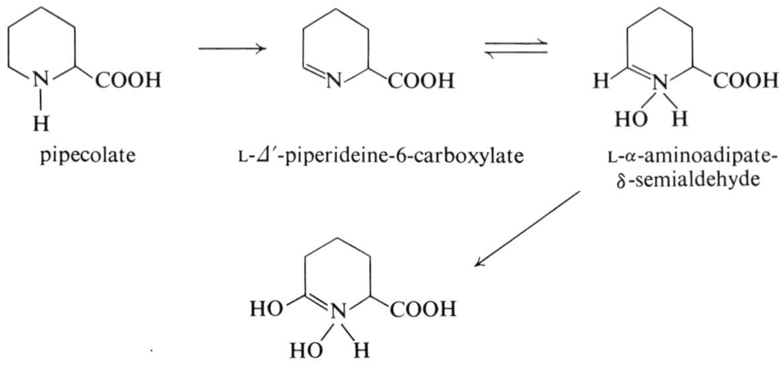

SCHEME 9.11. Metabolism of pipecolic acid by *Pseudomonas putida* (reprinted with permission of the American Society of Microbiology).

Pipecolic acid is a further aromatic compound metabolized by *Pseudomonas putida*(3) (see Scheme 9.11). D,L-Pipecolate is converted to L-Δ'-piperideine-6-carboxylate(5) under the catalyzing action of "*Pseudomonas* P 2 electron transport particle (P2-ETP)"(3), which may be a pipecolate dehydrogenase. A nonenzymatic reaction converts this compound further to L-α-aminoadipate-δ-semialdehyde. The function of a L-α-aminoadipate-δ-semialdehyde: NAD oxidoreductase(12) finally produces L-α-aminoadipate(123). It is suggested that the further metabolism leads to glutamate. The enzyme P2-ETP also contains FAD, FMN, iron, copper, and both b- and c-type cytochromes.

Hydroxyproline Metabolism

Hydroxyproline can be metabolized by some strains of *Pseudomonas* forming 2-oxoglutarate as their key intermediate for the entry into the TCA cycle (see Scheme 9.12). The first reaction from hydroxyproline to D-allo-hydroxyproline is a reversible function of an 2-epimerase (hydroxyproline 2-epimerase, E.C. 5.1.1.8) which is followed by an oxidase reaction with the formation of the intermediate Δ'-pyrroline-4-hydroxy-2-carboxylate(1). The latter undergoes an enzymatic deamination, which is catalyzed by the enzyme Δ'-pyrroline-4-hydroxy-2-carboxylate deaminase(128) to form 2,5-dioxo-valerate(129). The last step is a dehydrogenation of 2,5-dioxovalerate to 2-oxoglutarate which requires NADP as a cofactor.

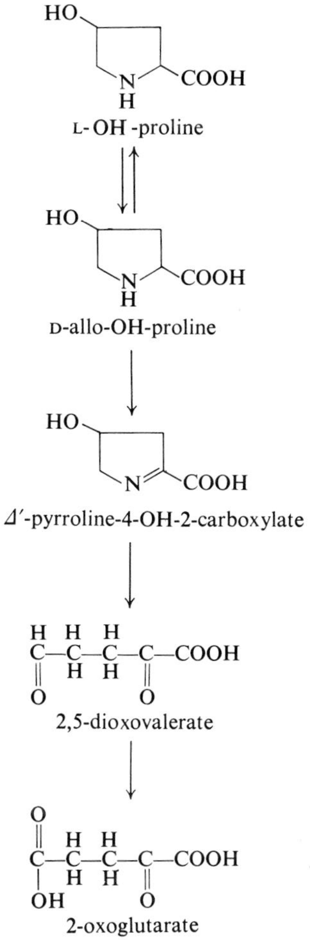

L- OH -proline

D-allo-OH-proline

Δ'-pyrroline-4-OH-2-carboxylate

2,5-dioxovalerate

2-oxoglutarate

SCHEME 9.12. Individual enzymatic steps and intermediates in the inducible oxidation of hydroxy-L-proline by extracts of *Pseudomonas striata* (reprinted with permission of the American Society of Biological Chemists).

Tryptophan Metabolism

Three categories of pseudomonads have been proposed(9) according to their pathways of tryptophan metabolism:

(1) the aromatic group, which degrades L-tryptophan via anthranilic acid(9);

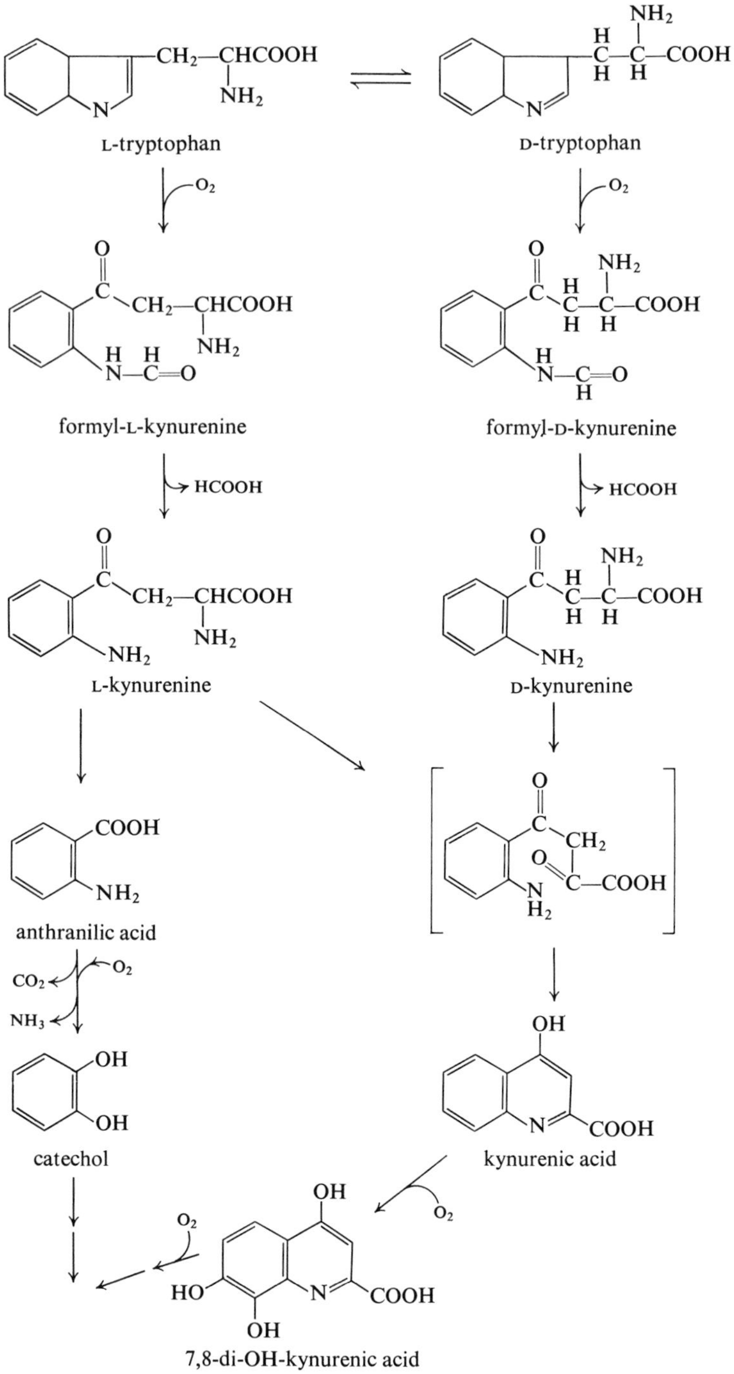

384

SCHEME 9.13. (Reprinted with permission of *Nature*, London.)

(2) the quinoline group, which degrades D- and L-tryptophan via kynurenic acid (7, 143); and

(3) the racemase–aromatic group, which degrades D- and L-tryptophan via anthranilic acid (9, 101).

The overall degradation of all three groups is outlined in Scheme 9.13.

The first group, which metabolizes L-tryptophan to anthranilic acid via L-kynurenine and catechol, from where they follow the α-ketoadipate pathway mentioned earlier, has been known for the longest time. The major gaps in our knowledge, however, still lie in the quinoline pathway. D-Tryptophan is possibly attacked in the same way as L-tryptophan (98). A D-specific tryptophan pyrrolase would convert D-tryptophan to D-formyl kynurenine in the same way as a L-specific tryptophan pyrrolase (98) (tryptophan oxygenase, E.C. 1.13.1.12) converts L-tryptophan to L-formyl kynurenine. The latter compound is metabolized by an kynurenine formamidase (aryl-formylamine amido-hydrolase, E.C. 3.5.1.9) to L-kynurenine. D-Kynurenine is subsequently oxidatively deaminated to kynurenic acid by D-kynurenine oxidase (143). In contrast, L-kynurenine is acted upon by kynureninase (L-kynurenine hydrolase, E.C. 3.7.1.3) forming anthranilic acid. Whereas anthranilic acid is oxidatively decarboxylated, kynurenic acid is metabolized to 7,8-dihydroxy-kynurenic acid with the aid of kynurenate hydroxylase (kynurenate, reduced NAD(P): oxygen oxidoreductase (hydroxylating), E.C. 1.14.1.4). Whereas catechol follows the β-ketoadipate pathway, the quinoline pathway has not been elucidated sufficiently but also yields intermediates of the TCA cycle.

These two pathways are not followed by all pseudomonads. Some strains of *Pseudomonas* (8) are able to racemize D-tryptophan to L-tryptophan and follow the pathway via anthranilic acid, whereas others are able to form kynurenic acid from L-kynurenine as indicated in the general scheme (Scheme 9.13). The degradation of tryptophan by *Pseudomonas* and *Flavobacterium* (101) is thus completely different from the metabolism of tryptophan in mammalian-tissue (48), possibly because of the availability of an oxygenase in these microorganisms.

Coumarin Metabolism

Arthrobacter metabolizes coumarin via a pathway which has not been fully elucidated as yet (see Scheme 9.14). Since coumarin is in fact the lactone of *cis*-coumarinic acid, a *cis-trans* isomerization on the double bond in the side chain of the aromatic ring is assumed to occur, giving rise to an *o-trans*-coumaric acid (88). This isomerization is produced by enzymatic hydrolysis between the oxygen and carbonyl carbon atom of the pyrone ring. *o*-Coumaric acid is reduced by the enzyme NADH: *o*-coumarate oxidoreductase to melilotic acid. In the presence of atmospheric oxygen and reduced NAD, a hydroxylation

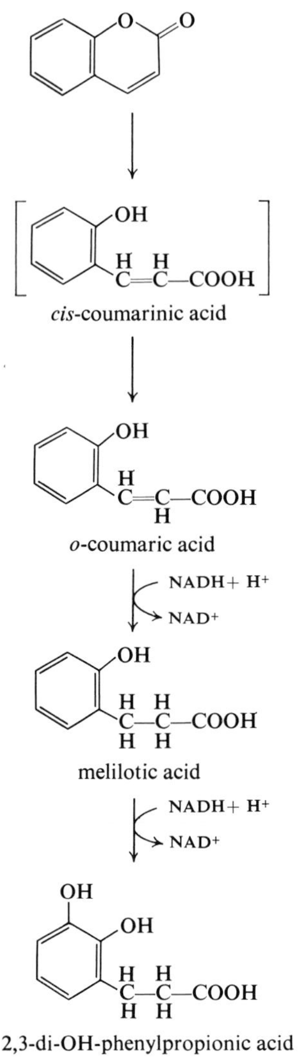

SCHEME 9.14. Degradation of coumarin by *Arthrobacter* (reprinted with permission of the American Society of Biological Chemists).

takes place which is mediated by an enzyme similar or identical to melilotate hydroxylase(89). This hydroxylation step produces 2,3-dihydroxyphenyl-propionic acid which is assumed to enter the catechol pathway possibly at the salicyclic or catechol level.

Allantoate Metabolism

The conversion of allantoate to glyoxylate and urea has been shown to be a two-step mechanism with ureidoglycolate as intermediate:

$$
\begin{array}{ccc}
\underset{\text{allantoate}}{\overset{\displaystyle \substack{H_2N \\ | \\ O{=}C \quad\quad COOH \quad C{=}O \\ | \quad\quad\quad\; | \quad\quad\quad | \\ HN\!\!-\!\!\!-\!\!\!-\!\!C\!\!-\!\!\!-\!\!\!-\!\!NH \\ | \\ H}}{}}
& \xrightarrow{\hspace{1cm}} &
\underset{\text{ureidoglycine}}{\overset{\displaystyle \substack{H_2N \\ | \\ O{=}C \quad COOH \\ | \quad\quad\; | \\ HN\!\!-\!\!C\!\!-\!\!NH_2 \\ | \\ H}}{}}
\quad + NH_3 + CO_2
\end{array}
$$

allantoate → ureidoglycine (+ NH₃ + CO₂)

↕ (solid line)   ⋮ ↓ (broken line)

$$
\underset{(-)\ \text{ureidoglycolate}}{\substack{H_2N \\ | \\ O{=}C \quad + \quad COOH \quad C{=}O \\ | \quad\quad\quad\quad | \quad\quad\quad | \\ H_2N \quad HO\!\!-\!\!C\!\!-\!\!\!-\!\!\!-\!\!NH \\ \quad\quad\quad | \\ \quad\quad\quad H}}
\qquad
\underset{(+)\ \text{ureidoglycolate}}{\substack{H_2N \\ | \\ O{=}C \quad COOH \\ | \quad\quad\; | \\ HN\!\!-\!\!C\!\!-\!\!OH \\ | \\ H}} \quad + NH_3
$$

(−) ureidoglycolate   (+) ureidoglycolate + NH₃

$$
\substack{COOH \\ | \\ HC{=}O} \quad + \quad \substack{NH_2 \\ | \\ C{=}O \\ | \\ NH_2}
$$

Pseudomonas aeruginosa converts allantoate to (−)ureidoglycolate and urea in a single step with the aid of the enzyme allantoicase (allantoate amidino-hydrolase, E.C. 3.5.3.4). A second molecule of urea together with glyoxylate is produced by the action of ureidoglycolase (E.C. 3.5.1 group) on (−)ureido-glycolate. The same organism is also able to metabolize (+)ureidoglycolate to glyoxylate and urea with allantoicase(145).

Pseudomonas acidovorans, on the other hand, follows a different pathway for allantoate metabolism. It appears that *P. acidovorans* lacks the enzyme allantoicase (E.C. 3.5.3.4), but possesses an enzyme called "allantoate amido-hydrolase"(146), which metabolizes allantoate to ureidoglycine with the liberation of ammonia and carbon dioxide. A ureidoglycine aminohydrolase converts ureidoglycine to (+)ureidoglycolate, which in turn is metabolized to its end products urea and glyoxylate by (+)ureidoglycolase. In the above general scheme the pathway of *Pseudomonas acidovorans* is indicated in a broken line.

It may be noted here that the aforementioned enzymatic reactions do not agree with the Enzyme Commission Report of the IUB. In this report the enzyme allantoicase (E.C. 3.5.3.4) still catalyzes the reaction of allantoate to glyoxylate. The lack of knowledge is also reflected in the assumption that (+)ureidoglycolate is metabolized by allantoicase to glyoxylate and urea by *Pseudomonas aeruginosa*, whereas the same substrate is metabolized by (+)ureidoglycolase to exactly the same end products in *Pseudomonas acidovorans*.

Pesticide Degradation

   Pesticides have become more and more a subject of active research. Modern pest-control research has been mainly concerned with the finding of potent organic compounds to control either a broad or narrow spectrum of pests, chiefly insects, weeds, and plant pathogens. The degradability of these pesticides therefore is of great practical importance since the toxicity of these chemicals can endanger the life of man. Although pesticides may be destroyed or detoxified by various mechanisms in the soil, the major means of degradation is a consequence of biological activity. The most resistant pesticides are the chlorinated hydrocarbon insecticides such as aldrin, chlordane, DDT, and dieldrin and phenoxy herbicides such as 2-(2,4-dichlorophenoxy)propionic acid (2). There appears to be a distinct influence of chemical structure on the persistence and rate of decomposition of phenoxyalkyl carboxylic acid herbicides. Compounds naving a chlorine on the aromatic ring meta to the ether linkage and alpha-substituted phenoxyalkyl carboxylic acids are more resistant to biodegradation than those having no meta halogen on the aromatic ring and ω-substitution on the side chain. Most of the work has been done with the dichlorophenoxyacetic acid compounds, these were known to be degraded by soil microorganisms, yet their pathways are still obscure.

   The first step in the degradation of 2,4-dichlorophenoxyacetic acid seems to be the oxidation of the acetic acid moiety of substituted phenoxyacetic acid to give the corresponding phenol, 2,4-dichlorophenol (136) (see Scheme 9.15).

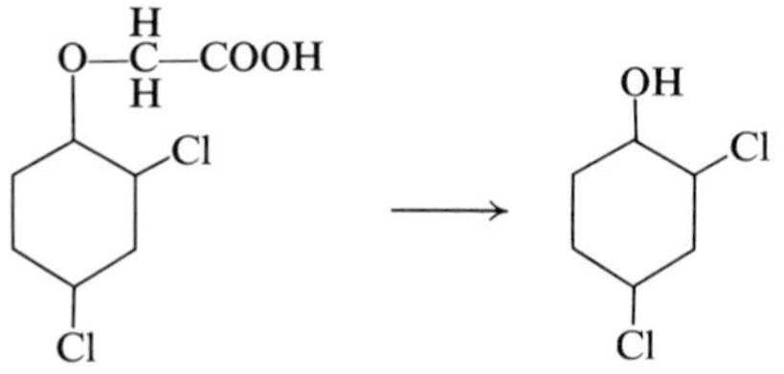

SCHEME 9.15

It is assumed that 2,4-dichlorophenol is converted next to 4-chlorocatechol although it is not known whether the microorganisms *Flavobacterium peregrinum* and *Achromobacter* sp. can use the β-ketoadipate pathway although the finding of p-chloromuconic acid(39) appear to support such a pathway. A similar degradation step was observed with 4-chlorophenoxyacetic acid, which was metabolized via 4-chlorophenol to 4-chlorocatechol. There are reports that *Corynebacterium* could also oxidize 2,4-dichlorophenol(126).

In using 4-chloro-2-methyl-phenoxyacetic acid as substrate, the first degradation steps appear to be identical to the one obtained with 2,4-dichloro-phenoxyacetic acid, as the corresponding phenol compound, in this case 5-chloro-2-cresol was formed (see Scheme 9.16). This adaptation of the microorganism to the oxidation of above-mentioned chlorinated hydro-carbons was only achieved by growing the cultures on peptone media with small quantities of either of the substrates present(137). By using the method

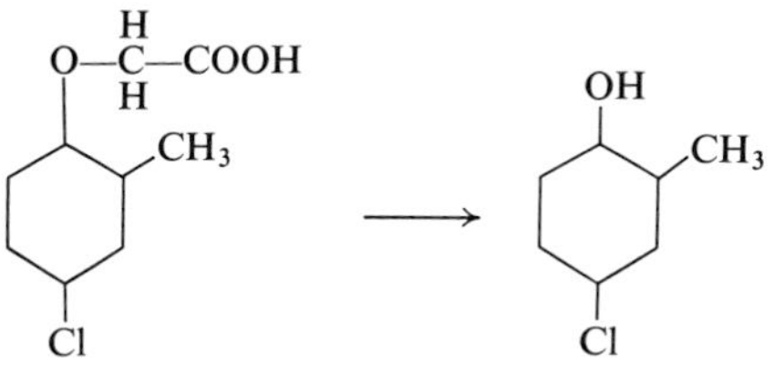

SCHEME 9.16

of simultaneous adaptation(133), it was possible to obtain microorganisms capable of degrading chlorinated hydrocarbons.

The mechanism of the initial oxidation of phenoxyalkyl carboxylic acids, however, is still in question. Whereas some investigators (40, 135, 136, 137, 144, 155) suggest that the aliphatic moiety of these acids is metabolized by β-oxidation, studies with the decomposition of 4-(2,4-dichlorophenoxy)butyric acid by *Flavobacterium* sp. give evidence for a degradation by cleavage of the ether linkage rather than β-oxidation of fatty acid(97) (see Scheme 9.17). This

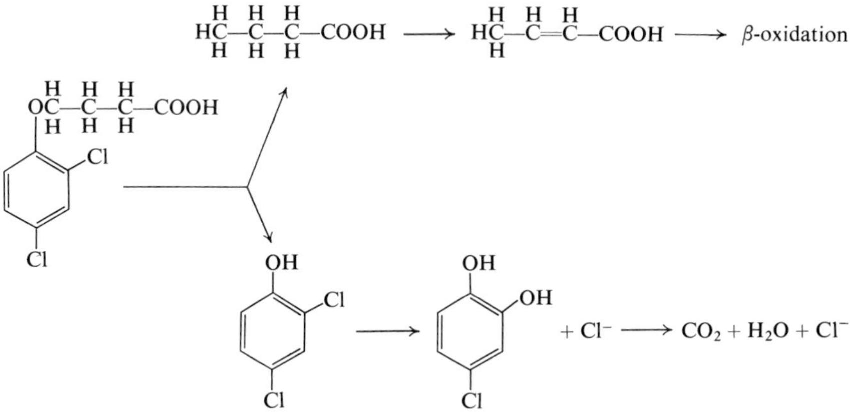

SCHEME 9.17

cleavage of the ether linkage results in the formation of 2,4-dichlorophenol and butyric acid. The 2,4-dichlorophenol is then dehalogenated at the *o*-position, and the resultant 4-chlorocatechol is readily and completely degraded, possibly with the formation of β-chloro-*cis,cis*-muconic acid.

It therefore appears that two pathways exist in the metabolism of these phenoxyalkyl carboxylic acids(96). The first pathway is used mainly by *Nocardia*. It involves a β-oxidation of the aliphatic moiety(144, 155) and leads to the production of phytotoxic intermediates from the original substrate, whereas the second pathway is initiated by a cleavage of the ether linkage, which leads to the immediate detoxication of the herbicidal activity.

OXYGENASES

Oxygenases are a group of enzymes which catalyze the incorporation of molecular oxygen into various organic compounds(53). They are recognized

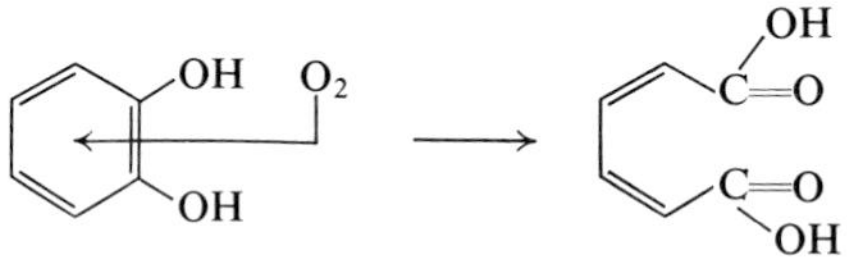

SCHEME 9.18

by the Enzyme Commission of the IUB as enzymes catalyzing the addition of molecular oxygen across a double bond between two carbon atoms. While doing so they add both atoms of the oxygen molecule to the substrate (see Scheme 9.18). It is important to note that both oxygen atoms are added to

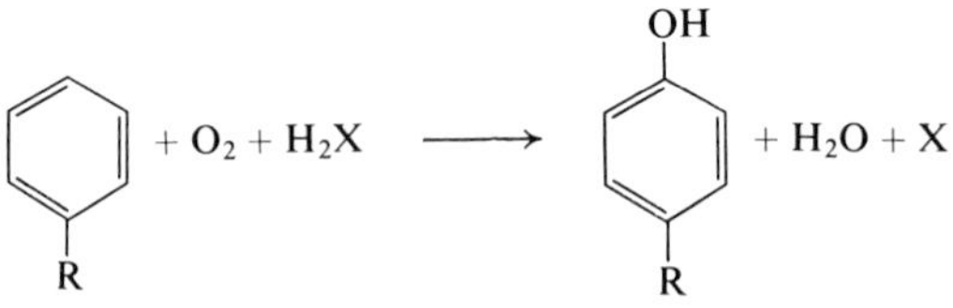

SCHEME 9.19

the substrate and none of the added oxygen atoms arises from solvent water. Hayaishi(53) uses the term "dioxygenases" for this type of enzyme.

In the same subgroup of enzymes belong the enzymes called "hydroxylases." These are enzymes which also catalyze the addition of molecular oxygen to a substrate, but only one atom of the molecular oxygen is incorporated into the substrate with the second atom forming water (see Scheme 9.19). In this reaction H_2X represents an electron donor. Hayaishi(53) uses the term "monooxygenase" for this type of enzyme.

An oxygenase should be distinctly separated from an oxidase. The latter are enzymes which use molecular oxygen as an electron acceptor and therefore form hydrogen peroxide as product. They do not incorporate oxygen into the substrate.

Oxygenases are widely distributed in nature. They are important in both catabolic and synthetic reactions generally involving aromatic compounds. They may account in part for the wide versatility of the pseudomonads with respect to utilizable substrates. In these pathways they are often the first enzyme and transform a generally nonreactive hydrocarbon such as benzene and naphthalene to one which can be utilized by the common metabolic pathways. In the case of n-alkanes oxygenases oxygenate these compounds to give the fatty acids which are then metabolized by ω- or β-oxidation.

Further references on this subject in regard to the detailed mechanism of the oxygenases can be obtained in a number of excellent reviews and papers available (51, 52, 54–57, 69, 75, 104). The oxidations of anthracene and phenanthrene seem to be via catechol and continue as demonstrated in the general scheme. There are, of course, still a great number of cyclic compounds of which the metabolism has not yet been clarified.

REFERENCES

1. Adams, E. (1959). Hydroxyproline metabolism. I. Conversion to α-ketoglutarate by extracts of *Pseudomonas*. *J. Biol. Chem.* **234**, 2073.
2. Alexander, M. (1965). Biodegradation: Problems of molecular recalcitrance and microbial fallibility. *Appl. Microbiol.* **7**, 35.
3. Baginsky, M. L., and Rodwell, V. W. (1966). Metabolism of pipecolic acid in a *Pseudomonas* species. IV. Electron transport particle of *Pseudomonas putida*. *J. Bacteriol.* **92**, 424.
4. Bailey, E., and Hullin, R. P. (1966). The metabolism of glyoxylate by cell-free extracts of *Pseudomonas* sp. *Biochem. J.* **101**, 755.
4a. Barrett, J. T., and Kallio, R. E. (1953). Terminal respiration in *Pseudomonas fluorescens*: component enzymes of the tricarboxylic acid cycle. *J. Bacteriol.* **66**, 517.
5. Basso, L. V., Rao, D. R., and Rodwell, V. W. (1962). Metabolism of pipecolic acid in *Pseudomonas* species. II. Δ'-Piperideine-6-carboxylic acid and α-amino-adipic acid-δ-semialdehyde. *J. Biol. Chem.* **237**, 2239.
6. Bayley, R. C., Dagley, S., and Gibson, D. T. (1966). The metabolism of cresols by species of *Pseudomonas*. *Biochem. J.* **101**, 293.
7. Behrman, E. J. (1962). Tryptophan metabolism in *Pseudomonas*. *Nature* **196**, 150.
8. Behrman, E. J., and Cullen, A. M. (1961). Enzymatic racemization of tryptophan. *Federation Proc.* **20**, 6.
9. Behrman, E. J., and Stella, E. J. (1963). Enrichment procedures for the isolation of tryptophan-oxidizing organisms. *J. Bacteriol.* **85**, 946.
10. Breed, R. S., Murray, E. G. D., and Smith, N. R. (1957). "Bergey's Manual of Determinative Bacteriology," 7th ed. Williams & Wilkins, Baltimore, Maryland.
11. Brisbane, P. G., and Ladd, J. N. (1965). The role of microorganisms in petroleum exploration. *Ann. Rev. Microbiol.* **19**, 351.

12. Calvert, A. F., and Rodwell, V. W. (1966). Metabolism of pipecolic acid in a *Pseudomonas* species. III. L-α-aminoadipate-δ-semialdehyde: NAD oxidoreductase. *J. Biol. Chem.* **241**, 409.

13. Campbell, J. J. R., and Norris, F. C. (1950). The intermediate metabolism of *Pseudomonas aeruginosa*. IV. The absence of an Embden-Meyerhof system as evidenced by phosphorus distribution. *Can. J. Res.* **C28**, 203.

14. Campbell, J. J. R., Norris, F. C., and Norris. M. E. (1949). The intermediate metabolism of *Pseudomonas aeruginosa*. II. Limitations of simultaneous adaptation as applied to the identification of acetic acid, an intermediate in glucose oxidation. *Can. J. Res.* **C27**, 165.

15. Campbell, J. J. R., Ramakrishnan, T., Linnes, A. G., and Eagles, B. A. (1956). Evaluation of the energy gained by *Pseudomonas aeruginosa* during the oxidation of glucose to 2-ketogluconate. *Can. J. Microbiol.* **2**, 304.

16. Canovas, J. L., and Stanier, R. Y. (1967). Regulation of the enzymes of the β-ketoadipate pathway in *Moraxella calcoacetica*. I. General aspects. *European J. Biochem.* **1**, 289.

17. Cartwright, L. N., and Hullin, R. P. (1966). Purification and properties of two glyoxylate reductases from a species of *Pseudomonas*. *Biochem. J.* **101**, 781.

18. Cartwright, N. J., and Smith, A. R. W. (1967). Bacterial attack on phenolic ethers. An enzyme system demethylating vanillic acid. *Biochem. J.* **102**, 826.

19. Clagett, C. O., Tolbert, N. E., and Burris, R. H. (1949). *J. Biol. Chem.* **178**, 977; as cited by Cartwright and Hullin (17).

20. Claridge, C. A., and Werkman, C. H. (1954). Evidence for alternate pathways for the oxidation of glucose by *Pseudomonas fluorescens*. *J. Bacteriol.* **68**, 77.

21. Clarke, P. H., and Meadow, P. H. (1959). Evidence for the occurrence of permeases for tricarboxylic acid cycle intermediates in *Pseudomonas aeruginosa*. *J. Gen. Microbiol.* **24**, 144.

22. Cline, A. L., and Hu, A. S. L. (1965). The isolation of three sugar dehydrogenases from a pseudomonad. *J. Biol. Chem.* **240**, 4488.

23. Cooper, R. A., and Kornberg, H. L. (1964). The utilization of itaconate by *Pseudomonas* sp. *Biochem. J.* **91**, 82.

24. Cooper, R. A., Itiaba, K., and Kornberg, H. L. (1965). The utilization of aconate and itaconate by *Micrococcus* sp. *Biochem. J.* **94**, 25.

25. Dagley, S., and Trudgill, P. W. (1963). The metabolism of tartaric acid by a *Pseudomonas*. A new pathway. *Biochem. J.* **89**, 22.

26. Dagley, S., Chapman, P. J., Gibson, D. T., and Wood, J. M. (1964). Degradation of the benzene nucleus by bacteria. *Nature* **202**, 775.

27. Dawes, E. A., Ribbons, D. W., and Large, P. J. (1966). The route of ethanol formation in *Zymomonas mobilis*. *Biochem. J.* **98**, 795.

28. DeLey, J. (1960). Comparative carbohydrate metabolism and localization of enzymes in *Pseudomonas* and related microorganisms. *J. Appl. Bacteriol.* **23**, 400.

29. DeLey, J. (1964). *Pseudomonas* and related genera. *Ann. Rev. Microbiol.* **18**, 17.

30. DeLey, J., and Doudoroff, M. (1957). The metabolism of D-galactose in *Pseudomonas saccharophila*. *J. Biol. Chem.* **227**, 745.

31. DeLey, J., and Vandamme, J. (1955). The metabolism of sodium 2-keto-D-gluconate by microorganisms. *J. Gen. Microbiol.* **12**, 162.

32. Dixon, M., and Webb, E. C. (1964). "Enzymes," 2nd ed. Longmans, Green, New York.

33. Eagon, R. G. (1958). Localization of glucose, gluconate, and glucose-6-phosphate oxidation systems in extracts of *Pseudomonas fluorescens*. *Can. J. Microbiol.* **4**, 1.

34. Eagon, R. G. (1962). Pyridine nucleotide-linked reactions of *Pseudomonas natriegens*. *J. Bacteriol.* **84**, 819.

35. Eagon, R. G., and Cho, H. W. (1965). Major products of glucose dissimilation by *Pseudomonas natriegens*. *J. Bacteriol*. **89**, 1209.

36. Eagon, R. G., and Wang, C. H. (1963). Dissimilation of glucose and gluconic acid by *Pseudomonas natriegens*. *J. Bacteriol*. **85**, 879.

37. Entner, N., and Doudoroff, M. (1952). Glucose and gluconic acid oxidation by *Pseudomonas saccharophila*. *J. Biol. Chem*. **196**, 853.

38. Entner, N., and Stanier, R. Y. (1951). Studies on the oxidation of glucose by *Pseudomonas fluorescens*. *J. Bacteriol*. **62**, 181.

39. Evans, W. C., and Moss, P. (1957). The metabolism of the herbicide, *p*-chlorophenoxyacetic acid by a soil microorganism—the formation of a β-chloromuconic acid on ring fission. *Biochem. J*. **65**, 8P.

40. Evans, W. C., and Smith, B. S. W. (1954). The photochemical inactivation and microbial metabolism of the chlorophenoxyacetic acid herbicides. *Biochem. J*. **57**, XXX.

41. Forney, F. W., Markovetz, A. J., and Kallio, R. E. (1967). Bacterial oxidation of 2-tridecanone to 1-undecanol. *J. Bacteriol*. **93**, 649.

42. Fossitt, D. D., and Bernstein, I. A. (1963). Fructose-1,6-diphosphatase from *Pseudomonas saccharophila*. *J. Bacteriol*. **86**, 598.

43. Fossitt, D. D., and Bernstein, I. A. (1963). Biosynthesis of ribose and deoxyribose in *Pseudomonas saccharophila*. *J. Bacteriol*. **86**, 1326.

44. Foster, J. W. (1962). Hydrocarbons as substrates for microorganisms. *Antonie van Leeuwenhoek, J. Microbiol. Serol*. **28**, 241.

45. Frampton, E. W., and Wood, W. A. (1961). Carbohydrate oxidation by *Pseudomonas fluorescens*. VI. Conversion of 2-keto-6-phosphogluconate to pyruvate. *J. Biol. Chem*. **235**, 2165.

46. Fredericks, K. M. (1967). Products of the oxidation of *n*-decane by *Pseudomonas aeruginosa* and *Mycobacterium rhodochrous*. *Antonie van Leeuwenhoek, J. Microbiol. Serol*. **33**, 41.

47. Fuhs, G. W. (1961). *Arch. Mikrobiol*. **39**, 374; cited by Foster (44).

48. Gholson, R. K., Nishizuka, Y., Ichiyama, A., Kawai, H., Nakamura, S., and Hayaishi, O. (1962). New intermediates in the catabolism of tryptophan in mammalian liver. *J. Biol. Chem*. **237**, PC2043.

49. Gibbs, M., and DeMoss, R. (1954). Anaerobic dissimilation of ¹⁴C-labelled glucose and fructose by *Pseudomonas lindneri*. *J. Biol. Chem*. **207**, 689.

50. Gilvarg, C., and Davis, B. D. (1956). The role of the tricarboxylic acid cycle in acetate oxidation in *Escherichia coli*. *J. Biol. Chem*. **222**, 307.

51. Guroff, G., and Ho, T. (1963). Induced soluble phenylalanine hydroxylase from *Pseudomonas* grown on phenylalanine and tyrosine. *Biochim. Biophys. Acta* **77**, 157.

52. Hayaishi, O., ed. (1962). "Oxygenases." Academic Press, New York.

53. Hayaishi, O. (1966). Crystalline oxygenase of *Pseudomonads*. *Bacteriol. Rev*. **30**, 720.

54. Hayaishi, O., and Stanier, R. Y. (1951). Bacterial oxidation of tryptophan. III. Enzymatic activities of cell-free systems from bacteria employing the aromatic pathway. *J. Bacteriol*. **62**, 691.

55. Hayaishi, O., Katagiri, M., and Rothberg, S. (1955). Mechanism of the pyrocatechase reaction. *J. Am. Chem. Soc*. **77**, 5450.

56. Hayaishi, O., Katagiri, M., and Rothberg, S. (1957). Studies on oxygenase-pyrocatechase. *J. Biol. Chem*. **229**, 905.

57. Hayaishi, O., Rothberg, S., Mehler, A. H., and Saito, Y. (1957). Studies on oxygenases, enzymatic formation of kynurenine from tryptophan. *J. Biol. Chem*. **229**, 889.

58. Hegeman, G. D. (1966). Synthesis of the enzymes of the mandelate pathway by *Pseudomonas putida*. I. Synthesis of enzymes by the wild type. *J. Bacteriol*. **91**, 1140.

59. Hegeman, G. D. (1966). Synthesis of the enzymes of the mandelate pathway by *Pseudomonas putida*. II. Isolation and properties of blocked mutants. *J. Bacteriol.* **91**, 1155.

60. Hegeman, G. D. (1966). Synthesis of the enzyme of the mandelate pathway. III. Isolation and properties of constitutive mutants. *J. Bacteriol.* **91**, 1161.

61. Hobbs, D. C., and Koeppe, R. R. (1958). The metabolism of glutaric acid-3-C¹⁴ by the intact rat. *J. Biol. Chem.* **230**, 655.

62. Hosokawa, K., and Stanier, R. Y. (1966). Crystallisation and properties of *p*-hydroxybenzoate hydroxylase from *Pseudomonas putida*. *J. Biol. Chem.* **241**, 2453.

63. Hullin, R. P., and Hassall, H. (1962). Butane-2,3-diol metabolism in *Pseudomonas*. *Biochem. J.* **83**, 298.

64. Iwasaki, K. (1965). The 6-phosphogluconolactonase in *Pseudomonas fluorescens*. *Seikagaku* **37**, 788; *Chem. Abstr.* **64**, 16211 (1966).

65. Jacobson, L. A., Bartholomans, R. C., and Gunsalus, I. C. (1966). Repression of malic enzyme by acetate in *Pseudomonas*. *Biochem. Biophys. Res. Commun.* **24**, 955.

66. Johnson, P. A., and Quayle, J. R. (1964). Microbial growth on C₁-compounds. 6. Oxidation of methanol, formaldehyde and formate by methanol-grown *Pseudomonas AM1*. *Biochem. J.* **93**, 281.

67. Juni, E., and Heym, G. A. (1956). A cyclic pathway for the dissimilation bacterial of 2,3-butanediol, acetoin and diacetyl. I. General aspects of the 2,3-butanediol cycle. *J. Bacteriol.* **71**, 425.

68. Juni, E., and Heym, G. A. (1956). Cyclic pathway for the bacterial dissimilation of 2,3-butanediol, acetylmethyl-carbinol, and diacetyl. III. A comparative study of 2,3-butanediol dehydrogenase from various microorganisms. *J. Bacteriol.* **74**, 757.

69. Katagiri, M., Maeno, H., Yamamoto, S., Hayaishi, O., Kito, H., and Oae, T. (1965). Salicylate hydroxylase—a mono-oxygenase requiring FAD. II. Mechanism of salicylate hydroxylation to catechol. *J. Biol. Chem.* **240**, 3414.

70. Katagiri, M., Takemori, S., Nakazawa, K., Suzuki, H., and Akagi, K. (1967). Benzyl-alcohol dehydrogenase, a new alcohol dehydrogenase from *Pseudomonas sp.*

70a. Katz, J., and Wood, H. G. (1960). The use of glucose-C¹⁴ for the evaluation of the pathways of glucose metabolism. *J. Biol. Chem.* **235**, 2165. *Biochim. Biophys. Acta* **139**, 173.

71. Klein, H. P. (1953). Some properties of the hexokinase of *Pseudomonas putrefaciens*. *J. Bacteriol.* **66**, 650.

72. Koepsell, H. J. (1950). Gluconate oxidation by *Pseudomonas fluorescens*. *J. Biol. Chem.* **186**, 743.

73. Koepsell, H. J., Stodola, F. H., and Sharpe, E. S. (1952). Production of α-ketoglutarate in glucose oxidation by *Pseudomonas fluorescens*. *J. Am. Chem. Soc.* **74**, 5142.

74. Kogut, M., and Podoski, E. P. (1953). Oxidative pathways in a fluorescent Pseudomonas. *Biochem. J.* **55**, 800.

75. Kojima, Y., Itada, N., and Hayaishi, O. (1961). Metapyrocatechase—a new catechol cleaving enzyme. *J. Biol. Chem.* **236**, 2223.

76. Kornberg, H. L. (1958). The metabolism of C₂-compounds in microorganisms. 1. The incorporation of 2-C¹⁴ acetate by *Pseudomonas fluorescens*, and by a *corynebacterium*, grown on ammonium acetate. *Biochem. J.* **68**, 535.

77. Kronberg, H. L. (1959). Aspects of terminal respiration in microorganisms. *Ann. Rev. Microbiol.* **13**, 49.

78. Kornberg, H. L. (1966). The role and control of the glyoxylate cycle in *Escherichia coli*. *Biochem. J.* **99**, 1.

79. Kornberg, H. L., and Elsden, S. R. (1961). The metabolism of 2-carbon compounds by microorganisms. *Advan. Enzymol.* **23**, 401.

80. Kornberg, H. L., and Gotto, A. M. (1961). The metabolism of C_2-compounds in microorganisms. 6. Synthesis of cell constituents from glycollate by *Pseudomonas* sp. *Biochem. J.* **78**, 69.

81. Kornberg, H. L., and Krebs, H. A. (1957). Synthesis of cell constituents from C_2 units by a modified tricarboxylic acid cycle. *Nature* **179**, 988.

82. Kornberg, H. L., and Madsen, N. B. (1958). The metabolism of C_2-compounds in microorganisms. 3. Synthesis of malate from acetate via the glyoxylate cycle. *Biochem. J.* **68**, 549.

83. Kornberg, H. L., and Sadler, J. R. (1960). Microbial oxidation of glycollate via a dicarboxylic acid cycle. *Nature* **185**, 153.

84. Kovachevich, R., and Wood, W. A. (1955). Carbohydrate metabolism of *Pseudomonas fluorescens*. III. Purification and properties of a 6-phosphogluconate dehydrase. *J. Biol. Chem.* **213**, 745.

85. Kovachevich, R., and Wood, W. A. (1955). Carbohydrate metabolism by *Pseudomonas fluorescens*. IV. Purification and properties of 2-keto-3-deoxy-6-phosphogluconate aldolase. *J. Biol. Chem.* **213**, 757.

86. Kusunose, M., Kusunose, E., and Coon, M. J. (1964). Enzymatic ω-oxidation of fatty acids. II. Substrate specificity and other properties of the enzyme system. *J. Biol. Chem.* **239**, 2135.

87. Kusunose, M., Matsumoto, J., Ishihara, K., Kusunose, E., and Nosaka, J. (1967). Requirement of three proteins for hydrocarbon oxidation. *J. Biochem. (Tokyo)* **61**, 665.

88. Levy, C. C. (1964). Metabolism of coumarin by a microorganism: o-coumaric acid as an intermediate between coumarin and melilotic acid. *Nature* **204**, 1059.

89. Levy, C. C., and Frost, P. (1966). The metabolism of coumarin by a microorganism. V. Melilotate hydroxylase. *J. Biol. Chem.* **241**, 997.

90. Lewis, K. F., Blumenthal, H. J., Weinrack, P. S., and Weinhouse, S. (1954). Glucose catabolism in *Pseudomonas fluorescens*. *Abstr. Proc. Am. chem. Soc.* p. 18c.

91. Lockwood, L. B., and Nelson, G. E. N. (1946). The oxidation of pentoses by *Pseudomonas*. *J. Bacteriol.* **52**, 581.

92. Lukins, H. B., and Foster, J. W. (1963). Utilization of hydrocarbons and hydrogen by mycobacteria. *Z. allgem. Mikrobiol.* **3**, 251.

93. MacDonald, D. L., Stanier, R. Y., and Ingraham, J. L. (1954). The enzymatic formation of β-carboxymuconic acid. *J. Biol. Chem.* **210**, 809.

94. McFadden, B. A., and Rao, G. R. (1964). Enzymes of the TCA cycle in *Pseudomonas indigofera*. *Can. J. Microbiol.* **10**, 503.

95. McKenna, E. J., and Kallio, R. E. (1965). The biology of hydrocarbons. *Ann. Rev. Microbiol.* **19**, 183.

96. MacRae, I. C., and Alexander, M. (1963). Metabolism of phenoxyalkyl carboxylic acids by a *Flavobacterium* species. *J. Bacteriol.* **86**, 1231.

97. MacRae, I. C., Alexander, M., and Rovira, A. D. (1963). The decomposition of 4-(2,4-dichlorophenoxy) butyric acid by *Flavobacterium* sp. *J. Gen. Microbiol.* **32**, 69.

98. Maeno, H., and Feigelson, P. (1967). Spectral studies on the catalytic mechanism and activation of *Pseudomonas* tryptophan oxygenase (tryptophan pyrrolase). *J. Biol. Chem.* **241**, 596.

99. Malesset-Bras, M., and Azoulay, E. (1964). Degradation bacterienne da naphthalene. *Ann. Inst. Pasteur* **109**, 894.

100. Mamkaeva, K. A. (1966). Formation of 2-ketogluconic acid by *Pseudomonas*. *Tr. Petergofsk. Biol. Inst., Leningr. Gos. Univ.* **19**, 104; *Chem. Abstr.* **65**, 19267 (1966).

396   9. PSEUDOMONADACEAE

101. Martin, J. R., and Durham, N. N. (1966). Metabolism of D-tryptophan by a species of *Flavobacterium. Can. J. Microbiol.* **12**, 1269.
102. Menon, G. K. K., and Stern, J. R. (1959). Enzymic synthesis and metabolism of coenzyme A esters of dicarboxylic acids. *Federation Proc.* **18**, 287.
103. Morris, J. G. (1965). The assimilation of 2-C compounds other than acetate. *J. Gen. Microbiol.* **32**, 167.
104. Nakazawa, T., Kojima, Y., Fujiwasa, H., Mazaki, M., Hayaishi, O., and Yamano, T. (1965). Studies on the mechanisms of pyrocatechase by ESR spectroscopy. *J. Biol. Chem.* **240**, PC3224.
105. Narrod, S. A., and Wood, W. A. (1954). Gluconate and 2-ketogluconate phosphorylation by extracts of *Pseudomonas fluorescens. Bacteriol. Proc.* p. 108.
106. Norris, F. C., and Campbell, J. J. R. (1949). The intermediate metabolism of *Pseudomonas aeruginosa.* III. The application of paper chromatography to the identification of gluconic and 2-ketogluconic acids, intermediates in glucose oxidation. *Can. J. Res.* **C27**, 253.
107. Numa, S., Ishimura, Y., Nishizuka, Y., and Hayaishi, O. (1961). β-Hydroxybutyryl-CoA, an intermediate in glutarate catabolism. *Biochem. Biophys. Res. Commun.* **6**, 38.
108. Numa, S., Ishimura, Y., Nakazawa, D., Okazaki, T., and Hayaishi, O. (1964). Enzymic studies on the metabolism of glutarate in *Pseudomonas. J. Biol. Chem.* **239**, 3915.
109. Olson, J. A. (1954). The d-isocitric lyase system: the formation of glyoxylic and succinic acids from D-isocitric acid. *Nature* **174**, 695.
110. Ornston, L. N. (1966). The conversion of catechol and protocatechuate to β-ketoadipate by *Pseudomonas putida.* II. Enzymes of the protocatechuate pathway. *J. Biol. Chem.* **241**, 3787.
111. Ornston, L. N. (1966). The conversion of catechol and protocatechuate to β-ketoadipate by *Pseudomonas putida.* III. Enzymes of the catechol pathway. *J. Biol. Chem.* **241**, 3795.
112. Ornston, L. N., and Stanier, R. Y. (1964). Mechanism of β-ketoadipate formation by bacteria. *Nature* **204**, 1279.
113. Ornston, L. N., and Stanier, R. Y. (1966). The conversion of catechol and protocatechuate to β-ketoadipate by *Pseudomonas putida.* I. Biochemistry. *J. Biol. Chem.* **241**, 3776.
114. Palleroni, N. J., and Doudoroff, M. (1957). Metabolism of carbohydrates by *Pseudomonas saccharophila.* III. Oxidation of D-arabinose. *J. Bacteriol.* **74**, 180.
115. Palleroni, N. J., Contopoulou, R., and Doudoroff, M. (1956). Metabolism of carbohydrates by *Pseudomonas saccharophila.* II. Nature of the kinase reaction involving fructose. *J. Bacteriol.* **71**, 202.
116. Peterson, J. A., Basu, D., and Coon, M. J. (1966). Enzymatic ω-oxidation. I. Electron carriers in fatty acid and hydrocarbon hydroxylation. *J. Biol. Chem.* **241**, 5162.
117. Quayle, J. R. (1963). The assimilation of 1-C compounds. *J. Gen. Microbiol.* **32**, 163.
118. Quayle, J. R. (1963). Carbon assimilation by *Pseudomonas oxalaticus* (OX 1). 7. Decarboxylation of oxalyl-coenzyme A to formyl-coenzyme A. *Biochem. J.* **89**, 492.
119. Quayle, J. R., and Keech, D. B. (1959). Carbon assimilation by *Pseudomonas oxalaticus* (OX 1). 1. Formate and carbon dioxide utilization during growth on formate. *Biochem. J.* **72**, 623.
120. Quayle, J. R., and Keech, D. B. (1959). Carbon assimilation by *Pseudomonas oxylaticus* (OX 1). 2. Formate and carbon dioxide utilization by cell-free extracts of the organism grown on formate. *Biochem. J.* **72**, 631.

121. Quayle, J. R., and Keech, D. B. (1959). Carboxydismutase activity in formate- and oxalate-grown *Pseudomonas oxalaticus* (OX 1). *Biochim. Biophys. Acta* **31**, 587.

122. Racker, E. (1954). Alternate pathways of glucose and fructose metabolism. *Advan. Enzymol.* **15**, 141.

123. Rao, D. R., and Rodwell, V. W. (1962). Metabolism of pipecolic acid in a *Pseudomonas* species. I. α-Aminoadipic and glutamic acids. *J. Biol. Chem.* **237**, 2232.

124. Robbins, K. C. (1961). Enzymatic omega oxidation of fatty acids. *Federation Proc.* **20**, 273.

125. Roberts, R. B., Abelson, P. H., Cowie, D. B., Bolton, E. T., and Britton, R. J. (1955). Studies of biosynthesis in *Escherichia coli. Carnegie Inst. Wash. Publ.* **607**; as cited by Kornberg and Gotto (80).

126. Rogoff, M. H., and Reid, J. J. (1956). Bacterial decomposition of 2,4-dichlorophenoxy acetic acid. *J. Bacteriol.* **71**, 303.

127. Saz, H. J., and Hillary, E. P. (1956). The formation of glyoxylate and succinate from tricarboxylic acids by *Pseudomonas aeruginosa. Biochem. J.* **62**, 563.

128. Singh, R. M. M., and Adams, E. (1965). Enzymatic deamination of Δ′-pyrroline-4-hydroxy-2-carboxylate to 2,5-dioxovalerate (α-ketoglutaric semialdehyde). *J. Biol. Chem.* **240**, 4344.

129. Singh, R. M. M., and Adams, E. (1965). Isolation and identification of 2,5-dioxovalerate, an intermediate in the bacterial oxidation of hydroxyproline. *J. Biol. Chem.* **240**, 4352.

130. Sistrom, W. R., and Stanier, R. Y. (1954). The mechanism of β-ketoadipic acid by bacteria. *J. Biol. Chem.* **210**, 821.

131. Skerman, V. B. D. (1967). "A Guide to the Identification of the Genera of Bacteria," 2nd ed. Williams & Wilkins, Baltimore, Maryland.

132. Sprecher, M., Berger, R., and Sprinson, D. B. (1964). Stereochemical course of the isocitrate lyase reaction. *J. Biol. Chem.* **239**, 4268.

133. Stanier, R. Y. (1947). Simultaneous adaptation: A new technique for the study of metabolic pathways. *J. Bacteriol.* **54**, 339.

134. Stanier, R. Y., and Tsuchida, M. (1959). Adaptive enzyme pattern in the bacterial oxidation of tryptophan. *J. Bacteriol.* **58**, 45.

135. Steenson, T. I., and Walker, N. (1956). Observations on the bacterial oxidation of chlorophenoxyacetic acids. *Plant Soil* **8**, 17.

136. Steenson, T. I., and Walker, N. (1957). The pathway of breakdown of 2:4-dichloro- and 4-chloro-2-methyl-phenoxy acetic acid by bacteria. *J. Gen. Microbiol.* **16**, 146.

137. Steenson, T. I., and Walker, N. (1958). Adaptive patterns in the bacterial oxidation of 2:4-dichloro- and 4-chloro-2-methyl-phenoxyacetic acid. *J. Gen. Microbiol.* **18**, 692.

138. Stern, I. C., Wang, C. H., and Gilmour, C. M. (1960). Comparative catabolism of carbohydrates in *Pseudomonas* species. *J. Bacteriol.* **79**, 601.

139. Stevenson, I. L., and Mandelstem, J. (1965). Induction and multisensitive endproduct repression in two converging pathways degrading aromatic substances in *Pseudomonas fluorescens. Biochem. J.* **96**. 354.

140. Stewart, D. J. (1959). Production of 5-ketogluconic acid by a species of *Pseudomonas. Nature* **183**, 1133.

141. Stewart, J. E., and Kallio, R. E. (1959). Bacterial hydrocarbon oxidation. II. Ester formation from alkanes. *J. Bacteriol.* **78**, 726.

142. Stodola, F. H., and Lockwood, L. B. (1947). The oxidation of lactose and maltose to bionic acids by *Pseudomonas. J. Biol. Chem.* **171**, 213.

143. Tashiro, M., Tsukada, M., Kobayashi, S., and Hayaishi, O. (1961). A new pathway of D-tryptophan metabolism: Enzymic formation of kynurenic acid via D-kynurenine. *Biochem. Biophys. Res. Commun.* **6**, 155.

144. Taylor, H. F., and Wain, R. L. (1962). Side chain degradation of certain ω-phenoxyalkane carboxylic acids by *Nocardia coeliaca* and other microorganisms isolated from soil. *Proc. Roy. Soc.* **B268**, 172.

145. Trijbels, F., and Vogels, G. D. (1966). Allantoicase and ureidoglycolase in pseudomonas and penicillium species. *Biochim. Biophys. Acta* **118**, 387.

146. Trijbels, F., and Vogels, G. D. (1967). Allantoate and ureidoglycolate degradation by *Pseudomonas aeruginosa. Biochim. Biophys. Acta* **132**, 115.

147. Trippett, S., Dagley, S., and Stopher, D. A. (1960). Bacterial oxidation of protocatechuic acid. *Biochem. J.* **76**, 9P.

148. Trudgill, P. W., and Widdus, R. (1966). D-Glucarate catabolism by *Pseudomonadaceae* and *Enterobacteriaceae. Nature* **211**, 1097.

149. Tustanoff, E. R., and Stern, J. R. (1960). Enzymic carboxylation of crotonyl-CoA and the metabolism of glutaric acid. *Biochem. Biophys. Res. Commun.* **3**, 81.

150. Tustanoff, E. R., and Stern, J. R. (1961). Oxidation of glutaryl coenzyme A to glutaconyl coenzyme A. *Federation Proc.* **20**, 272.

151. Van der Linden, A. C., and Thijsse, G. J. E. (1965). The mechanisms of microbial oxidations of petroleum hydrocarbons. *Advan. Enzymol.* **27**, 469.

152. von Tigerstrom, M., and Campbell, J. J. R. (1966). The tricarboxylic acid cycle, the glyoxylate cycle, and the enzymes of glucose oxidation in *Pseudomonas aeruginosa. Can. J. Microbiol.* **12**, 1015.

153. Wagner, C., Lusty, S. M., Jr., Kung, H. F., and Rogers, N. L. (1966). Trimethylsulfonium-tetrahydrofolate methyltransferase, a novel enzyme in the utilization of 1-carbon units. *J. Biol. Chem.* **241**, 1923.

154. Warburton, R. H., Eagles, B. A., and Campbell, J. J. R. (1951). The intermediate metabolism of *Pseudomonas aeruginosa.* V. The identification of pyruvate as an intermediate in glucose oxidation. *Can. J. Botany* **29**, 143.

155. Webley, D. M., Duff, R. B., and Farmer, V. C. (1957). Formation of β-hydroxy acid as an intermediate in the microbiological conversion of monochlorophenoxybutyric acids to the corresponding substituted acetic acids. *Nature* **179**, 1130.

156. Weil-Malherber, H. (1966). Some properties of mandelate racemase from *Pseudomonas fluorescens. Biochem. J.* **101**, 169.

157. Williams, A. K., and Eagon, R. G. (1959). Oxidation of 2-deoxy-D-glucose to 2-deoxy-D-gluconic acid by extracts of *Pseudomonas aeruginosa. J. Bacteriol.* **77**, 167.

158. Williams, J. P., Mayberry, W. R., and Payne, W. J. (1966). Metabolism of linear alcohols with various chain lengths by *Pseudomonas* species. *Appl. Microbiol.* **14**, 156.

159. Wolfe, J. B., Ivler, D., and Rittenberg, S. C. (1954). Malonate decarboxylation by *Pseudomonas fluorescens.* I. Observations with dry cells and cell-free extracts. *J. Biol. Chem.* **209**, 867.

160. Wolfe, J. B., Ivler, D., and Rittenberg, S. C. (1954). Malonate decarboxylation by *Pseudomonas fluorescens.* II. Mg^{2+} dependency and trapping of active intermediates. *J. Biol. Chem.* **209**, 875.

161. Wolfe, J. B., Ivler, D., and Rittenberg, S. C. (1954). Malonate decarboxylation by *Pseudomonas fluorescens.* III. Role of acetyl-CoA. *J. Biol. Chem.* **209**, 885.

162. Wood, W. A. (1955). Pathways, of carbohydrate degradation in *Pseudomonas fluorescens. Bacteriol. Rev.* **19**, 222.

163. Wood, W. A. (1957). Metabolism of carbohydrate and related compounds. *Ann. Rev. Microbiol.* **11**, 253.

164. Wood, W. A. (1961). Fermentation of carbohydrates and related compounds. *In* "The Bacteria" (I. C. Gunsalus and R. Y. Stanier, eds.), Vol. 2, p. 59. Academic Press, New York.

165. Wood, W. A., and Schwerdt, R. F. (1953). Alternate pathways of hexose oxidation in *Pseudomonas fluorescens. J. Cellular Comp. Physiol.* **41**, Suppl. 1, 165.

166. Wood, W. A., and Schwerdt, R. F. (1953). Carbohydrate oxidation by *Pseudomonas fluorescens.* I. The mechanism of glucose and gluconate oxidation. *J. Biol. Chem.* **201**, 501.

167. Wood, W. A., and Schwerdt, R. F. (1954). Carbohydrate oxidation by *Pseudomonas fluorescens.* II. Mechanism of hexose phosphate oxidation. *J. Biol. Chem.* **206**, 625.

168. Yamada, E. W., and Jacoby, W. B. (1959). Enzymatic utilization of acetylenic compounds. II. Acetylenemonocarboxylic acid hydrase. *J. Biol. Chem.* **234**, 941.

169. Yamada, E. W., and Jacoby, W. B. (1960). Enzymatic utilization of acetylenic compounds. V. Direct conversion of malonic semialdehyde to acetyl-coenzyme A. *J. Biol. Chem.* **235**, 589.

170. Yano, K., Yoshinaga, F., and Arima, K. (1963). *Koso Kagaku Shimpoziumu* **15**, 192; as cited in Hosokawa and Stanier (62).

171. Zelitch, I. (1953). *J. Biol. Chem.* **201**, 719; as cited by Cartwright and Hullin (17).

SUPPLEMENTARY READINGS

Adams, E., and Rosso, G. (1967). α-Ketoglutaric semialdehyde dehydrogenase of *Pseudomonas. J. Biol. Chem.* **242**, 1802.

Anthony, C., and Zatman, L. J. (1967). The prosthetic group of the alcohol dehydrogenase of *Pseudomonas sp. M 27*; a new oxidoreductase prosthetic group. *Biochem. J.* **103**, 19P.

Arima, K., and Nose, K. (1968). Studies on bacterial urate:oxygen oxidoreductase. I. Purification and properties of the enzyme. *Biochim. Biophys. Acta* **151**, 54.

Aurich, H., Kleber, H. P. and Schöpp, W. D. (1967). An inducible carnitine dehydrogenase from *Pseudomonas aeruginosa. Biochim. Biophys. Acta* **139**, 505.

Baginsky, M. L., and Rodwell, V. W. (1967). Metabolism of pipecolic acid in a *Pseudomonas* species. V. Pipecolate oxidase and dehydrogenase. *J. Bacteriol.* **94**, 1034.

Blackmore, M. A., Quayle, J. R., and Walker, I. O. (1968). Choice between autotrophy and heterotrophy in *Pseudomonas oxalaticus.* Utilization of oxalate by cells after adaptation from growth on formate to growth on oxalate. *Biochem. J.* **107**, 699.

Blackmore, M. A., and Quayle, J. R. (1968). Choice between autotrophy and heterotrophy in *Pseudomonas oxalaticus.* Growth in mixed substrates. *Biochem. J.* **107**, 705.

Blakley, E. R., Kurz, W., Halvorson, H., and Simpson, F. J. (1967). The metabolism of phenylacetic acid by a *Pseudomonas. Canad. J. Microbiol.* **13**, 447.

Bollag, J. M., Helling, C. S., and Alexander, M. (1967). Metabolism of 4-chloro-2-methylphenoxyacetic acid by soil bacteria. *Appl. Microbiol.* **15**, 1393.

Cain, R. B., Trauter, E. K., and Darrah, J. A. (1968). The utilization of some halogenated aromatic acids by *Nocardia.* Oxidation and metabolism. *Biochem. J.* **106**, 211.

Cain, R. B., and Farr, D. R. (1968). Metabolism of arylsulphonates by microorganisms. *Biochem. J.* **106**, 859.

Canovas, J. L. (1968). Regulation of convergent pathways for shikimate and p-hydroxybenzoate oxidation by *Moraxella. Biochem. J.* **106**, 30P.

Canovas, J. L., Wheelis, M. L., and Stanier, R. Y. (1968). Regulation of the enzymes of the β-ketoadipate pathway in *Moraxella calcoacetica.* 2. The role of protocatechuate as inducer. *European J. Biochem.* **3**, 293.

Canovas, J. L., Johnson, B. F., and Wheelis, M. L. (1968). Regulation of the enzymes of the β-ketoadipate pathway in *Moraxella calcoacetica*. 3. Effects of 3-hydroxy-4-methylbenzoate on the synthesis of enzymes of the protocatechuate branch. *European J. Biochem.* **3**, 305.

Canovas, J. L., and Johnson, B. F. (1968). Regulation of the enzymes of the β-ketoadipate pathway in *Moraxella calcoacetica*. 4. Constitutive synthesis of β-ketoadipate succinyl-CoA transferases II and III. *European J. Biochem.* **3**, 312.

Delafield, F. P., Doudoroff, M., Palleroni, N. J., Lusty, C. J., and Contopoulos, R. (1965). Decomposition of poly-β-hydroxy butyrate by pseudomonads. *J. Bacteriol.* **90**, 1455.

Farr, D. R., and Cain, R. B. (1968). Catechol oxygenase induction in *Pseudomonas aeruginosa*. *Biochem. J.* **106**, 879.

Fewson, C. A., and Kennedy, S. I. T. (1968). Regulation of enzymes of the mandelate pathway in *Bacterium* N.C.I.B. 8250. *Biochem. J.* **106**, 31P.

Fujisawa, H., and Hayaishi, O. (1968). Protocatechuate 3,4-dioxygenase. I. Crystallization and characterization. *J. Biol. Chem.* **243**, 2673.

Gaudy, E. T., and Wolfe, R. S. (1965). Ureidoglycolate synthetase of *Streptococcus allantoicus*. II. Properties of the enzyme and reaction equilibrium. *J. Bacteriol.* **90**, 1531.

Hegeman, G. D. (1967). The metabolism of p-hydroxybenzoate by *Rhodopseudomonas palustris* and its regulation. *Arch. Mikrobiol.* **59**, 143.

Hofham, J. B., Burgus, R. C., Ing, S. Y. S., and Pfiffner, J. J. (1968). Microbial degradation of corrinoids. VI. Reduction of hydroxocobalamin by cell-free particles from *Pseudomonas rubescens*. *J. Bacteriol.* **95**, 947.

Jeffcoat, R., Hassall, H., and Dagley, S. (1968). The metabolism of D-glucarate by a species of *Pseudomonas*. *Biochem. J.* **107**, 30P.

Kennedy, S. I. T., and Fewson, C. A. (1968). Enzymes of the mandelate pathway in *Bacterium* N.C.I.B. 8250. *Biochem. J.* **107**, 497.

Kohn, L. D., and Jakoby, W. B. (1968). Tartaric acid metabolism. III. The formation of glyceric acid. *J. Biol. Chem.* **243**, 2465.

Kohn, L. D., and Jakoby, W. B. (1968). Tartaric acid metabolism. IV. Crystalline L-malic dehydrogenase from *Pseudomonas acidovorans*. *J. Biol. Chem.* **243**, 2472.

Kohn, L. D., Packman, P. M., Allen, R. H., and Jakoby, W. B. (1968). Tartaric acid metabolism. V. Crystalline tartrate dehydrogenase. *J. Biol. Chem.* **243**, 2479.

Kohn, L. D., and Jakoby, W. B. (1968). Tartaric acid metabolism. VI. Crystalline oxaloglycolate reductive decarboxylase. *J. Biol. Chem.* **243**. 2486.

Kohn, L. D., and Jakoby, W. B. (1968). Tartaric acid metabolism. VII. Crystalline hydroxypyruvate reductase D-glycerate dehydrogenase). *J. Biol. Chem.* **243**, 2494.

Maeno, H., and Feigelson, P. (1968). Studies on the interaction of carbon monoxide with tryptophan oxygenase of *Pseudomonas*. *J. Biol. Chem.* **243**, 301.

Mann, S. (1967). Chinazolinderivate bei Pseudomonaden. *Arch. Mikrobiol.* **56**, 324.

Nozaki, M., Ono, K., Nakazawa, T., Kotani, S., and Hayaishi, O. (1968). Metapyrocatechase. II. The role of iron and sulfhydryl group. *J. Biol. Chem.* **243**, 2682.

Peterson, J. A., and Coon, M. J. (1968). Enzymatic ω-oxidation. III. Purification and properties of rubredoxin, a component of the ω-hydroxylation system of *Pseudomonas oleovorans*. *J. Biol. Chem.* **243**, 329.

Peterson, J. A., Kusunose, M., Kusunose, E., and Coon, M. J. (1967). Enzymatic ω-oxidation. II. Function of rubredoxin as the electron carrier in ω-hydroxylation. *J. Biol. Chem.* **242**, 4334.

Shuster, C. W., and Doudoroff, M. (1967). Purification of 2-keto-3-deoxy-6-phosphohexonate aldolases of *Pseudomonas saccharophila*. *Arch. Mikrobiol.* **59**, 279.

Smith, A., Trauter, E. K., and Cain, R. B. (1968). The utilization of some halogenated aromatic acids by *Nocardia*. Effects on the growth and enzyme induction. *Biochem. J.* **106**, 203.

Stachow, C. S., Stevenson, I. L., and Day, D. (1967). Purification and properties of nicotinamide adenine dinucleotide phosphate-specific benzaldehyde dehydrogenase from *Pseudomonas. J. Biol. Chem.* **242**, 5294.

Stalon, V., Ramos, F., Pierard, A., and Wiame, J. M. (1967). The occurrence of a catabolic and an anabolic ornithine carbamoyltransferase in *Pseudomonas. Biochim. Biophys. Acta* **139**, 91.

Stanier, R. Y. (1968). Control of the enzymes of the β-ketoadipate pathway in bacteria. *Biochem. J.* **106**, 25P.

Stevenson, I. L. (1967). Utilization of aromatic hydrocarbons by *Arthrobacter. Canad. J. Microbiol.* **13**, 205.

Stoolmiller, A. C., and Abeles, R. H. (1966). Formation of α-ketoglutaric semialdehyde from L-2-keto-3-deoxyarabonic acid and isolation of L-2-keto-3-deoxy-arabonate dehydratase from *Pseudomonas saccharophila. J. Biol. Chem.* **241**, 5764.

Treccani, V., Galli, E., Catelani, D., and Scorlini, C. (1968). Induction of 1,2- and 2,3-diphenol oxygenases in *Pseudomonas desmolyticum. Z. allg. Mikrobiol.* **8**, 65.

van der Linden, A. C. (1967). Dissimilation of 1,6-hexanediol and 1,8-octanediol by a hydrocarbon-oxidizing *Pseudomonas. Ant. v. Leeuwenhoek J. Microbiol. Serol.* **33**, 381.

van der Linden, A. C., and Huybregtse, R. (1967). Induction of alkane-oxidizing and α-olefin-epoxidizing enzymes by a non-hydrocarbon in a *Pseudomonas. Ant. v. Leeuwenh. J. Microbiol. Serol.* **33**, 381.

Wedemeyer, G. (1967). Biodegradation of dichlorodiphenyltrichloroethane: Intermediates in dichlorodiphenylacetic acid metabolism by *Aerobacter aerogenes. Appl. Microbiol.* **15**, 1494.

Wheelis, M. L., Palleroni, N. J., and Stanier, R. Y. (1967). The metabolism of aromatic acids by *Pseudomonas tetosteroni* and *Pseudomonas acidovorans. Arch. Mikrobiol.* **59**, 302.

10

NITROGEN METABOLISM AS AN ENERGY SOURCE FOR ANAEROBIC MICROORGANISMS (*CLOSTRIDIUM*)

The ability to break down proteins to peptones, polypeptides, and amino acids is not shared equally by all groups of bacteria. Since, however, the majority of these organic nitrogenous compounds are at an oxidation level between carbohydrates and fats, they are potentially useful as a source of carbon, nitrogen, and energy for both aerobic and anaerobic microorganisms. There are two possibilities open for the cell which metabolizes these large molecules that are normally outside the cell. There is plenty of evidence(17) available to show that the passage of molecules across the cell membrane is not determined solely by size, although size is certainly an important factor. Mechanisms for the passage of large molecules seem to be not as frequent as for small molecules (permeases!). This is particularly so for bacteria where nearly all the enzymes liberated outside the cell seem to be concerned with the metabolism of large molecules. These enzymes are called "exoenzymes" in contrast to the endoenzymes. Very little work has so far been directed to the problem of exoenzymatic liberation in bacteria. Pollock(17) states the reason for this as follows: "The only method of formally proving an enzyme to be extracellular according to the definition would be to demonstrate its liberation from a series of individual cells subsequently shown to be capable of normal growth and metabolism. So far, this has not been attempted . . .". Pollock continues: "In most reported work on exoenzymes little effort is made to control or estimate the extent of cell autolysis. There are, however, relatively simple, although indirect, ways of measuring the degree of lysis in a bacterial culture, and it should not be difficult to investigate the liberation of enzymes under conditions where the possibility of autolysis is minimized." Too often, exoenzymatic studies are done with old cultures, whereas young cultures in the logarithmic phase of growth should be used.

The bacteria involved in protein metabolism therefore must have proteolytic enzymes in order to break these polymeric compounds into their monomeric components before they can enter the cell and be used either as building blocks or as fermentative substrates.

The present discussion will be limited to the decomposition of nitrogenous compounds by bacteria under anaerobic conditions without the intervention of inorganic oxidizing agents such as sulfate, nitrate, or carbonate. It also will exclude such processes as denitrification. Proteolytic enzymes fall into two classes, endopeptidases and exopeptidases, according to their mode of action on a polypeptide chain. Such a chain can be attacked in two ways—at either ends or at random points along its length:

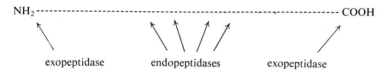

NH_2 - COOH

exopeptidase   endopeptidases   exopeptidase

The enzyme pepsin (E.C. 3.4.4.1), for example, is a typical endopeptidase, attacking polypeptide chains wherever aromatic R groups (L-phenylalanine or L-tyrosine) occur.

A further basis for their differentiation lies in their activation by metals such as Fe, Mn, and Mg and by reducing agents such as –CN or –SH. Exopeptidases are subdivided as follows:

(1) aminopeptidases, which require a free terminal $-NH_2$ group and are dependent on metal ions for their activity, and
(2) carboxypeptidases, which hydrolyze peptides with a free terminal –COOH group.

Both types of enzymes can break down the chain, liberating amino acids until the di- or tripeptidases complete the task of hydrolysis forming free amino acids. These monomers are now able to diffuse into the cell and be utilized. For further biochemical details the reader is referred to appropriate textbooks.

The catabolism of amino acids is carried out by a great number of anaerobic or facultative anaerobic bacteria. This is done either with single amino acids or pairs of amino acids or one amino acid in combination with one non-nitrogenous compound.

SINGLE AMINO ACID METABOLISM

All processes which liberate ammonia from amino acids are called "deaminations." Bacterial deamination proceeds in several ways, which differ according to the enzymatic constitution of the organism and to the conditions prevailing in the medium.

Oxidative deamination is a reaction whereby the products of the process are a keto acid and ammonia:

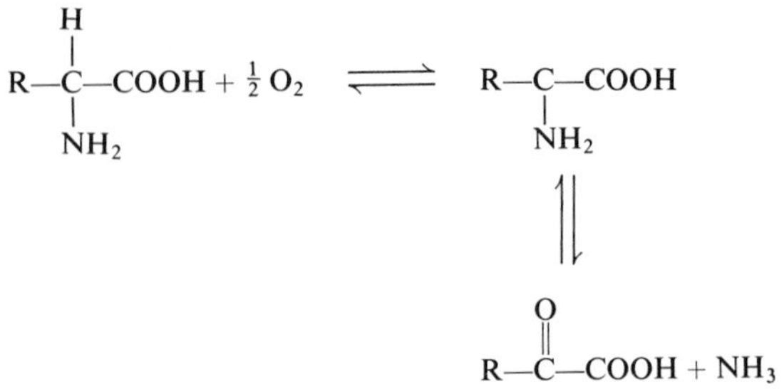

$$R{-}\underset{NH_2}{\overset{H}{C}}{-}COOH + \tfrac{1}{2}O_2 \rightleftharpoons R{-}\underset{NH_2}{C}{-}COOH$$

$$R{-}\overset{O}{C}{-}COOH + NH_3$$

An oxidative deamination of D,L-alanine, for example, results in the accumulation of pyruvate.

In the case of a desaturation deamination, the end product is an unsaturated fatty acid:

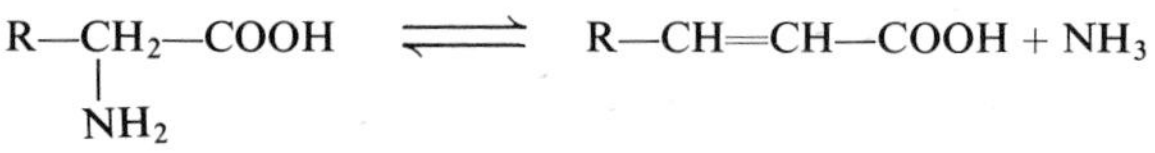

$$R{-}\underset{NH_2}{CH_2}{-}COOH \rightleftharpoons R{-}CH{=}CH{-}COOH + NH_3$$

In general, however, the compound resulting from deamination by a strict anaerobe or by a facultative anaerobe acting anaerobically is the corresponding saturated fatty acid, which is obtained by a reductive deamination:

$$R{-}CH_2{-}\underset{NH_2}{CH}{-}COOH + 2 H^+ \longrightarrow R{-}CH_2{-}CH_2{-}COOH + NH_3$$

This reduction deamination can be clearly demonstrated when the organism contains dehydrogenase (E.C. 1.12.1.1) and hydrogen acts as the hydrogen donor.

Clostridium tetanomorphum exhibits an anaerobic oxidative deamination which is accompanied by the evolution of hydrogen. This type of reaction may perhaps be regarded as an anaerobic device for obtaining energy from amino acids without the use of a hydrogen acceptor. Stickland(21–23) established the following reactions and end products:

$$alanine \rightarrow acetic\ acid + NH_3 + CO_2$$

$$glycine \rightarrow acetic\ acid + NH_3$$

$$proline \rightarrow \alpha\text{-amino valeric acid}$$

Cohen-Bazire *et al.* (4) added to these the end products derived from suspensions of *Clostridium caproicum* and/or *Clostridium valerianum*

$$\text{valine} \rightarrow \text{isobutyric acid} + CO_2$$

$$\text{leucine} \rightarrow \text{isovaleric acid} + CO_2$$

$$\text{isoleucine} \rightarrow \text{valeric acid} + CO_2$$

Arginine Metabolism

Arginine metabolism is a significant metabolic step for species of *Mycoplasma* which have been isolated from cell cultures. The conversion of arginine is rapid and appears to be the major source of ATP (1, 19):

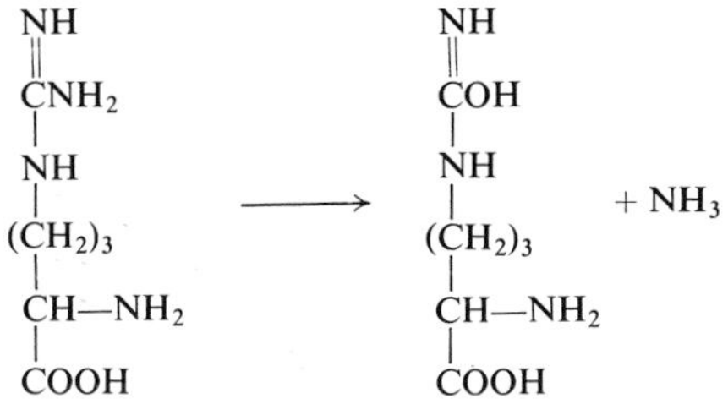

L-arginine L-citrulline

L-Arginine is deaminated first by an arginine deaminase (L-arginine iminohydrolase, E.C. 3.5.3.6) which is followed by a reversible transferase reaction, converting L-citrulline to ornithine:

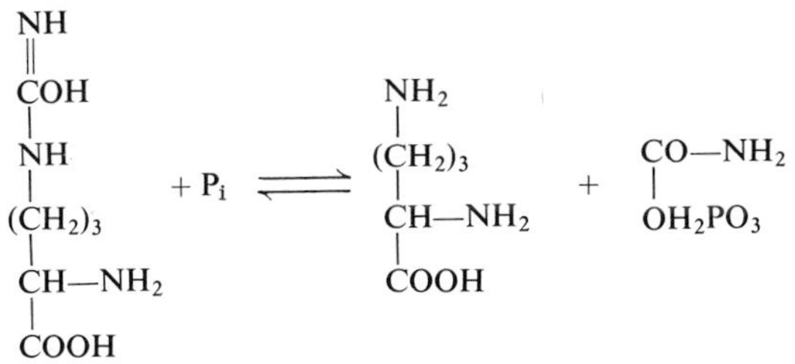

L-citrulline L-ornithine carbamoyl phosphate

The responsible enzyme for this reaction is ornithine carbamoyltransferase (carbamoyl phosphate: L-ornithine carbamoyltransferase, E.C. 2.1.3.3) and requires inorganic phosphate. This is followed by the vital energy-yielding reaction—the degradation of carbamoyl phosphate to ammonia and carbon dioxide with carbamate kinase (ATP: carbamate phosphotransferase, E.C. 2.7.2.2), which is an ATP-dependent reaction.

$$CO-NH_2$$
$$|$$
$$ADP + OH_2PO_3 \rightleftharpoons NH_3 + CO_2 + ATP$$

For earlier work on the energy metabolism of PPLO and L- forms of bacteria, the reader is referred to the review by Smith[20]. The reaction sequence of this arginine metabolism was also found in *Halobacterium salinarum*[5] and *Clostridium botulinum*[15] up to ornithine. *Clostridium botulinum* degrades ornithine further to volatile acids. All evidence suggests that L-ornithine is first reductively deaminated to δ-aminovalerate and from here into the various end products acetate, propionate, valerate, and butyrate. The proper sequence is, however, not known as yet.

Histidine and Glutamic Acid Metabolism

Clostridium tetanomorphum converts histidine to butyrate, acetate, CO_2, ammonia, and formamide[2] (reprinted with permission of John Wiley and Sons):

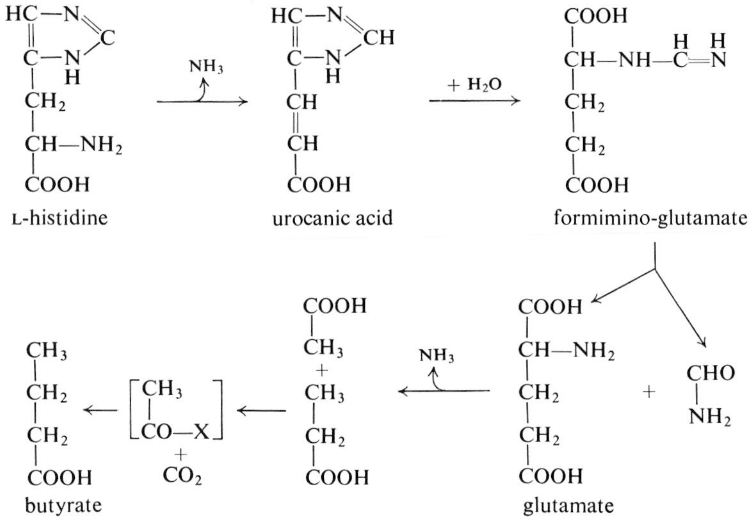

The first reaction is a desaturation deamination catalyzed by L-histidine ammonialyase (E.C. 4.3.1.3), which is followed by an urocanase system. The step to glutamate is still obscure, but it is assumed that a tetrahydrofolic acid–dependent reaction may be involved. The breakdown of glutamate, on the other hand, is a reductive deamination. *Clostridium tetanomorphum* grows very well on glutamate and rapidly utilizes this amino acid via mesaconate:

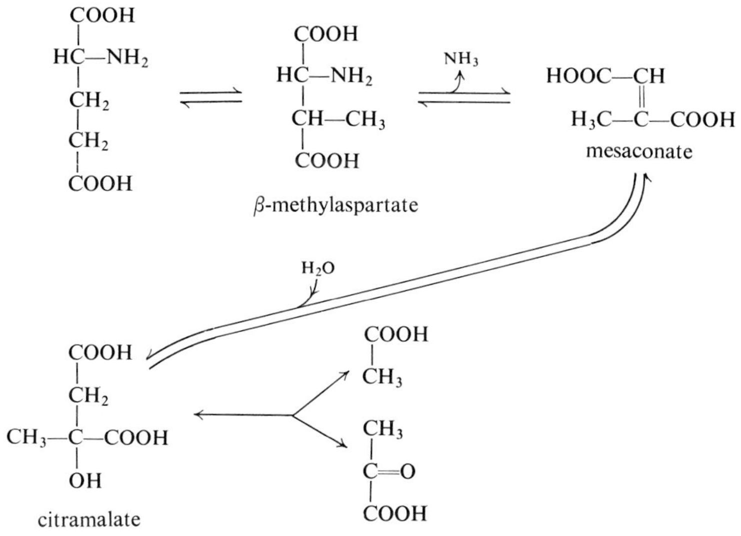

$$
\begin{array}{c}
\text{COOH} \\
| \\
\text{HC—NH}_2 \\
| \\
\text{CH}_2 \\
| \\
\text{CH}_2 \\
| \\
\text{COOH}
\end{array}
\rightleftharpoons
\begin{array}{c}
\text{COOH} \\
| \\
\text{HC—NH}_2 \\
| \\
\text{CH—CH}_3 \\
| \\
\text{COOH} \\
\beta\text{-methylaspartate}
\end{array}
\xrightarrow{\text{NH}_3}
\begin{array}{c}
\text{HOOC—CH} \\
\| \\
\text{H}_3\text{C—C—COOH} \\
\text{mesaconate}
\end{array}
$$

$$
\begin{array}{c}
\text{COOH} \\
| \\
\text{CH}_2 \\
| \\
\text{CH}_3\text{—C—COOH} \\
| \\
\text{OH} \\
\text{citramalate}
\end{array}
\xleftarrow{\text{H}_2\text{O}}
\left\{
\begin{array}{c}
\text{COOH} \\
| \\
\text{CH}_3 \\
\\
\text{CH}_3 \\
| \\
\text{C=O} \\
| \\
\text{COOH}
\end{array}
\right.
$$

The deamination reaction is a desaturation reaction and is catalyzed by L-threo-3-methylaspartate ammonialyase (E.C. 4.3.1.2). A mesaconase, which is different from fumarase (E.C. 4.2.1.1) or aconitase (E.C. 4.2.1.3) hydrolyzes mesaconate to L-(+)citramalate(3,25). A Mg^{2+} requiring citramalase splits citramalate in an aldolase-type reaction into acetate and pyruvate. A different way of L-histidine degradation has been reported(11) from studies with *Escherichia coli* B. It seems from these results that L-histidine is oxidatively deaminated to imidazol pyruvic acid, which is followed by a reduction to imidazole lactic acid and then further to acyclic compounds. The reduction that immediately follows the oxidative deamination indicates a cofactor requirement, which may possibly be reduced NAD or NADP.

Glycine Metabolism

The only anaerobic bacteria known which carry out a true glycine metabolism are *Diplococcus glycinophilus*, *Micrococcus anaerobius*, and *M. variabilis*

$$4 \text{ glycine} + 2 H_2O \rightarrow 4 NH_3 + 2 CO_2 + 3 CH_3COOH$$

In addition to this reaction, the two *Micrococcus* species also evolve hydrogen (3). The pathway of glycine metabolism in *Diplococcus glycinophilus* was found (12, 18) to involve tetrahydrofolate, pyridoxal phosphate, and NAD^+, as well as an acetate-generating system:

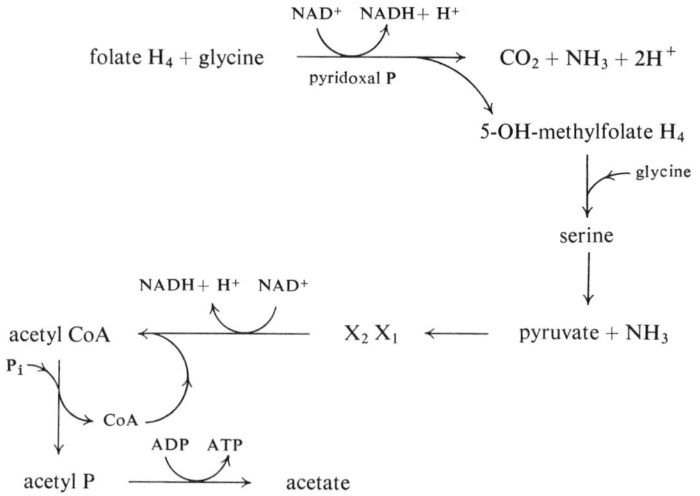

$$NAD^+ \quad NADH + H^+$$

folate H_4 + glycine $\xrightarrow[\text{pyridoxal P}]{}$ $CO_2 + NH_3 + 2H^+$

5-OH-methylfolate H_4

$\longleftarrow$ glycine

serine

$$NADH + H^+ \quad NAD^+$$

acetyl CoA $\longleftarrow$ $X_2 X_1$ $\longleftarrow$ pyruvate + NH_3

P_i

CoA

ADP ATP

acetyl P $\longrightarrow$ acetate

The first reaction is an oxidation–reduction step, whereby CO_2, NH_3, and hydrogen are formed with the help of pyridoxal phosphate and NAD^+ as cofactors:

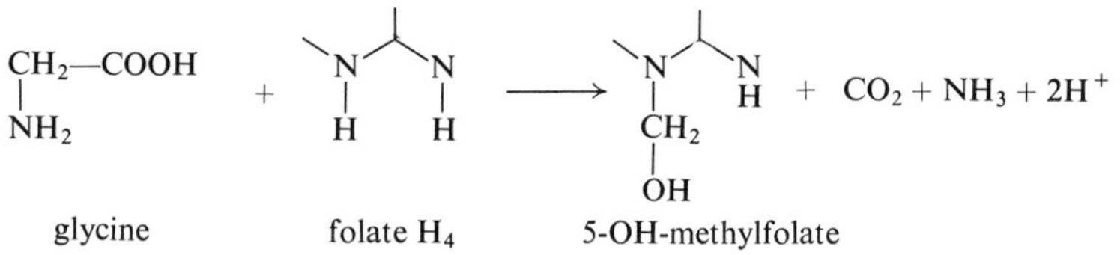

CH$_2$—COOH   +   (N–N, H, H) $\longrightarrow$ (N–N, H, CH$_2$, OH)   + $CO_2 + NH_3 + 2H^+$
NH$_2$

glycine   folate H_4 5-OH-methylfolate

A second molecule of glycine is now necessary to react with 5-hydroxymethyl-folate H_4 to form serine and reoxidize 5-hydroxymethylfolate H_4:

folate H_4—CH$_2$OH + CH$_2$COOH $\longrightarrow$ CH$_2$CHCOOH + folate H_4
                     NH$_2$ OH NH$_2$
                                                     serine

Methylfolate H_4 is used by this organism simply for the transfer of a methyl group from glycine to a second molecule of glycine thus producing serine. A deamination step follows with the production of pyruvate. The reduction

CH$_2$—CH—COOH $\longrightarrow$ CH$_3$—C—COOH + NH_3
OH   NH$_2$ O
        serine   pyruvate

of pyruvate to acetate may well involve a phosphoroclastic split with the formation of acetyl CoA, followed by a phosphotransferase (E.C. 2.3.1.8) and acetokinase (E.C. 2.7.2.1):

$$CH_3-\underset{\underset{O}{\|}}{C}-COOH \quad \xrightarrow{}_{CO_2} \quad CH_3-\underset{\underset{O}{\|}}{C}-SCoA \quad \longrightarrow$$

$$CH_3-\underset{\underset{O}{\|}}{C}-OPO_3H_2 \quad \longrightarrow \quad CH_3COOH$$

Serine Metabolism

The metabolism of serine to pyruvate is found frequently in anaerobic bacteria(6) and is catalyzed by serine deaminase [L-serine hydrolyase (deaminating), E.C. 4.2.1.13]. It is believed that serine deaminase is sometimes

$$CH_2OH-\underset{\underset{NH_2}{|}}{CH}-COOH \quad \longrightarrow \quad CH_3-CO-COOH + NH_3$$

specific for L-serine and can also act on L-threonine. When these cases occur, a second enzyme would be necessary for the degradation of D-serine and D-threonine.

Threonine Metabolism

Organisms like *Clostridium propionicum*, *Micrococcus aerogenes*(26), *M. lactilyticus*(27), and *Clostridium tetanomorphum*(28) require a threonine dehydratase [L-threonine hydrolyase (deaminating), E.C. 4.2.1.16] for the utilization of threonine and production of α-oxobutyrate:

$$CH_3-CHOH-\underset{\underset{NH_2}{|}}{CH}-COOH \quad \longrightarrow \quad CH_3-CH_2-CO-COOH + NH_3$$

Micrococcus aerogenes carries this step further and forms butyric acid

$$CH_3-CH_2-CO-COOH \rightarrow CH_3-CH_2-COOH + CO_2 + H_2$$

with the evolution of hydrogen. Taking all these reactions together in a general scheme, one arrives at the following mechanism of threonine metabolism:

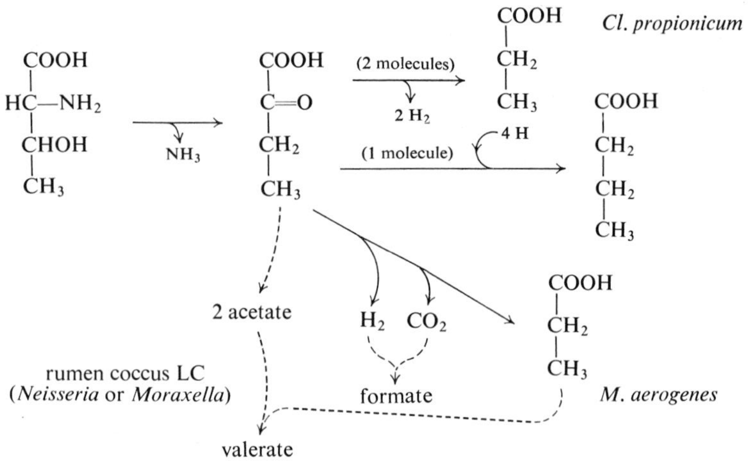

COOH   *Cl. propionicum*
CH$_2$

COOH   COOH (2 molecules) CH$_3$
HC—NH$_2$ C=O   ↓ 2 H$_2$ COOH
CHOH —NH$_3$→ CH$_2$ ⌐4 H   CH$_2$
CH$_3$ CH$_3$ (1 molecule) CH$_2$
                                    CH$_3$

                                    COOH
2 acetate   H$_2$ CO$_2$ CH$_2$
                                    CH$_3$
rumen coccus LC   *M. aerogenes*
(*Neisseria* or *Moraxella*)   formate

valerate

With these different products from threonine, a differentiation of the organism can easily be obtained metabolically.

Tryptophan Metabolism

Tryptophan is only slowly fermented by *Clostridium sporogenes* with the formation of indole propionic acid (see Scheme 10.1). The degradation of

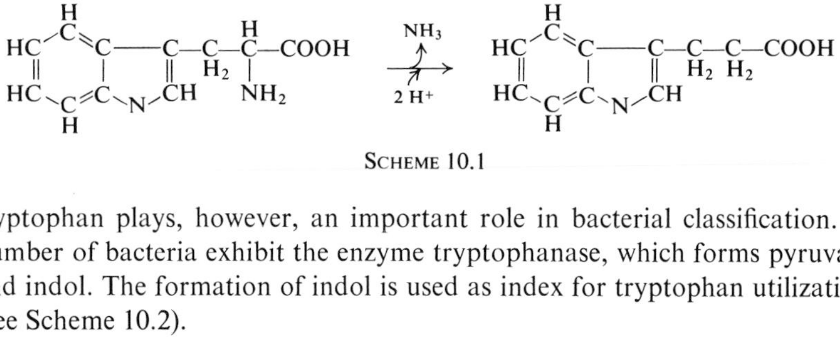

SCHEME 10.1

tryptophan plays, however, an important role in bacterial classification. A number of bacteria exhibit the enzyme tryptophanase, which forms pyruvate and indol. The formation of indol is used as index for tryptophan utilization (see Scheme 10.2).

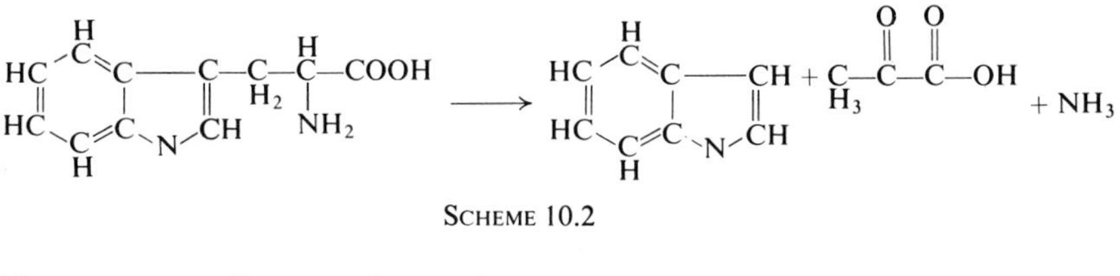

SCHEME 10.2

METABOLISM OF PAIRS OF AMINO ACIDS

Many clostridia, growing on protein hydrolysates or amino acid mixtures, appear to obtain most of their energy by a coupled oxidation–reduction reaction between suitable amino acids, or amino acids and non-nitrogenous compounds. The coupled decomposition of amino acids is commonly referred to as the "Stickland reaction." The characteristic feature of this Stickland reaction is that single amino acids are not decomposed appreciably, but appropriate pairs are decomposed very rapidly. One member of the pair is oxidized while the other is reduced.

Evidence for this formulation was initially obtained by studying the interaction between amino acids and suitable redox dyes in the presence of cell suspensions of *Clostridium sporogenes*. Bacteria using this Stickland reaction are mainly the proteolytic clostridia: *C. acetobutylicum*, *C. aerofoetidum*, *C. bifermentans*, *C. botulinum* (A + B), *C. butyricum*, *C. caproicum*, *C. histolyticum*, *C. sporogenes*, and *C. sticklandii*, etc.

The mechanism of individual oxidation and reduction varies according to the individual acid involved. Alanine, for example, is oxidized in a deamination process, whereby glycine is reduced to acetate and also in a nondeamination process, whereby proline is reduced to δ-amino valerate. All amino acids, which function as reductants, can be divided into three groups(16)

(1) aliphatic amino acids, which are more reduced than α-keto acids: alanine, leucine, isoleucine, norleucine, and valine;
(2) aliphatic amino acids in the same oxidation state as α-keto acids: serine, threonine, cystine, methionine, arginine, citrulline, and ornithine; and
(3) other amino acids; histidine, phenylalanine, tryptophan, tyrosine, aspartate, and glutamate. These amino acids have mostly an oxidation state below that of α-keto acids.

The oxidations of the amino acids is via the α-keto acids, which are then oxidatively decarboxylated. The following sequence is well established:

$$R\text{—}\underset{\underset{NH_2}{|}}{C}H\text{—}COOH + H_2O \longrightarrow NH_3 + R\text{—}\underset{\underset{O}{\|}}{C}\text{—}COOH \longrightarrow R\text{—}COOH + CO_2$$

The most difficult reaction mechanisms, which are not yet completely resolved, are involved in the group (1) amino acids. It has been suggested that they

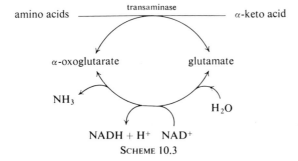

SCHEME 10.3

undergo either a direct oxidative deamination, which would be similar to glutamate dehydrogenase reactions, or a transamination followed by a oxidative deamination of the new amino acid (see Scheme 10.3). This reaction cycle would involve a transaminase and glutamate dehydrogenase (E.C. 1.4.1.2). In *Clostridium saccharobutyricum*, a species that does not catalyze Stickland reactions, the oxidation of alanine, valine, and leucine requires the presence of α-oxoglutarate.

Working with extracts of *Clostridium sporogenes*, Stickland himself found the coupled reaction of glycine-alanine and proline-alanine and established the over-all mechanism as follows:

$$\underset{\underset{NH_3^+}{|}}{R-CH-COO^-} + 2\ \underset{\underset{NH_3^+}{|}}{R'-CH-COO^-} + H_2O \longrightarrow$$

$$R-COO^- + CO_2 + 2\ R'CH_2COOH + 3\ NH_4$$

The two acids formed may then be metabolized further(14). Kocholaty and Hoogerheide(13) demonstrated the reduction of proline and glycine by hydrogen in cell suspensions.

The present evidence suggests that the Stickland reaction is composed of a number of steps, whereby the first step involves NAD^+ as primary hydrogen acceptor and an amino acid dehydrogenase system and the second step

$$\underset{\underset{NH_3^+}{|}}{R-CH-COOH} + NAD^+ + H_2O \longrightarrow \underset{\underset{O}{\|}}{R-C-COO^-} + NH_4^+ + NADH + H^+$$

involves the reoxidation of $NADH + H^+$ by the acceptor amino acid together with an amino acid reductase system:

$$\underset{\underset{NH_3^+}{|}}{R'-CH-COO^-} + NADH + H^+ \longrightarrow NAD^+ + R'CH_2-COO^- + NH_4^-$$

This latter reaction could be quite independent of the oxidation step in step (1). The oxidation step on the other hand could be a multi enzymatic step as outlined earlier, also involving a transaminase system. One could therefore arrive at the over-all mechanism for the Stickland reaction shown in Fig. 10.1. The numbers in parentheses represent the action of the following enzymes or enzyme systems: (1) amino acid dehydrogenase system; (2) 2-oxodehydrogenase with lipoamide, TPP, and HSCoA requirement; and (3) phosphotransacetylase. During the Stickland reaction three main enzyme systems are involved:

(1) an *l*-amino acid dehydrogenase system,
(2) an α-keto acid dehydrogenase system, and
(3) an amino acid reductase system of a hydrogenase type.

The hydrogen transfer proceeds anaerobically to an enzyme system whereby the acceptor amino acid is reduced.

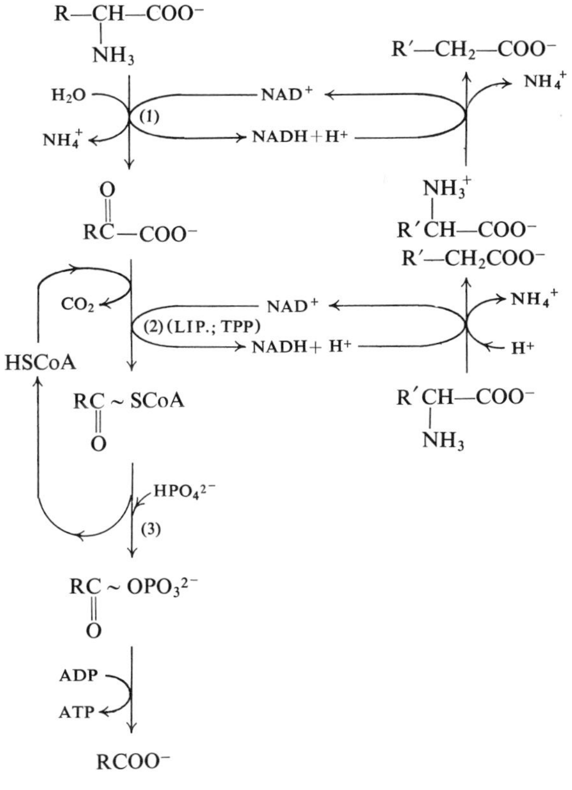

FIG. 10.1. Overall mechanism of the Stickland reaction.

METABOLISM OF A SINGLE AMINO ACID TOGETHER WITH A KETO ACID

Alanine Metabolism

Clostridium propionicum(7) uses the Stickland reaction to metabolize β-alanine to propionic acid with pyruvate playing a key role in the catalytic functions of the two cycles (see Fig. 10.2). The amino group of β-alanine is first transferred to pyruvate for the formation of α-alanine and malonate semialdehyde:

$$\begin{array}{ccccccc}
\text{H}_2\text{N}-\text{CH}_2 & & \text{CH}_3 & & \text{CH}_3 & & \text{OCH} \\
| & & | & & | & & | \\
\text{CH}_2 & + & \text{C}=\text{O} & \longrightarrow & \text{H}_2\text{N}-\text{CH} & + & \text{CH}_2 \\
| & & | & & | & & | \\
\text{COOH} & & \text{COOH} & & \text{COOH} & & \text{COOH} \\
\beta\text{-alanine} & & \text{pyruvate} & & \alpha\text{-alanine} & & \text{malonate} \\
& & & & & & \text{semialdehyde}
\end{array}$$

This transamination reaction is the function of β-alanine aminotransferase (L-alanine:malonate semialdehyde aminotransferase, E.C. 2.6.1.18). Both starter substances can be regenerated by two different systems.

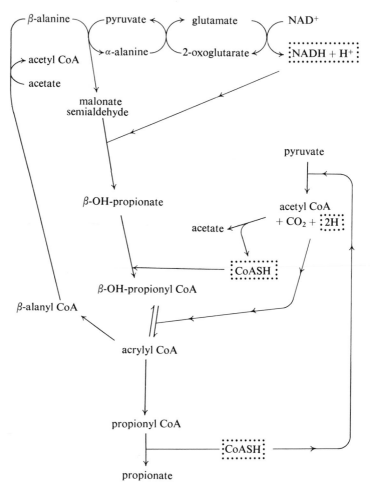

FIG. 10.2. Alanine metabolism by *C. propionicum.*

(1) Regeneration of pyruvate. The first transamination is followed by a second one, whereby the amino group from α-alanine is transferred to 2-oxo-glutarate for the formation of glutamate and pyruvate:

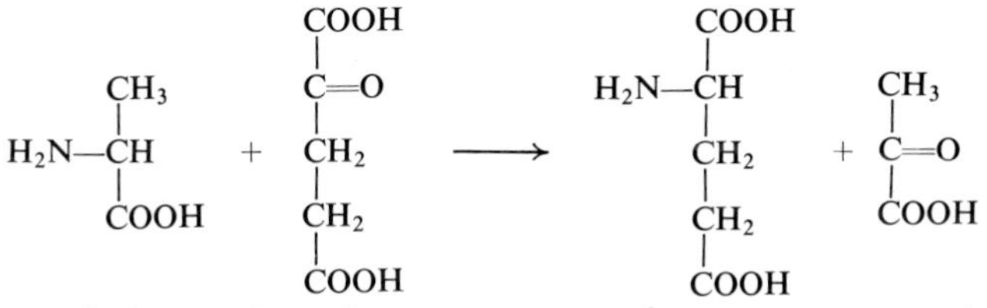

$$
\begin{array}{ccccc}
& \begin{array}{c} CH_3 \\ | \\ H_2N-CH \\ | \\ COOH \end{array}
& + &
\begin{array}{c} COOH \\ | \\ C\!=\!O \\ | \\ CH_2 \\ | \\ CH_2 \\ | \\ COOH \end{array}
& \longrightarrow
\end{array}
\quad
\begin{array}{ccccc}
\begin{array}{c} COOH \\ | \\ H_2N-CH \\ | \\ CH_2 \\ | \\ CH_2 \\ | \\ COOH \end{array}
& + &
\begin{array}{c} CH_3 \\ | \\ C\!=\!O \\ | \\ COOH \end{array}
\end{array}
$$

α-alanine   2-oxoglutarate   glutamate   pyruvate

This transamination requires an α-alanine aminotransferase (L-alanine: 2-oxoglutarate aminotransferase, E.C. 2.6.1.2). The final step of this first cycle is brought about by the function of glutamic dehydrogenase [L-glutamate: NAD oxidoreductase (deaminating), E.C. 1.4.1.2] on glutamate in the presence of NAD^+:

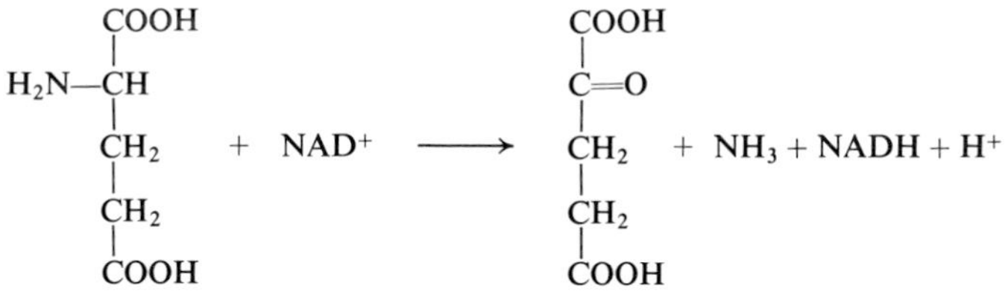

$$
\begin{array}{c} COOH \\ | \\ H_2N-CH \\ | \\ CH_2 \\ | \\ CH_2 \\ | \\ COOH \end{array}
\quad + \ NAD^+ \ \longrightarrow \quad
\begin{array}{c} COOH \\ | \\ C\!=\!O \\ | \\ CH_2 \\ | \\ CH_2 \\ | \\ COOH \end{array}
\quad + \ NH_3 + NADH + H^+
$$

glutamate   2-oxoglutarate

This reaction completes the first of the two cycles in β-alanine metabolism.

(2) Regeneration of β-alanine and formation of propionic acid. The reduced NAD produced in the last reaction of the first cycle is used to reduce, in a NAD-linked process, malonate semialdehyde to β-hydroxypropionate:

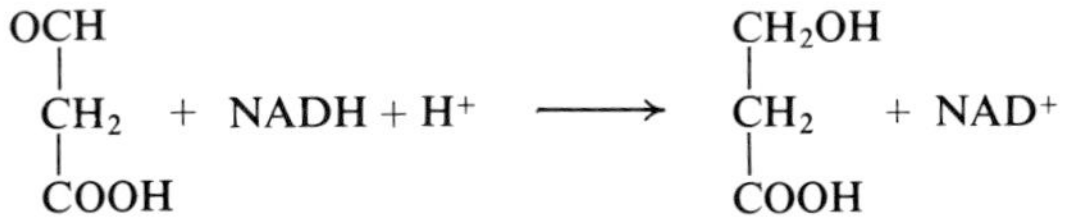

$$
\begin{array}{c} OCH \\ | \\ CH_2 \\ | \\ COOH \end{array}
\quad + \ NADH + H^+ \ \longrightarrow \quad
\begin{array}{c} CH_2OH \\ | \\ CH_2 \\ | \\ COOH \end{array}
\quad + \ NAD^+
$$

malonate semialdehyde   β-hydroxy propionate

The enzyme responsible for this reaction may be 3-hydroxypropionate dehydrogenase (3-hydroxypropionate: NAD oxidoreductase, E.C. 1.1.1.59), which reoxidizes the reduced NAD. β-Hydroxypropionate now takes up CoA and forms its CoA ester:

$$
\begin{array}{l}
CH_2OH \\
|\\
CH_2 \quad + HSCoA \\
|\\
COOH
\end{array}
\longrightarrow
\begin{array}{l}
CH_2OH \\
|\\
CH_2 \\
|\\
C{=}O \\
|\\
SCoA
\end{array}
$$

β-hydroxy propionate   β-hydroxypropionyl CoA

The required coenzyme for this reaction comes from the pyruvate degradation to acetate by this organism

$$CH_3COCOOH \rightarrow CH_3COSCoA + CO_2 + 2H^+ \rightarrow CH_3COOH$$

The liberated hydrogen in this side reaction is used in the next reduction step, whereby β-hydroxypropionyl CoA is reduced to acrylyl CoA:

$$
\begin{array}{l}
CH_2OH \\
|\\
CH_2 \\
|\\
C{=}O \\
|\\
SCoA
\end{array}
+ 2H^+ \rightleftharpoons
\begin{array}{l}
CH_2 \\
\|\\
CH \\
|\\
C{=}O \\
|\\
SCoA
\end{array}
$$

Acrylyl CoA itself can go two different ways. It can form β-alanyl CoA with the help of an aminase [or possibly β-alanyl CoA ammonialyase (E.C. 4.3.1.6)] and regenerate β-alanine with an acid and a CoA transferase, or it can be converted into propionate via propionyl CoA.

The conversion of acrylyl CoA to propionate is suggested to be similar to that described under the propionic acid bacteria. Pyruvate is necessary in this reaction sequence in two steps, where it has a catalytic function in the deamination of β-alanine and later in the dissimilation of β-hydroxybutyrate.

$$
\begin{array}{l}
CH_2 \\
\|\\
CH \\
|\\
C{=}O \\
|\\
SCoA
\end{array}
+ NH_3 \longrightarrow
\begin{array}{l}
H_2N{-}CH_2 \\
|\\
CH_2 \\
|\\
C{=}O \\
|\\
SCoA
\end{array}
$$

acrylyl CoA   β-alanyl CoA

$$
\begin{array}{l}
H_2N{-}CH_2 \\
|\\
CH_2 \\
|\\
C{=}O \\
|\\
SCoA
\end{array}
+ CH_3COOH \longrightarrow
\begin{array}{l}
H_2N{-}CH_2 \\
|\\
CH_2 \\
|\\
COOH
\end{array}
+ CH_3COSCoA
$$

β-alanyl CoA   β-alanine

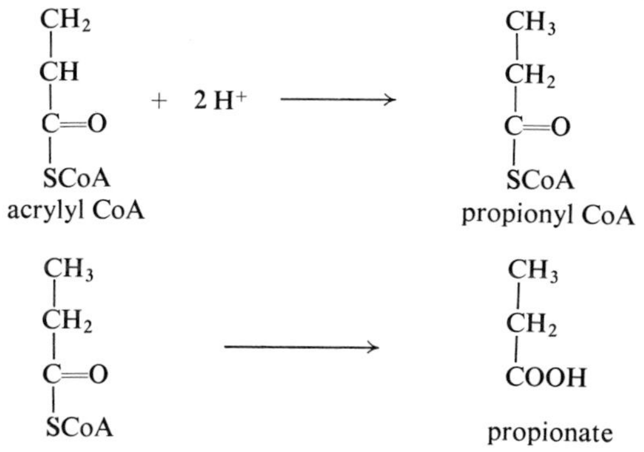

$$
\begin{array}{c}
CH_2 \\
| \\
CH \\
| \\
C{=}O \\
| \\
SCoA \\
\text{acrylyl CoA}
\end{array}
\; + \; 2\,H^+ \; \longrightarrow \;
\begin{array}{c}
CH_3 \\
| \\
CH_2 \\
| \\
C{=}O \\
| \\
SCoA \\
\text{propionyl CoA}
\end{array}
$$

$$
\begin{array}{c}
CH_3 \\
| \\
CH_2 \\
| \\
C{=}O \\
| \\
SCoA
\end{array}
\; \longrightarrow \;
\begin{array}{c}
CH_3 \\
| \\
CH_2 \\
| \\
COOH \\
\text{propionate}
\end{array}
$$

In *Clostridium kluyveri*(24) it appears that β-hydroxypropionate is not formed, but malonyl CoA which is converted via malonyl semialdehyde CoA to β-hydroxypropionyl CoA. There seem to be two differences:

(1) the level where CoA enters the cycle, and
(2) the dependence on $NADP^+$ instead of NAD^+.

γ-Aminobutyric Acid Metabolism

A very similar degradative system to that of alanine exists in the metabolism of ω-amino acids such as γ-aminobutyrate by *Clostridium aminobutyricum* (see Fig. 10.3). The initial steps in the catabolism of γ-aminobutyrate by *Clostridium aminobutyricum* are balanced oxidation–reduction reactions whereby γ-aminobutyrate is converted to succinic semialdehyde:

$$
\begin{array}{c}
H_2N{-}CH_2 \\
| \\
CH_2 \\
| \\
CH_2 \\
| \\
COOH \\
\text{γ-aminobutyrate}
\end{array}
\; + \;
\begin{array}{c}
COOH \\
| \\
C{=}O \\
| \\
CH_2 \\
| \\
CH_2 \\
| \\
COOH \\
\text{2-oxoglutarate}
\end{array}
\; \longrightarrow \;
\begin{array}{c}
CHO \\
| \\
CH_2 \\
| \\
CH_2 \\
| \\
COOH \\
\text{succinic} \\
\text{semialdehyde}
\end{array}
\; + \;
\begin{array}{c}
COOH \\
| \\
H_2N{-}CH \\
| \\
CH_2 \\
| \\
CH_2 \\
| \\
COOH \\
\text{glutamate}
\end{array}
$$

$$
\begin{array}{c}
COOH \\
| \\
H_2N{-}CH \\
| \\
CH_2 \\
| \\
CH_2 \\
| \\
COOH \\
\text{glutamate}
\end{array}
\; + \; NAD^+ \; \longrightarrow \;
\begin{array}{c}
COOH \\
| \\
C{=}O \\
| \\
CH_2 \\
| \\
CH_2 \\
| \\
COOH \\
\text{2-oxoglutarate}
\end{array}
\; + \; NH_3 + NADH + H^+
$$

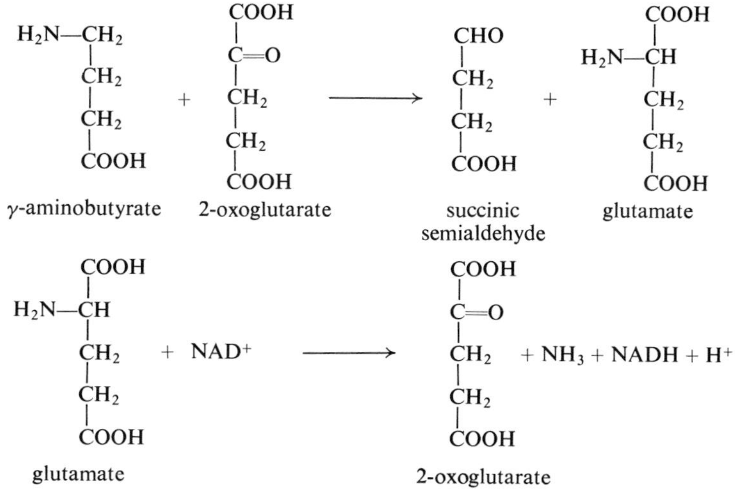

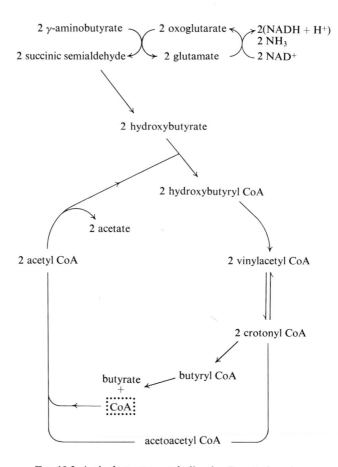

FIG. 10.3. Aminobutyrate metabolism by *C. aminobutyricum.*

These reactions are catalyzed by an γ-aminobutyrate transaminase(8) and glutamic dehydrogenase (E.C. 1.4.1.2). The formed succinic semialdehyde is then reduced to γ-hydroxybutyrate by γ-hydroxybutyrate dehydrogenase and $NADH + H^+$:

$$
\begin{array}{ccc}
\text{CHO} & & \text{CH}_2\text{OH} \\
| & & | \\
\text{CH}_2 & + \text{NADH} + \text{H}^+ \longrightarrow & \text{CH}_2 \quad + \text{ NAD}^+ \\
| & & | \\
\text{CH}_2 & & \text{CH}_2 \\
| & & | \\
\text{COOH} & & \text{COOH} \\
\text{succinic semialdehyde} & & \gamma\text{-hydroxybutyrate}
\end{array}
$$

In this process $NADH + H^+$ is reoxidized to NAD^+. The second part of the pathway starts with a CoA transferase reaction, which converts γ-hydroxybutyrate to γ-hydroxybutyryl CoA and acetyl CoA to acetate:

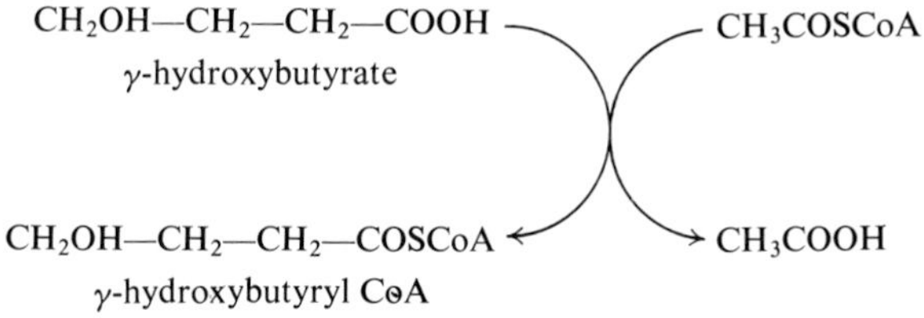

$$CH_2OH-CH_2-CH_2-COOH \quad\longrightarrow\quad CH_3COSCoA$$
$$\gamma\text{-hydroxybutyrate}$$

$$CH_2OH-CH_2-CH_2-COSCoA \quad\longleftarrow\quad CH_3COOH$$
$$\gamma\text{-hydroxybutyryl CoA}$$

The CoA transferase has been given the name "acetyl CoA:γ-hydroxybutyrate CoA transferase"(9). The unsaturated compound vinylacetyl CoA is formed under the action of a dehydrase, and vinylacetyl CoA is held in equilibrium with crotonyl CoA by an isomerase:

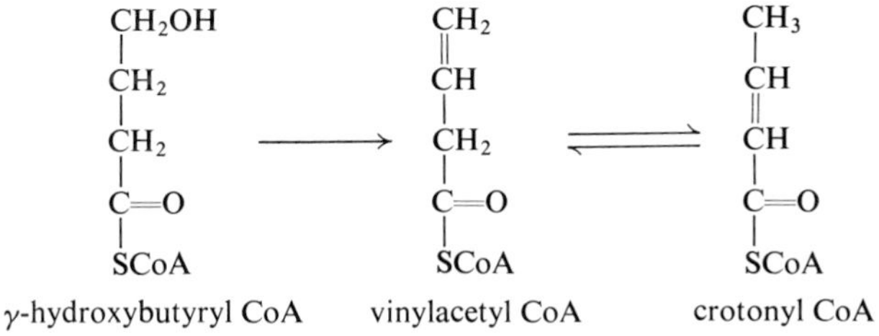

$$
\begin{array}{ccccc}
CH_2OH & & CH_2 & & CH_3 \\
| & & \| & & | \\
CH_2 & & CH & & CH \\
| & & | & & \| \\
CH_2 & \longrightarrow & CH_2 & \rightleftharpoons & CH \\
| & & | & & | \\
C{=}O & & C{=}O & & C{=}O \\
| & & | & & | \\
SCoA & & SCoA & & SCoA
\end{array}
$$

$$\gamma\text{-hydroxybutyryl CoA} \qquad \text{vinylacetyl CoA} \qquad \text{crotonyl CoA}$$

The intermediate crotonyl CoA undergoes, in analogy with fatty acid synthesis, a dismutation, whereby one mole is reduced to butyryl CoA and the second mole oxidized to acetoacetyl CoA:

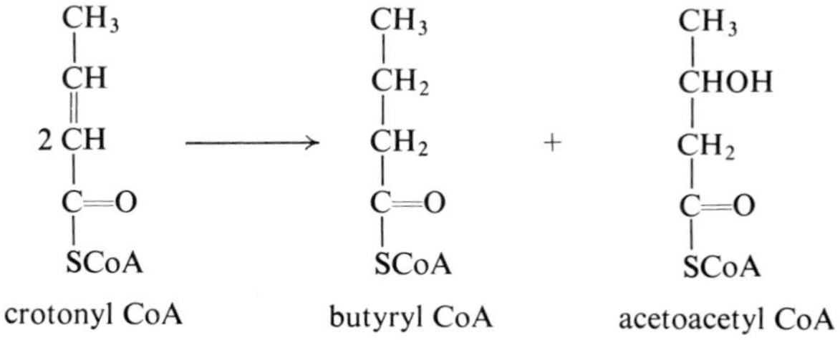

$$
\begin{array}{ccccc}
CH_3 & & CH_3 & & CH_3 \\
| & & | & & | \\
CH & & CH_2 & & CHOH \\
\| & & | & & | \\
2\ CH & \longrightarrow & CH_2 & + & CH_2 \\
| & & | & & | \\
C{=}O & & C{=}O & & C{=}O \\
| & & | & & | \\
SCoA & & SCoA & & SCoA
\end{array}
$$

$$\text{crotonyl CoA} \qquad \text{butyryl CoA} \qquad \text{acetoacetyl CoA}$$

A NAD-linked butyryl CoA dehydrogenase [butyryl CoA (acceptor) oxidoreductase, E.C. 1.3.99.2] is responsible for the butyryl CoA formation, which in turn is converted to the end product butyrate:

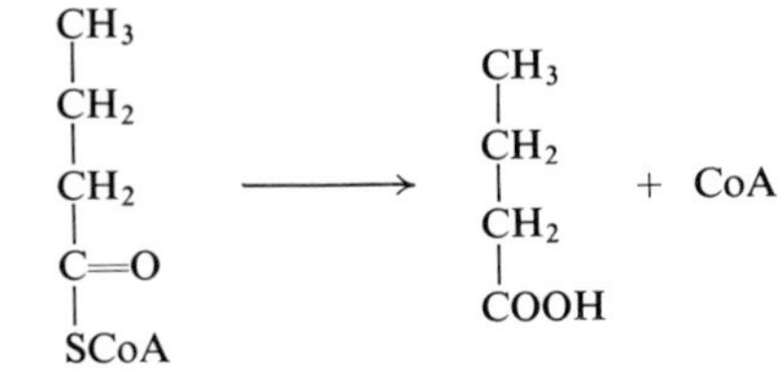

$$CH_3-CH_2-CH_2-C(=O)-SCoA \longrightarrow CH_3-CH_2-CH_2-COOH + CoA$$

butyryl CoA   butyrate

The oxidized dismutation product acetoacetyl CoA, on the other hand, is cleaved to 2 moles of acetyl CoA with an acetyl CoA thiolase (acetyl CoA: acetyl CoA C-acetyltransferase E.C. 2.3.1.9):

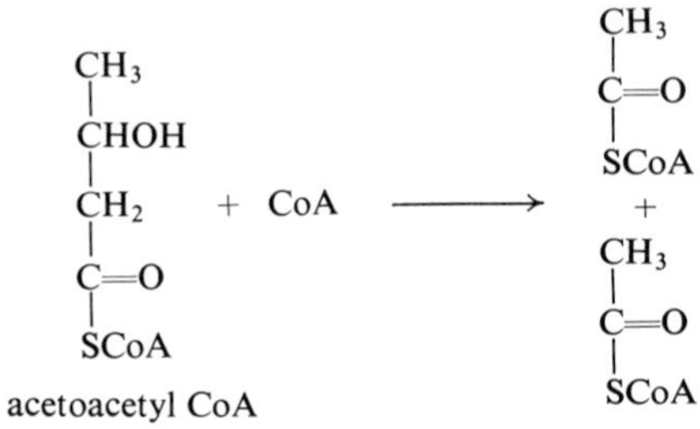

$$CH_3-CHOH-CH_2-C(=O)-SCoA + CoA \longrightarrow CH_3-C(=O)-SCoA + CH_3-C(=O)-SCoA$$

acetoacetyl CoA

Acetyl CoA reenters the cycle in the first CoA transferase step of this system. The net result of energy is 1 mole of ATP per 2 moles of amino acids fermented (10). An additional mole comes from the reduction of crotonyl CoA by $NADH + H^+$ to butyryl CoA, which is sufficiently exergonic to be coupled to ATP synthesis.

REFERENCES

1. Barile, M. F., Schimke, R. T., and Riggs, D. B. (1966). Presence of the arginine dihydrolase pathway in *Mycoplasma*. *J. Bacteriol*. **91**, 189.
2. Barker, H. A. (1956). "Bacterial Fermentations." Wiley, New York.
3. Barker, H. A. (1962). Fermentations on nitrogenous organic compounds. *In* "The Bacteria" (I. C. Gunsalus and R. Y. Stanier, eds.), Vol. 2, p. 151. Academic Press, New York.
4. Cohen-Bazire, G., Cohen, G.-N., and Prevot, A.-R. (1948). Nature et mode d'formation des acides volatiles dans les cultures de quelques bactéries anaérobies protéolytique du groupe de *Clostridium sporogenes*. Formation par reaction de Stickland des acides isobutyrique, isovalérianique, et valérianique optiquement actif. *Ann. Inst. Pasteur* **75**, 291.
5. Dundas, I. E. D., and Halvorson, H. W. (1966). Arginine metabolism in *Halobacterium salinarum*, an obligately halophilic bacterium. *J. Bacteriol*. **91**, 113.
6. Foulbert, E. L., and Douglas, H. C. (1948). Studies on the anaerobic Micrococci. II. The fermentation of lactate by *Micrococcus lactilyticus*. *J. Bacteriol*. **56**, 35.

7. Goldfine, H., and Stadtman, E. R. (1960). Propionic acid metabolism. V. The conversion of β-alanine to propionic acid by cell-free extracts of *Clostridium propionicum. J. Biol. Chem.* **235**, 2238.

8. Hardman, J. K., and Stadtman, T. C. (1963). Metabolism of ω-amino acids. III. Mechanism of conversion of γ-aminobutyrate to γ-hydroxybutyrate by *Clostridium aminobutyricum. J. Biol. Chem.* **238**, 2081.

9. Hardman, J. K., and Stadtman, T. C. (1963). Metabolism of ω-amino acids. IV. γ-Aminobutyrate fermentation by cell-free extracts of *Clostridium aminobutyricum. J. Biol. Chem.* **238**, 2088.

10. Hardman, J. K., and Stadtman, T. C. (1963). Metabolism of ω-amino acids. V. Energetics of the γ-aminobutyrate fermentation by *Clostridium aminobutyricum. J. Bacteriol.* **85**, 1326.

11. Hedegaard, J., Brevet, J., and Roche, J. (1966). Imidazole lactic acid: An intermediate in L-histidine degradation in *Escherichia coli* B. *Biochem. Biophys. Res. Commun.* **25**, 335.

12. Klein, S. M., and Sagers, R. D. (1962). Intermediary metabolism of *Diplococcus glycinophilus.* II. Enzymes of the acetate-generating system. *J. Bacteriol.* **83**, 121.

13. Kocholaty, W., and Hoogerheide, J. C. (1938). Dehydrogenation reactions by suspensions of *C. sporogenes. Biochem. J.* **32**, 437.

14. Lamanna, C., and Mallette, M. F. (1965). "Basic Bacteriology," 3rd ed., p. 840. Williams & Wilkins, Baltimore, Maryland.

15. Mitruka, B. M., and Costilow, R. N. (1967). Arginine and ornithine catabolism by *Clostridium botulinum. J. Bacteriol.* **93**, 295.

16. Nisman, B. (1954). The Stickland Reaction. *Bacteriol. Rev.* **18**, 16.

17. Pollock, M. R. (1962). Exoenzymes. *In* "The Bacteria" (I. C. Gunsalus and R. Y. Stanier, eds.), Vol. 4, p. 121. Academic Press, New York.

18. Sagers, R. D., and Gunsalus, I. C. (1961). Intermediary metabolism of *Diplococcus glycinophilus.* I. Glycine cleavage and one-carbon interconversion. *J. Bacteriol.* **81**, 541.

19. Schimke, R. T., and Barile, M. F. (1963). Arginine metabolism in pleuropneumonia-like organisms isolated from mammalian cell culture. *J. Bacteriol.* **86**, 195.

20. Smith, P. F. (1964). Comparative physiology of pleuropneumonia-like and L-type organisms. *Bacteriol. Rev.* **28**, 97.

21. Stickland, L. H. (1934). The chemical reaction by which *Clostridium sporogenes* obtains its energy. *Biochem. J.* **28**, 1746.

22. Stickland, L. H. (1935). The oxidation of alanine by *Clostridium sporogenes. Biochem. J.* **29**, 288.

23. Stickland, L. H. (1935). The reduction of glycine by *Clostridium sporogenes. Biochem. J.* **29**, 896.

24. Vagelos, P. R., and Earl, J. M. (1959). Propionic acid metabolism. III. β-Hydroxypropionyl-Coenzyme A and malonyl semialdehyde coenzyme A, intermediates in propionate oxidation by *Clostridium kluyveri. J. Biol. Chem.* **234**, 2272.

25. Wang, C. C., and Barker, H. A. (1967). Private communication.

26. Whiteley, H. R. (1957). Fermentation of amino acids by *Micrococcus aerogenes. J. Bacteriol.* **74**, 324.

27. Whiteley, H. R., and Ordal, Z. J. (1957). Fermentation of alpha ketoacids by *Micrococcus aerogenes* and *Micrococcus lactilyticus. J. Bacteriol.* **74**, 331.

28. Whiteley, H. R., and Tahara, M. (1966). Threonine deaminase in *Clostridium tetanomorphum.* I. Purification and properties. *J. Biol. Chem.* **241**, 4881.

SUPPLEMENTARY READINGS

Ammann, E. C. B., and Reed, L. L. (1967). Metabolism of nitrogen compounds by *Hydrogenomonas eutropha*. I. Utilization of uric acid, allantoin, hippuric acid and creatinine. *Biochim. Biophys. Acta.* **141**, 135.

Bridgeland, E. S., and Jones, K. M. (1967). Formation of dicarboxylic acids and phosphoenolpyruvate in *Arthrobacter globiformis*. *Biochem. J.* **104**, 9P.

Burus, R. O., and Zarlenger, M. H. (1968). Threonine deaminase from *Salmonella typhimurium*. *J. Biol. Chem.* **243**, 178.

Dart, R. K. (1968). The presence of threonine and serine dehydratase activities in *Pseudomonas*. *Biochem. J.* **107**, 29P.

Hodgins, D., and Abeles, R. H. (1967). The presence of covalently bound pyruvate in D-proline reductase and its participation in the catalytic process. *J. Biol. Chem.* **242**, 5158.

Klein, S. M., and Sagers, R. D. (1966). Glycine metabolism. I. Properties of the system catalyzing the exchange of bicarbonate with the carboxyl group of glycine in *Peptococcus glycinophilus*. *J. Biol. Chem.* **241**, 197.

Klein, S. M., and Sagers, R. D. (1966). Glycine metabolism. II. Kinetic and optical studies on the glycine decarboxylase system from *Peptococcus glycinophilus*. *J. Biol. Chem.* **241**, 206.

Leadbetter, E. R., and Gottlieb, J. A. (1967). On methylamine assimilation in a bacterium. *Arch. Mikrobiol.* **59**, 211.

Maeno, H., and Feigelson, P. (1968). Studies on the interaction of carbon monoxide with tryptophan oxygenase of *Pseudomonas*. *J. Biol. Chem.* **243**, 301.

Sokatch, J. R., Sanders, L. E., and Marshall, V. P. (1968). Oxidation of methylmalonate semialdehyde to propionyl coenzyme A in *Pseudomonas aeruginosa* grown on valine. *J. Biol. Chem.* **243**, 2500.

Stadtman, T. C., and Renz, P. (1968). Anaerobic degradation of lysine. V. Some properties of the cobamide enzyme-dependent β-lysine mutase of *Clostridium sticklandii*. *Arch. Biochem. Biophys.* **125**, 226.

Tsai, L., and Stadtman, T. C. (1968). Anaerobic degradation of lysine. IV. Cobamide coenzyme-dependent migration of an amino group from carbon-6 of β-lysine (3,6-diaminohexanoate) to carbon-5 forming a new naturally occurring amino acid, 3,5-diaminohexanoate. *Arch. Biochem. Biophys.* **125**, 210.

Wright, D. E., and Hungate, R. E. (1967). Metabolism of glycine by rumen microorganisms. *Appl. Microbiol.* **15**, 152.

AUTHOR INDEX

Numbers in parentheses are reference numbers and indicate that an author's work is referred to, although his name is not cited in the text. Numbers in italics show the page on which the complete reference is listed.

A

Abe, S., 74(81), *83*
Abeles, R. H., *401*, *422*
Abeliovitz, A., 311(5), *326*
Abelson, P. H., 357(125), *397*
Abiko, Y., 39(1, 2, 3, 4), *44*
Abraham, R. C., 113(104), *123*
Ackrell, B. A. C., *305*
Adair, F. W., 223, *243*
Adams, E., 382(1), 383(128, 129), *391*, *397*, *399*
Adams, G. A., 298(1), *300*
Adams, M. E., 96(24), *120*
Adelberg, E. A., 221(178), *251*, 260(53), *303*, 330(65), *350*
Adelson, J., 95(21), *119*, 239(42), *245*
Ahrens, J., 212(2), *243*, 261(2), *300*
Aiba, S., 259(3), *300*
Ailhaud, G. P., *303*, *304*
Ajl, S. J., *305*
Akagi, J. M., 101(23, 156), 102(1, 3, 156), 103(2), *119*, *120*, *126*, *127*, 272(66), *303*
Akagi, K., 378(70), *394*
Albury, M. N., 331(12), *347*
Aleem, M. I. H., 201(9, 10), 202, 205(5, 6, 7, 13), 206(2), 207, 208, 211(9, 10), 215, 219(4), 226(5, 6, 8, 9, 11), 227(5, 11), 228(8), 229(9), *243*, *244*
Alexander, M., 106(4), 110(4), *119*, *127*, 201(209), 235(18), 241(17), *244*, *252*, 388(2), 389(97), 390(96), *391*, *395*, *399*
Alico, R. K., 103(5), *119*
Allan, A. M., 118(178), *127*
Allen, M. B., 65(1), *79*
Allen, M. J., 240(19), *244*
Allen, R. H., *400*
Allen, S. H. G., *252*, 262(6), 264(4), 266(4, 5, 69), 267(4), *300*, *303*, *304*

Allison, D. P., 181(98), 186(3), *188*, *192*
Altermatt, H. A., 181(2), *188*
Amarger, N., *127*
Ambler, R. P., 236(20, 21), *244*
Amesz, J., 60(2), *79*
Ammann, E. C. B., *252*, *422*
Anderson, A. W., 243(62), *245*
Anderson, D. G., 175(10), *188*
Anderson, J. H., 201(23), 202, 204(24), *244*
Anderson, R. L., 180(83, 97), 181(97, 98), 185(4), 186(3, 4, 5), *188*, *190*, *191*, *192*, 268(7), *300*, *351*
Andiffren, P., 298(60), *303*
Androes, G. M., 61(23), *80*
Anthony, C., 218, *244*, *399*
Arcus, A. C., 182(6), 183(6), *188*
Arima, K., 381(170), *399*
Arnon, D. I., 48, 49(4), 52, 53(8, 92), 54(8), 55(8), 62(7, 42), 64(6), 65(21), 71(19), 72(91), 73(91), 75(91), *79*, *80*, *81*, *83*, *86*, 88, 102(158), *126*, *128*, 157(114), *193*, *197*
Arscott, L. D., *255*
Asano, A., 107, *119*, *127*, 240(27), *244*
Asato, R. N., *305*
Ashwell, G., 67(119), *85*
Atkinson, D. E., 112(72), 113(73, 93, 94), *122*, *123*, 147(7), 163(7), *188*, 211(29), 214(28), *244*, 311(1, 3), 313(2), *326*
Atzpodien, W., *197*
Aubert, J. P., 199(30), *244*
Aurich, H., *399*
Averbach, B. C., 113(104), *123*
Avigad, G., 316(3a, 4), 316(21, 22), *326*, *327*, *350*
Avron, M., 60(25), *80*, *86*
Azoulay, E., 110(8), *119*, 375(99), *395*
Azova, L. G., *304*

423

432 AUTHOR INDEX

Lees, G. J., 339, *349*
Lees, H., 62(88), *83*, 201, 202, 205(13, 121), 206(12, 47), 210(47), 215(15, 120), 221 (119, 120), *243, 248, 523*
Le Gall, J., 95(86), 102(87), *122*
Lehninger, A. L., 19, 20, 24(17), 37(17), 38, *44*, 61(89), *83*, 97(88), *122*, 177(156), 178, *195*, 231(122), 239(122), *548*
Leifson, E., 307(46a), *328*
Leininger, K. R., *253*
Leinweber, F. J., 100(89), *122*
Le John, H. B., *253, 254*
Leloir, L. F., 160(109), *193*
Lemberg, R., 114(90), *123*
Lerner, S. A., 182(165), *195*
Lester, R. L., 212(123), *248*
Levin, N., *350*
Levisohn, S. R., 179(61), *190*
Levy, C. C., 385(88), 386(89), *395*
Levy, J. B., 113(38, 39), *120*
Levy, L., 312(6a), *326*
Lewis, K., 240(124), *248*, 353(90), *385*
Li, L.-F., 273(34), 290(34), *302*
Lichstein, H. C., 338(3, 4, 5, 6), *347*
Liegey, R. W., 103(5), *119*
Lim, R., 185(10), *193*
Lin, E. C. C., 182(151, 165), 187(94), 188 (111), *192, 193, 195*, 235(87), *247, 304*
Lin, F.-J., *254, 305*
Linday, E. M., 213(125), *248*
Lindeberg, G., 112(91), *123*
Lindstrom, E. S., 64(90), 76(29), *81, 83, 88*
Linnane, A. W., 113(165), *126*, 147(173a, b), *196*
Linnes, A. G., 353(15), *392*
Lipmann, F., 175, *193*, 263(11), *301*, 343(40), 344(40), *349*
Liss, M., 182(113), 183(113), 184(113), *193*
Lizotte, C. L., 212(162), *250*
Loach, P. A., *87*
Lockhart, W. R., 148(185), *197*
Lockwood, L. B., 353(91, 142), 356(91, 142), *395, 397*
Lode, A., 112(91), *123*
Loesche, W. J., 115(92), *123*
Lohmann, K., 175, *194*
London, J., 200(175), 226(126), 227(128), *248, 251, 254, 350*
Lopez, J. A., 160, *193*

Losada, M., 52(7), 53, 62(7), 64(6), 72(91), 73(91), 75(91), *79, 83*, 157(114), *193, 197*
Low, I. E., *350*
Lowry, O. H., 160, 162(135, 136), *193, 194*
Lukins, H. B., 373(92), *395*
Lundegardh, H., *87*
Lundgren, D. G., 215(61), 216, *245, 249, 255*
Lusty, C. J., *400*
Lusty, S. M., Jr., 368(153), *398*
Lynen, F., 264(21, 52), 266(38, 42, 52), *301, 302*

M

McAllister, J. K., *255*
McBee, R. H., 47, *83*
McBride, B. C., *252*
McCleskey, C. S., 217(43), *245*, 342(51), *349*
McComb, B. B., 159(116), *193*
McCormick, D. B., *45*
McCormick, N. G., 287, 288(35), *302*
Machida, Y., 332(52), *349*
MacDonald, D. L., 380(93), *395*
McDonald, M. R., 161(117), *193*
McDonough, M. J., 187(184), 188(184), *197*
McElroy, W. D., 112(133), *124*
McFadden, B. A., 211(29), *244, 523*, 357(94), *395*
McGarry, J. D., *304, 305*
McGilverey, R. W., 97, *119*
McKenna, E. J., 371(95), *395*
Mackereth, F. J. H., 242(129), *249*
McLean, P., *198*
MacLennan, D. G., 205(131), 242(130), *249*
Maclosky, E. R., 113(66), *121*
McManus, D. K., 100(140), *125*
McNall, E. G., 113(93, 94), *123*
McNelis, E., 172, *189*
MacPherson, R., 103(95), *123*
MacRae, I. C., 112(144, 146), *125*, 389(97), 390(96), *395*
McSwain, B. D., 52(8), 53(8), 54(8), 55(8), *79*
Madsen, N. B., 358(82), *395*
Maeba, P., *198, 255*
Maeno, H., 385(98), 391(69), *394, 395, 400, 422*
Magasanik, B., *197*
Mahler, H. R., 291(36), *302*
Melavolta, E., 208(132), *245, 249*

434 AUTHOR INDEX

Malek, L., 242(133), *249*
Malesset-Bras, M., 375(99), *395*
Malhotra, O. P., *45*
Mallette, M. F., *122*, 201(113), 239(113), *248*, 273, 280(33), 281(33), 287(33), 289(33), 292(33), 294(33), *302*, 412(14), *421*
Mamkaeva, K. A., 353(100), *395*
Mandelstem, J., 375(139), *397*
Manderson, G., 178, *190*, *193*
Mann, S., *400*
Mansour, T. E., 163(119, 120), 164(120), *193*
Marcus, L., 183(121), *193*
Margalith, P., 216(134), *249*
Markovetz, A. J., 375(41), *393*
Marmur, J., 182(122), *193*
Marr, A. G., 59, 60, *82*, 183(121), *193*, 241(135), *249*, *304*
Martin, J. R., 385(101), *396*
Martinez, G., 170(81), *191*
Marunouchi, T., *254*
Marus, A., 146(13, 123), *188*, *193*
Marx, R., 61(17), *80*
Mastroni, P., 134(124), *193*
Mathies, A. P., 183(8), *188*
Matrone, G., *305*
Matsumoto, J., 372(87), *395*
Matsushima, K., 181(125, 126), *193*
Mauzerall, D., 114(47, 48, 96, 97), *121*, *123*
Mayberry, W. R., *254*, 374(158), *398*
Mayeux, J. V., *254*
Mayhew, S., *304*
Mazaki, M., 391(104), *396*
Mazarean, H. H., *122*, 345(55), *349*
Meadow, P. H., 357(21), *392*
Mechalas, B. J., 64(95), *84*
Medina, A., 113(106), *123*
Medrano, L., *197*
Meek, G. A., 113(123), *124*, 147(139a), *194*
Mehler, A. H., 177(146), *194*, 391(57), *393*
Melhorn, D. K., *304*
Mellin, D. B., 57(50), *81*
Meloche, H. P., 169, 170, 171(128), *191*, *193*, *194*
Menon, G. K. K., 366(102), *396*
Merrick, J. M., *87*
Meyerhof, O., 175, *194*
Michalska-Trenkner, E., *255*
Mickelson, M. N., *350*

Milhaud, G., 199(30), *244*
Miller, J. D. A., 103(95), *123*
Miller, S. J., 266(26), *301*
Millet, J., 101(98), *123*, 199(30), *244*
Millis, N. F., 129(1), *188*, 259(3), *300*
Mills, R. C., 147(91), *192*, *350*
Mitruka, B. M., 406(15), *421*
Miyajima, R., 243(144), *249*
Mizushi, S., 332(52), *349*
Mohler, B. A., 314(42), *328*
Monty, K. J., 100(37, 89), *120*, *122*
Moore, C. C., 147(130), *194*
Moore, R. B., *87*
Mori, T., 110(62), *121*
Moris, T., *254*
Morita, S., 55(60), 74(96), *82*, *84*, *85*
Morris, J. G., 103(78), 104(44), 105(43), *120*, *122*, 147(131), *194*, 363, *396*
Morrison, M., 114(157), *126*
Morse, M. C., *197*
Morse, M. L., *350*
Mortensen, L. E., 102(99), *123*, 272(37, 59), *302*, *303*
Mortlock, R. P., 184(132, 133), 188(58), *190*, *194*, *197*
Morton, R. L., 36, *44*
Moss, F. J., *198*, 241(136), 242(137), *249*
Moss, P., 389(39), *393*
Mossman, M. R., 115(50), *121*, 241(74), 242(75), *246*
Moulder, J. W., *198*
Mower, H. F., *304*
Moyer, R. W., *254*, *305*
Murphy, W. H., 182(134), *194*, *254*, *305*
Murray, E. G. D., 330(7), *347*, 353(10), *391*
Murthy, P. S., 240(138), *249*
Muto, A., 73(133), 74(81), *83*, *85*

N

Nadkarni, G. B., *350*
Naik, M. S., 109, *123*
Naik, V. R., *350*
Najjar, V. A., 108, *123*
Nakajima, O., *123*
Nakamoto, T., 100(166), *126*
Nakamura, S., 367(48), 385(48), *393*
Nakayama, T., 311(47), *328*
Nakazawa, D., 366(108), *396*

SUBJECT INDEX

A

Acetaldehyde
  cleavage with glyceraldehyde 3-phosphate, 339
    with pyruvate, 340
  conversion to ethanol, 278, 289, 340
  dehydrogenase, 334
  electron acceptor in lactic acid bacteria, 334
  formation from acetate, 288
    from acetyl CoA, 278, 288
    from pyruvate, 287
  product from threonine utilization, 339

Acetate
  conversion to acetyl CoA via acetyl adenylate, 65
    to citramalate by *Chromatium*, 73
    to glutamate by *Chromatium*, 73
    to poly-β-hydroxybutyric acid, 66
  as electron donor in methane formation, 116, 118
    in nitrate reduction, 106
    in sulfate reduction, 101
  end product in CO_2 reduction, 117
    in phosphoketolase pathway, 151
    of butanediol metabolism, 370
    of D-mandalate pathway, 380
  formation from acetyl CoA, 274, 275, 289 419
    from acetyl CoA via acetyl phosphate, 265
    from alanine, 404
    by *Clostridia*, 271, 274, 275
    from CO_2 and H_2, 273
    in *n*-decane oxidation, 374
    in *Enterobacteriaceae*, 289
    via formate in *Clostridium kluyveri*, 275
    from glycine, 404
    in homo- and heterofermentation, 335
    in photometabolism of succinate, 68
  photometabolic conversion to glutamate, 66

Acetate—*cont.*
  photometabolism of, 75
    in absence of CO_2 by *Rhodospirillum rubrum*, 65
    via TCA cycle, 66
  product in deoxyribose metabolism, 338
    in glutamate metabolism, 407
    in L-histidine metabolism, 406
    in lactate metabolism, 101, 310
    in ornithine metabolism, 406
    of β-oxidation of fatty acids, 372
    in photometabolism of acetone, 77
  replacing factor, 35, *see also* Lipoate
  as substrate for *Hydrogenomonas*, 213

Acetoacetate, 274, 275, 367
  conversion to 3-hydroxybutyrate, 67
  decarboxylation of, 278
  formation from acetoacetyl CoA, 277
  product in photometabolism of acetone, 77

Acetoacetate carboxy-lyase, *see* Acetoacetate decarboxylase
Acetoacetate decarboxylase (EC 4.1.1.4), 278

Acetoacetyl CoA
  conversion to acetoacetate, 277
    to acetyl CoA, 419
  formation from acetate, 276
    from acetoacetate, 274
    from acetyl CoA, 276
    from crotonyl CoA, 419
  intermediate in glutarate metabolism, 367
  reduction to β-OH butyryl CoA, 276
  thiolase (EC 2.3.1.9), 276

Acetoin
  conversion to L(+)-acetoin, 297
  endproduct of citrate metabolism, 335
  formation by acetic acid bacteria, 319
    from acetolactate, 295
    from 2,3-butanediol, 368, 369
    from diacetyl, 296
    via α-acetolactate, 319

443

Ferredoxin, 71
  association with sulfite reductase, 102
  catalytic action, 52, 53
  function in *Desulfotomaculum*, 102
    in *Desulfovibrio*, 102
  photochemical reduction, 53
  properties, 52
  as reductant in carbon assimilation, 71
  role in hydrogen lyase system, 272, 273,
    290
    in photochemical NAD reduction, 65
    in photosynthesis, 52, 53
    in pyruvate decarboxylation, 272
Ferredoxin-NAD reductase, 65
Ferredoxin-NADP reductase (EC 1.6.99.4),
  53
  similarity to green plant enzyme, 54
Ferric hydroxide, deposition by *Gallionella*,
  217
Ferric salt, as oxidizing agent, 9
Flavine adenine dinucleotide (FAD)
  comparison with NAD, 33
  as electron carrier in respiratory chain, 90,
    95
  formula, 33
  function as electron carrier, 33, 34, 210,
    211
  in soluble reaction of *Hydrogenomonas
    H 16*, 211, 212
  mechanism of reaction, 33
  reaction with oxygen, 33
  role in pyruvate dismutation, 344
Flavoprotein (FP)
  function in electron transport of chemo-
    synthesis, 90
  mode of action, 341
Flavoprotein NAD peroxidase (EC 1.11.1.1),
  341
Flavoprotein respiration in lactic acid bacteria, 340, 344
FMN, in soluble fraction of *Hydrogenomonas H 16*, 211, 212
Formaldehyde
  condensation with ribose-5-phosphate,
    219
  oxidation of, 217, 218, 290, 291
Formaldehyde: NAD oxidoreductase, *see*
  Formaldehyde dehydrogenase
Formaldehyde dehydrogenase (EC 1.2.1.1),
  218, 382

Formate, 71
  breakdown to carbon dioxide and hydro-
    gen, 290, 291
  as carbon source in *Pseudomonas oxalati-
    cus*, 361, 368
  as electron donor in sulfate reduction, 101
  oxidation of, 217, 361, 367
  production in heterolactic fermentation,
    335
Formate: cytochrome b_1 oxidoreductase,
  see Formate dehydrogenase (EC
  1.2.2.1)
Formate: NAD oxidoreductase, *see* Formate
  dehydrogenase, (EC 1.2.1.2)
Formate dehydrogenase
  (EC 1.2.1.2), 218, 290, 291
  (EC 1.2.2.1), 272, 361, 382
Formic hydrogenlyase system, 272, 273, 290
  in *Desulfovibrio*, 102
Formimino-glutamate
  conversion to glutamate, 406
  formation from urocanic acid, 406
Formimino tetrahydrofolic acid, formula,
  40
Formyl CoA, formation from oxalyl CoA,
  363
Formyl CoA hydrolase (EC 3.1.2.10), 274
L-Formylkynurenine, formation from L-
  tryptophan, 384, 385
Formyltetrahydrofolate
  role as active C_1 fragment, 40, 41
  role in formaldehyde oxidation, 218
11-Formyl undecanoic acid, formation of,
  372
FP-linked diaphorase, 341, 343
FP-linked menadione reductase (EC
  1.6.99.2), 341
FP-linked NAD oxidase, role in oxygen
  reduction, 343
FP-linked NAD peroxidase, role in oxygen
  reduction, 341
FP-linked oxidases of lactic acid bacteria,
  cytochrome c reductase (EC 1.6.99.3),
  341
FP-linked peroxidases
  atypical, 342
  in lactic acid bacteria, 243
  typical 342
Free energy, 5
  of acetyl CoA hydrolysis, 231

Hydrogenase (EC 1.12.1.1)—*cont.*
  coupled with oxidative phosphorylation, 212, 272
  in *Desulfovibrio*, 102
  function of, 212, 213
  in *Hydrogenomonas*, 211, 213
  mode of action, 211, 212, 290, 291
  properties of, 211
  role in hydrogen production by *Chromatium*, 63, 64
Hydrogenlyase system, in enterobacteria, 272
L-3-Hydroxyacyl CoA hydro-lyase, *see* Crotonase
L-3-Hydroxyacyl CoA hydro-lyase, *see* Enoyl CoA hydratase
p-Hydroxybenzoate hydroxylase, 380
p-Hydroxybenzoate, hydroxylation to protocatechuate, 380
3-Hydroxybutyrate
  conversion to CoA ester, 419
  formation from succinic semialdehyde, 418
  intermediate in poly-β-hydroxybutyrate formation, 67
3-Hydroxybutyrate dehydrogenase (EC 1.1.1.30), 67, 277, 418
D-Hydroxybutyrate-NAD oxidoreductase, *see* 3-Hydroxybutyrate dehydrogenase
D,L-β-Hydroxybutyric acid, formation from D,L-1,3-butanediol, 323
β-Hydroxybutyryl CoA, 367
  conversion to vinylacetyl CoA, 419
  dehydration to crotonyl CoA, 277
  formation from aceto-acetyl CoA, 276
    from crotonyl CoA, 367
    from 3-hydroxybutyrate, 419
α-Hydroxy-γ-carboxy propyl thiamine pyrophosphate, formation of, 234
12-Hydroxy dodecanoic acid, formation of, 372
α-Hydroxyethyl thiamine pyrophosphate
  conversion to 6-*S*-acetylhydrolipoate, 230
  intermediate in pyruvate decarboxylation, 43, 230
  product from pyruvate, 230
β-Hydroxyglutarate, 367
Hydroxylamine
  aerobic metabolism of, 203

Hydroxylamine—*cont.*
  oxidation of, 201–203
  product of ammonia oxidation, 201
  reduction by *Pseudomonas denitrificans*, 108
Hydroxylamine-cytochrome c reductase, 204
  electron transport of, 204
Hydroxylamine reductase, 107
  in *Micrococcus* sp., 108
ω-Hydroxylase, 372
Hydroxylases
  definition, 390
  mode of action, 390
5-Hydroxymethyl tetrahydrofolic acid, formula, 40
2-Hydroxy-4-oxopentanoate carboxy-lyase, *see* Acetolactate decarboxylase
Hydroxyproline, conversion to D-allohydroxy-proline, 382, 383
Hydroxyproline 2-epimerase (EC 5.1.1.8), 382
Hydroxyproline metabolism, 382, 383
β-Hydroxy propionaldehyde, intermediate in glycerol reduction, 298
β-Hydroxypropionate
  conversion to CoA ester, 415, 416
  formation from malonate semialdehyde, 415
β-Hydroxypropionate dehydrogenase (EC 1.1.1.59), 282, 415
3-Hydroxypropionate : NAD oxidoreductase *see* β-Hydroxypropionate dehydrogenase
Hydroxypropionyl CoA
  formation of, 282, 416
  reduction to acrylyl CoA, 282, 416
Hyponitrite reductase, 107

I

Imidazol lactic acid, formation from imidazol pyruvate, 407
Imidazol pyruvic acid
  formation from L-histidine, 407
  reduction of, 407
Indol, formation of, 410
Indol propionic acid, formation from tryptophan, 410
Infrared spectrum, for grouping lactobacilli, 335

Inosine diphosphate
  as phosphate carrier, 37, 265
  role in succinate formation, 292
Inosine triphosphate, 131
Intracytoplasmic membrane
  effect of light on formation of, 60
  formation in relation to chlorophyll
    synthesis, 60
Iron
  microbial transformation of, 214 ff.
  oxidase, 216
  oxidation by *Ferrobacillus ferrooxidans*,
    215
    permeability and, 216
    sulfate requirement and, 215, 216
    by *Thiobacillus ferrooxidans*, 217
Iron-cytochrome c reductase, 215
Isobutyrate, formation from valine, 405
Isocitrate
  aldo cleavage of, 358
  conversion to oxalosuccinate, 231, 233
  formation of, 231–233
Isocitrate dehydrogenase (EC 1.1.1.42), 233
Isocitrate lyase (EC 4.1.3.1), 358, 360
  as regulator, 358
Isoleucine, deamination to valeric acid, 405
Isopropanol, formation from acetone, 278
Isopropanol dehydrogenase, 278
Isovalerate, formation from leucine, 405
Itaconate
  conversion to itaconyl CoA, 364
  formation from aconitate, 363
  metabolism in pseudomonads, 363
Itaconate CoA transferase, 364
Itaconyl CoA
  conversion to citramyl CoA, 364
  formation from itaconate, 364
Itaconyl CoA hydratase, 364

K

Keto acids, effect on growth of thiobacilli,
  224
β-Ketoadipate
  formation from γ-carboxy-muconolac-
    tone, 379, 380
  product in mandelate pathway, 379
β-Ketoadipate enol-lactone, 380
β-Ketoadipate enol-lactone hydrolase, 380
β-Ketoadipyl CoA thiolase, 380

2,4-Ketoarabinonate
  formation from 2-keto-3-deoxy-arabinon-
    ate, 355
  hydrolysis of, 356
β-Keto-*n*-decanoic acid, β-oxidation of, 374
2-Keto-3-deoxy-D-arabinonate
  conversion to α-oxoglutarate, 355
    to pyruvate and glycollic acid, 355
  formation from arabinonate, 355
2-Keto-3-deoxy-D-galactonate
  conversion to pyruvate and triosephos-
    phate, 354, 355
  formation from galactonate, 354, 355
2-Keto-3-deoxy-galactonate-6-phosphate
  action of aldolase on, 355
  formation of, 355
2-Keto-3-deoxygluconate, 356
2-Keto-3-deoxy-6-phosphogluconate
  cleavage of, 142, 143
  distribution, 169, 170
  formation of, 142, 143, 170
    from 6-phosphogluconate, 142, 143
    of Schiff's base (azomethine), 170
2-Keto-3-deoxy-6-phosphogluconate aldol-
    ase (EC 4.1.2.14), 142, 143, 169, 332
  assay method, 171 ff.
  inducible enzyme, 332
2 - Keto - 3 - deoxy - 6 - phosphogluconate de-
    hydratase, 152
2 - Keto - 3 - deoxy - 6 - phosphogluconate : D -
    glyceraldehyde-3-phosphate lyase, *see*
    2 - Keto - 3 - deoxy - 6 - phosphogluconate
    aldolase
5-Keto-D-fructose, oxidation product from
    fructose, 316
2-Ketogluconate
  conversion to gluconate, 314
  oxidation of, 315
Ketogluconate dehydrogenase (EC 1.1.99.4),
  315
2-Keto-D-gluconate:(acceptor) oxidoreduc-
    tase, *see* Ketogluconate dehydrogenase
2-Ketogluconate reductase, 314
5-Ketogluconate
  conversion to gluconate, 314
  formation from gluconate, 314
5-Ketogluconate reductase (EC 1.1.1.69),
  314
5-Ketogluconokinase, 314
Ketohexokinase (EC 2.7.1.3), 159

α-Ketoisovalerate, 274, 275
Keto-1-phosphate aldehyde-lyase, *see* Aldolase
3-Keto-6-phosphogluconate, possible intermediate in dehydrogenase action, 167
Knallgas reaction, 211
Krebs cycle, *see* Tricarboxylic acid cycle
Kynurenate
    conversion of, 384, 385
    formation from D-kynurenine, 384, 385
Kynurenate hydroxylase (EC 1.14.1.4), 385
Kynurenate reduced NAD(P): oxygen oxidoreductase (hydroxylating), *see* Kynurenate hydroxylase
Kynureninase (EC 3.7.1.3), 385
Kynurenine formamidase (EC 3.5.1.9), 385
D-Kynurenine, oxidative deamination of, 384, 385
D-Kynurenine oxidase, 385
L-Kynurenine
    conversion to anthranilic acid, 384, 385
    formation in L-tryptophan metabolism, 384, 385
L-Kynurenine hydrolase, *see* Kynureninase

L

Lactate
    conversion to pyruvate in *Desulfovibrio*, 101
    endproduct in deoxyribose metabolism, 338
    fermentation to propionate, 268, 269
    formation in *Clostridia*, 279
    metabolism in acetic acid bacteria, 309
        by Group N streptococci, 339
    optical activity, 331
    oxidation in sulfate reduction, 101
    production by heterofermenters, 337
        by homofermenters, 337
        in mixed acid producers, 293
    photometabolism in *Rhodospirillum palustris*, 74
    stereospecificity, 331, 332
D-Lactate: NAD oxidoreductase (EC 1.1.1.28), *see* Lactate dehydrogenase
Lactate dehydrogenase
    (EC 1.1.1.27), 208, 268, 293
    (EC 1.1.1.28), 293, 332, 334
Lactate oxidase (EC 1.1.3.2), 33, 310, 344
Lactate racemase (EC 5.1.2.1), 332

D-Lactate: oxygen oxidoreductase, *see* D-Lactate oxidase
Lactobionic acid, formation from lactose, 356
Lactose
    oxidation of, 356
    substrate in homofermentation, 332
Lactyl CoA, intermediate in propionate formation, 268, 269
Lactyl CoA dehydrase, 268
Leucine, deamination to isovaleric acid, 405
Light reaction, role of chlorophyll, 50
Lipoamide dehydrogenase (EC 1.6.4.3), 231, 344
Lipoate, 35
    coenzymatical function in acetyl CoA formation, 230, 231
    definition, 35
    formula, 35
    as oxidizing agent in acetyl-transfer, 43
    role in oxidative decarboxylations, 35, 230, 234, 344
        in Stickland reaction, 412
        in thiosulfate reduction, 100
Lipoate acetyltransferase (EC 2.3.1.12), 231, 233, 234
Lyase, definition, 28
D-Lyxose isomerase, 186
D-Lyxose, isomerization of, 185, 186
D-Lyxose ketol-isomerase, 186
L-Lyxose, isomerization of, 186, 187

M

Malate
    conversion to fumarate, 231, 266
        to oxalacetate, 16, 231, 235, 312
        to pyruvate, 70, 292
    formation from acetate in *Rhodopseudomonas spheroides*, 72, 73
        from fumarate, 231, 235
        from glyoxylate, 357, 358, 362
        from oxalacetate, 231, 266
        from pyruvate, 361
    as hydrogen donor in purple bacteria, 63
    oxidation in *Azotobacter* and *Micrococcus*, 235
        in *Chromatium*, 236
        in *Escherichia coli*, 235
        to pyruvate in *Serratia*, 235

Oxygen—*cont.*
requirement for heme biosynthesis, 114
oxidation-reduction potential and, 48
as terminal electron acceptor, 47
toxicity in facultative anaerobes, 113
uptake in *Hydrogenomonas*, 214
during malate oxidation, 74
during α-oxoglutarate oxidation, 74
during succinate oxidation, 74
Oxygenases, 204, 216, 223, 225, 374
definition, 390
(EC 1.13.1.3), 380
mode of action, 390
system in *Nitrosomonas*, 204

P

Palmitic acid, 371
Panthotheine
formula, 39
as growth factor, 39, 40
Pantothenic acid, formula, 39
PAPS, *see* 3-Phosphoadenosine-5′-phosphosulfate
Pasteur effect, 147, 211
hexokinase and, 159
role of ADP and ATP, 147
of phosphofructokinase, 147
of 3-phosphoglyceraldehyde oxidation, 147
1,5-Pentanediol, oxidation to glutaric acid, 324
Pentitols, metabolism of, 184
Pentose
metabolism of, 184
phosphorylation of, 159
reductive cycle in phososynthetic bacteria, 76
Pentose cycle, *see* HMP pathway
Pentose-phosphoketolase pathway, 148, 173
Pepsin (EC 3.4.4.1), 403
Permeability, theory of, 200, 201, 221
Permeability barrier in photosynthetic bacteria, 74
Peroxidase (EC 1.11.1.7), 240
atypical, 341, 342
typical, 342
Pesticide degradation, 388
method of simultaneous adaptation, 389
Petroleum hydrocarbon oxidation, 373

Phosphatase in *Nitrosomonas*, 206
Phosphate acetyl transferase (EC 2.3.1.8), 275, 289
3-Phospho-adenosine-5′-phosphosulfate (PAPS), 96, 97
formula, 98
reductase, 96, 99, 225, 226
reduction via thiolytic split, 99
Phosphocozymase, *see* Nicotinamide adenine dinucleotide phosphate
Phosphoenol oxalacetate
conversion to oxalacetate, 292
formation from phosphoenolpyruvate, 292
Phosphoenol pyruvate
carboxylation of, 292
to oxalacetate, 157, 267, 361
conversion to pyruvate, 130, 134, 157, 265
formation from 2-phosphoglycerate, 130, 134
from pyruvate, 292
free energy of hydrolysis, 20, 21
produced in photometabolism of succinate, 69
role in "double CO_2 fixation" mechanism, 157
Phosphoenol pyruvate carboxylase (EC 4.1.1.32), 68, 157
Phosphoenol pyruvate carboxytransphosphorylase, 267
Phosphoenol pyruvate hydratase (EC 4.2.1.11), 68, 130, 134
Phosphofructokinase, (EC 2.7.1.11), 130, 132, 152, 162, 214, 318
assay methods, 164 ff.
influence by metabolites, 163, 164
as limiting factor in metabolism, 163
mechanism of action, 162, 163
occurrence, 162
properties, 162
role of ATP, 162, 163
in Pasteur effect, 147, 163
Phosphoglucomutase (EC 2.7.5.1), 7
6-Phosphogluconate
conversion by *Hydrogenomonas*, 214
to ribulose-5-phosphate, 136
dehydration of, 142, 143
formation of, 136
overall stoichiometry, 336
oxidation via EMP and ED pathway, 336
via EMP and HMP pathway, 336

MICROORGANISM INDEX

Numbers in parentheses are reference numbers and indicate that studies have been carried out with the particular microorgism, although the actual name is not cited in the text.

A

Acetobacter, 307, 309, 313
  aceti, 322
  acetigenus, 322
  acetosus, 322
  ascendens, 319, 322
  cerinus, 316
  industrium, 322
  kuetzingianus, 322
  liquefaciens, 310
  melanogenium, 171, 315
  mesoxydans, 308, 309, 311, 318, 324
  oxydans, 308, 309, 311, 318, 324
  pasteurianum, 310, 319, 322
  peroxidans, 307, 308–312, 318, 324
  rancens, 319, 324
  suboxydans, 169, 182, 300, 309
  xylinum, 172, 312, 313, 315, 316, 322
Acetomonas, 307, 309, 313
  melanogenum, 323
  oxidans, 325, 326
  suboxydans, 310, 311, 313–315, 317–324
Achromobacter, 112, 113, 388
  fisheri, 112, 113
  liquefaciens, 113
  stutzeri, 229
Actinomyces, 152
  naeslundii, 146
Aerobacter, 180, 188, 260, 284, 299, 368, 369
  aerogenes, 113, 115, 159, 180–182, 184, 242, 285, 293, 295, 296, 298, 299, 319
  cloacae (195, 304, 348)
Aeromonas
  formicans (304)
  hydrophila, 290
Agrobacterium, 353
  tumefaciens, 146
Alcaligenes, 180
  faecalis (190)
Anacystis nidulans, 76, 177
Arthrobacter, 147, 152, 385, 386
  atrocyaneus, 147
  globiformis, 147

Arthrobacter—cont.
  pascens, 147
  simplex, 147
  ureofaciens, 147
Aspergillus
  flavus-oryzae, 166, 168
  niger, 177
Azotobacter
  agile, 113
  agilis, 182, 235
  vinelandii, 171

B

Bacillus, 331, 368
  cereus, 114, 147
  lentimorbus (194)
  marcerans, 260
  megaterium, 166
  polymyxa, 260, 296, 298
  popilliae, 241
  stearothermophilus, 113, 177
  subtilis, 146, 166, 182, 184, 295, 296, 298
Bacterium
  anitratum, 109, 166
  tularense (192)
Bacteroides, 268
  ruminicola, 268, 269
Bifidobacterium, 148, 151, 152, 316, 333
Borrelia, 268
  recurrentis, 158
Brevibacterium fuscum (195)
Brucella suis, 177
Butyribacterium, 269, 279
  rettgeri, 270, 272, 331

C

Candida utilis, 176
Catenabacterium, 333
Cellvibrio polyoltrophicus, 182
Chlorella pyrenoidosa (84)
Chlorobium, 57, 62, 65, 66
  limicola, 62
  thiosulfatophilum, 58, 62, 66, 70